HEALING RESEARCH - VOLUME III

PERSONAL

SPIRITUALITY

Science, Spirit and The Eternal Soul

by

Daniel J. Benor, M.D.

ISBN 10 digit: 0-9754248-4-X
13 digit: 978-0-9754248-4-1

Printed in the United States of America

Wholistic Healing Publications
PO Box 502
Medford, NJ 08055, USA
(609) 714-1885   Fax (609) 714-3553
DB@WholisticHealingResearch.com

ACKNOWLEDGMENT OF PERMISSIONS TO REPRODUCE MATERIALS

I thank the many authors and publishers who have generously granted their permission to reproduce quotes in this book, in the spirit of healing.

I specifically acknowledge permissions for:

Tables on spiritual awareness in Chapter III-11 from David Aldridge, *Spirituality,
Healing and Medicine: Return to the Silence*, Philadelphia/London: Jessica
Kingsley 2000, with the kind permission of the author and publisher.

Library of Congress Control Number: 2006931437

Contents

Tables

Figures

Acknowledgments

I give thanks to Martina Steiger for her unstinting generosity in editing this work. Martina's warmth, centeredness, intuition, inner wisdom and Spirit have been and continue to be awesome inspirations to me.

I give thanks to Berney Williams, a true Renaissance scholar of amazingly broad and deep knowledge, for also providing editorial inputs and enormously helpful discussions, and for editing an earlier version of this book. I have yet to find a topic that Berney cannot expound upon from his encyclopedic knowledge of everything that is, was or could be.

I give thanks to the countless caregivers and careseekers who have been my teachers through a lifetime of studies about the human condition. I give thanks to the many authors of books, poems, pithy sayings, heartwarming and humorous quotes, and apt turns of phrasings that have given me information, insights, inspiration, pleasure, solace and spice to add to this book.

I give thanks to those who have treated me harshly, giving me the challenges that led me to seek out those who have offered me love, caring, support, wise teachings, and healings, all of them helping me find places of love, acceptance, forgiveness and healing within myself that I would not have found alone.

I give thanks to the Infinite Source and the spiritual intermediaries who have often wakened me in the wee hours of the morning with insights that furthered the writing of this book.

Dedication

This book is dedicated to the seekers of the meanings for life who have each contributed his or her own perceptions of and resonations with their higher self/ spirit/soul – each adding unique grains of sand to the ever-shifting figure that is the Infinite Source as we perceive and experience it and contribute to it.

I deeply admire the many explorers in the realms of spirituality who have bravely ventured into inner territories for explorations that are challenging on multiple levels. Acknowledging the difficulties of inner explorations, in Jewish tradition the question, "Who is the brave one?" is answered, "He who conquers his inner worlds." Overcoming the habits of repressing that which makes us anxious is a serious endeavor. It is not easy to open the doors behind which our unconscious minds have hidden our unpleasant, fearful and shameful memories and feelings. The locks and the "Beware of Tigers" signs on these doors also discourage inner explorations into intuitive realms that also open into spiritual awakenings. Connecting with the wisdom behind these doors strengthens our conscious awareness and connection to the Infinite Source.

The chorus of voices of people who have ventured into these realms is honored in this book through numerous quotes that acknowledge my debts to these brave explorers.

Western society (including many religious groups) denigrates, discourages, and disparages these explorations. Academics who research spiritual awareness and healing often have done so under peer censure, with the risk of curtailment of their funding and even dismissal from their university positions. They are indeed brave who have ventured to study these realms in the halls of academia.

I equally honor these explorers who have approached studies of the infinite through linear research methods. Their experiments and reports help to show that there is a consistency to accounts of spiritual explorations, providing linear reasons to accept these as valid observations.

I acknowledge here the many healers and other intuitives who have generously and often very patiently shared their experiences and views on topics that are difficult to describe – with a researcher who asks endless questions. Speaking with these people has helped me know enough about intuitive worlds to satisfy my personal doubts. This has been important not only in the gathering of information for this book but also in giving me courage to continue and deepen my own explorations of the Infinite.

Foreword

This landmark publication was written by Dan Benor, MD, a physician who has studied unconventional healing both as a researcher and as a participant. It clearly reveals Dr. Benor's several decades of immersion in this field and his commitment to it.

This is volume three of what will become a four volume set: the first volume summarizes research in what variously has been called psychic healing, remote healing, transpersonal healing, and spiritual healing; and the second thoroughly explores integrative care, self-healing and 'energy medicine.' This third volume of Dr. Benor's series can be read without the background provided by the earlier two. It is a complete work in itself.

It is unusual to find a physician involved in these topics, either as a researcher or as a practitioner. Dr. Benor addresses his explorations from the standpoint of an advocate, but one who is an open-minded explorer, neither from a religious nor a conventional medical perspective.

The breadth and depth of the research reports in this third volume, on the psychic, intuitive, and spiritual aspects of healing will engage even the knowledgeable reader. Dr. Benor brings an incredible wealth of detail to his discussions, taking an integrative systems approach, one that ties together disparate details into a coherent pattern.

For example, 'out-of-body' experiences (OBEs) have been explored in several different settings, from the anecdotal reports of the American business executive Robert Monroe on spontaneous and deliberate OBEs to the sleuthing of 'psychic spies' who were assigned to search for hidden Soviet military facilities. One would not expect that OBEs are relevant to healing, but Dr. Benor cites reports of shamans from traditional societies and other folk healers from around the world who claim that they travel 'out of body' in the course of their practice.

People who claim to have had Near-Death Experiences (NDEs) often return from these journeys across what is popularly known as 'the final divide' between life and death. They bring back with them stories of meeting deceased relatives, being greeted by angels (or other beings from another dimension), or an incredibly loving 'Being of Light.' They often recall reviewing their entire lives in a dispassionate scrutiny of the details of their earthly existence. Many doubters have dismissed these anecdotes as no more than wishful thinking or the products of a dying brain that is exhausting its supply of oxygen. This book, in contrast, marshals considerable evidence to support the notion that these reports are not just an acknowledgment that people are entitled to their subjective experiences, but that some aspect of the human psyche survives physical death. Some of the data presented in this book suggests that humans may 'come back' in repeated incarnations to implement the lessons that they seem to have learned in their current life.

Having established a basis in research and reason for some type of post-mortem survival, Dr. Benor finds what he considers compelling evidence for 'angelic' and 'spirit' involvements in human affairs. For instance, in the most thorough review I've read on the topic of so-called 'psychic surgery' in the Philippines and South America, Dr. Benor shows that this highly unusual form of healing is practiced in a variety of ways in several traditional cultures. Many of these healers purport to work with 'spirit guides,' and many of these healers believe that spiritual transformation is far more important than physical healing, and focus their efforts along these lines.

Next, Dr. Benor considers the implications of what he calls 'spiritual realities.' He brings his readers a rich review of a broad spectrum of religious, psychological, and philosophical speculations about the importance of spirituality in people's daily lives. In an overview that ranges from the dogma of Christian fundamentalism to the conjectures of so-called 'quantum theology,' Dr. Benor proposes that each model has a valid place in understanding the actualities that are beyond words in our current vocabularies. As a result, no contemporary hypothesis represents the 'entire picture.'

Western civilization does not differentiate between institutionalized spirituality and personal, individualistic spirituality, and the scientific community distances itself from both. In one of the most delightful sections of this book, Dr. Benor demystifies what have been called by many people 'mystical' experiences, suggesting that everyone can explore this area and enrich their lives as a result.

Overall, Dr. Benor's discussion is far from ponderous; it is enlivened by numerous humorous, provocative, and heartwarming stories, quotations, poems, and cartoons.

Readers of *Healing Research* might keep in mind that Dr. Benor is a physician, psychotherapist and researcher as well as a spiritual healer. He brings wise insights from every aspect of his broad knowledge and considerable clinical expertise to this book's data and discussions. Some readers will approach the tales he tells skeptically, perhaps asking themselves if there was a magician present during the treatments of 'psychic surgeries,' or if a distortion of memory could have clouded the details of a story about 'spirits.' Others will take the opposite point of view, that 'spiritual realities' are so obvious that laboratory research to verify them is a waste of time. Still others, especially those with a background in cross-cultural studies, will be amused at the hullabaloo raised by these accounts, many of which are everyday affairs to people who live in the world's few remaining traditional societies.

This book has much to offer readers of diverse pursuits and persuasions. And for those who have not given great thought to the issues tackled in these pages, *Healing Research* presents sufficient evidence and is written in a manner that invites you to apply your critical acumen to each chapter and make your own decisions as to the relevance for your lives of the wealth of material provided. This book is destined to take its place among the most influential and controversial in the field of claims, reports, and experiences of unconventional healing and spiritual awareness.

> Stanley Krippner, PhD
> Professor of Psychology, Saybrook Graduate School

Prologue

This prologue is written in an unexpected space of time created by delays in publication of volume III of *Healing Research*. During this interval I came upon a remarkable book: *A Leg to Stand On* by Dr. Oliver Sacks. Sacks is a neurologist with a marvelous gift for observation and narrative.[1] He describes how he broke his leg and injured its nerves while mountain climbing, underwent surgical repair, and then recuperating slowly and painfully.

Sacks felt a dissociation from his injured limb which appeared to result from a combination of pain, enforced immobilization and sensory deprivation in a small hospital room. When it came time to begin walking again, he felt he literally did not have a leg to stand on. He simply could not feel a connection with the 'white bit' that hung from his hip.

When two physiotherapists stood him up to take his first steps, he said, "I can't move... I can't think how to. I have no idea whatever how to take the first step." [2]

One of the physiotherapists had to move his leg for him in order to get him into a mode in which locomotion was conceivable. Next, he had to look at the leg and calculate visually each movement in his head, as he had no sensation in the leg and no awareness of its position without the visual inputs. This was not simple because his visual depth perception was severely distorted when he assayed to connect with the limb which had not been within the ambit of his awareness or under his control for several weeks. This was awkward and resulted in what he called a 'pseudo-walking,'

> And suddenly – into this silence, the silent twittering of motionless frozen images – came music, glorious music, Mendelssohn, *fortissimo*! Life, intoxicating movement! And, as suddenly, without thinking, without intending whatever, I found myself walking, easily, *with* the music. And, as suddenly, in the moment that this inner music started, the Mendelssohn which had been summoned and hallucinated by my soul, and in the very moment that my 'motor' music, my kinetic melody, my walking, came back – in this self-same moment *the leg came back*. Suddenly, with no warning, no transition whatever, the leg felt alive, and real, and mine... I *belonged* in the leg. I *knew* how to walk...[3]

...I was quickened into motion, my own perceptual and kinetic melody, quickened into life by the inner life of music. And in that moment, when the body became action, the leg, the flesh became quick and alive, the flesh became music, incarnate solid music. All of me, body and soul, became music in that moment...[4]

Sacks found other perceptual distortions. His visual fields, which had been limited to a small, windowless room for weeks, did not register depth perception beyond the several feet from his body that they were accustomed to dealing with. Anything beyond that habitual perimeter appeared flat. This distortion corrected itself with expanded use of his visual fields within a few hours.

Sacks is particularly appropriate to relate to these regressions in neuromotor and sensory functions because he studied patients who had been in coma for decades and were revived by a new drug. (This story was made into the movie, *Awakenings*.) He later went on to study hundreds of people who had had immobilizing injuries to their extremities. Many reported experiences similar to his own.

Sacks notes that twenty-five hundred years ago Hippocrates was aware of severe difficulties which could be experienced by those who broke a hip and were immobilized in bed for fifty days. By the end of their confinement they could not imagine how to move their leg, nor how to stand. If they were not forced to do so, they would remain bedridden all the rest of their lives.

Sacks speculates that this sort of regression could occur with immobilization of any sort.

In Western civilization we have broken our connection with nature, closeted ourselves from spiritual awareness – behind constructs built out of the bricks of scientific measurements – and immobilized that part of ourselves which connects directly with God[5] – through reductionistic, linear analyses, theories, and explanations. We started this process of immobilization of our intuitive and spiritual selves with the philosophy of Descartes and the industrial revolution, several hundred years ago, when our society adopted the agreement that body is separate from mind and spirit.[6] The process has been a self-reinforcing one. That which is distanced feels unfamiliar and is experienced as strange or even as alien. That which is alien is labeled 'mystical' or 'magical' and is avoided and denigrated, pushing it even further away.

No wonder it is difficult for us to return to awareness of our connection with the spiritual dimensions which are a part of us, yet for many are a part which is as distant and as difficult to connect with as was Sacks' leg for him.

My own awareness and experience of personal spirituality has reflected this same disconnection. To some extent, this book is a chronicle of my search for evidence to clarify whether I could have a basis in reason for accepting the spiritual as a real and valid phenomenon.

This book invites you to reconnect with your spiritual legs, to feel the wonderment of dimensions which are as real and legitimate as any physical reality.

Introduction

Everyone sees the unseen in proportion to the clarity of his heart, and that depends upon how much he has polished it. Whoever has polished it more sees more – more unseen forms become manifest to him.

– Jalaluddin Rumi

We are all part of a vast, magnificent web of spiritual consciousness that extends through infinite space and time. You may have felt this connection with the Infinite at special moments in your life, when your heart opened to the beauty of another person's smile, kind words or touch. You may have been touched physically or your heart may have been moved in gratitude, admiration, passion or pathos. You may have felt a oneness with nature in the vastness of a crystalline night sky sparkling with countless stars, or in the beauty of a flower, a hummingbird, an innocent child or some other creation sculpted by the Infinite Source.

At moments like these, you know with an absolute certainty that there is much more to life than just your physical being – without words to adequately or fully express this knowing. Your emotions may be deeply stirred; you may feel a love for others and for the community of all living things on this planet; your heart may swell till it feels like it is bursting with a joy that is overflowing the vessel of your beingness. And you know with a certainty that transcends any questioning that you have touched into or have been touched by the Infinite Source. You may know this as God, Christ, Buddha, Allah, the Goddess, Nature, Infinite Love and Acceptance, or any of myriads of forms that are known with our inner knowing that speaks to us with such clarity that we know its reality that is beyond the realities of our everyday senses and experiences. This is personal spirituality.

These experiences are common, accepted and deliberately cultivated in those individuals and societies living close to nature and open to spiritual realities. Western society has distanced itself from these personal spiritual experiences, suggesting that they are fantasies or wishful thinking, perhaps even delusions of deranged minds. Western science demands firm evidence before it will accept any such suggestions for realities extending beyond the physical world. This book brings you this very evidence.

Research now confirms what ordinary people, meditators and mystics have been reporting over many centuries: spirituality is a real, valid and vitalizing experience. A wide variety of studies also confirm that spirituality contributes to our health and well-being. Spirituality may also contribute to the wellbeing of our planet, helping us to look beyond our personal and collective immediate wants and needs – to consider the welfare of future generations. This third of the four-volume series, *Healing Research*, also explores many ways in which spiritual experiences and spiritual healing illuminate and inform our lives.

Let me first define a few important terms. (See below and glossary for more.)

Spirituality is our basic quest for cognitive understanding of ultimate meanings and values in life. We seek explanations for how we have come to be who and what we are. Spirituality is also a felt-sense; an inner, intuitive knowing of who we are; a deeper awareness about our place in relationship to the world of our senses; and an awareness of how we fit into a vaster world beyond our physical selves and sensory reality.

Spiritual awareness often evolves out of primary experience, *gnosis*, which may be stimulated by strongly positive, traumatic or transformational life occurrences – such as resonating to beauty and love in our lives; encountering dramatic loss and grief; awakenings at the boundaries between life and death, such as Near-Death Experiences, bereavement apparitions and channeled encounters with spirits; psychic or even psychotic episodes; and other encounters beyond ordinary experience, such as in unusual responses to spiritual healings. Any of these may include healing crises and transformations that awaken our spiritual awareness.

Spiritual healing, the focus of the *Healing Research* series of books, is the intentional influence of one or more people upon their own or another living system, beyond the use of known conventional mechanical, energetic, chemical, or social means of bringing about that influence.

The spectrum of healing approaches is as broad and varied as human experience and imagination can make them. The popular press tends to focus on rather rare, rapid physical changes that occur only occasionally with healing, the so-called *miracle cures*. This is unfortunate, as it leads many people to expect rapid results routinely with healing. Most commonly, healing produces gradual effects. These may be manifested not only in healees' physical bodies but also in their psychological and spiritual states.

Volume I, *Spiritual Healing: Scientific Validation of a Healing Revolution,* focuses on scientific studies of healing – both observational and randomized, controlled experiments. Out of 191 controlled studies – including healing for humans, animals, plants, bacteria, yeasts, cells in laboratory culture, enzymes and DNA – two thirds show statistically significant effects.

Volume I, Professional edition, provides a detailed, annotated bibliography and detailed discussion of these studies.

Volume I, Popular edition, has a lighter review of the research and includes three additional chapters:

1. A broad survey of anecdotal reports from healers around the world shows that healers have a very wide range of practices and explanations for what they do, how they do it, and how they believe it works.

2. A brief summary of *psi* [7] (parapsychological) phenomena shows that many effects reported by healers are supported by rigorous research in other contexts. Healers may know intuitively what is wrong with healees, even without being told. Research confirms it is possible to have communication by *telepathy* between people, and for one person to know intuitively by *clairsentience* what is going on in another living organism or in an inanimate object. Such knowledge may transcend the ordinary boundaries of time. Sensitive people may be able to obtain information about the past or future. Psi effects also include *psychokinesis* (*PK*), the direct influence of a person's mind upon an inanimate object. Psychic people have been able to move objects by mental intent, to influence electronic and mechanical random number generators, and more. PK is a clear parallel with healing. In fact, some parapsychologists refer to healing as *biological-* or *bio-PK*.[8]

3. Various healers may have some or all of these psi abilities; others have none of them. Studies show these abilities of healers are measurable and may contribute to their healing effects. Psi abilities are also relevant to the phenomena considered in this, Volume III of *Healing Research*. Psi may be involved in Out-of-Body and Near-Death Experiences, poltergeist effects, seeing spirits, and in having mystical/spiritual and healing experiences.

Wholistic energy medicine addresses people from the multiple dimensions of body, emotions, mind, relationships (with other people and with the environment) and spirit. It accepts that matter and energy are two sides of the same coin, and that people can be helped to heal through treatments of their bodies or through any of the other dimensions of their being.

Volume II, Professional edition, *Consciousness, Bioenergy and Healing,* considers how we can make ourselves ill or well through our perceptions and beliefs, through energetic aspects of our being, through complementary/alternative therapies and through spiritual dimensions. Numerous methods are available for self-healing. The mind has a vast array of mechanisms for interacting with the body. Any or all of these may be activated and augmented by healing.

Healers report that they interact with the biological energy fields that surround and interpenetrate the physical body. In this way, healing appears to be a common denominator among many of the complementary therapies. Volume II surveys a broad spectrum of these therapies such as yoga, acupuncture, craniosacral osteopathy, homeopathy, massage, yoga and more, to learn how each approach conceptualizes and addresses bioenergy aspects of health and illness, and how each identifies, addresses, explains and treats subtle bioenergy imbalances.

Volume II also reviews energy fields that are considered unconventional within the prevalent views of science, such as those encountered in dowsing and those postulated under astrology. These appear to have interactions with biological energies and to influence states of health and illness.

I am proud to have had Volume II acknowledged by The Scientific and Medical Network in the UK as their Book of the Year, 2004.

Volume II, Popular edition, *How Can I Heal What Hurts?* is a user-friendly version for the layperson, without the masses of references in the professional edition. A chapter on self-healing approaches introduces relaxations, meditations, cognitive behavior approaches, imagery, and more. Case examples illustrate ways in which these approaches can be helpful in dealing with stress, dis-ease and disease as well as in opening to spiritual awareness. Personal experiences of spiritual dimensions also open many avenues to healing, detailed in the next volume.

Volume III, this volume of *Healing Research*, surveys studies on spiritual aspects of healing and spirituality. You may again be surprised to see that a considerable body of research is available on these subjects. This volume confirms that personal spirituality is a real, valid and important part of our lives.

Expanding on my basic definition, I consider spirituality to include two facets:

1. Spirituality encompasses experiences in which people find their consciousness extends outside their physical bodies. This may be as simple as a vague, intuitive awareness that there is something vaster than yourself, in which you participate in an undefined manner. It may be much more specific, manifesting in intuitive or psychic perceptions; out-of-body experiences; near-death, pre-death, or deathbed experiences; reincarnation memories, seeing or hearing apparitions (ghosts and other visionary figures), nature spirits and angels; mediumistic (channeled) phenomena; deep meditative and mystical experiences; awareness which transcends present time – to past, future; and more. Research and anecdotal reports in all of these areas is surveyed and discussed in Chapters III-1 to III-6 and III-9.

Spirituality in this category also includes interactions with between people during spiritual healings. Healers and healees often feel heat, tingling, vibration and other sensations during laying-on of hand treatments. These sensations may occur with the healers' hands near to but not touching the body. Some healers also see *auras*, which are halos of color, around the body. All of these perceptions appear to be due to interactions of the biological energy fields of healers and healees. In other words, your bioenergy body extends beyond your physical body.[9]

This seems to be evidence for a biological energy body as described by healers and other intuitives. Healers and many CAM therapists believe this energy body animates the physical body during life. This also appears to be a vehicle for consciousness outside of the body during out-of-body and Near-Death Experiences and perhaps a vehicle for the spirit to continue beyond life, after physical death.

Not all experiences in (1) have a spiritual quality. People may have some of these, such as Out-of-Body Experiences or encounters with apparitions, without spiritual awareness. Out-of-Body Experiences, aspects of spiritual healing, and psychic experiences may have natural explanations, involving subtle biological energies and psychic awarenesses.

2. The Spiritual includes a sense of numinous ineffability, an awareness that is sometimes dim or fragmentary and sometimes thunderingly awesome – of being part of a vaster consciousness than is paradoxically contained also within any

single part of the whole. It is very difficult to find words that adequately describe spiritual awarenesses. Spiritual awarenesses come unbidden to some lucky people, through connecting with nature or with spirits, or through being challenged with a major crisis – such as illness or serious life challenges. For others the doorways into spiritual experiences may open through regular meditation, prayer and religious rituals. In addition, spiritual experiences may open people to awarenesses of transcendent realities from which they can draw inspiration.

Spiritual awareness often unfolds in one layer after another. My personal sense of the spiritual is that I am peeling a ginormous, Sisyphean[10] onion of life. I have been pleased to see that I am not alone in this awareness.

> *People with a high level of personal mastery live in a continual learning mode. They never 'arrive.' Sometimes, language, such as the term 'personal mastery,' creates a misleading sense of definiteness, of black and white. But personal mastery is not something you possess. It is a process. It is a lifelong discipline. People with a high level of personal mastery are acutely aware of their ignorance, their incompetence, their growth areas. Paradoxical? Only for those who do not see that 'the journey is the is the reward.'*
>
> – Peter Senge [11]

I have been drawn to the image of the nested series of Russian matryoshka dolls to illustrate the process of personal spiritual development. Each of us is a unit unto ourself and also a member of a family, community, nation and global village. Each of us has nested levels of experiences over many series of lifetimes. Each of us interacts with all of these levels in the worlds of physical, bioenergy, consciousness and spiritual realities.

Figure III-1. Nested series of matryoshka dolls

An interesting visual analog similar to this nested series is available on the Web.[12] Each of us is a pixel in the cosmic screen and can contribute to the All. More on this in Chapter III-13, Participatory spirituality.

Observations about nested hierarchies and their relevance to personal spirituality have been noted across many cultures, over many centuries.

> *To put the world right in order, we must first put the nation in order; to put the nation in order, we must first put the family in order; to put the family in order, we must first cultivate our personal life; we must first see our hearts right.*
>
> – Confucius [13]

Chapters III-9 and III-11 describe and discuss mystical and spiritual experiences, which also unfold in nested series of transcendent awarenesses.

Much of spiritual experience has frequently been claimed by religious authorities to be within their dominions, under their authority – often exclusively so. Religious affiliations, practices and attitudes may lead people towards or away from personal spiritual experiences. Chapter III-8 considers these issues.

Lest the reader consider that all of this exploration may be interesting but of little practical value, several chapters consider measurable effects of spiritual beliefs and practices upon states of health and illness.

Chapter III-7 reviews anecdotal reports of psychic surgery in which healers are said to be able to insert their bare hands into people's bodies and to remove or heal cancers, ulcers and other physical problems. This is viewed by many as an extreme form of subtle energy body manipulation. Practitioners of psychic surgery feel that the physical effects are not as important as the spiritual awareness which the surgery awakens. Many of these extraordinary healers also suggest that spiritual interventions surrounding the psychic surgery are the effective agencies for their dramatic results.

Chapter III-12 reviews research showing physical and emotional correlations between religious affiliation and practices with better health. Over 1200 studies are available.

Chapter III-13 considers participatory spiritual awareness, the connection each one of us has with the Infinite Source. Each of us is part of an all-encompassing consciousness which is so vast that it is beyond any possibility of our comprehension. In the same way that we participate in planning our own lives, our spiritual selves also participate as part of the collective consciousness in the planning of processes and events in the broader world beyond our personal boundaries. This includes, among other processes, the evolution of our species through participatory intelligent design. This chapter considers in detail the scientific evidence suggesting that Darwinian evolution is inadequate to explain many aspects of the genetic processes leading to development of new organisms and species. This is not to advocate teaching Biblical creationism in schools. It is an invitation to re-examine popular assumptions of Western science that have become so entrenched in our societal belief systems as to resemble a religion in their own right.

The Conclusion considers some of the implications and applications of personal spiritual awareness. Each of us participates in the vastness of all consciousness. Each of us is a spark of the Eternal Light, seeking our way home, guided by the light of the Infinite Source.

Science and spirituality

Many modern scientists have been quite happy to accept the claims of religious bodies to exclusive authority over spirituality because they feel that science relates to the physical world, in which observations are measurable and can be consensually validated. Science also works hard to develop systematic approaches for naturalistic observations, with methodical building and testing of hypotheses. Science had to work its way out of the Medieval dogmas which were accepted at that time as explanations for how the world worked. As these explanations were defended rather vigorously by the Church (at times even threatening the lives of scientists who were considered heretics), science has a long tradition of skepticism towards the teachings of the church.

Psychology has studied the functions of the mind for more than a century. Psychology has worked very hard to establish itself as a science and to be accepted within academic circles. This has been a difficult struggle because psychological phenomena in each individual person are unique, subjective and difficult to understand, much less to measure with precision. Psychology has dealt with this problem by focusing upon observations in large numbers of people, which are more easily quantifiable and can be subjected to statistical analyses. Within the confines of these numerical manipulations, psychological observations occur on average fairly consistently and repeatably, and qualify psychology for membership amongst the sciences which consider themselves to be the elite. (Never mind that the validity of observations of individuals are disqualified by psychologists in this quest for collective respectability.)

Western science has become firmly entrenched in its materialistic beliefs; so firmly that it has itself taken on the very same qualities of religious faith which science originally sought to question and replace with systematic, reasoned study.

Figure III-2. Certain uncertainties

Parapsychology studies experiences that touch on spiritual dimensions. Sadly, parapsychology has been a rejected step-child within psychology and within science as a whole, despite the fact that parapsychological research has been every bit as meticulous and rigorous as conventional science, and has produced and replicated highly significant results – again relying heavily on data from large numbers of subjects, or on large quantities of data from a few subjects. Psychology has not wanted to be tainted by the skepticism which is accorded to parapsychology and has generally distanced itself from psi research. In fact, some of the most trenchant critics of psi have been psychologists – often without any awareness of the impressive body of research on psi.

Sociology, investigating societal trends, has generally focused on large numbers of people with far less emphasis on the individual, and therefore finds it easier to be considered a science amongst the accepted sciences. Based largely in universities of Western, industrial society, sociology tended for many years to view traditional cultures as *primitive* – relative to the self-conferred assessment of superiority of its own Western culture. Spirituality, which is well established in traditional cultures, has been largely interpreted as magical beliefs which will, in the good course of time, give way to education in Western science. This is the *etic* view, assuming that Western science can provide 'objective' explanations for every phenomenon - within the frameworks of Western scientific paradigms. Even though greater respect is now given to traditional cultures as legitimate for their own people, most of Western sociology has been slow to acknowledge that traditional cultures might have great wisdom to offer to the West. This is the *emic* view, acknowledging that peoples from cultures other than our own, behaving in manners that are different from ours, usually have their own, entirely legitimate cultural explanations for their beliefs and behaviors.

Cultural anthropology has been a shade better than sociology, focusing often on individuals and examining the personal meanings of experiences within that culture. Anthropologists tend to be as limited, however, in perceiving possible relevance of such observations to spiritual experiences in Western society.

Thus, studies of spiritual experiences have tended to be step-grandchildren to all of these Western sciences. Spiritual experiences are viewed by many in the academic community as subjective, wishful thinking, denial of death fears, perhaps products of a drugged, diseased, or degenerating brain, or even delusional maunderings of misguided or deranged minds.[14]

Western science notwithstanding, spiritual experiences have been familiar to religious communities and individuals around the world, throughout recorded history. In monotheistic religions, there have been strong tendencies to view personal spiritual awakenings as the rare and exclusive experiences of saints (or their equivalents). Western religious teachings are given by clergy who are ordained after studying religious texts and the practice of prayer and rituals – not necessarily by people who are spiritually experienced or enlightened in a personal way. Flocks in such congregations rarely have immediate examples and little expectation of personal spiritual awakening. They may even be discouraged by their clergy from exploring personal spiritual paths that might deviate from doctrinal teachings. Such explorations may even be labeled heretical. Spontaneous encounters with angels or saints appearing in response to prayer, especially in times of crisis, may be acknowledged as spiritual interventions from on high, but are usually not seen as being invited by the people who have these experiences.

In polytheistic Eastern religions, particularly where meditation is part of spiritual practices, personal spiritual development is encouraged and nurtured. In these settings, spiritual awakenings are understood to be the results of the personal development of the individual. Spiritual experiences are accepted and validated within the cultural and religious norms of these societies.

Western society tends to be dichotomizing. We are *either* religious *or* secular; the world is *either* matter *or* energy; a theory is *either* right *or* wrong. Most European languages suffer the lack of a concept expressed clearly in Russian, where *da* is 'yes' and *nyet* is 'no' and a third possibility is *danyet* – where something is both a 'yes' and a 'no.' [15] Quantum physics has amply demonstrated that matter and energy are interconvertible. Whether an object is matter or energy depends on how we examine it. The same is true of matter and spirit. The world may be perceived and experienced as either – depending on how we address and relate to it.

In Western society, despite prevalent discouragements, most people who have personal spiritual experiences have no question about their validity. Their spiritual awakenings occur with a clarity, freshness, and intensity transcending awareness of ordinary life events. They know without question that these are not just stories they are making up to explain the mysteries of life: when they clearly sense the presence of someone dear to them after she[16] has passed on; when they encounter the Being of Light in a Near-Death Experience; when they sense a mystical awareness of their oneness with nature; or when an angel touches their life in a time of need. These spontaneous mystical experiences are also consistent with reports of meditators who have worked systematically for years to reach enlightenment. These potent inner experiences feel as real – sometimes even more real – than experiences in the everyday world perceived through our outer senses. They suggest that religious teachings may be based on realities which modern science has led us to discount or even to denigrate. Our acceptance of scientistic disparagements of spiritual experiences appears to be the result of our distancing ourselves from direct experiences of spirituality. We are led to believe that the way to study anything properly is to be *objective*, to not be personally involved in what we observe, lest we fool ourselves into believing something that is merely a product of our imagination. Many of us simply accept these societal opinions and don't take the time to explore spiritual dimensions ourselves.

> *The public buys its opinions as it buys its meat, or takes in its milk, on the principle that it is cheaper to do this than to keep a cow. So it is, but the milk is more likely to be watered.*
> – Samuel Butler

Those who have had spiritual experiences are transformed by them. Their clarity in describing their perceptions and in asserting the internal sense of their realness has invited a growing body of research on the phenomena covered in this book.

The studies reviewed in this book yield an impressively coherent picture of spiritual realms beyond our physical existence. This is all the more impressive as they include an enormous diversity of reports from researchers and mystics around the world and across many centuries.

Surprisingly, quantum physics, which one might expect to be amongst the most reductionistic of sciences – focusing as it does on identifying the smallest, most basic building blocks of the universe – suggests clear parallels and possibly con-firmations of observations of mystics and healers. It may even suggest mechanisms to explain aspects of psychic and spiritual experiences. Chapter III-10 reviews this subject.

I feel that one cannot but conclude that there is an underlying objective spiritual reality that is being experienced, reported and studied in these diverse fields.

Volume IV, *Theories and Practices of Spiritual Healing,* is a topical summary of the earlier volumes in this series, providing a broad overview and discussion of spiritual healing. It also presents my personal experiences as a medical doctor specializing in psychiatric psychotherapy and how I came to develop my own healing gifts. How I integrate spiritual healing in my clinical practice is discussed in Volume I-1.

My personal spiritual experience and views

It is essential to have some understanding of an author's background and opinions when one is considering his views on a subject such as spirituality – to know something about the life experiences that polished and others that tinted or scratched the lenses through which the author perceives the world. Let me there-fore share some of the unfoldings in my life which shape my current ideas on spirituality and spiritual healing.

When I ask people outside my circle of healing acquaintances about spirituality, I often draw a shrug. Most have little to do with this aspect of life. They may think of it in religious celebrations or be touched by it when they or someone close to them has a difficult time, or an unusual, fortunate experience, as they say to themselves, "Oh, God!" "Please, God!" or "Thank you God!" They might be uplifted by a sunset, an artistic creation, or an act of kindness – and feel glad to be alive. They might see or hear of a tragedy in the media and say, "There, but for the grace of God go I." For the most part, however, their spirituality is confined to their house of worship, and many complain that in this context, their spiritual-ity (such as it is) is not particularly nurturing, moving or in other ways satisfying. They find more of rigid ritual and restriction within their religion than upliftment and enhancement.

This was my own experience for the most part with my upbringing and affilia-tion in Jewish traditions. I was raised in a non-observant Jewish home, with religion experienced as a strong cultural and historical tradition rather than a spiritual influence. My parents preferred to observe the 'Thou shalts' of Judaism and to ignore most of the 'Thou shalt nots' of Jewish tradition. This was rein-forced by living in the secular sector of Israel for four years as a child and for six years as a husband, parent and counselor in various school psychology programs. For most Israelis the Bible is just their local history book. It is marvelously grounding, however, to live in a land in which one's people put down historical roots over many centuries. Though I attended a Jewish elementary day school in

New York through the eighth grade, I found little of the Spiritual in my childhood experiences in Judaism.

I have found the more Orthodox end of the Jewish spectrum concerned with rigidly preserving rituals and exclusivity of practices, and the more reform end of the spectrum too dilute for my tastes. I resonated more with the middle ground of Conservative and especially the Reconstructionist branches of Judaism, adapting traditional practices to modern life – but I still did not find within these anything like an enduring uplifting essence. The Hassidic branch offered marvelous access to limited aspects of spiritual awareness, particularly through the study of Kabbalah in Hebrew, but was again bounded by Orthodox Jewish beliefs and practices. All seemed to emphasize the social support and the preservation of the ancient traditions over the development of personal spirituality. I have felt far more of my personal connection with spirituality through being in nature, through practices of meditation, and through involvement with spiritual healing.

> *Religion asks you to learn from the experience of others.*
> *Spirituality urges you to seek your own.*
> – Neale Donald Walsch [17]

I gradually came to see that much of Western society's distancing from spirituality results from its focus on materialism and its emphasis on analytical explanations for Creation. We have lost much of our sense of immediate connection with the world around us. We have focused on building physical and social edifices to protect us against the unpredictable dangers of life and to provide food, education, medical and other services in the most cost-effective fashion. We have succeeded exceptionally well in the material sense. In other ways we succeeded too well for our own good. By placing many of the functions of life in the hands of specialists we have removed ourselves by many steps and stages from direct contact with the earth and sun, the winds and the rain – which are the sources of that which sustains us physically and stimulates and nurtures us spiritually. The very same efficiency which we hone to ever finer sharpness and consider the hallmark of our industrial society cuts out direct individual involvement with nature and to a large extent dehumanizes us.

Most of us distance ourselves from the natural processes of birth, illness and death. We relegate to specialists in hospitals, hospices and mortuaries the care of ourselves and our dear ones on entering and leaving the world of physical existence. We move to new homes with a frequency that leaves no time for our physical, social and energetic roots to plant themselves very deeply. Our relationships with extended family, friends, teachers, doctors, counselors and priests do not have the rootedness that comes with years shared in each others' company. We do not have long-standing neighbors who come to our rescue when we are disabled or distressed, nor are we there for them when they are in need. We may not have experienced a long-term relationship with a religious teacher, who would get to know us well enough to touch our soul and waken our spirit. Yet we relegate to this somewhat impersonal clergy the management of our spiritual selves, assuming they are experts – shepherds in this field, while we are meant to be their flocks. The clergy, inflated with their roles of leadership, and motivated (probably more unconsciously than deliberately) not only by spirituality but also by needs to survive in the material world, inculcate fears of the apostate, the infidel and the devil – which serve as fences to keep their flocks within the folds that they claim the expertise to define. Little wonder that individual spirituality is largely discouraged in such frameworks, as this might turn sheep into beings who think for themselves and no longer blindly follow spiritual shepherds.[18]

Little wonder that charismatic churches are growing. They provide sanctioned personal experiences of spirituality though these are still within a church setting. Sadly, however, they also discourage many parts of the spectrum of spiritual experience, such as *new age* thinking, or explorations outside their particular church beliefs and practices. Individualized spiritual experiences are discouraged.[19]

There are enormous losses in this divisiveness and antagonism engendered by the beliefs that a given religion holds THE valid and exclusive truth offers the only legitimate doorways into spirituality, revealed and explained by selected individuals and their interpreters – often in the dim mists of many centuries past.

Joseph Campbell,[20] a wonderfully wise sociologist, pointed out that monotheism has several distinct down-sides. Belief in a single, transcendent God biases us to an exclusivity of beliefs. Monotheism proposes that the God of the Jews, Christians, Muslims, or of others is THE only true god. All other gods are false. Monotheism thus pits one religion against another. Furthermore, if one finds it difficult to believe in the one God, then there is no other.

The belief in the transcendence of a one and only God has also distanced us from the immanent perception of God within us and in everything around us. This is reinforced by the power structures of the clergy, as mentioned above. Fortunately, in some churches there is a growing awareness of the Christ within; of the Native American (and other traditional views) of the Oneness of all creation.

> *All my relations.*
> – Native American invocation [21]

During my university and medical school years I became a Freudian agnostic, believing God was a father substitute, a creation of reluctance to give up childhood dependencies. This was confirmed by many experiences during my training and practice of psychiatry. I was impressed with how people defend against being aware of their hurts and fears through complex and elaborate mental and emotional avoidance mechanisms. I could readily support my arguments that God was an imaginary parent figure in a fantasy heaven, with these constructs helping people avoid facing their fears of the inevitability and absolute finality of death.

I also had difficulties understanding how a God, if he existed, could allow a Holocaust and other instances of genocide and natural disasters to happen. Why would God create human beings just to be slaughtered in such enormous numbers under the leadership of cruel dictators or by forces of nature – that He had also created? It was beyond any logical sense I could muster.

In these and many further ways, our spirituality withers from lack of first-hand familiarity and attention given to it. Sir Laurens van der Post states this well.

...for hundreds of years now all understanding of the spirit has been narrowed and restricted to what can be rationally expressed about 'the spirit.' The spirit is no longer seen as a gift that we hold in trust from life but as something that is narrowed to a conscious, willful, rational egoism. The spirit is not only reason – although it includes reason; it is not only feeling – and of course it includes feeling as well: but it is for me, above all, intuition, which is a profound compass, bearing on our origin and our destination. And this is ultimately what religion is about: 'origin and destination.' The result has been that the spirit has lost, for the moment, what made it one of the greatest of all human passions. So it has abandoned the human being in his narrowed, rational state, indulging the greatest pastime and specialty of our time, which is finding first-rate reasons for doing partial and wrong things.[22]

Figure III-3. What's what

My early personal awakening to spirituality developed through a gradual series of experiences. These included hatha yoga and meditation; undergoing psychotherapy with a variety of therapists over three decades; receiving healing and psychic readings; reading omnivorously – including many of the studies and observations I review in this book; being a psychotherapist, healer, lecturer and workshop leader; learning from clients, who synchronistically often teach me as much as I teach them; learning from people who are more spiritually awakened and intuitively gifted than myself; and studying and participating in healing research. All of these have led me to my current beliefs in spirituality, beliefs which are clear enough and strong enough that I feel confident in sharing them with others – not only in this book but in experiential workshops which I lead on developing creativity, intuitive and spiritual awareness, and healing gifts.

When I discuss spirituality, I most often end up in tangles of words and ideas *about it*. Our society distrusts intuitive knowing which recognizes the inner essence of spirituality from *experiencing it*. We prefer to study, define and have spirituality boxed into neat words and concepts, predictable and safe along with the rest of our ordered lives that are focused primarily on the material world.

Spirituality is the sense of being a part of something greater than the physical world, something transcending everyday reality. The fact that such awarenesses, as feelings and intuitions, are universally found throughout the world in every known culture does not sway the scientists, who demand research evidence to convince them that what is perceived is 'objective reality' and not fantasy, wishful thinking, mistaken observation, or delusional projections of deranged minds.

In our search for objective, verifiable assessments of personal spirituality we face challenging series of barriers. Investigations of spiritual domains rely on experiential reports sifted through religious and philosophical beliefs – brought back from realms where subjective reports provide the data, to realms where reasoned logic is always based on selected premises. We can listen to the experiences and ideas of various authorities but these do not give us a real taste of the spiritual. For more immediate appreciation of spirituality we must seek such experiences ourselves. Those who attain them report that these encounters are beyond human abilities to describe in everyday, linear language. Poetic and artistic renderings of these experiences begin to give small hints of their flavor, but the spiritual remains beyond full and accurate explication through any means we currently have to communicate – whether based on outer senses or on reason. I will use the term *to gnow* for these immediate, inner awarenesses of the spiritual.[23]

Spiritual healing is one of the avenues that opens us directly to experience our spirituality. Although healing is often sought primarily for physical or emotional problems, healers and healees find that the healing process naturally opens into spiritual awarenesses, immediate and personal gnowings[24] of being a part of the All. In fact, many healers believe that the spiritual aspects of healing are the most important part of what they offer. They suggest that spirituality is the essence of our lives and that illness is often a wake-up call to reconnect with it.

This volume considers claims of spiritual healers, mystics, philosophers, and others who report personal spiritual experiences. These suggest a spirit and soul survive the death of our physical bodies. The spirit is said to be the energy body which may detach from the physical body sometimes during life[25] and always after physical death. The soul is said to retain memory into eternity from the lessons of a person's life on earth.[26] Some religions and reports of many personal experiences suggest that aspects of the soul are reincarnated in a series of lives until it learns sufficient wisdom to move on to more refined levels of existence, beyond the physical world, where further lessons proceed. Such awarenesses have been reported throughout recorded history.

> *I shall not altogether die.*
> – Horace

My basic assumption is that we all have thinking, logical, linear ways of knowing about the world as well as intuitive, gestaltic, heart-based ways of gnowing the world through immediate perceptions and interactions with the world. Much has been written about right and left brain modes of relating to the world, and the wisdom of the heart.[27]

The research in this book

Having studied psychology, medicine, psychiatry, and research methodology, I have been cautious in accepting reports of spiritual experiences. Two sorts of evidence will be considered in this volume: anecdotal reports and scientific studies.

Individual, anecdotal reports of spiritual experiences provide qualitative information. They may move us to resonate with their beauty, intensity and subjective meaningfulness. They may point us towards practices to aid us in having similar experiences. The danger in these explanations of reality is that *they may lead us to accept as true something which is false*, something built more on the personal beliefs, fantasies and wishes of the reporter than on any objective reality.

Scientific method requires that theories should be stated and tested for their validity through a series of ordered examinations of the subject studied. The more rigorously the scrutinized variables are defined and the more meticulously hypotheses are built up and tested, the more credence is given to observations which support the hypothesis. A danger with this approach, however, is that *we might reject as false something which is true*. The very rigor of our experimental design may distort or rule out that which we are seeking to understand.

> *Initial analyses of the wingspans and muscles of bees demonstrated*
> *conclusively that bees simply cannot fly* [28]
> – DB [29]

We like to believe that science has brought us to understand our world and will ultimately completely explain all of reality. This is far from the case. One would be most unlikely to predict a snowflake from the study of water molecules, much less the myriads of forms of individual snowflakes. Even when we find scientific orderliness in the world, as in the laws of falling bodies and the motion of planets, which we label as the effects of *the force of gravity*, we have not begun to reach any true understandings of the mechanisms behind this universal force. What then, when we assay to examine our inner worlds? Most of us can attest to the existence of love. How can we measure and prove its existence? Are we to say that because it is beyond objective measures it does not exist?

Another advantage with research approaches is that they can produce results which may be quantified and analyzed statistically. We want to ascertain whether the results we got might simply have occurred by chance, in which case we assume our hypothesis is not supported by the study, or whether the results are significant and suggest that our hypothesis is correct. For instance, if we flip a coin (assuming it is symmetrically shaped and evenly weighted) we expect it to land half of the time on heads and half of the time on tails. In a series of tosses, if there occur sequences of many heads or tails in a row, it might be that the coin is unbalanced, or it might be that we simply have observed a rare but entirely chance event. Statistical analyses give us an estimate of how often the results gleaned from methodical studies such as 1,000 flips of a coin, are likely to occur by chance.

It is common knowledge that there is an equal probability that a head or a tail will face upward. How many times would a tail have to face upward before we could say that it is highly unlikely the coin is evenly balanced? Statistics would tell us how likely or unlikely it is that any series of head or tails has occurred. There will always be the possibility that a long series could occur by chance, but statistics will tell us whether this could be once in a hundred or once in a billion tosses.

Quantitative studies help us see correlations between religious affiliations and practices and health;[30] the percents of bereaved people who sense the presence of a departed person who was close to them[31] and correlations between events on earth and the positions of stars and planets in the heavens, relative to Earth.[32]

Numbers may provide some degree of assurance that we know what we are studying, but numbers do not describe fully or adequately the *qualities* of the objects they describe. Knowing that healers can ease or cure a given symptom or disease does not tell us why healing works for problems of various physical and emotional causes in some but not in all people. We need descriptions of subjective experiences of healers and healees to flesh out the bones which are weighed and measured, and to counterbalance and clarify the meanings of the resultant numbers that are statistically analyzed.

> *What if this new method were all wrong for the phenomenon – like trying to examine a snowflake on a hot stove? What if it promised only misunderstanding rather than understanding? What if the very point of an anomalous event were lost when it was not seen from the perspective of the experiencer, as an episode in his own life story? What if we had to develop a talent for listening to these experiences speak to us in their unique terms, rather than trying to fit them into narrow artificial boxes of cookie-cutter categories, our prefabricated concepts, and our controlled experiments?*
> – Joseph M. Felser [33]

In this volume we will examine anecdotal, qualitative and research evidence to make our way between the types of potential errors described above. We will review research on subjective reports suggesting that people may exist outside of their bodies for periods of time while their bodies are still alive. We will consider the existence of apparitions (spirits or ghosts) from reports of observers and from mediums. A surprising body of research evidence is available on reincarnation.

Angels and nature spirits have been described for thousands of years. While there is no scientific research of these entities, Chapter 4 explores numbers of reports that range from 'somewhat suggestive of credibility' to 'difficult to explain without resort to outside agencies'.

Personal spirituality

People who have had spiritual experiences may wish to know whether others have had similar experiences. If this is the case, it could validate what may appear strange when one first encounters the odd individual reports of mystical worlds. This book will suggest a variety of answers to such questions.

There may be readers who have never had a spiritual experience and may wish to know whether any credence can be given to such reports from other people who are unknown to them and whose word they may not feel they can trust. A thorough survey of the evidence is a vital first step in considering whether exploration of personal spirituality might be a valid and worthwhile endeavor. This will not be as convincing, however, as experiential explorations of these areas. In the many workshops I have led, it is consistently the *personal experiences* which are the most convincing that there are worlds of subtle energies and spiritual awarenesses, which we may know directly and can gradually learn to believe and to trust. Both the search for and the achievement of spiritual awarenesses are among the most rewarding experiences possible in life.

> *I have no doubt whatever that most people live whether physically, intellectually, or morally, in a very restricted circle of their potential being. They make use of a very small portion of their possible consciousness... Much like a man who, out of his whole bodily organism should get into a habit of using and moving only his little finger... We all have reservoirs of life to draw upon, of which we do not dream!*
>
> – William James

I should clarify that I am not advocating that we abandon analytical thinking in exploring personal spirituality. As we experientially investigate meditation, intuition, bioenergies, and other spiritual experiences it is important to keep a firm hold on our critical thinking. There are pitfalls, roadblocks and blind alleys of ego, emotional scars, beliefs and fears that could distort our perceptions and our interpretations of personal spiritual experiences. It is a challenge to develop and harmonize both spiritual and everyday world senses, to hold the delicate balance between gnowing and knowing. This book, along with Volumes I and II of *Healing Research*, can help you to find the balance that works for you.

Because spiritual awareness is an immediate experience, all of the research and discussions *about* spirituality are several steps removed from the personal experience of spirituality. To balance the analytical discussions, numerous heartwarming and humorous quotes, poetry and cartoons illustrate and counterpoint the text.[34]

In the near future, a workbook will be published to support individual explorations of personal spirituality. There are numerous approaches that can help us validate to ourselves that our intuitive awarenesses of the infinite All are not just products of our imagination.

This book is written not only as a theoretical discussion, nor just as a personal introduction to spirituality. It is an urgent call to awakening our awareness of our intimate interconnection with the world around us. We are a vital, essential part of the creation of our current planetary conditions – which threaten the continued existence of life as we know it on our planet.

Let us start with a relatively common experience leading to awareness of non-physical dimensions, the Out-of-Body Experience.

CHAPTER 1

Out-of-Body Experiences (OBE)

I am so afraid of error that I keep hurling myself
into the arms of doubt rather than into the arms of truth.
– Petrarch

Mystics and psychics through the ages have referred to an etheric or astral body. This energy body overlaps the physical body most of the time and extends in several layers outside the body. It may be detached to travel to distant places, especially during sleep. There may be several such bodies, each relating to its particular dimension of reality. This might also be the vehicle we inhabit after death as the spirit and soul survive physical existence.

  Knowledge about out-of-body travel goes back many centuries

> *Remember him – before the silver cord is severed, or the golden bowl is broken; before the pitcher is shattered at the spring, or the wheel broken at the well, and the dust returns to the ground it came from, and the spirit returns to God who gave it.*
> *– Ecclesiastes* [35]

Ordinary people have been reporting for centuries that occasionally they are conscious of themselves *outside their physical bodies*. An Out-of-Body Experience (OBE) often occurs spontaneously during states of sleep (natural or due to anesthesia) or in crisis or trauma situations. People typically feel themselves floating in the air above or standing by their beds. They might initially think that they are dreaming until they observe their physical bodies, still in bed, peacefully asleep. They might experience themselves as having ghost-like astral bodies or might feel themselves to be a ball of light or a totally disembodied point of consciousness. Commonly, they see a silvery cord connecting their astral head to their physical head, or astral to physical solar-plexus. While traveling out of body, many people perceive this etheric silver cord stretching and continuing to connect them to their physical body. It is said that people will always find their way back to their physical body as long as the silver cord remains intact. If they are in an astral body, they might choose to locomote with arms and legs, moving very much as they would in a physical body but passing *through* material objects like doors and walls. Alternatively, they might think of going to a certain place and discover that the mere thought results in their rapidly being transported through space to the desired location or instantaneously appearing there. While in an OBE they may observe events (even in distant locations) which they can later verify. Occasionally, they may be able to move objects at the distant location. Then, either with the thought that they are uncomfortable outside their bodies or without their volitional intent, they find themselves suddenly back in their physical bodies.[36]

Several Out-of-Body Experience reports include meetings with spirit entities while in the OBE state. Robert Monroe reports that some of the entities he encountered were wise beings who seemed to have only good intentions and were helpful. Some seemed neutral. Others felt negative, frightening and even menacing or dangerous. The various types of entities appeared to inhabit different levels or dimensions of being. Monroe developed very detailed descriptions of specific levels or dimensions that one can visit in OBE and the Monroe Institute continues his work, offering training in developing OBE abilities and in visiting these realms. Shafica Karagulla reports that some OBEers meet other OBEers for activities such as classroom-like spiritual learning in the OBE state. Students of the Spiritual often report meeting their spiritual Masters in an OBE state. Such encounters may occur sometimes well before they meet their Master in the flesh and also while they are engaged in the student/Master relationship. Healers may sometimes experience OBEs during healings.[37] Psychics and healers report that they sometimes find themselves in OBE states, ministering to spirits of people who have just died, helping them to adjust to being in new dimensions, and aiding these spirits in finding their ways into the helping hands of spirits who come to minister to them. They call this *rescue work*.[38]

Anecdotal evidence for OBEs

The OBE has been reported anecdotally over many centuries. The OBE was described by the ancient Egyptians, both as a subtle body during life and as a spirit surviving death.[39] Shamans and esoteric Masters in traditional societies[40] and luminaries in Western societies have been reported to travel by OBE to distant locations and to bring back observations which were later verified. For this reason the OBE is sometimes called *traveling clairvoyance*. Saints and Hassidic rabbis have been reported to appear in locations distant from where they were physically present. This has sometimes been labeled *bi-location*.[41]

The OBE is a relatively common experience. OBE reports have been found in 17 to 27% of populations surveyed in several countries.[42] OBEs commonly occur also in death-threatening situations like actual or near-accidents, surgery or other instances of danger or distress. For instance, patients undergoing surgery have observed activities in the operating room, where their physical bodies were being surgically treated under anesthesia. Doctors and nurses were later able to verify their observations, down to the minutest details. (This has sometimes been very embarrassing for doctors or other members of a surgical team!) Some of the details were definitely outside the potential field of vision of patients' physical eyes.

There are many reports of OBEs occurring during crises, particularly with physical trauma.

Case: Lora was driving home during rush hour traffic. A car came through a red light and hit her broadside. Her head was slammed against the side window and she immediately lost consciousness. She found herself floating above the scene of the accident, watching as people removed her from the car and laid her on the sidewalk. She observed the ambulance crew bandaging her bleeding head, and heard one of them mutter, "I've never seen someone hit this bad who survived yet!" The next thing she knew, she was back in her body in the ambulance, feeling the worst headache she had ever experienced. She asked the ambulance attendant if he really thought she wouldn't make it because her baby son and husband really needed her. The ambulance attendant was surprised and perturbed, because he couldn't believe she had heard him make his dire prediction.

Supporting the possibility that the OBE is more than a dream or imaginary experience are reports of OBEs from the blind. Kenneth Ring and Sharon Cooper interviewed four people who were blind from birth, two who were blind from below the age of five (so that their memories of visual perceptions are nil), and another four who were severely visually impaired (could not see forms clearly) – all of whom reported OBEs. During their OBEs they were able to see immediately and to make sense of what they saw. They reported seeing objects in their environment and could identify colors that they had not seen before.[43] This is highly unusual, not only for the fact of their being able to perceive visual images but also for their being able to make sense of what they are seeing. People who have been blind from an early age due to defects in their corneas or lenses, which were later corrected, have had great difficulty learning to make sense of the visual stimuli to their eyes, and in many cases found this impossible to do.

One can also learn to have OBEs by choice, although this is often as an invitation to let it happen (which is not always successful) rather than the implementation of a decision to leave one's body.[44]

Laboratory studies of the OBE

In France in 1908, H. Durvill explored whether a person could make his presence felt during an OBE by touching an observer in an adjacent room. Observers reported being touched at the times of the OBE. They also noted that the room appeared to grow markedly colder around the time they felt the touch. This is an unusual report, as most people experiencing OBEs under spontaneous or experimental conditions state that it is impossible to interact with physical matter while in an OBE.

In the 1980's, at the Stanford Research Institute in California, subjects gifted with OBE ability were challenged to project their consciousness to locations selected at random from a pre-designated pool of possibilities.[45] Observers on the research staff left the lab as the subjects arrived, physically visited these locations, recorded what they saw. Later, the researchers compared notes from the outside observers with OBE subjects' reports from the lab. In repeated experiments, independent judges were able to correlate reports of OBEers and observers on a double-blind basis with a very high degree of accuracy. In several cases the OBEer was able to see objects that were not visible to the physical observers, such as trees behind a house.

Similar studies were reported by Robert Jahn, Emeritus Dean at the Princeton School of Engineering, with Brenda Dunn.[46] Their conceptual model is of clairvoyance, which they term *remote viewing*. In some studies, subjects described the target locations *prior to the outward bound experimenter's arrival at those locations*. That is, the subjects were precognitive as well as clairvoyant. Jahn and Dunn's studies had highly significant statistical results.

Karlis Osis performed a series of experiments in New York with people claiming voluntary control over OBE travel.[47] He explored first whether they could perceive objects in a specific laboratory room, unfamiliar to them, at a distance of miles from their homes – where their corporal bodies were resting while they were in the OBE. Objects were set up on a partitioned table. A person standing on one side of the lab could see only part of the objects on that side of a partition. Osis wanted to see if OBEers were perceiving from the same perspectives as would a person standing in the room. He postulated that the OBEers could be picking up the information clairvoyantly and interpreting it as information obtained via an OBE, in which case they ought sometimes to report information impossible to observe from a single physical location in the laboratory.

A few of his more talented subjects described objects in terms of shapes and colors but the objects were sometimes difficult to identify specifically from the descriptions. One reported what appeared to be a view from the ceiling, right above the table. From this vantage point it was possible to see all four portions of the table divided by a double partition in the form of an X. Results were not consistently positive. Furthermore, OBEers would often pick up information extraneous to the designated targets, such as descriptions of people in the room.[48]

Osis then devised a special viewing box to differentiate between the possibility of clairvoyance and actual OBE. A series of prisms unified three separate images when a viewer peered through a peephole. A form, color and quadrant of a circle, in which the form and color appeared, could be viewed individually by clairvoyance or as a combined unit if one were perceiving it through the peephole. If the OBEers could travel to the experimental room and look through the hole, they would see a single image of a certain color in a particular quadrant. If they obtained the information clairvoyantly, they would have totally different information. Data were obtained again suggesting that the perception of the

OBEer was sometimes that of the view through the peephole. However, the results were not consistent.

In further experiments, Osis challenged psi-sensitive observers who were in the lab to see or sense the presence of the OBEers when they were visiting the room in the OBE state. Perceptions of the OBEer were sometimes noted merely as a 'feeling that someone is present in the room.' Occasionally, sensitives in the lab would glimpse 'something' out of the corner of their eye. An identifiable image of the OBEer was sometimes seen. The timings of the perceptions in the lab were highly correlated with the timings of the OBEs reported by the subject.

Further work seems warranted to clarify whether there is overlap in OBE reports between visualization/psi and OBE experiences. For instance, Sheryl Wilson and Theodore Barber describe people who are very vivid visualizers and often gifted with psi abilities.[49] It might be that some OBE reports are derived from clairsentient perceptions in persons who visualize them so vividly that they feel they are actually at the site they perceive through extra-sensory perception (ESP).

John Hartwell et al. monitored the physical body of OBEers for physiological changes when the OBEers were 'out' at distant locations. He found significant decreases in skin potential and increases in pulse and respiration, while electromyogram (EMG, measuring muscle tension), electroencephalogram (EEG) and electro-oculogram (EOG, used to identify eye movements during dream states) showed no significant changes.

Tart found that OBE brain wave patterns on EEGs were distinctly different in certain respects from dream patterns. In one subject, the OBE state produced "a non-dreaming, non-awake brain wave stage characterized by predominant slowed alpha activity from her brain and no activation of the autonomic nervous system."[50] In a second subject he reports, "OBEs seem to occur in conjunction with a prolonged, deliberately produced hypnogogic state (Stage 1 EEG). Such prolonged states are not normally seen in the laboratory." [51] Systolic blood pressure dropped roughly during the time that the OBE occurred.[52]

In contrast with Tart's findings, John Palmer[53] found theta waves during OBEs. These are much slower waves than those reported by Tart.

A last series of studies is in a different category. The US military studied *remote viewing*, in which a support person sits by the subject and guides him in his psychic explorations of distant locations. This was explored as a spying technique for a while but reportedly was abandoned for reasons that are not clear.[54] This appears to be more in the realms of clairsentience though some of the subjective reports of the remote viewers look a lot like the reports from OBE reports.[55]

Carlos Alvarado[56] cautions that while some studies of OBEs focused on gifted subjects,[57] in other studies unselected subjects were used.[58]

Is the OBE an aberration of mental functions?

OBEs could represent aberrations of brain or mind function such as delusions or hallucinations. These could be caused by organic brain disease as in a fever, in toxic or in other stress states. John Todd and Kenneth Dewhurst[59] briefly review the OBE literature and consider a range of more conventional explanations for the OBE. They explore in psychodynamic terms the roles of narcissism, super-normal powers of visualization, archetypal thinking and brain disorders with autoscopic (seeing a double of one's self) phenomena. In all subjects having such conditions, their awareness was of being in their physical body, viewing a 'double' apparently projected outside themselves. Most of the described cases occurred during waking or epileptic states. This is in direct contrast with reports of OBEers that they view themselves as being outside their bodies, most frequently during sleep.

N. Lukianowicz reviewed 101 references on these subjects. He found cases in which mentally disturbed patients with depression or schizophrenia and/or epileptics saw images that were duplicates of themselves. He briefly compares and contrasts these with cases of traveling clairvoyance and other instances in which a person might see a 'double' of herself. These others include:

1. *Imaginary companions*;
2. *Eidetic images*, or extremely realistic images that are clearly understood to be imaginary;
3. *Self-images*, which occur commonly in drowsy states;
4. *Hypnogogic imagery*, which is a vivid, dream-like state preceding sleep;
5. *Sleep hallucinosis*, or extremely vivid dreams; and
6. *Other states*, such as phantom limb phenomena, in which only parts of the body which were accidentally or surgically removed are perceived as duplicated.

Self-images (3) sound like brief dream images, or perhaps glimpses of an OBE image seen from the physical body. The various other states are clearly distinct from the OBE in several regards. Some involve ritualized, involuntary actions of the double. Others are total dream states, which appear as real experiences at the time but do not correspond with external reality and are perceived on awakening to have been imaginary. In autoscopic phenomena, which typify mental or brain disorders, he also found that the subjects usually do not find their consciousness in the projected body but rather view the double from their physical body.

These surveys point to distinct differences between the typical OBE report and products of emotional problems, electrophysiological brain disorders, sleep or dream states, and intense visualization experiences. They contradict the suggestion that the OBE represents a hallucination caused by organic brain disorders or emotional problems. Supporting this view is a survey by Jones and Twemlow, who found that people reporting OBEs were not different from people who did not experience them.

Is the OBE a state of mind?

Charles Tart[60] suggests a series of hypotheses which could explain OBEs:

1. *Mental aberration* – No evidence supports this hypothesis. The vast majority of those reporting OBEs are without remarkable psychopathology.

2. *The OBE is a dream* – Those who experience OBEs report their state of awareness in an OBE is like ordinary consciousness, with full reasoning abilities. This is distinctly different from dreams. Several investigators[61] found that during the OBE, EEG brain wave patterns were distinctly different in certain respects from dream patterns.

3. *The OBE is a special dream state, perhaps a lucid dream* – In lucid dreams people feel they are in their ordinary states of awareness though they are aware that they are dreaming. During lucid dreams it is possible to alter the events of the dream and create new ones.[62] In OBEs one finds oneself in situations where one cannot alter the conditions merely by wishing them to change.

4. *The OBE is a subjective state* – This may be accurate for some OBEs. However, in OBEs one may perceive actual situations as they exist at distant locations, which implies that they are more than subjective states of awareness.

5. *The mind is actually able to move outside the physical body* – This is supported by observations by people during OBEs, about physical conditions and events at locations distant from their bodies and subsequently confirmed during their waking state. There may be some distortions of their observations or observations that do not match with physical reality.

6. *The OBE is purely a coincidence of mental processes which happen to correlate with outside events* – Though this may be true in some instances, the correlations between OBE perceptions and the real world are sometimes so striking as to make this hypothesis unlikely. Tart notes such an example from a research study[63] in which a subject identified a five digit number correctly while in an OBE state.

7. *The OBE is an elaboration to present psi perceptions in a way which is more comfortable to the subject* – People might perceive information telepathically, clairsentiently, or precognitively without actually traveling outside their bodies.

8. *The OBE may include perceptions of physical reality and non-physical reality simultaneously* – Tart gives the example of a person traveling in OBE state to visit an acquaintance. He observed him in a particular place and conversed with him. The acquaintance later verified he had been in that particular location but he had no recall of having seen or spoken with the person who had the OBE.
   Another example is when a person in OBE state visits a location that is distinctly different from the ordinary world in which he lives, finds that this place has stable characteristics, and might return to visit there repeatedly on different occasions.

9. *There might be* "at least one world that is objectively real in its own right, that appears physical in some ways but is accessible only by OBE..." or "worlds that are 'nonphysical,' whatever that means, but that objectively exist and are accessible by OBE..." This hypothesis is suggested by the second example in (8).

Discussion

What can we say we know about the OBE?

We know it is relatively common in many cultures around the world. It can be consciously controlled by only a few gifted individuals. Shamans often claim to be able to exercise this ability at will. In most Western cases it is an unwilled, spontaneous occurrence, generally taking place during sleep, anesthesia or life-threatening situations. It can also be experimentally induced by techniques that bring about alternative states of consciousness. The OBEer can often bring back objectively verifiable information relating to the places 'visited'.

The fact that the blind may experience OBEs in which they see and comprehend what they are seeing suggests that these are not dream experiences, as the dreams of blind people mirror their usual daily experiences and perceptions. They dream of auditory, tactile and emotional experiences.[64]

One could postulate, as in Tart (7), that the OBE is merely a special case of psychic perceptions, in which the OBEers elaborate a visualization of themselves at the selected site. This makes sense from a psychological standpoint. The information which people obtain via psi channels appears to enter and/or is processed in the unconscious portions of the mind. As the information works its way into consciousness, it might be translated into images from the distant location, *including the subject in the picture*. This would be a mechanism that could remove, or at least reduce, anxiety associated with concerns about psi information.

Problems arise with the simple 'traveling clairvoyance' explanation when we must include independent observers sensing the presence of the OBEers at the distant location. One could again propose that the mechanisms of psi are applicable. Observers could be telepathically or clairsentiently perceiving the alleged OBEers. The observers could construct images of the OBEers via similar mechanisms of interpretation of psi perceptions from unconscious levels of the mind in order to translate less familiar into more familiar and therefore, less threatening constructs. This would also allow us to reject the somewhat alien, hard-to-digest concept of a separate, *astral* body that can travel to a distant location.

Several rare OBE-related occurrences would yet remain to tease us. OBEers are on rare occasions able to move objects at distant locations. One could still avoid the astral body explanation by invoking the hypothesis that PK is being employed in addition to clairvoyance and/or telepathy.

A single case is reviewed by D. Scott Rogo,[65] in which the astral son of an experimental OBEer was observed at the distant target location where his astral parent was also observed. The son had not been invited to participate but was aware of the experiment. Again, one could invoke the classical, basic mechanisms of telepathy and/or clairvoyance, saying that the observers connected via ESP with the OBEer, and either from her or from her son picked up the image of her son and projected it as though seen at the distant location. This stretches these psi explanations considerably, although it is conceivable.

Hart and Hart, who were investigating reports of apparitions (ghosts), found several cases of OBEs of living people, where several observers simultaneously saw the person in their OBE state.

The remote viewing experiments of Jahn and Dunne produced highly significant effects, when the subject described the distant location *prior to the arrival of the experimenter at that location*. This lends support to the psi explanation for OBE perceptions. It need not, however, rule out the OBE. It may be that in the OBE dimension *time* is not experienced in the linear fashion we are used to when we are in our bodies. The well-supported studies of pre- and retro-cognition in parapsychology confirm that perceptions transcending present time are possible and can be verified.[66] Experiments and theories of quantum physics also confirm that interactions across space and time are possible.[67]

While it is not necessarily true that the most economical explanation for a set of phenomena is the correct one, this principle would clearly simplify our explanations of the OBE. This would lead us to propose either that:

1. Human beings have an astral body which can separate from the physical body in certain circumstances; or

2. Consciousness may separate from the body – and subjects then fantasize themselves in a body because this is their usual experience of existence. The perceived OBE may represent one's mental self-construct in other dimensions of reality.

The OBE hypothesis would also be consistent with aura phenomena and Kirlian photography[68] – wherein apparent energy bodies or biological energies are perceived extending beyond the physical body. It may be this extended energy body that can be detached to travel to distant locations.

An obvious question arises when explanations for all of these observations are attempted under the psi hypothesis alone. It is unclear why OBE projections generally appear either as identical to the physical body in shape and size or smaller and not at all in the form of a body. This may mean that the OBE is a separate phenomenon and not a case of psi perceptions. Several psychic sensitives assert this is the case.

Further searches for altered physiological findings, guided by clairsentients, appear warranted. For instance, investigations of clairsentients may clarify whether the OBE involves detachment of the biological energy field, or aura, from the physical body during the OBE.

Spiritual healing and the OBE

The OBE parallels diverse observations of healers. A number of healers report they find themselves occasionally out-of-body when making diagnoses and/or healing. Healees sometimes report that they see the healer in a spirit body near them during distant healings. Again, these may be no more than the mind's way of interpreting to consciousness some of the spiritual healing experiences or these may represent an actual phenomenon of a spirit body being at a distant location.

The separation of an astral body from the physical body perceived at the time of death seems to lend further support to belief in the existence of an energy body which can travel about separately from the physical body – though this may differ substantially from OBE experiences during life.

> *I am not I.*
> *I am this one*
> *Walking beside me whom I do not see,*
> *Whom at times I manage to visit,*
> *And whom at other times I forget;*
> *Who remains calm and silent while I talk,*
> *And forgives, gently, when I hate,*
> *Who walks where I am not,*
> *Who will remain standing when I die.*
>
> – Juan Ramon Jimenez

Psi research supports reports that people may know information at a distance without inputs from their physical senses, and healers often diagnose conditions clairsentiently from any distance. Shamans regularly report they travel to other worlds to obtain information and inspiration for guidance and healings. OBEs may thus be a link with spiritual realms and spiritual healing.

My personal experiences with the OBE

Robert Monroe suggests it is possible to develop the ability to experience an OBE by staying in the in-between sleep and wake state. One way to do this is to lie on your back in bed, holding an arm up from the elbow. If you start to fall asleep, your arm falling down to the bed will wake you.

Very early in my studies of psychic phenomena, before I started exploring spiritual healing, I did this. I soon found myself sitting up in bed. I looked back, and the me that was sitting up was not the same me that was still lying down behind me. I panicked and let out a blood curdling scream, then found myself waking with a jerk. My wife, sleeping next to me, had not stirred, and neither had our children across the hall, nor the neighbors in the apartments facing us.

I surmised that I had screamed in my out of body state, not in my physical body. I have never had another such experience and have not repeated this exercise.

In summary

The Out-of-Body Experience is reported by 17 to 27 percent of people who have been surveyed. The evidence appears to favor the existence of an astral body but research support is weaker here than for many other psi phenomena.

If an independent astral body can be proven to exist, this would strongly support the contentions of mystics and healers that the true essence of human existence resides outside the physical body. These sensitives state that the soul detaches a spirit portion of itself to animate a physical body in order to experience lessons in the physical world. Daskalos, a very gifted Cypriot healer explains:

> ...the psychic body is not identical with the psyche of a person or the soul. The latter is eternal and beyond all manifestations. The psychic body eventually dies just like the gross material body and the noetic body. With every incarnation the self-conscious soul mandates itself with a new noetic, psychic and gross material body. The three bodies are the garment that the self-conscious soul wears to express itself from one incarnation to another.[69]

Research suggests that the OBE can be an invited, repeated experience and that valid information can be retrieved by a person who is traveling out of body. Overlaps are obvious between the OBE and psi communications - including telepathy, clairsentience, precognition and retrocognition. The perception of traveling out of one's body may be a mental construct rather than a physical or energetic reality. This may be our everyday reality consciousness attempting to normalize an unfamiliar psi experiences.
We shall see many points of correspondence between the OBE and reports of the near-death-experience (NDE), reincarnation, and with spirit and spiritual aspects of healing.

In following chapters we will consider further the question of existence not only beyond the physical body, but also beyond physical death.

CHAPTER 2

Near-Death and Pre-Death Experiences

"What happens to an enlightened person at death?" a student queried
Master Hakuin.
"Why ask me?"
"Because you're a Zen master!"
"Yes, but not a dead one!"

– Zen Parable

The Near Death Experience (NDE) has been acknowledged across many cultures, over many centuries.

I saw a point that radiated light
Of such intensity that the eye it strikes
Must close or ever after lose its sight...

– Dante Alighieri

Scientists have studied experiences of people who came close to death, or were actually declared dead (on the basis of total lack of responsiveness and flat EEGs) but returned to life. Many were cases of cardiac arrest, accidents or complications of surgery. Most of these people did not report an NDE.[70]

Some NDEs occur under a perceived threat of danger, without actually losing consciousness. Melvin Morse calls these Fear Death Experiences.[71]

In a composite picture of the Near-Death Experience (NDE), people typically feel they are moving out of their bodies in spirit form, passing through a long tunnel towards a light at the end. They may hear strange and beautiful music; may meet angels or other spirit-like beings who welcome them warmly; and may see or in other ways sense the presence of relatives who had died earlier.[72]

There is a tremendous sense of well-being and calmness; of knowing and understanding about one's own life and relationships as well as about the meaning of existence in general. These experiences peak in an encounter with a blinding white or golden light that appears to embody an all-knowing, non-judgmental, all-accepting, all-loving being. Many experience an instantaneous but complete review of all the events in their lifetime, under the guidance of the Being of Light. The review is totally accepting and non-judgmental on the part of this Being, but people may feel regrets and criticisms of themselves over errors or poor choices around things they did or did not do.

> *We are punished by our sins, not for them.*
> – Elbert Hubbard

Some NDEers plead that they wish to return to physical life to complete unfinished business. Others are led to understand – in words or just by some inner 'knowing' that a higher authority requires that they return to their physical bodies. Many feel great disappointment upon being told this. The next awareness is usually of being back in the body, with only a partial recall for the NDE.

Experiences that appear identical with the NDE may occur without being close to death, for example, when undergoing surgery.[73]

Just to confuse the picture, there are also reports of recall of conscious experiences during periods when people had been declared dead – on the basis of total lack of responsiveness and flat EEGs. These reports did not include the typical components of NDEs, but were more similar to OBEs.[74]

In and of itself, the NDE is frequently experienced as a healing. NDEers return from death's door with a markedly different, more peaceful and accepting attitude towards themselves and the world around them.

Research

Kenneth Ring, a professor of psychology at the University of Connecticut, has studied the NDE extensively. He points out that

> Following their experience, NDEers are likely to shift towards a
> universalistically spiritual orientation. This shift is not found... for...
> persons who have not had NDEs but who are otherwise comparable...
> I have found seven essential elements of this coherent world view...
>
> 1. A tendency to characterize oneself as spiritual rather than religious...
> 2. A feeling of being inwardly close to God.
> 3. A de-emphasis of the formal aspects of religious life and worship.
> 4. A conviction that there is life after death, regardless of religious... belief.
> 5. An openness to the doctrine of reincarnation (and a general sympathy...
>   toward Eastern religions).
> 6. A belief in the essential underlying unity of all religions.

7. A desire for a universal religion embracing all humanity.[75]

Ring emphatically characterizes the transformation the NDE creates in the lives of NDEers as the distinguishing hallmark of the NDE. People who return from an NDE no longer fear death and their lives are transformed by the broader perspectives and deeper meanings they perceive. Other researchers also emphasize transformative effects of the NDE.[76]

> *When Plato was dying, it is said that he went into something of a coma and then came out of it again, and all his students around him asked what was his last teaching before he died. And he said, "Practice dying."*
> ` – Stephen Levine [77]

An outstanding report of transformative effects of an NDE is described by Mellen-Thomas Benedict, an artist who died of cancer in 1982.[78] He went into the light, and in his NDE he asked questions about the universe and the meaning of life. Following his return to life an hour and a half after he was declared dead – with flat EKG and other body function monitors – he went on to study cellular communication and the influences of light upon life, particularly for healing.

The content of Benedict's NDE report is remarkable for its scope. He asked the light to explain the meaning of life. Telepathically he was led to perceive that the Higher Selves of all of humanity – of every individual – are joined in a matrix, and that all are connected to the Source.

> [W]e are actually the same being, different aspects of the same being. It was not committed to one particular religion... And I saw this mandala of human souls. It was the most beautiful thing I have ever seen. I just went into it and, it was just overwhelming. It was like all the love you've ever wanted, and it was the kind of love that cures, heals, regenerates...
>
> I was astonished to find that there was no evil in any soul. I said, "How can this be?" The answer was that no soul was inherently evil. The terrible things that happened to people might make them do evil things, but their souls were not evil. What all people seek, what sustains them, is love, the light told me. What distorts people is a lack of love.

Benedict's consciousness expanded to encompass all of creation, through all of time. He found it was without beginning or end.

> I came back with this understanding that God is not there. God is here.[79]

Surveys in numerous cultures reveal the NDE is a very common experience.[80] A survey of clergy reveal that 70% are told of NDEs by their parishioners.[81] The earliest collection of NDE reports I found is from mountain climbers who had scrapes with death, a few of them experiencing the NDE while falling.[82]

Some postulate that the NDE might simply be a manifestation of death of parts of the brain as perceived by other parts of the brain that are still alive.[83] J. E.

Owens et al. compared NDE reports of 28 people judged to be medically close to death with NDE reports of 30 people who thought they were close to death but were judged medically to have been in no danger of dying. Significantly more patients who were judged really close to death reported enhanced light perception and enhanced cognitive powers. Other variables did not distinguish between the groups. The experience of enhanced cognitive powers would suggest that the NDE is not a product of a dying brain, since cognitive powers would presumably be declining rather than markedly sharpened if NDE awareness was produced by activities of the physical brain..

Pim van Lommel and colleagues, in a prospective 12-year study of 344 people who had cardiac arrests, found that 18 percent had NDEs. This report is of particular interest because subjects were selected for study prior to having their NDE and because it was published in *Lancet,* a prominent medical journal.

> We compared demographic, medical, pharmacological, and psychological data between patients who reported NDE and patients who did not (controls) after resuscitation. In a longitudinal study of life changes after NDE, we compared the groups 2 and 8 years later.
>
> Findings: 62 patients (18%) reported NDE, of whom 41 (12%) described a core experience. Occurrence of the experience was not associated with duration of cardiac arrest or unconsciousness, medication, or fear of death before cardiac arrest... Significantly more patients who had an NDE, especially a deep experience, died within 30 days of CPR...[84] The process of transformation after NDE took several years, and differed from those of patients who survived cardiac arrest without NDE.

The probability that this could have occurred by chance is less than one in 10,000. Van Lommel et al. conclude that physical factors of oxygen starvation, medications and fear of death cannot account for the experiential or transformative effects of the NDE.

This is a particularly impressive study because it was prospective and included a control (comparison) group. All the other studies have been retrospective, with selection of subjects by their *a priori* report of having had a NDE.

The fact that more people died following the NDE may have several explanations. The NDE helps people to not fear death, so they may not cling to life when it is their time to make their transition back to spirit life. The NDE may occur more often as death approaches. The NDE may be a part of a spectrum of similar phenomena, including deathbed visions and apparitions, and perhaps also bereavement apparitions.[85]

Other studies have found between 12[86] and 50[87] percent of people who are resuscitated report NDEs. The variability may relate to selected populations and to how an NDE is defined.

There have also been reports from people returning after NDEs that they met relatives who had died previous to their NDE but whom they had never previously met or heard of. They were subsequently able to confirm descriptions of the physical appearance, personality characteristics, or information related by the deceased. In some cases they did know the deceased but had not known they were dead.[88]

Skeptics have suggested that the NDE is no more than wishful thinking to counter people's fears of death. To test this hypothesis, Michael Sabom compared reports of 32 people who survived cardiac arrests and had NDEs but previously had been unfamiliar with this phenomenon, with 25 medically sophisticated people who had not had an NDE. He asked the subjects in both groups to describe what they imagined would occur when a medical resuscitation team attempts to restart a heart. All of the naïve NDE survivors provided accurate descriptions of these procedures but only two of the 25 subjects familiar with NDEs did so.

Others postulate that over-stimulation of parts of the brain might cause people to have what appear to be spiritual awarenesses. New computer imaging techniques are providing some support for this theory, discussed in Chapter 8, under *neurotheology*.

Further impressive evidence comes from reports of children who have had NDEs.[89] Children under the age of eight usually have little understanding of death and are unlikely to have been primed with prior expectations that would lead them to the core experience of the NDE. Yet children report identical experiences when they return from their NDEs.

Numerous researchers[90] observe that with right brain temporal lobe abnormalities such as seizures, and tumors, and with electrical stimulation of the right temporal lobe, people have experiences that closely resemble the NDE. These include sensations of being outside one's body, and numinous experiences (often interpreted as religious experiences), such as hearing heavenly music and sensing the presence of God. Skeptics may use this evidence to support an argument that the NDE is simply a product of abnormal brain functions. Morse suggests the alternative hypothesis that the right temporal lobe is the mediator for awarenesses that are non-local. He relies on quantum physics to support this possibility.[91] P. M. H. Atwater[92] points out that such stimulation produces only "*a generalized pattern* of imagery... This was also true with similar states caused by temporal lobe seizure, centrifuge pilot training, and excessive stress." Penfield[93] also notes that people who had brain stimulation maintained dual awareness – of the operating room and of the stimulated perceptions, which had an 'as if' quality to them. The lasting, transformative effects of the NDE were not reported with brain dysfunctions.

Most remarkable are the NDEs in blind people who were identified by Kenneth Ring and Sharon Cooper. Of 21 people interviewed, 10 were blind from birth and another 9 were blind from before the age of five years. Fifteen of the 21 subjects (71 percent) reported they were able to see during their NDE. Their vision was typically clear, organized, and immediately comprehensible. In a few cases it was possible to confirm the accuracy of what they reported they had seen. This is very different from blind people whose vision is restored surgically.[94] In such cases it takes a long time for people to make sense of their perceived visual patterns.

What is clear is that the NDE is a very common experience. An estimate from a poll from *U.S. News & World Report*[95] suggests there are fifteen million people who have experienced NDEs in the United States. This represents approximately one-third of those who 'died' but then returned to life. Children's NDEs were not included in this survey. Melvin Morse[96] estimates that 70 percent of children who come close to death have NDEs.[97]

It is also of note that there is no correlation between experiencing an NDE and age, sex, race, culture, social class, religious affiliation, conscious beliefs, or educational level.[98] Wade notes that the following correlations have been observed: 1) people who easily experience altered states and have strong tendencies for psychological absorption may be more likely to experience and recall their NDEs; 2) fewer children than adults experience a life-review or encounter spirits of dead relatives; and 3) women are more likely than men to encounter spirit guides or spirits of deceased relatives. Beliefs are unlikely to influence the general experience of an NDE, but may affect its interpretation.[99]

Pre-death experiences

Melvin Morse[100] collected many stories of psychic and spiritual experiences preceding the time of death. Although these did not occur when people died and were resuscitated, they had very broad overlaps with NDEs in many respects. These include people who are close to death or in the process of dying, having precognitive awarenesses in dreams and waking visions that their deceased relatives were near or present; simultaneous perceptions by living relatives and medical staff of the visions that those close to death perceived; and angelic presences that conveyed helpful information or even intervened physically to prevent tragedies.

In addition, people reported knowing that relatives or friends close to them were approaching death (even when this was not obvious from any ordinary signs).

People with pre-death experiences often dismissed some of these as ordinary dreams or coincidences. Because the experiences were new and alien to their cultural norms, these individuals would question whether they hadn't imagined them out of wishful thinking or fears of death. Many were anxious that they might be losing their minds and for this reason would not tell anyone about their experiences. Morse suggests the following reassurances:

There is no reason to believe one is mentally unbalanced because one has such experiences. Most people who have these experiences are mentally healthy. People who are losing their minds tend to have multiple experiences of this sort, numerous fears in a variety of situations, with negative feelings and hallucinations, and loss of control over their emotions and behavior.

These experiences have a reality that is as valid as any other life experiences. They are not made up fantasies.

Spiritual experiences are transformative, producing more positive outlooks and beliefs about life and death and leading to commitments to work for the highest good of all. Those who have pre-death experiences are likely to have less anxieties, to feel more positive about the meaning of their life, to have increased spiritual awareness, to feel more certain that there is an afterlife, and to live more comfortably with their physical and emotional problems.

The quality of death is vastly improved for the dying, as well as for family, friends and caregivers who are able to listen to and accept their experiences.

Skeptics and those who are not reassured by the above may continue to query whether these experiences are real. In Morse's experience, criteria which appear to differentiate psychic and spiritual visions from ordinary dreams and fantasies include two or more of the following:

Visions and voices are superimposed over ordinary perceptions. They may appear as solid and sound as real as ordinary perceptions, or may have qualities that immediately distinguish them as visionary – such a mistiness or inner source to the perception. The inner experience feels absolutely real, often even more real than everyday experiences. Dreams and visions have a quality of uniqueness, clearly distinguishing them from ordinary experiences.

The visions and dreams convey information that is coherent, useful, and relevant to others in addition to the one perceiving them.

The experiences often include a unique white light or a Being of Light.

Morse presents excellent discussions on the very positive effects of these experiences, with a treasure trove of examples from people he treated and people who reported their NDEs to him after reading his books. The pre-death experiences often ease the processes of parting between those who are dying and those still alive. They soften the pains of bereavement. Most importantly, they open people to spiritual awarenesses. People approaching their death, along with those close to them, find peace in the reassurance that death is a transition rather than an end to existence. Death of a child or other person who is particularly dear to us may be shifted from being a complete tragedy towards also being a spiritual awakening.[101]

Deathbed experiences

Deathbed experiences, resembling the NDE and pre-death experiences, have been well documented in countries around the world, including the US, UK, Iceland and India.[102] Typically, people approaching their death become calm and have a peaceful smile. They may report that they see visions of various apparitions (angels, Christ or relatives who had passed on previously) coming 'to take them away.' These apparitions explain that there is an afterlife and that they need not fear death. They may hear celestial, ethereal, 'beautiful music of the spheres.' Often, following these visions, their pains and other distressing symptoms either abate or no longer bother them as much. A Gallup poll survey[103] in 1982 found that 5 percent of dying people were reported to have experienced deathbed visions.

Deathbed experiences from America, England and India are very similar to each other. Some have queried whether NDEs and deathbed experiences might be produced by processes of brain death or of emotional disturbances. Karlis Osis and Erlunder Haraldsson, both experienced parapsychologists, summarize the possible alternative explanations for deathbed visions in Table III-1. These point to a distinctness in the deathbed vision from physiological conditions that may produce hallucinations and the like.

Table III-1. Model of the two basic hypotheses of deathbed visions	
SURVIVAL	**DESTRUCTION**
Death is the transition to another mode of existence.	Death is the ultimate destruction of human personality.
1. Source of deathbed visions	
<u>ESP</u>	<u>Sick Brain + Morbid Reaction</u>
There are visions based upon ESP that are not caused by malfunctions of the nervous system and the dying brain. a. Telepathic impressions from other worldly visitors – for example, deceased relatives and religious figures. b. Clairvoyant or precognitive glimpse of that mode of existence where life after death takes place.	 a. Visions of the dying are caused by malfunctions of the nervous system and the dying brain. b. Visions are schizoid reactions to alleviate severe stress and social deprivation in the hospital through escape into otherworldly imagery.
2. Influence of medical factors in deathbed visions	
Malfunction of the brain, medication such as morphine, uremia poisoning, high temperature, hallucinogenic drugs, etc.	
<u>Relatively independent</u>	Dependent on Medical <u>Conditions</u>
a. The presence of hallucinogenic factors will not increase frequency of phenomena related to postmortem existence. b. Conditions detrimental to ESP will decrease the frequency of the phenomena.	The presence of hallucinogenic factors will increase the frequency of the phenomena related to postmortem survival; the more disturbed the brain processes, the more numerous the otherworldly fantasies.
3. Contents of Deathbed Visions	
<u>Perceptions</u>	<u>Hallucinations</u>
Contents of the visions will be of two kinds – either hallucinations or true perceptions of external reality via ESP. a. Hallucinations will be less coherent, rambling, expressing the concerns of this life, memories, desires and conflicts. b. True perceptions will be more coherent, oriented to the situation of dying and the transition to another world. They will try to portray otherworldly messengers and an environment of which we have no adequate image or conception.	Contents of all visions will be hallucinations and will portray no information that is not already stored in the brain. They will express the memories, expectations, desires, conflicts, and fears of the individual, as well as his cultural conditioning by family, society, and religious institutions.

Table III-1. (Continued)

4. Influence of psychological factors on deathbed visions

Clarity of consciousness, belief in life after death, belief in 'another world' (religion), person's expectations of whether he will die or recover

Conditions Related to Awareness of Another World	Conditions Related to Hallucinations of This World Or Other-World Fantasies
a. Clarity of consciousness. Normal or such altered states where contact with reality is intact will facilitate awareness of another world and its messengers, while states where contact with external reality is absent will impair such awareness.	a. Clarity of consciousness. Normal or such altered states where contact with reality is intact will be less conducive to all kinds of hallucinations than states where contact with reality is lost.
b. Openness to, and belief in, life after death and another world (religion) will facilitate deathbed visions, especially of the kind that cut across individual, national, and cultural differences.	b. Openness to, and belief in, life after death and another world will facilitate hallucinations of another world, but they will be specific as to the beliefs of the individual and of his culture.
c. Patients' expectancy of recovery from illness will not influence the occurrence of deathbed visions.	c. Patients' expectancy of recovery will facilitate this-life hallucinations, while expectancy of death will generate hallucinations of after-life fantasies.
d. Severe stress as indicated by a patient's mood before hallucination will not generate ESP and therefore will not affect the frequency of seeing afterlife-oriented apparitions.	d. Severe stress will release schizoid coping reactions and thus increase the frequency of afterlife-related hallucinations.

5. Variability of Contents across Individuals and Cultures

Little variability. Perceptions involving basic characteristics of the other world will be essentially similar for men and women, young and old, educated and illiterate, religious and nonreligious, American and Indian, Christian and Hindu. Only modest differences will be expected.	Much variability. Hallucinations, unlike perceptions, have little or no foundation in external reality. They will vary with dispositions, dynamics, and the cultural background of the individual. Hallucinations of an afterlife will portray the belief system of the patient – be it based on the Bible or on the Vedas.

In Buddhist traditions, death is a crucial state of transition. People prepare for their death over many years, through living their lives unselfishly, with regular prayer and meditation practices. At the time of death and in the days immediately following, if the spirit is properly guided and assisted through the prayers of the mourners it may transition to higher levels of advancement.

John Bockris points out that the descriptions of the dying process in *The Tibetan Book of the Dead*[104] have several overlaps with the NDE.

1. At the very moment of death, the Clear Light (*ground luminosity*) dawns in splendor. Buddhists believe that a dead person's consciousness is unified with this luminosity. This description resembles the experience of encountering the Light, which is the feature most commonly reported during NDEs.

2. Descriptions of the state between incarnations (Life in the Bardo) resembles the state reported at the beginning of an NDE: the surviving consciousness perceives its physical body from a perspective of being above the body.

3. Both descriptions report that attempts to communicate with living people are unsuccessful. The living cannot feel the touch nor hear the voice of the surviving consciousness. This is often a frustrating experience, often leading to the realization that the person has died.

4. Both descriptions report encounters with relatives who died earlier.[105]

5. Both report that the surviving body is restored to its form during its best years. Relatives and friends who are encountered in these realms are also in the forms they had during their prime years.

6. Both report that you can shape the appearance of your surroundings and can travel anywhere instantly just by thinking of being there.

7. Experiences in the Bardo reflect the quality of a person's previous life. For those who are spiritually advanced, Celestial visions are seen in the Bardo. Regardless of one's previous life, in some NDEs people feel they are in Paradise and hear celestial music.

8. Following a life of selfishness and cruelty, the Bardo may be an experience of isolation, fear even to panic proportions, desolation and gloom. Similarly, in up to 15% of NDEs one may experience images reminiscent of the classical descriptions of hell

Difficulties and challenges surrounding NDEs

Not all NDEs, pre-death or deathbed experiences are positive. After several years of glowing NDE experience reports in the modern literature, reports of negative experiences during NDEs began to appear.[106] People found themselves in places that resembled Dante's descriptions of Hell, with souls writhing and screaming in agonies of horrible tortures. Rather than a pleasant experience, this type of NDE was one of fear, even to panic proportions.

A Baptist cardiac surgeon named Morris Rawlings[107] witnessed and participated in many resuscitations. His patients' reports of NDEs also included negative experiences. He speculates that as a surgeon he might have been more likely to hear negative reports because he was present during the resuscitations. He believes that people may be more likely to report negative NDEs immediately following their experiences, relative to people who relate their stories of NDEs months or years after their experience. He believes that the pleasanter NDE experiences would be more readily remembered than those of nightmarish quality, which are likely to be repressed and forgotten.

Elizabeth Kübler-Ross, who devoted her life to helping people deal with death, also reported several negative NDEs.[108] These were usually in men 40-50 years old, fundamentalists who sinned (for example in deceiving their wives), despite acknowledging to themselves that what they were doing was wrong. She speculates that people who perceive themselves to be sinners may find that their NDE life-review is a negative experience: if they are critical of themselves, the whole NDE may become negative when viewed from self-critical perspectives.

I would add my own speculations here. Because industrial culture is a death-denying one, many experience difficulties in assimilating these Near-Death Experiences. While these death-related experiences can diminish the severity of grief reactions, they may stimulate emotional releases of old, buried hurts and may stir relational conflicts.

Melvin Morse observes that counseling by sensitive and knowledgeable caregivers can help to sort out fears, as well as to help in the life adjustments from strongly positive reactions to these experiences. He notes:

> These visions can restore dignity to the process of dying. Dying can be a dehumanizing and spiritually degrading process. Patients often die alone, stripped of personal dignity. They feel that they are useless and a burden to their families, often draining financial resources for expensive care that is of little benefit.
>
> Just knowing about death-related visions can change this. Family members who know about the visions of the dying are known to spend more time at the dying person's bedside. This factor alone alleviates much of the guilt they might feel after the loved one's death.
>
> Spiritual visions can empower dying patients as well. For one thing they realize that they still have something important to share with others. For another just hearing the reports of others who have almost died gives them courage in knowing that the dying process is not a painful one.
>
> As a caregiver it is important to know that even the sadness of death can be life-affirming and healing when it takes place within a spiritual context.[109]

I see many ways in which these experiences can be helpful to people other than those who experience them. Near-death and pre-death visions can be enormously beneficial to doctors, nurses and other caregivers. They can alter the perceptions of death as a frustrating failure to preserve life and a reminder of the caregivers' own mortality, shifting these into an awareness of death as a portal to new awarenesses. Instead of feeling helpless, caregivers can take these experiences as opportunities to help people into deeper connections with their spirituality. Caregivers will similarly benefit from their own resonations, becoming aware of their own spirituality. Societal attitudes towards death may also be shifted, with vast improvements in hospital care for the terminally ill and dying.

Explanations for the NDE from conventional science

Several explanations have been proposed for the NDE within conventional science.

One is that it is a physiological mechanism associated with particular sorts of pathology of the brain. Of all body tissues, the brain is most sensitive to oxygen deprivation. Therefore it might show symptoms of dying before the heart and other organs die. An analogy might be the spot of light seen on an old-style television tube when it is turned off. In a state of anoxia, an electrochemical 'turning off' of the brain could occur, with a release of all memories as the person approaches death. The NDE may likewise represent perceptions, fantasies or hallucinations produced by the electrochemical fading of the brain. A related alternative hypothesis is that physical trauma or oxygen starvation trigger epileptic discharges in the temporal lobes, which might produce panoramic memories.[110]

Numerous researchers have presented evidence that with right brain temporal lobe abnormalities such as seizures and tumors, and with electrical stimulation of the right temporal lobe, there are experiences that closely resemble the NDE.[111] These include sensations of being outside one's body, and numinous experiences (often perceived as religious experiences) such as hearing heavenly music and sensing the presence of God. Skeptics may use this evidence to support an argument that the NDE is a product of abnormal brain functions.

Mitigating against this argument is the absence of transformative changes in people's lives following electrical stimulation of the brain. It is possible, however, that those who studied the electrophysiology of the brain did not consider the possibility of transformative changes and did not inquire about them, and/or did not follow the people whose brains were stimulated long enough to observe transformations.

P. M. H. Atwater points out that direct electrical stimulation of the brain produces only "*a generalized pattern* of imagery... This was also true with similar states caused by temporal lobe seizure, centrifuge pilot training, and excessive stress." [112]

Morse suggests an alternative theory: the right temporal lobe could be the mediator for awarenesses that are non-local. He relies on quantum physics to support this possibility.[113]

Andrew Newberg[114] and colleagues identified parts of the brain that became more active during deep meditation. This lends support to the possibility that a particular part of the brain may be stimulated around the time of death, causing these spiritual experiences.

One might also postulate that the NDE is a response to the release of opiate-like hormones in the brain such as endorphins,[115] associated with the death of parts of the brain. Endorphins might produce a natural 'high' feeling that is interpreted as a mystical experience. Such 'highs' are commonly seen with hallucinogenic drugs. I know of no research, however, to suggest that endorphins are released in the brain at the time of death.

Ring and van Lommel et al. emphasize that a theory of 'fading brain' does not seem tenable. People who had periods of unconsciousness (with physical trauma as severe as those who had NDEs) but who did not have NDEs, do not demonstrate any transformations in attitudes.

Roberts and Owen point out that there are many reports of NDEs without trauma, as in mountain climbers who experienced these during their falls – prior to the trauma. The explorations of Osis and Haraldsson of deathbed experiences likewise contradict the fading brain theory. These may occur hours and days prior to death.

Psychological theories could also be suggested to account for NDEs.

While dreams might appear a logical explanation for the NDE at first thought,[116] on closer consideration this does not appear a likely hypothesis. Ordinary dreams are usually distortions of everyday experiences and usually do not give the dreamer a sense of being in ordinary physical space as does the NDE. The NDE perceptions appear to be absolutely real. *Lucid* dreams – which include a strong sense of being totally real – would then seem a possible explanation.[117] Some of the hallmarks of the lucid dream are that dreamers know they are dreaming and can control their actions.[118] Lucid dreams occur during sleep, or in transition from waking to sleeping, and it is possible to cultivate their happening more frequently. In contrast, NDEs cannot be deliberately invited to happen, occur specifically at a time of stress or death, have a numinous, transpersonal quality, and are transformative – qualitatively different from lucid dreams.

The dreams of the blind, contrasted with NDE experiences in the blind, particularly suggest that the NDE is a distinct experience from a normal dream. Those who have been blind from birth or before the age of five experience their dreams as very similar to their everyday life experiences.[119] Visual images are simply not a part of their spectrum of reality. In fact, they have no concepts of what colors, light, or other visual terms mean. Their dreams are of auditory, tactile and emotional experiences that reflect their waking lives. Yet in their NDEs the blind report clear and immediately comprehensible visual perceptions.

Dreams therefore appear an unlikely explanation for the NDE.

Simple, mental reconstructions born out of the expectations and imagination of the perceiver could explain the NDE.[120] Religious teachings and popular culture suggest that Christ, angels, or deserving relatives and friends might be waiting on the other side of the pearly gates to welcome us when we die. Assuming these are folk tales, it is conceivable that people who die and are resuscitated create such stories as part of their ways of dealing with physical and psychological traumas of their ordeals. While logical, this hypothesis is not supported by the evidence. People with no particular religious upbringing or affiliation have NDEs that include meeting a Being of Light, a life review without blame from this Being, and finding their lives are transformed by these experiences. The congenitally blind may report seeing specific objects during their NDE, with objective confirmations of the accuracy of such observations – and these would hardly be likely if they occurred solely on the basis of their imaginations. So again we have a hypothesis that, although logical, is not borne out by the evidence.

NDEs could be extreme psychological reactions to coming close to death, such as wishful thinking regarding an afterlife. Though the NDE is transformative, one could also postulate that those experiencing an NDE may be people who need to create such fantasies because of fears of death.

Greyson[121] found that there was a higher degree of dissociation in people experiencing NDEs compared to people coming close to death but not experiencing NDEs. On the one hand, this could suggest that the NDE is the product of the minds of people who tend to 'split' themselves off from aspects of their experiences. On the other hand, this could suggest that the general ability to dissociate facilitates awareness of the NDE.

Thus it appears that the psychological explanations of the NDE as a defense against fear are of mixed merit. The usual psychological reaction to a frightening experience is anxiety, avoidance, phobias, repression and a variety of other defense mechanisms. If the NDE were only a psychological reaction to a brush with death, I would expect substantial numbers of patients to report these other reactions. That they do not report these reactions suggests a uniqueness in the NDE which requires further explanation. Extreme denial of life-threatening circumstances might be postulated to produce a total denial of the associated fear. One would then expect the majority of NDEers to have denial patterns of dealing with stress or possibly even severe emotional pathology or personality disorders to begin with, as a basis for such extreme reactions. This bears investigation, although anecdotal reports do not point in these directions. Typical NDEers are sober, ordinary citizens, often people who are not particularly engaged in religious practices or beliefs, and who are very surprised by the experiences. They are far from being afraid in the NDE. They are calm and report that they come to know with absolute assurance that there is a life after death. As a result of the NDE they no longer fear death. This brings us full circle, as the commonly stated 'no longer' implies that there were fears of death beforehand – but not following the NDE.

> *[D]eath is not the enemy.*
> *It is our lack of self-trust.*
> – Stephen Levine [122]

The conventional theories also do not explain the core perceptions of meeting previously departed relatives, a Being of Light, or other religious and spirit entities, which are reported in nearly identical descriptions in cultures around the world.

Relevance of the NDE to healing

The existence of a 'spirit body' is supported by evidence from the NDE, pre-death and deathbed visions, and other phenomena reviewed in this book. A spirit body appears to coexist with the physical but seems able to transcend the space and time limits of the physical world as we know it in sensory reality. It may be a vehicle through which healers can give and healees can receive healing. It may be an aspect of life that survives physical death. During incarnations the spirit body may bring with it elements that participate in creation of diseases and also may include potentials for healing them.

> *The importance of the near-death studies is not what they teach us about life after death, but rather the spotlight they shine on the spiritual impoverishment of our own lives.*
> — Melvin Morse with Paul Perry [123]

In summary

Between 12 and 50 percent of people who are resuscitated report Near-Death Experiences. While a variety of hypotheses suggest ordinary explanations, such as biological shutdown of the brain or seizure disorders, these do not hold up under careful scrutiny. The most impressive feature of the NDE is its transformative effects on people who have this experience. They no longer fear death, are more spiritual, and have a clearer sense of purpose in life. The fact that little children report these experiences also suggests that they are real and not fantasies of wishful thinking. The reports of NDEs in people who have been blind from birth add further credibility to these as real experiences

Within the context of evidence from other research in spiritual dimensions, the NDE appears to be one of the most powerful in its effects, along with other mystical and spiritual experiences.[124] The NDE may actually be a part of a spectrum of similar experiences, along with bereavement apparitions and deathbed visions and apparitions.[125]

Let us look next at research on reincarnation.

CHAPTER 3

Reincarnation

Our birth is but a sleep and a forgetting:
The Soul that rises with us, our life's Star,
Hath had elsewhere its setting,
And cometh from afar:
Not in entire forgetfulness,
And not in utter nakedness,
But trailing clouds of glory do we come
From God who is our home:
Heaven lies about us in our infancy!
Shades of the prison-house begin to close
Upon the growing boy.

— William Wordsworth

Eastern religions, traditional cultures and healers around the world maintain that the spirit of man survives to an afterlife and returns to live again. It appears that early Christianity included this concept, as suggested by John 3:3, "Except as a man be born again, he cannot see the kingdom of God." Helen Greaves[126] points out that there was a 500 year tradition of belief in reincarnation in the Alexandrian school, including such proponents as Clement, Justin Martyr, St. Gregory of Nyasa and Origen: "The Council of Constantinople in AD 553, at which it seems a corrupt form of Origen's teaching was anathematized, is held by many historians to have been imperfectly constituted – the Pope himself refused to be present – and even Roman Catholics contest its validity as a General Council."

Though Western society has generally been skeptical about reincarnation, many well-known personalities have shared this belief, including Beethoven, Emily Dickinson, Henry Ford, Benjamin Franklin, J. W. von Goethe, Oliver Wendell Holmes, Harry Houdini, Aldous Huxley, Jack London, Thomas Moore, Mark Twain, and many more.[127]

Several lines of evidence suggest that reincarnation may, in fact, occur as people are reporting. A variety of approaches may bring forth memories of alleged previous lifetimes. Studies with hypnosis and a range of psychotherapies report that immediate symptom relief may be obtained when some patients relive experiences or release emotions from traumas they report they experienced in previous lifetimes.

Some of the most dramatic evidence comes from individual cases in which clear memories of apparent previous lives are reported spontaneously. In a few exceptional instances there is even recall of languages unlearned in the current life, with ability to converse in those languages.

Spontaneous reincarnation memories

Ian Stevenson, a psychiatrist at the University of Virginia, has pioneered the exploration of spontaneous reincarnation reports from India, Lebanon, Sri Lanka and other cultures around the world. He meticulously collected first-hand accounts of witnesses who corroborated the telling and/or demonstrating of such memories.[128]

Some cultures fully accept the concept of reincarnation, such as the Druse, who live in Southern Lebanon, Northern Israel and Syria. They welcome reincarnation memories as links between the family of the reincarnated person and the new person. If the new person can clearly describe the previous identity, he or she is welcomed into the folds of their recalled family. In such cases, however, extra precautions are taken (especially by the prominent and well-to-do) to guard against possible fraud by persons who might seek social or monetary advantages in this way.

Cases under such circumstances have been found, in which multiple witnesses verify the reported events. Particularly impressive are the cases of children who recall a previous life, in societies where there is little access to the media and little mobility. Here is a composite example.

> Four year-old Ahmed reported that he was really Shari, and lived in a small town 300 miles from his own village. His parents at first thought this was childish imagination, but the persistent and detailed descriptions of persons, places and events, along with altered personality styles in the child, piqued their curiosities to the point that appropriate inquiries were made.
>
> Ahmed, who had never visited the recalled town of his alleged past-life memories, nor had contact with anyone from there, was taken to the edge of the town. He led witnesses by the most direct route to his alleged former home. Along the way, he pointed out a place where a tree had stood (where no sign of a tree was then evident) and other changes in the houses and surroundings of the home where he claimed he had lived. On arrival at the home of his previous life, he identified relatives of Shari by name and kinship ties. He went on to disclose intimate details relating to his family's experiences that no one outside the family could possibly have known.

The family of the deceased Shari verified that Ahmed's statements were almost entirely accurate.

Stevenson has collected a large series of such witnessed reports.

Xenoglossy, an even more extensive form of recall, is reported in a few rare cases by Stevenson.[129] This is the speaking of a language unlearned by people during their current lives. Sometimes only a few phrases are spoken. Children might spontaneously use a strange name for an object, inappropriate in their mother tongue. Their family or outsiders might recognize such phrases as belonging to a distant dialect or language. In more developed cases, entire languages are apparently recalled, with the ability to converse freely in these languages (termed *responsive xenoglossy*). Past-life therapists have also reported cases of xenoglossy, though I know of no published reports with careful investigations to rule out present-life sources as explanations for these.

Stevenson[130] found astounding physical evidence supporting reincarnation. He searched out confirming evidence that birthmarks and other physical deformities appearing in the bodies of the current person corresponded to documented traumas on body parts relevant to trauma recalled from previous lives. A high percent of people who died violent deaths have such birthmarks. For example, a person who recalls having been killed by an arrow through their chest in a previous life finds a birthmark on their chest in that spot. These findings were replicated independently by Pasricha.[131]

Even more fascinating are cases where relatives placed charcoal marks on the body of a dead person, with the intention that a birthmark would appear on the same spot of his body when he reincarnates. Stevenson[132] reports several cases where relatives claimed this had succeeded. If verified, this phenomenon would add a new dimension to our understanding of reincarnation phenomena.

In Western society, where reincarnation is not a familiar phenomenon to most of the population, reports of past life memories are more rare than in societies where it is well accepted. Nevertheless, there is an increasing awareness about past life recall and more people are now speaking about it. For instance, Rabbi Yonassan Gershom[133] has an enormous collection of stories of people who recall previous lives as Jews during the Holocaust. Many of these people are not Jewish, and have had no significant connections with Jews or Judaism in their current lives. Gershom reports that those who recall past lives find great meaningfulness in these memories, some of which have been verifiable as relating to actual events.[134]

Past life memories from hypnosis and psychotherapy

> *Not the power to remember, but its very opposite, the power to forget, is a necessary condition of our existence. If the lore of the transmigration of souls is a true one, then these souls, between their exchange of bodies, must pass through the sea of forgetfulness. According to the Jewish view, we make the transition under the overlordship of the Angel of Forgetfulness.*

> *But it sometimes happens that the Angel of Forgetfulness himself forgets to remove from our memories the records of the former world; and then our senses are haunted by fragmentary recollections of another life. They drift like torn clouds above the hills and valleys of the mind, and weave themselves into the incidents of our current existence.*
>
> – Sholem Ash [135]

Hypnotic regressions to previous lives have been reported for decades. Morey Bernstein explored the classic case of an American housewife who recalled a life as Bridey Murphy, an Irish woman, near the end of the eighteenth century. With careful research, he found fascinating evidence in Ireland to support the accuracy of her memories. Numerous such cases have been reported, but few as well documented.

Psychotherapists may regress people to past lives in order to help them resolve emotional and relationship problems. Typically, people will present themselves to their therapist with a persistent pain, phobia, anxiety or interpersonal conflict that has not responded to conventional counseling approaches. The therapist helps them awaken relevant experiences apparently lingering in their unconscious mind from previous lifetimes. People will frequently experience intense emotional releases as they recall traumatic past-life experiences (such as the death of a dear one) or their own deaths. Bringing out the related memories and feelings often frees people of their presenting problems.[136]

Brian Weiss, a Florida psychiatrist, was surprised to find one of his patients reporting past lives during a hypnotherapy session. Though he considered at first that this might just be a fantasy, he became convinced of the validity of these memories. He has since gone on to conduct past life therapy sessions with numerous clients, with great success in alleviating an enormous range of physical and emotional problems.[137] One of his many cases illustrates how regression can relieve a troublesome symptom.

Kathy had had a successful hypnotic regression session in which she cleared residues of psychological trauma from an automobile accident in her childhood. She returned for further help, wishing to focus on her inability to lose weight. She had struggled with this for as long as she could remember, with only brief, temporary weight losses through dieting.

In a hypnotic trance, she was invited to go back to any memories that might be relevant to her weight problem. She immediately returned to memories of being as thin as a skeleton when imprisoned in a Nazi concentration camp, where she had been the subject of various inhumane medical experiments. She found release in death, recalling how she was welcomed into the white light with love. Spontaneously, she also returned to an earlier life when she had suffered a sexually transmitted disease, again wasting away to a skeleton before her untimely death.

> ...Once again, Kathy floated above her body. And, once again, she found the brilliant light that did not hurt her eyes.
>
> "I never found someone to love in that life," she wistfully observed. Her spirit had starved as had her body.

In both of these past life memories, she had died in a state of starvation. She was literally just skin and bones.

"Is there a connection between these two lifetimes and your current weight problem?" I asked...

The answer came quickly and effortlessly. "In this life, I needed the extra weight for protection. I needed to guarantee that I would not starve again." After a pause Kathy added, "But now I no longer need this protection."

Because Kathy had remembered the traumas of starvation, she no longer needed layers of fat to protect her.

Over the next six or eight months, Kathy slowly and steadily lost all of her extra weight. At the time of this writing, she has sustained the loss. Perhaps even more significantly, Kathy has started a wonderful new romantic relationship since losing the weight. Feeling good about herself and liking how she looks definitely played an important part in Kathy's ability to let this new relationship into her life.[138]

Morris Netherton, a psychotherapist, achieves similar results without hypnosis. He carefully attends to key phrases his patients use that suggest trauma in previous lives. By having them free-associate to these phrases, he helps them bring back the relevant memories from those lives, together with the emotions that appear to have been repressed across the boundaries between life, death and rebirth.

Past life events are often reported by psychics and mediums. Denys Kelsey, a psychiatrist, was a noted past life therapist who was married to the late Joan Grant, a gifted psychic. They worked as a team. When Kelsey had patients, whose problems were not resolved in psychoanalytic therapy, he called in his wife. She psychically read their past lives for traumatic events that seemed relevant to their current-life conflicts. They found that numerous problems and symptoms, unresponsive to conventional psychotherapy, were rapidly resolved in this way. A particularly impressive example is that of a phobic man, who made only limited progress in psychotherapy with Kelsey over a period of eight years. In one session with Grant, the memories and emotional pain of trauma in a previous lifetime were re-experienced, with dramatic improvement in the man's symptoms.

Research on past life hypnotic regressions has produced some fascinating results. Helen Wambach gathered two large groups of past-life memories under group hypnosis in Southern California. One series had 850 cases; the other had 350. Wambach sorted them first by century and within each century distributed them geographically. In each geographic area she sifted the cases into their apparent socio-economic groups. These sortings produced percentages of upper, middle and lower classes that closely parallel what is known of population distributions in the respective historical periods. Gender distribution in past lives was split 50 percent male/female in both groups, although the real-life distribution in her first series was 78 percent female. She also studied clothing, food and other items mentioned in past-life recall. There were cases in which verified types of historical items were mentioned that the subjects claimed they had had no conscious knowledge of prior to the hypnotic regressions. There were very few cases of objects misplaced in time.

With the growing interest in this area, there is now an International Association for Regression Research and Therapy (IARRT) in Riverside, CA.

Interestingly, Wambach also explored future life memories, finding considerable overlaps in the reports of her subjects from the 1980's.[139] While these are interesting, they are difficult to assess when predictions are made for the distant future. Most troubling in Wambach's series, paralleled by those of others, is that only about five percent of subjects were able to identify lives in the years 2100-2200, suggesting the possibility of a major decrease in planetary population.

Numerous explorers in these realms have come to the conclusion that reincarnation appears to be the process of spirits and souls taking the equivalent of elective courses in the material world, with a major in spiritual development. Explorations through reincarnation and near-death studies, along with evidence from channeled reports[140] and possession[141] provide glimpses of what it is like to be alive in spirit between earthly lives.[142]

Alternative theories to explain reincarnation

Stevenson[143] considers several possible alternative explanations for apparent reincarnation memories.

1. *Deliberate fraud* seems unlikely, considering the many and varied witnesses to the better documented spontaneous reincarnation memory reports and the fact that most of the cases are children under ten years old. Unconscious fraud may have contributed to some of the cases, perhaps motivated by wishes for attention, especially in cultures where reincarnation is accepted, such as in India and Burma. This would not hold true in subcultures where Hindu and Buddhist superstitions are prevalent, discouraging reincarnation memory reports by suggesting that those who recall previous lives are unfortunate and may be destined to die young. Western disbeliefs in reincarnation would similarly mitigate against the suggestion of unconscious motivation to produce these memories.

2. *Cryptomnesia*: Subjects could easily hear of certain persons, events, and even words or phrases in a foreign language, could retain them, and could have them appear in an appropriate context years later.[144]

The possibility of cryptomnesia is strengthened by a study, in which a post-hypnotic suggestion was given to subjects that they would recall a previous life.[145] The subjects complied in a very plausible manner, without recall of the hypnotic suggestion that stimulated their simulation. Under hypnosis again, they were able to recall the various sources for their concocted memories.

Stevenson took two steps to rule out this possibility in his cases. First, he investigated young children in small-towns in countries such as India. In many instances their past life recall began prior to their learning to read. Mobility is limited there and exposures to radio, television or other sources of distant information were nil. Second, he exhaustively questioned relatives and acquaintances to rule out all possible contacts with sources of information related to the past-life recall.

Satwant Pasricha considered this possibility of cultural sources for reincarnation memories as well, and explored parental influences upon children that might have produced these. He came up with negative findings.

3. *Collective consciousness*, or racial memories, have been proposed to explain the similarities in dream symbols, myths and legends across diverse cultures. If the memories are passed on as genetically transmitted information, this explanation would not hold. In most of the cases Stevenson investigated the persons recalled in past life memories were not of the same family. In fact, most were from different towns and many were from different cultures.

Ervin Laszlo proposes that what survives after death is the consciousness of the individual.

> Nothing in this world is evanescent; all things continue to exist through the traces they leave in the cosmic information field. We humans, too, create an Akashic record of our lifetime experiences, a record that can be retrieved by others. Our individual experience is not limited to ourselves and to our individual lifetime. It can be re-experienced and thus relived at any time and at any place, today and at all times in the future.[146]

The next possibility may also be relevant to collective consciousness.

4. *Extrasensory perception* (*ESP*) could theoretically provide details of the life of another person in an earlier time. This is unlikely, as very few of the children who reported past life recall exhibited general psi abilities. Their unusual memories were focused on a single previous life. Some adults reporting memories of previous lives have had broader psi abilities.

ESP as an explanation also appears unlikely because the information reported in many of the reports of past life recall is detailed and highly organized, with frequent additional items of recall over periods of years. It would be highly unusual for a person to have psi abilities that were restricted to such a narrow focus.

Motivation to use ESP in this fashion, should this have been the source for the memories, appeared to be lacking in the cases studied by Stevenson, both in the subjects and in their families. However, the families of the persons recalled in past life memories may still have been in mourning, which may have provided motivation to transmit such memories telepathically.

Clairsentience seems an unlikely explanation, as many of the subjects reported memories of buildings and other objects as they had been during the life they recalled, rather than as they appeared at the time of their reports.

Retrocognition is a fairly common aspect of psi abilities. In many instances this occurs either when the subject is at the scene of the recall, is stimulated by proximity to an object that belonged to a person or place in the past (*psychometry*), and may be in an alternative state of consciousness. None of these conditions applied to the majority of cases in Stevenson's studies or in the majority of other reincarnation reports. This is particularly true of children in rural locations who spontaneously report past life memories.

Precognition could be suggested to have provided information – from the verifying investigations following the reincarnation reports. However, none of the reports were given in ways suggesting that the perceptions were of future events, and this hypothesis would still have to explain the motivation for people doing this in a single case and not using precognition in other aspects of their lives.

ESP also cannot account for demonstrations of skills that were not learned in the current lifetime.[147]

5. *Communications from surviving spirits* could be suggested to provide the information reported as past life recall. The communicating spirits need not have been those whose lives were reported. Most mediums (channels) report that spirit communications occur in an altered state of consciousness, and in many cases they occur during an obvious trance state. This occurs over a period of minutes and the subjects retain a clear awareness of the distinctness of themselves from the spirits manifesting through them. The people reporting spontaneous past life recall did not appear to experience this in an altered state of consciousness, and their memories continued over several years.

6. *Possession* of the subject by a discarnate spirit could produce similar memories and even skills. (To Stevenson's observations I would add: Psychic surgeons often claim that they are channeling spirits who were surgeons or have spirit knowledge of medicine;[148] and other skills have been alleged to originate from spirit artists and musicians – producing artistic and musical creations that were unusual for the living person who created them.[149]) The temporary possession occurring with mediumship (channeling) differs distinctly from the cases of reincarnation recall. With mediumship there is an altered state of consciousness, in which the subject chooses to allow a discarnate entity to take over their mind and body. There were no reports in Stevenson's series of a discarnate entity taking over the person who reported past life memories. Stevenson feels that the reincarnation hypothesis is supported more than the hypothesis of pathological possession by the fact that his subjects would often recall extra details of their previous lives upon visiting the sites where they allegedly lived.[150]

Stevenson cannot find a suitable alternative to explain away the birthmarks and congenital defects that mirror injuries and deformities in past lives.

After considering all the feasible alternatives to explain these reports, Stevenson concludes that reincarnation is the most reasonable and economical hypothesis, although it is impossible to state that the evidence is conclusive for this.

Others have investigated various aspects of reincarnation memories. Vladimir Raikov claims he can enhance artistic abilities by suggesting under hypnosis that living artists are reincarnated famous artists from the past. Their paintings were dramatically improved following these suggestions.[151]

A further line of evidence comes from religious traditions such as Tibetan Buddhism, where highly evolved persons may predict their reincarnation after death, sometimes describing in some detail the future person they will be.[152] Other members of their religious order will then seek out the child into whom these avatars have reincarnated, testing for specific memories of his previous life. Objects belonging to the deceased persons are placed among a variety of other objects and the child is required to pick out those belonging to his previous incarnation. Such children are given special training in meditative methods, and they often demonstrate great facility in learning these. They may report clear recall of having known such skills and other information from their previous lives, or may simply learn with a degree of alacrity, which makes it feel to them more like remembering than learning new material.

Discussion

One of the strongest lines of evidence supporting a belief in reincarnation comes from Stevenson's carefully documented cases[153] of past life recall. I have great admiration for Stevenson's dedication to this research. He started at a time when reincarnation was a very poorly supported subject and has done more than any other person to investigate reincarnation in a thorough, scientific manner, and to bring the evidence to the attention of Western science. Stevenson's work has been replicated independently, validating spontaneous past-life recall – especially in children, in many countries around the world.

I believe that cryptomnesia may still explain some instances of apparent reincarnation memories. Reincarnation memories reported from industrial countries cannot be free of the suspicion that they were obtained in the present lifetime. Since the human memory is a capacious, omnivorous recorder, the possibility always exists that what appear to be past life memories were imprinted from books, news or entertainment media. We know from hypnotic regressions that present-life memory can be remarkably detailed even for events in the distant past. As mentioned above, minutiae of seemingly inconsequential nature, even from early childhood, are stored away in the memory banks of the unconscious mind. Names of childhood friends, specific clothing, decorations in a childhood home, and even intrauterine existence and unusual incidents during the process of being born[154] may be verified after they are reported spontaneously, under hypnosis or during other forms of psychotherapy. Recent research has also demonstrated that learning is possible in-utero.[155]

Stevenson argues that the xenoglossy cases are particularly convincing for reincarnation. It is conceivable that a child might learn occasional unusual names for objects from a nursemaid, visitor or other speaker of the foreign language. In some instances such sources for limited linguistic abilities were, in fact, identified. It seems less likely that an ability to respond to simple questions in a foreign language could be learned in casual, overheard conversations. In the cases where the subject was able to converse freely in a language unfamiliar to their family, such an explanation certainly would not hold, and the reincarnation hypothesis would remain the most likely explanation.

The instances of birthmarks and deformities in current lives that correlate with physical injuries and deformities in previous lives are also difficult, though not impossible, to explain away as fantasy when they occur in traditional cultural settings. There always remains a possibility that a person with a birthmark or birth defect might be motivated to assuage their injured self-image, or some other need for attention, by connecting via ESP with another person in a previous lifetime – in effect, glamorizing their defect or finding solace in communion with another person who suffered in a manner similar to their own. Though a logical possibility, this hypothesis is hard to support through evidence. Most of the past lives recalled are of ordinary people who lived very simple and unromantic lives. There would seem to be little glamour to gain through connecting one's birthmark, birth defect or low self-esteem via ESP with such a previous life. Why solace should be sought with persons in the past rather than persons currently living would be equally difficult to explain. In my opinion, the birthmarks and deformities appear to be fairly strong evidence suggestive of past life resonations.

If we accept the possibility of reincarnation, the presence of birthmarks and birth defects corresponding to fatal injuries in previous lives suggests that mental and emotional residues imprinted in a spirit may carry over from one life to another.

The evidence from hypnotic recall may be open to serious questions in individual cases. One cannot rely absolutely upon the validity of hypnotic recall. Hypnotic reincarnation memories might be induced unwittingly by investigators in 'false memories,' as has been amply explored with people claiming to have experienced physical, emotional and sexual abuse. People under hypnotic trance respond readily to suggestions. They might be led to fabricate past-life stories from bits of material garnered in their present lives – in essence, representing hypnotically induced cryptomnesia. Therapists studying past lives and reincarnation memories have generally not bothered to rule out present-life sources for the reports. Morey Bernstein is an exception. He did a very detailed investigation, ruling out present-life sources for the specific memories reported and verified.

What then of Netherton's report that he obtains similar past life memories without hypnosis? Several sources show that the psychotherapeutic setting is especially prone to the effects of suggestion, which may account for his results. Reincarnation memories could readily be suggested by reincarnation-believing investigators or therapists in a manner similar to (if not identical with) hypnotic suggestions.[156] Such suggestions are especially potent in clinical and experimental situations.[157]

It may seem an exaggeration to propose that Netherton could produce reincarnation memories by suggestion alone, without hypnotic induction. However, Milton Erickson and his followers have used many suggestive techniques from hypnotherapy without putting people into trance states.[158] We find a spectrum of suggestions from the deliberate, Erickson type, to the presumably unintentional ones of therapists of particular persuasions, who subtly encourage their patients into a particular mold of behavior, and on into the deliberate manipulation through suggestions, as in Neurolinguistic Programming.[159] It is commonly found that Freudian therapists' patients dream Freudian dreams and Jungian therapists' patients dream Jungian dreams – presumably to a great extent as a result of therapists' reinforcing patients' reports, thereby increasing the frequency of particular types of dreams.[160] Some reincarnation memories could conceivably be produced by subjects to satisfy the subtle expectations and demands of the therapist.

The success of Raikov in enhancing artistic abilities may not be as evidential for reincarnation as might appear at first reading. In my opinion this experiment has more in common with suggestion than with reincarnation. Suggestions may be given by experimenters in many subtle ways.[161] The subjects presumably knew the works of the artists who were mentioned by the hypnotists. The subjects could simply have incorporated in their subsequent work elements of styles of these artists. The suggestion of reincarnation may simply have made the experiences under hypnosis more vivid.

I agree with Stevenson that the psi powers of telepathy, clairsentience, pre- and retro-cognition must be very carefully considered as possible sources for apparent reincarnation memories. There could conceivably be motivations for using psi in this way. In some cultures, past-life recall is greeted with much interest and attention, plus occasional benefits accruing from association with well-to-do families. This psychological motivation might be sufficiently powerful to activate latent, unconscious psi powers in these particular cultures. Contradicting this explanation is the fact that many cases have been identified in cultures where no apparent reward exists for using ESP to acquire past life details, and in many instances it is actually negative attention that results from such reports.

ESP could also be considered as an explanation for xenoglossy. This could easily explain the use of a few words or even phrases in a foreign language. However, this explanation for the ability to converse freely in a foreign language would be stretching the psi hypothesis unreasonably far beyond what are generally accepted as the limits of psi abilities.

On rare occasions gifted mediums, including some healers, have reportedly spoken in trance state in foreign languages. Many mediums say they are guided by spirits. Could some or all apparent reincarnation memories are actually cases of unconscious 'possession' of some people by spirits rather than reincarnation memories of their own lives? This explanation is not without difficulties either. In cases of possession people often are disturbed by the interference in their lives by one or more spirits. The possessing spirits feel alien and distressfully intrusive. In reincarnation reports, individuals may find traumatic reincarnation memories jarring. However, as they absorb the impact of the traumatic memories upon their present lives, they often resonate very positively with the lessons of their past life experiences and their impact on their current lives and world views. These memories may help them to understand quirks of their present personalities, life styles and relationships, and help to resolve psychological tensions and existential questions. The positive psychological adaptations seen with past life memories do not occur with possession.[162]

One might ask whether psi can be better demonstrated under hypnosis, and might therefore be more suspected as a factor in past life regressions. The answer is a qualified yes. Although some people have been known to develop psi abilities in hypnotic trance, this approach has very limited success. Psi powers are usually evident in the laboratory as so slight a tendency that multiple trials and sophisticated statistics are needed to confirm that they were demonstrated at all.[163] The early Mesmerists reported psi as a frequently occurring phenomenon. Their good results might be explained by a selection of patients who were unusually good visualizers and psi-gifted[164] or by the prolonged hypnotic inductions they used (sometimes over several hours)[165] that could have produced results we do not see today.

Challenges in validating reincarnation reports

To verify alleged memories of previous lives is very difficult. The vast majority of lives reported are prosaic simple existences in agricultural communities. No written records or human memories of such lives survive more than a few generations. Most reported details cannot be verified.

Some reports of previous lives of prominent people can be verified. They might be from recent centuries or from well-known people in earlier centuries. The difficulty here is that the more prominent the person, the more likely the subjects in their current lives may have come across reports, articles or dramatizations of such a life. These memories are therefore suspect of being based on information obtained in current lifetimes and manifested as cryptomnesia.

If obscure records in some archive or museum are found to support the information, questions remain of psi as the source for the alleged past life memories. The psi hypothesis cannot be refuted in any single example. People have been known to screen their environment successfully via psi for specific information of interest to them, as in the remote viewing experiments.[166]

I again agree with Stevenson that the psi hypothesis has several serious weaknesses. The numbers of verified details reported in many reincarnation memories would require a highly developed psi ability. It is usually only the rare, very gifted psychics who show a capacity to obtain numerous details via psi powers. Such psychics do this in a wide variety of situations, not restricted to just a single or a few past life stories. They can use their psi powers to find lost objects or people; see glimpses of future or past; read aspects of others' minds; and so on. This is very different from the isolated, narrowly focused reincarnation memories.

Another strong piece of evidence can be seen in the statistical findings in Helen Wambach's group hypnotic regressions. These studies seem to make the memory tricks and psi hypotheses even more unlikely. That any one of a few individuals would recall a few historical details from studies or entertainment media, or respond to hypnotic suggestions and fabricate reincarnation memories seems plausible. That 1,100 people would do so with equal distribution of sexes and with details conforming to archeological, anthropological, sociological and historical data seems extremely unlikely.

If a typical, unhypnotized group of 1,100 Southern Californians were asked to fantasy past-life memories, I would anticipate a very skewed distribution. First, they would be more likely to create memories of persons of the same sex as themselves. In Wambach's first series 78 percent of 800 subjects were women. Still, they reported 50 percent of past lives as males. Second, I would expect most such memories, if fabricated, to portray middle- or upper-class existences, because this is what is familiar to such people today. I would expect that average Americans would be unlikely to spontaneously imagine themselves as peasants or slaves.

Wambach found that between 59 and 77 percent recalled lower-class existences, many of them in destitute poverty. Third, if imagination were the source for Wambach's case memories, then I would expect that geographic distribution would include far more memories from early America, Europe and Mediterranean countries (i.e., those more familiar to the American subjects). Wambach reports geographic distributions that correspond closely with historically known population pictures. Fourth, I would expect many errors of detail, especially objects out of place in time and location. Such errors were extremely rare. These points seem to effectively counter the cryptomnesia hypothesis in Wambach's series.

> ...ESP does not reach my boggle threshold, but survival takes me well beyond it, so I boggle and take any explanation involving ESP, however far-fetched, rather than one involving survival, at the very suggestion of which I blanch.
>
> – Michael Perry

Psi sources of information could still be present. Clear limits have not been found to psi in terms of distance, time or the complexity of tasks. Still, to produce distributions such as Wambach's with psi powers would be an extraordinary accomplishment, involving multiple manipulations of collective perceptions. Wambach herself would naturally be the first suspect as the source of such psi effects. She would have to keep mental track of a very large number of factors in order to organize her subjects into the appropriate distributions. She would have to suggest to them in telepathic or subliminal ways that they 'recall' the information needed, while working with a dozen or more subjects at a time. She does mention that she had a research assistant, but even with the help of another person the mental task of organizing such a mass of data is staggering. That any or all of the subjects might be responsible for organizing the data via psi seems even more unlikely. Although the psi (or super-psi) hypothesis cannot be ruled out definitively by these arguments, it does seem unlikely.[167]

An examination of Wambach's series by sub-groups that met for hypnotic sessions would be of interest in this regard. If Wambach or any other individual(s) used psi or suggestion to produce the results, there might occur clusterings of lives from particular periods in some sub-groups. However, believers in reincarnation could counter that clusterings represent present-life friends, or even synchronistic acquaintances, attending the same groups and that these friendships represent reincarnations of groups of people who return together to work through karmic debts or to continue lessons together – per reported agreements that people make between lives regarding their future incarnations on earth.

Replications of Wambach's study would be helpful.

The transformative effect of past-life recall

It is impressive that recall of traumatic events from previous lives can have a releasing effect upon disturbing symptoms in present lifetimes. This type of

evidence is the same as that presented by psychotherapists in conventional ther
apy. They find their patients are often relieved of their symptoms when repressed
memories of early traumas from their current lives are released, along with associated emotions,. Weiss,[168] in particular, parallels my views regarding the
evidential nature of the transformative effects. Psychotherapists often find that
recall of traumas and release of the related emotions, which were buried earlier in
a current lifetime, can relieve symptoms that develop later in life as a result of the
earlier traumas. Let me share a composite example of how this can work.

Tom developed panic attacks for no apparent reason. These began when he was
driving his wife home from the hospital with their newborn son. They persisted
and worsened, leading him to sweat even at the thought of driving and having
numerous panic attacks whenever he was behind the wheel of his car. Ordinary
counseling was getting nowhere, and he was advised to take medication. The
panic attacks were interfering to such a degree in his life that he agreed to take a
medicine known to help with panic disorders. When he developed impotence as a
side effect of this medication, and was excessively drowsy on several different
tranquilizers, he naturally refused to continue with this treatment route. His counselor suggested hypnotherapy, to which he skeptically agreed.

When the hypnotist asked him, in trance, to look inside to identify what might
be behind the panic attacks, he came up with memories that had long been buried
and forgotten. When he was 16 years old, Tom had been in an auto accident, in
which he was severely injured and two other teenagers were killed. Though not
responsible for the accident, he felt a mixture of guilt, anger and hurt that he had
survived while his buddies had died. Unable to deal with this, he simply put it out
of his conscious mind. When the hypnotist had him relive this traumatic experience, he cried and raged and felt the terror of the experience – all of the feelings
he had not allowed himself to express following the accident. Within two sessions
his panics cleared, never to return.

Tom came to understand that the panics had started because his unconscious
mind worried that he might have an accident, in which those nearest and dearest
to him would be killed. The feelings of responsibility towards his wife and newborn child had triggered the buried feelings from the accident.

This is a common experience in psychotherapy. Feelings that are buried can fester for years – outside of conscious awareness. Later in life, triggered by some
current-life situation, they come to a head and erupt into symptoms that lead a
person to uncover the buried hurts and drain the emotional pus pockets. Having
done this, the clients' symptoms clear.

Logic dictates that some credence be given to evidence of past life therapy if it
too produces relief of symptoms. The implication of traumatic events in previous
lives affecting people in their current lives is that the past life memory actually
has some validity. This is an empirical observation that can support, but does not
prove, the existence of reincarnation.

Alternate hypotheses are again possible. Past life recall in therapy may represent
fantasy memories rather than actual ones. This sort of fantasy (technically called a
'screen' of false memory) sometimes is found in conventional, current life therapy. A person may develop a screen memory for early events that never actually

took place. She may do this in order to justify or assimilate unacceptable feelings or circumstances that were experienced.

For example, 'Joan' reported that she had felt angry towards her parents for many reasons during her childhood. The anger was based on jealousy towards her six brothers and sisters, who she felt were receiving more from her parents than she was. This was so severe that she felt like a Cinderella, and often wondered whether she hadn't been adopted. When she explored her feelings and memories with various family members in later life, they all reported that she and her sisters and brothers had each received equal care and attention. She was astonished to have family members contradict specific instances of public mistreatment by her parents that she recalled quite clearly.

Joan had grown up feeling that she wanted and needed more. In order to justify her anger and salve her conscience, she apparently unconsciously invented memories of mistreatment and neglect.

Such occurrences of fictionalized, *screen memories*, are well known in psychoanalytic therapy and have also been identified more recently in instances of false memories over alleged sexual or physical abuses. In a similar manner, so-called past-life memories could conceivably be fantasies developed by the unconscious minds of people seeking to explain various conflictual situations.[169] The cases Stevenson has collected, in which a birthmark (or other physical defect present from birth) correlated precisely with an injury recalled in a previous life memory, might fit in this category. The birthmark could serve as a stimulus to the creation of fantasies of traumas that could explain these blemishes. However, in many instances Stevenson's investigations of the persons alleged to have lived the previous lives produced clear evidence of injuries precisely in those places where the birthmarks occur. This weighs heavily against the hypothesis of fantasy as an explanation in these instances. We are returned yet again to the reincarnation hypothesis as a more likely explanation for these and related phenomena.

> *A bodily disease may be but a symptom of some ailment in the spiritual past.*
>
> – Nathaniel Hawthorne

Even more impressive is the fact that most of the past life recall subjects were young children. Most of the elaborate psychological explanations suggested above would be highly unlikely in these instances.

Other psychological explanations for past life reports

Brugh Joy suggests that apparent reincarnation memories may represent patterns in the unconscious mind that represent various aspects of the inner self. For instance, a person's sub-personalities may be interpreted as manifestations of past lives. That is, one or more parts of a person may become split off from their primary consciousness. Such fragments could then be mistakenly perceived as representing past life personalities.[170]

Joy's views are based upon the experiences of having various sensitives report their impressions of his own past lives to him. Each sensitive might identify themes that overlapped with themes reported by other sensitives but the details they described were very different.

> Through these experiences with many different readers, I suddenly became aware of the Pattern Level of Reality. I saw the eternal dance of but a limited number of themes and plots, combining and recombining, dancing us generation after generation and having nothing to do with the personal self, that self which is but an illusion of consciousness and has only limited resources and options in relation to the forces that are actually manifesting us. Instead of seeing karma as personal and individual, I suddenly saw it as collective, impersonal, and immortal.
>
> All the patterns being read by the reader are those of impersonal forces manifesting through us. Each individual has a unique combination of the immortal patterns, determined by the energetics at conception. Life incarnates us and needs us. These patterns renew themselves in each generation and are present now, not somewhere in the past! We are only the latest vehicles acting out the forces in the great Mystery Play called Life. Our only spiritual responsibility is, to the best of our ability, to fully live out those patterns that relate us to the wholeness of Life.[171]

Although Joy's hypothesis is a possible explanation for past life memories, I do not accept his evidence on the varied reports of past life readers as relevant. Various psychic readers often report differing impressions when reading the same subject. The reasons for this rest more likely simply in the fact that different people will resonate with different aspects of whatever they are observing, in the psychic realms[172] as much as anywhere else.

A case might be made for past life recall representing unrecognized incidents of multiple personality disorder. I consider this highly unlikely because this disorder is typically found in people with severe abuse in childhood, is persistent, is often highly intrusive and disruptive to people in their adult lives, and is most difficult to treat. There is absolutely no indication that such was the case in the children or adults investigated by Stevenson and others.

In helping people with *post-traumatic stress disorders* (PTSD) to work through severe emotional traumas, it is sometimes found that the traumas did not occur to the person who claims to remember them. Francine Shapiro, who developed the remarkably effective methods of Eye Movement Desensitization and Repatterning (EMDR), reports an interesting instance of this sort.

> ..[A] client asked for help with PTSD symptomatology that included flashbacks of having been killed at Auschwitz during the Holocaust. While two specific scenes had repeated themselves in nightmares and flashbacks for many years, the client had no idea of their genesis. In fact, he was not old enough even to have been in the Holocaust. The first scene, of standing in line to enter the concentration camp, was targeted for reprocessing, and

the client reported a rapid reduction in SUD [*Subjective Units of Distress*, a measure of symptom severity] level... It was not until the second memory, of being gassed in a chamber, was treated that the client suddenly exclaimed... "It's not me, it's my uncle!" He then remembered all the stories he had been told as a child about his uncle dying in Auschwitz during the war. The impact of the *vicarious traumatization* [italics added] was sufficient to cause the client's pronounced symptomatology, although the actual trauma happened to someone else. It is vital for clinicians to remember that the genesis of a symptom may be masked by a representation or screen image that may never be penetrated...[173]

In effect, this appears to be a form of cryptomnesia. Another possibility exists. Such memories could come from actual past life recall but may be rationalized away as vicarious traumatization. I know personally of a number of people who have past life recall for Holocaust deaths, and Gershom chronicles many others, where it is highly unlikely that they experienced vicarious traumatization from experiences in their families. Vicarious traumatization cannot be ruled out, however, in these days of graphic media presentations on the Holocaust.

Another possible motivation for subjects to activate complex psychological and/or parapsychological mechanisms is the fear of death. This is a widespread, potent factor in most cultures. All the stories of life after life (as detailed in Chapters 2, 3, 5 and 6) could merely represent wishful fantasies, which would allay anxiety regarding the unknown that lies behind the final closing of a person's eyes in death. The super-psi hypothesis may be somewhat less far-fetched in the light of this potent motivation.

Benjamin Franklin's epitaph is a poignant example of such wishes and beliefs:

The Body of B. Franklin
Printer
Like the Cover of an Old Book
Its Contents Torn Out
And Stripped of its Lettering and Guilding
Lies Here
Food for Worms
But the Work shall not be Lost
For it Will as He Believed
Appear Once More
In a New and more Elegant Edition
Revised and Corrected
By the Author

Countering this last alternative are instances of childhood memories of past lives. Children under the age of eight have not developed the awareness of the finality of death that adults have. They are less likely to be motivated by fears of death and to fabricate stories about survival as a way of dealing with such fears. However, this factor has not been researched to rule it out.

Preview to discussion of spirituality

Roger Woolger[174] suggests that an incarnating soul may be attracted to parents who resonate with the soul's unresolved karmic issues. These parents may replicate the incoming soul's patterns, providing opportunities to all parties to work them through and resolve them. If this is so, it appears likely to me that in many cases the attraction for a soul would be strongest with souls with whom there had been earlier relationships – because the points of correspondence in unresolved conflicts would be most similar among these souls.

An alternative explanation is that while each of us has our individuality, we are parts of group collective consciousness. Each of us is thus exploring our own individual issues but also participating in group explorations of group experiences. Just as body, emotions, mind, and spirit are nested layers of overlapping bio-energy fields, so the individual, family, clan and national consciousnesses may be nested layers of experiences.

Looking at this from the other side: if we are reincarnated beings, then speculating on life between physical lives may be looking at it from the wrong perspective.[175]

> *We are not human beings having a spiritual experience. We are spiritual beings having a human experience.*
> – Pierre Teilhard de Chardin

It may be that our more long-term place of being is in spirit worlds, with brief sojourns in physical existence. More on this in later chapters.

Reincarnation memories as healing

Consider another possibility. Reincarnation could be a useful myth that permits healees to release their investment in their dysfunctional habits. This could be a stage for a fantasy play on which the subjects rework their conflicts in the mythic reality,[176] acting within rules that apply to that reality but are excluded from the sensory reality. This would be a real-life analogy to the physicists' theoretical use of the term 'i' (the square root of minus one), a nonexistent, mathematically impossible, imaginary number. Certain calculations in physics require the use of this otherwise nonsense number. Without its use, calculating formulae and predicting certain events in the real world would be impossible. During the time that they manipulate certain figures, physicists go into a nonexistent reality in order to handle the real world better. The healer and/or healee may similarly use the myth of reincarnation and spirits to create a place, where mind/body changes can take place in new and different (from sensory-reality) ways.[177]

> ...Reincarnation, like heaven, is a metaphor.
> The metaphor in Christianity that corresponds to reincarnation is purgatory. If one dies with such a fixation on the things of this world that one's

spirit is not ready to behold the beatific vision, then one has to undergo a purgation, one has to be purged clean of one's limitations. The limitations are what are called sins. Sin is simply a limiting factor that limits your consciousness and fixes it in an inappropriate condition.

In the Oriental metaphor, if you die in that condition, you come back again to have more experiences that will clarify, clarify, clarify, until you are released from these fixations. The reincarnating monad is the principal hero of Oriental myth. The monad puts on various personalities, life after life. Now the reincarnation idea is not that you and I as the personalities that we are will be reincarnated. The personality is what the monad throws off. Then the monad puts on another body, male or female, depending on what experiences are necessary for it to clear itself of this attachment to the field of time.

– Joseph Campbell [178]

Another analogy, closer to conventional imaging techniques in therapy, comes from the 'directed daydream' (Le rêve éveillé dirigé) of Robert Desoille. Mary Watkins briefly describes Desoille's method:

> He believed that psychological disturbances were the result of habitual vicious circles that make varied movement impossible. By introducing new symbols and symbolic modes of movement into the patient's waking dream the therapist could offer 'new lines of force,' alternatives to the patient's habitual modes. Desoille attempted to teach the patient not only how to participate with the various 'archetypes' that arise but how "to control," "to be free from them and thereby to lose his fear of them..." [179]
>
> Desoille had the patient repeatedly insert himself into six archetypal imaginary situations (for example, a descent into the ocean or a cave, meeting with a dragon) until the anxiety provoking images which appeared were drained of their painful effective charge. Each of these situations (as well as descension and ascension) were attempts to couch in symbolic terms specific questions i.e. what is the patient's relation to the parents, the unconscious personality, to the society). The contents of the waking dream were considered to answer symbolically the specific question... [180]
>
> Desoille attempted to borrow from myth and fairytale not only the images he suggested but ways of moving among the images. For example, to help make the patient secure when faced with threatening imagery Desoille would sometimes suggest that he see a hand reaching to help, that he have a magic wand that can produce desired metamorphoses of the images, that he could make an ascension to a level with more pleasant imagery. [181]

In this practice people project their problems onto the images and situations suggested by the therapist. This is often done without verbalizing or consciously conceptualizing the connections. For example, a man who has difficulty in being assertive with people may work-through this problem in a mythic story. He may gain confidence and assertiveness via tales that he weaves with the help of the therapist – climbing mountains and conquering villains. These successes enhance his self-confidence, which carries over into his real-life situations.

Another analogy can be drawn from EmotionalBody Process, another imagery therapy technique.[182] In this approach, people are instructed to create an image to represent something that bothers them, and to invite this image into a space within themselves where there is love, healing, acceptance and forgiveness. They strengthen the energetic qualities of this space by connecting to a series of supporting energies, including the Infinite Source.[183] They are then told to ask the image what it wants of them, and to freely give whatever is requested. By not battling the negative image, they stop feeding it energy. Being in this space of enormously positive energies, the image transforms at least into a less threatening one, and often shifts into a positive one. The experience of the person who is doing the imagery exercise is one of profound psychological growth, as they themselves enter this wonderfully positive, healing space and experience its transforming energies.

A reincarnation memory may be a similar experience, in which a person may face horrendously fearful experiences, often including their own death. Because they come through this and survive – as a spirit entering the tunnel of light, the experience in its totality becomes a positive one. Whether the reincarnation recall is a fantasy, such as in EmotionalBody Therapy, or whether it is a real memory, the strong positive ending may be transformative.

Similar analogies may be drawn from other therapies, such as psychodrama, gestalt therapy (particularly when focused on dream analysis), archetypal dream analysis, music therapy and art therapy. With these techniques, inner conflicts are worked out through projections onto contrived and invented stages and dramas.

For instance, Carl Jung is known for his awareness and use of imagery in therapy, such as the drawing of complex, symbolic mandalas. These function in the same way as the directed daydream, but also draw on potent collective unconscious images that Jung labeled *archetypes*. Reincarnation memories could be archetypal myths.

Personally, I favor the economy of the reincarnation hypothesis, supported as it is by evidence from the numerous and varied sources reviewed in this chapter.

> ...The splintered aspects of the soul, the aspects that require healing, need to interact in physical matter so that each part of the splinteredness can become whole. The personality is like a complex mandala that is formed from these splintered parts in addition to the parts that are not splintered. It comes directly from the parts of the soul that the soul has chosen to work on in this lifetime to heal, that need to experience physical matter, and these parts that the soul has given to the process of healing in which you are involved. Therefore, you can see within a person's personality the splintered suffering of the soul from which it was formed, as well as the grace that the soul has earned, which is the loving part of the personality.
>
> – Gary Zukav [184]

With respect to spiritual healing, I propose that the healer and/or healee may nevertheless simultaneously use the imagery of mythic reality to rework problems.[185] Once creating their new reality, the healer and/or healee may then be able to use PK and other powers that exist in this reality. An effective application of such techniques is described by Iris Owen and Margaret Sparrow, from their séance group that created a mythic reality named Philip.[186]

D. Scott Rogo,[187] a noted parapsychologist, reviewed most of the evidence I have sorted here and reaches a different conclusion. He proposes that some memories of individuals may survive death, but that they exist as part of a larger 'group mind.' Parts of such memories can then become available to one or more individuals, who appear to recall them as their own. This hypothesis explains why occasional memories, alleged to derive from past lives, may become available when the deceased person died several years after the birth of the person, who later recalls the previous life memories. It also provides an explanation for rare instances of recall of the same past life by several persons in concurrent lives. I would point out, however, that Rogo's analysis does not take into account the psychologically reparative effects of past life therapy.[188]

Relevant here are the wonderful worlds of collective consciousness detailed by Carl Jung and his followers. Jung had a phenomenal memory for details of myth and folklore. He identified mythic images in the dreams of people he treated in psychotherapy – often from sources the dreamers themselves had not learned about. Yet the images that came to them, when interpreted according to their mythological origins, were perfectly suited to represent aspects of their deepest inner conflicts and of the struggles of their unconscious minds to unravel these.

In a simple but telling example Jung[189] reports,

> I vividly recall the case of a professor who had had a sudden vision and thought he was insane. He came to see me in a state of complete panic. I simply took a 400-year-old book from the shelf and showed him an old woodcut depicting his very vision. "There's no reason for you to believe that you're insane," I said to him. "They knew about your vision 400 years ago." Whereupon he sad down entirely deflated, but once more normal.

The more surprising examples of collective consciousness come from Jung's notes of children who reported dreams with elaborate mythic imagery that precisely correlated with the ancestral stories of primitive tribes on distant continents – of which they could have had no direct or indirect knowledge. They simply could not have known of the historical origins of their dreams. In today's Western culture, we could hypothesize that such images came from TV or other media. In Jung's time, this did not apply and access to such images was highly unlikely.

Jung and his followers have helped us appreciate the collective unconscious – in addition to helping troubled people unravel their inner conflicts and turmoil.

If we accept that a collective consciousness exists and that each of us potentially can tap into this cosmic library, then reincarnation memories may represent elaborate myths that we humans create from this awareness. One cannot rule out this possibility. However, the specificity and discreteness of the past life memories, the physical and psychological residues that come to light as the results of a recall that resonates with symptoms – which are then resolved – suggest to me that while archetypal, collective consciousness exists, it is a separate phenomenon from reincarnation. People with reincarnation memories, in my experience, do not need to relate them to mythological images from the collective consciousness in order to make sense out of them and in order for them to be profoundly meaningful and transformative as they often are.

Jung himself observed:[190]

> I could well imagine that I might have lived in former centuries and there encountered questions I was not yet able to answer; that I had to be born again because I had not fulfilled the task that was given to me. When I die, my deeds will follow along with me – that is how I imagine it. I will bring with me what I have done. In the meantime it is important to insure that I do not stand at the end with empty hands...

I very much resonate with Brugh Joy's[191] associations of a collective consciousness with reincarnation memories. My personal belief is that reincarnation memories are a part of our awareness of belonging to a vast collective consciousness that is beyond our full comprehension while we are in the flesh, and only dimly perceptible through alternative states of consciousness.

Jane Roberts, in poetry[192] and in a series of fictional stories on spirit guidance across several lifetimes,[193] suggests ways in which experiences in one life may resonate with other reincarnations. Lessons in one life may be relevant to lessons being learned in another life – both forward and backward in time.[194]

Others have suggested that reincarnation is far more complex than can be conceptualized in linear, sensory reality terms. They propose that our lives on earth are a very small (though still important) portion of our vaster selves, which exist in other dimensions beyond ordinary space and time.

> [D]eath appears less an extinction than an awakening to 'where one was all along.' At death, the center of awareness shifts from the physical to higher planes... We don't go somewhere at death, we are already there. As this view becomes real in our lives, fear of death disappears. We couldn't non-exist if we wanted to.
>
> – Willis Harman [195]

> The spiritual path represents the process of becoming whereby the soul remembers itself and the Self discovers its true identity as Spirit. The spiritual journey can also be perceived as a healing journey that is completed in the recognition of wholeness...
>
> – Frances Vaughan [196]

Once considering reincarnation a reality, our lives may be drastically altered. If karmic debts incurred in this life have to be repaid, we ought to weigh carefully all of our actions.[197]

If you want to know about your past lives, look at your present condition.
If you want to know about your future lives, look at your present actions.
— H.H. the XIVth Dalai Lama

More on this in later chapters and in Volume IV of *Healing Research.*

I tramp a perpetual journey, (come listen all!)...
Not I, not any one else can travel that road for you,
You must travel it for yourself.
It is not far, it is within reach...
And as to you Life I reckon you are the leavings of many deaths,
(No doubt I have died myself ten thousand times before.)...
This day before dawn I ascended a hill and look'd at the crowded heaven,
And I said to my spirit, When we become the enfolders of those orbs and
*   the pleasure and knowledge of everything in them, shall we be fill'd*
*   and satisfied then?*
And my spirit said, No, we but level that lift to pass and continue beyond.
You are also asking me questions and I hear you,
I answer that I cannot answer, you must find out for yourself.
— Walt Whitman

Each of us must decide how to interpret the evidence and how to apply it in our lives.[198] More succinctly:

You lay your cash and conviction on any of a number of altars of assurance;
you pay your person and you take your choice.
— Paris Flammonde [199]

Regardless of the validity of reincarnation memories, the experiences and perspectives provided through a belief in reincarnation may contribute to healing. Consider, for instance, Robin Norwood's suggestion: "Every problem is an assignment from your soul." [200]

Fuller spiritual implications of reincarnation will be considered later in this book.

My personal experience with reincarnation memories

In exploring inwardly for psychological contributors to a persistent pain in my left hip that started with a fall when I was bike riding, I unexpectedly came upon what felt like a past life memory in a dream. I was a Native American or Eskimo, walking with a group of families up a snowy hill. I had injured my left hip and could not keep up with the pace of the rest of the clan. It was decided that we would have to say our farewells because they could not slow their pace anywhere near enough to let me keep up with them. This was done as a matter of course, with no recriminations on my part because sacrificing the injured individual was the accepted way for the clan to survive. I simply sat in the snow by the side of the path and waited for the cold death that would end my suffering.

Although I had no bad feelings towards the clan, I was angry at God for having left me to die in this way, sorely missing my wife who had died in childbirth shortly before. This had left me feeling I had no good reason to be with this clan, into which I had married in order to live with my wife.

I am not given to vivid, realistic dreams of this sort. My usual dreams are usually clear distortions of recent or past experiences from my current life.

This dream has been very meaningful to me, resonating strongly with my frequent feelings in childhood that I did not belong in the company of many of my childhood school and play mates. I have also had a recurrent sensitivity in my life to feeling abandoned or neglected by family and friends – often out of all proportion to the realities of the situation. The dream, whether it was only a dream or was a real past life memory, helped me confront my unreasonable projections and distortions of others' behaviors towards me.

In summary

Reincarnation memories may be reported by young children, often in communities where there are no media that could have provided the information about lives they claim to have lived – in places that are many miles away, which they have not visited. Research has validated numerous details in past life reports from such sources.

Adults may recall past lives spontaneously, during psychotherapy or as part of a deliberate quest for such memories. Here, too, research has validated a variety of reports. Particularly within the context of psychotherapy, reincarnation memories may be transformative – similar to Near-Death Experiences.

Survival of the spirit with reincarnation is made more credible by anecdotal reports and research on OBE, NDE, apparitions, mediumistic/channeled experiences, mystical and spiritual experiences, and spirit possession.[201]

The existence of reincarnation has the potential to bring an inspiring light into our lives at several levels. Psychologically, it provides windows into past traumas that may leave their emotional scars in our spirit, which brings these into our current lives. These residues from past lives may create emotional problems just as psychological traumas from our present lives can; and similarly may be cleared with the help of a therapist who understands reincarnation residues.

Spiritually, reincarnation is a lesson and a caution about behaving ethically and responsibly. Our behaviors in one life carry over into future lives – acknowledged historically as *karma*. When we behave in negative ways, we create relational scars that carry over into future lives and require the same sorts of clearing as our psychological residues of reincarnation memories.

Reincarnation also sheds light on questions of theodicy, the philosophical pondering on the reasons that God allows evil to exist in the world.[202]

If a spirit does survive death, then sightings of ghosts may be more than fantasy. Next, let us examine anecdotal reports and research on apparitions.

CHAPTER 4

Apparitions, Nature Spirits and Angels

But even though the spirit world exists,
however it may act,
it cannot prove itself as fact.
And even though God shows himself
upon his throne of might,
the thought will out despite:
'hallucination!' some will insist.

— V. Rydberg

Apparitions

Spontaneous sightings of apparitions (ghosts; spirits) are common. Usually these are unplanned, unpredictable occurrences. Apparitions typically have an ethereal, filmy, partly transparent appearance, although they may in some instances seem as solid as material objects. They may appear suddenly in a space, come through a wall, cross a given space, and then disappear into thin air or through another wall. They will often behave in a stereotyped manner, as though they are images in a film that is replayed. For instance, an apparition may be observed by a variety of people over months or years, traversing a particular hallway, opening a certain door, repeating various noises or words and then disappearing. In other cases they may interact with one or more observers. This is more typical of crisis or bereavement apparitions, associated with danger, trauma or death. Occasionally there are 'haunting' apparitions who seem to interact with the deliberate intention to frighten or even harm observers.

In most instances, apparitions appear to be (by clothing, information conveyed in words and use of language, etc.) the spirits of people who died previous to the encounter. Apparitions of the living may occur, especially around times of danger, crisis or death. It is not uncommon around the time of an accident that someone closely related to the person in danger would see an apparition of that person, occasionally perceiving the specific danger as well, with no normal means of communication that could have conveyed the perceived information. Apparitions of dying people may appear to their dear ones around the time of their death, announcing their departure and saying farewell.

Perceptions of apparitions may be cinematographically accurate in their details of the spirit's appearance, clothing and voice (later verified by the person in crisis) or may be altered in the sorts of distortions that fading memories impart to sensory impressions or that dreams introduce to inner knowledge and psi perceptions. The more distorted perceptions tend, in fact, to occur during dreams. A person may, for instance, dream that the president has died, and learn soon thereafter that their own father has died.

In cultures that have unbroken traditions of spirit awareness, the living may continue relationships with the spirits of those who have left physical existence. Kay Cordell Whitaker, a woman in California who was under the tutelage of a South American shaman, reported the following vision she perceived in the course of developing her shamanic awareness.

There was a forest with redwood trees along a field. Four Native American men, dressed in clothing typical of a local tribe of more than 200 years earlier, walked up to a deer they had just shot. The deer seemed to have given its life willingly and graciously, making no efforts to escape. The first man tenderly reached down and stroked the deer's head as it was breathing its last breath. He appeared sad over the deer's death. He gazed into its eyes just as one might peer into an old friend's eyes. He seemed to be thanking the deer for having given itself to them. He gestured to something in the air above the deer, his eyes returning to this area several times. The others took out herbs from small bags they carried around their waists. One scattered his herbs around the deer while the second put herbs into the animal's mouth. Two took out knives. In a way that appeared to honor the deer, they spoke to it, then softly sang to it as they turned the body over and removed its entrails. One dug a shallow hole. The first held the organs briefly, then put them into the hole. Branches were gathered for a carrying device. Their preparations and song completed, they carried the deer away. Whitaker continues:

> I felt very strongly that all five of them, the four men and the deer, formed some kind of a team, and that there had been no violence in this entire interaction. A sense of dignity and honor surrounded them...
>
> There was no remorse or guilt. There was honor and grief as one would show for a family member who had passed on...[203]

This scene was replayed several times when she moved from one vantage point to another. With each repetition of the vision, Whitaker opened to deeper awarenesses of the interactions between the men and the deer.

When the deer died, I saw a wispy, shimmering shape rise from the deer's chest and head and float into the low branches of the tree above them. It was two-legged and looked vaguely like a combination between a deer and a man. It was curious and attentive, looking carefully at each of the hunters. As the first hunter watched the shape rise, light streaked between them. And as the second man placed the herbs in the deer's mouth, the spirit deer took a special interest and moved closer. Light flashed between the second man, the deer's body, and the spirit deer's mouth.

The men lifted the deer when all was finished, and the leader looked back at the spirit deer in a gesture of invitation to join them. Keeping a distance, the spirit deer slowly followed them down the field toward their village.[204]

Apparitions appear very frequently to the bereaved. Vargas et al. published a survey of bereaved people in *The American Journal of Psychiatry*, a conservative professional publication, not given to featuring ghost stories. Two thirds of those surveyed reported they perceived the person who had died, either seeing them, hearing them, or intuitively sensing their 'presence.' [205] Apparitions are also relevant to spirit healing, in which it is claimed that spirits assist in healings.[206]

Research

The great strength of science is that it is rooted in actual experience. The great weakness of contemporary science is that it admits only certain types of experience as legitimate.
– Russell Targ and Jane Katra [207]

There is evidence that apparitions may be more than fantasies woven as tall tales on dark and stormy nights around campfires, or dreamed up in heads buried under pillows and blankets when the darkness stirs the imagination to do its worst.

Several approaches have been taken to confirm the existence of apparitions.

Concurrent observations of the same ghost by several observers
Hornell Hart and E. B. Hart[208] surveyed numerous reports of ghost sightings over many years. They distinguish between apparitions of living persons (who may or may not recall having experienced themselves in the situations reportedly viewed by others), of persons at the time of death, closely after death, or more than twelve hours after death. They found 165 apparitions that were perceived collectively (simultaneously) and reciprocally (details of individual sightings were corroborated by the several observers) which seem particularly evidential.

Here are two examples.[209]

*&

On Sunday, 28 June 1903, a little boy lay dying in a Yorkshire town. His mother had died some years previously. At the foot of the bed watched his eldest sister and a friend of his mother. At about 9 o'clock the boy was unconscious. Suddenly the friend saw the mother distinctly, bending over her boy with a look of intense love and longing, but not seeming to notice the two watchers. The apparition was in her ordinary dress, as when living, and was entirely natural in her appearance. After a minute or two she quietly and suddenly was not there.

The friend said nothing to the sister at the time. Two days later the boy died. After they had performed the last offices to the body, the sister and friend were standing as they had two days before. The friend said, "I had a strange experience on Sunday evening here." The sister quickly replied; "Yes, mother was here; I saw her." [210]

Apparitions sometimes are reported to come to the aid of the living.

On Christmas Eve 1869, after locking their bedroom door and retiring, both Mr. and Mrs. P. saw an apparition of a naval officer, whom Mr. P. recognized as his father. The apparition spoke his son's name reproachfully, cast a deep shadow as it moved past a lamp, and "disappeared, as it were, into the wall." The door of the room was found to be still locked. Mr. P. later admitted to his wife that at the time when the apparition occurred he had been intending to take the advice of a man who would certainly have led him to ruin or perhaps to disgrace.[211]

You might tend to think that evidence from 1933 is stale and perhaps not up to modern standards of observation, investigation or reporting. Numerous more recent reports have been published. Here is a similar experience taken from one of the books of Brian Weiss, MD,[212] a Harvard-trained psychiatrist in Florida who is now a past-life therapist:

A husband and wife, both respected physicians in Miami, came to see me in order to describe an unusual phenomenon they had both witnessed. The wife's father had recently died. About a week after his death, which had occurred in Colombia, both she and her husband saw her father's body, glowing brightly and somewhat translucent, waving to them from their bedroom door.

Both were wide awake at the time. They walked over to touch him, but when they did, their hands went right through his body.

The father waved good-bye and suddenly vanished. There were no words.

When they later compared notes, both physicians discovered that they had seen the same physical form, the same radiant body, and the same wave good-bye.

The concurrences in the collectively and reciprocally validated reports are detailed and specific. They suggest that the people who simultaneously perceived the apparitions were observing the same events.

Serial observations by several observers of the same ghost in the same location
In a modern-day study, Thelma Moss, known for her research in Kirlian photog-

raphy, and Gertrude Schmeidler, a well known parapsychologist, invited six psi 'sensitives' individually to investigate the same haunted house. Statistical analyses of elements in the independent reports of the sensitives showed that there was a highly significant degree of correlation between the reports of three sensitives and of those of four independent witnesses who had previously sighted the ghost. (The results of the other three sensitives were not statistically significant.) Similar studies of other haunting sites have produced significant findings.

Apparitions may take the form of broad scenes with numerous participants. For instance, a person may observe a battle scene, complete with soldiers, armaments, horses and bloody frays. Some investigators refer to observations of such apparitions as 'time-slips' or 'time-warps,' because it may appear to the perceivers that either they have traveled back to when the apparitions were alive (especially when the apparent environment of the apparitions' lifetimes is visible to the observer) or that the apparitions have traveled forward in time to interact with the observers.[213]

Many and varied *non-human* ghostly figures have also been reported, including animals, ships, a London bus and aircraft.[214] They behave in manners similar to those of human-form ghosts. They appear briefly, are witnessed by one or more persons, may be observed intermittently over periods of years, may vary from solid forms to wraith-like appearances and may be accompanied by appropriate sounds, such as the noise of aircraft engines with the planes.

Photographic evidence of apparitions
Apparitions appear occasionally in photographs as unexpected *extras*.[215] The extras may or may not be familiar to the live subject(s) in the photographs or to the photographer.

The 'old hag'

David Hufford[216] describes a form of apparition appearing during the borderlines between sleeping and waking. People wake in the night and find themselves paralyzed for minutes or even hours, unable to move or to utter a word, with a strong fear that can reach proportions of panic and terror. Footsteps may be heard approaching, and an old hag approaches close to the petrified, immobilized person. The hag may speak to them or may touch them, sometimes pressing on their chest and making it hard to breathe. In some cases, people were said to be able to summon the old hag deliberately to annoy or disturb someone else.

Hufford systematically questioned 93 people who reported that they had experienced the old hag phenomenon, and methodically analyzed a variety of conventional hypotheses, all of which were inadequate to explain it away. These included: imagination, outright lies or possible errors of memory, hoaxes or pranks, visions from fasting or hallucinogenic drugs, or psychotic hallucinations. While this is not a commonly known form of apparition, I include it here because of Hufford's meticulous study and documentation of these reports.

Discussion

Apparitions challenge our conventional belief systems. Immanuel Kant commented on the difficulties in accepting reports of apparitions:

> Stories of this kind will have at any time only secret believers, while publicly they are rejected by the prevalent fashion of disbelief...[217]
>
> The same ignorance makes me so bold as to absolutely deny the truth of the various ghost stories, and yet with the common, although queer, reservation that while I doubt any one of them, still I have a certain faith in the whole of them taken together.[218]

Skeptics may claim that apparitions are projections from the unconscious minds of those reporting them. For instance, Carl Jung[219] suggested,

> Spirits are complexes of the collective unconscious which appear when the individual loses his adaptation to reality, or which seek to replace the inadequate attitude of a whole people by a new one. They are therefore either pathological fantasies or new but as yet unknown ideas.

Such psychological explanations cannot account for apparitions that are perceived by more than one person.

Believers are likely to be impressed by the reciprocally and collectively perceived apparitions of Hart and Hart and of Weiss. Many of the observers appeared to be sober, intelligent citizens with no apparent motives for fabricating such stories. In fact, many of them would have had every motivation for not revealing them, as by doing so they opened themselves to questioning of their veracity and even of their sanity.

Skeptics can point out that these cases were gathered from diverse sources, over many decades. They were recorded, in most instances, days and even years after the events so that distortions and more *apparent* than *real* similarities may have developed between correspondences in separate reports. States of mind of the reporters could not be assessed, leaving questions of whether some percipients may have been drunk or in other alternative states of consciousness.

Samuel Johnson,[220] discussing beliefs in ghosts, observed, "All argument is against it; but all belief is for it."

Such is the nature of field research of irregularly seen phenomena.

The statistically significant correlations of several observers in studies (e.g. Moss; Schmeidler) suggest the existence of intuitively perceived phenomena that may be more than subjective individual experiences. These consistent findings by multiple sensitives point to the likelihood that an objective, 'out-there' reality exists which is being perceived by diverse observers over a period of time.

The non-human apparitions and the repeated appearances of ghosts in particular locations suggest that it may not be a surviving spirit that produces some aspects of apparition phenomena. In some instances, perceivers may create apparitions in their minds out of telepathic and/or clairsentient perceptions. Clairsentient perceptions are often associated with particular objects. That is, a psychic will hold an object and obtain impressions from it that relate to its history. This has been given the name *psychometry* and is used in a practical way by psychics who may hold a piece of clothing or a photograph in order to obtain psychic clues on the whereabouts and condition of missing persons.[221] If a small object can be a connecting link with clairsentient perceptions, there seems to be no reason that a location could not serve in the same manner.

Why only particular people or vehicles should stimulate apparitions remains an unanswered question. Perhaps these images are imbued by an original observer or participant with psi and/or intense emotional energy of some sort, which then imprints the image either in physical objects at the particular location or within another level of reality associated with the location. Perhaps the apparitions are *thought forms*, created in the auric field around the body and then somehow detached, remaining in a particular location. Thought forms are perceived by sensitives who see the *aura*, or energy field surrounding living and inanimate objects. They appear to represent an energetic concretization of thoughts.[222]

Other questions are raised by interactive apparitions of the time-warp type, as in the Native American scene quoted above. These occurrences suggest that 'wrinkles' or 'holes' in the fabric of reality may occur, through which persons in different time frames may be perceived, and on occasions may even interact. If this is possible, then some apparent ghost sightings may be partial time-warps.

It is encouraging to find that experiences of bereavement apparitions, prevalent in two thirds of the population, are increasingly gaining awareness. I was taught during my psychiatric studies in the late 1960s that sighting ghosts of relatives during mourning is not a sign of psychosis. It was explained that mourners wish so strongly to maintain contact with the departed that they hallucinate the images they would like to see. I now believe that although this may be true in a small portion of cases, the mass of evidence from a variety of sources reviewed in this book suggests that the spirit survives and may be perceived by the living.

> *...The gross material body, Daskalos teaches, is in a very real sense the prison-house of the ego- soul and a central part of human growth is to transcend its limitations...*
> – Kyriakos Markides [223]

During investigations of apparitions of the deceased, Hart and Hart found cases of out-of-body appearances (OBEs) of living persons who were perceived by others. OBE apparitions are sighted more often during crises or at the time of death. A continuum exists for perceiving apparitions of persons from just prior to their death to soon afterwards. This suggests that we may be dealing with identical types of apparitional entities with the living and the dead. It seems likely that people may exist at times during their physical lives in spirit form as well as in the flesh. This lends credence to the theory that our primary existence may be in spirit form, with our existence in the flesh being but one expression of the spirit.

The crisis apparitions suggest that people under stress or at the time of death may project themselves out of body to particular perceivers for specific purposes.

There are numerous reports of such apparitions summoning help in time of danger or appearing at the precise time of death of the person perceived, apparently as a message of farewell.[224]

Alternatively, one may hypothesize that perceivers are clairsentiently observing the people who appear to be projecting themselves. If true, this would imply a much more close, subtle awareness between people than feels consonant with our experience of awareness in everyday physical reality. For instance, people who are constantly aware of others who are close to them on an unconscious, psychic level, may produce visions of one of these people when she is in trouble. Thus, what appears to be an apparition that is present of its own volition actually may be a projection of the perceiver's psychic awareness, a way for their unconscious mind to bring important information into conscious awareness.

At times, apparitions of the deceased interact in order to help the living. Numerous reports from grateful recipients of spirit communications testify to an enormous feeling of relief to know – following spirit contacts – that death is not the end of existence. Communications relating to practical matters have also been of frequent assistance, such as the location of the deceased person's last will and testament. There are other times when the apparitions express needs of their own, such as resolving unfinished issues in interpersonal relationships that were sundered by their physical death. Asking forgiveness for acts of commission or omission is a common communication, particularly with reassurances that the deceased did love those they left behind, or acknowledging they appreciated feeling they were loved. From the opposite side of these contacts, there is often also relief and gratitude at the opportunity for the living to express their feelings.

Apparitions and healing

Studies of apparitions support various healers' reports that:

1. A spirit body may be involved in healer-healee interactions;
2. A non-material aspect of Self survives physical death;
3. Some healings may occur via interventions of spirits; and
4. Cases of alleged spirit 'possession' [225] may have some validity,

If we accept the evidence that spirits of people and animals survive, there are vast implications for human relationships with the world. Injustices committed by one person against another are slated not only for redress in this world and in this life but also in spirit worlds. If spirits survive, then reincarnation finds support, along with karmic reworkings of relational lessons.[226] This would appear to apply to our relationships to animals as well as to humans. How different is the hunting of a deer (as described in the Native American apparitions above) from industrial society's slaughtering of animals for mass consumption! What might be the karmic implications of killings of animals without respect for their spirits?

Explorations of more interactive spirit phenomena are discussed more fully in the next sections.[227]

Apparitions confront us with the limited views that our materialistically focused society teaches us. They suggest that mystics' reports of deeper, spiritual meanings of existence may be relevant.

> *Man is the bobbin at weaving the vestment of God*
> *Who in His love requireth Perfection*
> *Wherein is reflected His own Countenance,*
> *And Man's kinship in full is declared.*
> > – Patience Worth/Irving Litvag [228]

The existence of apparitions supports mystics' and theologians' teachings that a Spirit survives physical death, that earthly existence is a lesson in life to the Soul,[229] and that the eventual goal of existence is return to unity with the All.[230]

Nature Spirits and Angels

> *Over every blade of grass an angel watches, saying, "Grow!" "Grow!"*
> > – Jewish saying

Nature spirits are accepted as real in traditional societies and as folkloric tales in industrial society.[231] Though descriptions vary from culture to culture, the basic patterns appear fairly consistent.

People who are extremely sensitive and open to communication with other realities may perceive hierarchies of nature spirits and angels. Dora van Gelder[232] describes a wonderful panoply of these entities, whom she saw and interacted with from childhood – just as she would interact with a live person. She explained that her perceptions were not through her outer senses but through clairsentience,[233] for these creatures are not directly of the physical world. She believed they are an evolutionary line of life forms existing in realms of more subtle substance than the physical world. Their life task is to support all aspects of nature in the physical world. There are very simple ones that support rocks and minerals. More complex fairies attend to subtle energy aspects of the air and of bodies of water. There are spirits of individual plants; of classes of plants; of particular geographic features (such as mountains and valleys); of geographic regions; of processes of nature (such as rain, wind and storms); and more.

A nature spirit may be very simple and literal-minded, with limited tasks and responsibilities – perhaps caring for an individual plant. A more advanced example would be a tree spirit. Each tree draws its life force from its individual tree spirit, which grows and eventually dies with it. Each tree species has typical features, and each individual spirit has its own personality.

> …This personality can emerge from the tree for a little distance when it so desires, usually assuming a form which is more or less human. When inside the tree, the form is much vaguer and practically invisible... Most tree spirits look alike to the extent that they all seem to have a tall, brownish

form which looks something like...a human figure – square, slightly thick, and suggestive of a papoose, with little eyes and nose...[234]

The spirit might emerge from its tree for various reasons.

..Often when I have sat under a tree the spirit has come out to express its affection, though, of course, in rather vague terms, and it may even follow one for a few yards. At night these beings seem to have more free time and opportunity for social life...[235]

On the whole...trees generally feel quite affectionate towards people... They have the same kind of feeling of loyalty as a dog does, but they are more dignified...[236]

Other spirits may tend collections of plants, as in a particular garden or forest.

Van Gelder befriended many of these spirits. She observes that they are particularly responsive to children.

Every time a child says "I don't believe in fairies" there is a little fairy somewhere that falls down dead.
— J. M. Barrie, 'Peter Pan'

Some of the fairies are more advanced, supervising lower forms of nature spirits or having responsibilities over broader processes.

At higher levels of awareness are angels with various levels of responsibilities, attending to the needs of people and of broader, more complex aspects of nature. Some minister to individuals and groups of people. Some oversee various other nature spirits, assisted by sylphs. Sylphs have a form identical with human shape and communicate telepathically. Their task is to help people as well as angels.

Robert Ogilvie Crombie (known as 'Roc') describes encounters with a nature spirit named Kurmos, who had the classic appearance of a faun.[237] He has furred legs, cloven hooves, pointed ears, and small horns on his forehead. He worked with trees in a particular garden. He explained that nature spirits had given up on humans because humans stopped communicating with them.

Roc also met the god Pan, the 'king' of nature spirits.[238] His appearance is that of a faun, but he is larger than human size and radiates incredible power of love, wisdom and peace. Pan indicated that he and his hosts of nature spirits are open to helping mankind if man will just approach nature and its spirits with respect.

Roc explains the place of devas and nature spirits in the world:

We may think of the Devas as angelic beings, and it seems that they design the archetypal pattern for each species and channel down the required energies for its manifestation on earth.

The Nature Spirits, on the other hand, may be regarded as the builders. Working according to the archetypal design, they form and build up what may be called the 'etheric counterpart' or 'body' of the plant from the energies channeled down by the Devas.[239]

Roc reports that nature spirits exist as whorls of subtle energies and intelligence. They are unable to interact in their ordinary forms with denser physical energies of plants and inanimate objects in the sensory world familiar to modern Western awareness. To do so they must assume an etheric body, shaped by their thoughts. Thus were created the forms of elves, gnomes, devas, fairies, and the various mythical gods of antiquity. They may take on human behavior, but they are not moved by emotions of their own. Though Pan also takes on such a form, he is not localized to a single place, even when he is interacting with a particular person or situation at a given location. He is a universal energy that permeates the entire realms of nature. He can interact with the material world in many places at once.

While it may sound like only the most highly gifted intuitives can connect consciously with nature spirits and guides, Machaelle Small Wright describes ways in which we can invite nature spirits to work with us in creating a garden. The garden can be a plot of land with vegetables and flowers; it can be a creative project for growing better relationships; it could be a community project that is nurtured by a group of people; or it could be an inward project for growing in our own inner wisdom. Wright suggests:

> In Co-creative science, the scientist acknowledges that there is an inherent intelligence within all of nature, builds a communication bridge that allows him to access that intelligence, and then asks nature directly to explain and provide experiential insight to him so that he may understand... how something works. In co-creative science, nature becomes a fully operational, functioning, conscious partner with the scientist. Together they create a team, with each member of the team providing specific and different information that is needed for understanding and solving a defined problem.[240]

Everyone's project will be individually designed by and for that person.

> When you are working directly in partnership with nature, you cannot simply announce, "Let's put in a garden!" and expect that you will get any information back from nature regarding the garden. You must supply the definition, direction and purpose of this garden. In other words, you must supply the evolution dynamic within the balance, and you are the only one who can do that. Nature will not do your job for you. It will only supply the evolution dynamic for objects that fall within its 'natural' domain: plants, rocks, deer, lightning, etc.[241]

Wright finds that the average class takes four years. You should decide how much time each week you will spend on this and set a time period as a study 'term.' Four to six months is a comfortable time in which to see significant progress on a project.

Wright advises that nature can sort out its lessons in a more structured and orderly way when you let the nature spirits know the parameters for your availability:

1. Verbally state your intention to nature. Out loud is best. For instance: "I would like to open a co-creative science classroom with myself as the student and nature intelligence as my teacher. My intent is to be educated and trained as a co-creative scientist. I am ready to learn."

2. Select your classroom. This can be anything that provides structure for action. "Pick something that you can do alone, and remember that whatever you choose will become a classroom and you will need to hand over all the activity, timing and rhythms to your teacher. So, don't choose something you are not willing to release control of and don't pick something that is life-threatening either to yourself or anyone else. Your classroom has to remain personal for the amount of time you and nature are using it..."

3. Wright offers a wealth of further suggestions in the Perelandra materials, especially the 2 workbooks: Keep detailed notes, a log for each day; be as complete as possible; keep notes organized, so you can review them periodically.

I highly recommend Wright's excellent self-help book, enriched by the author's sharing of her own path in opening to intuitive and spiritual awarenesses and learning to be a co-creative gardener.

Angels

Angelic beings have been reported over thousands of years. Some of the earlier mentions of angels in the Bible are well known. For instance, an angel wrestled with Isaac, after which Isaac was renamed Israel (meaning *struggled with God*). At first this angel appeared as a human, and it was only when questioned that he revealed his angelic form. Jacob dreamed of angels going up and down a ladder. The births of John the Baptist and of Jesus were predicted by angels.[242]

There are numerous versions of angelic and devic hierarchies – based on legends, folklore, religious teachings and personal encounters. Some of these are derived from ancient traditions whose origins have been forgotten through the centuries. Though such hierarchies may be valid to an unknown degree in otherworldly levels of reality, it is difficult to verify them other than through cross-references in dusty old tomes and through legends – of unknown value in their origins – or through sifting modern reports of personal encounters.

Malcolm Godwin, in one of the clearest and most organized summaries on angels, notes that classical sources, such as St. Jerome, Thomas Aquinas and St. Paul disagree on angelic choirs, and there is much more confusion amongst later theologians. Citing Dionysius and Aquinas, Godwin details nine angelic orders:

Highest Triad:	Middle Triad:	Lowest Triad:
1. Seraphim	4. Dominations	7. Principalities
2. Cherubim	5. Virtues	8. Archangels
3. Thrones	6. Powers	9 Angels

The functions of angels (from the vantage of earthly existence) appear to be to translate and transform the intentions and energies of the Infinite Source into acts of creation in the physical realms – including the nurturing of mineral, plant and animal kingdoms.

While it may seem a rather large and complex group to deal with, all of these helpers seem to combine their wisdom and speak with a harmonized voice when we call for assistance from on high.

Angels, the celestial messengers closest to humans in the hierarchy, are often perceived as six to eight feet tall, luminously radiant figures, often with wings, sometimes with halos around their heads, and sometimes carrying swords. Some are translucent, others look as solid as any object in the material world. Angels appear particularly at times of stress and crisis, and especially when someone prays for help. They may have clearly masculine facial and body features or may be androgynous in appearance. They may intervene in times of crisis to prevent accidents or to help people in distress. In the intervention reports, many 'angels' are described as looking like normal people who appear out of nowhere, give their assistance, and then disappear again into nowhere. They may communicate in gestures, words or telepathically. Their communications are clear to the perceiver and, if spoken, are in the appropriate language. They are experienced as being wise beyond human comprehension and infinitely *compassionate and loving*, but at the same time *dispassionately free of emotions of their own*. They may reassure people simply by their presence, or may intervene with information, advice, or even with a touch or with substantial physical assistance. Whatever their appearance, they radiate an overwhelming presence of calm, peace, love and power. Most people feel calm when encountering angels, even when their intervention is entirely unexpected and surprising. Lest their presence be too heavy an intrusion, they may often inject humorous notes in their communications. quipped,

> *Angels...can fly because they take themselves lightly!*
> – Alan Watts [243]

It is often said that each person has one or more guardian angels who accompany them everywhere, from conception to their transition back into spirit worlds. Some believe that these are actually aspects of a person's own *higher self.* [244] As with most aspects of other dimensions, our beliefs and expectations may shape our perceptions and experiences with them.

Examples of alleged angelic interventions

James Pruitt has a pleasant collection of angel stories, amongst them the following:

Terry Baldwin was a bush pilot for fifteen years, flying hunters and other adventurers all around the state of Alaska. He had learned to fly as a navy pilot during the Vietnam War, and logged many miles flying cargo prior to settling in his job in Alaska. In March of 1992, Reverend Paul Roberts asked to be flown from Fairbanks to Anchorage to greet his new pastor who was to start work at his church. As Terry had two hunters chartered to fly there in any case, he offered the Reverend Roberts a free ride.

Terry took off in his twin Cessna the next morning with his three passengers, knowing a storm was heading towards Fairbanks but anticipating they would be well away before it arrived behind them. An hour on his way, he was surprised to see storm clouds moving in out of the West. Contacting Fairbanks, he was informed that this was an entirely unexpected storm that had already covered Anchorage and was advised to turn back. All the passengers agreed with his turning back.

Terry informed the Fairbanks airport that they were turning back, and was warned that the other storm there was moving in swiftly. Thirty minutes out of Fairbanks, the airplane instruments became totally unstable, with the compass gyrating wildly. Terry was unable at this point to tell in which direction he was flying. The altimeter read 4,000 feet higher than they had been flying a few moments before, which was impossible. The storm clouds were closing in rapidly.

Doing his best not to alarm the passengers, he radioed Fairbanks, telling them he was having problems with his instruments and asking if they had him on their radar. They responded,

> "4Y Whiskey Delta Seven, this is Fairbanks Tower – Roger, I have you five-zero miles southsoutheast at ten thousand feet, over."
>
> Terry, still remaining calm, told the tower that his instruments showed him at fifteen thousand feet and southwest of Fairbanks.
>
> "Sounds like you have a problem, 4Y Whiskey Delta Seven. I suggest you abandon all reliability on your instruments and we'll talk you down. Do you roger this?"
>
> "Affirmative, Fairbanks." [245]

Terry was guided to a lower altitude and given a new heading. When asked by his passengers if he was flying blind, he reassured them that the radar was as good as a pair of eyes. Snow was soon covering the windshield, and they were truly flying blind. The tower radioed a course correction. Then they hit severe air turbulence that buffeted the plane. Terry worried silently, knowing their course must have shifted considerably. Radioing the tower, he received no reply to repeated calls. He pounded the instrument panel, without effect.

The hunters joined Reverend Roberts in whispering the Lord's Prayer.

The wind shifted to blow head-on and their fuel gauge, the only instrument apparently still working, showed only enough to reach Fairbanks. There was no alternative landing field.

Terry realized the situation was desperate. He didn't know his altitude, which direction to fly, or how far it was to the airfield. Reverend Roberts suggested they might radio the tower again. They were enormously relieved to have a reply, with directions for a heading to bring them in to the field.

The controller continued to radio instructions and Terry intently and carefully followed each direction. Reverend Roberts and the hunters were openly praying at this point. The calm voice of the tower on the radio helped everyone to stave off panic as they flew blindly through the rough storm, the fuel gauge moving towards zero.

> Suddenly the controller said, "You're coming in on the end of the runway. Ease it down... down. Okay, set it down... now!"
> With nothing but faith in a voice on a radio, Terry obediently dropped the Cessna down through the surrounding whiteness. Then, suddenly, as if by magic, Terry saw the beginning of the runway just ahead, with lights lining both sides. Within a few seconds they touched down and a wild cheer broke among the passengers.[246]

They all let out a big sigh of relief as they taxied to a stop, and offered a little prayer of thanks.

Terry, his muscles still taut from his intense concentration, radioed the controller.

> "Thanks tower. There's little doubt that you saved our lives today."
> The controller's reply cast a stunned silence over the men in the plane. "What are you talking about? We lost contact with you about forty miles out." [247]

The tower assumed they had gone down in the storm when they lost contact, and were surprised and relieved to pick them up on radar again just prior to landing. The controller speculated that they must have had some angels guiding them.

This story is unusual in its clarity of extraordinary circumstances that suggest an unexplained intervention from an unknown source. In many other stories of this sort, skeptics could suggest alternative explanations, such as simple coincidences of rescuers appearing at a roadside accident or phoning a wrong number and waking someone who discovered a fire starting.

Prayers are often reported to precede angelic appearances, both for those who pray and for others they pray for. Numerous prayers for help, safety, improved health or release from suffering are said to have led to angelic interventions.

Hope Price presents another collection of Angel stories, reported from a Christian viewpoint. Among them is this story: Bob and Vi, driving in Southwest England, passed an ordinary looking elderly man standing at the side of the road. They offered him a ride, and although he wanted to get to Redruth, which was half a dozen miles in the opposite direction, they happily agreed to take him there. Vi moved to the back seat to let him sit in the front. He spoke little, except to say, "Praise the Lord" occasionally. Arriving in Redruth, they asked him where he wanted to go. He said, "Just here will be fine," and simply disappeared. He had not opened the door, and neither Vi nor Bob could see where he could have gone. They were so astounded that neither felt they wanted to drive on. Instead, they drove to visit Bert, a friend living in Redruth.

Bert's wife was overjoyed to see them. She told them she had been phoning them all day, and, failing to connect, had asked the Lord if He would bring them there. They urgently needed a speaker for a religious meeting that evening and hoped that Vi would share her experiences of how God was active in her life.

Looking back upon the events leading them to come that way, Bob and Vi realized that their gentleman passenger must have been an angelic messenger. They had picked him up from the side of the road leading *away* from Redruth, but this was the right side of the road to be picked up by Bob and Vi.

> *Do not forget to entertain strangers, for by so doing some people have entertained angels without knowing it.*
> – Hebrews [248]

Here is another gem from Price. Peter and Sue were distraught on being told their unborn baby was diagnosed as having spina bifida. This is a severe congenital spinal deformity, which can lead to weakness or paralysis of the lower extremities, as well as bladder and bowel problems. Spina bifida is also associated with hydrocephalus, which requires surgery to drain excess fluid from the brain and can be associated with learning disabilities. Peter and Sue were advised to consider a therapeutic abortion. They refused this recommendation. One day, the expectant mother heard God saying, "Trust me." About two weeks later they prayed with several friends. Though uncertain what they should pray for, they experienced an enormous feeling of glory, deep happiness, and were swelled with feelings of praise. Sue saw the entire room light up with angels who were praising God. Another woman saw an angel filling the room behind Sue, his wings wrapped around her. They felt a joy they attributed to God's presence rather than to the angel's appearance. They all felt, without any doubt, that the baby was healed. Needless to say, the medical personnel were skeptical. They baby was born without any defect.

Pierre Jovanovic, a French reporter, became interested in angels after an unexplainable incident. Driving away from an interview, he felt himself flung to the side of the car by an unexplainable force. At that instant a bullet tore through the windshield, burying itself in the seat where he had just been sitting. Following this and other incidents that spoke to him of angelic guidance, he methodically gathered and published one of the most impressive series of encounters with angels from people around the world.[249] These include meetings at times of great danger; during Near-Death Experiences;[250] in states of religious practice (prominently in the lives of saints); during serious illness; and many more.

The stories above are some of the typical reports of interventions of guardian angels in human affairs.[251] Skeptics will suggest that one need not resort to angelic, nor even to psychic or intuitive hypotheses in order to explain these tales away. Plain old unconscious awareness of information obtained by ordinary means, wishful thinking, misdiagnoses of medical problems (such as the in-utero diagnosis of spina bifida) and other ordinary reasons can explain away these allegedly unusual events, and that attributing them to angelic or Divine interventions is superstitious nonsense or religious misinterpretation of events that have normal – though possibly obscure - explanations. Further possible explanations are elaborated below.

Collective prayers are sometimes reported to produce spectacular angelic responses – as related in this report by Hope Price.

In July 1918 the war was going badly for the Allies. The English troops to the north of Béthune in France were exhausted and outnumbered. Their lines were breached by masses of German troops and it appeared that they would very soon be overrun.

Around that time the British and Americans had been called to prayers for the troops. These prayers are credited for the ensuing events.

The German shelling had been directed mostly at the town of Béthune. Suddenly it shifted away to an area of open ground on the outskirts of the town. There were no military targets there whatsoever, yet the Germans fiercely poured shells and machine gun fire into this area. The British could not understand what was going on. Suddenly, the German fire ceased and the masses of German troops that had begun their advance halted. Without any apparent reason, the German troops then scattered into disorganized groups and fled the battlefield, dropping their equipment in their haste.

A captured officer gave this amazing report:[252]

Just after the German troops had been ordered to advance, they saw a cavalry brigade approaching through the open ground behind Béthune. The Germans speculated that these must be colonial troops because they were dressed entirely in white, riding white horses. They thought the cavalry were mad to attack in this way and anticipated these British troops would have no chance under German gunfire.

> …We saw the shells bursting amongst the horses and their riders, all of whom came forward at a quiet walk trot, in parade ground formation, each man and horse in his exact place. Shortly afterwards, our machine guns opened a heavy fire, raking the advancing cavalry with a dense hail of lead. But they came quietly forward, though the shells were bursting amongst them with intensified fury, and not a single man or horse fell. Steadily they advanced, clear in the shining sunlight; and a few paces in front of them rode their Leader—a fine figure of a man, whose hair, like spun gold, shone in an aura round his bare head. By his side was a great sword, but his hands lay quietly holding his horse's reins... In spite of heavy shell, and concentrated machine-gun fire, the White Cavalry advanced, like the incoming tide over a sandy beach. Then a great fear fell on me, and I turned to flee; yes I, an officer of the Prussian Guard fled, panic-stricken, and around me were hundreds of terrified men, whimpering like children, all running. Their intense desire was to get away from that advancing White Cavalry; but most of all from their awe-inspiring Leader. We are beaten. The German army is broken. There may be fighting, but we have lost the war. We are beaten – by the White Cavalry. I cannot understand.[253]

Interestingly, this appears to be a parallel with a Biblical report:

Ben Hadad, king of Aram, and his army laid siege to the Israelite city of Samaria. The population was starving. The prophet Elisha predicted that the siege would be lifted. The next day it was found that the Arameans had left their camp, apparently in great haste.

When they reached the edge of the camp, not a man was there, for the Lord had caused the Arameans to hear the sound of chariots and horses and a great army, so that they said to one another, "Look, the king of Israel has hired the Hittite and Egyptian kings to attack us!" So they got up and fled in the dusk and abandoned their tents and their horses and donkeys. They left the camp as it was and ran for their lives.[254]

They followed them as far as the Jordan, and they found the whole road strewn with the clothing and equipment the Arameans had thrown away in their headlong flight.[255]

I find the parallels of modern reports with those of the Bible of interest because they suggest that similar observations have been made over many centuries, in cultures very different from our own.

The credence one gives to reports of angels may be strained by several factors. Many reports come from people who espouse strong religious beliefs that they feel are supported by the existence of angels. It is not uncommon to read in such books that the angel encountered was Michael or Gabriel or some other prominent angelic figure of Biblical mention. I have to report, however, that non-religious intuitives I respect have told me of such encounters too.

In general, many helpful apparitions are reported, with the assumption that they must have been angels. Once one accepts the existence of apparitions that appear to be surviving spirits of people who have passed on, or of living persons, any assumption that such apparitions are angels must be questioned. However, a case can be made for the reverse argument, that apparitions, which are felt to be surviving spirits, actually may be angels. There is also the possibility that some of each – spirits and angels – appear in these unusual encounters.

What may distinguish between the two possibilities is the fact that encounters with angels are profoundly transformative.

> [T]he word 'angel' means 'messenger,' but... an angel does not usually *bring* a message in the sense of a particular announcement. This does happen from time to time, but only in a minority of cases. The angel is actually the message himself. His appearance is the message that heaven is intensely concerned with us, and that God cares for us...
>
> – H. C. Moolenburgh [256]

Moolenburgh notes that many of those who encounter angels felt, prior to the encounter, that they were different from the average person. They had been sensitive as children and lonely. In adult life they did not fit in fully, though they got along reasonably well with others. Following the encounters, most experienced bliss constantly over several weeks. A few reported anxiety and confusion. They found their lives fundamentally changed in these ways:

- Their faith in God and the Bible was strengthened. (Protestants related more to the Bible; Catholics more to Mary.) None felt a greater closeness to the Church, though regular attenders continued their attendance. "...it was as though they realized the relative nature of any human organization... The Church makes some very absolute statements about itself, and mystics tend to take such pronouncements with a pinch of salt." [257]

- Life held new meaning, with a sense of purpose, peace and inward invulnerability.

- They experienced unity, love, mystery and integration – actually words that attempt to describe a Godly essence that is beyond words; awareness of their cosmic duality of existence in the physical and spiritual worlds; increased capacity to love; acceptance of life's negative experiences as belonging to a Divine pattern rather than representing tragedies.

- Special gifts were developed, such as healing and precognitive abilities, as well as being able to tell whether people were being spiritually truthful.

- Fears disappeared, such as fears of death, illness, surgery and other frightening situations.

- A sense of direction in life developed, with a knowledge of when they were on the right Path.

- Changes in daily life included the "...courage to pursue their ideals regardless of the social consequences" and greater fulfillment in being of help to others.[258]

Many other reporters of angelic encounters note simply that these meetings brought immediate calming and long-term transformations in beliefs, even when these people had started out as non-believers. A typical instance of this sort is presented by Jovanovich. When Nancy Meier was about 30 years old, she fell and ruptured her liver, which resulted in peritonitis and a Near-Death Experience.

> … I...traveled through that tunnel at an unbelievable speed... When I reached the end I met three Beings of Light... I said to myself: "O.K., I'm dead, so where are the Angels?" They answered me by thought: "For you, we don't need to look like Angels because you don't believe in Angels." And I laughed because I knew in my heart that they were Angels, in truth. It was like a thought, a certainty that they had transmitted to me. 'Looking' at them, I had the impression that they constituted a welcoming committee. They resembled candle lights.[259]

Meier felt that each angel had his own distinct personality, though she could not see their faces. No words were exchanged, only telepathic communications. Then she found herself in the white light of infinite love. Every atom of her being quivered with passionate love. "To melt in that light is a little like coming home, falling in unconditional love. That was my experience of God..." [260]

Various angels appear to have duties that differ from those reported for guardian and messenger angels. Angelic supervision of broader processes in nature are described by Dora van Gelder. For instance, there are sometimes energy imbalances on the planet which require rectification through storms. A storm angel might organize a hurricane with the help of local air, water and land angels and other nature spirits. Such a destructive process might appear at first to be contrary to the nature of angelic purposes. However, it appears that the welfare of the planet is of greater priority than individual lives. Though angels minimize loss of life, they also perceive and accept death as a transition rather than a termination of life.

Even more diffusely general spirit or energy patterns may underlie physical and spirit realities.

Cosmic healing rays are mentioned by Alice Bailey; Alex Tansley; others. These are said to relate not only to individual healings but also to evolution and healing of society and the cosmos. They are of the order of abstraction at which astrological cycles of thousands of years are calculated.[261]

Theories explaining angelic interventions

One of the best books on angels is by Malcolm Godwin. His historical review is superb, richly illustrated with artworks through the ages. Godwin points out that up to and including the Middle Ages, encounters with angels were widely reported and accepted, starting in pre-Christian pagan times. The Christian church included angels in its cosmologies. These became increasingly complex until the end of the Middle Ages. Godwin is also one of the most sophisticated in analyzing psychological and other mechanisms whereby we might convince ourselves an angel had intervened in our lives when other causal factors are responsible for these events. He calls these 'heavenly hypotheses.' [262]

1. *We could create what we think, particularly from 'archaic memories.'* Through psi perceptions and psychological mechanisms of the unconscious mind we could create angels as fantasy mental projections. Godwin relies heavily on Jungian psychology, suggesting that memories from the collective consciousness of mankind[263] could be interpreted by individuals as angelic encounters. Godwin points out that modern civilization has lost its trust in its own perceptions, relying on various experts to tell it how the world really is. Since we build our beliefs on second hand information, we have lost touch with our gut feelings that can inform us about things that are true or false.[264]

2. *We are complex beings and one part of ourself could 'get over' on the rest of ourself.* Under this explanation we have the extreme example of multiple personality disorders, in which a part of the personality may split off from the rest and assume autonomous functions and actions.[265] Lesser examples occur in daydreams, where one part of the mind presents materials to another, observing part. "Human beings are sleepwalkers who keep bumping into unrecognized chunks of their own drifting personalities." [266] Jung points out that we collectively are feeling divided from our deeper selves, and there is a growing search for

wholeness to bring the parts back together again. The fragments of ourselves seek to communicate with one another and could produce images of angels and extraterrestrials in symbolic efforts to communicate between the parts.[267]

3. *Through ingestion of various drugs (such as LSD), through hypnosis, sensory isolation or meditation one could reach states of superconsciousness or cosmic consciousness in which angels are perceived.*[268]

4. *Esoteric traditions report that we are composed of several bodies, each existing in a separate dimension* [269] The densest is the physical body. The *astral* body can go on OBEs through a dimension in which expectations and beliefs actually create reality. This is said to be the dimension, in which dreamers visit and in which the spirit surviving death acclimates to non-physical existence. Spirits who are attached to desires and fears inhabit this region. Auras, etheric, astral or psychic bodies may bear resemblances to angelic 'wings' ' Astral 'flight' may enhance this suggestion.

5. *Esoteric historians suggest that modern human civilization may have been 'seeded' or in other ways initiated by races of vastly superior intelligence and technology.* Various origins for these superior beings have been suggested in earlier civilizations on the lost continents of Atlantis or Lemuria,[270] extraterrestrials (ETs), beings from other space-time dimensions, and the like. These could remain in cultural or collective unconscious memories as angelic beings.

Support for these theories is suggested by very sudden, simultaneous flowering of several civilizations in various parts of the world. For instance, around Lebanon there are Sumerian, Babylonian and Hebrew reports of the arrival of aliens who had advanced technologies. Statues meant to depict these beings include unusually large eyes, very similar to those described in some modern ET encounters. Tibetan writings mention 'luminous sons' who produce 'form from no-form'.[271]

Esoteric writings, such as the book of Enoch, speak of what could have been alien encounters. Another author, Josef Blumrich, suggests that the Biblical story of Ezekiel's chariot of fire could have been a primitive person's description of a space ship.

These superior beings were often described as being unusually tall, wise beyond all local understanding, interested in teaching moral and spiritual precepts, and being capable of flight.

Godwin compares Angelic encounters with UFO and extraterrestrial encounters, finding many similarities between them.

6. *Christian theological arguments of several sorts explain angelic existence.*

The Dominican order was founded in 1216 to combat heresy and to defend ecclesiastic authority. This path relied on intellect, reason, knowledge, scholasticism and communication, following Thomas Aquinas, Aristotle and Dionysius the Aeropagite (whose angelic hierarchies were eventually challenged as being a fraud). In 1231 this order initiated the dreaded Inquisition. Within this branch of Christianity the Angelic Host described in Biblical scriptures were put forward as the only legitimate descriptions of heavenly dimensions. Godwin labels this approach the 'human-like angel.'

Soon after this, the Franciscans began to advocate mysticism, intuition, love, direct experience and communion, following St. Francis of Assisi, Plotinus and William of Occam. Franciscans taught that the union of the soul with God was not achieved by mimicking angels, but by actually becoming angels and knowing Christ directly.[272] Godwin calls this approach the 'angel-like human.'

The black plague that wiped out half the population of Europe struck a severe blow to beliefs in angels. This, combined with the Inquisition, focused attention on the devil, a 'fallen angel,' rather than on heavenly angels.

The rise of modern scientific methods of studying the world further weakened beliefs in angelic hierarchies. "So now man was no longer a replacement angel for the Holy City of God in Heaven, but a living example of the Redeemer within the City of Earth. The man-like angel became the angel-like man who could reach out, beyond the angels, to Christ Consciousness." [273]

Godwin's excellent discussion of angels is also illustrated with a wonderful collection of artistic renderings of angels through many centuries.

Unlikely as this may seem, angels are discussed in parallel with the scientific world views of quantum physics – by Matthew Fox, a British Episcopal priest, and Rupert Sheldrake, a biologist who developed a testable theory of morpho-genetic fields that guide each species.[274] Both experts review and analyze writings of three historic experts on angels. For instance, in the sixth century Dionysius the Areopagite detailed nine orders of angels that mediate between God and man. His cosmology influenced many later generations of angelologists.   Fox and Sheldrake suggest that angels, messengers of God, were viewed as organizers of the cosmos prior to the development of scientific worldviews. Various celestial spheres within spheres each had their angels in the angelic hierarchy.

> In many ways the modern conception of fields has superseded the traditional conception of souls as invisible organizing entities. Up until the seventeenth century even electricity and magnetism were described in terms of souls, stretching out invisibly beyond the magnet or electrically charged body and capable of acting at a distance.[275]

Fox and Sheldrake do not distinguish in their analyses between evidence that is reported from personal experiences versus cosmologies that appear to have been devised from historic writings, particularly from the Bible and its commentaries. They give far more consideration to the latter.[276]

The credibility of evidence from personal reports of angelic encounters

Again, skeptics will suggest the reports of angelic encounters are no more than the products of pure fantasy, wishful thinking, religiosity or mental derangement.

This is all the more so as many angelic encounters occur during times of danger and emergency when emotions are heightened. Under stress or the shock of a near-accident or actual disaster, the focus of our attention is scattered so that a real, flesh and blood person might come to our aid and we could experience their appearance as 'coming out of nowhere' and their departure as a 'disappearance.' All of the psychological mechanisms suggested in the discussions above could contribute to creating fantasy images of an angel. In addition, people might enjoy the attention of friends and media when they report angelic encounters.

> *For what a man would like to be true, that he more readily believes.*
> – Francis Bacon [277]

Countering such criticisms are the encounters where there are multiple observers who report consensual experiences, and where impossible feats of strength or extraordinary communications occur.

> *Angels do not need bodies for their own sake but for ours.*
> – St. Thomas Aquinas

If publicity following an angelic encounter were a common motivating factor, one could expect multiple sightings by the same person. However, this is a rare exception rather than the rule. Most angelic encounters are single, unique events. Many keep these strictly to themselves, out of anxiety that others will consider them deranged, with the liability their family or doctors could suggest medication or hospitalization. Christian traditions hold that angels are sent, not summoned, further discouraging frivolous reports and multiple sightings.

On the other hand, synchronicities and the generosity of passing strangers can be interpreted by the religious as 'help sent by angels' – and perhaps in some or all instances this is true, but not apparent or '*reason*-able' within linear, logical, reductionistic frameworks of analysis.

> *If you make the Most High your dwelling, He will command His angels concerning you, to guard you in all your ways; they will lift you up in their hands, so that you will not strike your foot against a stone.*
> – Psalm [278]

I am personally impressed with the transformative nature of the encounters (similar to transformations in near-death, pre-death and mystical experiences). Further discussion below on believing or disbelieving in angels.

What is your personal understanding of angelic and spiritual realms?

Are you skeptical about all of these fairy stories? I cannot fault you if you are. If you were raised in an industrial culture, as I was, you have been taught to believe only what you see and hear with your physical eyes and ears, or what scientists tell us has been proved to be true in their laboratory experiments. While science has given us a more secure and predictable world thus far, I believe we may have lost something in the process.

There never was a merry world since the fairies left off dancing...
– John Selden

You may choose to answer questions about angels and other spiritual matters intuitively.

You do not have to take the word of others about the inner intuitive realms of gnowing this world. Using the deeper links of your emotions, mind, intuition and spirit – in addition to your physical senses – you can check your own connections with these hosts of advisors. You can use your muscles to connect with your unconscious, intuitive awareness for a *yes* and a *no* sign in answer to questions. This was recognized early in the last century by hypnotherapists as an *ideomotor response*. For instance, you can rub your index finger across your thumb nail, asking in turn, "What feels like yes?" and "What feels like no?" Another way is to link the thumb and little finger of your non-dominant hand in a ring, asking the same questions as you repeatedly pull to test the strength of the opposition of those two fingers. Most people will notice a distinct difference between their body's responses to a yes and a no mental focus. If your body cooperates in this way, you can then ask your higher self questions about your spiritual support team, about options you have for healing or about any other subject.[279]

It is important to recall that common sense must prevail. Our inner selves also contain all of our memories, unconscious beliefs, disbeliefs, wishes and fears. All of these may contribute to the answer our body gives us, so these methods are less than fully accurate. This is why meditative states, where we quiet our minds and open to higher awareness, may contribute to more accurate intuitive perceptions. This is also why we may do well to consult impartial practitioners of various healing modalities to arrive at our best choices for treatments.

Planetary wellbeing, angels and nature spirits

The focus of modern man upon controlling and exploiting nature for the immediate enhancement of the quality of life of industrial nations is rapidly depleting natural resources and polluting the planet. This is reaching the point where humanity may be committing collective suicide.

Godwin points out that since we lost the close contact we once had with our emotions and unconscious awareness, many people are feeling alienated as we come to rely on scientific knowledge.

No longer do rivers contain the spirit of the waters, otherwise we couldn't pollute them as we do. No voice speaks from the skies, otherwise we could not destroy the ozone layer, and no Pan or great Earth Goddess inhabits the soil to stay our hands from raping the lands. And no angel watches over every blade of grass, encouraging it to grow any more. This terrible loss of the numinous and the mysterious finds its desperate compensations through the archetypes which appear in our dreams, our nightmares and our irrational fears. Modern humans are a curious mixture of scientific convictions and ancient demons. We are so stuffed full of beliefs and outmoded habits of thought that we cannot deal with the emotional charge behind those dreams.

The angel archetype is the messenger of the higher self. It is the wise being, the advanced soul, the Shaman, the Enlightened master, Superman, or the saint. Our present fascination with highly evolved extra-terrestrial beings who have come to guide humanity, or the galactic messengers of peace and love who contact the chosen few (who will form the new Ark of earth when we blow ourselves up), appears to arise from this extraordinarily potent interior archetype.

Such symbols may represent an individual who is striving towards a full realization of his or her cosmic self...[280]

The depletion of natural resources and pollution, which are growing problems on our planet, are reflected in diminished numbers of nature spirits, reports van Gelder. There is also evidence of disruptions in the collaborations between the spirits that coordinate the subtle energy management in nature.

[E]ven if the whole of nature is undergoing changes the angels and fairies know there is an underlying unity in the universe. They are part of an organic whole and this they accept. Men are also becoming aware of this holistic approach as there is a greater understanding and more conscious cooperation with the increase in meditation and outdoor living. A link is being forged with the people and this other dynamic world. This will become a pattern of the future.[281]

Discussion

The nature spirits, elves, devas and the like reported in recent and ancient times along with the heroic gods of ancient Egypt, Greece, Rome and other cultures have all been presumed by most modern investigators to be fantasized, mythological images.

One must consider whether some of the reports of nature spirits and angels might be more than fanciful stories to express fears, hopes and religious beliefs. They might be apparitions. Alternatively, they could represent *thought forms*, created as was 'Phillip' in the table sitting experiments,[282] or other mediumistic phenomena described in the next chapter. They may be metaphors, collectively visualized archetypal images, or other mechanisms of the mind for bringing about healings on individual, collective, spiritual, planetary and cosmic levels.

The fact that these nature spirits and angels are reported by children[283] could be taken to point more to the possibilities of their being objectively perceivable entities, if one accepts children's reports as naive. On the other hand, children could be given to fantasy productions or be influenced by suggestions from the media or religious authorities.

It is often difficult to appreciate, which elements of angelic reports may represent objective observations, and which are projections of the cultural and religious beliefs of the observers and researchers who collected the reports. For instance, Hope Price presents an excellent spectrum of reports on angelic encounter. However, her Christian religious beliefs are clearly evident, and one must assume that her reports are shaped and possibly even censored (consciously and unconsciously) by these beliefs. An example is when she speculates that an assistant priest's feeling of foreboding when he was in Glastonbury could perhaps have been related to early pagan and recent New Age practices that are associated with Glastonbury

Suggesting that reports of angels may not be real:

- *Coincidences* could occur and be attributed to angelic interventions.

- *Psi powers* (telepathy, clairsentience, retro- or pre-cognition, and psychokinesis), activated unconsciously by the needs and/or prayers of people, could bring about some of the effects attributed to angels. (The converse could obviously be true as well. That is, effects which are attributed to psi powers could be mediated or caused by angels.) The guidance of the airplane to land safely could be in this category.

- *Other phenomena could be mistaken for angelic appearances.* For instance, if one has no knowledge or understanding of something one encounters for the first time, one would most likely interpret it in concepts and language which are familiar, but possibly totally inappropriate. Apparitions of deceased or living persons could be interpreted as angels. Josef Blumrich, analyzing the description of Ezekiel's chariots of fire, suggests this could be a description of a UFO. The exhaust flames could produce "...an immense cloud with flashing lightning and surrounded by brilliant light..." Wheels, which moved in any direction, could be multi-directional propellers; and so on.

> *There are no 'facts in themselves',*
> *there are only facts for someone...*
> *for whom the fact is a fact.*
> – R. Pannikar

Suggesting that reports of angels may represent observations of real beings:

- The vast majority of published reports are of single encounters over the lifetime of individuals.

- The vast majority of reports were told to authors with comments to the effect that the observers had kept these powerful experiences secret, sharing them with no one or only with most intimate relations. If these were spontaneous fantasies or deliberate imaginary creations to gain attention, one would expect them to be repeated encounters and experiences that are shared with others.

- Consensual validation of angelic appearances by more than one observer make it less likely that these were the products of fantasy.

- Many reports coincide with prayers, either of the person perceiving the angels or, more impressively, prayers of people close to those who report angel encounters *even when the reporters are unaware of these prayers*. Situations in which fervent prayers are sent appear to make such awarenesses more likely.

- Encounters with angels are powerfully transformative experiences, much in the same ways as are Near-Death Experiences and other mystical experiences.[284]

- Reports from many parts of the world contain consistent elements:
  Appearance and disappearance of the observed entities in unusual manners, such as fading in and out of existence;
  Classical images of many angels, especially when they appear without interacting with the observers – six to eight feet tall, dressed in white gowns which are floor length and cover their feet, blonde hair, faces radiating light, and wings;
  Atypical images of entities, which intervene to give information or physical assistance – looking like ordinary people, but appearing and disappearing in the twinkling of an eye, performing superhuman feats;
  Appearing at the foot of the bed of sick or dying people;
  Unusual light suffusing the room in which classical angels appear;
  Telepathic communication;
  Overwhelming sense of peace, even at times of illness, danger and crisis;
  Producing healings;
  Singing in very high voices, beyond human capacities.

Loving, accepting, supportive presences

If we accept that angels exist, what do they say about the world we live in?

First, they suggest there are realms in which intelligent beings exist that are far more spiritually advanced than humanity. It appears from the reports reviewed here that there are levels of development within nature spirits and angels. In Medieval times, there were extensive theological discussions, sometimes quite acrimonious, as to the levels and hierarchies of angelic beings. For the most part, these arguments were based on interpretations of scriptural readings, where the original sources were usually unknown. My own inclination is to rely more on reports of psychics, mystics, and others who have visited these realms personally.

Second, they suggest that the physical world may be just one of many levels of reality. Muldoon describes various spirit levels he visited while in various OBEs. He encountered different kinds of spirit beings in each, some pleasant and some negative. It is unclear whether these differed according to the levels in which they inherently found themselves, or whether they were attracted or confined to realms appropriate to their levels of spiritual awareness and development, or whether Muldoon's perceptions distorted them to appear as they did because of varying states of consciousness within each realm.[285]

My personal experiences of the spirit and angelic realms

I have had no direct, conscious communications with spirits or angels. However, I have spoken with innumerable intuitives, healers and ordinary people who have had remarkable direct encounters with these realms beyond physical existence.

I have consulted psychics occasionally out of curiosity and with the wish to maximize the information available to me in making important decisions in my life. Some have provided helpful insights; some not. (More on this at the end of the next chapter.)

There have been several times in my life when I felt, looking backward, that I must have been protected by outside forces. The most clear one occurred on a dark night when my motor scooter, going about 40 miles per hour, collided with a car that made a quick left turn in front of me. I demolished his rear hubcap and was catapulted over the car and about fifteen feet further down the road. I landed on my hands (protected by gloves) and knees (scraped through my torn pants) and my helmet protected my head as it hit the ground with some force. I stood up immediately and had no serious sequellae to this encounter with a car which was driven by a Catholic priest.

In the workshops I lead, I encourage people to call upon their guardian angels for help. Many participants report that this is helpful, often in highly unusual ways. In my own life I do the same. I believe that angels are there to help, but they respectfully wait for us to ask for their assistance, though they may intervene spontaneously in times of need. I agree that the most important message angels may bring us is that there are worlds of spirit and the All beyond our own.

In summary

Nature spirits have been part of folklore historically in all cultures, including Western ones, and continue today in traditional cultures. Angelic presences have been continuously reported in many cultures. Within prevalent Western beliefs, these may seem no more than fanciful folk tales. To people who experience encounters with these beings, they are very real. Nature spirits are said to work with all parts of the natural world, helping to bring in vital energies to support physical life. They communicate with humans mostly when humans are engaged and committed to work in nature.

Encounters with angels often come unbidden, commonly in times of danger or other need. More importantly, they are often profoundly transformative – as with NDEs and reincarnation awarenesses. Angels are messengers, bringing love, support and help from the Infinite Source, with reassurances that life in spirit continues after physical life. They are often present at the time of transition through death, most frequently visible to the dying, but may also be seen by those who are close to those who are dying.

The Medicine Angel

When you are lonely, empty and afraid, remember this:
That an angel who loves and cares for you
is somewhere looking for the medicine you need.
And it will not give up until it is found
however long and far it takes.
This medicine, although it can be found in the dawn
and sunset, is both rare and priceless.
For it is sacred medicine. Medicine of the heart.
And one day, when you are least expecting it
you will awake to find that the angel who
loved you has returned with your medicine.
For this medicine angel has come home
to dwell within your own soul.
And its medicine is the light pouring into
your heart in an invisible fountain of joy.
Yet to benefit fully from its healing
process, your heart has to be empty.
Just as the tree is stripped naked before
new buds form.
Remember this too in your pain:
to look for the medicine messages it sends you each day in its absence.
These sacred messages may come in a rainbow,
a dew-webbed spider's web,
a greeting from a friend,
or a stranger's smile.

– Stephanie June Sorrell

Let us look next at spirits who communicate through mediums (channels). The summary discussion about spirit survival at the end of the next section is also relevant to questions about whether there can be a rational explanation for angels and nature spirits.

CHAPTER 5

Mediumistic (Channeled) Experiences

Death does not make a saint of a sinner nor a sage of a fool. The mentality is the same as before and individuals carry with them their old desires, habits, dogmas, faulty teachings, indifference or disbelief in a future life.

– Carl A. Wickland [286]

Introduction

For those unfamiliar with these phenomena, here is a brief description of what occurs when information is relayed from spirit dimensions by a person in the physical world. This will be followed by a review of research and discussion of these fascinating communications.

A *medium* or *channel* is a person who reports the ability to communicate with the spirit worlds. I prefer the more classical term, *medium*, because it suggests that the intermediary person in the communication is a part of the communication. I believe this is very much the case, and very important to any consideration of these communications.

We must always consider the contributions of the person presenting the information along with the content. Anyone who has ever heard a simultaneous translator for a foreign language will appreciate how delicate is the task of conveying information from one cultural context to another. Mediumistic communications are ever so much more difficult to translate because they are perceived by the medium telepathically, with images and information transmitted directly, often without words. The medium must then translate this information into language that will be understood by the person for whom it is intended.

Often, the information comes as specific words or images. These may make no sense to the medium but may be very meaningful to the intended audience.

Dennis Barrett shares a lovely story about how he learned this lesson about trusting the channeled voices.[287] Barrett's channeling gifts manifest as voices rather than visual imagery. While he doesn't see the spirits who are communicating to the people he is helping, his spirit guides provide descriptions of them.

He was the visiting speaker in a spiritualist church in Southwest England, doing well with spontaneous readings. He felt a message coming through from the mother (in spirit) of a woman in the congregation. His spirit helpers told him that this woman was going to need lots of evidence, so they provided a very detailed description of the spirit who was there for this woman.

> ... I described the woman's age group, her build and her way of dressing.
>
> Then I got to the necklace she was wearing and I described this almost bead by bead. I said: "She tells me she's proud of her beauties." Whereupon the congregation erupted into laughter. The woman smiled broadly along with the rest of them and it was a few moments before I could continue... The woman accepted that it was her mother and her mother was able to give her a moving message of love and comfort.
>
> When I sat down, I asked the chairwoman why there had been so much laughter earlier on about the necklace.
>
> "When we say 'her beauties' down here, we're not talking about 'her necklace,'" she said. "We're talking about *these*!" and she cupped her hands under her bosom. No wonder my words had prompted such laughter.[288]

After the service, the woman spoke with Barrett. She reported that this was the first time in several spirit communication readings that she felt able to believe her mother was really the one who was speaking. Although the previous mediums had said that her mother was speaking through them, they had given little information which was evidential. Barrett asked why her mother would mention her 'beauties.'

The woman explained that her mother had had a good figure and would spend a lot of time admiring herself in a mirror, being especially proud of her bust. She used to accuse her mother of being vain. Her mother would typically reply, "What's the matter with you, I'm proud of my beauties."

These were the precise words she had heard her mother say on many occasions.

This is a typical example of the type of communications that can be very meaningful to the person for whom the message is being transmitted, but totally ignored by the medium and anyone else in the audience.

The medium may work in a trance state induced by concentration, hypnosis or meditation. Gifted mediums may be aware of the spirit world constantly, either alongside or interpenetrating everyday reality.

I shall focus the following discussion primarily upon communications from spirits assumed to be entities that survived after having lived within living memory in the physical world. Communications from other sources, such as Christ, Mary, saints, God and extraterrestrial sources have also been reported, but these will be mentioned only briefly, as it is far more difficult to establish the validity of the latter sources.

Mediums were extensively investigated by researchers in America and England over the past century and some of the terminology in the classical literature originated nearly 100 years ago. Mediums call their consultations *sittings, séances, readings* or *channeling*. These may be held in a darkened room, with a group of people (termed *sitters*) seated around a table, seeking to communicate with spirits. In the early years of these investigations, the medium might sit through the entire session at the table or might withdraw to a curtained portion of the room (the *cabinet*) to sit in isolation from the sitters. Mediums today often consult in a room indistinguishable from that of a psychotherapist and may also work over the phone.

Mediums may receive spirit communications telepathically as words or images. Sometimes the medium visualizes the spirit and can describe physical details, such as stature, color of hair and eyes and other physical details that are verifiable by the sitter as having been characteristic of the channeled person prior to their passing from the physical world. In some cases the channeled words may be spoken in tones of voice and styles of speech very similar to those of the deceased. In such cases the medium is said to be *obsessed* or *briefly possessed* by the spirit(s). When psychokinetic (*physical*) phenomena are demonstrated, such as objects in the room moving or raps resounding from the table or walls, the guide is sometimes called an *operator*. A spirit channeled by the medium is referred to as a *guide* or *control* when this spirit acts as a mediator between the medium and other spirits. Substances seen to materialize outside the medium's body during the séance are called *apports*; those extruding from their body, *ectoplasm*.[289]

Some mediums transmit their spirit messages in writing (*automatic writing*) while in partial or full trance. A pencil is held in a relaxed manner and the spirits are felt to be writing the messages, using the mind and body of the medium as their vehicle for communication.

Spirits have been credited with passing vital messages through mediums to relatives and friends when such information was available to no one but the deceased.

Mediumistic readings are very similar to reports from some healers of interventions by spirits in healings. Healers may have spirit guides who inform them of the diagnosis and suggest treatments,[290] sometimes guiding healers in operations on the energy body or on the physical body.[291]

Some of the most impressive mediumistic phenomena involve psychokinesis (PK). These were much more common in earlier days of parapsychological investigations. Objects in the room were moved about by (apparently) the spirits, even when the investigators took elaborate precautions to prevent the medium or any hidden assistants from moving the objects by normal physical means.[292]

Several approaches allow ordinary people to communicate directly with spirits.

The most common is the *ouija board*, commonly available as a game for adults in toy stores. It contains a board with the letters of the alphabet and the numbers 1-10 on it. Several people sitting around the board place their fingers on a pointer, letting their hands move together spontaneously. They focus together on a given question, and let the pointer move to the letters, spelling out the answer. While I have heard of some positive results with the ouija board, I have also heard many cautions from knowledgeable intuitives: it is possible to open oneself to possession by negative entities and spirits through using the ouija board.[293]

Raymond Moody has been exploring how ordinary people can develop their abilities to contact spirits, using variations of *scrying* – gazing at a mirror in a meditative state.[294] This is similar to crystal ball gazing.

Allan Botkin is a psychologist who specializes in treatment of post-traumatic stress disorder (PTSD) with Eye Movement Diazotization and Reprocessing (EMDR).[295] He discovered that people who had been traumatized through the death of another person will spontaneously connect with the spirit of that person when that is relevant to their self-healing. He calls this Induced After-Death Communications (IADC). People report that the IADC includes the sensation of going through a tunnel towards a bright light that emanates love and acceptance, and encountering the people with whom they had unfinished business; they are able to converse with the spirit of the deceased to clear up old angers, guilts and hurts; they nearly always come away from the IADC encounter with an immense immediate sense of relief; and unresolved grief from bereavements or traumas that may have been carried for many years are usually cleared in a single session.

People who have undergone the IADC who have also had an NDE report that the two experiences appear to be very closely similar – with the obvious difference that in the NDE one is experiencing one's own death and in the IADC one is encountering another person in spirit. These IADC experiences are much more vivid than after-death communications (ADCs) which occur spontaneously. In the IADC, however, no Being of Light is encountered.

During the IADC, the living person may witness the death process of the deceased, though the life review and encounter with a Being of Light are not perceived. As with spontaneous ADCs, the appearance of the spirit is often more healthy and robust than when they died, with adults often appearing younger, while young children may appear older. In all cases, Botkin's clients report the spirits appeared to be at peace, serene, happy and contented.

Similar to NDEs, the IADC experience is always imbued with a very strong sense of love and acceptance. The spirits that are encountered appear to have learned the lessons they needed to in their previous lives, such as taking responsibility for their negative treatment of others. They have resolved their issues about the conflicts which had existed between them and the person undergoing the IADC, often showing concern about residual negative feelings from their previous life. This is sometimes quite striking, as in cases where the spirit had been killed by the person who is having the IADC and forgives him.

While some come to the IADC experience with trepidations that they may find the spirit in hell and might have to suffer some aspect of that horror, none has ever reported such an experience. When anyone who was presumed to still be alive was encountered during an IADC, it was subsequently found that this person had in fact already passed on. No live persons have been encountered during IADCs.

There is a loving reconnection with the deceased, dramatically erasing questions about the existence of an afterlife.

Summarizing the experiences of the first 84 people whom he treated, Botkin reports:

> [P]eople who experience an ADC no longer believe their friend or loved one is really gone. Grief work from this perspective, therefore, is not a matter of saying good-bye, but hello."
>
> Out of 84 patients for whom an ADC induction was offered, 83 (99%) were willing to participate in an induction. Of the 83 patients who partici- pated in an ADC induction, 81 (98%) achieved an ADC, defined as any perceived sensory contact with the deceased. Of the 81 patients who achieved an ADC, 78 (96%) reported full resolution of grief following the ADC, and 76 (94%) believed their ADC was an actual spiritual contact. Of those 76 patients who believed their ADC was an actual spiritual contact, only 6 (8%) had believed prior to the ADC that actual contact was possible.

Edie Devers, a psychotherapist, also reports on IADCs, from research for her MSN and PhD degrees. While she generally echoes Botkins' positive reports, she notes that some IADCs may have negative components. People may be retrauma- tized by encounters with spirits, through arousing negative feelings afresh or with renewed disappointment over losing the deceased. She finds that extended psy- chotherapy usually leads to positive resolutions of these feelings.

Research

Many are the tales of ghostly figures of departed relatives communicating meaningful messages to those left behind. These are matched by tales of hoaxes exposed, where fake mediums were caught manipulating objects via levers or by other means in the darkened séance rooms and passing on information gleaned from the purses of sitters by assistants who relayed messages by code or hidden electronic intercoms.

One's only recourse in individual reports is to have a measure of confidence in the observers, and if possible, in the integrity of the medium as well.

There are only a few scientific studies of channeled communications.

The content of mediumistic communications

Gary Schwartz[296] reports highly significant accuracy with careful content analysis of readings by five prominent mediums.[297] The probabilities that these could have occurred by chance are less than one in two and a half billion.

There are no other systematic assessments of mediumistic readings. While the remaining evidence presented here lacks the rigor of Schwartz's study, it conveys the flavor of these readings – through the reports of people who considered carefully and critically these messages that appeared to come from spirits.

Jane Roberts was a typical modern medium who wrote numerous books explaining spirit world cosmologies and relationships to the world of the living. Her information was received through automatic writing, in which she felt the spirits guided her hand while she was in trance. There is much wisdom in her writings, whatever the source.

I find particularly interesting her writings on the transcending of ordinary boundaries of time,[298] as spirits, angels and those who have Near-Death Experiences are said to report that time is not the same in these dimensions:

> In certain terms time intervals are jumped, as when a 'past' smell or sight is suddenly perceived with present vividness, though you would say it has already occurred in the past. Under particular conditions a memory may suddenly become more real than... the present moment...
>
> This could not happen if your physical structure did not have built-in mechanisms allowing it... In the same way, a future experience may also be physically perceived in your present. Now beneath your usual consciousness, your physical organism can react to future events without your knowledge, as it can to past ones...
>
> If you are aware of such a future episode, you will be forced to react to it as a conscious being. In any case your temporal structure will respond whether or not you are aware of the reasons for such behavior. The future incident may then occur in its time sequence, and you recognize it through memory, in which case your reactions in that future present will be altered because of the seemingly past memory.
>
> In your terms that event may never come to pass, however, because it may be arising from a probable past that was once your present, but from which you have diverged. This is one of the reasons why psychics' predictions often do not seem to bear out, for at every point you do indeed have the free will, through your beliefs, to alter your experience.
>
> Your beliefs form the pivot of your present experience.[299]

Roberts also wrote several fictionalized stories of lives interconnected through reincarnation backwards and forwards across time, and of a spirit guide called Oversoul 7. These suggest ways that life's lessons may be learned in one life when they have been misunderstood in a previous one, and how healings may occur across time through relationships of people with their own past and future reincarnations.

Many mediums have presented cogent channeled communications that were much beyond their cultural and educational backgrounds. Much prosaic drivel has also been received. Sorting the one from the other may not be easy.[300]

Gardner Murphy[301] was a distinguished American psychologist who taught at Columbia and Harvard Universities in the middle years of the last century. He was also an expert in parapsychology. He carefully investigated mediumistic reports, including dreams, automatic writing and mediumistic trances. He focused especially on *cross-correspondences*, in which separate mediums, who did not know of each other, obtained fragmentary messages from two spirits. Amazingly, the fragments made sense only when combined later by investigators. This process was allegedly utilized by the spirits to convince earthly skeptics of the spirit origins of the communications.

Murphy points out that the existence of spirits is also suggested by the fact that the initiative, purposes and motivations in many such spirit communications resides on the spirits' side of reality rather than on the physical side. For instance, spirits may convey messages asking forgiveness for errors of omission or commission during their previous lives on Earth. Murphy openly admitted he had considerable difficulty integrating these observations with his sensory reality view of the world.

Annie Besant and C.W. Leadbeater[302] channeled or clairvoyantly perceived the particle nature of atoms, detailing many of the elements in the periodic table years before they were identified by conventional science.

Of particular relevance to healing is the experience of George Chapman, a healer in Wales who channels the spirit of Dr. William Lang, who died in 1937.[303] Chapman's healing is in the form of psychic surgery in the aura, or biological energy field, of his healees.[304] Members of Lang's family and others, who knew Lang while he was alive, confirmed that the channeled voice, mannerisms and knowledge of intimate details of interaction of Lang with others were most accurate to their own memories of Lang.

Another unusual channel is Rosemary Brown, who claims she is given compositions by famous composers such as Liszt, Chopin, Mozart, Bach and others. Critics have been impressed with the versatility of Brown in creating pieces in these different styles, while not being able to comment on whether these represent authentic, channeled compositions.

Allan Gauld[305] reviews evidence for survival with the clear alternative hypothesis that these may be examples of *super-psi* abilities rather than communication from a spirit world.[306] That is, living people might obtain information through telepathy or clairsentience and translate it into alleged messages from spirits. He concludes that the continuity (of life after physical death) hypothesis is supported by the facts that mediums often reveal information that was not known to any of the sitters; that they often reproduce personality styles of the deceased in minute detail, without ever having known the deceased; and that they can produce cross-correspondences that require cooperative efforts of several mediums who have no knowledge of each others' messages. He also discusses the apparition evidence he considers too weak to withstand the criticism that it may represent super-psi.

Gauld also considers arguments against survival. On this side of the debate he notes that many of the mediumistic communications have the distinct flavor of the mediums' personalities, suggesting that they may be creations of their unconscious minds. Furthermore, much of the material communicated seems petty and hardly worth the efforts involved. Clairsentience could account for a major portion of the alleged communications, as the mediums frequently psychometrize (read clairsentiently) objects belonging to the deceased that are brought by sitters.

Others have objected that different readers may provide very different channeled impressions for any given person. Marie Louise von Franz,[307] a Jungian analyst, finds a different interpretation for such disparities in readings.

> ... I...had many hand readings made for me, many horoscopes made, if possible by people I more or less knew and I found out that they were all true... But if you were to read them, you would see that they are *most* different and if you read them with more understanding you would see that it is typical for *that* person to notice *that* in me and it is typical for that other person to notice something else. So the information is filtered by the personality of the medium, of the diviner or the horoscope maker or the palmist and so on; they get within the area of another's psychic constellation that is akin to theirs. All are true but all are only partial.

Physical phenomena of mediumship

The appearance of ghostly figures has been termed *physical phenomena*. The figures may be those of a whole person, or just a head and torso or a symbolic image may appear.

An example is the report of Gordon Turner,[308] who was a gifted English healer and an astute observer. In a séance he saw a life-like materialization of a human figure that spoke for the medium. At the end of the séance Turner shook hands with the figure. It literally melted away in his hand and appeared to be reabsorbed by the medium.

More rigorous studies of physical phenomena introduced electronic equipment to measure and record the physical effects.

Eugene Osty was a French physician and Director of the Institut Metapsychique Internationale. He describes a series of experiments using infrared (IR) photometers to measure the mediumistic materializations of a gifted subject, Rudi Schneider. IR light is invisible to the unaided eye. Osty also used IR devices positioned so that any physical movement of the medium would set off an IR camera and record any attempts at cheating. As a further precaution, the medium's hands and feet were held by the observers who could thus sense any movement he might make.

The photometer positioned to measure materializations registered occlusions that faded in and out, blocking the light by gradual degrees. Partial occlusions were recorded when no visible occlusion could yet be seen. There was a marked rhythmicity in the degree of occlusion, with oscillations ranging from 120 to 420 per minute. These were noted to be twice the frequency of the respirations of the medium, who was breathing very rapidly. Blood acidity (pH) was normal immediately after a sitting in which prolonged periods of rapid breathing occurred. This is unusual because rapid breathing lowers the carbon dioxide content of the blood and ordinarily would change the blood acidity. Darkness was the condition most conducive to the occurrence of this phenomenon, although weak red light would not interfere if the materialization was already in progress when the light was turned on.

Gross PK events, where objects moved without physical interventions, were observed in only about one tenth of the medium's attempts to produce them. In one of these, Osty observed an ethereal, foggy materialization moving from the medium towards the object to be moved by PK, prior to its moving.

Another researcher, W. J. Crawford, who was a lecturer in mechanical engineering at Queen's University, Belfast, made extraordinary observations of mediums. These included a series of table levitations on the demand of the experimenter performed during séances. Crawford found that if the medium was required to levitate a table that exceeded a certain weight, she was drawn to fall forward out of her chair. He reasoned that this might be caused by a cantilever. (See Figure III-4.) Asking the spirit operators if this were so he obtained an affirmative answer.

> On some occasions (I made the experiment many times) while I was pressing strongly downwards, the medium's body tilted forward and on other occasions it did not. She told me that when she did *not* move forward, she felt no inclination to tilt at all and when she *did* move forward, she simply could not help her body. This alternative tilting and non-tilting of the medium's body (the two phases occurred in alternations with succeeding levitations) took place so often that I suspected the operators were trying to bring something to my notice, so I asked them if the levitating structure was sometimes a true cantilever, i.e., no part of it touching the floor and sometimes *not* a true cantilever, i.e., with the free end resting on the floor under the table. They vigorously assented to this and demonstrated for my benefit...
>
> The operators say that at demonstration séances they rest the end of the cantilever upon the floor immediately under the table so that when a strong man stands over the levitated table and exerts a great pressure upon it, the medium is protected from the large reaction forces, the latter in this case being on the floor instead of on her body.
>
> The operators also say, that they much prefer to work with a true cantilever, for, when they have to rest the end of it upon the floor, the structure is badly strained and much *energy* is required to maintain its rigidity.

Crawford placed soft clay on the floor under the table. He asked the operators to levitate the table with a supported cantilever, resting its supported portion on the clay. (See Figure III-4.)

> In a very short time the table levitated immediately above the clay, the levitation lasting about a dozen seconds. At its conclusion I examined the clay. There was a large irregularly shaped impression on it, the length one way being about 3 inches and the other 2 1/2 inches.[309]

Crawford also explored the impression that ectoplasm, extending from the mediums' feet, might be producing the table levitations. He coated the feet of mediums with a light layer of clay, in their shoes, to see if he could trace the pathways of extrusion of ectoplasm. Following physical phenomena, he found streaks of clay on the outside of the shoes, some of these streaks bearing patterned impressions identical with the weave of the cloth of the medium's sox.

Figure III-4. Crawford's suggestions of ectoplasmic cantilevers

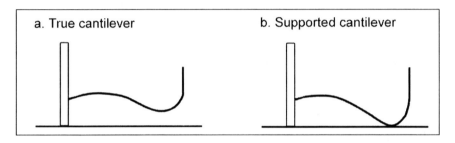

Crawford's observations imply that PK phenomena may be produced through extensions of materialized matter from the body of the agent.[310]

Mediums sometimes facilitate communication from spirits through coded raps on the séance table or from tilting of the table. One rap or a tilt in one direction indicates 'yes,' and the opposite, 'no.'

Iris Owen and Margaret Sparrow worked with a group of experimenters who deliberately created a ghost story. They fabricated the tale of a person named Philip who died a tragic death, throwing himself from the parapets of his castle over disappointment with unrequited love. They utilized the format of the séance room and obtained ostensible communications via table tiltings and table rappings. Careful scrutiny of transcripts of their sessions showed that the information obtained was limited to the knowledge available to the participants. These studies demonstrate that the séance room atmosphere is conducive to the occurrence of psi phenomena, *produced by the sitters.*[311]

Of special note is research on raps heard in the Philip-type séances.[312] When these sounds are translated into visual images on an oscilloscope, they have characteristics distinguishing them clearly from raps produced by normal objects tapping each other. The PK sounds either drop off in a decrescendo much more rapidly or actually start with a low intensity and build to a crescendo. The latter is the opposite of the pattern seen with sounds produced by normal means. With a normal rap, the initial jar of the tap creates the largest vibrations, which then decrescendo to silence. These electronic images of the mediumistic raps provide distinct 'signatures' by which such PK sounds may be identified. No normal tap or rap can produce such an oscilloscope pattern.

Spirits have been reported to produce sounds and images on audio and video recording tape.

Ernst Seknowski, a German physicist, collected a variety of spirit communications on both audio and video tapes. These were created by having the tape recorders running with a microphone and/or camera attached in the normal 'record' mode, with no medium participating to channel the information. Senkowski discovered that having a source of random (*white*) noise in the background facilitates the appearance of mediumistic messages. The most commonly used are ambient street sounds or static type sounds from between radio stations.

Senkowski[313] reports:

> There have been many reports from private persons showing the 'paranormality' of 'voices on tapes' (VOT) or 'electronic voice phenomena' (EVP). These are instances in which words appear on audio tapes – when there was no known source for the words – interposed on an otherwise normal recording. In many cases the messages purport to be from spirits of deceased people. Most of the publications[314] indicate intersubject reliability in interpreting the recorded words, with the exception of D. Ellis.[315] The consensus is that these represent spirit messages, though no theory accounts for how these might be generated in the recording systems.
>
> Oscilloscopic analyses of the EVP[316] such as recorded by Friedrich Jurgenson[317] were consistent with signals of speech quality. Later, anomalies were noted in the electronic analyses of the recorded speech:
>
> 1. At least in some examples, VOT signals are not of the 'glottal' type. That is, some formants are missing.[318]
>
> 2. There is a strong tendency for 'compressed speech.' Grammatical rules are disregarded, apparently to press maximum content into a minimum number of syllables. The distribution of duration of the 'sentences' has a clear maximum around 1.5 seconds.[319]
>
> 3. In a great number of cases the VOT show sort of 'computerization' of the speech, sounding similar to 'robot voices.'
>
> In a limited number of cases,[320] the VOT have been surpassed by electroacoustic direct voices coming from loudspeakers of different electronic systems. Fluent two-way communication has been realized and documented.[321] Images on TV have been observed as well as messages through computer systems, apparently not of normal origin. Such 'spectacular' effects seem tightly bound to 'special faculties' of living people (who may be psychics or mediums) and depend upon unknown parameters for the most part. Under these circumstances, consistent production of effects cannot be achieved. Since these observations were made in similar forms and contents independently in different countries with different devices and experimenters, a common background should be accepted and the whole complex scientifically researched.

Mark Macy and Rolf-Dietmar Ehrhardt have an informative website on a spectrum of these phenomena.[322]

What do we know about the spirit worlds?

Assuming the spirit does survive physical death, what mediumistic reports do we have on the nature of spirit existence?

There is general agreement that much depends on one's state of mind at the time of death. With peaceful deaths, with time to prepare psychologically and spiritually for the transition, we have seen in the Near-Death and Pre-Death Experiences the numerous reports of spirits coming to welcome and assist people in their transitions to the spirit world. They are encouraged to seek the light, experience the review of their lives under the unconditionally accepting guidance of the Being of Light, and move on to spirit existences (or to return to physical existence in the NDE).

Eastern traditions place enormous emphasis upon preparations for this transition.[323] Meditation masters say that much of their teachings serve to prepare people for spiritual awareness that will make their transition to the spirit world an easier one. Advanced meditators and spiritually enlightened people are said to be able to choose the time and manner of their transition to the spirit world.

In contrast, those who are unprepared for the transition may experience various difficulties. People who die sudden, unexpected deaths, or have strong disbeliefs about spirit survival, may actually transition to spirit existence without being aware that they have done so. They may wander about as spirit entities with human physical form, persisting in seeking to interact with the living. Mediums may be of great help to such spirits. Joan Grant reported that she did *rescue work* with spirits of this sort when she was still a child during World War I:[324]

> ...I knew that as soon as I was asleep, instead of being a child I would again be a responsible adult, who had been allotted a specific kind of 'war work.' This work consisted of convincing men who had died in battle that they had no reason to fear dying, for this familiar transition which they had so needlessly dreaded had already taken place.
>
>   Sometimes this proved to be easy, and I woke happy in the knowledge of a job well done. But if I had been sent to help someone who had allowed dogma to infect him with grotesque terrors, or who had clung to the agonies which had affected his physical body because he thought them the only alternative to oblivion, the task of releasing him could be arduous...
>
> [T]his type of work entails so intimate a degree of identification with the other person that instead of feeling "This is happening to him," one feels, "This is happening to me." So I would wake feeling that it was I who had been entangled in barbed-wire, or had been trying to cram glistening coils back into my belly, or drowning in mud, or choking with phosgene gas.

Why the living are appropriate for this work rather than spirits is unclear. There is speculation that the subtle life vibrations and mental states of those still in the flesh resonate more readily or more fully with those who have made only partial transitions, and that therefore they can help the surviving spirit more easily.

Rescue work is very much like helping the living who have had severe emotional traumas. It requires reassurance, unconditional acceptance, and sorting through whatever trauma has been experienced. The spirit is then encouraged to ask for help from other spirits, perhaps relatives who are eagerly waiting to assist, perhaps spirit rescue workers, or angelic presences. Sometimes it is enough to suggest that they "Look to the Light." This is truly spiritual healing.

When people who have made such transitions believe that they are still alive, they may create far more than their physical forms in the spirit world. Paul Beard[325] gathered channeled reports indicating that spirits in afterlife may create whole environments for themselves through their expectations and visualizations. A person who disbelieves in life after death may, upon entering the world of spirits, congregate with others of similar beliefs. Together they may visualize into existence whole earth-like suburban communities. Such a person may go on for a long time mowing his astral turf before he reaches enlightenment.[326]

> *I don't like to commit myself about heaven and hell – you see, I have*
> *friends in both places.*
> > – Mark Twain

In some instances, it is said that spirit guides encourage visualizations of such communities. Rabbi Yonassan Gershom reports on a woman who has reincarnation memories from having died in the Holocaust. She was a spiritually aware person and her transition to spirit life was with full awareness. She had studied psychology and medicine in Germany prior to her death, and as a spirit she was assigned to rescue work with other Holocaust victims. Many of them were eased through their horrendously traumatic transitions to spirit existence by being placed in spirit environments that mimicked earthly Jewish communities which were familiar to them from their lives prior to their deaths. There, they were encouraged to come into a gradual awareness of their spirit existence over a period of months and sometimes years.

> *You become what you believe you are, and you will remain that until*
> *you realize and become what you really are.*
> > – Rosalind McKnight

A healer I know who has done a lot of rescue work reports she has visited similar spirit communities of Holocaust victims many times, over several decades. Initially, she found they were gray and bleak, but over time she noted that grass and trees were growing there and were bringing healing vibrations to these severely traumatized spirits.

And what is the continued existence of a spirit in the spirit worlds? Relying again on mediumistic reports, we are told that various spiritual lessons and growth continue on the spirit planes, on levels that are spiritually more advanced than we can comprehend from our vantage of earthly existence. Mystics through the ages have said that we are sparks of the Eternal Flame, seeking our way back to that Divine Source. It is said that the ultimate in spiritual development is to be reunited with the All.[327]

It appears that spiritual healing extends well into the realms of death and the afterlife.

Coming from the opposite direction, another perspective is that the primary place of beingness is in spiritual existence, and that life in a physical body is an excursion outside of those realms of our true selves.[328]

> *We are not human beings having a spiritual experience. We are spiritual beings having a human experience.*
>
> – Teilhard de Chardin

Mediumistic communications with nature spirits, angelic beings and the Being of Light

In addition to spirits of departed humans, sources for spirit and mediumistic communication may include:

1. *Nature spirits (fairies, devas, sprites, wee folk, elves and gnomes)* – There appear to be energy medicine awarenesses relating to aspects of nature. These are perceived by some humans as spirit forms of beings or merely as various forms of spirit-level consciousness. Most of these appear highly specialized in energy world tasks. Garden fairies tend the energy needs of plants in a given area. Trees have their own spirits, as do mountains and bodies of water.[329]

   This type of spirit being gives the impression of limited awareness and limited intelligence in human terms. This should not in any way imply that their consciousness is of lesser importance or value in the grand scheme of nature.

2. *Beings that appear as angels in various shapes and guises* – Luminous, wise beings have been reported to appear, especially at times of crisis, to provide advice as well as emotional and physical assistance. Some of these are described as guardians of complex realms of nature, creating and supervising the spirits of type (1). People are said to have guardian angels, in addition to having spirit guides. The angels appear to constitute a higher level or order of consciousness than the guides. Their vision is more deep and broad in scope across space and time, and also more impersonal.[330]

3. *Archetypal images of animals, mythical characters and gods* – These spirit guides and guardians are reported particularly in cultures with unbroken traditions of healing through many centuries.[331] Some of these may be archetypal and/or culture-specific descriptions of type (1) entities, while others sound like concretizations of group awarenesses. The latter may represent projections of mythical imagery from the collective awareness of the people, or may represent nature spirits that are specific to given species of animals. Another possibility is that we may be able to tap into the morphogenetic fields of various species, and interpret or translate this into our conscious awareness as a nature spirit.

4. *Disembodied voices or presences* – Numinous presences that communicate as voices or awarenesses may be perceived by people in times of need or during

meditation and prayer. It is unclear whether these deserve a category of their own. It may be that these are any of the entities of (1-3) that are only partially perceived in conscious awareness. It is also possible that these are projections of a person's own intuitive awareness,[332] transformed through personal and cultural beliefs and expectations into voices or images as a way of allowing them to reach conscious awareness.

5. *A Being of Light* – An amazing presence is reported, particularly during Near-Death Experiences or as physical death is nearing. The Being of Light appears infinitely wise, compassionate, non-judgmental, unconditionally loving and totally accepting. Approaching the presence of this being is described as being like approaching a light that is so bright that it is impossible for a person to look at it directly.

It is most difficult to assess how much of the descriptions of the entities in categories (1-4) are influenced by cultural and religious conditioning, and how much may relate to perceptions of objective presences in other dimensions. Many of the entities described in these categories are perceived by individuals during crises, who had no previous experiences of these sorts and would in no way consider themselves to be channels or mediums, yet in these specific experiences appeared to have acted as such. Many who have these encounters are without religious affiliations and may be agnostic or atheistic. Often these experiences are transformative, bringing people towards beliefs in powers greater than themselves.

Space does not permit more detailed analyses of this subject here.

Responses to mediumship

Regardless of the source of mediumistic messages, many find that they are helped by such information. They seek the consultation of mediums for advice on business, relationships, health, and all of the challenges of life over which one may ponder and agonize.

Mediumship/channeling is growing in popularity and acceptance in the Western world. It is difficult to know how many people might avail themselves of such interventions, since much of this is done in the privacy of people's homes and at holistic health exhibitions, with no surveys of usage available.

Judao-Christian attitudes towards mediumship vary widely.

The Bible cautions against contacting the dead through mediums. Jewish tradition takes the view that consulting mediums is a forbidden, pagan practice that should definitely be discouraged. Saul paid with his life when he sought contact with the medium of Endor.[333] However, allowances in seeking mediumistic advice were made for people who were sick. Many Christians consider mediumistic communications to be suspect of the work of the Devil. Nowhere in the Bible, however, is there an injunction against paying attention to spontaneous communications from spirits.

Figure III-5. Religious prohibitions

POT-SHOTS NO. 768

Some things
are so forbidden,
they can't even
be mentioned on
lists of
forbidden things.

©BRILLIANT ENTERPRISES 1975

A polar opposite view is held in Christian Spiritualist churches, which abound in England – with estimated membership of over a million. Mediums regularly appear at services to channel messages from spirits of departed relatives and friends of congregation members and of visitors to the church. Casual observers criticize these mediums for presenting trivial data that could be so general that nearly anyone in the audience would find them relevant. Trained critics, such as stage magicians, further criticize the mediums for using feedback from their subjects to sharpen these 'readings,' which the magicians believe are no more than clever reworkings of what such mediums obtain through their normal senses.

My own observations of psychic readers[334] showed that they establish a deep rapport very rapidly through these trivial data that the subject finds impressive precisely because no one outside the family is likely to have known them. Though details are occasionally general, with the better readers they are more often unusual, highly specific and psychologically very meaningful. To an outsider, mention of a particular ring worn by the deceased may seem to be no more than a likely guess. Such mention may resonate deeply with a person who knows that the deceased had particular emotional associations with a particular ring,.

After establishing rapport with the person whom the spirit is wanting to contact, the spiritualist mediums give messages that are meaningful in informational, emotional and spiritual content.

Health advice, including warnings about impending illness and recommenda-tions to seek medical treatment are also given. Healing as the laying on of hands and prayer healing is also given in spiritualist churches, with the perception that spirits are usually participating or primary agents in giving the healings.

Information about the spirit is often conveyed, in general terms or in great detail. A major component of the proceedings is to heal the church members of fears of death and to alert them to the participation of spirits in earthly affairs.[335]

Initiations for shamans (medicine men) in many parts of the world often include long apprenticeships, with meditations, fasts and other procedures for inducing spirit visions. Even within traditional cultures there is a need for intense experiences in order for an initiate to relinquish sensory reality, to overcome fears of death and to become open to shamanic realities. Spirit guidance is sought for healing as well as for suggestions for dealing with problems of living – great and small.[336] Another aspect of some shamanic practices is *soul retrieval*, in which aspects of the person's soul or spirit are felt to have separated from the person and need to be brought back.[337]

Descriptions of the realms beyond the portals of death vary widely. It is difficult to know how much of the variance is due to difficulties in translations across boundaries between realities and how much to cultural and individual colorings imparted by different mediums. This is complicated further by the fact that in spirit dimensions people's visualizations may create that which they believe, wish or fear.[338] Thus, both mediums and spirits may be reporting widely varying worlds because these are actually created by those who are reporting them.[339]

To go into these cosmologies in detail would be a book in its own right, so let us suffice with a few common denominators. Mediums report that after death the spirit of a person goes through a period of adjustment. There is a spirit equivalent of a hospital, where one absorbs all the lessons learned and unlearned in the recent earthly life and to the broader horizons of spirit levels of existence. Spirit helpers are present, along with family members who have preceded one, to give comfort and to teach.

After the period of transition, there are spirit schools in which lessons are reportedly learned that bring the spirit and soul into increasingly more advanced levels of understanding and being. Highly evolved spirits supervise less evolved spirits in hierarchies that are ever more refined as one ascends towards unity with the Creator.[340]

Mediums, psychics, those who have Near-Death Experiences and the like report that the conventional Western views of a hell where people are tortured for their sins does not seem to exist. However, people who have hurt others may experience serious self-criticisms during the life review, and may be brought through other ways in the spirit world to feel the pain they have caused others.[341]

Discussion

The question of the existence of spirits is a difficult one. Though numerous mediums and healers report that their work is based on communications with and assistance from spirits, the inability of the average person to validate such reports leaves many people skeptical. Let us examine the evidence from two perspectives: If spirits exist and if they do not.

If spirits exist, we must ask why only a select few amongst the vast majority of us are able to hear and/or see them.

Mediums confront us with the question: Are the mediums in an altered state of consciousness that allows them to communicate with spirits or are we, the majority of people in industrial society who have no awareness of spirit worlds, in an altered, limited state of consciousness (that is validated by our societal beliefs and disbeliefs as the 'normal' state of consciousness)?

In traditional, non-industrial societies, spirits are more commonly accepted and more generally believed to communicate with the living. Although I know of no reliable studies on percentages of people in non-industrial societies who communicate with spirits, the general impression one gets from anthropological and sociological literature is that this is a much more frequent occurrence than in Western, industrial society.

From the point of view that spirits exist, we may postulate that Western cultural belief systems which exclude spirits may discourage people from experiencing communication with them or from reporting these. Yet a high percentage of people in Western society have experiences with spirits. For instance, two thirds of those surveyed in a study in the *American Journal of Psychiatry* reported bereavement apparitions – sensing the presence of departed persons who had been close to them.[342] This included seeing and/or hearing the departed and strong intuitive impressions that the deceased was present. This is not often spoken about or investigated in Western culture. The fact that so many people were willing to admit this appears to me impressive.

Further testimony on this reticence comes from repeated stories of gifted healers and psychics who saw spirits frequently in their childhood.[343] As children, they were confused at times between disembodied and embodied visitors in their homes. Joan Grant related that in childhood the apparitions she encountered appeared so real that she often had difficulty distinguishing that they were not solid.[344] "When I was a child, mistakes of this nature frequently got me into trouble, so I usually pretended not to see strangers until I had made sure that they were visible to everyone else." In some cases the parents of these gifted children reacted very negatively to their mention of seeing spirits. Olga Worrall saw a female spirit in her bedroom that frightened her. Her mother came to comfort her. Olga described the apparition and her mother felt the details matched a relative named Julika, who lived far away. Her mother was quite distressed when Olga mentioned that the spirit had said she had 'passed over.' Her mother told Olga never to say such things again. Several days later, news arrived that Julika had indeed died.

Because of such experiences, many sensitive children learn not to mention seeing spirits. They may begin to repress these perceptions below the threshold of consciousness in order to spare themselves conflicts with skeptics and disbelievers. Ultimately, they end up not seeing spirits as much, if at all. Later in life, upon maturing to the point of being able to assess realities independently of parental and societal censoring, some of these sensitives become more able to see spirits again. It seems likely that many children who see spirits may entirely block and repress these experiences forever under injunctions from family and peers to not mention them.[345]

There is an active avoidance in Western society of the subject of seeing spirits and great discomfort with the entire area of personal spiritual awareness. Part of the problems may be a fear of the unknown. Part of it may be a materialistic frame of mind that is uncomfortable with that which contradicts linear reality and points to the independence of mind/spirit from body. Still another part may be a discomfort with phenomena that lie outside people's control. Western society has become specialized in sensory reality. This creates the anticipation that one can control one's environment, a goal too often carried to sad extremes. A final part of the discomfort may relate to the fear of death.[346] Evidence for the existence of spirits challenges all of these beliefs and fears.

Mediums may help to bridge between the worlds of the living and those of spirits. They may decrease fears of death and may ease the way for all of us who will pass over sooner or later, preparing us for our continued development in the realms beyond the physical. Spirit assistance may include deathbed visions, in which the perceivers are themselves the mediums.

Nurses and healers who work in hospices tell of the joy and beauty in helping people make their transitions to the spirit world. This is often possible when fear is not present. The more sensitive caregivers can actually see the spirit body separating from the physical and can often see other spirits or angels coming to help and guide the departing spirit. Many report this is as exhilarating an experience as being a midwife at a birth – and, in fact, this is another birth, back into a spirit existence.

Popular films are now featuring these themes, as in 'Ghost' and 'Always.' Healers and psychics tell me the images in 'Ghost' are close to what they observe when a spirit departs the flesh. A misty vapor rises and separates from the physical body, sometimes maintaining the form of the dying person and sometimes being formless, like a wisp of smoke. Spirits or angelic beings may appear to guide the form away, or it may dissipate and become invisible.

The question still remains – why some persons see and hear spirits while others do not, even in traditional societies. Healers and mediums say that this is because only some persons are open or attuned to the spirit worlds. It is much the same as with any other human ability. Not everyone can sing, write, see auras or dance equally well. Some are gifted in particular areas and others are not.

From the other side, mediums report that not every spirit can make itself known to the conscious mind of every human. They report that certain vibrations or resonations must be precisely right and that this does not occur with many spirit/person pairs. Even where it does occur, it may vary according to unexplained cosmic conditions and requires intense (sometimes inordinate) efforts on the parts of the spirits. For these reasons, a particular spirit (*control* or *guide*), whose vibrations are harmonious with those of the medium, may be an intermediary in making the link for a medium with other spirits. The other spirits may be able to communicate through the resonation of the control with the medium, whereas they would not be able to achieve this directly themselves with the medium.

Why should spirits bother themselves with mortal beings? Opinions vary, but most agree that spirits feel an interest and even an obligation to help those of us who have chosen a course of lessons in being in the flesh because these are special and difficult lessons.

Even on spirit planes of existence there are allegedly ever more and more advanced levels of development, leading ultimately to being close to or reuniting with God.[347] This is consonant with mystical teachings in Judaism, Christianity, Islam and religions of the East.

> *For in that sleep of death what dreams may come,*
> *When we have shuffled off this mortal coil,*
> *Must give us pause.*
>
> – Hamlet

How do particular spirits select particular humans with whom to communicate? Again opinions vary. The following are representative samples of explanations for the pairings of spirits with living communicators:

- Humans can summon spirits as needed for their work on Earth or for help in their inner, spiritual development.

- The help of spirits and of guardian angels is available to all who ask, but without the request of the person they will rarely intervene to *change* events, though they may choreograph happenings and 'coincidences' which challenge people to higher awareness.

- It is the spirits who choose the humans they will help, often a choice made when the deceased wishes to continue helping friends and relatives from previous lives.

- These choices are made on the basis of affinities or 'vibrations' which have no exact description in human language, experience or concepts.

- This is a task either assumed willingly or assigned by the spiritual teachers of spirit-guides for the spiritual advancement of the spirits.

- Only a portion of a soul-like entity is incarnated in humans, while the rest of their being remains in spirit form and it is this other portion of themselves, which is sensed by humans as the spirits that helps them.

- Combinations of the above are possible.

Almost certainly these explanations suffer from difficulties in translations and interpretations between one plane of being and another. Mediums may also distort information unintentionally during channelings. This would not differ greatly from divergent reports we get from several witnesses and commentators who observed the same events in the physical world yet tell very differing stories about them.

Spirits were and are 'only human.' Caution is warranted in giving credence to information obtained through mediums. A spirit communicator quoted by Paul Beard[348] warned,

> Do not accept everything we advise you as the only possible solution to matters in your lives. Remember that we judge differently than you on earth. Certain points we do not see as clearly as you because with us the big issues are in the foreground, whilst with you small things may spoil or help. We rely on your judgment and good sense particularly as we rarely see the bad points. You must not think that our views which are based on spiritual existence are unfailing. Act through your own wisdom.[349]

A Native American put it more succinctly: "Dead no make smart."

It can be most confusing, puzzling and paradoxical when we realize that our expectations can create realities. One has to learn to negotiate other levels of reality and to trust one's inner awarenesses. Laurens van der Post[350] summarized this well:

...This potential of modern man on a quest of soul and a resumption of the dynamic dialogue between himself and the greater self is there always, like a star in the mirror of another self within, if only he would look not just with a blink of one-eyed science, as Blake named it, but with both inner and outer eyes.

The channels and recipients of the communication must also be cautious in *interpreting* what they are told. They must guard against the tendency to read into spirit messages what they expect or wish to hear, as Macbeth and others[351] learned to their chagrin.

Evidence supporting the various views of spirits is clearly different from evidence normally acceptable to Western science. It is not based on objective, 'out-there,' measurable-by-anyone types of data. Western materialistic science therefore rejects it because it is unmeasurable. In the eyes of many, such 'evidence' could be considered only a fantasy or a deliberate effort to defraud gullible people who are suffering from bereavement and longing for those they have lost. Margot Asquith[352] observed, "I always knew the living talked rot, but it's nothing to the rot the dead talk."

Eastern religions, which include a strong belief in survival of the spirit, do not present as dogma their cosmologies which suggest that there is more to existence than physical life.[353] They present these as truths that any who are interested can investigate and verify for themselves by looking inward. Multitudes of such investigators have found and validated these inner truths of so-called mystical awareness. The main difficulty seems to be in translating inner experiences into linear language in order to share them.[354] Furthermore, even if we accept the validity of the reports, we cannot be sure of consensual validation in our sensory reality state of what is experienced by separate individuals in alternative states of consciousness (ASCs). Charles Tart,[355] a parapsychologist who has written extensively on ASCs, suggests we conduct investigations while in these ASCs and develop ASC-specific terminology, concepts and perhaps even discrete branches of state-specific science. Although it might seem at first that this is unscientific, it is only so in sensory reality terms. I feel Tart's suggestions are valid and worth pursuing – as has been started in OBE studies.[356]

At the leading edges of modern physics there may be convergences or meeting points between these apparently disparate worlds of the physical and the mystical.[357]

Whether you accept the evidence or not is, in the end, a decision deriving from how you wish to relate to the world and what evidence you are willing to consider as relevant and real.

If spirits do not exist, we must assume that healers' and psychics' reports of spirits are fantasy or illusion. Here we are on firmer ground for *linear* arguments. In sensory reality[358] we can postulate many motivations for such fantasies, entirely consistent with familiar psychological mechanisms.

Psi phenomena may be unsettling to those of us raised in our materialistic culture because they require reordering of Western assumptive realities.[359] Saying, "The spirits told me so," to explain psi perceptions might lessen the queasy feelings many people get when they encounter such unfamiliar experiences. Spirits could provide a convenient fantasy vehicle, external to mediums, psychics, healers (who report they often communicate with spirits) and ordinary folk (who may have occasional spirit encounters), to allay their discomfort at experiencing psi phenomena. This view is supported by the 'Philip' type experiments. Furthermore, should mediumistic predictions be verified, the mediums can claim that they are allied with knowledgeable spirit authorities, thus enhancing their image in the eyes of sitters. Better yet, should the reading not be successful, mediums can *hedge* and claim that it was not their fault; that the spirits were inaccurate; or that cosmic conditions were not propitious for accurate communications.

By shifting responsibility in their own minds for the accuracy of their psi perceptions, mediums or healers might increase their effectiveness. Attributing the source of information to spirits could help them release their watchfulness over what they are doing and diminish anxieties about success or failure, both of which might distract them from their concentration on the readings or healings. That is, in watching and worrying over their accuracy while channeling information, they could distract themselves from focusing on the *content* of the communications. Believing in spirits, they can 'leave matters in the hands of higher authorities' – in this way leaving their unconscious minds free of linear concerns and anxieties.

Other rationales for invoking spirit explanations suggest themselves. People who have strange powers are sometimes viewed with suspicion, apprehension and even hostility by those who are blind to these dimensions. By attributing the powers to outside agencies, healers and mediums may disown some parts of that strangeness.

The notion of spirit intermediaries also may help maintain distance between the healer and healee. It can help preserve the sensory reality view of discreteness and intactness of individual boundaries for both parties. Some people experience a subjective loosening of their sense of self even upon coming into physical proximity and normal social interactions with others. They fear that others will 'take control' of them or, conversely, that they will take control of the others.[360] In spiritual healing, these anxieties may be even worse. The unconscious might reason, "If I can alter the physical condition of another when I work as a healer, might I also inadvertently alter their physical condition sometimes in undesirable ways?" Conversely, for the healee, "Can I trust a healer not to impose their will (desires, preferences, views) on mine; to not change me in ways I would not wish them to; to not harm me in some other ways?"[361] Healees often request assurances that healers will only do positive things for them. Having heard of black magic and voodoo curses by medicine men, healees are apprehensive about healers' credentials and intentions. A fantasied spirit intermediary, presumed to be of higher moral fiber because of being 'on high,' may lessen such anxieties.

The fear of death is very powerful in Western society. A fantasy belief in spirits could provide a measure of relief from this fear. Spirit communications, especially those of departed relatives, inherently promise an afterlife for the healee. This, in and of itself, gives a potent motivation for the invocation of such images. Spirit communication may relieve the healee or sitter of some of the painful emotions involved in grief reactions. When the deceased departed quickly or unexpectedly, people are often left with guilt and anger over what was or was not said or done in haste, in distress, or in error. How many of us are left with guilt over having been too late with an apology or an affirming word? Who has not had some distress or anger that led to difficult interactions with someone who departed this physical existence before these unsettled issues could be resolved? How helpful to feel one is able to make amends through a medium.

Letting go of a beloved person is difficult. I was taught as a student in psychiatry[362] that the internalized image of the loved *object* (psychological jargon for person towards whom one has feelings) is so hard to relinquish that the bereaved may hallucinate the presence of the departed shortly after their death. This is not a sign of psychosis, though the bereaved may fear it is. Thus psychiatry acknowledges this type of occurrence and recognizes it as being of benign prognosis, hypothesizing it is a mere projection of a wished-for presence.[363] And who is to say this may not be the way it happens in some instances?[364]

Mediumistic fraud for profit is a caution to everyone investigating the spirit world, as documented by Lamar Keene. The wish to contact the departed is so strong that any hope, however slim or flimsily presented, is likely to be eagerly grasped by the bereaved. There are unscrupulous shysters who regularly bilk people of large sums in phony mediumistic séances. Mediums who demand expensive fees should be approached with the greatest caution.

Even without deliberate fraud, one must carefully consider the possibility of deception in claims of seeing spirits. Motives for deception might start with personal gain or in ego aggrandizement for the channel. By clothing their work in images that are appealing, fraudulent mediums could increase their prestige and their business. This is a difficult contention to support with the more gifted mediums. They do not lack for clients. Many work very long hours and are unable to keep up with their normal social and family activities because of their workload. One could hypothesize that early in their career they might invoke images of spirits for such purposes. Later, through force of habit or expectations of their clients, they might continue using them. In reality, the reverse seems more often the case. Sensitives and healers frequently start out without any sense of spirit guides and gradually develop this awareness.

Mass hallucination might account for at least part of the mediumistic phenomena. If the projection of telepathic thoughts is possible, there is no logical reason that vivid images might not be similarly projected. Hypnotic induction via telepathy has been demonstrated.[365] Though it appears conceptually possible that telepathic hallucinations might be induced, there is little evidence to show that this occurs. It cannot be ruled out as an explanation for some mediumistic phenomena but appears rather an unlikely one for most, as the sitters rarely report they experienced an altered state of consciousness, and photographs of mediumistic apports (mediumistic materializations) have been confirmed by electronic devices.[366]

These are a few possibilities. You, dear reader, will have to decide for yourself which feels to be the truth.

> *...Our views of reality are maya, illusions, but these 'illusions' constitute our reality... The 'one' hidden reality expresses itself and it seems to be approached in many different representational ways, in mythologems that vary with different individuals, cultures, times and locations. They all circumambulate the 'truth,' each telling the story from its unique angle in a manner comparable to the trigonometric 'shooting' of a star from different positions. The more angles taken into account, the closer the approximation to accuracy.*
>
> – Edward Whitmont [366]

Personally, I have difficulty considering conscious deception a likely possibility when ethical healers report spirit interventions. The majority of those with whom I have talked and worked have a solid reverence for their healing gifts and works. They are very much in tune with themselves, the healees and the cosmos. They are used to reporting many psi or spirit impressions and/or messages (concerning healees) that they themselves do not understand but that have deep personal meaning for the healees. If they say they perceive their impressions as coming from spirits, I believe they are reporting their experiences honestly.

I must add, however, that I have also encountered the opposite. There are mediums and healers who cannot resist the aggrandizement of ego, enhancement of power, and boost to income potentially inherent in their work. Claims of prestigious spirit guides support these selfish motives.

So if you're seeking sensitives to help you explore your personal spiritual awareness, look for those who have done the work of 'clearing the vessel through which intuition pours,' [367] do not pressure you to accept their beliefs, and are respectful of your remaining in control of decisions in your life.

Mediumistic phenomena help to understand aspects of healing

In mediumistic physical phenomena we find that matter appears to be manipulated and/or materialized through acts of will – both by mediums and by sitters. Miraculous cures, in which instantaneous healings occur, may include the closing of chronic wounds, instantaneous mending of fractures and other bodily changes that require apparent materialization of living tissues and bone.[368]

In Psychic surgery the healers apparently open up the body with a touch of their hands, removing tumors and repairing damaged tissues.[369] Psychic surgery involves the seeming dissolution or dematerialization of tissues or permeability of these tissues in the initial phase of the surgeon opening the body and materializations in the closing phase.

Some seek to explain the occasional dissolving of tissue samples from psychic surgery in their preserving fluids as evidence that they consisted of materialized ectoplasm.[370] Though this hypothesis may seem theoretically plausible, it meets difficulties when we look more closely at reports of mediumistic materializations.

Mediums almost always request that the materialized figures should not be touched by the sitters, lest harm be done to the medium. Turner's report on the materialization of a completely real-looking person with whom he shook hands is an exception to this séance room routine. It may be that the hands-off tradition is one derived from mediums of the fraudulent type, who wish to protect their faked illusions from exposure. In any case, materializations of the séance room are always confined to that place. They do not leave the room to accompany sitters or the medium. Thus it is hard to compare these phenomena with those of healings – which persist and are often permanent changes in the healees.

Mind-matter interactions are complicated in healing by the contributions of healees and observers – in addition to those of the healers. Healers and healees have reported that when healees disbelieve in healings, they may block or reverse the effects of healing. I have seen many healees who had marked relief of pain, for instance, but then find the pain returning over the days and weeks following the healing treatments. While this might be attributed to a weak or incomplete healing effect in some cases, the fact that many of these healees do not return to get further healing suggests that they have unconscious motivations to hold onto their pains and other symptoms. Healers and psychics regularly observe that the presence of a skeptic can also impede or block healing and psi effects

It could be that healees materialize their own flesh and bone. There would then be no contradiction with the analogy with mediumistic materializations, as these would remain with the persons producing them.

Mediums teach us about healings of emotion through overcoming fears of death and of spiritual growth through awareness of spirit and spiritual levels of development. The greater proportion of healers (by my informal estimate) teach that the spiritual awareness that is opened up through healing is the most important aspect of a spiritual healing encounter. This is not to say that healings for physical and emotional problems are unimportant. It is to emphasize that such problems are, in themselves, invitations to healees to explore their relationships with themselves, their significant others, and the many levels of the cosmos around them.[371] There appears to exist a growing consensus that the task of mankind is evolving towards a spiritualization of matter. More on this in following chapters.

My personal experience with mediumistic phenomena

It took me a long time to accept spirit levels of existence, coming from my training in psychology, medicine, psychiatry and research. Although I have not had direct, conscious communications with spirits or angels, the collective evidence in this book leads me to accept the existence of a transcendent reality that includes these beings. However, I also remain cautious about individual reports and studies. I always keep in mind that the human instrument, the most sensitive computer known on earth, suffers from distortions of *noise* – the intrusion of extraneous mental activity – and the 'hard-wired' programs of genetically determined perceptual organs with extremely complex neurological wiring that transforms sensory stimuli into meaningful perceptions; overlaid by personal experiences, habits of perception and belief, and cultural conditioning. Thus, any individual report must be carefully scrutinized to filter out as many of these possible distorting factors.

My confidence and trust in the worlds and processes of intuitive perceptions are further enhanced through my own meditative practices, along with engaging in and receiving healing. These first-hand experiences provide immediate awarenesses of bioenergies that appear to be related to the spirit body. My deliberate explorations of transpersonal consciousness through muscle testing and spontaneous intuitive awarenesses contribute further to my gnowing and trusting of these realities. Just being able to touch the edge of spirit awareness in this way strengthens my beliefs in the spiritual dimensions.

In summary

Mediumistic/channeled communications with spirits have been reported through-out recorded history, and continue to be found in most cultures around the world. Modern Western society tends to denigrate and dismiss these as old wives' tales and wishful thinking of those who cannot release their links with the deceased.

Research on mediumship has been conducted for more than a century by scientists around the world. The evidence from studies where separate pieces of inter-related information were channeled through different mediums is particularly impressive.

If the spirits in mediumship and spiritual healings were taken in isolation, I might tend more towards the psychological and super-psi explanations rather than giving credence to the actual existence of spirits. Considering the sum of evidence from research on auras, OBEs, NDEs, pre-death experiences, reincarnation, appa-ritions, mediumistic phenomena, possession[372] and mystical experiences,[373] I find a disbelief in a surviving energy body and/or spirit logically hard to maintain.

Not having seen a spirit, however, my rational mind and gut-feelings still maintain reservations and raise questions. I have to admit it is strange, inasmuch as I have never observed an atom or an electron either, yet I find those latter entities easier to entertain as being actual bits of 'something' existing in my universe. I find my disbeliefs in spirits and mediumistic phenomena fading with increasing encounters with others who have strongly evidential, first-hand spirit encounters. It is fascinating to observe my shifts in beliefs through explorations of others' descriptions of distant lands they have visited. I somehow more easily accept black holes and the panoply of subatomic worlds, which scientists assure us that their instruments and experiments confirm, inhabiting the vastness of empty space, and that this invisible but objectively measurable world is the greater portion of sensory reality.

Let us turn now to spirit possession and exorcisms – further aspects of spirit manifestations and healing.

CHAPTER 6

Possession

He cast out the spirits with his word, and he healed all that were sick.
— Matthew [374]

Throughout the world, in cultures of many varieties, there is a commonly held belief that spirits can mischievously, misguidedly or maliciously interfere in the lives of men. Some medical traditions hold that many aspects of existence, including many conditions of health and illness, are due to spirit interventions. In such cultures the cures of disharmonies in one's body, and in relationships with people and nature require negotiations with and propitiation of the spirits.

   In this section we shall consider reports that a specific discarnate entity has taken over (*possessed* or *obsessed*) the mind and/or body of an individual for its own purposes. (This is in contrast with mediumistic experiences, described in the last chapter, in which the channeler may *invite* a spirit to communicate by taking control of the channeler's body.)

   William Blatty described the possession of a young girl named Regan in his book, *The Exorcist*, now even more famous through the motion picture. Regan started having episodes of strange behavior, with outbursts of anger and violence that were totally out of character and completely inappropriate. Benign (tapping noises in the walls) and violent poltergeist activity[375] accompanied these episodes, including levitation of her bed and physical harm to one of the priests participating in an exorcism. In this instance the psi spirit interventions seemed to have the intent of deliberately scaring and even harming others. Medical and psychiatric consultations were of no avail. An exorcism was required to rid the girl of the symptoms through a casting out of the possessing entity.

   There is evidence that such tales may be more than simply tales of horror created by authors who write scary stories. A number of scientific explorations of possession are reviewed here.

D. Scott Rogo described the syndrome of possession which includes: telepathy, precognition, xenoglossy, displays of super-human strength, vile language, vicious and malicious behavior, poltergeist-type phenomena, aversion to religious matters and other behaviors that are totally unusual and out of character for the individual who is possessed.[376] Rogo examined three possible explanations for such occurrences: hysterical (conversion) reactions, poltergeist phenomena and possession – summarized in Table III-2. In conversion reactions, people's unconscious minds produce physical symptoms that appear to be beyond their control. In poltergeist activity, objects are moved about by psychokinesis, sometimes forcefully and even violently. Rogo argues cogently for the distinctness of the possession hypothesis. Though accepting that discarnate entities are the most likely explanation, he stops short of extrapolating from the available evidence to any hypotheses on the nature of such entities.

Table III-2 clearly indicates distinct patterns for each of these possible explanations. Possession includes great fear, vicious behaviors, equal distribution among males and females reporting possession, xenoglossy, multiple voices, levitation, copious vomiting, feats of superhuman strength, personality disintegration, and extreme tenaciousness of the symptoms.

Individual cases of possession can be quite varied in their presentations and symptomatic manifestations. In some cases, overlaps between the various possibilities in the table may present a challenge to clear assessment of the cause of the symptoms.

W. F. Prince was a parapsychologist and psychotherapist, previously a minister. He described two cases of apparent paranoia, in which psychiatric patients complained that voices inside their heads were commanding them to do things that they found distasteful and contrary to their habits and wishes. Prince observed that these patients were different from most paranoid patients – who do not identify the voices they hear and what these voices tell them to do as alien. Prince took their assertions of possession at face value. He exhorted the alleged spirits, both directly and under hypnosis, to reconsider their actions and to look for better means of occupying themselves. He was successful in completely curing both cases in a relatively short time. One of the most remarkable aspects of Prince's paper is that it was published in the conventional journal, *The Psychoanalytic Review.*

Numerous anecdotal reports from healers and intuitives parallel this report. Psychotherapy is done with the healees on why they allowed the possession to occur and with the spirits on why they are lingering on material planes. Entities then are encouraged to 'turn to the light,' to seek the aid of relatives who passed over, to call for Christ or God to help, and so on. Cures of emotional and physical symptoms occur rapidly when the possessing spirits depart.

Uninvited spirit guidance

I. O. Azuonye reports a case in which a woman heard voices in her head and thought she was insane. One psychiatrist put her on antipsychotic medication, which banished the voices for a while. They returned, however, and directed her to go to an address that proved to be a computerized tomography department of a hospital. To everyone's surprise, a brain mass was seen, suggesting a tumor. No

Table III - 2 Alternative explanations for possession phenomena*

Factor	Hysteria (pseudo-possession)	Poltergeist	Possession
Decreasing trend in 20th Century	Yes	Unknown	No
Hysterical personality traits	Yes	Not prominent	No
Reactions of subject to symptoms	Passive, indifferent	Anxious, upset	Horrified
Directions of psychological intent	Guilt, self-punishment	Seemingly random	Vicious towards others; murderous
Sex distribution	90% Female	85% Female	50% Female
Physical symptoms	- - - - - Can be similar in all three categories - - - - -		
Psychokinesis (PK)	Uncommon	Same phenomena but limited in distance	Can occur over great distances, persecutory
Religious objects are targets of PK	- - - - - Can be similar in all three categories - - - - -		
Xenoglossy	Never	Never	Common
Voices	Never	Rare, few words	Prolific, independent voices
Levitation	Never	Rare	Usual
Vomiting	Rare, normal amounts	No	Gallons (!) of foreign material
Strength	Normal	Normal	Superhuman
Personality disintegration	No	Occasional dissociation	Yes
Violence	Occasional	No	Common, extreme
Duration	Brief	Brief or episodic	Tenacious, persistent

*From Rogo 1974(a) with amendments in consultation with the author

subjective or objective evidence of the tumor was found on neurological exam. In brain surgery, a meningioma measuring 1.5 x 2.5 inches was removed from the left posterior frontal lobe, extending across the midline to the right hemisphere. The tumor was removed completely. The voices said, "Goodbye" following the surgery. Antipsychotic medication was discontinued, and at 12-year follow-up she was free of auditory hallucinations. Again, this article is notable for its publication in a conventional periodical, the British Medical Journal.

A variety of explanations have been proposed for such phenomena of intuitive self-diagnosis. Some attribute this knowledge to uninvited channeled material, or a benign or positive case of possession. Others suggest that the unconscious mind projects the information on the screen of conscious awareness, under the guise of a need to deal with problems of medical or other urgency, and people who experience this believe it comes from outside themselves.

Multiple personality and possession

Another alternative explanation to possession is that people reporting another entity inside themselves are suffering from fragmentation of their personalities. Personality *splits* typically occur when children suffer extreme abuse and shut off a part of themselves in order not to suffer emotional pain. Once a split like that occurs it tends to persist. Furthermore, the psychological defense of splitting off parts of oneself that are uncomfortable becomes a habit and additional fragmentations can occur subsequent to the original trauma.

Ralph Allison is a psychiatrist who has specialized in treatment of patients with multiple personality. This gives him a unique perspective on questions regarding possession. He found numerous cases in which alternate personalities developed as a coping mechanism when a person faced unbearable stresses in childhood. The alternate personality permitted the primary personality to escape having to face and recall very difficult emotional traumas. Surprisingly, Allison found additional alternate personalities that had no evidence for trauma as a cause for their originating within the primary personality's life. These often claimed to be possessing spirits. The other, split-off personalities within the same person would often confirm this assertion. He found that he could free the patients of these possessing spirits relatively rapidly by exhortations to leave or by helping the patient to fight them off. In some cases the aid of a higher intelligence within the patient, which Allison terms the 'Inner Self Helper,' could also be invoked to aid in sorting out the various personalities, possessing spirits and emotional turmoil. This is distinctly different from the psychotherapeutic methods required to heal the fragmented personality that take many months and even years to produce results.

Allison distinguishes five gradations or levels of possession:

Grade 1. Obsessive-compulsive neurosis – "In such cases the patient is controlled by an idea, obsession, involuntary act, compulsion, or addiction to alcohol or drugs." [377]

Grade 2. Multiple personality – "...the result of the influence of a negative alter personality developed by a person with a hysterical personality structure." [378]

Grade 3. "...*possession* occurs when the controlling influence *seems to be the mind of another living human being...* witchcraft may be involved." [379]

Grade 4. "...*possession* is control by the *spirit of another human being.*" [380]

Grade 5. "...*possession* is control by a *spirit that has never had its own life* history and identifies itself as an *agent of evil.*" [381]

Grade 5 possession responds to religious ritual exorcism, while the other grades respond to psychotherapy and exhortation, often with the aid of hypnosis. [382]

Possession Treated by a Medium

Carl Wickland, a physician, describes many years' work with a medium (his wife) who helped him treat numerous cases of apparent spirit possession, which caused a wide variety of emotional and physical problems.

Wickland reports that spirits explained some of the whys and hows of possession.

> They stated that there is in reality no death, but a natural transition from the visible to the invisible world and that advanced spirits are ever striving to communicate with mortals to enlighten them concerning the higher possibilities which await the progressing spirit. But death – the freeing of the spirit from the body – is so simple and natural that a great majority do not, for a longer or shorter period, realize the change, and owing to a lack of education concerning the spiritual side of their natures they continue to remain in their earthly haunts.
>
> They maintained that many such spirits were attracted to the magnetic aura of mortals – although the spirit, as well as the mortal, might be unconscious of the intrusion – and thus, by obsessing or possessing their victims, they ignorantly or maliciously became the cause of untold mischief and misery, often producing invalidism, immorality, crime and seeming insanity... [383]
>
> ...Purity of life and motive, or high intellectuality, do not necessarily offer protection from obsession; recognition and knowledge of these problems are the only safeguards.
>
> The physical conditions permitting this impingement are varied; such encroachment is often due to a natural and predisposed susceptibility, a depleted nervous system, or sudden physical and/or emotional shock. Physical derangements are conducive to obsession, for when the vital forces are lowered less resistance is offered and intruding spirits are allowed easy access...
>
> This encroachment alters the characteristics of the sensitive, resulting in a seemingly changed personality, sometimes simulating multiple or dissociated personalities and frequently causes apparent insanity, varying

in degree from a simple mental aberration to and including, all types of dementia, hysteria, epilepsy, melancholia, shell shock, kleptomania, idiocy, religious and suicidal mania, as well as amnesia, psychic invalidism, dipsomania, immorality, functional bestiality, atrocities and other forms of criminality.

Humanity is surrounded by the thought influence of millions of discarnate beings, who have not yet arrived at a full realization of life's higher purposes. A recognition of this fact accounts for a great portion of unbidden thoughts, emotions, strange forebodings, gloomy moods, irritabilities, unreasonable impulses, irrational outbursts of temper, uncontrollable infatuations and countless other mental vagaries[384]

Wickland presents detailed discussions between himself and the possessing entities. In many cases he did counseling of an simple nature, helping spirits to accept that they were dead and could find better things to do than trying to hang on to life in the physical world. In some cases, he helped them process unresolved feelings lingering from physical life. Advising them to turn towards the white light and to ask for aid from other spirits also helped. In essence, he helped the spirits to resolve residual earth-existence emotional problems as well as confusion engendered by transition to spirit planes of existence.

Wickland applied additional techniques to convince obstinate spirits to relinquish possession of their subjects. One was to confront the possessing spirit, in the body of its host, with a mirror. This revealed to the spirit that it was not itself, not in the right body. Another was to use a charge of static electricity to dislodge them. This was empirically discovered to be extremely uncomfortable to spirits. As a psychiatrist, considering these reports, I am given pause to wonder whether some successful electroconvulsive treatments (ECT) of schizophrenia represent eliminations of possessing entities.

Physical symptoms and possession

C. W. M. Wilson, a Scottish physician, found that many people with severe allergies suffer from possession. He reports that when he did a diagnostic test by dowsing,[385] asking whether possession is a factor in a given person, this would often bring on the characteristic allergic symptomatology. Such people are also sensitive to heavy metals. He reports that hypnotic therapy, with exhortation of the possessing entities to depart, is highly successful in relieving the allergies. Regretfully, the possibility of suggestion effects was not explored.

Christopher Bird describes a dowser named Jastram, who identifies possessing entities that allegedly cause physical and emotional disorders of unusual, unexplainable nature. He then enters an altered state of consciousness, suggesting to the possessing spirits that they leave. Jastram notes a resemblance of his interventions with those of Hawaiian Kahuna healers.[386]

Andree Samuel and Julika Kiskos are clinical psychologists in Sao Paulo, Brazil. Their psychotherapy includes consultation with psychic sensitives who identify extraneous personalities (*theta agents*) who are influencing the patients in various ways. Removal of the theta agents contributes substantially to the improvement of their clients. They report on a series of patients who were in psychotherapy but did not know that the theta agents were being identified and dealt with through absent healing.

They identify four types of theta agents:

1. Those unaware that they died, who are often in a state of confusion, manifesting at least two of the following characteristics:

- Not knowing where they are or what is going on
- Feeling they are in total darkness
- Complaining of physical pains
- Being apathetic, weak, drowsy or tired
- Complaining of existential problems
- Worrying about or seeking family members whom they cannot find
- Complaining that people ignore their presence and that they cannot contact anyone
- They seem fixated with dramatic moments in their lives such as illness, accidents and quarrels and have no motivation to continue living, with suicidal ideation

2. Those pressured to harm patients by black magic, characterized by:

- Being aware of their condition
- Rendering services in certain places
- Being amoral
- Being mercenary – i.e., having contracted to do harm in return for certain rewards or to avoid punishments by black magic
- Being willing to draft the help of other entities who are unaware they are dead in order to achieve the objectives of the theta agents
- Being emotionally uninvolved with the patient

3. Those intentionally trying to harm the patients, characterized by:

- Being aware or unaware they have died
- Being motivated by wishes for revenge
- Being emotionally involved, reporting having been victimized by the patients
- Harming the patients unintentionally, remaining close to the patients and claiming to love them but interfering in their lives

4. Those sharing and enjoying patients' activities, characterized by:

- Being aware or unaware they have died

- Developing symbiotic relationships with the patients
- Being interested in pleasures enjoyed vicariously through the patients, but not being interested in the patients themselves

Though responsibility of the *influencing agent* has been stressed in most of the literature, Samuel and Kiskos point out that *the patients* often contribute to or are predisposed to the possessing influences.

To explain the fact that *distant healing* eliminated theta agents and helped their patients, Samuel and Kiskos considered the following alternatives:

1. Mediums simulated trance;
2. Theta agents were products of the sensitives' unconscious;
3. Patients' improvements were merely coincidental with the distant healings;
4. Patients were improved through self-healing, by auto-suggestion;
5. Telepathy;
6. Clairvoyance; and/or
7. "This-world ESP was used by the healers to produce the information about the healees."

To sort out the alternatives, these hypotheses were analyzed in relation to three types of treatment:

A. with patients who were unaware that they were given absent healing.
B. with patients who knew that they were being given absent healing.
C. with patients who were being treated in the presence of sensitives.

Samuel and Kiskos present the following analysis:

> *Concerning (A)*: alternatives (1) and (2) are eliminated when a patient is unaware of absent healing. The sensitives' perceptions coincided with patients' mental and/or physical states and a significant improvement was observed. Coincidental improvement alone (3) does not explain the many cases observed during these years, some with chronic symptoms (cured at the time of the healings). Improvement due to autosuggestion (4) can be eliminated as the healees did not know they were being treated by absent healing. In (5), (6) and (7), it is natural for sensitives to obtain information by telepathy, clairvoyance or 'this-world ESP.' However, we are reporting here a gradual improvement occurring in patients that had been presenting psychological disorders. The mere perception by the sensitives of their emotional states or symptoms by means of telepathy, clairvoyance or 'this-world ESP' would not have removed them. Improvement only happened after our work with the theta agent or agents involved in the case.
>
> *Concerning 'B' and 'C'*: After the above discussion the only thing that might be said is that patients improve due to autosuggestion (4). However, when the patient does not know he is being treated and still improves, autosuggestion is eliminated. When patients are aware of the absent healing

then autosuggestion cannot be totally eliminated, but it would be only one single component of a group of factors responsible for his improvement.

Unfortunately, Samuel and Kiskos did not gather convincing evidence in terms of numbers of cases or statistical analysis of controls vs. treated patients to support their claims. In personal communication, Kiskos[387] answers this criticism with the observations that healer and other variables contribute to the experimental equation and

> [O]ur present scientific methodology is not able to translate well what goes on with healing... There are a number of variables [which] do not remain stable during experiments...are not always easy to interpret...and sometimes we are not even aware of them... Many things also depend on the type of 'guides' you work with...and who would contribute, joining efforts with the group, to harmonize the individual under treatment.

It is also conceivable that in option (2), in which symptoms are produced by a person's unconscious mind, absent healing brings about improvements. They also mention no blinds, so experimenter-effects in the form of clinical suggestion is a possible alternative explanation. Though they discount the *super-ESP hypothesis* (that mediums may have used a combination of psi abilities) to explain their results, this too remains a possibility.

My personal impression from reviewing the literature and talking with healers who deal with possession is that *each of the mentioned mechanisms* may create clinical pictures of possession. Each individual therefore presents a challenge to a healer to sort out which factor or combination of factors is creating the problems.

Stanley Krippner and Alberto Villoldo[388] describe Hernani Guimares Andrade, a Brazilian parapsychologist who has extensively investigated many aspects of healing. He is also credited with being a healer of great repute himself. He discusses obsession, and possession:

> In 'obsession,' it is felt that the magnetic fields[389] of the healees are in disequilibrium due to poor mental control and disharmonious thoughts. As a result, they assimilate magnetic forces from the environment of the same poor quality, exaggerating the condition and producing a mental pattern diagnosed as mental illness. The environmental forces which are attracted include those of discarnate 'spirits' of a lower order. These entities attach themselves to the person, creating various mental 'imbalances' and illnesses. The ailments that characterize an entity in its previous incarnation have a certain 'vibration' which often matches the 'vibrations' of the healee who frequently manifests physically the ailment of the 'spirit.'
>   A 'healing' service arranged to assist an 'obsessed' person begins with a series of inspirational readings which encourage the mediums to direct their thoughts to God. A 'spirit guide' is then called upon to serve as 'mentor' for the group. The 'obsessing spirit' is then asked to express itself through a medium in all of its anguish, pain and ignorance. One of the mediums

holds a dialogue with the 'obsessing spirit.' Gradually, the entity is encouraged to leave the ailing person. If no dialogue with the 'spirit' is possible, the medium purportedly hypnotizes the 'spirit' and coaxes it to leave.

In order for 'psychic healing' to be effective, the healees must change their behavior so as to develop an affinity for higher vibrations. 'Magnetic passes' can temporarily remove the lower 'energies' that have accumulated in the 'perispirit' due to the entities' attachment. But if the healees are to be free from future 'obsession' both from lower entities as well as from their own psychological complexes, they must direct their will towards a 'reinvestment' of their personalities. This can be done by 'investing' their efforts in higher thoughts rather than in overindulgence in tobacco and liquor and other bad habits. As a result of the 'reinvestment' process, the healees will develop affinities for the more highly evolved 'spirits' who can serve as guides and as sources of inspiration.

Once the ties are broken to the lower entities, the physical manifestations of the illness should begin to disappear. If not, a healee would be taken to a medium who can 'see' the 'obsessing' entities and persuade them to leave the healee. The entities are told they, too, are on an evolutionary path and they will do better to break their attachments to the earthly plane.

'Possession' is a more serious matter. In this case, the 'spirit' entities have taken over a person's body and will. Andrade has taken part in many 'exorcisms' in which the healee would be placed in a circle of mediums, one of which could 'incorporate' the offending entity. Another medium, the 'indoctrinator,' would stand outside the circle and would speak to the 'spirit.' The entity would be lured out of the healee's body and told to enter the body of the 'incorporator.' The healee would then be sent to a different room. At this point, the 'incorporator' would expunge the 'spirit' from his or her own body, firmly telling the entity not to return.[390]

Villoldo and Krippner[391] describe the work of Eliezer Mendes, a Brazilian surgeon. He now works with healers of the Umbanda tradition (derived from African shamanism) who heal while in ecstatic trances, reporting that they are under spirit influences.

> ...He observed that when a person first became a medium, he or she often would have epileptic-like seizures. At other times, certain aspects of the medium's personality would become exaggerated; he or she would begin to hear voices and see visions, and would demonstrate some of the symptoms of schizophrenia or multiple personality disorder.
>
> In both cases these symptoms would result from the first shocking contact with a disembodied spirit, when a foreign intelligence entered the novice medium's body and created epileptic-like seizures, loss of contact with external reality, or a 'double' personality. All of these symptoms were said to stop as soon as the medium developed his or her psychic abilities and learned to regulate his or her 'open window' into the spirit world. Mendes

claims that these symptoms could also be caused when one suffered a shock in death. These personalities from one's past could act as foreign entities that intrude on one's psyche, and must be dealt with as intrusive spirits...

Mendes claims an 85 percent success rate in curing epileptics by teaching them to develop and control their psychic abilities, utilizing Umbanda techniques – though not within a religious setting. He has a lower rate of success with schizophrenics. In both types of patients he requires family members to participate in the therapy.

Possession as a generic concept

This concept of possession, whether by witchcraft or unconscious conflict, is what psychotherapy is about. All healers, including psychiatrists, strengthen people's life force by helping to remove destructive debris; some healers call it exorcising devils. I've discovered that this kind of healing always works better when you use more than words.

– Carl Hammerschlag [392]

There is a growing awareness in some psychotherapy traditions[393] that dissociative disorders are far more common than has been generally appreciated. In the mildest cases, all of us constellate parts of our personality and split off other parts when we relate to particular people or situations in ways which differ from how we relate to other people or situations. We are different people in relating to a spouse, our children, grandchildren, various friends and colleagues, employers and so on. While generally this is not a problem, it is on the same spectrum as the splits that can be pathological.

In moderately serious instances, we might have emotional scars that lead us to exclude some of our potentials in particular situations. 'Jane' was upset in first grade when she forgot some of her lines in the Christmas play. Her mother was embarrassed and scolded Jane, saying, "How stupid you are!" Jane found herself so fearful of speaking in public when she grew up that she avoided many social situations that might have been enjoyable. "Tom' found it impossible to handle simple arithmetic after his school teacher ridiculed him for making a minor error in a problem he was doing on the blackboard in second grade. We might say that Jane and Tom were *possessed with fears.*

The removal of such generalized fears in the art and science of psychotherapy may often involve rituals that are not dissimilar to exorcisms. Alternative states of consciousness such as relaxation, meditation, imagery and hypnosis may be used. The therapist may help Jane and Tom by exorcising their fears through such rituals. She may suggest to them, as a strong authority figure, that they engage in activities which they would otherwise have avoided, helping them to overcome their fears by acting on her advice, with her support.

A psychotherapeutic exorcism of this sort of fear may also be approached through unconditional love rather than through exhortation and resort to religious rituals.[394]

Perfect love can never be defeated because it is infinite.
                                                – Mother Meera [395]

In my own practice of psychotherapy combined with spiritual healing I might do a laying-on of hands to help relieve pain, anxiety, or depression. I might pray with clients for strength to deal with problems, for greater understanding of their situation, or for Divine guidance and help.

In all of the above there appears to be a place for exorcising (metaphorically) old hurts, poor self-images, and habits. While there are these similarities between conventional psychotherapy and exorcism, I believe that classical exorcism for entity possession is a distinct and separate category of intervention.

Skeptics' views of possession

He who believes in the devil already belongs to him
                                                – Thomas Mann

Carlos Trevino, a physician, summarizes 2,000 interviews with people referred by the Catholic Archdiocese in Mexico City for evaluation of being bothered by evil spirits or being 'possessed.' The investigators considered these reports from perspectives of psychiatry, psychology, theology and parapsychology. In all cases, psychiatric diagnoses were assigned. These included paranoia, schizophrenia, manic-depressive psychosis, senile cerebral arteriosclerosis, hysteria, epilepsy, drug or alcohol intoxication or other organic disease. In 85% of cases, psi accounted for alleged possession. In 15% it was attributed to hallucinations.

Several examples are given of the psychotherapeutic treatment that alleviated these apparent cases of psi and psychological difficulties.[396] The authors do not report any cases in which possession per se appeared to explain the phenomena. They also do not report rates of success with psychotherapy. Trevino does not state whether his group believed in or allowed for the possibility that spirits might have actually been involved in any of their cases. The tone of his writing implies that a strong disbelief in this possibility was maintained by his group.

Yet another skeptic is William Sargant, a psychiatrist, who worked in World War II with soldiers who had severe emotional reactions in combat and were helped with hypnotic drugs to facilitate release of repressed traumatic experiences. He noted that in order to be cured, patients had to re-experience the full intensity of original emotional traumas.

In subsequent years, Sargant traveled widely around the world. He observed local shamans and medicine men, noting that in many cases their treatments resembled the above therapy, with strong emotional releases. They utilized intense, loud, rhythmic chanting and dancing; suggestive techniques; group process and moralizing or other invocations of social and religious belief systems to induce trance states in which emotional releases occurred.

In many cases the local diagnosis was spirit possession and the ceremonies utilized were to drive out spirits. Sargant found that the dancing, chanting, drumming and emotionality appeared to bring the patients into very suggestible states wherein the healers could authoritatively inject new ways of viewing their conditions, thereby aiding them to relinquish maladaptive beliefs and behavior patterns.

These treatments seemed very effective in more acute conditions of neurotic nature, especially in hysterical (conversion) symptoms. They were not as effective in long-standing personality disorders or in psychoses.[397]

Discussion

The similarities in numerous details between the above reports of believers in possession are striking. They suggest that there is some common basis in life experiences for the phenomenon of possession.

An alternative explanation is that there was some common source of instruction in clinical assessments for these diverse healers – other than in the healees and spirits from whom they appeared to have learned these ideas, or that one therapist learned from the other. I find this unlikely when we have very similar reports from around the world. Furthermore, the neat dovetailing of reports on possession with those of diverse spirit phenomena, reviewed in other chapters of this book, lends the hypothesis of spirit possession greater credibility.

If the Trevino group's findings are verified by other investigators, this would constitute a most helpful contribution to an understanding of how magical beliefs may be perpetuated by persons uneducated in the intricacies of psychopathology and psychotherapy. Other reports of alleged possession would then be open to the criticism that the investigators were probably not attuned to the underlying psychological problems that produced psi or other phenomena – which were misinterpreted as possession. However, this could not be the case with Prince, Allison, Kiskos or Samuel, who were trained in psychotherapy, so one may just as well ask the opposite question: Did Trevino's apparent disbelief in possession lead him to miss the sorts of evidence that others have reported? In my opinion this seems the more likely explanation.

Sargant makes a convincing argument for his thesis, marshalling a wealth of clinical observations to support his contentions. It seems very likely that the processes he proposes do occur in some cases. Some Kahuna healing treatments in Hawaii are even clearer examples of the use of suggestion to bring about such cures and further support Sargant's hypothesis. However, other Kahuna healings are reported to be related to interventions of spirits.[398]

There is a one-dimensionality about Sargant's book that is disappointing. Although noting that local healers are often more effective for certain illnesses than Western doctors, Sargant does not seriously consider other explanations, such as spiritual healing, for any of the unusual cures he observed.

How to know when possession is a causal factor in illness is a difficult problem, without the help of a gifted intuitive who can perceive the spirit entities and communicate with them. I know healers whose judgment and integrity I trust, in whose word I would have a high degree of confidence. I know of other healers who suggest that possession may be lurking behind almost every problem. Some of the latter healers work in secular settings, others through churches. From the strongly negative, even frightened reactions of healees to proclamations that they are possessed, I have strong doubts both about the accuracy of the diagnosis and about the judgment of these healers who suggest that possession is the cause of most problems. Particularly in some religious settings it appears to me that the fear of possession, of "the dark side" and of the devil are used to frighten people into staying within the fold, and may be grossly over-diagnosed.

Even if possession were only a cultural metaphor for malaise, or a spiritistic invention to explain illnesses that are beyond the medical understanding of a culture, possession may still be a valid construct – for caregivers and careseekers within those cultures. In sociology, there are two broad approaches. The *emic* view acknowledges that peoples from cultures other than our own, behaving in manners that are different from ours, usually have their own legitimate cultural explanations for their beliefs and behaviors. The *etic* position suggests that modern science can provide 'objective' explanations for every phenomenon - within the frameworks of Western scientific paradigms. The emic/etic sword cuts with two edges. We may find that people in other cultures use images in ways that are different from our own, and that for them the concept of possession is a useful explanatory and healing metaphor within their world view. Even if spirits do not exist and do not possess people, shamans may relieve healees of symptoms by invoking this imagery within their cultural healing frameworks. Conversely, we might find that etic disbeliefs in possession lead us to miss a valid phenomenon, more prominent and more accepted in traditional cultures, and explainable through phenomena that are not yet understood or accepted in Western culture.

In summary

Research on possession is rare, as this is perceived on the one hand to be a subject for intervention by clergy and on the other hand is so strange as to suggest mental derangement and therefore is left to psychologists and psychiatrists – who are unfamiliar with spirit phenomena and tend to dismiss any possibility of their validity.

Numbers of reports from physicians, hypnotherapists and clergy indicate that releasing possessing spirits can bring about improvements in physical symptoms that were apparently being caused by the spirit possession. A survey of people who appear to be possessed demonstrated distinct differences between possession, poltergeist activity and hysterical (conversion) reactions and on a number of variables.

The skeptic may dismiss any belief in possession, suggesting perhaps that it is a convenient myth to facilitate psychological acceptance of change in one's life.

There is considerable research on the OBE, NDE, reincarnation, apparitions, and mediumistic communications to support a belief in a spirit that survives death. Derived from a variety of sources around the world, the evidence forms a coherent pattern. This suggests that it is derived from an objective underlying reality which is perceived intuitively and therefore difficult to put into words, to measure with instruments, or to validate objectively. Within our Western society, which focuses on linear interactions with the world, this has been used as a reason to reject a belief in spirit. Within the worlds of healing, intuition is a valid way of relating to the world, and intuitive reports can be highly evidential and convincing. My personal impression is that possession is a valid explanation for problems that have been resolved in the reports cited in this chapter.

Let us examine in the next chapters some of the lessons on healing derived from practices involving spirits and from various religious traditions.

CHAPTER 7

Psychic Surgery

> *If she knows for one moment that the body
> is not in or of matter, it will cease to utter
> its complaints.*
>
> — *Mary Baker Eddie*

Psychic surgery (PS) is a form of healing found in various traditional cultures, such as in Brazil and the Philippines. PS has been described by numerous Western observers. Two varieties are prevalent.[399] To correct physical problems, psychic surgeons appear either: (1) to perform manipulations within the aura or biological energy body of healees, or (2) to insert their hands, with or without instruments, inside healees' bodies.

I shall label as PS-I manipulations by the healers only in the aura or astral body, which is secondarily presumed to effect changes in the physical body.[400] The healers may be in their normal state of consciousness, in meditative states, or in mediumistic trance, with or without being temporarily *obsessed* or *possessed* by guiding spirits.

PS-II is a manipulation by the healers of the healee's physical body. They may do this in various ways. They may simply point to the body without touching it, mimicking an injection or a cut with a scalpel, and needle marks or fine incisions may appear in the skin. They may press their fingers on the body, apparently making incisions without any use of surgical instruments. Some healers do use a knife or other instruments. No antiseptic techniques are used. Red fluid (often, but not always, confirmed as blood) appears, and tissues or various objects may be removed from the body. Upon completion of their treatments, the healers remove their hands, sometimes massaging the area of the surgery, and the wound close immediately, often leaving no mark or only a slight, fresh scar after the skin is wiped clean. The scar may disappear within minutes or may persists for several days. Healees report that they feel no pain or that pain was present but did not bother them. In other instances, knives are used for what appears to be very crude surgery. The wounds may be stitched but heal much more rapidly than with ordinary surgery. Healees may be weak or groggy after PS procedures, but usually are able to walk away from the operating table, even following major PS interventions, evidencing little or no pain, and recover within a few hours.

There is much controversy regarding the legitimacy of these phenomena, especially regarding PS-II. Sleight-of-hand or other frauds were observed in some cases.

PS is discussed here, after the various sections dealing with spiritual healing[401] psi,[402] the energy body and energy medicine,[403] and spiritual experiences because PS would be totally unbelievable and incomprehensible without this background. This is not to say unequivocally that PS, per se, is an established fact, but to make a case for examining the available reports with an open mind. PS is also discussed in this volume because many of the healers practicing these methods claim that the physical manipulations are of secondary importance relative to the spiritual effects of their healing interventions.

Many anecdotal reports have been written about PS but few first-hand observations have been made by researchers familiar with surgery and sleight-of-hand. I have made no attempt to be comprehensive in my review of this literature. A few select books and articles are reviewed in detail.

Overview

Numerous people from Western countries who were suffering from illnesses incurable by conventional medicine have found help from Philippine psychic surgeons. Not everyone reports a cure and some responses are only partial.

Various scientists have studied the operations of the psychic surgeons on visitors from foreign lands, as well as observing local people undergoing these unusual healings. Research in the local settings where psychic surgeons work is not conducive to rigorously controlled conditions, and in fact may be quite difficult. The surgeons often live in small remote villages. They speak local dialects and translators are needed for the researchers to understand the healers and the local healees. The local traditions of healing are so totally accepting of healing that there is a cultural divide between the outsiders who are incredulous and often skeptical and locals who may have difficulty understanding the need for controlled conditions. Fakery is also a problem that seriously concerns the researchers but may not bother the local populace as much.

I review these reports in some detail because they seem to demonstrate remarkable cures that are activated by faith and spiritual healing. Psychic surgery is an unsolved mystery on many levels, so you, the reader are invited to explore some of the evidence with me and to decide for yourself.

Lyall Watson is an expert on animal and human behavior and a popular writer on explorations at the leading edge of science. He has traveled around the globe, studying animals and humans in cultures and habitats very different from our own. He is open-minded and willing to consider unconventional explanations for unusual observations.

Watson describes PS that he witnessed during his visit to the Philippines.[404] He observed hundreds of healings given by a variety of healers. While each differed somewhat in their interventions, the operation Watson describes below is seen across a broad spectrum of psychic surgeons.

The patient was a middle-aged local woman who reported through an interpreter that she suffered from chronic stomach pains. She lay down on a wooden table that Watson had examined with great care to assure that there was no possibility the healer had concealed anything either on or under it.

Watson watched the surgical procedure very carefully. For instance, he examined the towel used to drape the woman, noting it was not very clean but contained nothing whatsoever that could be used to fake psychic surgery.

The woman seemed to be completely trusting. The healer was simply dressed and wore a short-sleeved shirt that would have made it difficult to conceal anything he might have used in sleight of hand manipulations. He laid his bare hands gently on the woman, holding them there in silent prayer, with his eyes closed, after he recited a prayer in his local Ilocano dialect. He began the psychic surgery, swabbing her abdomen thoroughly with a piece of cotton from a roll that Watson had provided, after dipping it into a plastic bowl that Watson had filled from a water tap. He massage the stomach with both hands, his fingertips sinking into her abdomen and suddenly a red color appeared that looked like blood. At first watery, it soon darkened as it seeped up between his fingers.

Watson could see no wound at first, but then the healer pulled his hands a little way apart and Watson saw what looked like "connective tissue, thin, almost transparent, obviously elastic, red and bloody." The healer massaged her abdomen a bit more, his left hand seeming to penetrate into her flesh to the depth of the second joint of his fingers. He pulled his hands apart and Watson was able to examine the surgical area more clearly. The cotton had been entirely transformed into what appeared to be flesh. Touching it with his hand, Watson found it warm and wet, starting to congeal into "little liver-like chunks on the surface." It was sticky and clearly smelled like blood.

The healer continued pressing into her abdomen, with blood collecting in pools where he was pressing. Watson glimpsed "a fan of capillaries attached to what looks like a part of the small intestine." The healer pressed even harder and a large round lump began growing between his fingers. In seconds it was tennis ball size and shape, still connected to her body. The assistant gripped the ball with forceps and cut it loose with a pair of scissors, dropping it in Watson's hand, "much like a serving of blancmange." It was warm and hard, with just a little blood seeping out. He dropped it into the basin and returned to observe.

The healer's hand was still sloshing around in her abdomen, but his gaze was turned to the ceiling. Less blood was evident at this point. Watson was no longer able to see the subcutaneous tissue. Suddenly the healer stopped, lifted his empty hands, and turned to wash. An assistant mopped up the blood with more cotton and with the towel. No wound was evident upon completion of these procedures.

The woman's abdomen was hot to Watson's touch, but he could see no sign that she had had any surgery. She opened her eyes, pulled her clothes together, climbed off the table, and walked away with the assistance of an old man.

Watson again studied the ball of tissue that had been removed, which had the appearance of a tumor but had shrunken, although no one had touched it in the mean time. Watson cut it open and "found the inside partly filled with a mass of fibers laced through the tissue." He was shown several Polaroid photos taken by an American woman who had witnessed the operation too, catching the tumor on film as it appeared out of the body and as it was being cut. The entire procedure had lasted only ten minutes.[405]

Watson notes that the Luzon healers seemed especially "adept at dealing with diseased tissue, blood clots, and pus. I have seen them remove an appendix, excise growths from the breast, open cysts, shrink bladder stones, varicose veins and hemorrhoids, and even treat several types of cancer with excellent results." They treated varieties of cancers, apparently with positive outcomes. In all of these cases, it seemed the cures were authentic and from what Watson could determine, the majority of their healings seemed both legitimate and had permanent effects.

People have suggested that the Philippine healers regularly use sleight of hand to make it appear as though they have removed tissues from their patients. If this is so, they feel justified in questioning and discounting all of the PS phenomena. Countering this hypothesis, Watson reports that he witnessed several apparent materializations during operations that were done in a Manila hotel room without prior scheduling or preparations.

Not all reports of Philippine PS have been positive. Hans Naegeli, a Swiss psychiatrist, found that three blood samples from PS did not match those taken from the patients themselves. While two of the samples were identical to each other, they were not from the PS patients, and a third sample was reported to be sheep's blood. This is peculiar, because there are no sheep in the Philippines.[406] However, this still suggests that the blood which appeared during PS could have been produced by sleight of hand.

Watson took blood samples from one of his friends prior to, during, and following a PS operation to remove a simple cyst on her arm. He later personally monitored the blood typing of these samples in a Manila laboratory. All of them were reported to be the same blood type.

Watson reports on some other examples of PS:

An American biochemist came to Tony Agpaoa in the Philippines after losing his vision as a consequence of the growth of a brain tumor that was diagnosed as being inoperable in the US. After two sessions with the healer he could see again, and upon returning home there was no longer any sign of the tumor that his doctors could identify.[407]

An American woman was paralyzed due to "a disease involving progressive deterioration of the bone marrow in her head and shoulders." The diagnosis had been made through biopsy at a hospital in Los Angeles. Using PS, Agpaoa extracted a large amount of cartilage and blood. When she returned home, her surgeon could not understand how the condition had been cured, leaving only scar tissue.[408]

Another Philippine healer, Juan Blance, actually cuts the flesh of people on whom he does PS. The amazing thing about his operations is that he does not use a knife. He points a finger at the patients and a small, superficial cut appears in their skin. Watson put a sheet of plastic over a patient's skin and the cut still appeared in the skin. Watson observed the same effects on himself, under a sheet of plastic, and to this day has a white scar attesting to the fact that this actually happened. (Watson does not specify in these cases whether the plastic was cut as well, but seems to imply that they were not.)[409]

In a similar manner, Watson notes that Jose Mercado, yet another Philippine psychic surgeon, administers 'spirit injections.' He will treat a long row of patients, simply pointing with a finger as though shooting at each one as he walks by them. Patients report they feel like they have been pricked by a pin wherever Mercado was pointing, and they often find blood oozing from that point on their skin. Watson notes that this could be the effects of mass hypnotic suggestion, similar to demonstrations he had observed in India. Through such suggestion, a fakir produced stigmata (wounds similar to those of Christ) on the hands of people in his audience.[410]

Watson cites a report of Stephen Black on a person who could be made to reproduce the puncture mark and the swelling he had experienced with an ordinary injection he had received twenty years earlier in a conventional medical setting. This would occur simply by reminding this person of the experience.[411]

Watson notes that Mercado's spirit injections appear to be more than just suggestion, however, because when Watson covered his own arm with a sheet of plastic and Mercado gave him a 'shot,' a hole appeared in the plastic right over the pinprick in his arm.[412]

Watson speculates on the nature of healing – considering the balance of influence of the healer and the healee. He suggests that the healings produced by psychic surgeons simply activate latent self-healing abilities in the healees. All of the messy, gory procedures may simply be grand placebos that shock people out of their states of illness, and are thus figuratively as well as literally immaterial. In support of this view, he reports that tissue samples sometimes vanished a few hours after he had sealed them into specimen jars with preserving fluids. He speculates that their disappearance is due to the fact that they weren't completely materialized.[413]

Watson believes that the healers act from natural instincts, without comprehending the processes that are involved in PS. He suggests that this phenomenon may actually be a doorway into new aspects of realities yet to be explored and explained in Western concepts. He shares that his experiences and those of other scientists with the Philippine healers is shattering to conventional understandings of reality. Naturally, when our cherished beliefs are challenged, we tend to retreat behind barriers of intellectual defenses such as denial that PS could actually happen, or that any such phenomena could exist. However, as Watson amply witnesses and musters evidence from other observers, PS actually brings about dramatic healings.

Watson wisely points out that reality, which we tend to feel is a fixed item – according to the explanations and understandings of our own culture – can be described in different ways by different cultures. Watson cites similar ponderings by George Meek about the difficulties of accepting new concepts about realities: "Twentieth Century Man is so physically and materialistically oriented that he is totally incapable of thinking of himself in terms of his own individual etheric, astral, mental, and causal or spiritual bodies. Even a very well educated patient is totally incapable of visualizing himself and all living matter as a complex inter-locking series of scintillating and pulsating energy fields." [414] Watson speculates that more educated people may have greater difficulties in these regards, since they have had more thorough indoctrinations, over longer periods of time, in par-ticular views and explanations for reality. This produces a more rigid belief in the validity of one's beliefs.

Clearly, the Philippine healers' greatest challenge to Western beliefs is in their startling materializations of blood and various tissues. Watson notes that the spec-trum of healing phenomena, such as spiritual healings in England that involve prayers and laying-on of hands, the proceedings are typically routine and repeti-tive to the point of being boring after one has seen more than a few of them. Though all healings may, basically, be self-healings, and while just as many heal-ing changes may occur with these Western approaches, they cannot compare with the drama of Philippine PS. So it may be that Philippine healers succeed in cases that are considered hopeless by Western medicine because they shock people out of their illness reality into a new reality where dramatic healings can occur.

And, after all of these acknowledgments of the self-healing aspects of spiritual healings in general, Watson acknowledges that evidence also suggests that healers transmit something to their healees, be they plants or patients, which facilitates healings. We are just at the beginnings of our journeys of explorations and expla-nations and have much to learn. [415]

Watson's observations are clearly described. He only passingly discusses alter-natives such as sleight of hand and does not venture more than the generalized hypotheses above in explanation.

Gert Chesi, [416] a German journalist, provides the most comprehensive visual overview of Philippine psychic surgery. In an oversize volume, he gathers an im-pressive series of black-and-white and color photos of many psychic healers at work. He also provides very helpful descriptions and discussions on the reported phenomena:

1. Josephine Sison performs psychic surgery much in the same manner as her Philippine colleagues, apparently inserting her hands within the body and materi-alizing blood and tissues. In addition, she has the unique ability to heal via the insertion of cotton wool swabs into the body apparently by psychic means. She will rub the swab against a portion of the body and it will enter the body through the intact skin. Sometimes she withdraws the swab immediately, either at the same spot on the body or from a distant spot. Sometimes she leaves it inside the body. The swabs are alleged to absorb the disease, allowing it to be removed from

the body. Occasionally she leaves swabs in the body to dematerialize on their own.[417]

> Josephine once allowed a team of Swiss scientists to investigate her method of treating disease with cotton wool... By using a Geiger counter, the scientists were able to locate the exact position of radioactive cotton wool in the body... The team's cameraman filmed the process of dematerialization in frequencies of 1/25 seconds. The cotton wool gradually disintegrated until it became completely invisible. Sleight of hand was therefore out of the question.[418]

2. Dr. Antonio Araneta, formerly a journalist, was president of the Philippine Society for Psychic Research. He specializes in investigation of healing and psychic surgery. He observes from the perspective of an educated native of the Philippines:

> Ours is a completely different plane of thinking. We do not think in terms of time or space as Europeans do. We are often accused of unpunctuality, but this is because we are simply not conscious of time. We have a different concept of space and time, and our thinking is based on faith and trust. The European way of thinking is based on rationalism, and so Westerners come to us demanding an explanation. Why? They should try to understand our point of view rather than adhering to their own. It is not so much a question of one way of thinking being superior to another but rather of two conflicting points of view. It is impossible for a healer to explain his work in terms of rationalism...
>
> A faith healer scratches his belly if he wants to and eats with his hands. Yet when he heals, he takes out eye-balls and cures terminal cancer cases your fine medical celebrities have failed to heal. And they live as they want to. They go to movies if they feel like it, they get drunk and they womanize.
>
> A Westerner will ask: Is this compatible with spiritualism, is it compatible with Christianity? But these people do not think of themselves as Christlike. All they know is that they believe in Christ and want to help other human beings. You Europeans are the ones who propagate the concept of Christian purity and sanctity. You must learn to accept the fact that there are other ways of living up to one's religion.
>
> I recall that when I began to study the phenomenon myself thirty years ago, I was also led by this idea of collecting evidence before drawing conclusions. But then a healer told me that I was putting the cart before the horse: I should try to arrive at conclusions first, the evidence would come later. That is exactly what I did. I put my faith into it and did not ask for evidence; the evidence came later of its own accord...
>
> I am convinced that the documentation of psi-healing is no longer of any importance. The problem today, as I see it, lies in assessing the basic attitude toward the phenomenon. In a way, it is a question of history repeating

itself. Galileo's theories were repudiated by the scientists of his era. Many scientists today refuse to believe in the existence of certain phenomena for which they know no explanation because according to the school of thought to which they adhere, these phenomena are simply not possible. In other words, they are incapable of revolutionary thought.

Many doctors are reluctant to accept the phenomenon of Philippine faith healing just as they were reluctant to accept acupuncture. And, in fact, there are records made by the PMA in 1965 which state that acupuncture is of no therapeutic value whatsoever. So, to me, it is not a question of proving or disproving the phenomenon itself, but of determining the belief concepts of those concerned with the problem. Just because your pattern of thinking cannot comprehend the phenomena, it does not mean that they do not exist...

All peoples of the world have to fight this handicap. I myself had to fight it too. There finally comes a point when you have to repudiate all this 'evidence first' business and handle the problem from a completely different angle. You must reconstruct your mental frame, your attitudes. Without realizing it, you undergo a kind of spiritual transformation. This is how I, without really wanting to, became a healer. Two years ago I was utterly amazed to discover that I could actually heal through thought-projection...

The physical angle is simply one angle among many. As soon as we begin to understand that energy and matter are interchangeable, we shall discover that not everything can be regarded as matter. There may be a fourth medium, not just solid, liquid and gas. And if you see the problem as we see it, as a question of energy and matter, you suddenly realize that everything is possible.[419]

3. Chesi describes a broad spectrum of opinions among Philippine healers on the nature of their work. Even among healers themselves there are often disagreements on such things as the need to live a life of purity (some eschew smoking, liquor and sex; others do not); the involvement of spirits in healings; and more.

4. A wonderful feast of observations is scattered throughout Chesi's anecdotes, descriptions, graphic photos and theories about the healers. Many, however, are presented without the support of evidence. It is therefore somewhat difficult to know how much credence to give to these – to know whether they are gems or costume jewelry.

Chesi does an excellent job of documenting PS through witnesses, personal experiences of the author and others, and photographs.

John Fuller[420] describes Jose Pedro de Freitas, popularly known as Arigo. Arigo was born in 1918 in Brazil. He was a marvelous clairsentient diagnostician, healer and psychic surgeon. He claimed he worked with the help of a German spirit guide, Dr. Adolfo Fritz, who died in 1918. He saw about 300 patients daily for many years. His routine was to walk down the waiting line, writing prescriptions with incredible speed, never asking what the problems were. Dr. Fritz knew and prescribed appropriately, often in doses and combinations that make no sense, or even seem dangerous, to a conventional physician.

Arigo himself was a simple, uneducated man. He never charged for his services, earning a living for himself and his family as a receptionist in a State Welfare Office. He reported that he did not recall what occurred when he was writing prescriptions or performing PS on the long lines of patients who flocked to see him.

Most remarkable of all were his surgical operations.

The late Andrija Puharich, an American physician trained at Northwestern University with a specialty in Bio-Engineering, observed and filmed Arigo on a number of occasions. He also allowed him to operate in his usual fashion on a lipoma (fatty tumor) on his own arm. His operation and others were filmed.

Fuller reports:

> ... The length of time from Arigo's incision to the removal of the tumor: it was closer to five seconds, not ten. Instead of a direct surgical incision, Arigo seemed to scrape the blade across the surface of the arm, moving the knife so fast that it was almost impossible to discern exactly how he did it. If the tumor had not completely disappeared from his arm, and if Puharich did not have the lipoma in a bottle, he would almost think it had been sleight of hand – a device some charlatans in the Philippines had used. Within the brief seconds involved, the lipoma was out, and a thin trickle of blood rolled down the arm.
>
> The film was effective as proof of the event, and it was enough to rule out any possibility of unconscious hallucination, which, of course, had been practically ruled out earlier. What's more, the wound had continued to heal cleanly, no pus formed, no systemic poisoning was evident. Two wildly improbable medical events had taken place; the removal of the tumor, and the total absence of infection...[421]
>
> In... the eye operations, there was no question, as they had also noted in person, that the blade of a sharp knife was scraped down over the open eye, was plunged deeply up into the sinuses, was manipulated with force, was used as a lever to extrude the eyeball partly out of the socket; and that no injury or damage resulted, after careful examination. Under normal conditions, the pain involved would have been literally unbearable. A cataract was removed in a matter of seconds from a fully conscious unflinching patient. A later medical examination by a fully qualified ophthalmologist confirmed the success...
>
> Another unusual sequence followed. Arigo operated on a large but relatively uncomplicated abscess on a patient's back. As usual, he plunged the knife in brutally, cut deeply into the flesh of the small of the back – a sector heavily served with blood vessels, and therefore inclined to bleed profusely. Very little blood flowed out, but the abscess was drained, and Arigo turned the patient over to Altimiro to complete the draining, and extract the remaining matter. Although the patient was totally calm and without pain during the time Arigo was operating, he screamed in pain as soon as Al-

timiro touched him. In other words, whatever power it was that permitted Arigo to cut painlessly into...the body, it was apparently not transferable to his assistant.[422]

Fuller adds that the knife used by Arigo was extremely dull. Despite this, no pain was experienced. Unusual procedures were filmed during his PS. An operation on an infected sebaceous cyst of the scalp is described (recorded on film):

[H]e said he would squeeze the capsule out of the head. You see that the sebaceous material is being expressed from the wound which is really an almost impossible feat from a surgical point of view. He...was asking his spirit guide, Dr. Fritz, to please pull out this capsule and he would get through with the cleaning out of the inside of the capsule. Now you will see him squeeze this capsule out and shortly he will actually pull it out without having surgically dissected it from the scalp or from the periosteum [surface membrane] of the skull...whenever he had anything like a bleeder, he would again pick up his dirty cotton cloth and wipe the wound and invariably stop the bleeding...[423]

Puharich[424] provided more first-hand observations of Arigo:

Arigo's diagnostic abilities were phenomenal. Puharich found he could arrive at extremely accurate diagnoses either by clairsentience or via information he reported was transmitted through his spirit guides. For example, he announced that the blood pressure of a healee was 230/70 and this was indeed found to be correct; he precisely named the diagnoses of healees' eye diseases (e.g., retinoblastoma, retinitis pigmentosa, etc). Puharich reports that of 1,000 cases his percentage of correct diagnoses was very high.

Arigo did not engage in distant healing.

Arigo wrote prescriptions with extreme rapidity, in a handwriting that was illegible other than to Altimero,[425] a man who worked with him. These included preparations that were alleged to be successful in treating a wide variety of diseases, including leukemia and schizophrenia.

Arigo treated cancer patients with prescriptions by preference, but also used PS. Occasionally he removed tissues by PS with his hands, without the use of a knife.

He would reject patients for a variety of reasons:

1. If they had an illness that their regular physician could heal;
2. If the illness was too far advanced; or
3. If Arigo sensed malingering or a faking of illness in order to entrap him (per efforts of the Brazilian Medical Association to obstruct his work).

Puharich hypothesizes that there may be a

... parallel to the known genetic programming of cells that reproduces an organism and sets up all the instructions for developing it to a full grown organism. There may be equivalent parallel genetically coded instructions which are not actual molecules but some kind of parallel mind effect, an isomorphic field, which I call psi plasma... which may in fact give rise to the phenomena that we see in healing...[426]

Discussion: Puharich was viewed by some Western scientists as a questionably reliable reporter because of his beliefs in UFOs and other such phenomena. Inasmuch as he was a physician, and his reports tally very closely with those of many others who have observed the psychic surgeons, I feel the above details are probably credible.

It is interesting to note that Altimero was the only person able to decipher Arigo's prescriptions. The range of abilities of such healers' assistants warrants further investigation. Altimero may have had some mediumistic, clairsentient or healing abilities himself.

Puharich is not alone in proposing a theory of healing via a healer's influence over an organizing field.[427]

Arigo died in an auto accident in 1971 before well-controlled studies could be done on how he performed his healings. Proper documentation of Arigo's work, especially his prescribing, is not available. The accounts of physicians mentioned by Fuller, in addition to the brief observations of Puharich, are tantalizing. There was never a serious question of fraud with Arigo, as he was vindicated several times when the local medical authorities and government prosecuted him for practice of medicine without a license.

Sidney Greenfield and Elizabeth Rauscher[428] provide sequels to the Arigo story. Edson Cavalcante de Queiroz, a Brazilian gynecologist, reported he had been elected by the spirit doctor Adolf Fritz to perform PS, after the death of Arigo. Rauscher describes his techniques, which are similar to Arigo's.

I (DB) have seen a film of Arigo and a videotape of Queiroz performing PS-II. Arigo inserted a pocket knife at the side of a healee's eye, levering it out of the socket to scrape out material behind the eyeball. Queiroz inserted needles at the margins of healees' eyes and scraped the corneas with a knife. None of the healees flinched or showed any signs of pain or distress. Both films are impressive and seem unlikely to have been produced in a fraudulent manner.

Queiroz was tragically murdered by a dissatisfied assistant.[429]

George Meek edited an excellent early book reviewing healing.[430] He and others in his book discuss Philippine PS in considerable detail:

Meek and his colleagues observed Josefina Sison working under rigorously controlled conditions. Meek reports on his own experience of undergoing PS. The placement of the healer, healee, all observers and equipment is shown in Figure III-6.[431]

As I had been suffering from a slight urinary tract problem, it seemed like a good opportunity for some personal research with the transparent table and the other equipment and research personnel as shown in [Figure III-6].

Figure III-6. Placement of observers and equipment

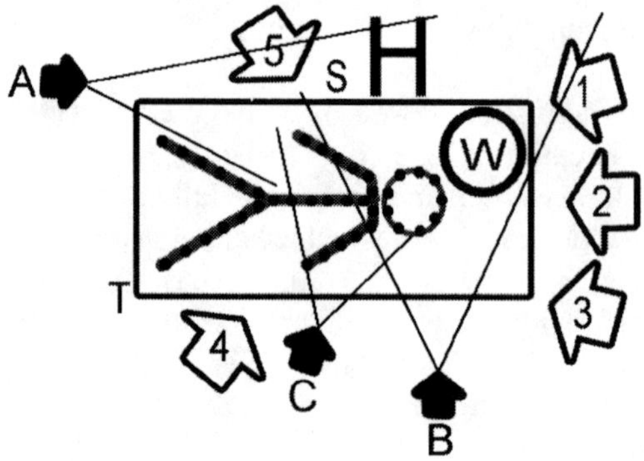

The healer (H) – the key figure in the action – stands beside a patient... who is lying on a specially constructed transparent operating table (T) made of half-inch thick clear plexiglass. Movie cameras (16 mm. with wide angle zoom lenses, electric drive, and 400 ft. magazines to permit uninterrupted filming for the entire sequence) are positioned at (A) and (B) to cover all action from two directions. Motorized still color camera (C) with adjustable intervalometer and 250 frame back is capable of taking photos as fast as two per second. Positions (1) through (5) are occupied by qualified observers. A transparent plastic basin (W) contains water for healer to wash hands as needed. Sterile cotton (c) is handed to the healer by observer in position (1) from sealed box purchased by observer in his home city. Specimens (S) are promptly handed by the healer to observer (5) who stores specimen in glass bottle with suitable preservative.

... The observers making up this team were as follows [432]:

Position   Qualification
(1) M.D. (Member of American College of Surgeons)
(2) M.D. (psychiatrist, ophthalmologist on staff of large U.S. hospital)
(3) M.D. (Doctor of emergency medicine [in] large U.S. hospital)
(4) Bio-medical engineer (clairvoyant and student of occultism)
(5) Clinical psychologist (hypnotherapist and clairvoyant, a native of
        the Philippines who has studied the healers for many years)
(A) Cameraman (who is also a hypnotherapist)
(B) Psychical researcher on his 4th trip to study Filippino healers.

I climbed onto the table and fully exposed my abdomen. Josefina held her hands for inspection and then placed them to the left and slightly below my navel. Within seconds 'blood' appeared under her fingers. (In the movie, this 'blood' seemed thicker than was sometimes observed.) Soon the fingers of both hands were colored red and there was a small pool of 'blood' formed by the depression in the skin where her hands were resting. She signaled for a piece of cotton which was given to her from the box of J & J sterile cotton I had purchased in my home town. Taking the cotton in one hand, while holding the other hand in place, she soaked up some of the 'blood' and then threw the cotton into the waste basket. She returned the hand to its original position. From my line of sight – only sixteen inches from her hands – and looking horizontally across the surface of my abdomen, I could see the 'blood' was still accumulating. She pressed in at one small spot so hard that I felt an intense localized pain. (It persisted for thirty minutes after the 'operation.') After several seconds the pressure staunched the flow which seemed to come through the skin. Then with more cotton she cleaned up the remaining blood.

There was not the slightest chance that this 'blood' was manufactured on the spot by fakery. I was just one of a long series of patients. Every motion of Josefina as she stood beside the transparent table had been under the closest scrutiny of the movie cameras and the medical doctors and scientists who were standing shoulder to shoulder with her and surrounding the patient on the table. As the patient, I had the advantage of having previously observed many hundreds of 'operations' by 23... healers and had long since passed the 'Gee-whiz' stage.[433]

Meek speculates on the nature of blood and tissue specimens produced during PS, feeling these may be:

1. Animal tissue and blood reconstituted from dried animal blood, in some form easily concealed and within reach of the healer, or
2. Animal tissue and blood apported [brought by PK] from an unknown source, or
3. Human tissue actually removed from the patient, by
   a. opening and closing the body, or
   b. dematerialization and rematerialization.

Another mystery may also be closer to solution – why have some specimens disappeared from tightly closed glass specimen bottles within hours or days, even when close surveillance was maintained? In case (2) we might speculate that since the apporting process involves the steps of dematerialization, transporting, and rematerialization, some molecular *instability* has been introduced in the apported matter...

To complicate the mysteries still further is a previously unmentioned fact that blood actually taken from a patient in a healer's presence undergoes chemical changes so extensive that it may test out as 'non-human' blood...

Detailed analysis of some 16mm. color film sequences indicates there may be still another factor contributing to the 'blood' specimen mystery. In many cases it seems that the thin pale red liquid is being *drawn through* the skin of the patient. In a few film sequences it is observed that the healer has to actually put her finger over the spot where the liquid is issuing and press hard to stop the flow. In such cases the liquid looks more like blood. Immediate close-up inspection does to disclose any change in the surface of the skin.[434]

Meek acknowledges that deception and sleight of hand may be practiced by all of the Philippine healers. He excuses this on grounds that they are pressed with heavy demands to treat large numbers of patients since their abilities have become more widely known. He feels that even the best healers cannot sustain such a pace. This has led to diversion of some healers' interests to materialistic goals, served by introducing sleight of hand manipulations to impress healees.

Meek discusses hypothetical, potential dangers of Philippine PS:

> 1. *Precious time could be wasted* in the diagnosis and treatment of a problem that might easily be amenable to orthodox medical therapy.

> 2. *Infection might be transmitted* through the use of unsterile instruments... Thus, at this time, we cannot preclude the possibility of an already debilitated patient contracting a serious infection such as hepatitis from the use of an unsterile instrument.

> 3. *Further damage might occur as a result of injudiciously applied pressure.* If a patient suffered from a detached retina, pressure on the eye might cause serious progression of the problem. A patient with infectious mononucleosis and a fragile spleen might sustain a rupture if heavy pressure were applied over the left upper quadrant of his abdomen.

> 4. *The long arduous journey* could further impair the health of already seriously debilitated patients.

> 5. *The financial burden* imposed could greatly tax the already dwindling monetary resources of a chronically ill patient.
>
> The ultimate hazard of 'psychic surgery' is its separation from orthodox medicine. The tragedy is that the medical profession is reluctant to discuss or investigate this phenomenon and the patient is fearful of discussing this topic with his physician at all. The result is that the patient in search of a ray of hope is forced to step outside of the protective confines of orthodox medicine and take the attendant risks.[435]

The late Sigrun Seutemann's chapter in Meek is of special value.

Meek points out that Seutemann is in a unique position to report on this facet of paranormal healing because:

> She has a medical background [homeopathy].
> She herself has been psychic since childhood.
> She has received help from Filipino healers for her own very serious ailments.
> She observed the 'operations' of 29 healers on more than 3,000 patients during her more than 20 trips to the Philippines.
> Here she reflects on her experiences in personally accompanying... patients from Europe to the Philippines for visits with native healers.

[I] gradually developed these psychic abilities to the point where I could use them to diagnose illness. By observing the effect of minerals as well as herbs and homeopathic remedies on the human aura, I have been able to prescribe these in a way that is most effective for the patient...[436]

During my medical studies I was subjected to considerable stress. I was concentrating on educating my intellectual self but my spiritual and psychic self constantly told me that some of the intellectual teachings in the medical texts were in error. Adding to my personal problems was the fact that since childhood I had suffered from a congenital heart disease. As I grew older this caused increasingly serious limitations on my work until finally it became such a limiting factor that I was faced with the complete stoppage of my medical practice.

Having heard of Philippine 'psychic surgery,' I made a decision to travel to the Philippines, even though at this time some very negative publicity came out in Germany against the work of the Filipino healers. In July, 1971, I put myself in the hands of Tony Agpaoa and that act changed my life. The recovery was so quick and so complete that I just could not believe what had taken place. Back in Germany again, I was so completely astonished at what had happened, that after a few weeks I decided to return to the Philippines to verify what was taking place. What I found convinced me that I could render great service to many European patients for whom neither I nor my German medical colleagues could provide relief...[437]

The first thing I had to do was to take further steps to assure myself against fraud. Tony collaborated fully. This involved working in a room which was bare except for a plain table for the patient to lie on. Tony put on clothes we supplied. My assistant held a new package of cotton and the plastic bowl with water. Tony had to repeatedly show his hands for inspection. I myself assisted. This type of test was repeated several times.

Of course as a physician I was able to see that this type of 'surgery' had nothing to do with conventional Western medical surgery. Often the 'operations' were performed in cases where there was no medical indication for surgery, for example: organic dysfunctions, diabetes, skin diseases, nerve inflammation, etc. Occasionally I would see the ends of Tony's fingers disappear, or even much of the hand, but the great majority of the 'operations' were entirely on the surface of the patients' body.

Often when I wanted to observe closely, I reached down between Tony's hands and touched what seemed to be a tight membrane. On occasion I could verify parts of organs, but they did not seem specific.

Of course this was very puzzling. Once I asked five scientists to observe an 'operation' and then tell me what they had seen. All agreed in the description of having seen how Tony put the cotton (handed to him by one of the scientists) into the bowl of water and then put the water-soaked cotton on the body. They agreed upon the movement of his fingers. But each had a different description of the red blood-like liquid and the membrane-like tissue. There began the frontiers of the unbelievable.

We of course took blood and tissue specimens, but these only added to the confusion. In some cases the laboratory tests confirmed the blood and tissue specimens. In other cases there was no confirmation by the laboratory.

I detected another curious thing. In those cases where Tony knew the blood and tissue were going to be examined, he worked longer to produce the phenomenon and he seemed to concentrate more deeply and then seemed to be more exhausted after the 'operation.' [438]

... I had been taught that a healer is a spiritually developed person with negative and positive potentials, and that he must continuously change negative potential for positive, for the benefit of the patient seeking his help. Certainly some of the 'escapades' in Tony's life do not square with this concept...[439]

Discussing the mechanisms of PS, Seutemann suggests:

[T]he etheric body influences all functions of, and controls the metabolism of, the physical body. The etheric body reacts to all the thoughts and emotions of the individual.

It is my conviction that most of the work done by the healer is at the level of the *etheric* body. Only after this body is restored to normal balance can the healing result in the organs of the *physical* body.

After the experiences I had in my own clinic in West Germany I got so I could trust my knowledge of what it was I seemed to 'see' around the physical body. This ability helped me greatly in my observations of Tony's work. However, his technique of diagnosis is quite different from mine. He says that at first it is like seeing a reflection of his own body, but he has learned to protect himself by concentration so that the patient's problems will not be transferred to him. While he is thus concentrating, his whole metabolism is changing and the reactions in his nervous system are completely different. He says that he works to concentrate the power in his brow chakra and in his hands... The scientists and other researchers... have often been heard to observe, "Tony seems to be in trance only from his shoulders down. He appears to be entirely unconscious of the movement being made by his hands." His invisible work appears to me as being of far more importance to the healing than anything which is visible. The criterion for successful healing is not the effect on the physical body but the changes brought about at the patient's etheric level of existence.

It is obvious to me that Tony can 'see' the etheric body or the aura, because he can tell if other healers had touched a patient without his knowledge, and in fact he can give the other healer's name...[440]

Of a series of 1,200 patients she observed, Seutemann reports:

No patient in my groups ever came home worse than when he went. No patient in my groups died while under the care of Tony.

A few times I saw him refuse a patient in other groups, saying that he could do nothing.

Two percent of the patients were healed instantly.

Ten percent could be adjudged as healed in a medical way at the end of their ten-day or two-week stay in the Philippines.

Thirty percent had at least partial success within the first month.

Thirty percent felt better and some medical tests confirmed improvement in three to six months.

Eighteen percent were patients on which no follow-up was possible.

Ten percent seemed to have no benefit...[441]

... A patient cannot be made to get well or to stay well if for any of many reasons he does not have such a desire.

I must say that I never saw a vertebral paralyzed patient completely dispense with the use of a wheel chair. Myelitis patients showed limited improvement. Cancer in the last stages could not be stopped. Multiple sclerosis cases often showed considerable improvement.

In some cases where subsequent surgery was still indicated – for example the actual removal of kidney stones, and certain heart operations – the surgery took place with none of the complications which had been initially anticipated. The healing procedure was fast and without complications.

[I]n many instances the patient got a whole new outlook on life in general and his illness in particular. The empathy of the healers, the understanding of the other people's illnesses, and the group spirit all helped to improve the emotional well-being of many patients...[442]

Meek is obviously a firm believer in PS. His enthusiasm is apparent in his reluctance to discuss the deceptions of the healers squarely as possible fraud in at least some of the cases. Despite the danger under these circumstances of Type I errors, much of his material appears to have been gathered under rigorous conditions and is a major contribution to the PS literature. The original is highly recommended.

Seutemann's observations are of special value because of her qualifications as homeopathic physician and gifted sensitive.

Meek's cautions against dangers of PS appear prudent though not substantiated in fact. Seutemann's estimates of responses to PS (including no negative effects) suggest there is little actual danger in PS. I have found no reports of harm done to patients by Philippine healers.

Further observations by Seutemann are helpful.[443]

In Tony Agpaoa's case I have learned to differentiate several types of treatment:

The magnetic treatment: In this case Tony Agpaoa passes his hands along the body, the patient feels warmth and something like soft electricity. Sometimes he holds his hands for a short while at the solar plexus or head chakras. He also uses a kind of acupuncture without needles to investigate the reflexes and to balance the Yang and Yin, touching the acupuncture points at the toes; this can be painful for the patient. Sometimes he holds his hands about 20 centimeters away from the body; the patient experiences a kind of warm vibration but no temperature difference can be detected.

Astral materialization: In this type of treatment Tony Agpaoa usually places wet cotton wool on the body. After this red liquid comes out of the cotton wool and then tissue material appears, which usually has a smooth form. When the tissue has appeared the cotton wool can no longer be seen. Sometimes Tony Agpaoa throws off some of the cotton wool, sometimes he has some again in his hands at the end of the operation. He or one of his assistants takes some specimen from the materialized tissue; the red liquid coagulates around his fingers. The time of the operation is usually 3-7 minutes, but his left hand is usually in contact with the body for longer than this. When the operation is completed only some blood is to be seen on the skin. This type of operation seems to be an astral materialization. Examination of the specimens that have been removed and of the blood show them to be human or animal; the blood is difficult to investigate because it is always mixed with water from the beginning of the operation... I have investigated all possibilities of fraud and could find none. Whatever the conditions I have imposed on Tony Agpaoa he has always been able to perform his treatment. I can say that in more than 4,000 operations which I have observed him to carry out I have never seen any trickery.

Body opening: The third and most interesting type of treatment is the opening of the body. This seems to proceed at first in the same way as for astral materialization, but then Tony's fingers disappear inside the body. This only happens when the indications are that a conventional surgical operation is necessary. Examination of the specimens removed and of the blood show that these come from the patient. He does not open the body with his fingertips, but with the first joint of his fingers. This could give the impression that he was hiding something in his hands...

Not all of the tissue that is removed comes from the physical body of the patient. The potentials of the energy body of the healer also seem to be involved in the materialization of some kind of psycho-kinetic phenomenon. In some cases when the body is opened it seems that this force is used to balance up the forces of the body of the patient.

Twice I saw Tony close wounds that had been caused by accidents. In other cases he explained he could not close such wounds. I think he needs another type of vibration to do this than the one he uses in materializations.

One case was reported by an American citizen of a brain tumor of his sister where Tony left the wound open for about three days. Tony could not explain why he did this, but there was complete healing. Tony said that he had done the same thing with a few other cases.

Often I observed a complete change in the way of life of these patients. Depressions disappeared, people became more satisfied and happy, they tried to overcome fear and hate. This psychological effect is also very remarkable.

I think these phenomena cannot be explained in terms of the science of today. Comparison with normal surgery is pointless. Even examination of the blood and tissue specimens removed with body opening does not relate to the results of normal surgery because the protein seems to change as a result of the healer's vibrations...

One of the next problems is to try to find out why the healing is not successful with some patients and what basic conditions are necessary for this type of healing to... help a patient. It has already been found that the patient can be sceptical and be objective and non-believing and that this does not prevent healing. Equally it is unwise for the patient to have absolute faith and confidence in this type of healing as his case may not be curable.

Discussion: Inasmuch as there are so many reports of fakery, one must wonder at Seutemann's never having observed this. Is it a case (on both sides) of seeing only what one expects to see? Creating or eliciting the expected effects? Seutemann's naiveté? Were the Philippine psychic surgeons kept 'straight' by Seutemann, who could see auras, and who would therefore accurately observe whether they produced legitimate effects? Could Seutemann see energetic healing effects which conventional observers missed? Where fakery was detected, had healers been inhibited by skeptical observers, forcing them to use sleight of hand as a 'backup' procedure to help healees?[444] Even when using sleight of hand as a tool to impress the healee, could they produce PS effects as well?

Hiroshi Motoyama[445] is a Japanese physiologist, raised in a blend of Shinto Buddhist, Taoist and Hindu traditions. He visited the Philippines many times and shares here several vignettes on Agpaoa:

At the Annual Convention of the International Association of Religion and Parapsychology in Tokyo in 1977, Agpaoa repeatedly demonstrated his ability to cut through thick wads of adhesive tape using the endpoint of his small finger. He claims that the energy that he ejects from the endpoint of this small finger to cut the tape is the same sort of energy he uses to make incisions in his patients. As most psychic healing is 'bloodless,' I asked why he finds it necessary to produce immediate, physically apprehensible results (such as blood) during the operation. Tony said that it is actually unnecessary to produce blood or tissue to cure a person, but he held that people will become more convinced of the existence of the higher dimensions of being if they witness the materialization of physical objects through nonphysical means, and that such immediate experience is necessary to shock materialistically oriented people into spiritual growth.

Motoyama reports his observations of PS in the Philippines.

The operations were not so much 'surgery' as a kind of psychic healing often seen in Japan. Tony first says a short prayer while laying his hands on the diseased part of the patients' body. When Tony placed his hands over the swollen part of a nettle-rash patient, the reddish swelling gradually disappeared and normal coloring returned to the affected area. This I observed with my own eyes. I was surprised to see the swelling disappear so quickly. In the case of internal troubles such as stomach disease, one cannot discern if the stomach is really cured. However, in external cases such as nettle rash the change is quite obvious. After performing similar treatment on 95 out of 100 patients, Tony rested for about 20 minutes. He spent only one or two minutes on each patient...

[I]n 1968 and in 1972 I went again to the Philippines to inspect operations by psychic surgeons, including Tony, and I observed that the surgeon's hands... entered the body in only a few cases. Furthermore, I came to realize that even when the surgeon's hands did enter the patient's body he did not actually touch the tumor as in conventional surgery. Thus it gradually became apparent that the physical hands are not the most important instrument in psychic surgery, but that a kind of mental-spiritual energy – the energy of the astral body – is more important...

The energy of the astral body which emanates from the middle finger and the center of the palm penetrates the physical body and reaches the diseased part to be removed far more easily than radio waves or magnetic force. Thus directed, the astral energy first removes the part which is diseased in the astral dimension, bringing it to the surface of the body and then rematerilizes it in the physical dimension. Once materialized, it can be seen by the physical eyes. This constitutes one form of psychic surgery...

One may wonder why a psychic surgeon uses water or oil on the skin surface at the point where the operation is to be performed. None of the surgeons I interviewed gave a fully scientific answer. They usually explained that a better 'connection with the patient' seems to be established when water or oil is used, although it is possible to perform operations without water or oil...

Operation in the astral dimension and materialization constitute the main part of this type of surgery (Type I). In other cases, the surgeon's hands enter the patient's body to remove the tumor or diseased tissue in the physical dimension (Type II)... Type III... is a combination of Types I and II...

Bleeding of some sort is always involved in any of the three types of psychic surgery. In the case of Type I, one observes the materialized manifestation of what may correspond to the blood of the astral body, whereas in Type II and III what appears to be the blood of the physical body is observed.

Motoyama reports on blood-type analyses of seven blood and tissue samples taken from PS sent by Seutemann along with venous blood samples from the same patients. Three pairs of samples matched; the other four were questionable. Motoyama notes:

Tony, who had been invited to speak, gave a succinct explanation of how he performs psychic surgery:

Guided by the Holy Spirit, a psychic surgeon transmits a beam of spiritual energy or magnetic power into the astral as well as the physical bodies of the patient at a particular point and thus effects a holistic healing. The essence of psychic healing lies in the promotion of the patient's spiritual evolution by infusing the patient's spirit with spiritual energy.

Tony Agpaoa felt that the ultimate purpose of psychic healing or surgery is not merely to provide a cure for the disease of the physical or the astral bodies, but primarily to help the patient's spiritual evolution. This comment encompasses a profound message, which should not be taken lightly.

In performing actual psychic surgery, it is said that spiritual energy or magnetic power is sent into the patient's astral body through a particular point in his physical or astral body. It seems to be that these entrance points are in fact the chakras, as described in yogic teachings, and the acupuncture points of Oriental medicine. The acupuncture points are located on the meridians through which vital energy flows. The chakras are the centers of the nadi-system and nadis correspond to the meridians of the physical body. The astral energy, lying in planes of existence higher than the physical, flows through the nadis. The vital or spiritual energy in the astral plane flows in and out through the chakras, where the transformation of the higher dimensional vital energy into the energies of the physical dimension (vital energy of the physical body) takes place.

According to Tony, a disease cannot be thoroughly cured unless the karma of the reincarnating astral body and its mind (*Manas*) are somehow dissolved. Therefore, he says the most important task of the psychic surgeon is to give spiritual energy to the patient's soul, thereby assisting, if possible, the soul's evolutionary process to reach the state of Satori (an enlightened state).

Motoyama hypothesizes mechanisms for PS that could be associated with chakra energy changes. He was able to confirm such changes through recordings with his specially designed instruments.[446]

Also, another instrument for detecting changes in the earth's magnetic field showed that the magnetic field inside the room was slightly changed. This fact suggests that the energy originally belonging to the dimension of the spirit or astral body was first converted into various forms of physical energy and then emitted into the physical environment through the Anahata [heart] chakra. In other words, the spiritual energy or the energy of the astral body in the higher dimensions, uninhibited by the space-time of the physical dimension, was converted and recreated into the energy of the physical dimension. When this astral body energy is locally accumulated, matter in the physical dimension, e.g., tissue, tumor, blood, etc., can be created. In my opinion this is the phenomenon generally referred to as 'materialization.' Then, it may be presumed that the majority of psychic surgeons must have awakened Anahata chakras. This presumption is also supported by their subjective experiences – abnormal functioning of the heart, energy emission from the heart area, etc., as well as by various measurements performed at our institute.

In the process of psychic surgery, it is then possible that the psychic surgeon emits astral energy from the Anahata chakra or the 'seiketsu' point of the heart and heart constrictor meridians. (These meridians have their seiketsu points at the tips of the middle and little fingers, respectively.) The energy... transforms the original cancer, tumor, blood, etc., in the astral dimension into their counterparts in the physical dimension, thus causing a phenomenon of materialization which can be witnessed by all observers.

In psychic surgery, cancerous tissue, tumors, etc., are first removed in the astral dimension and then materialized in the physical dimension. The objects removed and materialized from the astral body are discarded, and in several days or sometimes in several months the cancerous tissue, tumor or other diseased parts of the physical body disappear to bring about a complete cure. One might say that there is a sort of light and shadow, or real shadow-like relationship between the astral and the physical body. (The astral being the real, the physical the shadow.) Therefore, when the defect in the real is repaired, the defect in the shadow automatically follows toward repair thus bringing about the complete cure of the physical body. Nevertheless, just as the relationship between light and shadow is not direct, with shadow having a certain degree of independence, perhaps for the same reason it takes a certain number of days for the change in the astral body or the real, or appear in the physical body or the shadow.

Motoyama provides a starting point for conceptualizing what might be happening in PS. His speculations on materializations need much further clarification and verification. They are consistent with many healers' observations that the bioenergy body is a template for the physical body.

Alfred Stelter, a German professor of physics and chemistry, has extensive experience with Philippine healers.

In four years I made five trips to the Philippines. During the last one, from October 1974 to March 1975, I worked especially closely with Dr. Hiram Ramos, the most experienced observer of psychic surgery in the Philippines... I have met almost all the interesting healers of the Northern Philippines, have observed many of them for several years, and have conducted experiments with several of them recently.

Stelter marshals a host of observations to support his conviction that spiritual healing[447] is legitimate. Much of the literature he cites is in German. Only a few of the author's many fascinating reports and observations are summarized here.

Tony Agpaoa, the most famous of the Philippine healers, was born of poor parents in 1939. In his early years he experienced a peculiar kind of sleep walking. He was repeatedly pulled out of trees by his family in early morning hours.

Even as a small boy he sensed there were states of consciousness about which people around him knew nothing; he was aware of many things long before he was able to put them into words. He felt at one with his natural surroundings, and nothing seemed alien to him. He seemed to remember much that should by rights have been new to him.

He felt from an early age that there is a spiritual being watching over him. He called this being his 'comforter.' He had well-developed abilities of visualization and meditation.

He was able to sit in the woods, meditating to the point of self-forgetfulness and filling himself with the invisible.

The most important event of Tony's childhood occurred when he was eight or nine. His playmate Pedro Gonzales, engaging in some horseplay, fell on a sharp object, and a large, bleeding wound gaped in his thigh. The boy's parents and others came running and did not know what to do. Tony saw his friend's bloodied skin and pain-distorted face. "You will open and close wounds," he heard a voice saying inside himself and felt a warm pulsing in his hands. Slowly he placed his hands over Pedro's wound, and when he pulled them away a few seconds later, the deep wound had closed. Only a little coagulated blood remained.

The news of this 'miracle' spread like wildfire. When Tony returned home, neighbors were already waiting for his touch. He touched them, and all immediately felt cured or at least improved. Tony Agpaoa began to believe in his power to heal.

Tony believes that in internal illness something in the patient's body reacts to his touch. He claims to see dark, eerie clouds or shapes within the patient's body, which he can move around and remove through the natural openings and mucous membranes. A pathologist examining the singular substances that emerge would have to report; 'Not human tissue.'

Presumably the processes at work here belong in the category of materialization. Such internal diseases are probably on an incipient, perhaps preclinical, level, and have close connection with the bioplasmic body alleged by the Soviets. Today Agpaoa himself says he works on patients' astral bodies.

Stelter continues, describing the development of Tony's gifts. A woman came to Tony with a disorder he could not heal by moving the 'formation' to body openings. The formations kept slipping back. Tony later explained that he had said to himself:

"I can't get it to a body opening. If I were a surgeon, I'd just cut the place open." He gnashed his teeth and, lost in thought, ran his fingertips over the woman's body. Horror seized him as he saw the raw flesh of an open wound, as if he had cut into the body with a knife. Blood streamed out.

He heard a voice behind him. "Make the bleeding stop or you'll kill the woman."

Tony was deathly afraid. "How can I stop the bleeding?"

"You opened the body with your fingertips. Try to close it by rubbing your hand across it," said the voice.

Tony passed the flat of his hand across the wound without touching it directly. The other spectators' eyes followed him. The wound had closed; only a little puddle of coagulating blood remained. No scar could be seen. Tony wanted to thank the person who had given him the… instructions, but could not see him. None of those present aside from Tony had heard him.

"Then I'm not the one who did this. You are," he said, meaning his protector.

"Neither of us, Antonio," came the answer, "but the Hand which is in all hands. For God is everywhere."

"But please, let me operate without blood. I can't stand it. The sight and the smell of it make me sick," Tony begged.

"Not only you, Antonio, the others as well. But without blood no one would believe, not even those who have been healed. But all right – perhaps a little less blood." In this way Tony arrived at the final stage of his training. He went from place to place, healing the sick.

Tony was known to transfer to other people his ability to heal, after suitable preparation on their part. Stelter describes one such example in detail, noting that the student healer, who worked with Tony for several years, could perform PS only when near Tony.

Stelter tells of other types and varieties of healing. Juan Blance is said to be a psychic surgeon who cannot psychically close the surgical wounds he makes. He lets the patients heal naturally by themselves.

Blance reached for my right hand and said he would transfer his power to me. I was told to ball my right hand into a fist and stretch out my index finger. Then, holding my hand about 8 inches above the patient's neck, Blance made a short jerky movement in the air and at the same time pointed to a spot on the patient's neck. I saw a delicate short incision, as if etched by a razor blade.

Now Blance applied a procedure known in Western folk medicine as cupping. The assistant handed Blance an old coin, which he placed on the neck incision, where no bleeding was to be seen. On the coin was placed some cotton soaked in alcohol or coconut oil. This was set alight, and the healer turned a small glass upside down over both coin and cotton and pressed it tightly against the skin. The flame under the glass went out quickly, since the oxygen in the air was used up almost at once. The suction thus produced under the glass produced a swelling, growing even larger, at the incision, and the wound began to bleed.

The blood rose in the glass until it filled about halfway. Then Blance tilted the glass away, some of the blood remaining in it. The rest of the blood, containing coagulated clots, was wiped off the patient's neck. Blance pressed the edges of the cut together and said that it would heal soon...

Blance again used my finger to make a 'cut from a distance,' this time not in the neck but in the patient's abdomen. I concentrated on looking at the place where the cut would appear, but as if he wished to trick me and to punish me for my curiosity, Blance moved his outspread left hand between me and the patient – definitely without touching the patient – so that I did not see the small, delicate incision until he removed his hand. He repeated the procedure with the coin and the cotton... When the glass was removed Blance used his fingers, still smeared with blood, to press against both sides of the wound. I could not trust my eyes: something came out of the wound which looked almost like a fat caterpillar. It was reddish brown, and it seemed to be a couple of inches long. Blance put it in a small bowl filled with water.

"The root," he explained. "The small cut, enlarged by the 'root's' passage, remained open. Blance said that it would have to heal by itself... "

I [Stelter] saw one patient who had obviously had leg ulcers, now closed, which still caused severe itching or pain. Blance's fingers touched the affected skin. Each time he removed his hands, small fusiform seedlike substances clung to his fingertips... Blance threw them into the washbowl with a little jerky motion each time, as if they tended to stick to his fingers.

This process seemed absolutely inexplicable, and I stared attentively at the healer's fingers. His nails were cut very short. The rim normally present on the nails was almost completely cut off – as I noticed among most Philippine healers, probably to prevent scratching. Blance could not have concealed the 'seeds' under his fingernails. Again, these strange substances sometimes seemed to emerge from the skin as if in slow motion. Blance moved calmly and deliberately, wearing a short-sleeved shirt. Such processes can probably only be explained on the basis of materialization...

In other cases – perhaps with less advanced diseases or ones not so sharply localized – Blance brings peculiar doughy or liquid substances out of the body without opening it. This looks like a process of diffusion, as if the body were exuding something naturally, as during sweating or skin rashes, but such natural procedures take much longer and are usually not so localized. Perhaps there is an analogy between this form of treatment and the second stage of Agpaoa's surgery...

Psychic surgeons perform a variety of unusual eye operations.

As for Jurgen S., suffering from an old head injury, Agpaoa took his right eye out of the socket and removed from it a remnant of blood that had not resorbed after the accident – a so-called hematoma – which had caused the patient great difficulties. Since then, Jurgen S. has been able to move his eye without difficulty. The deformation of the pupil, present before the operation, has disappeared.

Stelter presents generous excerpts of German newspaper articles skeptical and critical of claims for PS. He points out that in many of the cited cases the reports carried only parts of the results of PS and were clearly biased against the possibility that such a phenomenon could exist.

He cites a number of analyses of tissues and fluids from PS operations, in which lab reports showed that tissues were either not certainly of human origin; not blood; not analyzable; or that blood types of samples and patients did not match.

Stelter mentions that German news media reported that 'so-called psychic surgery' was done with a plastic film covering the patient's body. This film supposedly allowed psychic surgeons to fabricate fake blood and tissue samples on it. The methods for this fabrication are not explained.

Stelter continues to discuss negative reports on psychic surgery. He quotes Sigrun Seutemann:

> The television team... sought out the German ambassador in Manila, hoping for support in exposing Agpaoa. The embassy referred them to Dr. Lothar Lissner, a Filipino of German descent who practiced in Manila and whose publications had earned him a wide scientific reputation.
>
> Dr. Lissner had never heard of Agpaoa, but he was immediately willing to help expose a fraud. He refused the high fee he was offered, since – as he put it – he wanted to render a completely unbiased judgment. He accepted only payment of his expenses for one night in a Baguio hotel.
>
> Dr. Lissner observed several operations by Tony. He also asked him for help for himself.
>
> He had been suffering for a long time from nasal polyps. Agpaoa agreed.
>
> I assisted, and Dr. Lissner's wife was present. A large towel was placed around the patient's neck. Agpaoa opened the nose at the bridge and encouraged the somewhat stunned wife to look at the inside of her husband's nose. Then Agpaoa exposed the polyps and asked me to pinch them off with a small pair of pliers. I did so. Then Agpaoa removed his hands, and the nose closed again. The whole procedure may have taken two minutes.
>
> Dr. Lissner also observed operations by Mercado, another healer.
>
> Together with a few others, we looked up Mercado without a previous appointment. He was operating in his chapel, with about thirty patients waiting. After we had observed for some time, a young woman was carried in. Dr. Lissner immediately recognized her disease as a uterine abscess formerly called Douglas's abscess, a common and dreaded occurrence in the Philippines. He told me that in his opinion the patient was lost.
>
> Mercado immediately postponed all other surgery and had the woman placed on the operating table. She was very weak and could no longer stretch out her legs; her abdomen was hard as a board. Our eyes were hardly more than a foot away from the site of the operation, and we could observe minutely. Before Dr. Lissner's astonished eyes, Mercado pushed his hands into the patient's body, and after a little while pulled out a handful of poison-green pus. "Only one kind of pus smells like that," exclaimed the physician, "the kind with a Douglas abscess." A little while later Mercado closed the opening and the patient, who seemed utterly exhausted of course, was put on another cot. Mercado ordered an hour's rest for her. After that she would be able to go home.
>
> Dr. Lissner almost lost his composure during this event, since he was par-

ticularly experienced in treating this kind of abscess. "I don't want to see any more," he said. "I've seen enough. I have no more doubts."

When we returned to Baguio that Saturday, Dr. Lissner invited the television team to his room. A few others were also present while Dr. Lissner gave his final interview for German television. In this interview he summarized the experiences and events of the past few days. He pointed out that these operations involved phenomena which he could not explain. He could say with certainty, however, that there was no deception.

In 1968, Motoyama and Dr. Hiram Ramos of Manila,

> ...along with the pathologist Professor David de Leon, observed operations performed by the healer Juan Blance, including surgery on cysts on the nape of the neck, without using a knife. The doctors took blood and tissue samples during the operations. These were tested at the University of Tokyo and at Professor Leon's institute at Manila's Far Eastern University. Comparison with blood later withdrawn from the same patient showed that the operation blood was the patient's... In all, Dr. Motoyama collected and analyzed twenty blood and tissue samples; on the basis of the test results he judged Blance's operations to be genuine.
>
> In 1970 Motoyama analyzed blood from two operations, including a cardiac operation performed on a sixty-year-old Japanese woman by the surgeon Gonzales of Baguio. Both operations were proved genuine by the results of the analyses...
>
> In 1973 Dr. Werner Schiebeler observed as his German colleague, Professor Benno Kirchgassner, was given a magnetic injection by the healer Mercado. Mercado never touched the patient, although Professor Kirchgassner clearly felt a puncture, and blood began to well from the wound. The two scientists preserved the flowing blood: a forensic examination in Germany revealed that the fluid was human O-group blood. Professor Kirchgassner has B-type blood; nevertheless, there is no possibility that the healer committed any kind of trickery.

Stelter tells of Dr. Theo Lorcher, who reported (in a Swiss parapsychological bulletin) on the investigations performed by an Italian team.

> The application of spiritual injections by hand without touching the body... was confirmed... During these injections the seven European members of the team felt something like needle punctures or electric shocks at the affected sites. Three members of the team were bleeding. The analysis of one of these blood samples (studied at the University of Turin, Italy) revealed that it was not human blood. In spite of tele-cameras, infrared film, and other monitoring of the puncture site, it was not possible to ascertain anything suspicious. Analysis of the blood flowing down the leg of another member of the group revealed a substance that was not blood, which remained completely incomprehensible to the members of the research team.

> A piece of paper placed under Mr. Moser's shirt showed three small holes at the site of the injection, although the healer's hands were constantly monitored by the group's apparatus. The substances produced during Blance's eye operations turned out to be useless for scientific evaluation. They quickly dissolved in formaldehyde...

It is a challenge to know what to make of these reports from various people who observed the same healers but differ markedly in their impressions, some of which conform to conventional expectations and some of which do not.

Many have hypothesized that sleight of hand can explain alleged PS.

> [I]nvitations were extended to Dr. Tooquet, president of Paris Magician's Guild, as well as to a specialist from the Solon Cinema Society. They were shown the movies made in January and February 1971 during our visit in Baguio. The experts concluded that what they saw could not be a trick.

Stelter hypothesizes that PS involves materializations and dematerializations of matter. He cites a host of evidence to support this thesis. Again, only a partial summary is presented here. He starts with the East European concept of *bioplasma*. This is a suggested biological parallel with plasma from the world of physics. Plasma is a fourth state of matter (after solid, liquid, and gas). In physics, plasma is found only at very hot temperatures. In biology it is allegedly present at normal temperatures, and is hypothesized to be a basis for life.[448]

Stelter proposes:

> Dematerialization means a dissolution of organic matter, which probably turns into a fundamentally new state or energy beyond the four states of the material world – solid, liquid, gas and plasma. This form must be much more subtle than atoms – perhaps similar to elementary particles – and quasi-nonelectrical, so that it can easily penetrate solid material structures. Assuming that bioplasma is involved, as postulated by the Russian researchers Inyushin and Sergeyev, dematerialization would be the transition of normal organic substance into bioplasma. 'Rematerialization' or simply 'materialization' is used to designate the return or transfer of bioplasma to normal material condition.

Stelter reviews a few reports on physical mediums. These go into a trance state and produce apparent materializations or substances.[449] A number of careful investigations of some of these mediums could not demonstrate any deception. For instance,

> In 1915-16 the English physicist W. J. Crawford noted that an extension about 3 feet long extruded from the torso of his medium, Miss Goligher. Comparable to an elephant's trunk, it was able to 'suck fast' to objects, exert an attracting and repelling force, and – given the necessary hardening and firming – to function as a carrier for raising heavy objects.

Without the medium's knowledge, Crawford marked the objects to be moved with a dye. After the experiments were done, stains could be found *under* the medium's clothing, on the skin of her abdomen, as if the materialization had returned into the medium's body at these sites. Crawford, as well as other researchers, placed their mediums on scales during séances and checked their weight during the process. At times they noted a considerable loss of weight for the duration of the ectoplasmic exteriorization, amounting to a few pounds, sometimes more than a few. This suggests that substances are actually exteriorized from the medium's bodies.[450]

Stelter concludes:

Today we can assume that the extrusion occurs over the intermediate state of bioplasma, with consequent materialization into ectoplasm at the body surface... Anyone who has closely scrutinized existing photos... and who has seen enough of Agpaoa's operations, both in person and on color and black-and-white film, gains the impression that the substances Agpaoa extracts from patient's bodies[are]... ectoplasm...

Stelter describes PS instances that support his suggestion:

I saw Tony Agpaoa perform the operation in a Manila hotel room. The patient, a young woman, suffered from a brain tumor; various surgeons had been only partly successful in removing it... After an assistant put some wet cotton on the patient's head, Tony began lightly massaging the shaved scalp with his fingers spread wide, so that there was no way to conceal anything. As he worked, a little bloodlike fluid quickly appeared, and under his fingers some tissue became visible. It looked like raw flesh, seemed to restructure itself into a skin-like substance, and after a short while covered most of the scalp.

A layman might easily have spoken of a plastic sheet. It did look as if the skull were wrapped in the hard layer of a substance like a bat's wing. (The expression 'like a bat's wing' for such ectoplasmic formations has been used by Richet and other researchers.)

The ectoplasmic skin now seemed grown to the skull; Agpaoa pressed lightly against the edge of the skin, revealing the skin surface; at times, with his eyes closed, he concentrated heavily. Now, under this skin, processes seemed to unroll that made me understand why Richet, Crawford... and others often spoke of an 'embryogenesis of materializations.' Just as fetal tissue develops in the amniotic sac, so here, under the protective cover of an ectoplasmic skin, a paranormal growth process seemed to run its course. The protective skin became more taut, seeming to grow harder and more stretched. After a short while a colored dark mass glowed through it.

Agpaoa signaled his assistant, who cut through the surface of the thick, hard membrane with great care, extending the cut to half and inch or more. A small amount of bloodlike liquid and a large amount of coagulated and clotted blood gushed out, and finally a little piece of flesh came to the surface. At Agpaoa's instruction, the assistant grasped it with a forceps and – with some difficulty – pulled it out. It had to be severed with scissors. The soft, blood-smeared tissue was about the length of a little finger and somewhat thicker. Agpaoa treated the site with his fingers, getting slightly in the way of my observation; finally he threw a membranelike piece of tissue, mixed with many clots, into the garbage can. I can guarantee it was not plastic.

Stelter acknowledges difficulties in relating his hypotheses of materializations and dematerializations to the world of atomic physics. It is known that transformations of matter into energy release tremendous amounts of energy. This is not apparent in the case of PS. Therefore the proposed bioplasma transformations must involve different, as yet not understood processes.
  Stelter adds observations from other quarters to support his hypotheses:

1. He considers several reports of firewalking, in which people tread barefooted across coal beds which measure 800-1,200 degrees Farenheit.
  These incredible accomplishments make more sense if we presume that during certain spiritual states the bioplasmic body of the firewalkers can materialize an ectoplasm able to withstand high temperatures.[451]

2. Though ignored by the official sciences, French and German chemists have carried out numerous tests with plants and animals with significant bearings on problems of the energy released during materialization and dematerialization. Following the work of the German chemist Albrecht von Herzeele in the nineteenth century, Dr. Rudolf Hauschka, a contemporary German chemist, has observed the germinating process and the weight of plant seeds sealed in glass tubes with distilled water. The results show an unmistakable alteration in the mass that, according to Hauschka, far exceeds allowable margins of error. Can these changes be materialization phenomena in the realm of the biological processes?

3. The works of the French chemist C. Louis Kervran[452] are closely related. Kervran claims to have demonstrated transmutations of chemical elements in plants and animals, such as phosphorus into sulfur and potassium into calcium. These are not just changes on the periphery of atoms, as in the usual chemical reactions, but in the nucleus– which is possible in modern physics, but requires an energy expenditure millions of times greater than biochemical and biophysical processes that take place in living organisms, according to present knowledge.
  Kervran is not alone in such claims. Professor Pierre Baranger, director of the Institute for Organic Chemistry at the Ecole Polytechnique in Paris, has proved transmutations in the biological sphere based on the work of von Herzeele, and other researchers seem to confirm his results.[453]

Stelter's book is a gold mine of information and observations. He presents critical discussions of material reviewed. However, it is in some instances difficult to distinguish where his quotes end and discussions begin. He also seems to overstate his hypotheses in some cases, presenting them as well-demonstrated conclusions.

Walter and Mary Jo Uphoff report:[454]

> Frau Seutemann cited in a letter to us, October 23, 1973:
>
> In March 1972 I took a Swiss citizen in a wheelchair to Tony (Agpaoa). This 42-year-old man at that time had been unable to walk for 5 years after he had cortisone therapy to cure psoriasis. The treatment was toxic for him and the cartilages in his joints were necrotized [destroyed]. He had been in Swiss hospitals for 2 1/2 years without interruption and had paid more than 280,000 Swiss francs. Cartilages were removed; the bone was taken off at the hips and knees – so far had the necrotization gone. Of course, it was not possible for him to walk, or even to use his arms because the shoulders and elbows were also affected. His spine is one continuous scar. Five operations were done to fuse it because he could not live with the pain.
>
> Tony gave him treatment – the patient stood on his feet, and after two days began to walk again. Today he works all day in his big repair station (for trucks); he swims, walks many hours in the Alps.
>
> The invalid insurance (charged) him with being a fraud and for months there has been a fight. Now we have the clinic attests that the X-rays show no change (as a result of) Tony's treatment. The professors shake their heads. They just cannot understand why this man can walk. In their eyes, he is 100 percent an invalid. The insurance continues to be paid, but he can walk. You only notice that his spine is still a little stiff... Normal clinic tests are not enough to give a full picture of the effectiveness of spiritual healing or surgery. What kind of substance makes this man free of pain and able to walk? X-rays cannot show this.[455]

Harold Sherman, a popular author of books on parapsychology, wrote one of the first books describing the Philippine psychic surgeons.[456] In easy, discursive style, he clearly described many of the processes and effects of PS as well as the difficulties encountered in studying these healers:

1. Nelson C. Decker, a chiropractor from California, was a student of Tony Agpaoa. He related that Agpaoa told him he performed his operations in order to impress the patients that something had actually occurred during the healing treatments.

> One day, I asked Tony, "Why all the blood?"
> "Well, the Espiritistas are bloodless," he replied. "They have an organization, you have to go to their church and be a member, with all their rigamarole. I have to impress people that I am really doing something." [457]

Asking whether Tony needed to have such displays of blood, Decker relates,

The way he explained it to me – he is in and out of the body so fast, many patients and their friends and relatives don't believe he's done anything – but if they can go home with blood-spattered undergarments, they can prove they really had an operation.[458]

2. Decker was taught by Agpaoa to extract teeth with his fingers, anesthetizing the patient by merely pointing a thumb at the tooth. Decker found he could do this and other operations only in Agpaoa's presence.

3. To help Decker perform more extensive psychic surgery, Agpaoa used an induction procedure in which he blew in Decker's ear and on his hands. Decker felt a chill go through his body.

Decker describes what it feels like to perform PS:

I was awake enough to remain on my feet, I knew what I was doing, but I also knew that something working through me was doing it. I forced my eyes to stay open so I could see what was going on, but it was very hard to see.[459]

He reported these sensations were similar to ones he had experienced in deep hypnosis. With practice, Decker felt the 'trance' influence only in his arms and hands. Onset of trance was accompanied with heaviness and tingling in his hands. He explains that his hands appeared to function independently of his will, through directions of an outside agency. When he did PS, he deliberately did not think about PS. He would 'forget about everything' during these procedures.

... This is the way Tony does it. He never goes into an unconscious state to perform his operations. The power and intelligence is only in his hands and arms...

That first time, when I saw the body open up, under my hands, I froze, and my hands stopped operating. Tony said, "Look away. Get your mind off it. You're not doing this. Let the God power do it!" The instant I shifted my attention away, my hands and arms started moving and completed the operation and closed up the body![460]

4. Sherman mentions observing Tony cutting through a three-inch width of adhesive tape using his fingers, the side of his hand or his tongue. Tony said this was the same power he used in surgical procedures.

5. Sherman observed that psychic surgeons had difficulty in closing wounds or correcting procedures performed by regular surgeons, whereas most of them usually had no problems in closing openings they themselves created. Considerable variability is found between different psychic surgeons. One may open the body by merely pointing at it from a distance of several inches (with his own finger, or by holding the finger of another person); most open the body with direct

pressure from their own hands; others may leave PS wounds to heal by natural means.

Sherman's book is an excellent introduction to the topics, personalities, and controversies involved in PS.[461]

Jaime Licauco reports he has observed psi healing and PS for many years in the Philippines. He presents a variety of notes on many aspects of the Philippine healers' work, in a question and answer style:

1. Why are there so many unusually good healers in the Philippines?

> ... Filipinos are close to nature, generally relaxed and friendly[T]heir vibrations are higher and they are able to reach a heightened state of awareness faster and more easily than other people. This is especially true of the rural Filipinos.[462]
> ... Filipinos... believe... in spirits. It is therefore very easy for Filipinos especially those in the countryside to be in communion with unseen or spiritual forces which is necessary for healing. Because the Filipino's view of the world is not limited to the five senses his intellect is able to accept concepts beyond the purely rational.[463]

The Union Espiritista Christiana de Filipinas, a religious organization, teaches the arts of mediumistic healing.

> At the beginning of his training period, the would-be healer would go into a deep trance and then wait for the spirit to enter his body. Once the spirit is inside his body, the healer can then begin to heal. He does this in a totally unconscious manner. However, later on, the healer is able to go into that other state of consciousness while being fully conscious of the material environment. He no longer has to go into a deep trance to heal and to perform psychic surgery...[464]

2. Are some healers better at healing in general than others or able to help better with certain problems?

> We must realize that these faith healers are not doctors but mediums or channels of the spirit. Sometimes the spirit guide that enters their body may be good at treating some forms of illnesses and not others. At other times, a different spirit may enter his body...
>   Sometimes it happens that one healer will not be able to help a person suffering from an ailment that another healer can...[465]

3. What about claims of fakery by some observers?
 Licauco explains that the healers sometimes fake PS when their powers are weak. He condemns such fakery but explains that healers are human and some-

times given to false pride or other frailties. He adds a twist to the controversy on this subject:

> One faith healer, whom I asked about this problem, related to me how, when he was just getting the attention of the foreign press, some Americans came to observe him and asked for the tissues he had taken out to have analyzed in their laboratory. Naively, the healer consented to this. Without his knowledge, these Americans substituted his samples with chicken liver and other animal tissues and blood. When the results of the analysis came out, they revealed quite gleefully that the healers were not really removing human tissues. These reports were given wide publicity both here and abroad. And this in part accounts for the negative image of our healers. The story has persisted despite growing solid evidence to the contrary.[466]

4. What of karmic aspects of illness?

> ... I wish to emphasize here that most of our faith healers consider the curing of the patient to be secondary to their mission. What they believe to be the primary goal of their healing activity is assisting in the spiritual upliftment of the patient or the speeding up of his soul evolution. Unless this spiritual enlightenment or upliftment is achieved, they do not consider their healing to be a complete success. For they believe that all sickness stems from the spiritual levels of man's being, the physical manifestation being merely the effect.[467]

Licauco's little booklet is very readable and informative, reflecting his considerable experience with PS. Reports of others who visited the Philippines are also cited. A number of black and white photographs of healers at work are included. One is particularly striking, showing two index fingers of a healer inserted to the first joint in a healee's back, a pool of dark fluid around them. It appears highly unlikely such a photo could be faked by positioning of the hands. The skeptic will point out that doctoring of the photographs would still have to be ruled out.

> *If the man doesn't believe as we do, we say he is a crank, and that settles it. I mean, it does nowadays, because now we can't burn him.*
> – Mark Twain

Anne Dooley, a reporter, gathered interesting descriptions of psychic healers. Of special note are her descriptions of the Brazilian psychic surgeon, Lourival (also called de Freitas). Lourival began his healing career at age nine, following a near-drowning, in which he contacted one of his spirit guides for the first time. He also has extensive herbal knowledge derived from his gypsy grandmother. His PS techniques differ in some respects from those of other healers.

1. He often prepares the healee by making a shallow incision at the surgical site several days prior to the operation.

2. He uses razors and scissors to open the body. Healees usually enter an unconscious state and report surgery to be painless or only 'somewhat uncomfortable.'

3. He uses needle and thread to close the body, somewhat in the manner that a conventional surgeon would (minus sterile technique) but removes the sutures within minutes, leaving the wound closed. He warns the patients not to exert themselves for several days thereafter.

4. He often has observers assist in the surgery. Usually this is merely to manipulate a knife or needle in a small manner. Sometimes it is more. For instance, during an operation several of the spectators in the room went into a trance state. He explained that their energies were being used to help in the healing.

5. Dooley also reports on a rare case where psi gifts appear to have been used to bring about a merciful end to terrible suffering for an animal:

> Lourival was asked to give aid to an eight-year-old pedigree Guernsey cow suffering over a strangulated birth. It was her fifth calf.
>
> [T]he calf had come feet first and the head was too large to allow passage. Francis had been a helpless witness to the cow's 15-hour ordeal, which had included unsuccessful 'bleeding' by two veterinary surgeons called in. They had recommended that the animal should be destroyed.
>
> [W]e found the cow – a beautiful animal with heart rending lustrous brown eyes – lying on her side in a semi-open thatched byre, her head resting on straw. She uttered continuous pitiful moans. From her uterus two of the calf's legs extended grotesquely, one of them broken at the knee joint as a result of earlier manhandling. When we set eyes on her Lourival had shaken his head over her plight. After ordering that the farmhands be sent out of the byre he became entranced. Calling for a pad and pen he began to draw a diagram of the cow's womb, muttering to himself as he marked different sections. A pail of water was brought into the byre and after plunging his hand and arm into the cow's uterus he told us that the calf had died in the imprisoning womb. Tetanus, he said, had already set in. But I noticed with relief that although at one point he had pulled the cow right around, using the calf's dangling legs as a lever, the animal had ceased to groan. At intervals he washed his hands, sipped whisky, and smoked a cigarette.
>
> Appearing to abandon the idea of trying to save the cow by removing the calf, he then began timing some unseen process partly by checking with his wristwatch, which he had not removed during his earlier examination, and partly by checking off with his fingers. He seemed to be in touch with unseen forces and awaiting a certain signal. At all times, intensely, compassionately intent upon the quietly prone animal, he appeared to be able, by merely raising his hand, to control her slightest movement, for suddenly as if in obedience to his will, she raised her head and silently began – mouth open and tongue slightly extended as if to suck in maximum

air – to make weaving, snake-like movements in ever widening arcs. At maximum stretch her jaw hit a post near by with some force, but no sound came from her; the eyes were fixed and already slightly receding into her head. Then movement ceased as her head came to rest against a light fence which separated the byre from a small pen containing two piglets...

[H]olding a lighted candle for which he had asked, he voiced a brief noble invocation. It asked God's pardon for the mercy killing granted in the name of love, paid homage to death's liberation and expressed a plea for redemptive aid upon all suffering life.[468]

Lourival's techniques are interesting variations on the theme of PS. The apparent psi involvement of observers in the healing process (5) is unusual – perhaps more in its clarity than in the fact of its occurrence. Other healers often report that observers' rapport contributes to healing but support for this claim is nowhere as evident as here. A similar example may be found in a report that Boris Ermolaev, a Russian PK adept, may need friends nearby during experiments in order to avoid feeling sick and faint.[469]

Lourival's bringing about a rapid, peaceful death to an animal in fatal distress is unusual in the healing literature. It confirms that a healing may be effected by bringing release to incurable suffering through death.[470]

The next series of reviews describe PS-I, in which healers' interventions are in the aura, or energy field of the healees, and not directly on the healees' bodies.

Walter and Mary Jo Uphoff[471] report on the late Gerard Croiset, Sr. and on George Chapman:

1. Gerard Croiset, the internationally-famous paragnost from Utrecht who has helped locate many lost persons who have been victims of accidents or foul play, considers laying-on-of-hands healing his principal work... In an effort to determine if some form of energy flows from Croiset's hands, Prof. Tenhaeff [and others]... conducted an experiment in 1970. Solutions of nickel chloride exposed to Croiset's hands for 60-120 seconds were compared with untreated solutions of the same chemical by means of Beckman spectrophotometer readings taken every 24 hours for five days. The tracings showed significantly different readings for the treated sample which after five days had returned to normal... The experiment was planned and directed by G. H. van Leeuwen, president of Enzypharm... Solutions of organic substances (fructose and indigo) produced even more marked results than the inorganic nickel salt solution.

Mr. van Leeuwen concludes his report on the experiment, saying (in part): "The influence is a real, measurable one... the nature of this influence is not yet clear, more investigations are needed before attempting to make any postulations." [472]

2. The British medium, George Chapman, former RAF mechanic, and fireman...in trance, becomes the 'instrument' of the noted ophthalmologist,

Dr. William Lang, who died in 1937. Lang, through Chapman, is so convincing a diagnostician and surgeon that Dr. Robert Laidlaw, a New York psychiatrist, after observing him, testified: "There is no doubt I was talking to a medical man. No layman could be familiar with all the technical matters we [Lang and Laidlaw] discussed."

Maurice Barbanell,[473] reviewing Chapman's... book,[474] wrote: "George Chapman is regularly consulted by medicos on their own behalf for relatives and friends. Many sent patients to him. Medical etiquette prevents those in Britain from being named. They would be struck off for 'co-operating with an unregistered practitioner.'" However, in 1969 Chapman made public the fact that he is 'under contract' to a group of medical men. Some of them knew and worked with Dr. William Lang at Middlesex and Moorfields Hospitals before 1937. Chapman reports that when Lang first made his presence known, he [Chapman] contacted the hospitals where the surgeon said he had worked. Some of Lang's medical colleagues were intrigued and at a trance session Lang, during a strict cross-examination, accurately named many relatives and recounted facts known only to the doctors present. They then produced patients and after diagnosis were convinced enough to ask for a 'gentleman's agreement contract' to allow them to further investigate and consult with Chapman-Lang. [475]

Figure III-7 George Chapman holding photo of Dr. Lang, and his son, George Chapman Jr. who is also a healer

Photograph courtesy of Tony Sleep

Roy Stemman[476] describes mediumistic phenomena produced by Isa A. Northage, an English woman who materialized spirit forms in séances. Her spirit guide, Dr. Reynolds, guided her in establishing a healing clinic in which materialized spirits could perform psychic surgery. In 1949 Ernest Thompson, editor of the spiritualist newspaper *Two Worlds*, witnessed the following operation.[477]

> Eight people, including Isa Northage, gathered in the operating theatre... The door was locked, the light turned out, and the meeting started with prayer. Isa was in her cabinet, in a trance; soon a trumpet rose into the air, and the sitters were addressed by the spirit helper, Ellen Dawes. Dr. Reynold's materialized form then appeared, discernible as a "black silhouette against the red glow from the lamp on a trolley, on which were laid forceps, two red electric torches [flashlights], one white electric torch, and two luminous plaques."
>
> Dr. Reynolds picked up a torch, switched it on, and turned towards the operating table "on which lay a patient suffering from an acute duodenal pain. No anesthetic was used. Dr. Reynolds explained how he would 'freeze' the portions of the body to be operated upon and then pass his hand, which would become dematerialized, into the side of the body and ulcer." Two of the witnesses were not wearing masks, and the doctor asked them to put them on before he began operating. He then placed cotton wool swabs on the patient's abdomen and assured him that there would be no difficulty to remove the ulcer. His hands moved to the side of the body and as he did so he asked the patient if he felt any pain.
>
> The patient apparently replied that he did not. Then 'a gurgling sound' was heard, and Dr. Reynolds reported that "the ulcer was in a very bad condition and would not come away in a whole piece and that he was afraid of hemorrhage." This difficulty was overcome and "portions of ulcer brought through what Dr. Reynolds described as a temporary opening in the abdomen, and placed on the swabs on the surface of the body."
>
> When the séance ended Thompson retrieved the human tissue from the swabs and put it in a bottle of surgical spirit. A few days later he arranged to have it analyzed, and the verdict was: "It is an acute duodenal ulcer, contains Brunner's glands and shows from its condition that it was about to penetrate the intestine and would have proved fatal."

Isa Northage continued to heal with PS for several years but then stopped, following an automobile accident. A later article in the August, 1967 *Scottish Sunday Express*

> ... described how a bus driver suffering from a stomach ulcer visited Pinewoods. Before the astonished witnesses, Isa massaged his abdomen, which 'opened like a rose' and the ulcer was plucked out in two pieces. The patient told the newspaper: "Before the operation almost anything I ate gave me pain. An hour after, I was able to eat a five-course meal. I haven't had a twinge since."

This is a remarkable report. If it is accurate and if the PS actually occurred as described, one can only wonder why Isa Northage did not attract far more publicity. Unfortunately, mediums have been known to produce séance room phenomena by sleight of hand and other trickery. As no mention is made of any precautions to preclude these, and as the report does not even cite its sources, one can give little weight to this evidence.[478]

David St. Clair[479] describes a number of American healers whose techniques fall within the realm of PS-III.

1. The Reverend Harold Plume was born and raised in England. He was a soldier, worked in a factory, and managed a shop prior to being ordained a minister of the Church of the Good Shepherd in a London suburb. He saw spirits from the early age of three. He developed strong mediumistic abilities and did frequent public readings.

> It was at one of these, while he was in trance, that Hoo Fang appeared.
>
> Hoo Fang claimed to be a Chinese doctor who had died some twenty-five hundred years ago. He said he worked with a group of other doctors in the spirit world and his aim was someday to have Harold's vibration so high that he would be able to perform operations with Harold. But Harold wasn't that interested in healing – not until the first one happened in his own family.
>
> This healing through Hoo Fang came directly and surprisingly to the Plumes. Bertha was expecting their first child, and she developed a serious kidney infection. Doctors wanted to operate and take out the diseased organ, saying that it would cost the life of the baby but if allowed to remain it might even cost the life of the mother. Bertha, always independent, didn't want anything to do with medical doctors. She told Harold to ask Hoo Fang for guidance.
>
> The Chinese physician came through upon being called and asked Harold to trust him. When the young worried husband promised, the spirit asked him to go and place his finger tips on Bertha's body. He wanted the fingers placed directly over the area of infection. Harold was in semitrance at this stage, fully aware of what was happening yet still under enough to be a channel for Hoo Fang. Harold placed the fingers of one hand on the area and Hoo Fang ordered, 'Push!'
>
> Harold pushed and to his amazement saw his fingers slide effortlessly into his wife's body. He saw his fingers disappear, and Bertha jumped at the sensation.
>
> Through Harold's voice box, Hoo Fang explained that what he was doing was using Harold's physical body and cosmic energy to dematerialize his fingers as well as the area where Bertha's disease was located. This high vibration would dematerialize the diseased tissue of her kidney. Harold felt his fingers rub against a swelled inner organ. Bertha said she felt it too.
>
> At Hoo Fang's orders, Harold slid his hand out slowly. There was no hole

in Bertha's body. There was no blood. There was no pain. And, most importantly, there was no more diseased tissue in her kidney.[480]

He has practiced as a healer since that time. St. Clair discussed his techniques with him.

"Close the aura?" I asked. "How do you do that?"

"You make your passes over the body... from the head all the way down to the ground." He jumped up to show me how it was done, making downward motions with his outstretched fingers. "Never work on a patient and not close them off afterward. People will look at me and say, 'Well what's he waving his hands in the air for?' But I'm not. I'm closing off the aura."

"This is *after* you've gone into their body, right?"

"Well, I'll tell you something surprising. I don't know sometimes when I've gone in or when I haven't. There are times when I'm very conscious of it and other times when I'm not. I really don't know what happens. Hoo Fang told me that he disintegrates my fingers by vibrating them very rapidly. You know if you took this sofa and vibrated it fast enough it would disintegrate. So it's the same with my fingers. And when my fingers, in that fast state, touch another person's body they also feel that vibration and that part of *their* body disintegrates. That's why the energy is allowed to slip right in without a scar and without any blood. It's the darndest thing. Been filmed you know, but," he added, "often all the photographer gets is a blur or a black band across his negative. It's as if Hoo Fang didn't want anybody to take a picture of what's going on."

"And the patient has nothing to do with this?" I asked. "They can be complete skeptics and still receive a healing?"

"No, because it seems to depend upon the state of mind of the person sitting in the chair. Are they sitting there in a state of believing or are they sitting there in a state of doubt? Are they thinking 'I've heard of the work of this man but I don't believe it?' If so, their mind is affecting their whole make-up. If they come in and *doubt* me but *trust* God that's different. Even while they are doubting, if they will say, 'God heal me,' then they will be healed. It's not *me* doing this healing, you know. It's not me. It's God. That's who should be getting the praise. That's why some of these cases have been instantaneous healing and I feel the energy flowing and I know they are being healed."

"But there are some who will never be healed. And I've known when there was no possible chance... "[481]

"I don't dwell upon defects. People will come in wheel chairs and tell me they can't walk. Well I can see that! But I *know* that with God *nothing* is impossible. That's how I work. I *see* that person walking. I don't see the defect when I work on them. I only see it when they come in. As soon as they are sitting in the chair I see them as completely cured."

"You don't see the organs going back slowly to what they should be?"

"I see them *immediately* cured. They are, as far as I'm concerned in my soul's eye, perfect. Perfect as God made them. God creates them perfect and they *are* perfect. But imperfections do creep in, that I'm aware of... " [482]

2. Reverend William Brown is another healer who in trance state is "used by spirit physicians who perform healings." He too saw spirits since childhood. He uses PS-I.

"There are twenty-eight specialists who use this body," Reverend Brown said matter-of-factly; "some are heart specialists, others deal with bones, eyes, nerves, muscles, etc. Dr. Murphy is a diagnostician but he's also started to do some surgery. He's become fascinated with ophthalmology in the last few years; previously, he had turned all those cases over to another doctor, and he still defers to others when he comes up against a real tough case. But mostly he gives injections with invisible syringes and calms the patient down. He's got a great sense of humor."

"You make him sound as if he were still alive," I said. "He is dead, isn't he?"

"No! he is not dead!" Reverend Brown said sharply. "He does not have a physical body per se, but uses my physical body as though it were his own. He is, nevertheless, very much alive! How could a physically embodied person take over my body?" He glared at me and then continued. "There is Dr. Spaulding, who is my protector. He doesn't operate but stands by this body to see that no malevolent entity takes it over while I am away from it. There is Dr. Livingston, too. You know, the one that Stanley went looking for in Africa. Dr. Thorndyke works on abdominal problems. He's a very serious gentleman, almost the exact opposite of Dr. Murphy, who jokes around a lot. Dr. Chandler is an orthopedic. Dr. Fredericks is a heart specialist. Dr. Cushing is the most recent one to join the group. He was an American."

"Have you ever checked into their stories?" I asked. "Have you ever dug up information about them to prove that they were who they say they were?"

"What good would that do?" he asked quickly. "I don't think it matters one little bit who these people were or what they did while they were in human bodies. What matters is what kind of results they bring about now..." [483]

The doctors experimented with Bill Brown's body in fourteen different ways until they finally decided that they worked best by having him leave it so that they could work through it. Apparently he was chosen not because of his being a minister or his metaphysical studies but because the chemical make-up of his body was compatible to their purposes. He insists that he didn't ask for this and made no effort to obtain it. He was more surprised than Nancy [his wife] when he came out of it and she told him what had happened.

Then his teachers showed him the Akashic Records, the fabled books where each soul's life pattern is carefully recorded. "The healing work had to be resumed in this life," said Nancy, "because Bill had failed five times before."

"I didn't fail," he put in, "I just quit."

"The same thing!" she said quickly. "You failed in your Karmic missions because of the lack of understanding of the people around you in those various lifetimes. I was with him in each of them, that I know. They showed us that in the Records... " [484]

Patients coming for treatments rest overnight prior to treatment in the Browns' home.

He doesn't eat any breakfast before the operation, nor does Nancy, who acts as recording nurse. The patient is also not allowed to eat anything beforehand. He can have a little water or some fruit juice but the doctors want the body as light as it can be, without a lot of heavy undigested food in the stomach. Cigarettes and coffee are also forbidden.

There is a ritual before the operation. There is recorded sacred music and Reverend Brown asks the patient to repeat the Lord's Prayer with him, "slowly, so as to understand...each word." Then there is what he calls the 'Affirmation of Faith.' It too is said aloud and in unison.

The patient, dressed in a hospital gown, then gets onto a blue massage table that has been draped with a white sheet and made more comfortable with a pillow. Reverend Brown sits in a chair near the table and listens to the soft music playing in the room. Then he slumps over, his head hanging between his knees, and when he rights himself it is no longer Bill Brown but a departed entity who is inhabiting his body.

The first visitor is always Dr. John Geoffrey Spaulding. His job is to see that Bill Brown's body is protected from any outside, unwanted influences. He is introduced to those present in the room by Nancy. Then... a new entity takes over. The second visitor is always Dr. John Murphy, the Irish diagnostician. Dr. Murphy tells the patient what is wrong – where and what shall be done about it. He gives invisible injections to prepare the patient for the surgery that is to come. When he leaves, another doctor comes into the body and performs the actual operation.

Reverend Brown's hands never touch a patient. They are always working quickly in the air a few inches over the body. The surgery takes place on the etheric and not the physical level.

The etheric body is an exact copy of the flesh and blood body with every muscle, bone, organ, and nerve reproduced but in a finer density. The principle is that this body, being more basic than the physical, can be adjusted more rapidly and bloodlessly. Each condition corrected in the etheric body is reflected back into the physical body, thus adjusting the physical back into health.

While the doctors work, you can see Bill Brown's hands (powered by the entities) moving quickly. You watch as his hand picks up an invisible knife from an invisible side table and can almost see it sink into the flesh as it makes a rapid incision. You almost see the assistants standing on the other side of the table who take the used instruments and hand him the necessary new ones. You watch as the fingers remove something and toss it on the table, and you sit fascinated as the fingers stitch up the invisible wound with a needle and thread. All this time Bill Brown, the man, has his eyes shut tight, yet his voice makes comments about conditions, and he points with great accuracy to various sections of the anatomy.

Patients are encouraged to answer the surgeon's questions but are at the same time warned not to try and carry on any unnecessary conversation. His time in Bill Brown's body is limited and he has come for work, not for chitchat.

After the operation has been completed, a Dr. Davis shows up to give a closing prayer. The body is sitting down at this point and soon its head falls forward between its knees. This time when the head comes up it is Bill Brown once more. He sits calmly for a few minutes, then shakes his hands rapidly and opens his eyes. He says, "The hands feel larger than when I normally occupy the body."

After this the patient is allowed to get off the table and, putting on a bathrobe, is taken to a bedroom for several hours of rest and sleep. It is very important that this rest period be one of absolute repose, because once the etheric body starts reflecting the newly made changes into the physical, some discomfort, shock, or even pain will be felt. This reaction seems to depend on how far the patient has progressed spiritually in this lifetime. Nonbelievers, it appears, suffer much more than those who have accepted these things as a natural part of God's laws.[485]

Discussing why his patients feel pain, he says:

"I've given it a lot of thought... and it seems to me that there is no other way for the skeptic to be convinced that something has actually happened."[486]

Addressing Nancy,

"When you are helping him and his body had been taken over," I asked, "do you see the various doctors as they come and go?"

"No, I don't. If I saw a drawing of what Dr. Murphy looked like while he was on this earth, I wouldn't recognize him. I do see their hands and sometimes see the instruments and I can tell from their movements exactly what they are doing and what they are removing."

"When they cut out a tumor, for instance, and throw it aside, what happens to it?"

"That question has been asked many times. It simply disintegrates. There is a constant cleansing and cleaning up going on all the time in there. The parts and pieces are not left lying around on my level."[487]

St. Clair's presentation is easy reading, but is more valuable as anecdotal than scientific information.

A more recent psychic surgeon is Joao de Deus (John of God), who established a healing center called The Casa de Dom Inácio in Abadiania, Goias, Brazil. More than with most other psychic surgeons, the reports of Western visitors reflect a deep sense of spirituality in their visits to his center and in the healings they receive. It is unclear whether this is a factual observation of greater spirituality or whether it may be because people are more open to discussing spiritual awareness and healing in recent times.[488] While John of God does perform PSII operations, he emphasizes that spiritual preparation are essential to the success of his treatments, and his healees may spend several hours or days in prayers prior to their treatments.

Many have observed some of the same psychic surgeons but came away with negative impressions.

William Nolen, an American physician, visited the Philippines. He reports he saw healers' hands with fingers curled, pressed on the patient's abdomen up to the end of the bent fingers, but no further. A red fluid appeared, and cotton wads were applied. Nolen felt that the 'blood clots' removed by the psychic surgeons and thrown in a pail were actually the cotton swabs soaked in the red fluid. In some cases, yellow tissue was also flourished, the psychic surgeons claiming it had been removed from the patients. Nolen offered himself as a patient for such an operation. He observed his psychic surgeon palming a piece of yellow tissue prior to the 'surgery,' then producing it as though it had been extracted from his abdomen.

In other cases he observed 'cuppings' on patients' legs. The psychic surgeon first wiped the skin with cotton. He pointed his finger at the skin, making a slicing motion in the air, several inches away from the body. A scratch appeared on the skin within a few moments. The cups were then applied that led to a puckering of the skin within the cup, as the oxygen was used up. Dark blood oozed out, supposedly carrying the disease with it. At first this seemed to be true PS, even if of a minor sort. Nolen claims he found on repeated observation that the healers were scratching the skin with a sharp fragment of mica while wiping off the skin prior to pointing with their fingers.

In yet another procedure, a manipulation of a patient's eye in which the psychic surgeon appeared to pull the eye several inches out of its socket, Nolen reports the healer was palming a fake eye.

Nolen also talked with several Philippine physicians and a psychologist who confirmed his impression that all the operations were faked. One reported that Agpaoa had agreed a number of times to demonstrate his techniques in front of a group of doctors, but had made excuses each time, or had simply not shown up.

Nolen also describes a number of seeming evasions by healers when he disagreed with their diagnoses, and asked to have a tooth of his own extracted.

Nolen demonstrates the importance of having trained medical observers in such investigations. People unused to surgery are likely to be disturbed and distracted by the sight of blood to the point that they do not observe sleight of hand manipulations. Nolen believes that the finding of fakery makes all such PS questionable.

One must note, however, that negative observations in some instances do not rule out the possibility that other PS may be genuine.

Alfred Stelter criticizes Nolen severely. He presents damning evidence that Nolen distorted information presented to him, both by healers and by others who had observed them, in the process of supporting his skeptical views of Philippine PS.

The late David Hoy was both an expert in psi and in stage magic. He accompanied George Meek to the Philippines to investigate psychic healers, stating that he came with a genuine investment in exploration of psi phenomena but with a mind open also to the possibilities of sleight of hand. His report is sharply at variance with those of other researchers cited here.[489]

Hoy observed Brother Nemesio G. Taylor, Juan Blance, Placido and several other healers at work. He was disappointed to see them use generally crude methods of misdirection and sleight of hand to achieve the appearances of surgical procedures of various sorts.

He reports on his own replication of many of the effects of the healers:

> [B]y impregnating plain drugstore absorbent cotton with Burnt Sienna No.2 and Carmine (red) No.2 water colors (purchased at a Manila art supply shop) I was able to bring forth 'blood' when I mixed 'holy water' from the hotel water tap with the wads of cotton I had secreted in various out-of-the-way parts of my body. There was even a plus product from the mixture: I could see that some of the stained cotton wads could be passed off as 'tissue' from the body were they to be deftly palmed and introduced at the right psychological moment in a 'psychic surgery' performance.
>
> Faking an incision was another matter, I admit. Even the most courageous researcher might be reluctant to experiment with sharp instruments on his own hide. But the challenge had been made – that I would attempt to reproduce the effects used by the psychic healers whose performance my group of scientists had observed. With a little experimentation, I found that part of a standard double edge razor blade could be so sheathed and hidden beneath my thumb nail that a light, ever so light, cut on the skin of my right leg produced an incision that barely penetrated the subcutaneous layer. Moreover, the incision did not show for a full ten seconds and then a fine pinstripe of blood appeared and the flow continued to increase until a swipe with an alcohol-soaked swab stopped it.
>
> The pain, incidentally, was minimal – about what one feels when he scratches himself with a rough edge of his fingernail. Next, I placed a coin on one of the 'incisions,' then placed a burning piece of cotton on the coin and inverted a shot glass over the whole megillah. The vacuum created in the air space under the shot glass encouraged a more rapid flow of blood, and it soon soaked the cotton thoroughly and even overflowed rather dramatically. The effect was nothing short of spectacular! Given the

opportunity to create an air of mystery, something any competent magician can do quite easily, I felt that I could reproduce many of the more gory effects used by the healers. Actually, my only concern was for sterilizing my self-inflicted 'incisions' so as to avoid infection in the hot humid atmosphere of the Philippines.

What did my experiments prove? In my opinion and because I was a trained sleight-of-hand practitioner myself and because I had detected many classic misdirectional moves used by the 'healers,' I was forced to the conclusion that 'cures' produced by these means were at least suspect. Further, that if there were indeed supernatural forces at the command of these people, they weakened their credibility by using the crude methods of deception that I have described and can reproduce.

Hoy further reported on a number of instances in which actual surgical procedures were used. In one case he saw the cauterization of an abscess in a girl's mouth with a match stick wrapped in cotton and set afire. In another, a tumorous growth the size of a grapefruit was casually excised with a double-edged razor blade from the thigh of a woman. In both instances Hoy reports the patients winced in pain. He felt the healers were callous and insensitive. He did not sense any air of "meaningful psychic bridge between the 'surgeons' and their wretched patients."

Regarding filmed evidence, Hoy points out:

Time after time, the statement was made that 'the camera doesn't lie,' in reference to the photographic 'evidence' that several of my colleagues displayed. It was difficult, if not impossible, to explain that the camera's 'eye' is actually only the eye of the person taking the picture and that the tricks of misdirection, sleight-of-hand and palming of objects that are the main stock in trade of the 'healers' are in no magical way revealed by even the most expert photographic techniques.

He reluctantly concludes:

[T]hese men and women were simply creating magical effects to provide a level of hope to patients that in fact did not exist. And the hardest pill to swallow was that the techniques of sleight-of-hand, misdirection and palming were so crudely executed as to offend the professional standards of even a mediocre stage magician. Still, thousands of desperately ill and diseased were literally placing their lives in the hands of these crude practitioners of the healing arts.

I realize that this is a harsh judgment, and I make it very reluctantly. But I am forced to report the evidence of my own eyes because I sincerely believe that healing of this kind is a clear and present danger. It involves not only the deluded people who submit to the faked ministrations of the kind of 'psychic surgeons' I've described, but it threatens to totally undermine the serious attempts of thinking men and women to complete the bridge between orthodox medicine and the unknown potential for unorthodox methods of helping mankind to better physical and mental health.

Hoy's direct reports regarding sleight of hand used in PS must be taken with utmost seriousness. It puts in doubt much of the evidence reported by non-magician observers. It cannot be taken as proof, however, that *all* PS is fakery.

> *Some circumstantial evidence is very strong, as when you find a trout in the milk.*
>
> – Henry David Thoreau [490]

The qualitative differences between reports by Hoy and those of others regarding psychic surgeon-patient relationships and attitudes eludes definitive explanation. I can only hypothesize selective perception as a contributing, if not final cause, in observations of healers who sometimes perform actual psychic surgery and at other times use sleight of hand. I suggest that each observer may have brought to the situation a set of anticipations and beliefs about what s/he would see. This then becomes a self-fulfilling prophecy by an unconscious process of selective screening of observations.

Andrija Puharich,[491] who described his experiences with PS under the scalpel of Arigo, shared another PS operation he underwent. This one was for otosclerosis, that produced spongy bone growth in his middle ear on both sides, with progressive hearing loss. Pachita, a Mexican healer, treated him.

> I was not hypnotized before the operation, nor was any medication given. I lay down on the table, and some cotton pads were placed around the ear to absorb any bleeding. Three witnesses were present, one of whom took photographs. Holding the knife in her right hand, Pachita quickly inserted 3 inches (7.5 centimeters) of the knife blade into the right ear canal; the forefinger of her left hand guided the blade in. The pain was acute; yet I did not scream, or try to avoid the knife, even though it felt as if the tip of the blade had penetrated the eardrum. After holding the knife in the ear canal for about 40 seconds, Pachita withdrew it, and the pain ceased immediately. The left ear was operated on in a similar way; this time the pain was even greater – close to my breaking point. As soon as the knife was withdrawn however the pain stopped.
>
> The surgery had taken three minutes, no sterile procedure was used, and Pachita's bare hands were covered with blood from previous operations.
>
> After the operation there was only minimal bleeding. But a new complication appeared. My head was ringing with loud noises – so loud that I could not hear what people were saying to me. I was given a tincture (contents unknown) and told to put one drop in each ear daily; the noises decreased gradually, and by the eighth day after the operation had ceased altogether. In fact my hearing was now so acute that I suffered painfully from hyperacusis (abnormally increased power of hearing); this condition lasted for

about two weeks. One month after the operation my hearing was completely back to normal.

Puharich continues with several more cases treated by Pachita.

In the first, she treated a 46 year-old man who had suffered loss of speech for more than a year due to cancer of the larynx. Pachita made an incision in his throat and also inserted the knife in his mouth (apparently to the level of the vocal cords) without anesthesia. He was able to drive himself home after the operation; was drinking and eating normally within 24 hours; speaking hoarsely in eight days; and speaking normally after a month.

In the second, a 34 year-old woman came for treatment of severe damage to her kidneys that had resulted from recurrent infections since age 13.

> ... Pachita decided on a two-stage operation.
>
> In the first operation she inserted the knife in the lumbar region and made a transverse incision 4 inches (10 centimeters) deep across both lumbar muscles and the spine. The patient felt pain, but at tolerable level. Pachita laid open the cavity of each deformed kidney and its corresponding ureter and, as she said, 'cleaned them out.' Two hours after the operation the patient was able to stand, and three days later, when the bandages were removed (showing some signs of pus), the lumbar scar looked like a scratch mark. Six days after the operation, the scar was barely visible.
>
> The second operation took place 12 days later. For the transplant, Pachita obtained a human kidney from an unsterile post-mortem examination. The kidney was suspended in ordinary water in a large glass preserving jar; it was brought to Pachita by taxi some 12 hours before the operation and stored in a kitchen refrigerator. At the start of the second operation the preserving jar was brought to Pachita at the operating table and she lifted the kidney out with her blood-covered hands... she sliced it in two lengthways... to implant the two halves separately on the two sides of the patient. She then handed me the kidney to touch, so that I could be sure it was real.
>
> Pachita then plunged the knife deep into the right side of the patient's back, twisted it around, and asked me...to drop one half-kidney into the hole. I did so, and was surprised to feel the kidney being 'sucked into' the body of the patient... immediately afterwards, I found that the tissue had closed up and the hole was gone! Pachita then plunged the knife some 5 inches...into the patient's other side. She asked me to withdraw it, and I found it took about 20 pounds...of pulling force to extract the blade.
>
> The other half of the kidney was implanted in a similar manner; during the operation the patient experienced only a moderate level of pain. One hour afterwards she was able to stand, unsteadily, and three days after the operation she boarded a commercial airliner and flew back to the United States. She reported, by telephone, a complete and uneventful recovery.

Puharich reports that he saw the blood clot immediately after it left the blood vessels during Pachita's operations. She claimed that the power to control bleeding resided in her left hand, that often guided the tip of the knife which she wielded in her right hand. Postoperative shock, commonly present after ordinary surgery as a feeling of marked weakness and tiredness, was not present. Patients usually rested for a few hours and were then able to stand and walk. Scar tissue was minimal a week following surgery.

Puharich's report is a valuable contribution to the healing literature. It may help to explain some of the doubts of skeptics such as David Hoy regarding the treatments they observed that produced pain and were performed with apparent insensitivity on the part of the healers to the discomforts of the healees.

Tom Valentine, senior articles editor of National Features Syndicate, describes several Philippine psychic surgeons and their work. He takes an aggressive stand against the claims of possible fakery:

> [P]sychic surgery is *not fakery*. The incidents in which faking has been proved beyond the shadow of a doubt are few and far between. Fakery has been alleged many times but proved only rarely. Claims of fakery are as subject to skepticism as are claims of genuine operations...
>
> Skepticism can be overdone. The natives in the heartland of Morocco, living in a primitive desert tribal culture, consider the Apollo moon landings to be a hoax. Even those who saw the events on television considered the Apollo flights to be nothing more than 'Hollywood fakes.' Those desert people are as positive that they are right as you and I are that the landings truly did happen.
>
> When it comes to psychic surgery, the majority of Americans behave like the Bedouins of Morocco. Their narrow comprehension cannot assimilate the information; therefore, it must be a hoax.[492]
>
> Still another scornful allegation made by doubters of psychic surgery is that motion picture films showing the operations are tampered with to look real. This is absurd. The number of home movies of psychic surgery in existence is impressive. It's absurd to believe that persons with no motive other than a conviction about a healing would go to considerable expense to have a film doctored for the purposes of perpetrating a hoax diametrically opposed to their beliefs.[493]

Valentine discusses claims of various observers that the Indian rope trick is an induced mass hallucination.[494] These claims were based on photographs and movie films that revealed the performers to be standing still while the spectators reported they observed the fakirs throwing a rope into the air, climbing it and disappearing at the top, and so on?. Valentine contrasts this with PS, where films and pictures confirm the reported operations.

Valentine[495] points out how negative beliefs can influence scientific analysis:

> With the help of a Filipino-American medical doctor who was in Baguio when we were, I carried out an informal placebo test on a clinic. Two genu-

ine gallstones removed from a living patient were sent to a laboratory, but the clinic was informed that the stones had been removed by psychic surgery. The report came back without a detailed analysis, but it carried a flat statement that the stones were not organic.

Valentine reports several PS operations observed by Hiroshi Motoyama, Enrique Ramos (a Philippine physician) and David M. DeLeon (a pathologist). An epidermal cyst removed by the healer Juan Blance was examined by the laboratories of the Far Eastern University Hospital and the Tokyo University of Medicine. It was reported by both to be composed of normal fatty tissue, as expected.

Valentine[496] also reports cases in which blood samples from PS and healees did not match. He presents observations of Dr. Hans Naegeli (a Swiss psychiatrist who has studied PS extensively) on such problems:

> ...Dr. Naegali... said that he was quite confused when some blood samples of patients were reported by a Zurich laboratory to be 'animal.'
>
> I knew this could not be. I had witnessed the removal from the patient. I discovered that the albumin curves had been altered; to me this could have been due to radiation in the healer's hands, and it certainly did not justify the analysis as animal blood.

Valentine[497] then considers how PS might be understood:

> ... I asked Tony Agpaoa, David Oligani, and Joaquin Cunanan to explain the mechanics of psychic surgery as they understood them. Tony and Oligani are practitioners, but they differ extensively in the method and character (Cunanan is the vice-president of the Espiritistas Union, and he has been a student of yoga, spiritualism, and healing for more than thirty years).
>
> In essence the Filipinos explained that man is made up of many bodies: The 'Holy Spirit,' from a vantage point on high, works through the healers to operate and cure by effecting the necessary changes. Tony and the others accept the concept that our physical bodies fit a pattern, or matrix, formed on another level of existence. This second body is called by various names, including *vital body* and (etheric body).
>
> "If the vital body is opened by a spirit guide working through the healer (mediumship), the physical body will follow the pattern and open also. But this does not have to be so dramatic; many times vital surgery can take place without bleeding or incision. Our healers open the body primarily to dramatize the healing for the patient's benefit," Cunanan explained.
>
> "Yes, I merely plant the seed. The mind of the patient really provides the cure," agreed Agpaoa.
>
> Oligani, who has no education and only occasional contact with culture outside his village, said: "If the patient's higher self does not seek a cure, there will be no cure. Our angels know these things, and only God can cure."

Valentine presents views on spirit-world modes of influencing physical planes of existence. These involve various levels of vibrations and spirit entity interventions. He sees the teaching of PS as the teaching of mediumship.

Valentine excuses some of the eccentricities and observed fakery as due to:

1. Low level spirits that act via the mediumship of the healers and care more for the ego-trip of impressing their earthly audience than for the consequences of their actions; and

2. The fact that healers who go in and out of mediumistic trances cannot recall everything that transpires around them.

Valentine's book is thoughtful and his presentation generally well balanced. His excuses for fakery seem to me questionable.

Related phenomena

An interesting phenomenon, somewhat similar to psychic surgery, is the *deliberately caused bodily damage* (DCBD) taught by Sufi dervishes in Jordan.[498] The dervishes impart to devotees the ability to pierce their flesh with spikes without pain, bleeding or infection. Healing occurs rapidly, sometimes instantaneously.

Various other unusual human abilities have been documented, such as firewalking,[499] handling hot coals and other objects, ingesting strychnine, handling poisonous snakes.[500]

Under hypnosis, people can be without pain during and following surgery, cure their warts, enlarge breasts, and more.[501]

These observations suggest that people have a vast capacity to alter their body functions under alternative states of consciousness.

Discussion

Most of the researchers who observed PS operations were impressed positively with the unusual healings in selected cases, as well as with the legitimacy of the PS phenomena per se. Many investigators note that most of the psychic surgeons indulge in sleight of hand some of the time. Both the PS and the fakery are disturbing to Western observers.

The fact that blood samples in some cases matched those of the patients suggests PS may be legitimate.

That many instances of sleight of hand maneuvers have been observed and that the magician, David Hoy, was able to reproduce PS effects through sleight of hand techniques does not prove that *all* cases of PS are faked. The Philippine surgeons operate on many problems over many hours in a hot climate, where refrigerators are not available. Magicians have replicated such feats in single demonstrations. They have not replicated a long series of such operations under conditions similar to those of the Philippine psychic surgeons, who hasten to point out that a large store of body fluids and parts would be required if one were to be faking this over a period of time.

Cultural differences between Philippine and Western observers must be taken into account in discussing these issues. Western science holds honesty to be a virtue. In other cultures, honesty (at least in the practice of healers) does not have as high a priority relative to other values. I am not familiar with Philippine culture in particular but my years in Israel made me aware of ethical and moral systems with priorities very different from those I was raised with in the United States. In the Middle East, for instance, honor and chauvinistic adherence to nationalistic policies that may shift and sometimes even reverse from week to week are common. Honesty has a different meaning in such a context. I have to hypothesize that cultural practices and standards particular to their culture are present in the Philippines as well. Although such explanations do not make our evaluation of PS any easier, they may help us understand (although not necessarily condone) practices that in our culture would be far less acceptable. More on this shortly.

George Meek excuses the psychic surgeons' use of tricks. He notes that no psychic is able to produce psi effects one-hundred percent of the time and that Philippine healers are overwhelmed with large numbers of people seeking their help. Tony Agpaoa and Licauco's healers report that they produced physical effects primarily to convince their healees that something had actually been done, so that they would not 'undo' the healing effects. This is consistent with most healers' statements that disbelief on the part of healees in their ability to improve can retard or even block entirely either the receptiveness to healing, or can undermine the permanence of healing effects. This could explain their use of sleight of hand as merely another method to convince healees that a healing was effected.

While any number of cases of fakery do not prove that *all* PS is fakery, the fact that many of the Philippine psychic surgeons have been observed on some occasions engaging in sleight of hand makes a researcher suspect any single instance of PS. This is exactly the opposite of the effect that Agpaoa claimed the fakery is supposed to achieve, which is to confirm that something actually occurred.

One must deduce that the healers are concerned primarily with the responses of their healees and not with those of researchers.

One cannot help contrasting reports of PS from the Philippines with reports of PS done by Arigo in Brazil. Arigo did not hesitate to say to some that he was unable to help them. He was never noted to fake surgery or to attempt to impress through tricks. This is all the more certain, as the Brazilian medical community prosecuted and jailed him for practicing medicine without a license – but found no evidence that he faked his PS.

It is difficult to dismiss the PS performed under the rigorous scrutiny of Meek as fake. The personal reports of Puharich add support though they are not nearly as rigorous.

Possible mechanisms for PS

The whole of science consists of data that, at one time or another, were inexplicable.

– Brendan O'Regan

Assuming that some of the cases of PS are genuine psi manipulations of healees' bodies, we must ask how they might occur. Several types of healing appear to be possible.

PS-I, with surgery performed in the aura rather than on the body, was developed independently by Rev. Brown in the States and George Chapman in the U.K. Whether the etheric body is a template for the physical or whether these rituals are effective simply by impressing the patients needs further study.

The observations of sensitives who see auras would be helpful in assessing and understanding what occurs with PS-I.

PS-I may be involved in PS-II. Motoyama and Stelter hypothesize that PS-I (interventions through the aura) may be used during PS-II. The healer may remove a diseased portion of the astral body from within the patient and then materialize it outside the physical body. Healers elsewhere also state that treatments in the auric or etheric body transfer their effects to the healee's physical body.[502] Such procedures may involve resonance of the healee's and the healer's biofields. This could alternatively represent the healer's unconscious mind processing clairsentient diagnostic information from the healee and transmitting therapeutic suggestions telepathically to her, activating self-healing in the healee's body.

Barbara Brennan[503] suggests similarly that PSII involves alterations of the physical body through manipulation of the energy fields that control the body. The fields are influenced in such a way as to separate tissues of the body wall, remove growths and then to unite the tissues again at the end of the procedure. She also reported in personal observations of psychic surgeons in London[504] that with cuppings there appeared to be a drawing out of negative energies from the region around the incision.

Plume[505] and Chesi present similar hypotheses regarding the healer's hands vibrating in a different plane of existence so that penetration of the body becomes possible. Such explanations sound non*sens*ical in sensory reality but may have lost a lot in translation from other realities into linear concepts and language. Precisely what it means to vibrate on a different plane remains to be clarified.

It is likely that a combination of mechanisms is at play. The psychic surgeons have been reported to demonstrate clairsentient diagnostic abilities. Not only are some able to pinpoint illness within the body without being told the diagnosis and without needing to examine the body via normal sensory means, but they are also allegedly able to identify when another psychic surgeon gave healing treatments to the same healee and to identify who this was. Most do spiritual healing without surgery in addition to PS.

In PS-II, the direct alteration of the body, Stelter proposes that healers use PK to move a diseased part, growth, or stone (let us just call this an 'object') out of the healee's body via a body orifice. Though this may seem logical at first glance, it makes little anatomical sense to anyone familiar with the structures of the body.

I suggest that the most logical change in linear terms would be a temporary dematerialization of either the tissues to be removed or of the body surrounding it or both. That is, the involved tissues would be altered in some way so as to offer no obstruction to other matter they might encounter as they are removed. One can postulate that an etheric matter, of which auras, OBE bodies, ghosts and mediumistic materializations are made, or *bioplasma* might be a transitional state of the pathological tissues that the healer could produce.

Even without specifying the mechanism(s) involved, one can cite parallel evidence of PK in John Hasted's experiments, in which metal objects sealed in transparent containers were partially or totally removed from these containers by PK without any apparent tampering or damage to the containers.[506] In Cox's experiments, rubber and wooden rings in sealed containers were filmed linking and unlinking.[507] These observations suggest that objects can be moved through each other in some manner. Though it would seem that moving tissues through tissues would be far more complex a task (than moving metals through glass and plastic, wood through wood, or rubber through rubber), this is purely conjecture when the underlying processes are so totally obscure.

The added factors of the human elements in healing – involving biological fields, perceptions, beliefs, will, etc. of the healee – add further complexities. On the other hand, these complexities may also facilitate *biological* PK if the forces maintaining the healees' body integrity can be manipulated via changes in their perceptions and beliefs with the help of the healer.

Here we run into difficulties with the observed phenomena. If the object is dematerialized, it should logically make no difference where it emerges from the body. It would seem an easier route, in fact, to have it come directly, let us say, from the abdomen through the flank than to move it circuitously to a body orifice.

Stelter provides few details to clarify through which body orifices he observed these objects emerge, although he mentions the umbilicus in some abdominal cases and the nose in lesions of the nasal passages and sinuses. Logic of sensory reality does not seem to fit either of these two cases: The umbilicus is not an orifice; and, in the case of the nose, Stelter mentions that creating an opening at the bridge of the nose is frequent. Thus the linear logic of economy of dematerialization does not seem to apply.

Perhaps it is simply psychologically easier sometimes for healers and/or healees to facilitate (or not counteract) a dematerialization of the body through the aperture of a natural body orifice. More study is required.

The apparent opening of the body by PS with hands or knife, would seem to be a more difficult procedure to complete than a dematerialization for two reasons. First, by sensory reality reasoning, repairing a wound ought to require more meticulous work than effecting a rematerialization. That is, when the body is opened (by hand or instrument), it must then be closed again. Each tissue layer and blood vessel that was severed and separated must be reunited for the completion of the healing. Second, Stelter's description of Agpaoa's learning to become a healer indicates a progression from dematerializations to PS using the hands as instruments to enter the body. This may represent a hierarchical step in terms of procedural difficulty. Alternatively, it may only be a *conceptual* hierarchy of beliefs/disbeliefs that needs to be addressed as the student healer adapts to new realities.

The fact that mediums can produce materializations and dematerializations suggests modest support for reports that healers can do likewise or can facilitate healees' doing so on their own as self-healing.

Watson and others cite examples of PS incisions and injections that left needle-like marks. The incisions were made in some instances through a plastic sheet, when the sheet was not cut. The injections sometimes left small holes in the plastic but in other instances did not. The intact sheets demonstrate that hidden knives could not have been used in those instances; the pierced ones indicate that this is probably not produced by a mechanism similar to that of the appearance of stigmata, in which wounds are also known to materialize on the body.[508]

Confirming that healers can produce cuts in other materials, Motoyama[509] and Sherman witnessed the cutting of wads of adhesive tape by Agpaoa by his pointing a finger or other parts of his body at them. These observations make it evident that actual physical phenomena may be produced by healers – not just illusions or changes in the auric body.

Many problems make it hard to analyze these reports. Sensory reality logic may not be applicable,[510] and difficulties in analyzing procedures of which we have only second- or third-hand observations is a risky process at best.

Considering PS from the perspective of the healee, we have evidence from anecdotal and research reports that people can alter their pain perceptions and can profoundly influence their bodies in various ways through mental intent and alternative states of consciousness, including the production of stigmata – wounds that mirror the wounds of Christ. It is possible that part or all of PS may be produced by the beliefs of the healees under the suggestions of the healers.

Let us consider other aspects of PS. Philippine healers have stated that the effects they produce are not necessary for a healing but are done to impress the healee.[511] It may be that they understated the truth and that *all* of the apparent dramatic PS effects (without surgical instruments), including the surgeons' seeming insertion of their hands within the healees' bodies, are illusion.[512] This might be consonant with some of the reports of very strange-looking incisions and very strange, incomprehensible tissues and organs within the incisions, reported by competent, experienced surgeons. These may be telepathic projections or materializations from the imagination of the healer.

Numerous photographs and films of PS-II incisions have been made, in which it seems impossible that mass suggestion could have been used. It would be interesting to check whether strange tissues appear on these visual records and to have experts examine the films to assure that they have not been fabricated or altered.

A skeptic might seek to explain away the films as a product of PK on film (*thoughtography*).[513] This is extremely unlikely, based on several studies of *thoughtography*. Photographs produced by PK are fuzzy. It seems highly unlikely that sharp pictures would be produced on motion picture film or videotape only in the instance of PS – thus seeming to rule out thoughtography as an explanation.

> *A man receives only what he is ready to receive... The phenomenon or fact that cannot in any wise be linked with the rest of what he has observed, he does not observe. By and by we may be ready to receive what we cannot receive now.*
>
> – Henry David Thoreau

Laboratory examinations of tissues removed by PS

Laboratories have given mixed reports – some with matches between the samples and blood types of the healees and others with mismatches of blood typing and reports that the tissues were from various animals.

Motoyama and Stelter propose that in PS-II the psychic surgeon's hands enter the body to remove the tissue in a non-physical dimension, rematerializing it outside the body. Motoyama also uses such hypotheses to explain the fact that blood and tissues removed during PS-II do not always match those of the healee and sometimes are not even real blood (setting aside obvious cases where such tissues have been identified as having an animal source). Although such explanations may apply, they seem farfetched. When the psychic surgeon removes his hands from the surgical field, the body tissues are restored to complete integrity. One presumes that the closure has to involve materialization of tissue to bond at least the edges of the wound and seal severed blood vessels that nourished the cut tissues, if not also to fill or close a defect created by removal of tissues. As minimal scars are noted, it seems most likely that if dematerialization and rematerialization are involved, the psychic surgeon is able to produce normal human tissue with great precision. If he can do it in the instance of PS perfectly, it is hard to understand why he could or would not do it so well in the instance of blood and tissue samples.

The examinations of blood that were reported as sometimes matching the healees' and sometimes not[514] are perplexing. Granted that some instances may involve sleight of hand, we still have cases in which the fluid was found not even to be blood. In these instances, fakery must still remain high on the list of possibilities. It is interesting that an investigation of an American stigmatist, Sister Lucy, demonstrated blood that was reported by the laboratory to be untypeable.[515] Several physicians witnessed her phenomena, which suggests that fakery was unlikely, though the report of Starr is far from sufficiently complete to permit a confident conclusion.

On the other hand, it may be that the psychic surgeons concentrate more on visualizing the proper rematerializations of the healee's body than they do on rematerializing the specimens that are removed and discarded. The discrepancies between blood and tissue samples taken with PS and healees' blood drawn by scientists ultimately might prove to be evidence for the legitimacy of PS.

The need factor may be important in PS. It appears that psi phenomena, including healing, occur often in association with a true need on the part of the participants. In many cases the one responsible for the psi effects does not know how he brings them about. He merely hopes, wishes, asks or prays for the desired result, leaving the processes to occur as they may. If the desired result in PS is that a healing occurs and that the healee believes sufficiently it is possible she may be healed, the Philippine healers certainly have a method that works. The appearance of red fluid resembling blood would certainly be adequate for such purposes.

One might question whether the needs of the observing scientist to be convinced of the legitimacy of the phenomena would not be included in the aggregate of needs that shape the process of PS and that therefore this explanation is invalid. Since the scientists observing PS may actually be put off by the appearance of fluids that do not match the blood of the healee, the scientists' needs appear to be ignored in this process. Possibly, the unconscious needs of the scientist may be to understand the psychological and psi processes involved. Therefore, materializations of red fluid or blood which does not match the healee's blood types may point out important aspects of PS that would otherwise be ignored. More likely, the needs of the scientist may not be of as high priority as those of the healer and healee.

Yet another possibility is that skeptical scientists actually do contribute to the PS – by altering the tissues psychically so that the results conform with their skeptical beliefs. This has been found in many other studies of psi effects, and has acquired the name of *the sheep-goat effect.* Believers in psi (*sheep*) very frequently demonstrate psi effects significantly more often than chance expectations, while disbelievers (*goats*) score significantly less often than chance.[516]

Spiritual healing and PS

The PS and even the physical problem may not be the most important parts of the process. In the quoted reports of Licauco, Motoyama and Valentine this is clearly indicated. *The spiritual advancement of the healee is felt to be of higher priority.* This is echoed by healers around the world.[517]

My personal impression is that PS is most likely a legitimate psychic phenomenon some of the time, as supported by the reports of Meek and of physician observers of PS,. This would be the epitome of energy medicine, involving applied PK under volitional control of the healers.

As in any other aspect of healing, it is clear that more, carefully observed studies would be of benefit. Until we have these it is unlikely we will know the true value of such procedures.

As to comprehending their mechanisms, I am reminded of the quote from Lawrence Young:

> A combined group of our scientists have been studying bees and have made the following discovery - bees can't fly! Bees can't fly!
> Now, I know you find this difficult to grasp, but a study [detailed] the wing surface compared to body mass, the center of gravity, and drag ratio to airflow and lateral axis, [plus the facts that] they have no horizontal stabilizer and their aerodynamics are all wrong. The scientists gave the bees an aptitude test – the bee flying aptitude test or 'BFAT' and the bees failed. So what we see is an optical illusion or the bees refusing to be limited by what others conclude they cannot do.[518]

The most important aspect of psychic surgery is that it challenges us to consider in a fresh way our intimate, bioenergetic, and spiritual relationships with each other and with the world around us. We are far more intimately linked with others and with our environment through our resonations than we are taught to believe in Western science.

My personal experiences with PS

I was present when a Philippine psychic surgeon, Emilio Laporga, operated in London in 1990[519] on a woman's cheek to remove a parotid (salivary gland) tumor that had been treated surgically three times previously over many years. He used surgical instruments without anesthesia, removing the tumor with forceps in little chunks through a small incision. The woman had considerable pain during the procedure. I spoke with her about 20 hours later. She had two small adhesive strips over her cheek, with no apparent discoloration or swelling. She declared she was free of pain and had a good appetite. She estimated this compared to her state at about four or five days post-operatively in the three previous treatments of her tumor. She complained that she had not been warned the procedure would be painful, but asserted she would choose this procedure again over conventional surgery because of her rapid and painless recovery.

I know other healers whose healees self-correct their physical problems through various movements of their bodies (such as stretching, bending, and moving body parts in other ways) despite this being quite painful to do. The healees complain of the pain at the time, but comment that it feels like this was a necessary step towards healing, and is thus tolerable.[520]

It may also be that a measure of pain serves to convince the healee that actual treatment occurred. This would be similar to the production of copious amounts of blood and/or other apparent materializations that may serve the same purpose.

I saw a film in 1975 of Arigo at work. An eye that was exophthalmic (bulging beyond the eye socket) settled back into place immediately after Arigo plunged a knife blade into the orbit, forcing the eye to bulge even further, as he scraped out what looked like pus from behind it. The patient demonstrated no pain or discomfort during the procedure. It seems unlikely to me that this film could have been faked.

I also saw a videotape of the late Edson Queiroz, a Brazilian gynecologist, who claimed that Arigo's spirit guide, Dr. Fritz, was guiding him in his PS. He, too, manipulated eyes – rubbing the cornea, inserting needles in the orbits and excising growths from the sclera (white of the eye) without anesthesia. He used no sterile technique. These, plus other surgical procedures with knives and forceps, were performed by Queiroz rapidly and apparently without causing pain.

In summary

Psychic surgery has been reported by sufficient numbers of careful observers that it is difficult to dismiss it as fakery. This is particularly so in view of films that have been taken of the procedures and of reports of chronic conditions that were cured by PS.

Several of the psychic surgeons have stated that the gory procedures are actually unnecessary, but that these help to convince people dramatically that a change has occurred so that they can release their illnesses.

Skeptics have pointed out that sleight of hand could account for many of the reported effects of PS. I am impressed that while some effects might be reproduced through stage type magic tricks, effects such as eye operations without pain have never been reproduced in these ways.

What is glaringly missing is a series of people whose diseases were clearly diagnosed prior to PS and subsequently confirmed as cured following treatment – with objective laboratory studies before and after. This has been done with pilgrims at Lourdes[521] and there is no reason in principle that it cannot be done with PS. Having said that, however, one must acknowledge that thousands of reports are sifted at Lourdes to obtain only a handful of validated healings.

If we accept that PS is legitimate, and that the physical body can dematerialize and rematerialize during healings, then here is further support for a belief that spiritual and bioenergetic levels of reality are primary and physical reality is secondary. This view is consistent with reports from NDEs, reincarnation memories and mediumistic experiences, suggesting that physical existence is an educational excursion into the world of matter for a lifetime (or series of lifetimes), between lessons that are pursued in spiritual worlds of existence.

Having reviewed anecdotal and research reports on a broad spectrum of spiritual phenomena, let us now consider the place of spiritual awareness and healing in religious contexts.

CHAPTER 8

Religions and Healing

> In the floods of life,
> In the storm of work,
> In the ebb and flow
> In warp and weft,
> Cradle and grave,
> An eternal sea,
> A changing patchwork,
> A glowing life,
> At the whirring loom of time I weave
> The living clothes of the Deity.
>   – Goethe [522]

Introduction

Healing has been an integral part of most religions. Healing is often intimately linked and interwoven with religious practices. In religions of traditional cultures where mythical and clairsentient realities[523] are accepted aspects of everyday life, healing is a natural part of existence. All aspects of life are directly related to each other, to the physical world, as well as to spirits and/or gods in other dimensions. Illness is being out of tune with one's world. Healing in these cultures is a harmonizing of oneself with the total environment, including one's inner self, relationships with family and friends, and interactions with all of the cosmos. Healing is a return to wholeness and harmony on all levels of one's being.

In Western societies many of us have relegated religion to a portion of our lives that is largely separated from our everyday existence. Western religions are frequently practiced primarily as rituals of worship on particular 'holy' days of the week or year but bear little influence on working days or secular holidays. Religion in the West is no longer connected with medical treatment (which itself is also compartmentalized from the rest of our lives in a focus upon the physical body). Religion in Western society may thus be distanced or even devoid of spiritual awareness and spiritual practice.

In traditional societies, religion is an integral part of life. Living closer to nature, people sense the spirits in the land, the waters, the air, the growing plants and the animals that sustain their lives. They pray to spirits and to God for guidance, trusting their intuitive knowing of the responses they receive.

Joseph Felser[524] notes that the word *religion* derives originally from *relegare* or *relictio*, Latin for "the careful reading of the great book of nature." In the early years of the Christian church, religious authorities saw nature as fallen and evil and were displeased with this definition. They replaced it with a similar sounding word with a totally different meaning: *religare* or *religio*, which means "strict obedience to authority." For many centuries, when State and Church combined to rule the populace, this definition made the church the source of explanations for secular as well as for religious matters. Scientific methodology and explanations were opposed by the church as this contradicted their views of nature.

In Western society many have rejected religious authority as a source for explaining the physical world. In doing so, they have rejected religious explanations for spiritual matters. This is the reverse error – of applying the rules for dealing with the physical world to matters of the spirit.

At the same time, *scientism* has become in many ways the religion of the Western world, in an existence focused on and explained by materialistic theories. Science claims the ability to explain the workings of the world and all that it contains. It assumes that increasingly refined linear analyses of all matter and of all of nature's processes will ultimately explain every aspect of the cosmos.

> *Modern science itself is based on the idea that the universe is governed by invisible principles, the laws of nature. These laws are essentially intellectual because mathematical equations are things that exist in minds. They're not physical things you actually encounter in the world. You don't look through an electron microscope and see Schrödinger's equation among the molecules, or look through a telescope and see Einstein's equations written in the sky. They are invisible governing principles. But they are conceived of in an extremely limited and noncreative sense, as abstract mathematical equations rather than as living minds with creative power. Creativity is supposed to come into the evolutionary process through blind chance.*
>
> *[I]nsofar as people believe that mathematical equations are the ultimate truth, this is a form of idolatry. It treats manmade mathematical models as the ultimate reality.*
>
> – Rupert Sheldrake [525]

In traditional societies shamans embody in one person the priest, doctor and counselor.[526] In some societies a shaman may also provide an alternative to the functions of judge, jury, and police force.[527] Western society has split up these functions into sub-specialties. Physical problems are addressed by doctors;

psychological ones by social workers, psychologists, psychiatrists (and by default, bartenders, hairdressers, and other good listeners); and spiritual questions by clergy. Inevitably, this leaves people who need such services feeling fragmented.

There is a growing movement away from this fragmenting approach in segments of Western society. Wholistic medicine seeks to address body, emotions, mind, relationships, and spirit. Clergy are including counseling in their ministries and some churches are taking more seriously the spiritual healing component in their services. An occasional doctor will address spiritual issues.[528] Spiritual healing is becoming more accepted and more openly advertises its being a doorway to spiritual awareness. This 'S-word' can now be spoken in many medical, nursing, counseling, and educational forums – where previously this was uncomfortable.

> *Plus ça change, plus c'est la même chose.*
> *(The more things change, the more they are the same.)*
> – Alphonse Karr [529]

Western religions commonly include sorely attenuated elements of healing. Prayer, the primary agency for healing, is used in several fashions that are discussed below.

In its truest and deepest sense, healing is about connecting with spiritual awareness. Spirituality is a qualitative state of being that may be invoked and developed in religious, meditative, mystical, and healing practices. It may lead to or result from healings for physical and psychological problems. It may also be a subject for scientific research, that we shall consider shortly.

> *The cosmic religious experience is the strongest and noblest mainspring of scientific research.*
> – Albert Einstein [530]

> *I make a distinction between spirituality and religion. Religion is for people who are afraid of going to hell; spirituality is for people who have been there.*
> – Timothy J. Mordaunt

Spirit healing is another dimension of spirituality and religion. It is practiced in spiritualist churches, where members invoke aid from surviving entities of people who died ('passed on') and who are now living in spirit.

Some healers report they see and hear spirits and are aware of other dimensions while dreaming or in a normal, waking state. Other healers may consult with spirits while in mediumistic or hypnotic trances. Many spirit healers have spirit guides or advisors who assist them in their ministrations. Yet others feel they are taken over by or *channel* spirits temporarily. They report that the spirits effect healings directly through the healer's physical and/or bioenergetic bodies.

Theologians and philosophers have discussed and debated over many centuries the nature of spiritual worlds. Today, scientists and transpersonal psychologists debate whether spirit exists or is the product of wishful thinking, religious teachings, cultural beliefs or delusions. Earlier chapters review evidence suggesting that a world of spirits does exist and evidence for an energy body that may be a basis for healing[531] and may survive death.

The discussion of religions and healing in this chapter in no way presumes to be exhaustive. It considers a representative sampling of relevant views and reports from amongst the very rich traditions of healing within a spectrum of religions.

Spiritual awareness and healing will then be discussed in Chapter III-11.

A spectrum of religious views

> *Our whole hope for understanding our world is based on our faith and confidence that the world is orderly, that natural phenomena are dependable, repetitive, consistent, understandable and perhaps controllable. All that science has discovered confirms that events respond to analysis and synthesis, hypothesis and verification and that sure knowledge results from this approach.*
>
> *If natural phenomena are not consistent, if God can and does play tricks in His world at variance with His own laws, then the world can not be understood; then are we mere puppets... without freedom of thought and will to work out our problems and realize our potentials; then Jesus' faith in a Kingdom of evolving Sons of God is foolishness. For these reasons, we should not accept uncritically explanations of events that run counter to the existing structure of knowledge or the concept of an order unifying nature.*
> — Charles C. Wise, Jr.

> *... There are many good paths: Christian, Buddhist, Hindu, Sufi. I prefer brand names – the great traditions – because they've been tried by one or two hundred million people and they have the kinks worked out...*
> — Jack Kornfield [532]

Judaism and healing

> *According to Rabbi Nachman, prayer is a dialogue between humans and their Creator and is absolutely key in the repair of the world. The ultimate goal in Jewish teaching is to bring the world to a state of tikkun. Rabbi Weintraub explains that this word implies repair, correction, wholeness, and perfection. Tikkun repairs the Covenant relationship and bridges the separation between the people and God.*
> Linda L. Smith [533]

Being Jewish, I find it disappointing that Judaism has traditionally not emphasized healing in any major way. Through the past thousand and more years the practice of medicine has been a respected profession for Jews, yet healing has been viewed officially since Biblical times as a pagan practice, not to be encouraged. However, in the typical pragmatic acceptance of human nature, Jewish tradition allows that for treatment of illness a person is not to be censured if he seeks such help.[534]

A number of Orthodox and Hassidic rabbis have been gifted healers in centuries past and in modern times. Their practices have been based largely on ritual prayer and on prayers written on little slips of paper that are held by the healee as amulets.[535]

Persecution and possession by nasty spirits (called *dibbuks*) have been recognized more in folklore than in religious literature. I have not been able to find any serious writings on Jewish healing practices.

A number of Jewish healing centers are now offering various spiritual healing approaches in the US and UK.

It is encouraging that over the past few years a few innovative rabbis have been introducing healing services that invite the congregants to develop and practice their own healing gifts.

Christianity (in general) and healing

> *... they are quite incapable of filling the gap, because this infinite gulf can only be filled by an infinite and immutable object – that is, God, Himself. He alone is man's veritable good, and since man has deserted Him it is a strange thing that there is nothing in nature that has not been capable of taking His place for man: stars, sky, earth, elements, plants, cabbages, leeks, animals, insects, calves, serpents, fever, plague, war, famine, vices, adultery, incest. And since he has lost the true good, everything can equally appear to him as such -- even his own destruction, though that is so contrary at once to God, to reason, and to nature.*
>
> – Blaise Pascal

Christ was a potent healer[536] and Christianity has a rich tradition of spiritual healing. It is of note that modern English takes the word *healing* from the Anglo-Saxon *haelan*, meaning 'to cure or restore to wholeness,' used relating to spiritual as well as bodily ills.[537] In Old English writings, *haeland* was often used in place of the name, *Jesus*.[538]

Christianity provides some thought-provoking observations on healing.

Many have pondered why some are healed and others not. Carried beyond the physical and energy medicine levels, this leads to theological questions of good and evil, sin and punishment, justice in heavenly judgments, and other challenging issues.

Agnes Sanford[539] focuses on the beliefs and faith of Christian healers and healees as relating to success and failure in healing.

> "Prayer is only auto-suggestion," some people say.
>   Those who really experiment with prayer know from its results that it is far more than auto-suggestion. But even auto-suggestion, so far as it goes,

follows out the laws of God. For who is the 'auto' that makes the suggestions? It is the inner being that is part of God speaking to the framework of flesh...

When we realize that God is not only transcendent, He is also immanent – that is, He is not only in the heaven and the heaven of heavens, but also in our own small minds and bodies... We see that the lack of success in healing is not due to God's will for us but to our failure to live near enough to God so that He can accomplish His will in us. If we do not give Him an opportunity to accomplish perfection in our spirits and bodies, He will do the next best thing and endeavor with divine patience to teach us through suffering. In this case we are receiving as much of His life-giving spirit as He can get through to us, but not the full flow necessary to life...

God is standing before us with the answer in His hands. But unless we reach out our hands and take it by giving thanks for it, we are not apt to receive it. For while love is the wiring that connects our souls with His, faith is the switch that turns on the power...

When our electric lights work partially or not at all, we know that the lack of power is not in the universal and infinite and eternal flow of electricity in the universe, but in the wiring that connects us with that flow...

Sanford shares her vast experience in working out ways to get healees and their families to believe that they can get better; to visualize themselves being better; and to call upon higher powers to help them. I find her writings among the clearest on the powers of Christian faith in healing, without invoking blame, guilt and sin.[540]

Morton T. Kelsey presents an excellent history of the origins and evolution of sacramental healing in the Christian church. Here the healer deliberately and consciously invokes the spirit of God to act through himself. Kelsey views Jesus' attitude towards healing as an indication of God's attitude towards it.

If sin is understood as turning aside from God's way, failing to follow the way of wholeness or individuation, there is good reason for believing that this leads to illness. Men who lose their religious way or have found none to follow, find themselves exposed to destructive spiritual forces that often trigger emotional disturbances. Thus they are open to fear and hate; to mental distress, meaninglessness and despair; to destructive emotions that are almost a catalogue of the cardinal sins.

Yet although some illness is caused by sin, Jesus did not have any illusion that therefore it all originates in sin. Nor did he hold that once a man had stepped off the way and was suffering for it, he ought to be made to endure the full burden of his mistake.

The coming of Jesus, if indeed he was the incarnation of God, wipes out once and for all the notion that God puts sickness upon men because he is angry with them. Jesus' ministry of healing embodies the exact antithesis of this idea. He did not inquire whether a man was good or bad, whether he had repented or was reforming, before he healed him.

Kelsey discusses modern church attitudes towards healing, and summarizes succinctly some of the emotional factors that may be involved. He feels the church can provide the sick with help to understand their place in the cosmos via intellectual and theological frameworks; with a place for discussion; with a loving religious community; and with the healing sacrament.

Charles C. Wise, Jr., considers aspects of Christian healings.

> God does the actual healing, through the power of the collective hope, faith and expectation of those present...
>
> Not all illnesses should be healed. Some may be handicaps which encourage strength in their overcoming. Paul was a great healer, but Christ smote Paul and Paul was not healed of his 'thorn of the flesh' though oft he prayed for healing (2 Corinthians 12:7-10). The answer always was: "My Grace is sufficient for you." So it often is for us...
>
> It is dangerous to force the healing of an illness (which may be a set of symptoms rather than an entity) without curing the cause... '
>
> It is preferable to pray and to invoke healing, not for the cure of a specific ailment, but more generally for what is best for the whole person (the mind-body-spirit entity)...
>
> Physical healing should not be made the test of faith. It occurs best as the bonus or byproduct of love in action and is rather less 'healthy' when raised to the level of primary aim... '

Historical notes on Christianity and healing
The late Bruce MacManaway,[541] a British healer and teacher of healing, provides historical notes on ways in which the church disassociated itself from healers and healing in the early stages of its history.[542]

In the early centuries after Christ, the priests were healers as well as religious leaders. As the church grew, there were two groups involved in healing which evolved separately: the healers and prophets who dealt with the people directly and the priests and bishops who were church officials. The latter felt their authority threatened by the former.

> The crunch came over a group of churches in Phrygia in Asia Minor where Montanus and his followers, and in particular two very gifted women, were gaining a dangerous amount of influence by their prophesying and healing. According to the historian Tertullian, a priest called Praxeus was largely responsible for persuading the Bishop of Rome to excommunicate the affected churches and brand their members as heretics.[543]

This gradually led to a ban on lay healers, with the priests addressing themselves to theology and administration.

> With Constantine's conversion and the gradual adoption of Christianity as the predominant state religion, what had previously been a Church ban acquired all the penalties of secular law and for a layman to practice any of

the gifts of the Spirit became a very risky business. The practicing of the gifts within the auspices of the Church was allowed, and the Church had its 'saints.' Even they, however, were and are grilled pretty thoroughly before gaining acceptance. Anyone outside the Church's control ran the risk of the accusation of heresy or witchcraft... By claiming a monopoly of the gifts of the Spirit, the Church has alternately brainwashed and bullied the population into thinking that any person trying to heal without the proper qualifications must be in league with the Devil. I maintain that this is not in accordance with the teachings of Christ himself, who lived and taught amongst laymen. It is not surprising, however, that healing went underground.[544]

MacManaway points out that it was not until the early 1950s that the Witchcraft Act in Britain was laid aside. It carried the death penalty and could have been applied to healers.[545]

MacManaway also explores historical attitudes of the church to various spiritual issues reviewed in earlier chapters of this book, such as spirit contacts and mediumship. He points out that the early church was quite open to communication with God via such intermediaries although always adjuring that care be taken to distinguish good spirits from evil ones.

> *The altar cloth of one aeon is the doormat of the next.*
> – Mark Twain

Traditionally, Christians have held strongly negative views on reincarnation

[R]eincarnation represents a threat to the very essence of Christianity: the need for Christ's redemptive sacrifice for our sins. If we are to pay for the consequences of our sins ourselves in further lives and attain salvation through our own efforts, the sacrifice of Christ becomes useless and absurd. It wouldn't be the only way back to God, but only a stupid accident of history. In this case Christianity would be a mere form of Hindu Bhakti-Yoga.[546]

Helen Greaves points out that there was a 500-year tradition of belief in reincarnation in the Alexandrian school, including such proponents as Clement, Justin Martyr, St. Gregory of Nyasa and Origen. "The Council of Constantinople in AD 553, at which it seems a corrupt form of Origen's teaching was anathematized, is held by many historians to have been imperfectly constituted – the Pope himself refused to be present – and even Roman Catholics contest its validity as a General Council."

Henry Chadwick, former Regius Professor of Divinity at Oxford University, an acknowledged world expert on church history, stated, "I don't recall a Council condemning belief in Transmigration... Councils only dismiss and regulate when a serious group (led at least by a bishop) advocates a position contrary to the *consensus fidelium*." He feels that a pessimism inherent in reincarnation beliefs has been the reason for its rejection by the Church.[547]

There are a minority who consider reincarnation a theory compatible with Christian teachings. Hugh Montefiore points to concepts of spirit survival and reincarnation in the Old and New Testaments. They are compatible with a compassionate God, who would not condemn dead fetuses and unbaptized children to limbo and would give sinners more than one chance to redeem themselves.

Relationships with spirits have similarly seen a spectrum of Christian opinions. In the past few centuries, there has been a strong move away from spirit contacts in segments of the church, basing their doctrine largely on portions of Deuteronomy,[548]

> There shall not be found among you any one that maketh his son or his daughter to pass through the fire or that useth divination or an observer of times or an enchanter or a witch or a charmer or a consulter with familiar spirits or a wizard or a necromancer. For all that do these things are an abomination unto the Lord...

In recent years, there has been a resurgence of interest in personal spiritual experiences in some churches. In some instances this can include a respect for personal reincarnation memories.

Catholicism and healing

> *On the part of official pronouncements the most far-reaching of all the changes in understanding the sacraments went into effect January 1, 1974. The 'Anointing of the Sick' is now for the professed purpose of healing the whole man and is no longer primarily a preparation of the soul for death. In line with this reorientation of the sacrament's purpose, it is to be administered not just to those in danger of death, but to anyone suffering from a serious illness.*[549]
>
> – Catholic Conference (U.S.)

Francis MacNutt, influential in the Charismatic Christian renewal healing movement, presents Catholic historical perspectives and views on healing. Starting with Biblical quotations on healings by Jesus and his disciples, he traces the history of the initial growth, then the decline and lately the rebirth of awareness of healing in the Catholic Church. Marking the current day healing renaissance, MacNutt cites the above quote.

Considering suffering, MacNutt explains that illness is not 'a cross to bear,' because it comes from within and was never viewed as such in the Bible. (This is in contrast with external misfortunes.)

MacNutt distinguishes four kinds of sickness:

1. Sickness of our spirit, caused by our own personal sin;
2. Emotional sickness and problems (e.g., anxiety) caused by the emotional hurts of our past;

3. Physical sickness in our bodies, caused by disease or accidents; and

4. In addition, any of the above – sin, emotional problems or physical sickness – can be caused by demonic oppression, a different cause that requires a different prayer approach, namely, prayer for exorcism.[550]

MacNutt delineates four methods of prayer, respectively, for each of these:

1. Prayer for repentance;
2. Prayer for inner healing ('healing of memories');
3. Prayer for physical healing; and
4. Prayer for deliverance (exorcism).[551]

Complementing prayers, MacNutt further advises cooperation with physicians and surgeons.

Healing miracles are a prominent aspect of religious traditions. Many of the saints were beatified on the basis of their extraordinary healings. Modern science tends to view these with skepticism. The Catholic church has accommodated to its critics, now including doctors in its assessments of whether unusual recoveries from illness are truly miraculous.

Francois Leuret and Henri Bon explain how, as devout Catholics, they view *scientific research of miraculous cures*. They read in Genesis that the world was given to man for his use. For this reason humans were endowed with intelligence. It is their right and duty to explore nature in as far as it is possible. This is their way to find God. A precedent can be found in the story of Moses, who was drawn to examine the burning bush that was not consumed. In this action he came face to face with God.

> *Except ye see signs and wonders, ye will not believe.*
> – St. John

Leuret and Bon claim that it is similarly our right today to explore why healing eradicates illness, contrary to our modern understandings of the courses of infection and of other disease processes.

Leuret and Bon review the criteria applied by the Catholic Church in judging a healing to have been miraculous:

1. The treated physical problem must be serious;

2. At the time of response to the healing the patient's disease should be stabilized or worsening and not expected to improve;

3. At the time of response to the healing the patient should be free of other treatments;

4. The effects of the healing should be sudden and instantaneous;

5. The effects of the healing must be complete;

6. The healing must occur at a time when no other crisis was influencing the patient's life or illness; and

7. The cure must be permanent.

D. Scott Rogo[552] points out that saints are sometimes recognized many years, even centuries, after their death. Miracles are attributed to these saints on the basis that petitionary prayer directed to them seemed effective in producing miraculous cures. A case in point is that of Saint Martin de Porres, a holy man who lived in Peru from 1579 to 1639. He was beatified in 1837 after validation of two of his cures as miraculous in 1836. Here is one of these, authenticated by the patient's doctor, as reported by Rogo:

> [A] Lima housewife... sustained an eye injury when a sliver of an earthenware jar she had broken lodged in her eye. The fluid normally present in the eye leaked out, leaving the eye incurably blind. The master of a nearby monastery, however, sent the woman a small bone fragment, a relic of Martin de Porres and instructed her to hold it to the damaged eye. She did as she was directed and woke the next morning to find her eye and sight totally restored.[553]

In another instance, a middle aged man named Fagan underwent abdominal surgery in 1967. He was diagnosed as having advanced stomach cancer with multiple metastases that made it impossible to remove all of the cancerous tissue in the operation. His condition gradually deteriorated over the next half year to the point that a priest was called to administer last rites, advising him that the only thing left to do might be to pray to the Blessed John Ogilvie (a Scottish holy man who was executed by the Protestant authorities in 1614). Fagan lingered, deteriorating slowly over the next two months until he was in a moribund condition, barely able to do anything at all, finally bedridden, unable even to eat or talk.

> [H]e could only vomit repeatedly, since by now his stomach was literally dissolving itself. Then... several religious friends... visited and held a prayer session around Fagan's bed. Although they beseeched Blessed John Ogilvie repeatedly to intercede in the dying man's behalf, the situation didn't look very encouraging. [554]

Fagans' doctor predicted he would die before the end of the weekend. He could only provide an injection of pain medicine. The next morning Mrs. Fagan was amazed upon entering her husband's room to find her husband partially recovered and hungry. His vomiting ceased and his pain abated, with complete recovery following shortly.

Fagan's doctor and subsequent investigators felt that his recovery had been miraculous. This led to the canonization of Blessed John Ogilvie in 1976.

In cases described centuries ago, the skeptic may query whether proper observations were made or whether reports might not have been exaggerated. Rogo felt that

> ... because these healings resulted from the petitionary prayers offered by the patients' friends and relatives, it is a moot point whether the cures were

brought about by the saints whose intercession was sought or whether they were actually produced by the friends and relatives themselves.[555]

There is evidence to contradict Rogo's opinion. The importance of the participation of living people praying for healings in such cases of alleged posthumous influence of saints cannot be overlooked. From numerous controlled studies,[556] plus the anecdotal reports of healers and healees,[557] it is apparent that many people possess healing abilities. It seems possible that living persons attending the sick may be the agents for healings, although the use of the image of a saint may aid in boosting their confidence in their own healing abilities. Francis MacNutt[558] himself noted that "... it was much easier to believe that God could heal the sick *through prayer* than to believe he would heal *through my prayer*."

One might argue that the healing apparently produced by the relic, a bone of the dead saint, is proof of the saint's healing powers. However, this too might be merely an aid to the patient's *self* healing. The relic might have been no more than a placebo.

On the other hand, support of the assumptions of the church and Rogo may be found in methods of some healers involving the apparent imprinting of various materials with healing properties. Research confirms it is possible to convey healing through cotton, water, and other *vehicles*.[559] Tradition has it that relics of saints can convey healings. There is no reason why their physical remains or earthly possessions should not act as vehicles for their healing energies.

Yet it may still not necessarily be the saint who has done or is doing this. Any believer with healing abilities who came in contact with the object could contribute healing properties to it. Furthermore, if Sheldrake's[560] theory of morphogenetic fields and formative causation[561] is valid, the collective adoration and prayers of people through decades and centuries of reverence for the saint could create a healing morphogenetic field. This could then be available for those in need, accessible by invoking the thought, image, name, or relic of the saint. Rogo himself noted that locations such as Lourdes may represent repositories for healing energies contributed by numerous pilgrims, rather than the locations themselves possessing inherent healing properties.[562] This is also supported by the laboratory observations of *linger effects* of healing. Healers report and research has confirmed that healing effects linger in the locations where healing was given.[563] For instance, matched pairs of mice were wakened from anesthesia on a laboratory table, with the healer directing healing to one side of the table or the other with the intent of waking the mouse on that side more quickly. If mice were placed on the same side of the table within the twenty minutes following healing given to a mouse on that side of the table, they wakened more quickly than control mice - without the healer being present.[564]

Even if we discount many healings at shrines as linger effects of previous healings or as morphogenetic fields that were attached to the location, the early miracles at a given location would remain to be explained.

One may also hypothesize that supplications to saints could engage the saint in the flesh, across the years, during the time they were on earth. Evidence supporting this can be found in reports that linear time was transcended with pre-

and retro-cognition;[565] in experiments suggesting causality that transcends time;[566] in interactional apparitions appearing to represent time-warps;[567] and in anecdotal reports of distant healings that were reported by healees to have occurred at times prior to or later than the intentional healing efforts of the healer.[568]

The most common evidence for involvement of saints in healings is from the subjective impressions of the people involved with healings, who intuitively sensed the saints' presence or saw them. The saint, in spirit, could be the agent for posthumous healings. We find ample evidence for spirit survival and involvement with people who are still in the flesh, as reviewed earlier in this book. In cases where a vision of the saint is reported in association with the healing I would consider the likelihood of saintly involvement to be more credible. But even here one couldn't rule out the viewing of an apparition-saint as the product of the imagination of the living people who are fervently praying, rather than their having invoked an actual spirit intervention. Consensual validation of sightings of a saint would be an aid in this regard, though again not conclusive. Here again, a skeptic might counter with the reports such as that of the apparent mass hypnotic phenomenon of the Indian rope trick, which suggest that numerous people may perceive an image projected by one individual.[569] The creation of fantasy entities, as in *Conjuring up Philip*[570] also suggests that participants may bring about psychokinetic effects and, by extension, healings as well.

My personal impression is that there is validity to some of the claims of posthumous involvement of saints in cures. I trust that some of the intuitive impressions of participants in such miraculous healings are accurate. Hopefully, as intuitive impressions are increasingly accepted, intuitives may be invited to participate in research that would systematically validate these impressions within linear frameworks. This would help to weed the kernels of replicable truths from the chaff of individual colorings of the perceptions and beliefs about these truths. This is not to say that the individual colorings are not of importance to the individuals who perceive and/or produce them. This may also be more acceptable as personal spiritual awareness gains greater acceptance.

Angels
The Old and New Testament include nearly three hundred references to angels. Christian tradition holds that these are messengers or assistants under God's direction. Encounters with angels, along with other spiritual experiences, may be taken as confirmation of one's religious beliefs.[571]

The Devil is a 'fallen angel' who claimed to be as powerful as God and stirred a rebellion of angels against God. He and those who joined him were thrown out of heaven and have continued to battle against God, avenging themselves by seeking every way to subvert his creation, the world we live in. In some traditions, the rebellion is said to have started with the Devil's jealousy over God's creation of Adam and Eve. The Book of Enoch suggests that the fallen angels had lusted after mortal women and were punished for pursuing them.

Malcolm Godwin identifies several other theories accounting for fallen angels. According to one, they are the shadow side of God. A second, attributed to Origen (185-245 AD), is that angels drifted away from the Infinite Source of their own free wills, some taking on human form and other drifting further away to become demons. A third recounts a war in Heaven that occurred on the second day of creation between two angelic factions. One group was created with God's Grace, assigned to pursue good; the other was devoid of God's Grace and chose to pursue sin. Archangel Michael led the good angels to victory, banishing the bad ones from Heaven. The last asserts that the Devil, who had already been banished from heaven, was challenged by Jesus Christ as the embodiment of God. Christ vanquished him but Satan vows to continue to tempt humanity into sinning. Christ banishes him to Hell with the help of Michael.

Islam and healing

> *With each breath may we take refuge in the Living Truth alone, released from coarse arrogance and subtle pride. May every thought and action be intended in the Supremely Holy Name Allah as direct expression of boundless Divine Compassion and Most Tender Love. May the exaltation of endless praise arising spontaneously as the life of endless beings flow consciously toward the Single Source of Being, Source of the intricate evolution of endless worlds. May we be guided through every experience along the Direct Path of Love that leads from the Human Heart into the Most Sublime Source of Love.*
>
> – Sheik Lex Hixon

Islam has a rich tradition of healing, known in the West particularly through the Sufi tradition. Sufi teachings emphasize, "Know thyself and thou wilt know God." Sufi teachings are rich in stories and parables, chanting, dancing and meditation – bringing adherents into spiritual awareness experientially, rather than through scriptural or doctrinal teachings..

Fundamentalist religious views

> *Man is a Religious Animal. He is the only Religious Animal. He is the only animal that has the True Religion – several of them. He is the only animal that loves his neighbor as himself and cuts his throat if his theology isn't straight. He has made a graveyard of the globe in trying his honest best to smooth his brother's path to happiness and heaven.... The higher animals have no religion. And we are told that they are going to be left out in the Hereafter. I wonder why? It seems questionable taste.*
>
> – Mark Twain

Fundamentalists of various faiths believe that they have received THE word of God and know from this revealed information the way the world was created, the ways in which people are meant to behave, and the rewards and punishments that will be meted out by God for sins of omission or commission in this life and the hereafter. Scripture, as interpreted by their religious leaders, is the only acceptable source of information and guidance, a source that supersedes all other sources – be they from other religions, from scientific explorations of the world, or from personal spiritual awarenesses. They do not question whether their interpretations might be mistaken, in view of the fact that others have developed other variations on the theme of scriptural interpretations, derived from the same original source.

Because fundamentalists have only one valid source for information about the world, they often damn all others – including other religions, evidence from archaeology, genetics and any other scientific research – that might put any of their teachings in question. From an outsider's perspective, they live in a closed belief system that resists all scrutiny and analysis through any system of beliefs but their own. Considering their narrowly limited focus and their exclusion of any possible alternatives – no matter how logical or reasonable – a logical suspicion is that a major reason for the closedness of their system is to assure its own perpetuation.

> *He who discommendeth others obliquely commendeth himself.*
> – Thomas Browne [572]

The Barna Group is a Christian polling and researching organization that has conducted annual surveys of religious affiliation and practice in the US since 1991. In April 2005 their annual report found that "despite the media frenzy surrounding the influence of evangelical Christians during the 2004 presidential election, the new study indicates that evangelicals remain just 7% of the adult population. That number has not changed since the Barna Group began measuring the size of the evangelical public in 1994."

The Barna definition of fundamentalism is complex, narrow and precise. In addition, they found that 40 percent of those surveyed are 'born again' Christians. There is a significant overlap between these and the fundamentalists in many details.[573]

Fundamentalism and healing
There are fundamentalists who hold that illnesses are the consequences of sins. That is, if people are sick, they have brought it upon themselves through their sins.[574] Prayer to God, repentance and absolution are then the only legitimate means to cure. In this framework, healing would be viewed as the work of God and no other mechanisms need be sought.

> The difficulty with this is that people continue to be ill, despite their best appeals for surcease through religious avenues. These beliefs may inject a burden of guilt and despair by implication that those who remain ill are still sinners... The Most Merciful One does not allow for punishments. He allows only for lessons that will help us advance on the spiritual path.
> – Daskalos [575]

Some fundamentalists interpret any healing approaches outside their churches as questioning God's ways – or worse, even as the work of the Devil. This could include scientific investigations of healing; using therapies such as meditation, yoga or other CAM approaches; and even, in some religions, seeking conventional medical care.

Sadly, many fundamentalists are not content to practice their beliefs within their communities. They intrude in the affairs of others, imposing their views to the detriment of those too weak to oppose them. In the US there has been protection under the Bill of Rights against this. In England I encountered fundamentalists who blocked introduction of healers into NHS hospitals and into hospices because the healers were not practicing within the staff's religious belief system. In the recent history of the world, many indigenous people have been lured or coerced into abandoning their native ways and adopting the proselytizers' religions because the missionaries displayed superior technologies – which made it appear to the natives that the proselytizers must also have stronger or better gods.

Rational arguments, based on scientific evidence, are of no use in dealing with the firmly held and often stridently expressed views of fundamentalists. Bertrand Russell[576] suggests, "The opinions that are held with passion are always those for which no good ground exists; indeed the passion is the measure of the holder's lack of rational conviction." Fundamentalists base their arguments on totally different premises from those of the scientific community.

> *Religion is a magic device for turning unanswerable questions into unquestionable answers.*
> – Art Gecko

We are challenged to deal fairly and respectfully with religious groups that would treat us unfairly. Karl Popper[577] observes, "We should...claim, in the name of tolerance, the right not to tolerate the intolerant." We are fortunate in the US to have a Bill of Rights that protects us from religious oppressions. It is only through such legal safeguards that we can arrange for a fair co-existence among people with differing views and beliefs.[578]

Eastern religions

> *Your work is to discover your work and then with all your heart give yourself to it.*
> – Buddha

Healing has a recognized place in Buddhism, Hinduism, and other Eastern religions. Many gurus and priests are healers. Only a few drops from these rich cultural streams are considered here. Their cosmologies are too vast and intricate for adequate consideration in the present discussion, but those who are interested may enjoy Huston Smith's succinct summaries on a spectrum of religions.

I start this discussion with a brief overview of Buddhism because it has seen the most rapidly growing religious affiliation and practice in the US over recent years. While Buddhists accounted for only 0.5 percent of the population in 2001, there was an increase from 401,000 in 1990 to 1,082,000 in 2001, representing a 170 percent increase. This growth in Buddhism is a manifestation of the awakening to personal spirituality, which is the focus of this book. Buddhism invites us to explore our inner worlds of spiritual awareness in a methodical way that has been developed and honed over several thousand years.

The founder of Buddhism, Siddhartha Gautama, was born into a wealthy and powerful family in 563 BC in what is now Nepal. He grew up to be a handsome man and married a princess who bore him a son. Though lacking nothing, he became discontented with worldly life when he perceived the impermanence of life and the suffering of mankind. At age twenty-six he decided to leave his estate to seek spiritual wisdom. He studied with Hindu masters, explored ascetisicm, and practiced meditation. After six years, sitting in meditation under a fig tree, he finally achieved *Bodhi* (enlightenement) and was thereafter called Buddha. For the last forty-three years of his life he was a great teacher, founding an order of monks that evolved into Buddhism.

Buddhism broke with the then prevalent Brahmin Hindu traditions, emphasizing that each person must seek inner guidance rather than outer authority in evolving their understanding and practice of their religion. Direct experience of inner spiritual awareness is nurtured, furthered through life experiences.

Buddha emphasizes Four Noble Truths:[579]

I. Life is *dukkha* (suffering). Huston Smith explains that the origin for *dukkha*[580] is a bone joint that has slipped from its socket, or an off-center axle (relative to its wheel). Metaphorically, *dukkha* would then refer to a dislocation in life where you have slipped out of joint; have gotten dislocated; are spinning wheels on a pivot that is no longer centered and therefore are encountering friction, conflict, and pain. Buddha focused on six of life traumas in particular: birth, sickness, decrepitude of old age, fears of death, being chained to conditions that are intolerable and abhorrent, and being separated from one's loves.

Suffering may be experienced in body, senses, ideas, feelings and/or consciousness. Healing requires that we first understand our suffering.

II. The cause of suffering is *tanha* (craving) that originates in our lower self, that increase our separation from our true selves. We tend to tie ourselves in knots of self-indulgence that provide small pleasures and then we hold onto these with a tenacity that gets in the way of realizing our true Selves. Much of our craving is in the service of maintaining our perceived self (in Western terms, our ego), which we fear to relinquish.

III. The cure lies in overcoming our cravings. When we release our cravings, we can reach the state of *Nirvana* (enlightenment).

IV. We can overcome *tanha* through the Eightfold Path

1. *Right knowledge* provides a map for moving towards enlightenment; particularly the Four Noble Truths.

2. *Right aspiration* aligns our heart's desires with our right knowledge and focuses our energies behind our intentions that are formed through right knowledge. We must hold as our goals the highest possible levels of kindness, selflessness, and charity – towards *everyone*, not just towards those who are dear to our hearts or likely to reciprocate in kind.

3. *Right speech* aligns our actions with our knowledge and aspirations. This is achieved a step at a time.

4. *Right behavior* starts with awareness of our motivations, and includes Five Percepts, closely paralleling the second half of the Ten Commandments that prescribe an ethical life: Do not kill, steal, lie, be unchaste or drink intoxicants.

5. *Right livelihood* that promotes spiritual progress. For laypersons this requires an occupation which promotes and does not destroy life. For those seeking liberation from earthly attachments there is the discipline of belonging to a monastic order. It is not uncommon for men to leave their families at some point in their lives to follow this path, commonly after the birth of a grandchild.

6. *Right effort* requires the discipline of will that sets a steady pace and does not relent under the challenges of tedium, external temptations or internal obstacles of habit, personality or appetites.

7. *Right mindfulness* is the development of understanding of our habits of thoughts and behaviors. Once we understand ourselves, we are able to release our attachments to our everyday habits. Buddha felt that ignorance was worse than sin and that through exercise of will we can overcome our aversions of fearful and negative experiences. Positive, loving thoughts overcome negativity.

8. *Right absorption* follows the teachings of raja yoga, the path to God through psychological and spiritual experimentation. By quieting the mind's everyday chatter and refusing to pursue distractions, one withdraws one's energies from outer-world attachments and opens the inner doorways to spiritual perceptions. The body is disciplined through a series of yoga practices that maintain health and others that promote and deepen meditation. Breathing exercises both eliminate this body function as a distraction and deepen meditative focus. Concentration is strengthened so that sensory distractions no longer intrude upon one's mental focus. Focus is strengthened to the point that unwavering focus on the external or internal object of one's choice is achieved. Through diligent practice, meditative focus is deepened so that one loses all awareness of oneself. Eventually, when no distractions remain, the doorways to spiritual awakening open. All sense of earthly time and space disappear as one finds oneself being one with the Infinite All.

Buddhism teaches that every aspect of our earthly existence is transient. Sensory stimuli come and go. Pleasures and suffering may last for shorter or longer periods but must inevitably come to an end, as does life itself. Nothing is permanent.

Ken Wilber, a leading expert on meditation and transpersonal cosmologies[581] describes this view of reality, in which each of us is reborn again and again in every instant:

> ... In this moment and this moment and this, an individual is Buddha, is Atman...[582] *but*, in this moment and this moment and this, he ends up as John Doe, as a separate self, as an isolated body apparently bounded by other isolated bodies. At the beginning of *this* and every moment, each individual *is* God as the Clear Light; but by the *end* of this same moment – in a flash, in the twinkling of an eye – he winds up as an isolated ego. And what happens In Between the beginning and ending of *this* moment is identical to what happened In Between death and rebirth as described by the Thotrol.[583]
>
> This moment-to-moment phenomenon we call 'microgeny' – the micro-genetic involution of the spectrum of consciousness. Each moment, the individual passes through the entire Bardo sequence... and he remembers to the extent that he has *evolved*.[584]

Benjamin Franklin put it more succinctly: "Work as though you were to live a hundred years, and pray as though you were to die tomorrow."

Buddhism also teaches that the All is truly unknowable to humans. No description of the enlightened state would be adequate and therefore it is beyond description.

Karma is a concept widely held in Eastern traditions. Karma is the legacy one carries over from one life to another, including experiences; skills; emotional trauma; unresolved feelings towards particular people or relations – such as debts of gratitude for positive deeds, and vengeful angers for negative deeds, respectively of others; and 'credits' for positive and altruistic deeds towards others.[585]

> *[N]ext of kin... can be looked upon as the living representatives of one's inherited consequences of past lives...*
> – Nancy Gardner and Esmond Gardner [586]

Believers in reincarnation tell us that we either choose our parents and other family members or they are chosen for us (in consultation with our spirit guides and teachers prior to our birth) in order to work out relationships we have not mastered yet in our spiritual group collective series of incarnations. If I was a woman who was mean to my son or husband in a previous life, I may be reborn as a man who has a difficult mother – perhaps even my husband or son from the previous life – in order to learn the consequences of my previous behavior and to give myself a chance to repay my previous-life relative for my previous mistreatment, through better behavior in this life. The complementary lesson of my mother/previous son/husband will be to process her/his feelings of hurt and anger from the past life relationships, learning (in this lifetime or another) to forgive rather than to avenge.

Reincarnation gives meaning, or at least a firm promise of a long-term meaning, to the vocational mystery of each earth life. So many find themselves confronting unwelcome yet unavoidable tasks, which intrude themselves into the life pattern and seem the very opposite of what each would have chosen. This is most usually due to karmic bonds to be set straight between man and man, or arises from things springing from what had been left undone or done crookedly before. But this is not always so. It need not necessarily be based on ancient failings or guilt. The seeming burden can also spring from the principle of compassion. It may be an opportunity for the ultimately joyous creation of good karma. Tasks in life look forward as well as backward.

– Paul Beard [587]

Many people speak of *retributive* karma, in which we suffer the consequences of our sins from past lives. An early statement of this belief was made by Plato.[588]

O young man, who fancy that you are neglected by the Gods, know that if you become worse you shall go to the worse souls, or if better to the better... this is the justice of heaven, which neither you nor any other unfortunate will ever glory in escaping.

It is often more helpful to consider *restitutive* or *rebalancing* karma, in which we learn lessons in this life that help us to appreciate both sides of a situation or relationship, and make amends for our misdeeds in a future life. More on this in the discussion on spirituality in Chapter III-11.

In reincarnation research[589] we saw that past-life therapy may produce marked changes in symptoms, when apparent unresolved past-life traumas are recognized and the associated emotions are released. A difficult death in a previous life, for instance, might leave emotional scars – including fears of illness, death or circumstances resembling those surrounding that death. Once these memories are accessed and the buried feelings are released, the irrational fears can dissipate.

Some healers clairsentiently perceive karmic influences and can identify which karmic lessons people have sufficiently digested in order to be ready to relinquish their illnesses and which will not respond to healing because the lessons brought across the chasms of death have not been learned, nor the karmic debts repaid.[590] Most healers say that karmic illnesses cannot be healed but a few claim they sometimes can.[591]

Here's a test to find whether your mission on earth is finished:
if you're alive, it isn't.

– Richard Bach [592]

Beliefs in an afterlife and in reincarnation often arise spontaneously with NDEs and mystical experiences, even in people who previously were agnostics or atheists, or whose religious beliefs excluded reincarnation. This hints there may be validity to them though skeptics suggest they are more likely products of basic human psychology, such as a fear of death, or products of brain electrical or biochemical activity.[593]

If we assume reincarnation occurs, a logical question is, why would a soul reincarnate? The commonly held belief is that life in the flesh, on this planet, provides special lessons that advance one's spiritual development.

> *Each soul takes upon itself a particular task... Whatever the task that your soul has agreed to, whatever its contract with the Universe, all of the experiences of your life serve to awaken within you the memory of that contract, and to prepare you to fulfill it.*
>
> – Gary Zukav [594]

With the evidence from Western research in spiritual dimensions reviewed in this book, the Western world is coming closer to Eastern views regarding survival of the spirit and reincarnation.

Eastern explorations of spirituality are through personal research, primarily through meditation. The guidance of master teachers is helpful, based on meditative practices over many generations.

> *Do not believe in anything simply because you have heard it.*
> *Do not believe in traditions because they have been handed down for many generations.*
> *Do not believe in anything because it is spoken and rumored by many.*
> *Do not believe in anything simply because it is written in religious books.*
> *Do not believe in anything merely on the authority of teachers or elders.*
> *But after observation and analysis, when you find that anything agrees with reason, and is conducive to the good and benefit of one and all, then accept it and live to it.*
>
> – Buddha [595]

Eastern worldviews suggest that physical existence is temporary, or even an illusion. Through meditation and through other spiritual paths[596] we find our way back to personal awareness of our oneness with all of creation and with the infinite All. Healing – in its highest level – is to accept our situation, not letting illness or unhappy circumstances cast a negative pall on our existence.[597]

Meditation is healing, in and of itself. It can contribute to health through stress reduction, reducing blood pressure, controlling pain, and much more.[598]

Meditation is also a gateway into spiritual awareness and healing. By quieting our mind, we can access dimensions in which spiritual healing can occur.[599]

There are marvelous benefits in being able to transcend our problems. Pain may even become a reminder to return to your meditative and spiritual awareness.

There are also potential pitfalls in this application of spiritual practice. There may be psychological problems underlying our dis-ease or disease. In turning to spiritual awareness we may ignore pus-pockets of old hurts that are buried in our psyche and body memories.[600] While we will feel less pain through such spiritual practice, the old hurts may fester, continuing to seek release. This will be a drain on our energies at the very least, and may lead to disturbances of emotions and relationships, and can manifest as well in physical symptoms and illnesses. I call this problem a *spiritual bypass.*

> *We've longed to see the roses, but never felt the thorns, and bought our pretty crowns, but never paid the price.*
> – Martin Smith

One would think that enlightened spiritual teachers would have cleared such psychological dross or would have transcended it. This is not necessarily so. It is well known in the spiritual community that some of the most enlightened gurus have glaring psychological faults and hang-ups.[601]

The better way may be to combine the best of Western and Eastern approaches. You can release the old, buried emotional traumas through some form of psychotherapy, while also reaching for spiritual awareness. Where you are dealing with current stresses that cannot be resolved through changes in your circumstances or relationships, spiritual practice can help you transcend the suffering.

Having said all this, we must also accept human nature. Since we let a child program our lifetime 'computer guidance' programs, our tendencies are to sweep uncomfortable things under the carpet. Most of us learn in childhood to shut away worrisome or painful memories and feelings in the depths of our unconscious minds. As children, this is a good choice for avoiding pain and suffering, as we cannot leave, change, trade in or fire our parents when they are hurting us. Our unconscious gets used to protecting us from the distress of these old hurts by keeping them firmly buried and outside our awareness. It resists releasing these emotions in the caverns of our being – even when we are no longer in the painful situations that caused them; even when we are clearly in a better position to deal with them. While meditation and spiritual healing can help to release some of these well-hidden traumas,[602] our inner programs tend to resist such efforts. Often, it is only when the emotional pus from past hurts festers to the point of physical and emotional pain that we begin to become aware that something is awry inside us.

> *Illness is the doctor to whom we pay most heed; to kindness, to knowledge we make promises only; to pain we obey.*
> – Marcel Proust

Pain may thus be a call to meditation and an unexpected opening into spiritual awareness and healing.

Shamanism

> *I am not interested in learning your medicine. I don't need any machines in order to make a direct diagnosis. I can see into my patients with my own*

> *eyes. And my medicine is medicine from nature and spirit, which heals not*
> *only their bodies but their hearts and souls, too. I'm sorry but I'm not*
> *interested, because* your medicine does not have any magic in it.
>
> – Don Antonio

In traditional cultures, shamans serve as counselors, priests and healers, mediating between the everyday world and spirit worlds. They may offer healings through prayers, chants, rituals (dance, drumming, healing ceremonies) and herbal remedies.

Shamans come to their work through revealing natural gifts for healing or divination, through an inner calling or through being chosen by an experienced shaman. Learning to be a shaman may take years of apprenticeship, and may include rituals and exercises in communicating with spirit guides, astral travel and understanding the natures of humans, animals, and plants.

Shamanism teaches that each of us is intimately related to all of creation. Animals, plants and the earth, waters and air are all living entities that together create our collective reality. Harming any of these is causing harm to a part of ourselves. Healing ourselves is a contribution towards healing the whole world.

As traditional cultures merge with Western culture, shamanistic healers continue to offer various types of healings and spiritual guidance.[603]

Along with their folkloric and intuitive knowledge of herbalism, shamans often use psychedelic plants to facilitate spiritual awakenings. A rich literature is available on Western explorations of these drugs, sometimes dignified with the term *entheogens* - to distinguish the use of these drugs for spiritual explorations from their popular use in search of casual stimulation and 'highs.' [604]

Animism

> *Let the mountain speak through you. Let the bird speak through you. Let*
> *the river speak through you. Give them voice and in the deepest caves of*
> *understanding you will hear a song. It sings of your oneness, blessed in the*
> *eternal fragments of your mind. Let no separation come between you and*
> *nature and you will become the guide who will always find his way home.*
>
> Matthew Smith [605]

Animism is the belief that everything in the world has its own spirit – animals, plants, geographic locations, bodies of water and processes such as fire and storms. This is not actually a religion, rather a world view that contributes to many religions.

The *etic* anthropological approach views such beliefs as myths and superstitions, born out of 'primitive' people's wishes to explain and control a world that is beyond their comprehension (in terms of Western scientific conceptualizations). The *emic* approach accepts that traditional societies have explanations for the ways the world functions that are valid – at least within their cultures, for purposes of explaining nature and for communicating with each other.

I have spoken with many gifted intuitives who report that they see and can communicate with spirits of humans, animals, plants, rocks, geographic locations and more. Intuitive healers and herbalists have reported that when a remedy is needed, they focus in their mind on the problem needing treatment as they wander in nature, waiting for the appropriate therapeutic plants to call out to them to offer their help. Dora van Gelder[606] reported that she communicated with spirits of trees and angels who periodically choreographed storms – to rebalance various earth energies.[607]

Animism is an important aspect of personal spiritual awareness. When we are aware that the animals, the trees, the land, the waters and the air are alive and sentient then our relationship to all of our world is transformed. (More on this in Chapter III-13 and the Conclusion of this book.)

While the average person in Western industrial society is likely to question the validity of animistic observations, the more relevant question in my view is, "Why have people in Western society lost and forgotten their awareness of the spirits that animate the world?" Some of the answers to this question, I believe, have been provided in the Prologue and earlier chapters of this book, and further observations and speculations are offered in the following chapters.

Atheism

The numbers of Americans declaring they affiliate with no organized religion increased from 8% (14.3 million people) in 1990 to 14.1% (29.4 million) in 2001, according to a survey conducted by The American Religious Identification Survey (ARIS).[608] Over the same period, the numbers of Americans reporting they are Christians diminished about 10 percent, from 86.2% to 76.5%.[609] Should this trend continue, non-Christians will outnumber Christians in America by the year 2042.[610]

Many in our modern world have been turned off by religious teachings and rituals, which they experience as hollow words and practices, devoid of spirituality. Many have been discouraged by experiences with organized religion to the point that they doubt and reject any reality or validity of spirituality. Others have criticized churches that seem more concerned with perpetuating and expanding their power than with the welfare of their flocks, as in churches that oppose birth control in a world that is dangerously overpopulated, and churches based on religious teachings and liturgies that seem outdated and irrelevant to modern life. Marxism teaches that religion is simply a method for the clergy to control the populace.

> *The main object of religion is not to get a man into heaven, but to get heaven into him.*
> – Thomas Hardy

Reasoned disbeliefs in religious teachings are a natural product of scientific teachings that show the Biblical stories of creation are myths and not historical truths.

> *The philosophies of one age have become the absurdities of the next, and the foolishness of yesterday has become the wisdom of tomorrow.*
> – Sir William Osler

In our modern world, many have been raised without any religious teachings or experiences. Some suggest that a belief in God is wishful thinking or even delusional.

> *If you talk to God, you are praying; if God talks to you, you have schizophrenia.*
> – Thomas Szasz [611]

Philosophical arguments against a belief in God follow several lines of reasoning.

First and foremost is the observation that any religious belief must start with axioms that are unproveable within frameworks of logical arguments. These axioms must be accepted as articles of faith. They are therefore without objective validity. Because there is no logical way to prove that spirit exists within linear reductionistic frameworks, there can be no *reason*able proof of its reality.[612]

Many come to atheism through the belief that God, were He to exist, would be a caring and loving being. They are unable to reconcile this belief with the existence of immeasurable suffering and cruelty that exists in the world. They cannot believe that a loving God would allow such suffering to occur – as for instance in the Holocaust or in natural disasters in which thousands die and millions suffer. A classical observation was made by Richard Dawkins arguing that the universe was formed by purely chance:

> In a universe of electrons and selfish genes, blind physical forces and genetic replication, some people are going to get hurt, other people are going to get lucky, and you won't find any rhyme or reason in it nor any justice. The universe we observe has precisely the properties we should expect if there is, at bottom, no design, no purpose, no evil and no good, nothing but blind, pitiless indifference.[613]

Some atheists may still feel an intuitive connection with nature or with something outside themselves, without committing to a theology.

> *Do not stand at my grave and weep,*
> *I am not there, I do not sleep.*
>
> *I am a thousand winds that blow;*
> *I am the diamond glints on snow.*
> *I am the sunlight on ripened grain.*
> *I am the gentle autumn rain.*
>
> *When you awaken in the morning's hush,*
> *I am the swift uplifting rush*

Of quiet birds in circled flight.
I am the soft stars that shine at night.

Do not stand at my grave and cry.
I am not there; I did not die.
                         – Mary Frye [614]

For many who worship at the altar of reasoning, atheism is a logical conclusion that brooks no questioning or contradiction. The fact that a belief in the ultimate value and validity of logical reasoning is in and of itself an axiom is usually overlooked.

A little philosophy inclineth men's mind to atheism, but depth in philosophy bringeth men's minds about to religion.
                         – Francis Bacon [615]

Agnosticism

There lives more faith in honest doubt,
Believe me, than in half the creeds
                         –Lord Alfred Tennyson [616]

An agnostic believes that God or any other ultimate reality cannot be known or proven. This is a stance of neutrality in judgment about religious matters, not stating that they are not or cannot be present in the cosmos, but declaring it is impossible to know them.

Agnosticism need not be an all or nothing system of beliefs or disbeliefs. In delving into the mysteries of spiritual dimensions, we may reach a point of knowing that we cannot know beyond the point of our current psychospiritual development. We may likewise find that no matter how hard we work at everyday problems – a vital aspect of our spiritual development – we seem to be getting nowhere.

Rainer Marie Rilke advises:

Be patient toward all that is unsolved in your heart and try to love the questions themselves... Do not now seek the answers, which cannot be given you because you would not be able to live them.

And the point is, to live everything. Live the questions now.

Perhaps then you will gradually, without noticing it live along some distant day into the answer.[617]

Agnosticism can still provide an ethical basis for relating to others, starting with the Golden Rule, "Do unto others as you would have them do unto you." This can extend to wholistic healing, though many agnostics may well prefer not to go into levels of spiritual awareness.

I do not pretend to know where many ignorant men are sure – that is all that agnosticism means.

– Clarence Darrow [618]

Avoiding the spiritual, however, can become a vicious circle, as pointed out in the prologue to this volume: spiritual experiences are foreign to our experiences, so we are unfamiliar and feel uncomfortable with them, so we discourage and disparage them, so we experience them even less, so they become even more unfamiliar and even alien to us, and so on. We are then uncomfortable with the ways in which spiritual awarenesses and experiences differ from our linear world experiences. Gypsy Rose Lee suggested, "God is love, but get it in writing." This attitude makes it difficult for us to consider that there might be other realities in which valid experiences occur within frameworks and under natural laws that differ from those of our material world reality.[619]

Having struggled myself through a period of agnosticism and atheism, in which I formulated all sorts of psychological explanations and rationalizations for spirituality and beliefs in spirit survival, I can attest that life experiences and education may shift such beliefs. Conventional psychology, medicine and psychiatry were materialistic in the extreme and not in the least helpful in considering spiritual awareness. I was taught that spirituality was a cultural myth or a personal fantasy – born of fears of inevitable death and disintegration of the physical body. It was mainly through speaking with healers, learning healing, and practicing meditation that I opened into my personal spiritual awareness.[620]

Neurotheology

[M]ystical experience is biologically, observably and scientifically real.
–Andrew Newberg et al. [621]

Particular areas of the brain have shown increased activity during meditation and other spiritual states, using sophisticated brain imaging devices. This has led to speculation that spiritual awareness may be no more than a function of the activity of these brain cells.[622]

While this is a viable hypothesis, an equally viable hypothesis is that the brain is like a television receiver for information from spiritual dimensions, and this is the function of these particular brain cells.[623]

Quantum Theology

Although we can't see, with our naked eye, the space between the parts of the atom, we now understand through physics that an atom is mostly space. It's mostly emptiness and it's more of a pattern than a solid thing. Similarly, in our own self, in our own mind, when we see that we're not just a solid thing, that we are flowing, that we are part of the flow, then it under-

*mines a lot of the solidity of our self-concept, of our clinging to the reality
of external things and the reality of internal noumena or mind stuff and the
reality of the self. So there's a natural releasing of the grasping or clinging
or resistance. There's a natural letting go of who we think we are and being whatever is in the now.*

– Lama Surya Das

The road to spiritual awareness through quantum physics is so well traveled that
the next chapter is devoted entirely to this subject. Suffice it to say here that
numerous findings in modern physics suggest that non-local consciousness and
influences are verifiable, transcending space and in some instances transcending
time as well. From these perspectives, the physical reality of our everyday world
appears to be only a limited range of the total spectrum of the energetic and
conscious world. Transpersonal realities are entirely possible within the broader
range of the quantum world.

Scientism

Scientism, the religion of the Western world, teaches of an existence exclusively
focused on and explained by materialistic theories. Modern science can be the
equivalent of a religion when it assumes it has the ultimate answers to explain
life, the universe and everything; when it resists or even refuses to consider
alternative theories; and when it discounts out of hand many observations and
theories that are not currently popular, such as psi abilities and spiritual healing –
for which there are substantial bodies of research evidence.

  Science claims to have the sole and exclusive explanation for the workings of
the world and all that it contains. It assumes that increasingly refined linear
analyses of all matter and of all of nature's processes will ultimately explain every
aspect of the cosmos; that mind is the product of brain; and that when the brain
dies, mind ceases to exist. Sadly, like other fundamentalist religions, it is also
exclusive. At its worst, scientism may respond to challenges to its axioms with the
illogical venom of the religious fanatic attacking the heretic.

Some readers might feel that these statements are rather extreme. Consider how
many of the following statements you feel are accurate – according to the
teachings of modern science. Charles Tart, a transpersonal psychologist, has
written a Creed that states the prevalent Western scientific beliefs, following the
format of the Christian Nicene Creed.[624]

> I BELIEVE - in the material universe – as the only and ultimate reality - a
> universe controlled by fixed physical laws - and blind chance.
>
> I AFFIRM - that the universe has no creator – no objective purpose - and
> no objective meaning or destiny.
>
> I MAINTAIN - that all ideas about God or gods – enlightened beings –
> prophets and saviors – or other non-physical beings or forces – are super-
> stitions and delusions. – Life and consciousness are totally identical to

physical processes - and arose from chance interactions of blind physical forces. – Like the rest of life – my life – and my consciousness – have no objective purpose – meaning – or destiny.

I BELIEVE – that all judgments, values, and moralities – whether my own or others – are subjective – arising solely from biological determinants – personal history – and chance. – Free will is an illusion. – Therefore the most rational values I can personally live by must be based on the knowledge that for me – what pleases me is Good – what pains me is Bad. – Those who please me or help me avoid pain are my friends – those who pain me or keep me from my pleasure are my enemies. – Rationality requires that friends and enemies be used in ways that maximize my pleasure – and minimize my pain.

I AFFIRM – that churches have no real use other than social support – that there are no objective sins to commit or be forgiven for – that there is no divine or supernatural retribution for sin or reward for virtue – although there may be social consequences of actions. – Virtue for me is getting what I want – without being caught and punished by others.

I MAINTAIN – that the death of the body – is the death of the mind. – There is no afterlife – and all hope of such is nonsense.

Scientism is an insidious religious belief because it cloaks itself in a mantle of alleged knowledge that is supposedly based on objective findings from research. While many scientific theories have been systematically tested and confirmed, the rules of good science state that any theory can be amended or overturned by research evidence which contradicts the underlying hypotheses. Many in the field of science are not open to considering alternatives to popularly held beliefs, despite clear evidence suggesting new possibilities.

You may wonder, how can science become scientism? The answers to this question are many-layered. Great leaps of faith are commonly taken about the validity of basic mathematical hypotheses and their relevance to the real world. We tend to accept the theories we are taught as though they are firm and fixed truths about the way the earth and skies and everything between them are held together and function. There are mathematical formulas explaining how subatomic particles interact; how molecules of nutrients enter our cells and waste chemicals exit; how populations grow and decline in relationship to their environments, and how stars and galaxies were created and expand across the universe. However, all of these are just theories. The formulas are a best fit between the observations and how we presume the atoms, and body chemicals and stars actually relate to each other. If the theories predict new findings that are then confirmed, they are validated. The fact that there are different concentrations of chemicals inside our body cells, compared to their concentrations outside the cells suggested that there must be a pumping mechanism in the cell membrane that creates and maintains these differences. Sure enough, it was discovered that there are enzymes and biochemical 'pumps' that maintain the required concentrations of ions inside and outside the cells.

Often enough, new observations do not quite fit the explanatory hypotheses, so theories have to be tweaked and adjusted. In high school chemistry I was taught that the nucleus of the atom had tiny electrons circling around it like our planets circle around the sun. Subsequent findings demonstrated that electrons are more like waves and their paths around the nucleus are better described as clouds of probability positions where the electrons might be found. Sometimes the new findings completely invalidate the theories and we have to go back to the drawing boards. The Big Bang theory of the universe appeared to explain how the universe was created, throwing out an enormous quantity of matter that expanded across the universe, coalescing into stars and galaxies. Eventually, it was predicted that gravity would slow the expansion and that everything would then start to come back together. New findings show that galaxies appear to be moving apart at an accelerated pace that is incompatible with the Big Bang theory. A new theory will have to be proposed to explain this.

Scientists, however, often resist challenges to their theories. They may even defend them with vehement, irrational and personal attacks on opponents that differ very little from the sorts of in-fighting that are common between diverse religious authorities.

> *Insofar as the propositions of mathematics give an account of reality, they are not certain; and insofar as they are certain, they do not describe reality.*
> – Albert Einstein [625]

Practical considerations may contribute as well to the rigidities of scientism. Beyond the problems in building a world view on mathematical constructs, human nature may lead scientists to ignore the rules of their profession. Scientists often resist questions and have a hard time considering challenges to their theories. They may even mount bitter battles to defend them, refusing to accept new evidence. When one looks at the practicalities of working in science, these reactions are not surprising. Professors' jobs, professional status and even their careers may be threatened by a challenge to the theories they have developed and are researching. It takes several years to obtain a research grant. To have funds cut off by evidence suggesting that basic hypotheses are flawed may leave researchers up a creek of science without a way to crawl, much less paddle forward. So when their theory (= their livelihood) is threatened, they will be highly motivated to defend it and to attack the proponents of a new theory.

The whole grant application process is also biased towards resisting new ideas and innovations. Those who sit on research grant boards have established their credibility within popularly accepted frameworks of science. They are unlikely to approve funding for a study that might threaten their positions.

Journals have a peer review system that employs (can you guess?) similarly oriented and motivated scientists. Innovative authors are therefore likely to have their papers rejected.[626]

So while science teaches a method that requires intellectual clarity and honesty, these requisites for rigorous science are liberally ignored, and scientism becomes a fundamentalist religion.[627]

Interestingly, many senior scientists have come into mystical awarenesses and spiritual awakenings, after many years of participation in the church of scientism.[628]

> *I admire scientists in a way. They take the painfully exquisite slow boat to wisdom, while us lazy meditators and followers of the Eastern sciences take the superhighway of meditation and contemplation. Still, at the end of their lives the great scientists often sound like holy men.*
> – David Frank Gomes

Mystical teachings and mystical experiences

> *Mystics and sages have long held that Divinity is within us...*
> – Jan Phillips

Throughout human history there have been individuals who appear to have very deep awarenesses of mystical realms, often claiming to have received their knowledge from a Divine source. Their teachings have inspired many generations of followers. Believers find wisdom and guidance in these teachings. Skeptics can raise legitimate questions as to whether such teachings are more than the fantasies of charismatic leaders, or collective creative writings gathered over the intervening centuries. How might one decide between these two views?

Most religious teachings are based on fundamental beliefs from which various lessons are derived. These are usually attributed to information revealed to one or more inspired individuals, believed to have had an awareness of the Divine. There is no logical way to prove the truth or falsity of inspired knowledge, other than to point out its internal consistencies and inconsistencies and to assess whether it inspires and guides people to more ethical, healing and spiritual behaviors.

Figure III-8. Axioms of beliefs

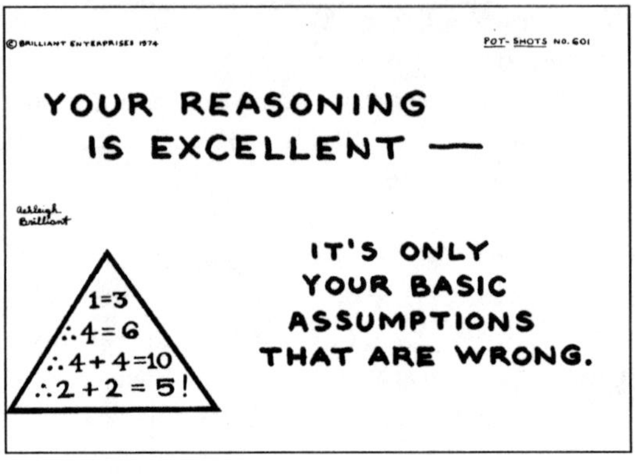

© BRILLIANT ENTERPRISES 1974   POT-SHOTS NO. 601

YOUR REASONING
IS EXCELLENT —

Ashleigh
Brilliant

IT'S ONLY
YOUR BASIC
ASSUMPTIONS
THAT ARE WRONG.

$1 = 3$
$\therefore 4 = 6$
$\therefore 4 + 4 = 10$
$\therefore 2 + 2 = 5 !$

One can, however, explore the spectrum of spiritual awarenesses that are available to many through meditative practices and other avenues for spiritual awakening.[629] These domains can be studied at more abstract levels by assessing the consistency of reports of multiple explorers in a given transpersonal domain, as well as consistencies across domains. The consistency and coherence of such reports through many centuries and in many cultures suggest that there is a measure of validity to transpersonal perceptions – although it may be difficult for mortal beings to comprehend or explain the nature of these domains. The picture that emerges from research in the various forms of transpersonal exploration covered in the first seven chapters of this book is even more impressive, as many of these observations and reports are based on rigorous studies.

Believers will point to the subjective knowing of being in an inspired state – an awareness that has qualities that are self-validating – of being in contact with some aspect of the Divine. Skeptics will say that transpersonal perceptions may simply represent subjective experiences of a quiet mind or particular electrochemical states of specific portions of the brain.

My personal experience in exploring these realms through the eyes of research is that logic alone cannot explain the transpersonal realms. Any logical reasoning I apply must be based upon axioms of belief that cannot be tested or validated (except for internal consistency). I cannot know the mind of God in order to answer the question, "Why would God allow evil to exist?" Any educated guesses I make are based on my mortal perceptions and experiences in the world of human flesh and spirit. Relying on the words of Christ, Buddha, Allah, or any other luminary is an arbitrary preference, usually due to the teachings in one's family of birth or to conscious selection.

For example, a logical question to ask is, "Why would a Divine consciousness want or need to create mortal beings in a physical world?" To put it more skeptically, "Isn't it more likely that God is the creation of man than man the creation of God?"

Grof[630] suggests that

> [T]he undifferentiated Absolute Consciousness/Void represents not only the end of the spiritual journey, but also the source and the beginning of creation. The Divine is the principle offering reunion for the separated, but also the agent responsible for the division and separation of the original unity. If this principle were complete and self-fulfilling in itself, there would not be any reason for it to create and the other experiential realms would not exist. Since they do, the tendency of Absolute Consciousness to create clearly expresses a fundamental 'need.' The worlds of plurality thus represent an important complement to the undifferentiated state of the Divine. In the terminology of the Cabala, 'people need God and God needs people.'

My current personal understanding[631] of this question is two-fold. First, my life appears to be a series of lessons in forgetting and re-acquainting myself with the Divine. Through having forgotten the Divine I come to many fine nuances of awarenesses of the Divine that would never have existed without the forgetting. To put it another way, I know *knowing* more thoroughly from the perspective of having come to it after having forgotten; more than I could possibly know *knowing* without the experience of having been in a state of forgetting. Light is known better for its contrast with darkness than for its existence as light alone.

Second, from the limited vantage point of my human awareness of four dimensions,[632] I am unable to appreciate a universe that probably includes many more dimensions than I can begin to imagine. Quantum physics suggests there may be eleven dimensions of reality, according to demonstrable experimental data and theories that are consistent with these data.[633] The same principle of contrasts applies here. The vastness of the awareness of the All is more appreciable because of the limitations of my awareness. The Infinite Source could not sing praises to itself without lesser beings who can appreciate its awesomeness. It is said, in fact, that one of the functions of angels is to sing the praises of the Divine.

Evil, as I similarly understand it, exists in order to give us an understanding and appreciation of good. Good would not be as good without the presence of evil.

From perspectives of mortals, moral behavior demands that evil be prevented, limited, and counteracted in every way possible. From the perspective of a loving All, evil may be a way through which we learn to appreciate good. Not that the All perpetrates evil but that we are allowed choices of acting through good or evil, knowing we will collectively achieve a balance that is for the highest good of all.

Evidence from research in NDEs, channeled wisdom, and reincarnation memories supports this view. People who return from NDEs report they have a wonderfully clear and enormously liberating sense that the universe is moving along precisely as it needs to, according to a plan beyond human comprehension. Channeled wisdom suggests that individual human beings are not just single entities but also parts of various levels of collective beingness.[634] Reincarnation memories include experiences of returning to physical life in varying relationships with the same souls. It is very common for reincarnation memories to include recollections of having been in very different relationships with people who are now in our lives in intimate ways. The Eastern concepts of *karma* suggest that we are given opportunities across many series of lifetimes to repay interpersonal debts of evil that we have perpetrated and of good that has been done to us.

Here is an illustrative case. Trevor's father was alcoholic and frequently abused Trevor, his mother, and his sister, both verbally and physically. In a past life regression, Trevor remembered a lifetime in which their roles had been reversed. Trevor had been the father to his (current life) father, and Trevor had himself been abusive towards him in similar ways. The spiritual healing he had, which opened him to these memories, helped him understand, with a longer time perspective, the lessons his soul is in the process of learning. The healing brought him to a place of forgiveness for his father.

Believers, particularly those who have personal reincarnation and NDE memories, will often say that these experiences are more real than anything they have known in physical life. Skeptics will say that such 'memories' are the creation of fantasy, a way for the unconscious mind to explain, justify, and make peace with difficult and painful situations.

A common awareness with past life memories is that there is often a choice in reincarnating into karmic relationships. A person who experienced evil from a person in one lifetime is invited, in the spirit world, to reincarnate and provide that other person opportunities of experiencing evil in a later lifetime. It is not as an act of revenge but as an opportunity for the other person to learn – through being on the receiving end of evil – what that experience is like in order to expiate the evil. Conversely, the initial perpetrator of evil agrees in the spirit world to come back and be a victim in order to work through that experience.

Some childhood victims of evil, including ritual abuse, have reported they were conscious of angels around them, reassuring them that all would be well – even during the worst of their abuse. I have spoken with several people who have had such awarenesses.

Personal spirituality

> *Christian civilization has proved hollow to a terrifying degree... Too few people have experienced the divine image as the innermost possession of their own souls.*
>
> – Carl Jung

> *[T]he evolution of the spirit... is gathering force in the wide prophetic soul of the dreaming of things to come... recognizing that our revelation will no longer come in one overwhelming and unchanging revelation from one great man.*
>
> – Laurens van der Post [635]

A USA Today/Gallup poll in 2002 found that 33 percent of Americans described themselves as 'spiritual but not religious.' This represents an increase of three percent from 1999.

Some people have doubts about spiritual matters but apply the principles of the well-known wager of Pascal. This 17th century mathematician made a major contribution to the development of probability theory. He had serious questions and doubts about the existence of God. However, he decided to continue praying regularly. He reasoned that if God did not exist, then only a few minutes would be wasted each day in prayers that, in effect, were to no avail. If God did exist, and he neglected his prayers, he would be sacrificing his salvation through all eternity.

> *As it is convenient that there be gods, let us believe that there are.*
> – Ovid

Others in Western society find that there is something palpably missing from their lives. Joseph Felser suggests that we may suffer from 'spiritual malnutrition,' a lack of spirituality in our lives. It may take a spiritual quest, an illness, a trauma or other major event to force us to look where we haven't explored before.

Until science challenged religious explanations of the world, nearly everyone found their spiritual identification within religious institutions. In modern Western society, people are developing their spiritual lives through meditation, communing with nature, and involvement in healing activities. Many are coming to trust inner gnowings that accompany spiritual awareness. This is seen most dramatically in the transformations that occur with NDEs and other strong mystical experiences. Less dramatic experiences, such as a moment of beauty or caring, can also be doorways to spiritual wakening. Spiritual healings commonly open into spiritual awarenesses. Many healers suggest that illness and other forms of suffering are stimuli from our higher selves to awaken us to our spirituality.

In January 2002, a USA TODAY/Gallup poll found that 50 percent of all American adults do not view themselves religious, down from 54 percent in 1999. One third of Americans considered themselves to be 'spiritual but not religious,' which was an increase of 3 percent in that three year interval.[636]

The growing movements towards individual, personal spirituality are in sharp contrast with codified religious practices. Personal spirituality may be expressed through many forms of meditation and contemplation, qigong, yoga and other practices, individually or in groups. These practices often lead away from materialistic, reductionistic attachments and into personal searches for immanent awareness of one's relationship to the All and of spiritual ways of living.

More on personal spirituality in Chapter III-13.

Religious healing rituals, ceremonies and prayers

> *Ritual is a way we perform ceremony... In Holy Communion, the wine and the bread and the passing of them is the ritual. The ceremony is the emotional vessel the holds all the ritual. Smoking the pipe is a ritual. The prayers that we send in the pipe create the ceremony. Rituals allow us the means to come into the mystery realms of being. When ritual is done well, with great care, it becomes ceremony. Ritual performed with careless hands and a distracted heart is just a bunch of 'stuff.'*
> – Susan Chernak McElroy [637]

> *Prayer is an ancient technology for implementation of one's intention. People may have been taught* prayers *but they have not been taught* how to pray,
> – John F. Rossiter Thornton

Most religions prescribe rituals and ceremonies as part of their healing practices. These may involve prayers, chants, dances, drumming, particular postures for prayer and meditation, anointing, immersion in water, as well as rites of passage at times of birth, attaining adulthood, marriage and death.

Western science has viewed rituals as aids to attainment of alternative states of consciousness (ASCs) through monotonous sensory stimulation (similar to hypnotic inductions) or as magical beliefs which have little more than placebo value. You may be surprised to learn that there is evidence to suggest that rituals can actually convey healings for body, emotions, mind, relationships and spirit.

Rituals and ceremonies

> *Ritual is used to create a transformation in the status quo. Ceremony is used to restore or reinforce the status quo. Ritual is the intentional, focused use of chaos directed to change the current order of things, like an illness or pattern of self-destructive behavior. Ceremony strengthens the individual or community by releasing that which stands in the way of harmony and grounding people in the right order of things (natural laws).*
> – Christina Pratt [638]

Rituals are prescribed procedures for smoothing our dealings with each other. They often acknowledge and invoke the presence of higher powers to help us deal with problems that are greater than any one person can master – such as illness that leads us to seek healing; life changes that are acknowledged individually and communally; and social wrongs that need redressing;. Ceremonies are combinations and series of rituals – often quite elaborate – that link the present landscape with teachings and traditions from the recent and archeological past, rooting our awareness in the history of our people, providing a common language for naming and dealing with the winds or challenge and change that blow gently or storm through our communities and nations, and teaching us strokes for paddling our communal canoe along the rivers and seas of life.

Patrice Malidoma Somé notes that ceremonies include:[639]

1. *Invocations* welcome and invite the participation of spirits, guides, religious luminaries, and God in the activities of the individual, group or community. The invocation is enhanced by solemnizing and consecrating the occasion through the presence of revered symbols including religious leaders who typically dress in ritual ways to accentuate these effects. Rituals and ceremonies may include lighting candles, burning incense, reciting particular prayers, singing and chanting, dancing and other actions. Symbolic objects may be used that evoke the spirit of the occasion or represent the spirits or deities who are invoked. Examples include: making the sign of the cross during prayers; reciting series of prayers to celebrate religious holy days and life events; holding a prayer vigil to bring about an effect (promote a cause, invite a healing); and baptism.

2. *Dialogues* with spirits and gods to ask for guidance and help or to give thanks.

3. *Repetition* of the rituals in a consistent, traditional manner may be considered essential to the success of the ceremony.

4. *Opening and closure* rituals and ceremonies create a sacred space – both in the physical procedures and in flow of time – within which a special atmosphere is created that facilitates connections with spiritual dimensions and their participation in the proceedings. The closure rituals round out the experience and close the door to the sacred space, acknowledging its special place in the house of life.

5. *Sacrifice,* "which... means 'making sacred,' is a form of devotion and worship in which people surrender a part of themselves, give up a comfort for a higher good, or make an offering to a divine power." [640] Sacrifices may include fasting, relinquishing unhealthy habits, or contributing a portion of one's food or drink to the ritual.

6. David Kertzer points out that power which is ordered through symbols and ceremonies enables us to deal with archetypes. Archetypes are collective patterns of awareness and relationships that are mostly unconscious. They take individualized form within each society.[641]

To these observations of Somé I add:

7. *Alternative states of consciousness* (ASCs) are created through prayers, chanting, drumming, dancing, meditating, psychedelics and sometimes also through physical ordeals such as fasting, prolonging the ceremonies, and undergoing painful rituals. On the one hand these invite participants to let go of ordinary consciousness, and on the other they open into the special realms where God can be sensed more clearly.

8. *Group process,* in which the energies of the collective are more powerful than those of any individual within the group.

9. *Sacred spaces* facilitate the spiritual awarenesses that are created through ritual and ceremony. These spaces may be physical (geographic power points, buildings such as houses of worship, a room or a consecrated table on which ritual objects are kept), or spaces consecrated by the leaders of the ceremonies for special occasions, where the sacredness is endowed by the presence of the leaders and participants rather than by the physical surroundings.
    While the ritual, in and of itself, may convey spiritual awareness, it is the quality of participation in the ritual that determine how successful it will be.

Research on rituals

The strongest research evidence to support the value of rituals comes from studies showing that healing can be transferred through various vehicles. Water and soil treated by healers significantly enhanced plant growth,[642] and treated cotton significantly retarded the growth of goiters in mice.[643] Ritual objects may act as batteries for spiritual awareness and healing energies.
    Another line of research was developed by Felicitas Goodman, an American psychological anthropologist. Goodman studied positions assumed by healers depicted in cave drawings, hieroglyphs, and photographs. Some postures appeared repeatedly in independent sources separated by continents and centuries. She then exposed naive, Western subjects to the rhythmic sound of a rattle for fifteen minutes while they assumed some of these postures. She found that each posture

revealed many common sensations and subjective psychological states, among a wide sample of participants. For example, some reported that with particular postures they experienced time distortions, seeing colors, stimulation of the base of the spine, heat or other sensations. Different clusters of elements were reported with different body positions.

The fact that different naive subjects reported similar experiences suggests that these are not due to cultural expectations. The researcher could not have caused the effects as she herself did not know what to expect. This research hints that humans may be able to activate or open themselves to various energies and/or subjective states of consciousness and experience through particular rituals. The postures may inherently produce these effects or they may have acquired their efficacy through species-specific, morphogenetic fields.[644]

Luciano Bernardi and colleagues explored the effects of rosary prayer and yoga mantras on heart rhythms. They found that "both prayer and mantra caused striking, powerful, and synchronous increases in cardiovascular rhythms when recited six times a minute." They speculate that the effects are mechanical ones, in that the mantra and prayer each took ten seconds to recite, and each would typically be spoken with a single breath. By enforcing a six-cycle per minute rhythm on breathing, they brought about corresponding effects on the cardiovascular system.

Eastern religions recommend yogic *asanas* (postures), exercises and *mudras* (ritual postures and gestures) that might also help to access ASCs and/or other realities. Sensitives who see auras report that the flows of energy fields in and around the body are altered with particular postures and movements.[645]

Healees sometimes spontaneously move in particular ways or assume peculiar postures during healing, without any suggestions from the healers. In many cases these are identical with yoga postures. This is surprising, in that most of the healers I have spoken with, who have had healees respond in these ways, have no knowledge of yoga or of Eastern healing traditions; and neither do their healees have such knowledge.[646]

All of these observations suggest that specific postures and movements may contribute to healing.

Discussion: Rituals and ceremonies may, in many cases, be no more than placebos, however elaborate they are. In fact, more complex ceremonies could strengthen suggestive effects. Within sensory, linear reality, they may simply give participants the confidence or enhance their beliefs and expectations that something extraordinary will happen, which then creates a powerful *feel-good* in the participants; confirms through group consensus that the spirits and God are or will be there for them; creates alternative states of consciousness in which participants are more suggestible, and encourages a self-healing to occur in those who are afflicted.

Extending into psychic dimensions, rituals and ceremonies can enhance confidence in individual psychic abilities – which then facilitate their producing stronger psi effects; combine individual psi energies to produce stronger, group psi effects; and invite the participation of greater numbers of spirit helpers.

Morphogenetic fields are hypothesized to form from aggregates of individual participants' life experiences.[647] Repeated experiences form stronger morphogenetic fields. Rituals and ceremonies that are performed precisely the same way each time may key into the morphogenetic fields more readily.

Particular postures appear to predispose people to experience unusual psychological states, and might enhance their abilities to access psi and spiritual dimensions. This might explain some of the Eastern mudras, which are ritualized positions of the hands and other parts of the body as depicted in religious art, and some yoga exercises. These might facilitate spiritual awareness. Support for this speculation may be found in the spontaneous yoga postures that healees assume when receiving healings from particular healers.[648]

The wonderful richness in rituals that enhance spiritual awareness is too vast to review more comprehensively here.[649]

Prayer

> *My words fly up, my thoughts remain below.*
> *Words without thoughts never to heaven go.*
> > – William Shakespeare [650]

The practice of contemplative and meditative prayer is a discipline. At first we may feel we are merely reciting words – perhaps even that these are words written centuries ago and not particularly relevant to our life today. To go deeper into prayer requires focused, regular engagement. At first, as with any meditative practice, the mind may wander. With repetition, prayers *deepen*. We reach into levels where we connect with personal inner resources that we didn't know existed. Prayer helps us to open into spiritual dimensions of reality. Those who engage in prayer find that their inner spiritual awareness is every bit as real to them as any proof that might be presented in the outside world.

> *Don't pray when it rains, if you don't pray when the sun shines.*
> > – Leroy (Satchel) Paige

Prayer is a form of healing. The origin of the word prayer is in the Latin *precari*, meaning *to entreat*. Prayers are commonly offered as *petitions*, asking for something to help oneself, or as *intercession*, asking to help others. Other prayers may be offered as *invocation*, asking for God's awareness and attention; for *confession* over sins or acts that are regretted; for *forgiveness* when one repents one's misdeeds; *lamentation*, when one cries out and asks that one's pains and anguish be heard and acknowledged; *adoration*, expressing awe, gratitude and praise; *thanksgiving*; and more.[651] In one of its deepest variations, as Larry Dossey[652] observes, "Prayer is not an innovation, it is a process of remembering who we really are and how we are related." Prayer is the most common intervention for healing, with an estimated corps of individuals and prayer groups[653] in the many millions using this healing modality.

Prayer also provides a binding ritual to maintain cultural cohesion, a rootedness that provides one with a sense of peoplehood that is nurturing and sustaining in times of major stress.

Prayer opens us to awarenesses of our connections with the Divine. Beyond the act of prayer, a deeper connection develops – of self with Self and the All.

In petitionary prayer the interventions of God, Christ, Mary and saints (or the relevant gods and saints of other religions) are *requested* for illness. In healing services the prayer itself is felt to facilitate Divine intervention through opening the petitioner to receive it, through invoking the presence of highly spiritual intermediaries (in flesh and spirit), and through acknowledging the unity of the people praying with the Deity.[654] I have also heard healers *command* God to responds to their orders to heal someone – which still feels to me a petition, as much as it presumes to be otherwise.

Meditative prayer may help people to find within themselves the states of mind in which deeper primary awareness of their unity with the Creator can be experienced. Some find that hymns and fervent chanting brings them to these states. Others prefer silent, inward meditations.

> *When you ask for something in a prayer you are really just praying to yourself, but when you sit in prayer with a willingness to listen, you receive God, you receive deeper and deeper levels of yourself – you may even discover that there is no such thing as 'strangers' but only a oneness that all share.*
>
> – Stephen Levine [655]

Another function of prayer is to consecrate rituals with healing power, such as in sprinkling with blessed water or anointing with oil.[656]

Suffering and prayer are experiences rich with lamentations, questioning and explanations within all religious traditions. For instance, these are addressed by Rebbe Nachman, a Jewish mystic from the early 19th century:

> When the crisis of faith is so great that even cries without words cannot help, one has to cry from the heart alone. The heart alone cries without our letting out a sound. And from the depths of the heart comes guidance, for "like deep waters, so is counsel in the heart of man…" [657]
>
> – Avraham Greenbaum [658]

Greenbaum[659] offers further observations:

> *Prayer is not just a matter of asking God for favors. It is our way to channel divine power and blessing into ourselves, our lives and the whole world. Through prayer the soul rises to God and is healed, and in turn sends healing power into the body.*

Though a full discussion on prayer is beyond the scope of this book, a few further observations may entice the reader to explore further.

In Jewish tradition, one must not pray on the High Holy Days for forgiveness from God before one has asked the forgiveness of one's fellow man. One prays to God directly.

> *Holy song is the paradigm of devotion to God. The entire creation is a downward emanation from God to Man, designed with the purpose of bringing man to connect with God. The climax of creation is when man attains his purpose and sings out joyously to God in recognition and thanksgiving... The downward chain through which God reveals Himself turns into an upward ladder of ascent on which we, his creatures, rise step by step beyond the bounds of the finite until we become totally merged within His unity.*
>
> – Avraham Greenbaum [660]

In Christian traditions one must have faith in Christ in order to be forgiven for one's sins. One may pray to Christ, to saints and to God.

In Eastern and many shamanic traditions, one may address prayers to a variety of gods or spirits associated with a wide range of aspects of nature.

Personal spirituality often presumes that everyone is part of the All – in which case, prayer is an acknowledgement of this unity and a search for inner guidance towards the best paths of acceptance and action.[661]

Jewish tradition holds that prayer can stave off death. An example is the story of Rabbi Yehuda Hanassi, who lay unconscious on his deathbed, barely clinging to life. His disciples were loath to see him leave this earth and kept a constant prayer vigil to prevent his spirit from departing. His wife, seeing him in distress, prayed that his soul might depart but as his disciples continued to pray for his soul to remain, her prayer was not answered. She then took a large jug and sent it crashing to the floor. This momentarily silenced their prayers and the Rabbi's soul departed.[662]

In many church services the more direct intervention of healing by laying-on-of-hands is gradually being reintroduced, combined with prayers. With some, this is merely another ritual. With others, spiritual healing is included and results are frequently observed in healees on the levels of body, emotions, mind, relationships and spirit.[663]

Prayer healing is practiced in most religious traditions, either as part of the routine prayer services or in prayer healing groups, which meet specifically for this purpose.[664] Prayer healers collectively constitute the largest group of healers in the world. Many of these groups function strictly within the confines of their own religion and some may consider prayer healing by all other prayer healing groups to be suspect of impurities in one way or another, or in some cases even potentially involving the work of the Devil.

The teachings of various religions that claim prayer is an actual force for good in the world are supported by healers and psychics, who report direct perceptions of the effects of prayers. Typically, they see white or golden light surrounding those who pray and those for whom prayers are being offered. As a potent intervention, it is therefore important to ask permission before sending prayers.[665]

Research on prayer

Prayer healing has produced significant effects in some studies addressing serious health problems, but no effects were noted in several other studies.

Randolph C. Byrd performed a double-blind study of intercessory prayer for treatment of patients in a coronary care unit (CCU). He randomized 192 patients to the prayer group and 201 to the control group. There were no differences between groups on admission in degree of severity of myocardial infarction or in numerous other pertinent variables. Those sending prayers were exclusively born-again Christian, praying many miles away from the hospital for the wellbeing of the experimental group and never having any contact with the patients. Significantly lower illness scores were recorded for the prayer group than for the control group, using a problems severity scale devised by Byrd. "Significantly fewer patients in the prayer group needed intubation/ventilation... or antibiotics... had cardiopulmonary arrests... developed pneumonia... or required diuretics... However, the average times in CCU and durations of hospitalization were nearly identical between groups." [666]

These results might actually be more significant than the figures indicate because, as Byrd noted, some of the control group patients may have been sent prayers from outsiders who were unassociated with the study. Presumably, this would reduce the differences between groups.

William Harris et al, replicating Byrd's study, randomized, 990 consecutively admitted patients on a CCU into a controlled, double-blind trial of prayer healing. There were 466 in the prayer group and 524 in the control group. Neither the patients nor the staff knew that this research was being conducted. Prayers were sent by volunteers of mixed religious affiliations.[667] Harris and colleagues developed another assessment scale because standard scales do not exist for assessing CCU cardiac status or clinical changes. The prayer group demonstrated significantly greater overall improvement on this scale than the control group.[668] In this study as well, no significant differences were found in length of hospital stay between the two groups.

AIDS was the subject of a third trial of prayer healing. Fred Sicher et al. arranged a randomized, double-blind study of distant healing on 40 volunteers with advanced AIDS. They were classified in AIDS severity category C-3, which meant that they had $CD4^+$ immune cell counts under 200, a history of at least one AIDS-defining disease,[669] and were taking prophylactic treatment against Pneumococcus carinii (causing pneumonia). "Volunteers were... randomly assigned to receive either distant healing or no healing. All received standard medical care from their own doctors, at several different medical centers."

Distant healing was sent for ten weeks by 40 healers in various parts of the United States. Healers sent healing for an hour each day, six days per week, over a 10-week period.[670] Healers were rotated randomly in weekly healee assignments so that every healee had ten different healers who sent healing over the course of their treatment. Healers' religious backgrounds included Christianity, Buddhism, Judaism, Native American and other Shamanic traditions, and healing traditions included several modern-day healing schools.

Subjects and doctors were blind to who received the healing and when the healing was sent. There was never any contact whatsoever between healers and patients. Assessment of severity of illness was also done on a blinded basis.

At six months following the initial assessment, the prayer group "had significantly fewer AIDS-related illnesses... and lower severity of illnesses... Visits to doctors were less frequent... as were hospitalizations... and days in hospital..." Mood showed significantly more improvement in the prayer group.[671] The authors point out that the overall improvements appear to indicate "a global rather than a specific distant healing effect."

These are three of the best healing studies published to date, showing effects of prayers. It is also of note that they are published in respected, conventional medical journals.

William Michael Green explored effects of ten people praying from a distance for reduced anxiety and enhanced recovery of 57 people undergoing pituitary tumor surgery. Strict double-blind procedures were maintained, with hospital staff not informed who was in the experimental group, subjects unaware of whether they were being sent prayer healing, and the people praying receiving no feedback during the study on the progress of the people for whom they prayed. A part of the study also explored whether *expecting prayer healing* or *just expecting a normal outcome of surgery* made a difference. Significant decreases in anxiety were found in the group of patients who had normal expectations and prayer.

In another study, Barbara Schutze addressed the question: "Does group counseling with the addition of intercessory prayer for psychological (inner) healing change self-esteem more than counseling without the intercessory prayer condition?" A Self-Esteem Inventory was used as the measure of change. Significantly greater improvement was found in the subjects who had intercessory prayer.

Prayer was also studied in a totally different context. P. M. H. Atwater studied several hundred reports of Near-Death Experiences in Children.[672] While the children were in the NDE state, they also reported awareness of prayers.

> Many of these youngsters actually *saw* prayers being said for them while they were out of body. They describe how the power of those prayers turned into beams of radiant, golden, or rainbow light that arched over from the one saying the prayers, no matter how many miles away, to where they themselves were 'hovering.' Once the prayer beam reached them, the feeling would be akin to a 'splash' of love or an incredible warming. Because they have seen and felt the effectiveness of prayer, child experiencers consider it a valid and real way to talk with God while sharing God's healing love with others.[673]

A number of other studies, several of these involving hundreds of subjects, showed no effects of prayer healing for people, for reasons yet to be clarified.[674] Prayer healing has been shown in a variety of studies to enhance plant growth.[675]

Discussion: The research suggests that prayer healing is an intervention which can have potent effects on other people's physical problems, even when they cannot know whether prayers were being sent for their conditions. The carefully controlled, double-blind studies, published in peer-reviewed, conventional medical journals, suggest it is highly unlikely that this is a placebo effect.

It is difficult to explain within conventional scientific paradigms how prayers from a distance could influence physical or psychological problems. This cannot be a placebo effect when people who were being prayed for did not know whether prayers were being sent. Nor is suggestion a likely explanation for prayers sent to plants, though in Loehr's reports it is not clear whether 'blinds'[676] were used in many of the studies, so preferential handling of plants could possibly have been a factor in the enhanced growth of those which were subjects for prayer healing. The findings are sufficiently impressive to suggest that there are aspects of our world which we need to study further, and theories yet to be proposed to explain these.

Intercessory prayer for the benefit of someone in need, is widely practiced around the world. Seán ÓLaoire suggests several common perspectives on intercessory prayer:

Theory One – The Charade: Since God is omniscient and we live in an omnidetermined universe, intercessory prayer is merely chatting about the inevitable.

Theory Two – The Satellite: Because of the 'curvature' of the space/time universe in which we live, God has to be the gateway and amplifier of all human interpersonal interactions. He behaves like a satellite dish in the heavens. One bounces one's prayer intention off Him and He redirects it to the specified target.

Theory Three – Abraham: In the book of Genesis, chapter 18, Abraham pleads with God over the fate of Sodom and Gomorrah, arguing that it is not fair to kill the innocent with the guilty. Initially, God agrees to spare the cities if fifty 'just men' can be found within them. Eventually, under Abraham's persistent haggling, God agrees to spare the cities if even ten 'just men' can be found within them. So the theory suggests that intercessory prayer is about bargaining with God.

Theory Four – Moses: In the book of Exodus, chapter 17, the Israelites are locked in battle with the Amalekites. Moses is praying, arms uplifted, on a hilltop overlooking the battle scene. As long as he can keep his arms aloft, the Israelites are getting the better of things, but when his arms tire and droop, the Amalekites gain the advantage. Finally, Aaron and Hur hold Moses' arms in the air and, thus, the ultimate victory goes to Israel. This theory suggests that there is some kind of formula or trick to intercessory prayer, and if only one can discover it, success is assured.

Theory Five – Seán ÓLaoire: We live in a universe which is evolving according to a loving blueprint. Humanity has unique abilities, through free will and self-reflection, to accelerate, inhibit or derail this process for planet earth. Intercessory prayer is the intention to align oneself with that process and thus become a channel for the loving energy of evolution to flow freely through the 5.8 billion humans who constitute the planetary 'SpiritBrain.'

It appears possible that the intent to heal may be an essential factor in distant Healings. This might be a crucial ingredient also in prayer healing. Many studies of intentional healing from a distance (not including prayer as an aspect of the healing) have shown significant effects on humans, animals, plants, bacteria, and yeasts.[677] While prayer healers are certain that prayers are more powerful than intent alone, this has yet to be confirmed in research.

The intent of the healer may vary in prayer healing, ranging from "Thy will be done." to "My will be done," or when ego is involved, to "Heal, damn it, heal!" *The Spindrift Papers* present a serious effort by a father and son team of Christian Scientists in the US to clarify whether 'qualitative thought' by a healer is superior to 'non-qualitative' thought.[678] Qualitative thought is not goal-directed, while non-qualitative thought seeks to 'push' a biological system towards a pre-conceived direction of change determined by the healer. Prayers and healing were sent to germinating seeds under various contingencies. For instance, the experimenters held a promise firmly in mind that if one set out of several sets of seeds germinated more quickly, they would be given more light. Measurable differences were observed in the predicted directions. The non-qualitative, 'Thy will be done' approach appeared to produce more significant effects.

Though the authors assert that these experiments support their hypothesis, the alternative of a simple experimenter effect, in which intention produces the expected effect, seems to me just as likely.[679]

It appears possible that *prayer for healing in all of its forms* and *spiritual healing as simple intent, done without deliberate invocation of formal prayers* (when it is not just a bioenergy intervention), may overlap so broadly as to be indistinguishable in their underlying processes and effects. I cannot see any way that an experimenter effect can be ruled out as the cause of healing in an experiment – which may make it impossible to confirm through experiments that prayer, per se, is an agent for healing. The same is true, of course, for every other healing modality that requires an agent to administer it and to study its effects.

It also appears possible that prayer which invites participation of Higher Powers could be more effective for psychological reasons. Anticipating the help of an omnipotent, omniscient God could add power to human prayers. If God is no more than a wished-for father figure, this may still enhance confidence in the likelihood that prayers will be answered. That would facilitate prayers that carry less doubt; which, in turn, would make the power of suggestion more potent and more likely to produce positive effects of prayers. Furthermore, if God is a construct of human creation, the very fact that people have been praying to God for many centuries could create a morphogenetic healing field.[680]

The formal research on prayer healing suggests that experienced prayer healers appeared to produce more marked effects than the (presumed) inexperienced healers who were praying for many of the patients, including those in the control groups. While it would be interesting to analyze which aspects of prayer healing contributed to make them more potent, and various religious groups might like to prove that their prayers are superior to those of other groups, such studies would be fraught with sectarian issues that discourage pursuit of these questions.

It is my personal impression that individual healer factors are far more important in determining the efficacy of healing than particular rituals, beliefs, practices or the name given to the divinity to whom the prayers are addressed.[681]

More easily understood are the personal beneficial healing effects of prayer practice, which appear to resemble those of meditation. [682] In addition, prayer helps to deal with life crises, to bond people with their praying community, and to open into spiritual awarenesses.

> *More things are wrought by prayer*
> *Than this world dreams of.*
>
> – Alfred Lord Tennyson [683]

Personal benefits of spiritual awareness and practice

Leaving for later in this book a review of the vast body of evidence which shows that religious affiliation and practices are correlated with health benefits,[684] there are immediate benefits in terms of spiritual enrichment. Exploring the world through this inner awareness, one can come to appreciate that each of us is a part of a vaster reality. This is the essence of spirituality as appreciated by traditional societies, such as the Native Americans, in their healing practices.

> *[I]n the context of traditional culture, the word medicine... means the presence and power embodied in or demonstrated by a person, a place, an event, an object, or a natural phenomenon. In some tribes, the word for medicine may connote spirit, power, energy, or mystic potency... Thus, the... medicine, whether a prayer or an herb, affects more than illness; it establishes or restores a state or harmony and positive thinking.*
>
> – Kenneth Cohen [685]

You don't have to be a believer in God or in any religion in order to experience personal spirituality.

> *[The] highest praise of God consists in the denial of Him by the atheist who finds creation so perfect that it can dispense with a creator.*
>
> – Marcel Proust [686]

My own experience is that it is possible to bring discrete specimens from observations of our inner spiritual experiences for analysis in the light of reason – both in personal explorations of spiritual awareness and in teaching others to develop their energy medicine and spiritual healing awarenesses. This helps us to feel reassured that we are not simply indulging in hopeful fantasies.

Here is an example of this type of investigation.

Experiential explorations of spiritual awareness
Seat yourself comfortably in a quiet environment where you will not be disturbed for about 45 to 60 minutes. If you have a familiar practice of meditation or prayer

then use that as a starting point for quieting and centering yourself. (The term *centering* comes from potters. If their clay is centered on the potter's wheel, it will stay there. If it is even a little off center, it will fly in all directions. It is the same with our minds.)

Step 1. Once you are centered, think of someone who could use spiritual healing and would not object to your sending him or her your healing wishes. Spend as long as feels intuitively right to you in sensing that you are projecting healing to that person. Write down how you felt during this portion of the exercise. The following footnote will give you further instructions for steps 2-4, but don't read these before you have completed Step 1.[687]

Going deeper through meditations

Meditation is the most common route for reaching personal spirituality, practiced through endless variations that are limited only by habit of limited practices or laziness. To a great extent, this is simply a way to quiet the chattering of the mind that distracts us from our awareness of our connection with the All.

In many meditations it is important to sit quietly and comfortably, with your back upright if possible. Don't hesitate to move if you become uncomfortable. This is not an endurance test but a journey of inward exploration. Do these meditations one at a time, for as long as they feel right to you. Most people find 5-15 minutes comfortable. With practice this may be extended to 30 minutes or much more.

Here are a few simple meditations:

1. Using the metronome that is always with you, your breathing:

a. As your breath comes in, simply welcome it quietly to yourself with the word 'In.' As your breath goes out, simply acknowledge it with the word 'Out.' Stay with this focus.

With this meditation or with any other one, if external sounds, thoughts, feelings, or anything else draw your attention away from your breathing, gently but firmly tell them that you can give them attention later but that now you are focusing on your breath.

b. Sense that with your in-breath you draw in spiritual, healing energy that spreads to every particle of your being. With your out-breath you release any tensions or other inner dross that you don't wish or need to carry around inside you any more.

c. Count your breaths, starting with 'and' on the in-breath, then '1' on the out-breath, then 'and,' then '2,' and so on up to 4, when you start back at 'and... 1.' If you get distracted in any way, simply return to '1.'

d. Repeat (c), matching 'and' to the out-breath, and the numbers to the in-breath. You might experience this as emptying your mind of ordinary reality, then inviting spiritual awareness in.

2. Pick an object you find pleasing to contemplate. Focus your full attention on it. Notice every detail of its beingness – its shape, its colors, its textures, and so on.

Explore this with plants or flowers as well as with inanimate objects.

3. Take an observer's position to your inner processes. As you notice anything coming up on the screen of your awareness, acknowledge it by naming it 'thought,' 'feeling,' 'memory,' and so on. Simply watch it, don't engage in analyzing or wrestling with it. When this is replaced by another mental visitor, simply repeat your observing and labeling.

4. Meditation does not have to be a separate activity. As you go through your day, pick an activity where you will constantly maintain your awareness of yourself as an observer to what you are doing. In other words, stay aware that you are conscious of doing what your are doing.[688]

5. If you find your mind is very chatty and distractible, then the following may be a useful meditation.
a. Picture to yourself that you are in a bubble that is as large as you wish it to be to feel comfortable. It can be as large as a room or as small and snug as a space-suit. It can be located wherever you wish it to be. It might be in your home, out in nature, or floating in the air. It can be opaque if you want privacy and solitude, or transparent if you wish to focus on the outside world. It could be mirrored on the outside to keep others from seeing in, but clear from the inside so you can look out. (I like to have mine floating in a coral lagoon, with transparent walls, so that I can see the play of sunlight on the water surface above and the shadows of waves on the sands below, with beautiful corals and fish to watch. Enjoy your privacy!
b. Start as above. As any thought or sound or other item enters your awareness, welcome it lovingly. Wrap it in its own bubble and then pop it through the wall of your own bubble and let it float away. You may disconnect your awareness of it as it passes through the wall of your bubble, or you may watch it as it floats away. Then return and wait for the next item to enter your awareness that you treat in the same way.[689] This form of meditation is helpful for dealing with distractions.

Meditation allows us to quiet the mind from its chatter and its focus on everyday, outer world matters. With prolonged practice, it helps us open into transcendent awareness.

Spirituality grows with our involvement in spiritual activities. Periodic retreats for more prolonged contemplation help to deepen meditative practice, as do meditations in the presence of others who are pursuing similar paths. Having a teacher who can sound a meditative note on their spiritual tuning fork to which we can resonate is also a help. Pir Vilayat Khan,[690] head of the Sufi Order of the West and an experienced meditation teacher, says,

> The purpose of life is to make God a reality... Making God a reality is the counterpart of one's realization, which means that awakening is overcoming the limitation of one's personal vantage point... [C]onsciousness functioning in a human being is focalized into what one calls the personal consciousness. It is really the Consciousness of the Universe, but it is functioning as though it were focalized, and consequently one is judging things from that vantage point. Awakening is

being able to change one's perspective from the personal vantage point and being able to see what is being enacted beyond the appearance of things.

The word *God* may be uncomfortable to some, particularly when they were taught that God is watching their every move and tallying every sin in a book that will be used on Judgment Day to determine their residence for the rest of eternity. Swami Satchidananda[691] suggests, "... God is an experience... God is not a person."

If personal acquaintance with God is universal, one would think that it could be possible to develop a universally acceptable religion. Because cultural differences shape perceptions and interpretations of inner awarenesses, this is highly unlikely.

> *A universal theology is impossible, but a universal experience is not only possible but necessary.*
>   – A Course in Miracles [692]

More on spirituality in the following chapters.

Problems of spiritual awakenings

Mystical traditions caution against rushing into spiritual awakenings without proper support from spiritual teachers and without appropriate preparations.

Hassidic Jewish mystics advise that in order to study the esoteric texts you must wait till you are over forty years old, must be married, and must be of the masculine gender. Even if you meet these criteria, you are warned that not everyone who enters the garden of mystical awareness is able to return. Some may become lost in inner worlds of delusions or psychoses.

There is a good measure of wisdom in this advice, however, though we may well suspect that some of these warnings are products of male-dominated traditions and that others perhaps were devised as fences to protect a particular religious turf. Nevertheless, there may be legitimate reasons for caution. In exploring new territory it is possible to wander into realms that are unfamiliar. Some of these are beautiful and peaceful but others may be alien and frightening.[693] The greatest danger may be from our own fears. If we panic while in an alternative state of consciousness, we may become so stressed that we have a nervous breakdown. Considering this possibility, it may be wiser to wait until one is mature, has the emotional support of a family, and is not likely to be emotional under stress before embarking on one's own into explorations of these inner realms.[694] The guidance of a meditation teacher may help to deal with these and any other issues that arise in the course of meditating.

One can also become entranced with the allure of visiting other worlds, avoiding dealing with the challenges of the everyday world. For some people it is easier to drop out into spiritual preoccupations than to face situations they find difficult. This is the *spiritual bypass*.[695] Among these are many who become *workshop junkies*, attending endless series of weekend spiritual experiences but devoting themselves to no one practice that could take them to deeper explorations of their inner self and their higher Self. We must finish dealing with earthly existence before we go off to dwell in other dimensions.

Intelligent design

The concept of intelligent design for living organisms has been discussed for several centuries, preceding Darwin by many years. William Paley,[696] an English theologian, suggested that if someone finds a pocket watch in a field, he would naturally infer it must have been produced by an intelligent, designing human rather than by natural processes that acted blindly. Similarly, he argued, a supernatural creator must be postulated to explain the complexity of the natural world. This *argument from design* was the generally accepted explanation for the natural world until Darwin published the *Origin of Species*.[697] Evolution through natural selection of the fittest appeared to be the better explanation. Darwin's theory, based on numerous examples from natural science, particularly archeology, was quickly adopted by scientists. Subsequently, various experiments, particularly in genetics, have confirmed that natural selection processes can produce changes in the forms and functions of a species.

In recent years, the theory of intelligent design has had a resurgence. Phillip E. Johnson initiated this movement with his book, *Darwin on Trial*. Closely following this publication, the Center for the Renewal of Science and Culture (CRSC) launched the intelligent design movement.[698] The 'Wedge' agenda of the CRSC and intelligent design movement is openly stated to be aimed at splitting science from 'atheistic naturalism' and replacing it with evangelical Christianity. Within this context, *intelligent design* is simply another term for *creationism* – the belief that the Bible provides the true and only acceptable explanation for the creation of the world.

Intelligent design is advocated primarily by Christian fundamentalists through two broad approaches:

1. Basing their arguments on Biblical scriptures, the first approach insists that Darwinian evolution is impossible because the Biblical timeframe for creation spans about 6,000 years.

Fundamentalist creationists base their arguments on faith in their interpretations of the Bible. No arguments or discussions, however reasoned and based on scientific evidence, can counter arguments based on creationist faith. (Nor do contradictions within various portions of Biblical scripture, nor contradictions between interpretations of scripture by various religious factions appear to bother fundamentalists.) The frames of reference for science and creationism are so basically different that I have difficulty seeing how there can be a meeting ground for resolution of their differences. It is like arguing that logic trumps love on the one side; or on the other side that God must have created the world because no logical theory can explain the ultimate source of the universe, since we can always continue to ask, "So how was the Big Bang (or any of its precedent processes) created?" There can be no compromise or consensus other than to agree that each system has its own, separate, and distinct foundation for belief, and each builds its arguments on these. Faith is discussed at great length in Chapter III-11 and will not be considered here.

2. The second approach argues that scientific evidence shows that Darwin's theory is too simple and inadequate to explain the complexity of the world as we know it. Evidence is put forward suggesting that evolution cannot have produced the enormous varieties of living organisms on this planet, even over spans vastly longer than 6,000 years. Arguments for intelligent design based on interpretation of scientific evidence can be reasoned without relying on religious faith and will be discussed here.

Before examining this evidence in detail, several observations must be made about scientific theory and methodology. Within the stated rules of science, if newly observed evidence contradicts existing theory, then the theory must either be amended to account for the new evidence, or a new theory may be proposed to explain the conflicting evidence. Sadly, the majority of scientists, while giving lip service to scientific methodology, do not adhere to these rules. Theories that are clearly contradicted by new evidence are tenaciously maintained and perpetuated by mainstream scientists, who often dismiss the contradicting evidence a priori as impossible, rather than re-examine and restructure their theories. Science has in many ways become the religion of the Western world.

Spiritual healing is an excellent example in this regard. Despite the publication of numerous controlled studies of healing,[699] most doctors and scientists still refuse to accept the possibility that healing could really exist – since it contradicts the currently accepted scientific paradigms.[700] The lack of acceptance is expressed as limitations and denial of funding for studies outside the box of accepted theories; blocking of institutional approvals for innovative research;[701] editorial biases that deny publication to reports of research that contradict prevailing beliefs; and severe peer censure and dismissal from teaching and employment positions for advocating and pursuing studies that might contradict or disprove currently popular and accepted scientific theories. This is no different from the biases of religious fundamentalists – who refuse to consider any views that differ from their own. The same scientistic attitudes (i.e., scientific beliefs held as irrefutable tenets) hinder studies of parapsychology, discussed below, and of bioenergy medicine, discussed in *Healing Research,* Volume II.[702] So the present discussion is based on the stated rules of scientific study, even though the majority of scientists do not adhere to or abide by these rules – when it comes to subjects that are outside their beliefs about acceptable scientific theories and evidence.

> *Nothing is sacred to the point where it should not be investigated or put under inquiry.*
>
> – Robert A. Monroe [703]

Scientific discussions of intelligent design in evolution begin with the observation that the multitude and combinations of absolute requirements for life to exist is utterly mind-boggling. These can be seen at many different levels of organization in nature. They suggest the work of a Creator.

The scientific evidence for Darwinian evolution and the questions raised about its adequacy are rather technical. If you are not keen to delve into the finer details of these arguments, you may accept the initial summary above is a sufficient explanation and skip the following analysis of arguments for intelligent design.

Detailed discussion of Darwinian evolution

Michael Behe[704] presents the following succinct arguments against Darwinism and for intelligent design.

> Darwin himself set the standard when he acknowledged, "If it could be demonstrated that any complex organ existed which could not possibly have been formed by numerous, successive, slight modifications, my theory would absolutely break down."

Behe begins by pointing out that there are systems that are irreducibly complex. It appears extremely difficult, if not totally impossible, to form such systems through successive modifications. He suggests we consider a mousetrap as a simple example of an irreducibly complex system.

> It consists of (1) a flat wooden platform or base; (2) a metal hammer, which crushes the mouse; (3) a spring with extended ends to power the hammer; (4) a catch that releases the spring; and (5) a metal bar that connects to the catch and holds the hammer back. You can't catch a mouse with just a platform, then add a spring and catch a few more mice, then add a holding bar and catch a few more. All the pieces have to be in place before you catch any mice.

Natural selection can only choose among the irreducibly complex living systems that are already working. Therefore, irreducibly complex biological systems pose a powerful challenge to Darwinian theory – as Darwin himself noted. It appears highly unlikely that small, successive modifications in earlier systems could produce irreducibly complex cells, organs and organisms we see today. Any precursor mutation that did not contain an element essential for the whole organism would not function in isolation for the advantage of the organism.

John O'M Bockris nicely summarizes the steps required for the evolutionary development of the eye, a classical example of the mousetrap analogy in living organisms. In its most primitive form, the eye is found in single-celled organisms as a light-sensitive spot that has pigment beneath it. This allows the organism to sense the direction of a source of light, without perceiving any images. In multicellular organisms, collections of light-sensitive cells are located in a cup-like depression. If this is deep enough, and the opening into the depression is narrowed, it forms the equivalent of a pinhole camera. The next improvement is to have a transparent film over the opening, which is a primitive lens. The fullest development, familiar in humans and other mammals, includes a lens combined with a muscular iris that widens or contracts to control the amount of light admitted to the eye.

It is difficult to imagine how each of the components of an eye could develop – prior to the existence of all of the complete eye. The chemicals, 11-cis-retinal and rhodopsin are sensitive to light and transform light entering the eye into nerve impulses that go to the brain, where they are interpreted for whatever meaningful information they convey. How could these chemicals have been synthesized at precisely the right spot in order to initiate primitive vision? The same is true of the development of the indentation that forms a primitive eye, and of the lens that then appears as an enhancement of the eye. It is difficult to explain how all of these pieces could have assembled themselves by chance, since each component alone would convey no advantage to the organism.

Bockris notes that natural selection occurs from living organisms that already exist, in their irreducible complexity. Jumping from one irreducibly complex system into another one appears to be a process unlikely to occur by chance. This is a strong challenge to Darwinian theory, which cannot explain how selection would produce the original irreducibly complex system.

Behe points out that a basic cell is an even more irreducibly complex system. Cells contain essential organelles that cannot be removed without bringing the function of the whole cell to a grinding halt. Behe suggests that we consider the structure and function of whip-like flagella that give certain bacteria their mobility. Flagella resemble the mouse trap in their irreducible complexity. These organs for locomotion resemble outboard motors, including a long, whip-like propeller which bacteria rotate using a molecular 'motor.' Proteins hold the motor in place like the stator of a mechanical motor. Other proteins function similarly to bushings, allowing the biological driveshaft to enter the bacterial cell membrane. Dozens of diverse proteins are required for a flagellum to function. If any of them is missing, the flagellum does not work or cannot even be built by the cell.[705]

It is difficult to imagine, Behe argues, how such complex combinations of structure and function could have evolved through selection.

Many scientists are utterly dismissive of such arguments for intelligent design. Kenneth Miller points out that the example of the mousetrap actually reveals the flaws in Behe's arguments. Parts of what appear to be an irreducibly complex machine can have various functions. If you remove the metal bar and catch of the mousetrap, you no longer have a mousetrap. However, you do have a structure with three parts which can be used as a paper clip or tie clip. Remove the spring, and a key chain remains. A fishhook could be fashioned out of the catch of a mousetrap; the base could be used as a paperweight; and innumerable other applications could be devised from other parts or combinations of parts from the mousetrap. The same may apply within nature. Various elements from an existing organic system may be adapted into a new system and could provide building materials for evolution.

Miller argues that evolution may replicate, modify and/or combine proteins from one place and apply them to other, new designs and purposes. For instance, he disagrees with Behe's assessment that the structure and function of flagella represent irreducible complex systems. Each contains components that are found in other biological contexts. As an example, he notes that a sub-group of flagellum proteins can function without the remaining parts of this motor. This sub-group is utilized by many bacteria to inject poisons into other cells. While the functions of this sub-group differs from its function within the flagellum, it could still be favored through natural selection.

Miller notes that the same pattern can be seen in blood clotting proteins. These are very similar to proteins found in the digestive system. Research has demonstrated how evolution could have replicated and modified the gut proteins into a vertebrate blood-clotting system.

Miller concludes, "*Behe's points are philosophical, not scientific.*" This observations succinctly summarizes the criticisms of many who argue against intelligent design. They point out that its proponents have not designed nor have they conducted any studies to support their theories. They have relied instead on polemics and politics to promote their views.

Returning to proponents of intelligent design, Stephen Meyer, in a cogent, detailed analysis of Darwinian theory, points out a further logical inadequacy in this explanation of evolution.[706] New types of cells require entire systems of proteins to work together in order to produce these advantageous new features. Darwinian selection can act on the organism as a whole. However, natural selection cannot play a part in the generation of information that builds the desirable features – until the information required to build the required aggregate protein system has already been created. In other words, one can't select the functional features that offer advantages until the advantages are demonstrated. There would be no obvious way that selection would act on a given protein – prior to that protein altering a gene and prior to that gene producing an advantageous effect. Only at the point of demonstrating the functional advantage can Darwinian survival of the fittest can come into play, but not before this.

I believe that this argument is the most telling one: Meyers' cogent criticism of the illogic of Darwinian selection at levels of genes, proteins, and cells. For Darwinian selection to prevail at these levels would require that selection must precede the demonstrated advantages of features that will later confer greater survival on the members of a species. Logically, within the materialistic and mechanistic frameworks of Darwinian theory, there appears to be no theory that would explain how the original complex elements of an eye could have been selected for any purpose, prior to their having demonstrated some advantage in survival.

Summary of problems with Darwinian selection of the fittest
There are various stages at which selection may take place:[707]

- Darwinian selection of the fittest has classically focused on the functional advantages conferred on organisms by their form and other capabilities. There will be greater numbers of survivors among those who are stronger, swifter, smarter, or in some other ways better than other members of their species. These will survive through natural selection of the fittest.

- Genes control development of form and function. The genes of those surviving to have progeny survive through their offspring. Therefore, selection acts also on the gene pools of species, weeding out the less beneficial genes and promoting the proliferation of the genes conferring fitness on the organism.

- Between the level of genes and the level of a functioning organism there are enormously complex combinations of biochemical processes. Genes are templates for DNA and RNA, proteins that control the activities of cells, hormones, growth, reproduction, and every other function of a living organism. The proteins must work together in the correct sequence, timing, and harmony. The organism must acquire and digest nutrients, transform the nutrients into protein building blocks, and then direct the transport and recombinations of these building blocks into bones, muscles, respiratory, circulatory, nervous system, hormonal, immunological, digestive, and excretory systems. Somewhere in the genetic programs there are also encoded instructions for when to stop building. (These have yet to be discovered.) Maintenance and repair continue after full growth, presumably also directed by genetic programs. As complicated as the above may appear, it is an enormously simplified summary of the very, very, very complex processes that make life possible.

It appears at first glance logical to suggest that Darwinian selection would act as well at the cellular and biochemical levels. Proteins that are more advantageous to the organism ought to survive more often than those which are less efficient. However, there are problems with Darwinism at these levels:

- *Biochemistry and evolution*
  Simple logic does not take into account the tremendous complexity of biochemical systems in living organisms. If one protein changes by mutation, it is highly likely that it will be out of harmony with the collective programs and will not function properly within the complex systems that involve countless other biochemical reactions. More likely than not, a mutated protein will be like a wrench arbitrarily inserted into the mechanism of an assembly line for producing automobiles. It will block various organismic functions rather than conferring an advantage to the organism.[708] If the mutated, non-functional protein is essential for life, the organism will not survive.

- *Mutation rates of proteins and evolution*
  The observed rates of development of new species through archeological history cannot be explained by selection of mutated proteins. The rates of mutation that would have to occur in order for a viable new organism to be created by selection of the fittest proteins are far too high, relative to the time periods in which we know that new species have appeared.[709] Darwinian selection therefore cannot explain – at the level of genes and proteins – how evolution could occur.

- *Mutation rates of cells and evolution*
  The same problems and limitations of complexity arise in the evolution of new cells. Each cell must cooperate in close harmony with other cells in the body if the organism is to survive. Randomly mutated cells will more often than not prove to be incompatible with other cells in the body. Again at this level of biological organization, the organism is likely to function more poorly, possi-

bly to a fatal degree, rather than more efficiently. Again, the amount of time required for advantageous new cells to be formed through chance alone would be uncountably longer than the observed rates of evolution.

- *Illogic of selection of the fittest genes, proteins and cells*
Darwinian selection favors features of structure and function that offer advantages in survival. This selection can only occur after the advantages are demonstrated. Natural selection cannot choose better genes, proteins or cells prior to their demonstrating their advantages in the full form and functions of the organism.

As mentioned above, intelligent design has been a euphemism for Biblical creationism. Christian fundamentalists have challenged the theory of Darwinian mechanisms for evolution, presenting the above arguments and proposing that the only viable alternative is that God, as described in the Bible, must have been the creator of our world.[710]

Problems with Darwinism are reviewed in Chapter III-13 in even greater detail, on many further levels, supporting an expanded theory of participatory intelligent design. This, combined with evidence from research in spiritual healing, bioenergies and transcendent dimensions of experience, suggests that there may be further alternative explanations for intelligent design that do not rely on Biblical beliefs. I propose therefore that each of us is a co-creator of all aspects of reality, including participation in evolution, a thesis I will expand upon in Chapter III-13.

Contributions of religions to healing

This chapter is focused on the relationships of religions to healing. Let us return our attention to ways in which this occur.

Regardless of our individual religious beliefs, I believe the highest contribution of most religions is in helping us to heal ourselves. Healing, in its broader sense, is the process of bringing love, acceptance and forgiveness into our lives – in relationships with ourselves and with each other. In addition to healing our own lives, this can encompass healing our community, our nation and the entire planet. To the extent that religions teach healing and lead us in these directions, they are contributing to healing on all of these levels. To the extent that they divide us and pit us one against another, they are un-healing in their direct actions, but offer challenges for healing at other levels. As discussed below under *good and evil*, were there no evil in the world, we would have fewer challenges to give us the opportunities to activate our healing awareness and energies. So in a backwards sort of way, those religions which promote divisiveness, self-centered prejudice and even hatred may actually present challenges for others (and hopefully themselves as well) to bring more healing into the world.

You can't have the joy of repentance unless you sin first.
– Ashleigh Brilliant

Religions teach values that enhance social order and quality of life.

The Golden Rule, "Do unto others as you would have them do unto you," and the ten commandments are well known examples. Those who are inspired by these teachings live lives that are blessings to their families, friends, and communities.

For many, however, the good of others is forgotten when temptations of immediate pleasures and personal gains are difficult to resist. For others of us, navigating the paths of life through our head – with goals of achievements and satisfactions based on acquisitions of material goods or power – may distance us from our immediate knowing of the rightness and wrongness of our actions, which are recognized by our heart and our intuitive awareness. For both of these groups, the promoters of religious institutions have developed restraints that are reinforced by social pressures to conform, backed up by promises of rewards in the hereafter on the one hand, and threats of Divine retribution on the other. To some extent, these religious constraints support the social order.

Those who feel the personal presence of the Infinite Source – through experiences such as mystical or religious awakenings, NDEs, spiritual healing, and the like – and who know they are one with the All, need no religious teachings to guide or restrain them. Being one with the All makes it impossible to hurt anyone or anything – because one would be hurting oneself in doing so.

This is the hope and prayer of healers who work to bring more spiritual awareness into the world. If everyone were to open to these awarenesses, then love and light would rule and negativity and darkness would no longer prevail.

Religion can help people deal with pain and suffering.

> ... Pearls are created from the oyster's pain. They are the valuable tears of the sea. Suffering is meaningful if man learns to answer this not with the question 'why' uttered in despair, but with the word 'wherefore,' uttered with faith... The word 'why' looks back, the word 'wherefore' leads to the future and can even give meaning to the most severe suffering.
> – H. C. Moolenburgh [711]

A belief in God brings hope that there is meaning to life's struggles. The reasons for life's mysteries may not be comprehensible within human frameworks of understanding, but it is presumed that the Infinite Source has a plan behind it all.

> We can worship God by studying the beauty of his handiwork.
> – Petrarch

Faith in the healer and in the treatment can enhance the effects of the treatment. [712]

> The Rebbe used to say that it is not the medicine that heals, but faith in God's loving-kindness.
> – Rabbi Kalonymus Kalman Shapira [713]

A belief in reincarnation opens suggestions that pain and suffering are challenges the soul chooses to experience, or is challenged by some higher intelligence to face, in order to learn deep lessons that serve to advance the soul in its spiritual advancement. Within this belief system, the challenges we are given are graded to our level of development. Such beliefs can help us face difficult situations that might otherwise seem overwhelming.

> *Nothing happens to anybody which he is not fitted by nature to bear.*
> – Marcus Aurelius

Within the limits of materialistic existence, anything that threatens or ends life is bad. In a world in which reincarnation promotes lessons over a series of lifetimes, physical death is merely a transition to the between-physical-worlds existence, where further lessons are learned and where one prepares for the next round of incarnation. Conversely, coming into physical existence is a between-spiritual-worlds experience that allows us to practice the lessons we have learned in previous physical and spiritual world experiences. Within such a framework, a struggle in which we do not succeed or even fail to survive may be a worthwhile and valuable lesson. Maintaining a spiritual awareness and healing attitude as we deal with our challenges seems to be the most important lesson.

> *What is to give light must endure burning.*
> – Viktor Frankl

Why do some prayers go unanswered, while others bring about dramatic results? The skeptic will say that those prayers that are answered are simply prayers recited prior to events that would have occurred in any case, even without the prayers. Our whole belief in prayer may therefore be due to such chance occurrences, which falsely reinforce our beliefs that prayer is a potent intervention.

This is a well-known learning process studied by behavioral psychologists. If pigeons are given bits of bird seed at random times, they start behaving oddly. One will turn repeatedly in circles to the right. A second may flap her wings and coo incessantly – for no apparent reason. Another may scratch his head repeatedly, even to the point of scratching away all the feathers. On careful observation it becomes apparent that these peculiar behaviors begin when a seed arrives just as the pigeon turns to the right, flaps her wings, or scratches his head, and the pigeon appears to believe that *these behaviors are what caused the seed to fall into the cage.* Repeating the behavior will eventually coincide again at some point with another seed appearing, and the behavior becomes *conditioned* to continue.

Our belief in the success of prayers may be no more than a randomly reinforced behavior of this sort. Have you ever had the experience of pushing some irrelevant button that 'made the elevator door close?'

Unanswered prayers would be expected if random reinforcement of occasional prayers were the only reason to believe in prayers.

You may be the answer to my prayers,
But you're not the answer I was hoping for.

– Ashleigh Brilliant

Those who have faith through acceptance of religious teachings, and even more so, those who have had their fervent prayers answered, especially in circumstances that were unlikely to have changed on their own, are convinced that prayers are indeed potent interventions, facilitated with the support of spirits, saints, angels, and the Divine. The research in spiritual healing begins to confirm this is possible even though we as yet cannot explain the powers of prayer.

If this is so, then why are some prayers unanswered? Several hypotheses are offered:

1. The prayers may not have been offered in a manner that is effective. In some cultures, such as in Native American and African traditions, it is held that elaborate rituals must be followed precisely if prayers are to be answered. When some prayers are not answered, it is assumed that there was an error in the performance of the ritual.

2. The prayers may not have been offered propitiously. There are innumerable factors that may combine to influence events, many of which may be beyond our awareness.

To every thing there is a season, and a time to every purpose under heaven:
A time to be born, and a time to die; a time to plant, and a time to pluck up;
A time to kill, and a time to heal; a time to break down, and a time to build up;
A time to weep, and a time to laugh; a time to mourn, and a time to dance;
A time to cast away stones, and a time to gather stones together; a time to embrace, and a time to refrain from embracing;
A time to get, and a time to lose; a time to keep, and a time to cast away;
A time to rend, and a time to sew; a time to keep silence, and a time to speak;
A time to love, and a time to hate; a time of war, and a time of peace.

– Ecclesiastes [714]

3. There may be differences in the efficacy or potency of some people praying relative to others. Some people are particularly known for the effectiveness of their prayers. In Medieval Europe, Choni Hame-agel (meaning: Choni, the circling one) was known for being able to pray for rain successfully. When there was a drought, people would send for this man, who would come and place himself in a field, marking a circle in the earth around himself. He vowed that he would pray constantly and would not leave that circle until rains came. Many are the tales of his successes.

When the prayers of people with greater or lesser prayer potency are unanswered, other explanations may be offered.

4. Human frailties may have contributed to the failure of the prayers to bear fruit. The person praying may have had a bad day. Her attention might have been distracted.

5. Unanswered prayers are to be expected some of the time. God might have not been ready to grant their prayers for reasons that only He knows. (This has waggishly been framed as: "God answers all prayers, but sometimes the answer is 'No'.")

6. The skeptic will say that people reported to be successful or unsuccessful in their prayers just happen to be lucky on some days, unlucky on others, or have some sense of pattern recognition that enables them to select those situations in which they will be successful. Their successes may also be selectively recalled, while their failures are conveniently forgotten. Furthermore, skeptics point out that folk tales from centuries ago are often embroidered in the telling and re-telling so that they are more valuable as myths than as anything approaching scientific evidence.

7. With healing, there are enormous varieties of factors that may contribute to success and failure.[715] Many of these factors may have to be present in order for healing to occur. The same may also be true of prayers for anything else.
   In Jewish tradition it is said that "... healing can only come about 'on a particular day, through a particular medicine and a particular doctor." [716]
   Within such belief systems, when a healing has not occurred, then one of these factors must have been awry.

8. A prayer unanswered may be an angel's gift.
   The limited vision of a person praying, particularly at a time of stress or crisis, may lead her to pray for something that would not be for the highest good of herself or of others – when all factors are taken into consideration. Many people look back at their unanswered prayers for success with a particular relationship, for some material gain or even for healing, and are grateful that these wishes and prayers were not granted. Had they been granted, the much better relationship or material object that was found, or the deeply healing unfolding of life through treatments of the disease or lessons which the problems brought would not have come about. I have repeatedly been surprised at the cases of unanswered prayers for healing, in which people reported that the relational and spiritual growth which occurred as results of the illness had brought them to feel grateful for having their illness.

> *Miroslav Volf writes of his anguish at infertility for nine years, especially painful at Christmas when everyone was rejoicing "unto us a child is born." He writes, "If God's son indeed was in charge, it seemed that he didn't care to move even his royal finger in our favor. At Christmas, I felt like the only child in a large family to whom the parents had forgotten to give gifts. Others' joy increased my sadness..."*

After the incredible joy of the adoption of his two sons, however, Volf realized he hadn't been waiting for a child who stubbornly refused to come. He was waiting for the two boys he now has. "Fertility would have robbed me of my boys.... Infertility was the condition for the possibility of these two indescribable gifts. And understanding that changed my attitude toward infertility. Since it gave me what I now can't imagine living without, poison was transmuted into a gift, God's strange gift. The pain of it remains, of course. But the poison is gone. Nine years of desperate trying were like one long painful childbirth, the purpose of which was to give us Nathanael and Aaron. [717]

9. Karma may require that certain situations be endured or suffered for the growth of the soul. In past life regressions, people may become aware of the lessons chosen by their soul when it agreed to incarnate into a particular family at this particular time.

Rabbi Yonassan Gershom[718] has collected stories of people who recall past lives in the Holocaust. He tells the story of Anna and her husband, Richard, who were students in Germany during the rise of Nazism.[719] Both were idealistic, Anna investing her energies in the study and practice of psychology and medicine, and Richard joining a dissident student group. Because of Nazi harassments they fled towards France. Richard crashed their car deliberately against a tree, choosing intuitively to die with his wife quickly rather than be captured and die apart. When she crossed into spirit existence, Anna was very angry with him for having made this choice without consulting her – even though he explained that he had seen in a flash of precognition that they would have been captured just after the point at which he crashed the car, that they would have been separated, and that one of them would die – leaving the other behind.

After a period of helping other spirits in the spirit world who arrived from Holocaust deaths, Anna related that

> ... With the help of her two spirit guides, Ruth and Isaac, she wrote the contract for her new life on earth. The first forty years would be filled with struggle, physical and emotional pain, mental and spiritual challenges, learning, and the repaying of karmic debt. After this period, she would prosper materially and be able to serve G-d as a healer once more. Her guides promised that they would remain active in her life, providing the opening for her to remain connected to the spiritual worlds.

Anna was reborn in 1953.

> As Abby, I spent over a decade consciously mourning and grieving the losses of Anna's life. I struggled to complete her goals and was met with obstacle after obstacle. Finally, I took control of my own life in this incarnation, for myself and for my son. I stopped grieving. I forgave myself and laid Anna's driven memories to rest. I kept my love for Richard on the soul level, but let go of my yearning for him in this life.

I decided to pursue a career in counseling and acupuncture, in order to continue being a healer in this present life. It was through my study and practice of these healing arts that my own physical, mental, and spiritual pain was also healed, enabling me to release the sorrow of Anna and the Holocaust.[720]

The obligations of such karmic lessons may supersede immediate responses to prayers. For instance, restitutive suffering – to learn lessons of pain after having inflicted pain on others in a past life – may prevent healing in response to prayers. As with Job, however, persistent prayers are believed to contribute towards resolution of even such difficult situations.

10. Some situations are beyond human ken to explain.[721]

> *Our prayers are answered not when we are given what we ask, but when we are challenged to be what we can be.*
> – Morris Adler

Good and evil

> *Violence is not only demonic but also daimonic. Also inspiring.*
> – Thomas Moore [722]

Understanding the presence of evil in the world, and developing ways to deal with it, are among the greatest spiritual challenges. For the purposes of this discussion I define evil as the use of influence to coerce others to do anything that is against their better interests or to deliberately harm others.

Religious teachings promote good and suggest ways to deal with evil. Religious responses to evil vary from condemnation and codification of revenge through forgiveness and healing.

As prevention of evil is far easier than cure, enormous investments are made in educating and reinforcing good behaviors while discouraging evil ones. Religious teachings in houses of worship and schools help children acquire beliefs, values, and behaviors that are meant to shape their lives to be good rather than evil. Religious beliefs, affiliations, and practices reinforce positive behaviors for adults.

While all of these efforts may be helpful, clearly they are not sufficient to prevent or eliminate evil. Unhappy and abusive relationships, selfish and antisocial behaviors, serious crime by individuals, and wars, genocide, and corporate misdeeds attest to the failure of many efforts to prevent evil behaviors.

In many cultural groups, religious teachings suggest that their particular flock is the chosen one and that outsiders are infidels, to be viewed as less than human – or worse, to be condemned and attacked as opportunity allows or can be engineered. Conflict is therefore generated by religious groups, often with the perpetration of what I define as evil acts against outsiders, but which they perceive as justifiable because of their definitions of recommended and acceptable actions towards outsiders. More people have died from religious persecutions and wars than from all other scourges known to mankind.

Difficult questions are raised about innocent victims of evil, especially children. I have known many people who say, "I can't believe in a God who would allow guiltless people to suffer and be hurt." This is all the more difficult to answer when their questions relate to genocide, with the suffering and deaths of millions of innocent victims.

Theodicy is the attempt to understand why a God who otherwise is perceived as benevolent would permit evil to exist, or even be culpable for creating a world that includes evil. Several answers to these questions have been proposed. For example, Gordon Sherman, who founded Midas Muffler, once wrote:

> There is a teasing irony: we spend our lives evading our own redemption. And this is naturally so because something in us knows that to be fully human we must experience pain and loss. Therefore, we are at ceaseless effort to elude this high cost, whatever the price, until at last it overtakes us. And then in spite of ourselves we do realize our humanity. We are put in worthier possession of our souls. Then we look back and know that even our grief contained our blessing.[723]

Another answer is that disasters created by man and nature are nature's way of reshuffling the ecobiological deck to produce new evolutionary (physical and social) outcomes. The tsunami in Southeast Asia in 2004, while killing many thousands of people and injuring even more, brought together much of the rest of the world in rescue efforts. Overall, the bonds built in the rescue work may help the global community build future bonds of cooperation that could overcome international tensions which might otherwise lead to worse disasters – ecologically and socially.

Each religion has explanations for innocent victims of evil, and I do not propose to elaborate in even a light way on such major questions that have absorbed theologians and philosophers for thousands of years.[724] I do expand, however, on understandings of evil from perspectives of personal spirituality.

Stanislav Grof, a psychiatrist who has explored transpersonal awarenesses through deep psychotherapy, observes that good and evil are intrinsic to life. God's creation of evil may be understood in the Creator's exploration of all aspects of knowing creation.

> …To the extent to which the divine creates to explore its own inner potential, not expressing the full range of this potential would mean incomplete self-knowledge. And if Absolute Consciousness is also the ultimate Artist, Experimenter, and Explorer, it would compromise the richness of creation to leave out some significant options…
>
> The existence of the shadow side of creation enhances its light aspects by providing contrast and gives extraordinary richness and depth to the universal drama. The conflict between good and evil in all the domains and on all levels of existence is an inexhaustible source of inspiration…[725]

Grof points out that if disease were totally eliminated, we would also eliminate medical research and the pioneers and heroes who advance medical knowledge, opportunities for compassionate care and love, and the miracles of healing,. We would not have doctors, shamans, miraculous healings or psychic surgeons and would not have had Mother Teresa, nor reasons to award her and others a Nobel Prize.

Considering a world without evil in oppression, wars, and genocide, Grof suggests that we would eliminate major portions of human history. We would never know the heroic acts of people fighting for liberty – people who dedicated their whole being and at times even sacrificed their lives for causes they believed just, and to advance the ideals of their fellow-man and their country. There would be no triumphs over evil empires, nor any real appreciation of freedoms because we would never know the experiences of oppression that make these so sweet.

Along with these losses, he observes, we would be missing the inspiration of story, poetry, song, theater, painting, sculpture, and other art that have been inspired by these struggles. The need for religion would be very much weakened, "...since God without a powerful adversary would become a guaranteed commodity that would be taken for granted." [726] We would have little need for ritual life and would be missing a major motivation for reaching into the spiritual dimensions.

In short, Grof concludes, we would lose many dimensions of the cosmic drama which energize and inspire our existence.

Others have put it more succinctly:

> *Although the world is full of suffering, it is also full of the overcoming of it.*
> – Helen Keller

> *In the depth of winter, I finally learned that there was within me an invincible summer.*
> – Albert Camus

> *No pain, no palm; no thorns, no throne; no gall, no glory; no cross, no crown.*
> – William Penn

I believe the drama of good and evil on the stage of the outer world fascinates us because it resonates with struggles on our inner stage between good and evil thoughts, feelings and impulses. Each of us faces challenges of desires, hurts, fears and angers, with pangs of guilt and shame. How we handle each of these innerworld tests – of our moral fiber, emotional fortitude, and willpower – is reflected in outerworld conflicts and struggles. We find inspiration to understand better and deal with our own inner conflicts through the struggles of outerworld heroes. Each of us then knows good immeasurably better because of our vicarious and personal struggles with evil.

Acknowledging that evil illuminates and intensifies our appreciation of good in no way condones evil or suggests that we must not do our best to avoid and eliminate it. It does, however, relieve us of a sense of wrongness about the universe and God's role in creating a world that includes evil.

Jenny Wade[727] observes:

> Jesus, explicitly given the ability to eradicate hunger, declined to do so and said that suffering and material hardship would continue as part of incarnate life.[728] Similarly Gautama did not use his powers to eliminate suffering, but taught that it could be overcome by volition directed toward the self rather than the circumstances. Enlightened leaders have abandoned positions of rank and temporal power to incite change through self-development and example.

These speculations on good and evil are not merely theoretical. The burgeoning field of conflict resolution addresses societal conflicts as manifested between individuals, between the law and the individual, between diverse groups of people within the same community, and between cultures and nations. Kay Pranis and colleagues, with a wealth of experience in facilitating peacemaking circles, point out that conflict is a natural and normal aspect of life which can be growth-promoting as we work through it. However, it is destructive when it festers over long periods and is not vented, processed and released.

> Conflict is not just inevitable, as we are prone to say wisely and with a sigh of resignation. Instead it is part of the divine plan, a gift. Disruption is integral to God's order. Conflict doesn't sometimes provide us with energy, insight, and new possibility as reluctant by-products; newness cannot come without conflict. It is not a price to be paid and endured, but a condition to be sought and welcomed and nurtured...
>
> To manage conflict then would be to allow it, not to suppress it; to open our doors and windows to its fresh wind. Following this line of thought to its ultimate conclusion, violence and war become not conflict run amuck, conflict out of all bounds, but the final outcome of conflict quelled. *They result when we will not allow the other to be different, when we deny our life-giving dependence on the different one with all our might and means.*[729]

Peacemaking circles invite as many people from both sides of a conflict as can be mustered to a series of discussions to hear the stories of each side. Through this process, empathy and understanding are fostered – to the point that victims and perpetrators can agree on the steps necessary for a just restitution. Surprisingly, even in cases of murder and rape, it is possible to achieve this.

In this process, there are often major healings of family and community conflicts, extending far beyond the original individual perpetrators and victims.

One may well ask whether a world of spiritual growth and learning is possible without the inner and outer struggles with negativity. I actually find such a world difficult to imagine. In my experience, most people (including myself) tend towards complacency, satiety and laziness when not challenged in some way to rise above themselves.

Reincarnation also shines light on questions of theodicy. It is reported by intuitives and by people who have reincarnation memories and NDEs that at some point in spirit existence we are invited by our spiritual guides to contract for a lifetime on earth. A contract is an educational program designed for the spiritual growth of our soul. It involves challenges of working out our relationships with others, who have similarly contracted to play roles in the nested hierarchy of spiritual dramas that are choreographed by a wisdom that is utterly beyond our human comprehension. In order for there to be dramas as we know them, there have to be villains and heroes. In other words, we must each take our turns in each of these roles, in various lifetimes. The challenge appears to be to graduate from the role of villain, and ultimately from participating in such dramas.[730]

Cautions against sharing spiritual and healing knowledge indiscriminately

It is apparent from studies of religious writings of East and West that religious leaders through the ages felt that methodologies for opening personal spiritual awareness must be earned through rigorous practices and guidance under expert tutelage rather than acquired through reading, casual questioning, or psychedelic drugs that are taken without proper ritual and expert spiritual guidance.

In Jewish tradition, the *Kabballah* provides a rich literature on mystical teachings. A part of the learning derives from mental gymnastics of sorting out vague references and becoming aware through this process of meanings hidden within rich numerological and metaphoric allusions. The process itself is a metaphor for hidden meanings in life behind ordinary occurrences – awareness of which brings one to appreciate the infinite wisdom of God.

The Bible itself encodes within the Hebrew writing extensive esoteric knowledge. Stan Tenen spent two decades numerologically decoding the first sentence of the Bible, assuming that the first sentence must provide clues to esoteric ciphers which would be used in the rest of the text. Hebrew letters are assigned numerical values. *Aleph*, the first letter is '1'; *bet*, the second letter is '2,' and so on. He found mathematical patterns in this sentence that are so regular in their sequence that the statistical probability of their numerical values displaying such an order merely by coincidence is way beyond chance levels.

Tenen puzzled over patterns that suggest a geometric regularity as a part of the pattern. These patterns become apparent when one takes the numbers in sequence and makes a spiral of them. This then led him to further amazing deductions that he details in a series of videotapes. We have yet to obtain further analyses of Biblical texts based on these ciphers.

Other traditions have protected their esoteric teachings in similar manners. Initially, this knowledge was transmitted from generation to generation through mystical teachings available to only a few chosen initiates. Often, this knowledge has been dissipated and much of it lost, as time flowed through seasons of conflicts and the mystery schools were unable to continue their teachings.

Considering the corruptions that power brings with it, it is understandable that religious teachers should wish to maintain secret the potent methods that can open up within people enormous psi powers. Safeguards against the misuse of psi powers have included requirements that students have close supervision from mentors or apprentice themselves to religious orders if they wish to be initiated into mystical transpersonal teachings. This allows the teachers to determine when a particular student may be stable enough and ready to acquire the deeper knowledge.

Shamans in traditional cultures may teach apprentices in similar manners, conveying esoteric knowledge as the students mature into their healing powers.[731]

Today these cautions have been largely ignored by governments which have invested considerable sums and efforts in studying psychic methodologies that could be applied towards espionage and military aims.[732] Even here, however, the psychic person is usually accompanied by a guide when engaged in remote psychic viewing.

I believe that there is still a definite place to caution those who might be unwise, rash or impetuous and to not make it easy to develop psi abilities for those motivated by wishes for power and material gains more than desires for enlightenment and healing. Sadly, commercialism in our materialistic society puts development of psi powers on sale through numerous self-development courses, where little or no screening of applicants is practiced. Worse yet, teachers of these subjects usually work in isolation, with no peer or mentor supervision and few if any traditions that teach cautions. They are themselves prone to ego inflation and open to the potentials of becoming psychologically destabilized or of abusing these powers.

Western relationships with death and its healing

> *Death is normal, is good, is not defeat and is not the end. Every person Jesus healed later died...*
> *Death is the best solution in many situations and, "if it is of God, it were better not to contend against it."*
> – Charles C. Wise, Jr.

Death is another topic traditionally addressed by religion. Recently, segments of the Western medical and psychological community have shown renewed interest in its psychological and emotional aspects.

Elisabeth Kübler-Ross,[733] a psychiatrist, probably did more than any other person to return this topic to the awareness of the public in general and of the caregiving professions in particular. She has delineated the processes and stages involved in mourning various losses. These include the deaths of others; deterioration in health; terminations of relationships; or loss of positions or possessions of great significance – up to and including one's own anticipated loss of life itself. In *Death, the Final Stage of Growth* she presents a collection of writings by several authors, offering suggestions for healing through understanding and acceptance. In a third book, she shares experiences of children approaching death.[734]

Western society is strongly death-avoiding and death-denying.

Men do not care how nobly they live, but only how long, although it is within the reach of every man to live nobly, but within no man's power to live long.

– Seneca

Health caregivers are often untrained in dealing with issues surrounding death. I was given very little instruction in my medical and psychiatric training about helping people prepare for death, helping families with bereavement, or dealing with my own feelings of impotence in the face of terminal illness and bereavements with the death of people I worked with.

This denial of death by caregivers can be distressing to people who are dealing with death and bereavement issues. For instance, parents of children with Sudden Infant Death Syndrome (SIDS) have premonitions about the impending death of their children significantly more often than parents whose children did not die of SIDS.[735] The parents whose children died were frequently frustrated and distressed by their physicians' failure to address their fears seriously.

Denial of the pain of bereavement is frequently encouraged in our society. Too often the bereaved 'put on a brave face,' while denying and holding in their feelings in order to not feel the hurt of grief themselves, and not to upset others. Feelings that are repressed tend to fester inside – rather like a carbuncle. The unconscious mind, seeking to protect a person from hurt, then builds various avoidance fences around the emotional pus to keep it from erupting into painful awareness. The protective inner fences tend to keep people away from a full enjoyment of life.

[T]he *fear of death* recoils as a *fear of life*...
– Abraham Maslow [736]

A frequent problem I see as a consequence of unresolved grief is the unconscious avoidance of close relationships, out of fear of further losses. Maslow called this *the Jonah Syndrome*, a "fear of being torn apart, of losing control of being shattered and disintegrated, even of being killed by the experience." So just by reducing our fear of death, healing can be of benefit, and healing can help well beyond this.

So many parts of ourselves we have pushed away come up in grief. That is why grief has this enormity of potential for healing.
– Stephen Levine [737]

Spiritual healing helps relieve depression. It can release emotions hidden under layers of denial. I have also seen healing aid in the various stages of grief, such as in aiding to relieve guilt and anger. Where it sometimes helps most is in introducing awareness of spirit survival, through which people reach out beyond the grave to resolve unsettled emotional business with their dear ones.

Lawrence Althouse presents the Protestant view of healing from the vantage point of a minister who conducts regular healing services. He ponders knotty moral dilemmas, like praying for someone who is severely injured and seemingly a hopeless case; helping people fight a potentially lethal illness; and more. His section on ministering to dying patients is especially helpful, as in the following quotations:

> So where does the experience of death fit in with the ministry of healing? It would seem that death would be an embarrassing reminder that this ministry is often not effective. Instead, however, it is a reminder that no participant in this ministry must ever forget: All physical healing, medical or spiritual or both, are only temporary!
>
> In the minds of many people, death is regarded as the ultimate tragedy. Yet in light of our Christian beliefs and expectations, death ought to be regarded as *the ultimate healing*. It is not a tragic and ignoble end to life, a 'rotten break that overtakes us,' but a blessed part of God's plan and purpose for this world. Death represents not the thwarting of his game plan but really the fulfillment of it.
>
> Often it is only through this ultimate healing of death that a person can finally know the wholeness for which he or she was created. A person who has had to struggle through life with the burden of amputation, loss of vision or some other vital faculty, will be fully healed only through that transition we call death.
>
> So, sometimes in our ministry of healing we must help people to learn to die 'rightly,' as Hammerskjold put it.
>
> Actually, strange as it may seem, one of the greatest privileges in the ministry of healing is that of helping someone to die![738]

For the conventional doctor, treatment stops with death – or perhaps with the mourning of relatives if the doctor feels competent and has the time to intervene with the family. Religious clerics are often left to deal with this portion of life's unraveling. Western medical world views tend to relegate beliefs about the afterlife to a realm they label *mystical*, meaning that they cannot substantiate it within linear systems of reasoning, do not understand it, are therefore uncomfortable with it, and consequently do not want to delve into it too deeply – leading them to avoid the subject of death for the most part.

Western society is caught in the vicious circle of being death-fearing because it is death-avoiding. Fears of death are self-reinforcing. For example, in fearing death, we encourage the dying to spend their last moments in hospitals and hospices – where we will not witness their passing out of this life. We avoid speaking of death with the dying, and they with us, lest we upset each other. We turn over to specialists the tasks of preparing the body for burial and of interring the remains. We may even elect over the phone to have the body transferred from the hospital to a mortuary and hold the funeral with a closed casket or urn so that we never even cast eyes on the body or even the ashes of the deceased. By dealing as little as possible with the dying person or body of the deceased, we remain distanced and unfamiliar with the process of dying. The unfamiliar is alien, discomforting, and even frightening. We therefore distance ourselves from it emotionally. So the fears become deeper and deeper. Such fears can bring about great suffering, not only from the buried hurts gnawing away inside, but also from restraints they impose on our lives. Having lost someone close and not having grieved properly for them, people will often avoid close relationships out of unconscious fears that they will again be abandoned.

> *Some people are so afraid to die that they never begin to live.*
> – Henry Van Dyke

Bernie Siegel,[739] a surgeon who works closely with cancer patients, points out "[I]f we can react to loss with personal growth, we can prevent growth gone wrong within us." When we don't avoid the grieving process, we can deepen our appreciation of life. As we work through the pain, anger, guilt of grieving, we grow more confident in our abilities to deal with painful feelings. We don't distance ourselves from our own mortality. We can then face the big question of how we are going to deal with the end of our own life.

We may find it difficult to deal with our fears of death and dying, as I did when I went into my practice of psychotherapy and was soon faced with these sorts of issues. Over the years I have found a number of further ways of understanding and helping those who are approaching death and those who are bereaved to understand and deal better with death.

Reports of spirits in pre-death and deathbed visions challenge conventional scientific beliefs about life and death. Rather than re-examine our fears – of the unknown; of having to abandon familiar beliefs; and of approaching the end of our own lives – it is easier to distance ourselves from, or even to reject the evidence of, survival of the spirit – sweeping it under the carpet of repression that covers our unconscious anxieties and fears. This is a child's way (programmed into our biocomputers when we were young) of avoiding what is uncomfortable. It succeeds admirably in immediately reducing anxiety.

> *Death – the last sleep? No, it is the final awakening.*
> – Walter Scott

Sadly, this is nearly always counter-productive in the long run. People with terminal illness are desperately eager to discuss their fears. By tacitly making a pact of silence with them, family and health care professionals often condemn them to carry their fears, unspoken and unshared, to their grave. Worse yet, collusion in avoiding their fears isolates the dying from those who ought to be closest to them in their last days, as the silence leads to tippy-toeing around issues that most people would feel better airing and clearing.

Similarly, it leaves the bereaved holding unspoken and unresolved feelings. These unresolved feelings about a death in the family may fester for years, leading to generations of maladaptive feelings and behaviors.[740]

My personal experience and that of others who work in care of the dying, is that most people are enormously relieved to be able to air their feelings about dying with those they love. Once the barriers of mutual anxieties and fears are removed, emotions come pouring out on both sides. A much greater closeness develops. Passing on becomes a sharing that is treasured by all.

Death may also be an incredibly rich and valuable lesson to those remaining alive – in relating to the awareness of worlds beyond the physical,. This may include deathbed visions of spirits or angels, or may simply be the sobering self-confrontation one has with one's own mortality, upon interacting others who are dealing with theirs.

Many healers view death as a stage of growth. Growth often occurs in the process of facing death. This is a healing unto death.[741]

> *Michelangelo found that whereas death inevitably killed every person, thoughts of death also made them.*
> – Irving Stone

Healing also may help a person to pass on peacefully, which is another stage of healing unto death.[742] It is often those left behind who have greater difficulties with separation and death than the dying persons themselves.

Often, death is also disturbing to us because it stirs a dim awareness deep in our beings of the little deaths we experience daily.

> *Religion is a wizard, a sibyl... She faces the wreck of worlds, and prophesies restoration. She faces a sky blood-red with sunset colors that deepen into darkness, and prophesies dawn. She faces death, and prophesies life.*
> – Felix Alder [743]

> *[D]eath is not what happens when you leave your body. Death is what happens when we live our lives in confusion and closed-heartedness, in anger and fear. In a sense, we are all partly dead, and there is nothing like the loss to make that evident, to make us see how unalive we have been, because it attracts our attention to the moment. Paradoxically, dying may be one of the few moments in life when we feel fully alive.*
> – Steven Levine [744]

> *[D]eath is not something that happens at the end of our life... It is imprisonment in one moment of time, confinement in one sharp uncompromising deed or aspect of ourselves. Death is exclusion from renewal of our present-day selves. Neither heaven nor hell are hereafter. Hell is time arrested within and refusing to join in the movement of wind and stars. Heaven is the boulder rock unrolled to let new life out: it is man restored to all four of his seasons rounding for eternity*
> – Laurens van der Post [745]

Views on suffering and death differ in Eastern religions compared to Western ones. Where reincarnation is an accepted fact, death is but another in a long series of rebirths – from physical life into spiritual life and then back again. In traditional societies, death is not an unfamiliar or distant experience. There may be elaborate rituals for helping people make the transition from physical existence; family members may consider it an honor to minister personally to the dead body; funeral rituals may graphically acknowledge the transmutation of body into spirit - as in burning the body on a pyre; and mourning rituals may encourage fervent prayers for the spirit's ongoing journey in the realms beyond.

> *When there is life there is death, and when there is death there is life. When there is possibility there is impossibility, and when there is impossibility, there is possibility. Because of the right, there is wrong, and because of the wrong, there is right... The 'this' is also the 'that.' The 'that' is also the 'this.' Is there really a distinction between 'that' and 'this?'... When 'this.' and 'that' have no opposites, there is the very axis of the Tao.*
> – Chang Tzu

Similar views were expressed by Abraham a Sancta Clara, a German Augustinian monk in the 17th century:

> *The man who dies before he dies, does not die when he dies.*

Similar echoes can be found here and there in Western spiritual teachings.

> *God knew that to split a perfect anything would make a magnet that would attract itself to itself, would create a lifetime search, and within each would be heartache and joy but rarely boredom.*
> – Alice Steadman [746]

Eastern religions[747] and mediumistic reports[748] indicate that one's mental, emotional and spiritual focus at the time of death may shape one's course in the afterlife, and that spiritual development continues after death.[749]

Personal transpersonal and spiritual awareness are growing in the Western world.[750] It is particularly satisfying to see increased awareness and sensitivity among caregivers in dealing with death and bereavement.[751]

> *Don't stand by my grave and weep,*
> *For I am not there.*
> *I do not sleep.*
> *I am a thousand winds that blow,*
> *I am the diamond's glint on snow,*
> *I am the sunlight on ripened grain,*
> *I am the gentle autumn's rain.*
> *In the soft hush of the morning light*
> *I am the swift bird in flight.*
> *Don't stand by my grave and cry,*
> *I am not there,*
> *I did not die.*

Author unknown

In summary

On the positive side, organized religions have been the cultural vehicle for teaching spiritual awareness through many centuries, throughout the world. Religions provide wonderfully rich treasures of prayers, past and living luminaries who can inspire spiritual awareness, and collections of stories, lessons and advice for connecting with spiritual dimensions and living an ethical and moral life.

On the negative side, religious authorities often claim an exclusive connection with the Infinite Source that they insist is the only acceptable avenue for their flocks to follow. Sanctions against those straying from accepted teachings are applied through social pressures, with promises of rewards and threats of punishments after death if one strays from prescribed paths. Personal spiritual explorations are often discouraged and denigrated, if not actually proscribed.

Eastern religions teach that personal explorations of meditative and devotional paths offer experiential roads to spiritual awakening. Personal spirituality will be explored further in the following chapters.

Let us continue with explorations of mystical aspects of spiritual healing.

CHAPTER 9

Mystical Experiences

The most beautiful and most profound emotion we can experience is the sensation of the mystical. It is the sower of all true science. He to whom this emotion is a stranger, who can no longer wonder and stand rapt in awe, is as good as dead.

— *Albert Einstein* [752]

A thing that is infinite and eternal hath no qualities, since it hath all qualities.

— *Carl Jung* [753]

Terminology

As with other areas of spirituality, terminology for mystical experiences is a challenge because different cultures, religious traditions, philosophical perspectives and scientific methods for examining the world and assessing evidence for spiritual phenomena are often contradictory.

The term *mystical* derives from the Greek mystery cults, in which the initiated were entrusted with knowledge kept secret from the general public. The word itself comes from the Greek root *mu*, meaning mute or silent. This knowledge was generally acquired through alternative states of consciousness (ASCs) rather than learned. The initiates were helped through rituals, meditation and other practices to develop in abilities to achieve these states of consciousness in which the knowledge could come to them. The ultimate purpose of these states was to bring the devotee closer to a union with the Divine.

The term *mystical* is often taken colloquially as being interchangeable with *magical*. From the perspectives of behavioral psychology, magical beliefs attribute spiritual/mystical qualities to certain experiences, when actually they are explainable by known mechanisms, which are outside one's realm of knowledge. To people in traditional cultures, a television or airplane might appear magical.

In these traditional cultures, religious rituals and ecstasies are often experienced as communications with their gods or with nature spirits. Westerners who study them from outside their culture may propose that these perceptions are all simply the results of altered brain mechanisms or self-delusion brought about by magical beliefs.[754] Interestingly, Western who experience these mental states (particularly with hallucinogens) often report that these open them to develop similar awarenesses. However, from the perspectives of the majority in industrial society, the spiritual realities of these mystical experiences are largely discounted – dismissed as complex psychological states that are psychologically or socially conditioned, perhaps induced biochemically in the brain by neurohormones, by ingestion of hallucinogenic plants or through various types chanting, fasting, meditating or other practices that promote alternative states of consciousness.

Magic is also used by practitioners of *Wicca* (witchcraft), based upon the reconstruction of pre-Christian traditions that originated in Scotland, Ireland, and Wales. In this context, magic is used to describe rituals and other practices that manipulate and control states of mind, body and spirit.

Spiritual is often used interchangeably with mystical. I see important distinctions that I trust will become clearer after reading this and the next several chapters. For present purposes, I define mystical experiences as transpersonal awarenesses that may arise spontaneously, may occur as a result of meditative or other practices that induce ASCs, or may be products of hallucinogens. In other words, what I am discussing here are *secular* mystical experiences. They are interpreted as non-ordinary states of consciousness by those who experience them and by observers and researchers, but not as products or reflections of a Divine presence. While they have a numinous, ineffable quality, and they may be transformative, they are explained as self-contained events. Spiritual experiences have all of the qualities of mystical experiences, but they are perceived, experienced, and interpreted as relating to a broader cosmological context, including archetypal, collective consciousness, spirit survival, reincarnation, soul-purposes and soul-lessons for being incarnated, and communion with a Divine presence. It is my impression that they are more often transformative than mystical experiences.

The usage adopted here contradicts the historic traditions of Christian mystics such as St. Augustine, Meister Ekhart, Francis of Assisi and Hildegard of Bingen, among others, who were clearly experiencing spiritual awarenesses – as defined above – which have been described as mystical experiences. In my terminology, I would call these spiritual experiences. As with the choices in using *spirit* and *soul*, these choices are the best ones I can see for the sake of clarity with modern common usage for these terms in the discussions in this book.

Most major religions have their gnostics[755] and mystics. The experience of gnosis, or personal inner knowledge, comes from meditative practices, spontaneous spiritual awakenings, and visions. Most religions have prescribed practices that facilitate the attainment of such inner gnowing. Secularized Western society has largely devalued gnostic teachings – which are unexplainable and alien in the material world, with its linear, reductionistic ways of analyzing and explaining life.

In Eastern meditative practices, mystical experiences are commonly reported. Anyone can experience these states, not just the highly gifted mystics. While these experiences are acknowledged as real and valid, they are usually discouraged as distractions along the path of true spiritual development. Mystical states are experienced personally, not just known through descriptions of the experiences of the Masters and advanced meditative adepts.

A growing number of people, intuitively recognizing the value of gnostic knowledge, are seeking the deeply moving alternative states of consciousness (ASCs) in which mystical and spiritual experiences occur. Those who hesitate to immerse themselves directly in such gnostic explorations may pursue linear, cognitive understandings of them (and to some degree, may still sense inner resonations) through encounters with practitioners of divination (astrology, tarot, I Ching, runes, and the like), psychic readings, mediumship, and through exploring the vast treasure troves of mystical texts and teachings.

Western views of mystical experiences

> *We may know immeasurably more about the universe than our ancestors did, and yet it increasingly seems that they knew something more essential about it than we do, something that escapes us.*
> – Vaclav Havel

Mystical experiences can have no validity in and of themselves if we are wedded to conventional, Western scientific thinking. Within this paradigm, we begin with the axiom that life is a coincidence of the coming together of chemicals in a primordial soup several billion years ago, evolving strictly through selection of the fittest into humanity as the pinnacle of evolution;[756] and we accept the promises of modern science that one day we will comprehend everything through ever finer analysis of the current combinations of chemicals that constitute our bodies and the rest of the world; and we accept that any thought everyone ever had is simply the product of electrochemical reactions in their brain, however responsive they may be to learning from their environment. Within these frameworks, mystical experiences are presumed to be fantasies, delusions, or products of electrochemical processes of neurons in the brain.

To represent this viewpoint I like the discussion of John Horgan. He comes from this Western scientific mind frame but is more open to considering various alternative explanations because he experimented himself with a wide variety of mind-altering drugs in personal explorations of Alternative States of Consciousness (ASCs). Unsatisfied with his own experimentations as his sole basis for deciding whether mystical awarenesses have any intrinsic validity, Horgan set out on an odyssey to explore and clarify the views of eminent philosophers, theologians, and scientists who have studied and written about mysticism. He feels that science cannot "reveal the mind of God," despite the promises of eminent scientists such as Stephen Hawking (an atheist) that science will ultimately be able to do so through ever more refined and sophisticated linear explorations of the cosmos.[757] However, Horgan's perspective remains firmly rooted in scientific methodology: "I see science, in spite of its limitations, as a polestar that we desperately need for guidance when we venture onto the perilous waters of mysticism." [758]

Here is a brief distillation of some of Horgan's explorations:

1. *Postmodernists* point out that religions rely on various texts that are many steps removed from the inexpressible mystery of transcendent experiences. In the extreme of this view, there is no way to express ultimate reality because it is beyond words. While Horgan details these arguments, he dismisses them on the grounds that many of postmodernists tend to present an exclusivist view that promotes a particular cosmology and denigrates all other perspectives and traditions. He also observes that if one claims these experiences are totally beyond words, then it seems a waste of time, even foolish, to be investing energies in wordy discussions about mystical experiences.

2. *The meditative path to mysticism* was explored by Horgan in an interview with Ken Wilber.[759] Wilber claims the highest meditative state is non-dual consciousness, where awareness of the void that underlies everything is completely integrated with worldly perceptions. Horgan accepts Wilber's observation that mystical and material science domains are separate and have differing methodologies appropriate for each. Wilber holds that Eastern approaches have been practiced for many centuries (particularly Buddhist meditation) as systematic explorations of mystical realms, and therefore meditation is a scientific method. Horgan disagrees because not everyone who engages in meditation perceives the same mystical realities. Furthermore, he notes that very few people reach the ultimate non-dual awareness which is the goal of Eastern meditative practice.

3. *Neurotheology* explores the activity of various parts of the brain that are activated during meditation (as imaged in PET scans). Widely popularized by Andrew Newberg, who studied the brains of eight nuns while they meditated in his laboratory, the consistent activation of frontal lobe activity is taken to be a validation that there is a reality to subjective mystical experiences.[760]

Horgan observes that it is doubtful that the nuns meditating in Newberg's laboratory achieved a deep mystical state. He also observes that another study with PET scans, focused on Danish meditators, demonstrated increased parietal lobe activity and decreased frontal activity, which is opposite to the findings in Newberg's study.[761] He concludes that we are just at the start of our neurological understanding of mystical processes.

4. Michael Persinger, a psychologist working at Laurentian University in Canada, theorizes that mystical experiences are caused by aberrant electrical activity in the brain.[762] He observed that people with brain injuries reported that they "sensed presences." If the damage was in their left hemisphere, this was a voice which

could be experienced as pleasant or even ecstatic. Damage to the right hemisphere more often resulted in frightening presences, sometimes interpreted as possessing demons or evil spirits. These experiences were also colored by the person's personality and cultural background.

Persinger developed the *Octopus,* an electrical device to stimulate the brain. This device has eight electromagnets, which are placed strategically on the skull so that specific parts of the brain can be stimulated. He found that up to 40 percent of the people he tested reported they "sensed a presence" as a result of this electromagnetic stimulation.

Horgan volunteered to experience the effects of the Octopus. He sat in a reclining chair in a sound-insulated room, observing his thoughts and mental imagery. After a period with neutral mental activity, suddenly a memory intruded in his thoughts. He recalled an earlier sensory isolation experience in which he had floated in an enclosed tank of water and had had a panic reaction. At the end of the Octopus session, Horgan was puzzled when he was invited to rank five pictures on their closeness to his mental imagery while being stimulated by the Octopus. They included "a herd of zebras, two men climbing what appeared to be a wall of mud, a crowd of men fighting, fish drifting through green-blue water, an elderly woman." [763] The underwater scene was his first choice.

Horgan was surprised to be told that this had been a successful test of ESP because the laboratory assistant had been staring at the water scene while Horgan was stimulated by the Octopus. Persinger reports that subjects stimulated by the Octopus have been scoring correctly 75 percent of the time, when the chance expectation is only 20 percent.

Horgan is utterly dismissive of psi, stating, "...psi has never been convincingly demonstrated in the laboratory..." [764]

In addition to the skepticism engendered by the psi portion of this experience, Horgan came away from his visit unimpressed that Persinger's research was worth considering as evidence for mystical experiences of any sort.

Horgan has several cogent observations on the difficulties in explaining mental experiences through neurological mechanisms. He points out that there is an explanatory gap[765] between theories explaining brain physiology and the subjective awarenesses the theories endeavor to explain. The experiences and qualities of mind seem to resist scientific explanations – a phenomenon which has been labeled *mysterianism.* He adds that "Neurotheologians face not an explanatory gap but a chasm." [766]

5. *Zen meditation* has been reported to lead to mystical experiences with advanced practice. Horgan interviewed James Austin, who is a neurologist and has studied and practiced Zen meditation for several decades. He thinks that mysticism can produce profound changes in personality but is skeptical about reports of metaphysical insights. Early in his meditative practice, he had an experience of what he calls absorption. "It was the most intense blackness imaginable... And yet it glistened, like being in an obsidian crystal." [767] The enchantment and bliss he experienced during absorption resembled a previous experiences when receiving morphine during a minor surgical procedure. This had led to such intense

pleasure that he promised himself he would never take an opiod again. He specu-lates that absorption may lead to release of endorphins, a person's own natural brain opioids. He notes that the experience of absorption is actually rare.[768]

Several years of meditative practice later, he experienced kensho.

> ... It was Sunday morning, and he was standing on the platform of a tube station waiting for a train that would take him to his Zen session. Abruptly, his ordinary sense of self dissolved. Nothing changed, and everything changed. Austin wasn't just seeing; he was *seeing*. The dingy station was still a dingy station... but it was also "profound, implicit, perfect reality." He understood "at depths far beyond simple knowledge" that "this is the eternal state of affairs." There is "nothing more to do" and "nothing what-soever to fear," since the world is "completely and intrinsically valid." Austin felt neither ecstasy nor any other emotion, only the "cool, clinical detachment of a mirror as it witnesses a landscape bathed in moonlight." He understood why Zen painters use the cold, pale moon to depict enlight-enment.[769]

During kensho people maintain their awareness of the external world, but their ordinary sense of themselves as individuals who are distinct from the world around them disappears. All motivation to influence or change the world also dis-appears and people simply perceive the world as the way it is. This was a transformative experience for Austin. He lost "the psychic, intellectual, emo-tional, visceral sense of ... egocentric self." [770] Ever since then he has felt a greater calmness and emotional stability, with no fear of death (which he had pre-viously felt). He was no longer interested in philosophy, theology, or metaphysics. He was able to accept paradoxes of life and live with them. He feels no sense of a God behind life and nature. Everything just is.

While Horgan is bothered by questions of theodicy, Austin simply accepts that the world includes suffering and death that may appear unfair and may not be explainable from our perspective. Austin speculates that this acceptance might have been partly the result of his experiences as a pediatrician. In this work he had experiences of treating children with terminal diseases, where all he could do was to minister to their suffering. Horgan marveled at Austin's equanimity, speculating with him that this may be due to Austin's age and life experiences as a physician. He admires Austin's open-mindedness about mystical experiences and his strong advocation for testing spiritual suppositions rather than taking them on faith.

6. *Hallucinogenic drugs* (*entheogens*) became popular in the 1950s and 1960s with the use of LSD, psilocybin and dimethyl tryptamine (DMT).[771] These syn-thesized chemicals were found to be components of naturally occurring hallucinogens, along with mescaline, that have been used in traditional cultures for a longer time than history can pinpoint. Wonderful hallucinatory visual ex-periences were reported by numerous people, often associated with transformative mystical experiences.

When psychotic and suicidal responses were increasingly reported in the 1960s, the US government restricted their use and for several decades there was a decline in such drug 'trips.' In recent years there has been a modest resurgence of hallucinogen use.

Horgan strongly favors the view that visions produced by drugs are from biochemical processes in the brain, and that the sense of the mystical accompanying these is also a product of the drugs. He cites numbers of researchers who share his views. Nevertheless, it is to his credit that he details the experiences and opinions of Stanislav Grof, a psychiatrist with a wealth of experience with LSD in clinical practice.[772] Horgan interviewed Grof with the expectation that he would find further confirmation of his own opinions. He was surprised that Grof is a firm believer in psi and in the validity of mystical experiences induced by LSD.

Grof has taken LSD numerous times himself, including very high doses, and has administered it clinically in over four thousand sessions to others. Grof firmly believes the spiritual, cosmic awarenesses experienced under LSD are real and not the product of altered brain chemistry. He points out, however, that it can bring out strongly negative, terrifying responses as well as very positive ones, even bringing out psychotic delusions and decompensations. Grof feels he has achieved a state of greater spiritual equilibrium from his LSD experiences and has come to terms with his relationship to death.

Horgan had a difficult time listening to Grof's views that LSD (and holotropic breathing, another technique extensively explored by Grof [773]) could bring back actual birth and past life memories. Grof has used these techniques to help clients uncover underlying psychological issues as a part of their psychotherapy.

Horgan concludes with mention of other LSD researchers who hold views similar to his own, reasserting the theory that the visions experienced with hallucinogens are explainable by memories from the media if not from personal experiences. However, Horgan also shares that he himself experienced very vivid imagery that was alien to his personal history, such as being transformed into an ape-man and an extremely intelligent cosmic computer. He notes that these visions had more archetypal and mythical qualities than his normal dreams.

7. *The perceived sense of the mystical* is both difficult to define and impossible to ignore. Horgan does a creditable job of presenting both sides of this challenge: "Mystical awe is the inverse of knowledge; it is a kind of anti-knowledge. Instead of seeing The Answer to the riddle of existence, you see just how impenetrable the riddle is."

Spontaneous spiritual experiences

Spiritual experiences have been reported over many centuries, often strongly flavored by their cultural contexts.

> *I know a man in Christ who fourteen years ago was caught up to the third heaven. Whether it was in the body or out of the body I do not know – God*

knows. And I know that this man – whether in the body or apart from the body I do not know, but God knows – was caught up to paradise. He heard inexpressible things...

Paul [774]

A more recent example is that of Richard M. Bucke, who was a Canadian doctor among the friends of Walt Whitman. He shares a classic description of what has been popularly described as a mystical experience (which in my terms is a spiritual experience in this instance),[775] written in third person, as was the style at the turn of the century:

It was in the early spring, at the beginning of his thirty-sixth year. He and two friends had spent the evening reading Wordsworth, Shelley, Keats, Browning, and especially Whitman. They parted at midnight, and he had a long drive in a hansom[776]... His mind, deeply under the influence of the ideas, images and emotions called up by the reading and talk of the evening, was calm and peaceful. He was in a state of quiet, almost passive enjoyment. All at once, without warning of any kind, he found himself wrapped around as it were by a flame-colored cloud. For an instant he thought of fire, some sudden conflagration in the great city; the next, he knew that the light was within himself. Directly afterwards came upon him a sense of exultation, of immense joyousness accompanied or immediately followed by an intellectual illumination quite impossible to describe. Into his brain streamed one momentary lightning-flash of the Brahmic[777] Splendor which has ever since lightened his life; upon his heart fell one drop of Brahmic Bliss, leaving thenceforward for always an aftertaste of heaven. Among other things he did not come to believe, he saw and knew that the Cosmos is not dead matter but a living Presence, that the soul of man is immortal, that the universe is so built and ordered that without any peradventure all things work together for the good of each and all, that the foundation principle of the world is what we call love and that the happiness of every one is in the long run absolutely certain. He claims that he learned more within the few seconds during which the illumination lasted than in previous months or even years of study, and that he learned much that no study could ever have taught.

The illumination itself continued not more than a few moments, but its effects proved ineffaceable; it was impossible for him ever to forget what he at that time saw and knew; neither did he, or could he, ever doubt the truth of what was then presented to his mind. There was no return, that night or at any other time, of the experience...[778]

Bucke spent many years clarifying for himself the meanings of his mystical experience, writing one of the early modern treatises on the subject.[779]

One of the most impressive qualities of the spiritual experience is its transformtive nature. People emerge from such states no longer the persons they were prior to these inner awakenings. New understandings suffuse their views of the world and of their place in it. They know ineffable truths on a deep level, with a certainty transcending all question – a knowing of a primary nature that derives from a total sharing of essences of Self with the All. They know the All from inside in deeper and clearer ways even than they have known their everyday selves from inside. Conversely, spiritual experiences bring people to an awareness of their Self – that part, deep within, that knows (and that knows it knows) truths which are beyond words. While the same may be true with mystical experiences, this is less often the case.

The mystical experience may also involve encounters with one or more beings who appear infinitely wiser and more able to comprehend and explain the nature, development and evolution of human and other-worldly states.

Experiences that may bring one to mystical states include prayer,[780] meditation,[781] crises,[782] experiential quests,[783] encounters with the psychic and spiritual,[784] peak experiences in athletics,[785] awakening of kundalini energies,[786] and more. The tutelage of masters experienced in the explorations of such realms may be helpful when one is deliberately seeking mystical experiences. Many such teachers work within religious traditions that have mapped alternative-reality territories and have specific paths that they recommend, practices that facilitate the journey, and cosmologies to explain the paths and territories. Huston Smith describes the more prominent of the world's religions, each of which has its own cosmologies but all of which share common denominators in their mystical experiences that we shall shortly consider in more detail.

Mind-altering drugs[787] may also lead to transformative experiences with mystical qualities, as mentioned above by Horgan. Though they have brought many into touch with creative and cosmic awareness, psychedelic drugs may lead to habituation, and occasionally even to acute psychotic decompensations. Sensitives and healers also warn that this route may have hidden dangerous effects entailing bioenergetic toxicities. Repeated use of such drugs, they claim, can leave long-standing scars in the energy body.

Many aspects of psi and spiritual healing overlap with mystical experiences. I do not begin to do justice to this transformative experience in the brief presentation that space limitations dictate. Just a small taste is provided, a few poetic morsels.

Analyses of mystical experiences

> *Metaphysics is the finding of bad reasons for what we believe upon instinct, but to find these reasons is no less an instinct.*
> – F. H. Bradley [788]

Two types of linear explanations are common for the mystical experience, the naturalistic and the religious approaches. The naturalistic approach agnostically fits reports of mystical experiences into a cosmology as free as possible from preconceptions about the observed phenomena. However, linear scientific systems, in manners similar to religions, must include assumptions about the way the world is to be divided into portions for analysis, and about the rules that are acceptable for analyses. While scientific investigations cannot be entirely objective, they can allow for modification of their theories in line with new observations or with alternative explanations for them. Evelyn Underhill wisely, if waggishly, stated, "The difference between mystic and unmystic is how large a part of reality would you like to unite with." [789]

The religious views start with various tenets that are usually taken as God-given, immutable and unquestionable. Much more could be said on religious views and interpretations of mystical experiences,[790] but limits of space dictate only brief mention of these here – except as they touch on issues involved in spiritual healing. In no way would I imply that religious views are unworthy of study. On the contrary, religious explorations through the ages have unearthed treasure troves of information on inner- or higher-dimension realms that we three-dimensional beings can only begin to conjecture and conceive of from our limited perspectives. Those who prefer to view the world through prisms cut and colored by particular visionaries may fit the mystical experiences into whatever perspectives and cosmologies they find comfortable. A variety of spiritual experiences from a spectrum of religious perspectives will be considered in Chapter III-11.[791]

I often have difficulty with those theologians and philosophers who presume that their views represent *THE* truth rather than *a* truth. I am especially bothered when they attempt to force others to abandon differing or dissenting interpretations, rather than reexamine their own views to find what might be similar or different and to ask questions that might be enlightening about the disparities in understandings about the transcendent. Here I ask of religious groups that they adopt my naturalistic approach, in effect hoisting myself on my own petard by suggesting that my way is a more valid way of exploring mystical and spiritual experiences.[792] And yet, I see no way around this.

Figure III-9. True believers

A word of caution is also in order. Much as we may find upliftment through mystical experiences, we must also be cautious and even wary in our mystical explorations. Our unconscious minds may sometimes trick us into believing we have had visionary experiences when we have actually projected our own fantasies, wishful thinking, or even delusions and hallucinations. We might then take these projections to represent guidance from on high, when it is actually the shadow side of our unconscious speaking. It may take a person experienced in spiritual matters as well as in psychotherapy to help us sort out the differences.[793]

> *Experience may be judged as invalidly mad or as validly mystical. The distinction is not easy.*
> – R. D. Laing

Qualities of the mystical experience

My naturalistic analysis assumes the existence of psi as a given fact.[794] Most of us possess a modicum of clairsentient, telepathic, precognitive and psychokinetic abilities. These, along with various psychological and neurological factors, may help to explain many elements of the mystical experience.

While many of the aspects of mystical experiences can be understood in the context of psychic awarenesses, these do not seem adequate to encompass the entire spectrum of the mystical. In addition to psi perceptions, there appear to be transcendent aspects of reality that are beyond linear observations and logic, perceived within psi and mystical awarenesses as valid in their own right. These awarenesses must be accepted and included in a consideration of what mystical experiences may be, just as other inner experiences (such as emotions and other psychological experiences) may be accepted and studied. I take the perspective here that mystical experiences include something that is beyond current human understanding, and perhaps even beyond human capabilities to understand, and may or may not include awareness of a Divine presence.

Similarly, all of the phenomena in Chapters III-1 to III-7 are taken to have a valid, naturalistic existence – regardless of the explanations people attribute to them.

Several authors have reviewed the mystical experience, extracting what they considered the essential common denominators.[795] (See Table III-3.)

1. *Imperceptivity* – insensitivity to external distractions during the mystical state:

> *And the slumber of the body seems to be but the waking of the soul.*
> – Sir Thomas Browne

Imperceptivity may represent withdrawal to focus on an inner consciousness, with a decrease of awareness of sensory stimuli. In those mystical experiences that are deliberately sought, this may be a way to reduce distracting 'noise' from the five external senses in order to concentrate on inner perceptions, over which people usually have very limited conscious awareness or control. Many techniques are employed to reach this state, including visual concentration on an object; mental concentration on a word or phrase; attention to the words of a luminary speaker; physical exercises such as walking a labyrinth; resonations with a developed soul; hypnosis; alpha or theta EEG feedback; fasting; psychoactive drugs; rhythmically or monotonously repetitive sounds or physical actions such as chanting, dancing,

Table III-3. Properties of the mystical experience

1. *Imperceptivity*	- insensitivity to external distractions during the mystical state
2. *Renunciation*	- detachment of the self from the external world, from material encumbrances and other ties which would distract and mislead us from connecting with the All
3. *Fusion*	- a feeling of unity with the cosmos and transcendence of time and space
4. *Noesis*	- self-evident, profound truths; "insightful knowledge or illumination felt at an intuitive, non-rational level and gained by direct experience." [796], with the authoritative feeling that the experience is real[797]
5. *Ineffability*	- beyond description in normal terms
6. *Paradoxicality*	- the 'I' both exists and does not exist
7. *Transiency*	- sustained for a limited period of time
8. *Ecstasy*	- bliss, joy
9. *Awe... fear*	- A profound awareness of a universe so vast that man is but an insignificant speck in its midst lies at one end of this spectrum of the mystical experience. This is an aspect of (4) noesis, (6) ineffability and (8) ecstasy. It shades by degrees into fear of the unknown
10. *Encounters with 'higher' beings*	- discarnate intelligences which are interested in assisting in man's development
11. *Love*	- the unconditional positive regard experienced in encounters with other-reality intelligent beings/awarenesses and felt by the person undergoing a mystical experience towards all of creation
12. *Trust... Surrender*	- the polar opposites to fear, develop with our acceptance of the mystical experience as utterly valid and transcending everyday reality
13. *Dualism of existence*	- awareness that our eternal soul exists in realities other than the sensory one, at the same time as we are plodding along our everyday, physical reality Path, born into flesh to learn the lessons of earthly existence
14. *Transformation*	- persisting positive changes in attitudes and behavior following the mystical experience

dream states; and more.[798] Such techniques are also reported to enhance psi abilities, though experimental evidence for this has been equivocal.

From the far side of barriers between transpersonal worlds and the world of everyday consciousness, imperceptivity may represent a total absorption in other dimensions to the exclusion of sensory reality. Perhaps, when we visit the inner spaces beyond the borders of ordinary consciousness, there are natural barriers to perceptions back across the border that are reciprocal to the barriers to perceptions from everyday reality into the mystical.

2. *Renunciation* – detachment of the self from the external world, from material encumbrances and other ties that would distract and mislead us from connecting with the All:

> *Nature does not have to insist,*
> *Can blow for only half a morning,*
> *Rain for only half a day,*
> *And what are these winds and these rains but natural?*
> *If nature does not have to insist,*
> *Why should man?...*
>
> – Lao Tsu

As an extension of (1) *imperceptivity*, renunciation enables concentration under any circumstances.

Renunciation of attraction to the world is recommended as an aid towards attaining mystical experiences and is often expressed in the lifestyle of those who follow these paths.

Renunciation of everyday beliefs and habits of perception is also required in order to move comfortably into the mystical experience. We must be ready to relinquish the anchors of sensory reality and trust our being to the mystical realms where thoughts, beliefs and feelings shape reality. If we become afraid, we can invite (or perhaps even create) negative experiences instead of positive ones.

> *Objects of sense draw back from a person who is abstinent; not so the taste for these objects. But even the taste departs from him when he has seen the Supreme.*
>
> – Bhagavad Gita

Meditators are also encouraged to ignore distractions via psi channels of perception in the same way they ignore the distractions of their five external senses in order to reach a full connection with the All.

3. *Fusion* – a feeling of unity with the cosmos and transcendence of time and space:

> *[A]nywhere is the center of the world.*
> – Black Elk [799]

The whole universe is one mathematical and symphonic expression, made up of finite representations of the infinite.
                                        – F. L. Kunz

The nothingness of fullness we name the PLEROMA. Therein both thinking and being cease.
                                        – Carl Jung [800]

[A]ll things are related, and in each action in the web of life influences everything else...
                                        – Steven McFadden [801]

If we are more connected with our psi awarenesses during the mystical state, this could explain the feeling of 'oneness' with the universe. Via psi we are intimately in contact with the whole of creation, irrespective of distance and time.

Mystics say we are part of the All and the All is perceptible by looking within ourselves. Mystical experiences often lead people to look inwards in new ways.

4. *Noesis* – self evident, profound truths; insightful knowledge or illumination felt at an intuitive, non-rational level and gained by direct experience,[802] with the authoritative feeling that the experience is real:[803]

When it comes, it doesn't come as thoughts, not at all, it's as if I were *BATHED IN IT*, and then... I don't know, it isn't something I 'see' – something outside of myself that I see – it's... I AM that, all of a sudden. And there is no longer me-you, no longer... I find no words to describe these experiences...
                                        – The Mother [804]

Those who have visited these realms say that they cannot be described, analyzed nor indeed known through language, reasoning or anything but personal experience. Illumination and knowledge gained via psi must carry with them a greater sense of assurance as to their validity than information obtained via the five senses. Though our senses appear to convey immediate knowledge of our environment, they are actually several analog steps removed from this. For instance, light bounces off an object or is emitted by it and impinges upon our eyes. Light produces chemical changes in photoreceptors of the retina and these are transformed into nerve impulses. The patterns of nerve impulses are interpreted by the brain as analogs of external reality, through matching with memories of experiences from the past with similar patterns.

If we are not familiar with the perceived patterns, we may not recognize or comprehend them. Natives in the Pacific reported that they could not see the large ships of the first White explorers because they had no mental references to these visual patterns, which were entirely outside of their previous experiences.

Psi perceptions can provide more deep awarenesses and more immediate understandings than outer, sensory perceptions of what other objects or people look or sound or feel *like*. It is a direct, immediate awareness of what they *are*. Via psi we may experience their state as they experience it. Full psi perception may open the doors to true consensual experiences of anything and everything, anywhere and anywhen.

How could we integrate such perceptions into our world-views? Quite likely, we would experience the remaining attributes of the mystical experience.

5. *Ineffability* – beyond description in normal terms:

> *An ideal is beyond explanation; to analyze God is to dethrone God.*
> – Inayat Khan

This is an extension of (4) *noesis*. How can qualities of information obtained non-verbally via psi be explained to someone who does not perceive them? It is like explaining color to a person who has been blind from birth.

> *It is easy to understand God as long as you don't try to explain him.*
> – Joseph Joubert

6. *Paradoxicality* – The 'I' both exists and does not exist:

> It is the duty of the human understanding to understand that there are things which it cannot understand, and what those things are.
> Soren Kierkegaard

Paradoxicality may be a linear reality analog and a gateway to the mystical. Through darkness we know the nature of light; through evil we appreciate good; through contrast with the profane we appreciates the holy. When we begin to contemplate the wholeness that is represented by these polarities, we find it is more than the sum of the parts.[805] We cannot adequately put into words the feelings that such awareness awakens. They are ineffable and as such, partake of the mystical.

I greatly admire the Oriental perspectives of yin and yang, polarities that are found in every single aspect of nature and action. Anything can be either yin or yang, depending on what it is being compared or related to. In focusing awareness upon these shifting relationships, depending upon their contexts, and in pointing out that we must balance them in our diets, environments and interactions, we are drawn through these polarities to the ineffable awareness that is hinted in the dance of their complementarities.

Poetry moves us in similar fashion, bringing us through transpositions of images of one domain upon another, to appreciate the multiplicities of our own beingness across several domains of existence.

> *The notes I handle no better than many pianists. But the pauses between the notes – ah, that is where the art resides!*
> – Artur Schnabel [806]

Paradoxicality also may be present as an initial confusion upon moving out of sensory and into psi perceptions. As we becomes increasingly comfortable with broadened horizons through psi perceptions and more able to accept their validity, a greater sense of fusion or unity can prevail. We may feel ourselves more a part of the world at large as we are more immediately in touch with it, receptively and actively.[807] At the same time, the world could be experiencing the perceiver as one with it and the perceiver could perceive this perception – leading to a fusion of simultaneously perceiving and being perceived, and possibly to feeling at first as both existing within and outside ourselves. It is like a wave aware of itself as an independent force at the same time that it is aware of being part of the vast ocean.[808]

We might also sense aspects of the self that are aware of survival of the physical body. This complementary aspect to paradoxicality is considered in (13) *the dualism of existence.*

7. *Transiency* – sustained for a limited period of time:

> *Many years ago, a Zen temple was renown for its magnificently carved and painted gate. People made pilgrimages just to contemplate its beauty.*
> *All were shocked when a Zen student set it afire one night and burned it down.*
> *Asked why he had done such a horrible deed, he replied, "The temple gates were so exquisitely beautiful, I could not tolerate their imperfection in one quality: transiency."*
> *The Master declared that he was to be forgiven and thanked.*
> *– Zen parable*

Transiency relates to two levels of awareness in the mystical experience. As with any other mode of perception, we are usually unable to focus for long on a single subject before incoming information from other subjects, or on other channels, distracts us. Mystics practiced in meditation learn to minimize the attention they give to their bodily senses, feelings and mentations. With prolonged practice it is possible to overcome these limitations and to maintain a constant meditative state. Shamans typically enter such states to seek answers to important questions. They may retreat into meditative, mystical states for days at a time. The mystical experience often entices us to wish to remain in that state but, inevitably, most of those who continue to live are forced to return to everyday reality.

Transiency brings us to "...what the Japanese call *aware*, the bittersweet, elegaic joy that encompasses both beauty and its passing; the poignancy of knowing that this moment is what it is like to be fully human, and that we must inevitably return to a narrower existence." [809] In the most advanced meditative states we may maintain awareness of dual realities.[810]

The enormous impact of a mystical experience, with its perspectives of life beyond life, may also impart a sense of transiency to our ordinary existence.[811] This may be a boon to those suffering from chronic illness.

In visiting the realms of the infinite, how insignificant become my daily, finite cares.
                                                – A Course in Miracles

In grasping at wisps of mystical awareness of transiency as perceived in everyday awareness, poets have suggested,

Exhaust the little moment. Soon it dies,
And be it gash or gold it will not come
Again in this identical disguise.
                                                – Gwendolyn Knight [812]

8. *Ecstasy* – deeply felt positive mood with a feeling of sacredness, transcending ordinary experience:

The soul should always stand ajar,
ready to welcome the ecstatic experience.
                                                – Emily Dickinson

Imagine our ecstasy if we have lived on the ground all or our life and we are suddenly given an aerial view of familiar surroundings. Awareness of selected aspects of the cosmos through psi perceptions may produce something of this feeling. How exhilarating to view these and all the rest of creation at one inner glance.

On psychological grounds, another element may contribute to ecstasy. We often feels far stronger and better for being part of a group, be it family, team, work or cultural unit. The group also imparts a feeling that it is more than the sum of its component parts. Would we not feel via psi a more intense exaltation at being part of a group – becoming 'one' with the others in the group? We would actually *be* far more than ourselves, as the group becomes one in perception and actions with ourselves.

Mystics say that the ultimate ecstasy is simply being in the presence of the All. More on this under (11) *Love*.

Eastern mystic Masters consider psi experiences during meditation (*siddhis*) to be distractions from the true object of meditation, which is the attainment of cosmic awareness. In Zen Buddhism this ultimate state is called *satori* or *kensho*; Hindus label it *Samadhi;* Taoists name it *absolute Tao*; Sufis speak of *fana*; modern Western mystics call it a *peak experience*.

9. *Awe...fear* – A profound awareness of a universe so vast that man is but an insignificant speck in its midst lies at one end of this spectrum of the mystical experience. This is an aspect of (4) *noesis*, (6) *ineffability* and (8) *ecstasy*. It may also shade by degrees into fear of the unknown:

If there is a universal mind, must it be sane?
                                                – Damon Knight [813]

In the mystical, as in the parapsychological, fear may intrude. Those who wish to enter the world of the mystic are cautioned that they should do this only under guidance of a Master.[814] Jewish mystics advise that a man should be married, over the age of 40 and mentally stable before he studies the Kabballah, but that even then he is in serious danger of not returning from the other side. I have heard and read many reports from people who felt severe anxiety and fear as a result of such mystical experiences, and from some who decompensated in phases of meditative experiences and other explorations of transcendent realms. Of drug freakouts I need hardly write. I myself experienced severe anxiety in my initial foray into an OBE.

Psychiatric theories suggest a variety of explanations for such fears.

In moving beyond our limited perceptions of our sensory self in the physical world, we may fear a dissolution of ourselves. Having lived for an instant in the consciousness of a wave upon the sea of eternity, we may fear a loss of identify in becoming aware that we are also an integral part of that infinitely large ocean.

To appreciate people's defensiveness, one need only look at their responses to what they do not yet understand. Take for example the wild and wonderful theories invented throughout history to explain eclipses of the sun and moon – ranging from imagined battles between these heavenly bodies, to attempts by cosmic demons to devour them, to proposals that the heavenly bodies were making love and creating stars, to projecting one's inner fears and worrying that one's sins of commission or omission may be to blame for the withdrawal of the moon – which require propitiation to bring back the sun or moon.

As nature abhors a vacuum, so humans abhor the unknown. Better an invented explanation than an admission that we do not know or understand. Worse yet, having accepted an explanation, man is ever so stubborn in relinquishing it for a better one. The early rejections of Galileo and Darwin are outstanding (but far from uncommon) examples of this rigidity in the face of newly discovered explanations.

With psi we see the same reaction, for it contradicts commonly accepted Western views of the world. If telepathy, clairsentience, precognition and psychokinesis exist, then common views of time, space and man's relationships with the world must change. We must begin to appreciate the influence of non-local mind.[815] But change engenders anxiety and not everyone is comfortable with a view from vastly expanded perspectives. Some suffer from fears of heights or open spaces that would make vast perspectives frightening.

'Mystification,' in the sense of attributing obscure, scientifically unproven causes to puzzling phenomena, may help both the religious person and the atheist get around these anxieties. Rather than face the fears of the unknown and learn to live with them, it is easier to declare such phenomena to be *mystical*. Placing this tidy label upon them seems to make them more understandable and acceptable, regardless of how vague the explanation of that label – or, perhaps precisely because it is vague, it can serve multiple purposes for various people in diverse situations.[816] 'Mystical' may invoke images of greater powers or of other agents or agencies which most people would agree that mortal men cannot completely comprehend. On the one hand, mystification places these phenomena in the vague but familiar contexts of religion (from common usage or ecclesiastically codified explanations) – and believers are satisfied. On the other hand, this label allows non-believers to reject mystical experiences as related to religious beliefs rather than to a body of hypotheses supported by experiential and experimental evidence. Once they have applied this label, people need not examine, much less alter, their views of the world with such mystifications. They can either blindly accept that there are phenomena which only God comprehends, or can reject the very existence of these unsettling occurrences out of hand – all with the help of this little label.

Looking more deeply into the complexities of psi and of man's psychological makeup, there are other reasons for fears associated with the mystical and parapsychological.[817] Most relate to fears of violations of one's personal boundaries via psi powers.

Meditation masters, mystics and others familiar with realms beyond the sensory world point out that what is termed *reality* from our everyday, sensory perspective is an illusion, a construct of such limited proportions that it cannot begin to encompass the vastness of cosmic reality.[818] People hold on tenaciously to their limited conceptualizations of reality, to their *little me*, and are fearful of letting go of the familiar to explore the unknown.[819] Yet to relinquish our stubbornly-held grasp on physical and psychological reality, we are told, is man's greatest challenge and offers the greatest and longest-lasting rewards through participation in advanced spiritual development in this world and in the worlds beyond.

Whether people respond with awe or fear as they open to mystical awarenesses may depend on non-specific factors such as their mood, general outlook on life, characterological flexibility, self-confidence, emotional stability and trust in their inner and outer guidance. If they are optimistic, then a positive, self-reinforcing, *sweetening spiral* may be produced by a mystical experience.[820] If fear creeps in, then a vicious circle of negative responses may ensue. This fear can at times escalate to panic of psychotic proportions. People may even permanently lose their hold on sensory reality.

There are now organizations with therapists available to help with such problems of spiritual emergencies.[821]

10. *Encounters with 'higher' beings* – discarnate intelligences that are interested in assisting in man's development:

> *My psychic initiation really began one evening... as I sat writing poetry. Suddenly my consciousness left my body, and my mind was barraged by ideas that were astonishing and new to me at the time... I experimented with a Ouija board... the pointer spelled out messages that claimed to come from a personality called Seth.*
> – Jane Roberts [822]

Though this would seem to be in the category of religious belief, it is reported repeatedly with mystical experiences and may have naturalistic explanations.

If the existence of reincarnation is accepted[823] as a naturalistic observation,[824] without religious interpretations, then some aspects of humans survive death on other planes of existence. These could be the entities described in mystical experiences. Mediums and mystics suggest that the surviving entity continues to develop, to study and to progress in understanding in these other dimensions.[825] Entities at progressively more refined levels are said to be available for instruction and guidance of those who are not as advanced. It is said that spirits evolve and grow in awareness and spiritual development. The ultimate consciousness is an omniscient, omnipotent, unconditionally loving and accepting *Being of Light*. The radiance of this Being is so strong that those who are not sufficiently refined in their development find it painful to gaze at it.[826] Mystics in several cultures have said, "We are sparks of the eternal flame, seeking our way back to that guiding light."

Angelic beings and nature spirits[827] may also be encountered, either spontaneously or through meditation and prayer. Such encounters may be part of mystical experiences.

Why have people through the ages developed such diverse, often divergent and even contradictory explanations for the between-lives and afterlife experience, and for encounters with angelic beings? Limitations of sensory reality language and concepts for describing other-dimension experiences is an obvious suggestion, as discussed under (4) *noesis* and (5) *ineffability*. Add to this the diversities of languages and cultures around the world, plus distortions with the transmission of these concepts from person to person for centuries after an illumined mortal experienced and described them, and there is little problem in postulating this process to explain the tower of Babel we have today.

Religion and philosophy have commonly assumed that there is an objective, 'out there' spiritual reality, and that God is an all-knowing, all-powerful being. They suggest that the diversity of views about the transcendent is due to distortions in perception of a unitary reality that is beyond mortal perception or understanding. Jorge Ferrer[828] points out that we may be co-creators of perceptions of the infinite All, so that our individual experiences of the All constitute a pixel on the Divine screen.

Others have suggested that what appear to be spirits as separate, independent entities may actually be aspects of our own spirit selves, as manifested in transcendent dimensions. If we contain some aspect of the All within ourselves, then the part of the All within us that is not usually relevant or apparent to our everyday consciousness may appear mystical to us because we are not familiar with it.

Why should most people be so profoundly unaware of other levels of existence? This is a question that is beyond our comprehension, to which the answers must be religious or philosophical. A plethora of meditational, mediumistic, philosophical and religious speculations have been made in this regard.[829]

11. *Love* – the unconditional positive regard experienced in encounters with other-reality intelligent beings/awarenesses and felt by the person undergoing a mystical experience towards all of creation:

> *...wonderful, wonderful feeling of this light... It's almost like a*
> *person. It is not a person, but it is a being of some kind. It is a mass*
> *of energy. It doesn't have a character like you would describe*
> *another person, but it has a character in that it is more than just a*
> *thing... And it totally engulfs whatever the horizon might be...*
> *...the light communicates to you and for the first time in your life... is*
> *a feeling of true, pure love. It can't be compared to the love of your*
> *wife, the love of your children, or some people consider a very*
> *intense sexual experience as love and they consider (it) possibly the*
> *most beautiful moment in their life – and it couldn't even begin to*
> *compare. All these wonderful, wonderful feelings combined could not*
> *possibly compare to the feeling, the true love. If you can imagine*
> *what pure love would be, this would be the feeling that you'd get from*
> *this brilliant white light.*
>
> – Tom [830]

Being enveloped in love is a common aspect of the NDE. The *Being of Light* is totally accepting, uncritical and loving. The impact of this acceptance may be heightened by a minutely detailed scrutiny of our earth-life experiences. Although people might be disappointed in themselves during this life review, regretting sins of omission or commission, the Being of Light is totally understanding and accepting in this moment of 'reckoning.' In actuality, the only judgment rendered is by the people of themselves.

This loving acceptance must also be contrasted with the misguided directions people commonly take and the challenging and difficult experiences they encounter as they steer through the stormy waters of life. Often, people seek to buy acceptance – pleasing others with behaviors that compromise their own wishes, beliefs and sense of self. This often starts in childhood, when parents unwittingly fall into judgmental patterns of criticism. The child who misbehaves is called a 'bad boy.' What the parents really mean is that they are angry at what he has *done*. Children, however, hear that it is *they* who are bad or wrong, not just what they have done. Religion can add its heavy toll of sinfulness, guilt and other blamefulness for deeds of commission or omission. Impersonal, regimented schools, unsatisfying jobs and the anomie of life in cities that foster anonymity add their barnacles of negative self-image in a lifetime of trials and challenges. Our negative self-image may eventually become our own worst enemy.

> *When we die and go to heaven, and we meet our Maker, our Maker is not*
> *going to say to us, why didn't you become a messiah? Why didn't you*
> *discover the cure for such and such? The only thing we're going to be*
> *asked at that precious moment is why didn't you become you?*
>
> – Hassidic story

In contrast with such earthly light, the Being of Light shines her unconditionally accepting love upon a person. It is no wonder that words are inadequate for the experience.

This aspect of the mystical experience suggests awareness of the existence of what is commonly called *God* through naturalistic explorations. The skeptic will point out that this is based on subjective reports. I venture that there are no better (indeed, no other) ones through which to explore the existence of the Being of Light.

> *Let the mind be enlarged... to the grandeur of the mysteries, and not the mysteries contracted to the narrowness of the mind.*
> – Francis Bacon

NDEers themselves, shedding prejudices and preconceptions, often feel unconditional positive regard for the transcendent world they left behind. Often enough, a measure of this positive attitude is retained upon their return to everyday reality. Thus the mystical experience becomes a transformative one.

12. *Trust... Surrender* – the polar opposites to fear, develop with our acceptance of the mystical experience and our trust that it is utterly valid, transcending everyday reality.

> *A man slipped off the edge of a cliff, managing to grasp a bush just below the verge. He looked down, and knew he could not survive a fall into the abyss. He looked up, and saw the roots of the bush slowly starting to tear loose. Though he had been an atheist, he called from the depths of his heart, "God, if there is a God, please save me!"*
> *A voice boomed out of the blue, "My son, I have only been waiting for you to ask. You only have to let go of that bush and I shall save you."*
> *He looked down again, and it was a long, long way to the rocks below. He looked up, and the bush was definitely coming loose. With a shaky voice he cried out, "Is anyone else about?"*
> – Sufi parable

Trust and surrender are made possible through encounters with loving, higher beings and through an acceptance of the intuitive validity of noetic reality. The relinquishing of habitual perceptions, beliefs and disbeliefs of everyday reality is usually very difficult. The more educated we are in Western culture, the harder this may be.

13. *Dualism of existence* – awareness that one exists in realities other than the sensory one, at the same time as one is plodding along one's everyday reality path, born in flesh to learn the lessons of earthly existence:

> *...I will not last too long any more. I am marked. But life has fortunately become provisional. It has become a transitory prejudice, a working hypothesis for the time being, but not existence itself.*
> – Carl Jung [831]

Reports from mystical experiences, supported by research on reincarnation, NDE, OBE, apparitions, mediumistic reports and possession all suggest that body and *mind* (i.e. the little 'i' or self) are separate. The brain appears not to be the *origin* of mind but more likely a transformer for *expression* of mind – from other dimensions into the material world. Mind seems more an essence that has an existence on other planes, expresses itself through the body, survives the body and may return at another time to another life in a different body.

Yet another aspect of dualism, on non-material levels, is the apparent separateness of self versus the awareness of being one with the All. This resembles our being a member of a work or game team, contributing to the team individually but also as part of a whole greater than ourselves. On a cosmic level, through psi, each of us is a brain cell in the collective consciousness.

This is the resolution of the confusion of (6) paradoxicality.

14. *Transformation* – persisting positive changes in attitudes and behavior following the mystical experience:

> *I was raised Protestant... I gave it up in my early teens... I researched Catholicism. I found that was worse... Essentially, at the same time of my accident, I was a ranting, raving atheist. There was no God... He was a figment of man's imagination... (Now) I know that there's a God. And that God is everything that exists, (that's) the essence of God... Everything that exists has the essence of God within it. I know there's a God now. I have no question.*
>
> – 'Janis' [832]

Mystical experiences can lead to striking, far-reaching changes in the lives of those experiencing them. Until recently such changes were found primarily in religious contexts. Lately, they have been sought for their own sake, via all of the methods for attaining Alternative States of Consciousness. Psychotherapies of many types now also introduce exercises leading to mystical experiences as a way of bringing about growth and change.

This aspect of the mystical also seems explainable once we see the vistas open to man via psi. Having glimpsed a broader and deeper understanding of man's interrelations with the cosmos, it would not be surprising that people experiencing the mystic would behave differently. Just as people from a non-industrial country who visit a country more materially developed have difficulty upon their return home in perceiving their native culture again as they saw it originally, so those who became aware of the world via psi might find it hard to see and live their lives as they had prior to the expanded and deepened vision of their mystical experiences.

This dissection and analysis of mystical experiences may seem forced, particularly when considers them outside the context of spirituality and religion. This endeavor to reduce all that has been labeled mystical into linear, scientific explanations might seem to ignore vast vistas introduced to us by religious visionaries, poets and others. Obviously they are extraordinary in their sensitivities and openness to transcendent awareness, and often gifted in being able to describe these dimensions in words and images that convey a deeper appreciation for the mystical. The point I wish to make is that one need not rely solely on religious explanations to understand the impact of these messages. The lives of these luminaries were punctuated with psi manifestations. Could it not be that mystic leaders in ages past were simply charismatic personalities who, in addition, had highly developed psi faculties?

Skeptics will ask, "Could it not be that their visions are mere fantasies?"

Let us consider several such alternatives.

Mystical perceptions as projections from the unconscious mind

Is the mystical experience a delusion, sometimes of psychotic proportions? This question is often asked – by those who have mystical experiences, as well as by those who hear of them. Unless those having mystical experiences are psychotic to begin with, the answer in most cases is an emphatic "No!"

As a psychiatrist, I have examined and treated thousands of psychotic and delusional people. Most psychotic experiences that seem at first glance to overlap with mystical experiences are found on closer scrutiny to be of a clearly different quality from the mystical. Psychotics are often confused, delusional people with poor psychological boundaries. Their psychotic experiences serve immediate personal needs of distancing them from uncomfortable emotions, situations and relationships, and serve defensive interactional needs and processes of other family members as well. In some cases there is a grandiosity, in which the psychotic person claims he hears or is himself God, Christ or The Holy Spirit. In very few of these psychotic experiences is *transformation* or *transiency* evident. In most of them, signs identified by Bleuler early in the last century as characteristic of schizophrenia are found, including extreme ambivalence, autistic preoccupations, inappropriate affect and looseness of associations.[833] R. D. Laing, who was unusually adept at communicating with schizophrenics, observed: "Mystics and schizophrenics find themselves in the same ocean, but the mystics swim whereas the schizophrenics drown."

It is possible for someone with an overwhelming mystical experience to decompensate, as well as for a psychotic person to have growth-promoting mystical experiences,[834] but both of these are relatively uncommon, by no means representative of the much larger group of non-psychotic people who have mystical experiences. Some would suggest that it is society's negative reaction to psychotics and rejection of them that converts their experiences from transformative into negative ones.[835] While there may be a few instances in which this is so, my clinical experience suggests that most psychoses are inherently far from the mystical.

It is not uncommon, however, for psychotic people to have psychic experiences. As mentioned above, however, these are usually incorporated in their psychoses defensively, and are rarely illuminating or inspiring. There can be exceptions, however, in which the psychotic experience is accompanied by transpersonal awarenesses that are transformative. In these cases, *breakdown* becomes a *breakthrough.* This can be facilitated by a transpersonal psychotherapist.

Yet another instance of psychopathology may be accompanied by spiritual awakenings. In multiple personality disorders (currently termed *dissociative disorders* by psychiatrists, psychologists and insurance companies), there is often a personality fragment that is identified as a guiding light.[836] This part of the person may be psychic as well as spiritual, speaking the inner soul wisdom of the person's higher self.

Mystical experiences are commonly achieved through systematic meditation practices. Again the question must be asked: *Are meditative mystical experiences projections from the minds of the meditators rather than perceptions of anything from beyond themselves?*

Ken Wilber[837] is a leading authority on meditative states. He has excellent descriptions of the levels of consciousness that one may attain through the dedicated practice of meditation. These have been described with a general consistency in meditative traditions across numerous cultures. His answer to the above question is also a clear and firm "No!" Mystical experiences are well understood within these traditions and are universally attributed to awareness of and participation in a transcendent reality rather than being a projection of the meditators. [838]

Neurological explanations for mystical experiences

The mystical experience may represent an altered physiological state of the nervous system. When we open up psi modes of perception and action we may in some way also open up the pleasure centers in the brain to greater neuronal self-stimulation or to psi stimulation from outside. People who had electrical stimulation of their pleasure centers incidental to brain surgery reported that this was the most intense pleasure they had ever experienced. Many who achieve ecstatic experiences spontaneously, via meditation, during sexual encounters[839] or via psychedelic drugs say the same thing.

Other evidence supports this hypothesis. During drug-induced ASCs, crossed-sensory experiences called *synesthesias* are common. For example, people may hear color; may feel color with their fingertips; may see colors when they taste certain foods; or may taste something that they smell. A presumed explanation for these chemical-induced synesthesias is that new connections are formed in the brain while under the influence of drugs, or that inhibiting feedback loops of nerves that normally suppress and prevent such confusion are themselves inhibited. By analogy, during mystical experiences the pleasure centers may similarly be stimulated via new or newly-unsuppressed connections in the brain, or the veils may be lifted that separated ordinary consciousness from mystical awareness.[840]

The brain can produce morphine-like substances called endorphins. The ecstasy reported during mystical experiences may be related in some measure to chemical self-stimulation with these natural opiates.

It would be relatively easy to give chemical antagonists for opiates to meditators to see whether these block all or parts of their meditative mystical experiences. It would be more difficult but still of great interest to see if people who had experienced electrical stimulation of their pleasure centers could be taught meditation, or conversely, if experienced meditators requiring brain surgery would permit stimulation of their pleasure centers, allowing comparisons between these experiences.

Recent studies with sophisticated brain imaging devices show that during deep meditation, particular portions of the brain are activated.[841] Meditation leads to altered EEG brain wave patterns.[842] Though we do not yet understand the basis of these EEG changes, it seems reasonable to suggest that they represent new pathways established in the brain, perhaps amongst them connections with the pleasure centers.

Contradicting these neurobiological theories are mediumistic reports that spirits (who have no brain or nervous system) experience ecstatic states, for instance, in the presence of the Being of Light.[843]

We saw earlier[844] that unconsciousness without an NDE is not a transformative experience, while with an NDE it is. This would point away from organic hypotheses to explain mystical experiences.

The images perceived during meditative and ecstatic experiences may provide further clues to the question: Are mystical perceptions awarenesses of the world outside or are they projections created by the perceiver from within herself? Eastern art includes stereotyped images such as the *bindu* point, symbolizing the ultimate center of the cosmos; and recurrent images of circles; triangles and spirals.[845] Phosphene images from pressure on the eyeballs, from electrical stimulation of the brain and from hallucinogenic drugs strongly resemble drawings of preschool children,[846] meditative images[847] and meditative art.[848] This suggests a common underlying process. Commonalities in perceived images of the mystical experience (and perhaps other aspects of it as well) may relate more strongly to projections due to the wiring of the nervous system rather than to the world outside.

The opposite could equally be postulated. The hardware of the brain may channel perceptions of other realities, from outside the individual, into a limited range of stereotyped images – due to the limitations of the nervous system to translate transcendent awarenesses. This is consistent with reports of mystics that words are inadequate to describe their experiences.

I see no way to distinguish definitively between these two broad possibilities. Interpretations will depend on the type of evidence one is willing to accept. The reductionist will insist on limiting considerations to neuronal pathways and chemistry, while the healer and mystic will accept intuitive, subjective evidence as well.

Perhaps a meeting ground can eventually be found in an energetic or vibrational conceptualization of the world. The fact that reductionistic theories do not account for much of the evidence reviewed in this book suggests to me that such theories are limited-case explanations of reality, like classical physics is in relation to quantum physics.[849]

The relevance of mystical experiences to healing

I am not I.
I am this One
Walking beside me whom I do not see,
Whom at times I manage to visit,
And whom at other times I forget;
Who remains calm and silent while I talk,
And forgives, gently, when I hate,
Who walks where I am not,
Who will remain standing when I die.
                                                    – Juan Ramon Jimenez

A common denominator among healers is 'being one with the healee and with the All.' [850] Many healers, practicing many varieties of healing, feel that even an instant of contact with the All suffices to bring about a healing.

Positive effects of healers probably derive in part from their bringing healees to taste mystical experiences. Healees often become more spiritual following spiritual healings, regardless of whether they experience dramatic cures or only moderate relief of symptoms. Even with no physical healings, healees may begin to sense their connection with the All, either through resonance with the healer or through the experience of the healing. Many healers feel that this spiritual awareness is an even more important aspect of healing than physical effects of their treatments.

Healers obtain their information from internal cues and perceptions that have the strong, noetic quality of mystical experiences. This may be how the term *clairvoyance*, meaning *clear vision*, originated. Healers often report they intuitively know information such as: a the physical and emotional causes behind a problem; when, where and how to apply bioenergies; when a treatment is completed; early life experiences creating chronic physical tensions leading to illness; past-life roots of physical and inter-personal disharmonies; whether a particular therapeutic intervention will help or not; and more.

To uninitiated observers and skeptics these may appear to be fanciful claims, as they are unsupported by objectively observable data, and little research has yet been published to support these claims.[851]. We may begin to give more credence to these reports if we also take into account the subjective qualities of the perceptions involved in mystical experiences. Many healers learn to know and trust these inner awarenesses. In one study of healers' abilities to sense bioenergy fields, they were able to identify with greater accuracy when their perceptions were on target than when their perceptions were in error.[852]

I find that there is a distinct quality of engagement with transcendent realities in my personal use of intuition in psychotherapy and of offering and receiving spiritual healing. It resembles the sensory experience of perceiving a distinctive odor that identifies a particular experience. There are times when this is strong and unmistakable, and other times when it may be weak to the point that it is difficult to be certain whether it is actually there.

My clinical impression is that a rough consensual validation among healers can often be achieved regarding such perceptions of the transcendent. More formal studies on consensual impressions of multiple healers from diverse healing traditions are needed, however, to provide firmer assessments of the reliability of observations associated with these noetic impressions. It may be that those assessments and interventions with a noetic quality are the more accurate or successful ones.[853]

Are mystical experiences identical with spiritual experiences? I invite you to consider the evidence for both. My impression is that both represent an opening of awareness into the transcendent realms, with people from secular backgrounds or agnostic and atheistic beliefs interpreting and labeling these experiences as mystical, while those who are open to religious beliefs and who trust in their personal awareness of the transcendent identifying these as spiritual.[854]

Intuitive statements about the mystical

Dissecting the non-linear mystical experience may help us to begin to comprehend its elements, but this is like analyzing the molecular structure of ice in order to understand the nature of snowflakes or lemon-ices, or to appreciate our responses to seeing and tasting them. One may appreciate the snowflake more for the linear analyses, but one must view many snowflakes in their entirety to grasp their essence.[855]

Accepting that metaphoric statements about the transcendent may do these realms more justice than linear dissections, here are some crystals and polished gems of observations from explorers in transcendent dimensions.

> *As one's hand held before one's eye conceals the greatest mountain, so our little earthly life hides from our vision the immense lights and mysteries which fill the world. He who can draw it away from before his eyes, as one draws away a hand, beholds the great shining of the inner worlds.*
> – Rabbi Nachman of Bratzlav

> *Just as a white summer cloud, in harmony with heaven and earth freely floats in the blue sky from horizon to horizon following the breath of the atmosphere – in the same way the pilgrim abandons himself to the breath of the greater life that... leads him beyond the farthest horizons to an aim which is already present within him, though yet hidden from his sight.*
> – Lama Govinda

> *In that hour came the disciples unto Jesus, saying: Who, then, is the greatest in the kingdom of heaven? And he called to him a little child and said: Verily I say unto you: except ye turn and become as little children ye shall in no wise enter into the kingdom of heaven.*
> – Matthew [856]

*And being asked by the Pharisees when the kingdom of God cometh he
answered them and said: The kingdom of God cometh not with
observation; neither shall they say, Lo, here! or there, for lo, the kingdom
of God is within you.*

– Luke [857]

Student: *Can I know God?*
 Krishnamurti: *Is belief necessary to find out?*
 *To learn is far more important than to know. Learning about belief is the
end of belief. When the mind is free of belief then it can look. It is belief, or
disbelief, that binds; for they are the same... The question, 'Is there a
God?' has quite a different meaning. The word God with all its tradition,
its memory, its intellectual and sentimental connotations – all this is not
God. The word is not the real. So can the mind be free of the word?*

– Krishnamurti

*Compare the wild, free paintings of the child with the stiff, pinched
'pictures' these become as the painter notices the painting and tries to
portray 'reality' as others see it; self-conscious now, he steps out of his
own painting and, finding himself apart from things, notices the silence all
around and becomes alarmed by the vast significations of Creation. The
armor of the 'I' begins to form, the construction and desperate assertion of
separate identity, the loneliness: "Man has closed himself up, till he sees
all things through the narrow chinks of his cavern." [858]*

– Peter Matthiessen

*Hast never come to thee an hour,
A sudden gleam divine, precipitating, bursting all these bubbles, fashions,
wealth?
These eager business aims – books, politics, arts, amours,
To utter nothingness.*

– Walt Whitman

*As in a swoon, one instant,
Another sun, ineffable full-dazzles me,
And all the orbs I knew, and brighter, unknown orbs;
One instant of the future land,
Heaven's land.*

– Walt Whitman

*Until I knew the shape of the Hua Mountain, how could I paint a picture of
it? But even after I had visited it and drawn it from nature, the 'idea' was
still immature. Subsequently I brooded... One day I was resting... I leapt
up and cried 'I have got it!' Then I tore up the old sketches and painted it
again. This time my only guide was the Hua Mountain itself.*

– Chinese painter, 14th Century [859]

> *The TAO that can be expressed*
> *is not the eternal TAO.*
> *The name that can be named*
> *is not the eternal name.*
>
> – Lao Tsu

My personal experiences with the mystical

My most intense experience was the one and only time I took LSD. This was in the context of a research project to clarify several reports that autistic children could respond better to other people if they were given LSD. I requested this experience so that I could better appreciate what the children we were to study might be experiencing. On a summer day in 1963, between my second and third years in medical school, I lay down on a couch in a hospital room appropriated for the occasion. Two psychiatric residents had volunteered to administer the drug and observe. Both had had 'bad trips' and felt to me rather like snoopy playing vulture on the edge of his dog house – just waiting to see me have my bad trip.

Within minutes of the IV injection of 200 micrograms of laboratory grade LSD I began to see vivid colors streaming from between the ceiling tiles. I started to describe what I saw, but simply could not do so because the vibrations of my voice stimulated more intense color experiences. In any case, words came too slowly. What I started to describe was very quickly a long way down the river of expanding time, with floods of new colors constantly arriving.

Then the rough, green texture of the couch drew my attention. As I ran my hands over it, I could feel the green through my skin. For an indefinable period of time I was nothing but green and cold, grateful for the faint awareness in some recess of my mind that this was an experience that was time-limited and would end eventually. At one point I was lonely, totally alone in the universe. At another point I laughed a cosmic laugh, resonating with the laughter of an All that took pleasure in the pleasure of those experiencing pleasure.

Externally, my life was not altered by this marvelous, mystical experience. But somewhere inside me there remains a stronger awareness of my connection with the All.

This awareness waned in the weeks and months and years of medical and psychiatric studies and practice that followed. It has only gradually built back up through my spiritual practices of meditation, personal prayer, and spiritual healing. Teaching and writing about these subjects has deepened my understandings and appreciations for them.

In summary

Mystical experiences are sought in various quests, or may come unbidden and totally unexpectedly. They are profoundly moving openings into a cosmic awareness of being part of the vastness of the All.

From the vantage of modern Western culture, they may be seen as no more than fantasies. From the vantage of anyone who has had a mystical experience, they often appear more real than physical reality, and certainly more attractive – as they include a strong sense of timeless, infinite love, ecstasy and awe. They are beyond adequate description in linear language, making it difficult to bridge this divide in ways of viewing the world.

There are broad overlaps between the perceptions of mystical experiences and reports of NDEs. Both are profoundly transformative, often leaving those who experience them with an inner certainty that spirit life continues after physical death, and often bring on major changes in the lives of those who are fortunate enough to awaken to spiritual realities in these ways.

The descriptions of mystical experiences suggest a major awakening of psi awarenesses – including telepathy, clairsentience, pre- and retrocognition. On the one hand, this provides a way of demystifying mystical experiences; on the other hand, it suggests that everyone may have the capacity to touch upon the mystical, since it appears that everyone has a measure of intuitive abilities.

Too often, the mystical is misunderstood within Western frameworks only as an escape from reality; an avoidance of engagement with the real (i.e. physical) world. While for some it may be an escape of this sort, for many others it is an inspiration that gives meaning and purpose to life. My own belief is that connecting with our awareness of the spiritual purposes for our being on this earth may be the only way through our modern society's current materialistic, suicidal self-absorption.

> *Great ideas, it has been said, come into the world as gently as doves. Perhaps then, if we listen attentively, we shall hear amid the uproar of empires and nations, a faint flutter of wings, the gentle stirring of life and hope Some will say that this hope lies in a nation; others in a man.*
>
> *I believe rather that it is awakened, revived, nourished by millions of solitary individuals whose deeds and works every day negate frontiers and the crudest implications of history. As a result, there shines forth fleetingly the ever-threatened truth that each and every man, on the foundation of his own suffering and joys, builds for all.*
>
> – Albert Camus

Continuing our demystification of mystical experiences, let us now turn to the world of quantum physics.

CHAPTER 10

Quantum Physics Converges with the Mystical

[W]e all know that our own reality depends on the structure of our consciousness; we can objectify no more than a small part of our world. But even when we try to probe into the subjective realm, we cannot ignore the central order or look upon the forms peopling this realm as mere phantoms or accidents.... in the final analysis, the central order or the 'one' as it used to be called and with which we commune in the language of religion, must win out.
— *Werner Heisenberg* [860]

The mystical experience includes a feeling that one is part of the All. Mystics claim this is the true reality and that our everyday, sensory reality is an illusion. Such reports are viewed by many with great skepticism. In the last few centuries, Western society has elevated observation of external reality and reason above internal observation, intuition and feeling. We assume that science has an objective way of measuring reality. We overlook the fact that even scientists must interpret what their instruments indicate. Scientists who are observing nature are also interpreting nature through the labels and properties they attribute to nature and through the theories they use to explain nature.

Modern physics, the most basic of material sciences, appears to be bringing us full circle back to a mystical view of the cosmos – as in the statement above by Werner Heisenberg, who developed the uncertainty principle in modern physics. Explorations by quantum physicists of the essence of physical reality appears to be verifying many of the observations that mystics have been reporting for millennia. A few excerpts from writers who have explored the overlap of physics and mysticism will help us appreciate this re-emergence within science of basic intuitive truths that have long been familiar within mystical traditions.

> *The observer is never entirely replaced by instruments; for if he were, he could obviously obtain no knowledge whatsoever... The most careful record, when not inspected, tells us nothing.*
> – Erwin Schrödinger [861]

To the layman, it appears that scientists have worked out THE basic measurements of the universe, or are close to being able to do so. Arthur Eddington[862] points out that this is not so:

> *Quantities like length, duration, mass, force, etc. have no absolute significance; their values will depend on the mesh-system to which they are referred... There is no fundamental mesh-system... The systems used in current physics are arbitrary.*

Moving from measurements to theories built upon these investigations, we introduce yet another level of observer participation.

> *The system of concepts is a creation of man together with the rules of syntax, which constitute the structure of the conceptual systems... All concepts, even those which are closest to experience, are from the point of view of logic freely chosen conventions, just as is the case with the concept of causality...*
> – Albert Einstein [863]

> *Useful as it is under everyday circumstances to say that the world exists 'out there' independent of us, that view can no longer be upheld. There is a strange sense in which this is a 'participatory universe.'*
> – John Wheeler [864]

Quantum physics has confirmed that nonlocal interactions between widely separated particles are possible, through the Einstein, Podalsky and Rosen (EPR) theory, substantiated by experimental evidence after elaborations of Bell. The EPR theory states that one particle may shift its orientation in one part of the universe and a second particle, which has been linked ('entangled') with the first, but which is located anywhere else in the universe, no matter how far away, will shift simultaneously in response to the shift in the first one.

A variety of other authors discuss the growing convergence of modern physics with mysticism.[865] They point out that both in mysticism and physics the studied object and the persons/instrument(s) studying the object interact in many ways, the definition of which depends upon the conceptualizations and interpretations of the observers and the ways in which they study the object. Classical statements of philosophers and mystics over many centuries, both from East and West, are strikingly similar to those of modern physicists.

I share here a few observations from the books of my favorite authors on this subject, Gary Zukav and Fritjof Capra. Both suggest that the study of quantum physics is leading us to appreciate the nature of the world in ways that appear to parallel very closely the descriptions of the world provided by mystics.

Zukav: Professor G. F. Chew,[866] Chairman of the Physics Department, Berkeley, remarked, in reference to a theory of particle physics:

> ...Our current struggle with [advanced physics] may...be only a foretaste of a completely new form of human intellectual endeavor, one that will not only lie outside physics but will not even be describable as 'scientific.'
>
> We need not make a pilgrimage to India or Tibet. There is much to learn there, but here at home, in the most inconceivable of places, amidst the particle accelerators and computers, our own Path without Form is emerging.[867]

Capra: "...In the words of Henry Margenau [a physicist],"

> The central recognition of the theory of relativity is that geometry...is a construct of the intellect.[868] Only when this discovery is accepted can the mind feel free to tamper with the time-honored notions of space and time, to survey the range of possibilities available for defining them, and to select that formulation which agrees with observation.[869]

> Eastern philosophy, unlike that of the Greeks, has always maintained that space and time are constructs of the mind. The Eastern mystics treated them like all other intellectual concepts; as relative, limited, and illusory. In a Buddhist text, for example, we find the words,[870] "It was taught by the Buddha, oh Monks, that...the past, the future, physical space...and individuals are nothing but names, forms of thought, words of common usage, merely superficial realities." [871]

Capra points out that if we carefully analyze the processes of observation developed in atomic physics, we find that subatomic 'particles' actually have no meaning in terms of being isolated entities. The concept of particles is taken from our everyday experience of the world of gross matter and transferred incorrectly to the world of quantum phenomena. We are misled to believe we can interpret the subatomic domain through experiments that involve instruments that we manipulate and from which we derive various measurements. Quantum theory, being a realm that is beyond separations between particles "reveals a basic oneness of the universe." Within the quantum universe we cannot separate and divide our cosmos into independent bits of matter. There are actually no isolated, elementary building blocks in nature. What appears to exist in the quantum domain is a complex web of interrelationships between the diverse parts of the whole. The human observer is always included in the observations in essential ways. "The observer constitutes the final link in the chain of observational process, and the properties of any atomic object can only be understood in terms of the object's interaction with the observer." What this means is that the scientific ideal of objective descriptions of nature can no longer be held to be valid. The classical Cartesian separation between the observer and that which is observed in the outside world cannot be made in analyses of atomic matter. "In atomic physics, we can never speak about nature without, at the same time, speaking about ourselves." [872]

Capra continues, observing that traditions in both China and India suggest that an ultimate, inner reality exists, underlying and unifying the outer, worldly objects and events that we observe:

> There are the three terms – 'complete,' 'all-embracing,' 'the whole.' These names are different, but the reality sought in them is the same: referring to the One thing. [873]

As Capra points out, this understanding of reality is called the Tao, meaning *the Way*. This signifies the flow or process of our universe, the inherent order within nature. As times passed, the Confucianists developed a new interpretation for the Tao as the inherent nature of man, or as societal Tao, explaining this as the proper ways of life within moral frameworks rather than as a cosmology to explain the universe. The doctrine of impermanence in Indian Buddhism held to similar views, but perceived the inherent nature of the universe as a basic human premise with various psychological consequences. In contrast, the Chinese identified changes and flows in the cosmos that are essential features of nature, and that we as humans are sensitive to patterns within these changes. The sage can recognize these natural patterns and will guide his actions in accordance with their flows. In this way, the wise person lives in harmony with nature, becoming 'one with the Tao,' and succeeds in everything he undertakes.

> The universal interconnectedness of things, and events, however, seems to be a fundamental feature of the atomic reality which does not depend on a particular interpretation of the mathematical theory. The following passage from a recent article by David Bohm, confirms this fact most eloquently. [874]

> One is led to a new notion of unbroken wholeness which denies the classical idea of analyzability of the world into separately and independently existing parts... We have reversed the usual classical notion that the independent 'elementary parts' of the world are the fundamental reality, and that the various systems are merely particular contingent forms and arrangements of these parts. Rather, we say that inseparable quantum interconnected-

ness of the whole universe is the fundamental reality, and that relatively independently behaving parts are merely particular and contingent forms within this whole...[875]

Capra notes this is the way Eastern mystics have reported their experiences of the world. This is nearly identical with the interpretations of the world offered by atomic physicists, as witnessed by the following two examples:

The material object becomes...something different from what we now see, not a separate object on the background or in the environment of the rest of nature but an indivisible part and even in a subtle way an expression of the unity of all that we see...[876]

Things derive their being and nature by mutual dependence and are nothing in themselves...[877]

If these statements could be taken as an account of how nature appears in atomic physics, the following two statements from atomic physicists could, in turn, be read as a description of the mystical experience of nature:[878]

An elementary particle is not an independently existing unanalyzable entity. It is, in essence, a set of relationships that reach outward to other things...[879]

The world thus appears as a complicated tissue of events, in which connections of different kinds alternate or overlap or combine and thereby determine the texture of the whole.[880]

The reader is warmly recommended to the fuller discussions of remarkable parallels of quantum physics and mystical writings in Capra and Zukav.

Connections between mind and matter are found in the dual nature of matter, describable as both particles and waves. We are all familiar with Einstein's theory that mass (an attribute of matter) and energy are interconvertible, $E=MC^2$ but we have not yet digested the profound meaning of this observation.

Sir James Jeans[881] notes:

...In this progress towards the truth...each step was from particles to waves, or from the material to the mental; the final picture consists wholly of waves, and its ingredients are wholly mental constructs...the cumulative evidence of various pieces of probable reasoning makes it seem more and more likely that reality is better described as mental than as material...

...Mind no longer appears as an accidental intruder into the realm of matter; we are beginning to suspect that we ought rather to hail it as the creator and governor of the realm of matter.

Robert Jahn and Brenda Dunne[882] go so far as to state that, "[W]e...suggest that it is consciousness that is the ultimate metaphor for quantum mechanics, or for any other theoretical model, for that matter." [883]   Others consider these same issues from a different perspective. The holographic world view propounded by neurophysiologist Karl Pribram and physicist David Bohm may also describe aspects of healing and psi. The three-dimensional photographic image of a hologram has unusual properties. If the negative is cut into pieces, each piece maintains the whole original picture though with somewhat less clarity of detail. This is an apt analogy and a useful way of visualizing the unity that seems to underlie our universe.[884]   Our psi perceptions may be examples of direct experiences of the unity of the cosmos.[885]

>   *As above, so below.*
>   – A. Huxley

Famous physicists who have come to appreciate the mystical side of science include David Bohm, Niels Bohr, Louis de Broglie, Sir Arthur Eddington, Albert Einstein, Werner Heisenberg, Sir James Jeans, Brian Josephson, Wolfgang Pauli, Max Planck, Erwin Schroedinger, Henry Stapp, Baron Carl Friedrich von Weizsacker, and Eugene P. Wigner.[886]

To this list I add the special mention of William Tiller, who has written extensively over the past thirty-five years about the metaphysics suggested by quantum physics.[887] Even more interestingly, he has been exploring the overlaps of consciousness in quantum physics and in spiritual healing.[888]

Tiller suggests that in each scientific generation we tend to presume we possess the ultimate and final knowledge and explanations for our world – only to discover that there are deeper and more fundamental ways of understanding the universe. Changing our ways of explaining the cosmos is, however, a slow and painful process, often resisted because of habitual ways of conceptualizing the universe.

In a series of experiments, Tiller[889] demonstrated that conscious intent can be imprinted in materials which can be shipped to a distant laboratory, where they bring about the intentional effect that is imprinted on them. Tiller developed an Intention Imprinted Electrical Device (IIED) which can change the acidity of water, alter the action of enzymes (chemicals that facilitate physiological processes) and accelerate the growth rate of fruit fly larvae. "By comparing the separate influence of two physically identical devices, one unimprinted and the other imprinted via our meditative process, we were able to demonstrate a robust influence of human consciousness on these materials..." [890]

An unexpected finding was that each of the laboratories in which these experiments were conducted became 'conditioned' to enhance these effects, even after the devices had been removed from the laboratory for several months.

Tiller likens this conditioning effect to the spiritual 'field of consciousness' that appears to fill a room where people have gathered regularly to meditate or pray together. Tiller found preliminary evidence suggesting a validation for this intuitive 'feeling of spirituality,' demonstrating that the space used by a husband and wife healer team had the same 'conditioned' effects as the laboratories where the IEEDs were used.

Other experiments by Tiller produced further, highly unusual results. The IIED was placed in a beaker of purified water within a Faraday cage (shielding it from electromagnetic radiation). A number of thermometers that were placed in a line, extending radially from the IEED, showed a specific pattern of temperature gradient that remained constant despite strong fans blowing on the thermometers. The fans would be expected to dissipate any heat differences between the thermometers, but they did not do so. This is a highly anomalous finding, inexplicable in conventional physics. Continued anomalous effects were noted when the IEED was removed from the room.

Recent advances in theoretical physics suggest that the space between atoms and molecules is not inert.[891] Tiller speculates that this 'vacuum' may be where the intent is imprinted.

Tiller suggests that as human beings we are spirits dressed in 'biobodysuits' that are composed of four layers, spanning the physical and vacuum dimensions. He discusses consciousness as an aspect of the biobodysuit, representing spirit as it exists in matter, and relates these layers to theories of physics.

Further discussions on quantum physics and consciousness are presented by Ervin Laszlo, a brilliant French former professor of philosophy, systems theory and futures studies, who holds the highest degree awarded by the Sorbonne (State Doctorate) and four Honorary PhDs. In his outstanding book, *Science and the Akashic Field,* he presents a wholistic view of the world from the vantage points of quantum physics and systems theory. He does not hesitate to question the commonly held beliefs within quantum physics, pointing out facts that do not fit within currently popular theories explaining the universe. For instance, he summarizes evidence that the so-called 'empty' space between stars is not really empty, but contains enormous amounts of energy and provides the medium for the transmission of light throughout the universe.

Coming from the opposite direction, Laszlo suggests that living organisms have similarities with quantum systems:

> The 'music' of a higher organism ranges over more than seventy octaves. It is made up of the vibration of localized chemical bonds, the turning of molecular wheels, the beating of micro-cilia, the propagation of fluxes of electrons and protons, and the flowing of metabolites and ionic currents within and among cells through ten orders of spatial magnitude.
>
> The level of coherence discovered in the organism suggests that in some respects it is a macroscopic quantum system. Living tissue is a ... form of matter in which quantum-type processes, hitherto believed to be limited to the microscopic domain, occur at macroscopic scales.[892]

Laszlo argues on the one hand that all matter is conscious, and on the other, that we are hard put to define exactly what consciousness is. He marshals cogent arguments to support his thesis that the entire universe is conscious, interconnected through a universal field. He cites scientist after scientist who postulate theories that can explain a universal, collective consciousness which has been called in mystical tradition *the Akashic field*, and which Laszlo calls the A-field.

Varieties of broader speculations have been offered to explain these unusual findings. H. Everett proposes that many worlds co-exist, and that consciousness determines which is in existence at any one time. John Wheeler suggests that channels between parallel three-dimensional universes (*wormholes*) enable interactions between them.[893] Larry Dossey[894] wonders, "Is the outward reaching of subatomic particles a form of prayer? If so, the entire universe is prayer."

Peter Russell,[895] who has studied theoretical physics and experimental psychology, suggests:

> God is Light. God is said to be absolute – and in physics, so is light. God lies beyond the manifest world of matter, shape, and form, beyond both space and time – so does light. God cannot be known directly – nor can light.

The discussions on a convergence of modern physics with the mystical have stirred much controversy in the community of physicists. Many physicists are convinced that ever finer and more detailed analyses of the physical world will ultimately yield a complete explanation for the workings of nature, including the phenomena of consciousness.

Ken Wilber[896] argues that evidence from quantum physics should not be presented in support of a belief in the mystical, and certainly not as *proof* of its existence. Quantum physics explores mathematical constructs of the world, based on highly sophisticated machines that record interactions of subatomic particles. Wilber believes that mystical experiences stem from intuitive, inner awareness and cannot be studied or compared with the methods of quantum physics. He acknowledges, however, that the most eminent of quantum physicists also believed in the mystical, and that the mystical has its own, valid, inner-perception reality.

Drew Leder has an different perspective. He proposes a theory of *compatiblism*, contending "the phenomena involved in psi and distant healing are not explained by, but are interestingly compatible with, the paradigms of modern physics. That is, the evolving world views of physics suggest how such 'spooky actions' might be possible (even plausible) and provide frameworks with which to interpret them in a way that earlier mechanistic science did not."

Discussion

> *A little science estranges men from God, much science leads them back to Him.*
>
> – Louis Pasteur

I assume that the majority of physicists are similar to the majority of doctors and others in modern Western science who have little awareness of the intuitive or mystical, and who would apply Procrustean, reductionist, linear yardsticks to the mystical and dismiss it as irrelevant.

I presume that those physicists who consider the mystical to be a legitimate reality, which can be appreciated from within quantum physics, are relating to phenomena we are considering in this book. If this is true, it is a marvel that we may arrive at similar conclusions through very different paths of investigation.

Mystics have stated that man is one with the universe. They claim the evidence is available to all through looking inward in meditative states.[897]

From the point of view of intuitives, healers and mystics, the universe is a cosmic mind, manifesting through various levels of vibrations, with matter being the most dense of vibrational states. Kyriakos Markides,[898] a Sociologist from the University of Maine, details the views of the gifted Cypriot healer, Daskalos:

> [A]ll matter is Mind in various forms of 'vibrations.' Mind...is not the Absolute, as he [Daskalos] preferred to call what people understand as God, but the means by which the unmanifest Absolute manifests Itself. Mind is the 'supersubstance' with which the 'universes' are created. There is no 'dead matter.'

Modern physics arrives at a similar point through complex mathematical analyses of various measurements of subatomic particles. Modern physics is finding a unity of relatedness underlying our universe from evidence of interconnection of particles across space and time, from the indivisibility of observer from the observed, and from a validation of energy as a basis for reality equal with matter.

Discussion on alternate realities and quantum physics

It is fascinating to me how indoctrinated I find myself in Western, linear, Cartesian, left-brain views of the world. Despite all my reading, meditating and experience with multidetermined psychiatric thought, with healing and other psi phenomena, some small part of me still hopes to find linear maps of the mystical. Better yet, perhaps, might be to find ways to boost myself via sensory reality into the dimensions of the mystical, which would allow me to travel there on familiar paths and feel more of a sense of control on this journey into unknown territory. It is difficult to overcome my indoctrination in the sciences, which prejudices me to favor the evidence of physicists. I have a habitual preference to rely more on the registrations of dials and screens of linear accelerators and computers and on the conclusions derived from them via what appears to me to be mathematical magic and theoretical speculations of 'hard scientists' that are beyond my capacities to decipher directly. A part of me simply hesitates to rely on the inward observations of countless mystics through the ages. The very word 'mystic' connotes non-linear thinking that I am conditioned to respond to with skepticism.

It is only as I start to trust the growing, non-linear, inner 'knowing' I experience personally in being a psychotherapist, healer, meditator and healee that I begin to appreciate the possible legitimacy and validity of direct intuitive perceptions and comprehensions of the world. I have resonated with the mystical experiences described by others. I have sniffed the fragrance of mystical experiences in exploring nature and through intense and moving human experiences, and can imagine their full marvelous taste as described by others who have visited these realms. But I have yet to relish their fullness experientially, as in a near death experience or a full mystical awakening in order to know them with the intensity described by mystics. I expect I shall have difficulty relinquishing my sensory reality beliefs until I am so blessed. Yet in order to reach the mystical, I must let go of the bush at the verge of the cliff of linear reality and trust that I shall not be dashed upon some rocks in the infinite chasm of my inner connections with the All.

I am comforted at the same time that I am frustrated by the fact that I am among the majority of humanity in my hesitations to explore these realms. I was recently helped by Wendy Hurwitz, a remarkable intuitive, to understand that within the world of my senses I should not expect to find a full awakening to the mystical experience, which I frame as "knowing the love of the Infinite Source." Within sensory reality, my experiences of this love can be learned from my interactions with the physical world. I can deduce logically that there must be a guiding hand behind the miracles of creation and existence as I perceive and experience them. I can feel a part of the All in my gratitude for the many blessings of my physical world. I can equally, and often more powerfully, give thanks for this knowing that I am a cared-for part of the All with the healing lessons learned through adversities and pains. But I may not be able to reach the fullest possible depth of mystical experience from this vantage point.

As I move deeper into meditative, prayer and healing experiences, I begin to experience the inner gnowing of the mystical that I crave. It is in these realms that the fuller sense of the mystical can be more fully experienced.[899]

Alternate realities and quantum physics

As far as the laws of mathematics refer to reality, they are not certain. And as far as they are certain, they do not refer to reality.
– Albert Einstein

To the still skeptical reader I will pose these questions: Have you ever seen an atom? An electron? What basis do you have for any confidence in your belief in their existence? Is this more valid than the basis you might have for believing a meditative adept who explains the nature of the world? I challenge you to study either subject yourself!

Quantum physicists say that matter can be conceptualized either as particles or waves. Their equations allow us to specify characteristics in one or another aspect of matter but not both simultaneously. Louis de Broglie[900] speculated:

May it not be universally true that the concepts produced by the human mind, when formulated in a slightly vague form, are roughly valid for Reality, but that when extreme precision is aimed at, they become ideal forms whose real content tends to vanish away?

Physicists tell us that their complex equations disclose eleven or more dimensions to the world, each at a level of abstraction beyond the next lower one. The worlds of physicists are shrouded in clouds of mathematical equations that few can penetrate. We can just sniff a whiff of rudimentary understanding of higher dimensions through Edwin Abbott's lovely description of an imaginary world called Flatland. In this imaginary world, two-dimensional creatures would experience serious difficulties understanding what is happening when they encounter three-dimensional intrusions into their world. As an example, imagine that we all live in a world that is absolutely flat, and we are attached to the surface of a sheet of paper on which we can move but we have no awareness of anything outside the surface of the paper. A pencil poking through the paper would appear to be a dot, widening into a circle for a period of time, then disappearing. It would be extremely difficult to get an image of a pencil from the experience of perceiving these circles appearing and disappearing.[901] It may be that healing and other psi effects will one day be perfectly comprehensible through better analyses and understandings of these dimensions that physicists assure us are really there.

Now, my suspicion is that the universe is not only queerer than we suppose, but queerer than we can suppose... I suspect that there are more things in heaven and earth than are dreamed of, in any philosophy.
– J.B.S. Haldane

Theoretical physicists suggest that everything may be connected to everything else. This is what mystics also claim. Depth psychologists such as Jung have postulated that there is a collective unconscious in which we all share. Jung never quite explained how the collective unconscious could operate. Modern physics may provide the necessary theories and proofs.[902]

The dilemmas of a system's attempts to analyze itself are manifold.[903] There are additional problems in the study of subjective reports of mysticism. The brain is subject to emotional, chemical and metabolic factors. These shifting influences may produce distortions in a mind's self-observations, especially unfamiliar ones such as in alternative states of consciousness. Thus it is difficult to trust reports of mystical experiences because they may, in some cases, represent subjective sensations or fantasies resulting from biochemical or psychological processes.

Against the above I place the weight of evidence of research from OBE, NDE, mediumistic, reincarnation, mystical and psi interactions with the world reviewed in this book. A coherent picture of other realities is beginning to emerge from these diverse avenues of investigation. Though the mind may in some part mislead or drug itself, it also can experience directly other realities and ultimately can help us to comprehend the cosmos.

It is time we accepted these limitations as unavoidable – both in examination of the outer world, where observers are part of the system they observe and may create those realities they expect, and in examination of inner worlds, where the same applies even more clearly and pervasively. In modern science we require verification of observations by several investigators before we accept them. The same can be done with inner investigations.[904] Discussions with healers and healees convince me we have partially *similar* subjective experiences in the course of facilitating and receiving healing. Further systematic studies of subjective reports can help clarify in linear terms (to the extent possible) consistently perceived aspects of other realities – while keeping in mind that individual experiences may be validly idiosyncratic and may differ in minor or even major ways from the 'average' report.[905]

Jorge Ferrer takes this argument a step further. He suggests that it is actually impossible to distill a valid common denominator from diverse reports of transpersonal experiences that will accurately describe spiritual dimensions. Each person's perceptions are unique. Therefore, Ferrer argues, each person is actually co-creating transpersonal reality through her or his perceptions and descriptions of these dimensions.

> Though we seem to be sleeping,
> there is an inner wakefulness
> that directs the dream,
> and that will eventually startle us back
> to the Truth of who we are."
>
> – Rumi [906]

Modern Western society has denigrated the term mystical as being 'unscientific,' 'un-*reason*-able,' or 'merely intuitive' and often has dismissed it outright as 'non-*sense*.' It may be time to let the pendulum of investigation swing back from its traverse into materialism and return towards exploring the mystical – not abandoning our reason but allowing reason to be open to the richness of inner worlds.

We must be careful in riding this pendulum into mystical worlds not to make a Type II research error. It may be impossible to draw accurate *linear* maps of inner observations, especially of their qualities. One needs to experience them oneself in order to comprehend them. Practice in entering ASCs, including telepathy and clairsentience, may eventually lead to the consensual experiences in other realities needed to confirm the validity of the territory. My personal experience with healing has convinced me of the impossibility of describing fully a healing experience to anyone who has no similar frames of reference.

I propose that for purposes of analysis in sensory reality terms we adopt an *alternate reality uncertainty principle*: We are limited to partial explanatory statements when we seek to qualify the nature of other realities in linear terms. Because these are each of limited scope and suffer from errors of translation from the realities of other dimensions into sensory reality conceptualizations, our explanations will necessarily represent only approximate truths. In linear terminology we will find contradictions between various statements. These are not due to misperceptions of observations but rather to the impossibility of explaining fully the realities of other dimensions in linear terminology. The apparent contradictions are a function of applying linear logic to non-linear dimensions. We must accept the experiences reported by travelers in other dimensions, just as we have learned to accept the explanations of quantum physics as having a logic that is counter-intuitive when judged by the yardsticks of classical, Newtonian physics.[907]

Contrasts with other cultures may enlighten us. For instance, Marie-Louise von Franz points out that the Chinese emphasize the qualities of numbers more than their quantifying functions. She illustrates this with a story of eleven Chinese generals who were debating whether to attack or retreat. After lengthy analyses of the relative strengths and weaknesses of the opposing forces, their vote was eight for retreat and three for attack. They therefore attacked *because three is the number for success.*

As noted earlier, in Russian, *da* means 'yes' and *nyet* means 'no.' In German, it is *ja* and *nein.* In both of these languages, the single word that encompasses both polarities, *danyet* and *jein* are accepted concepts. These terms are not equivalent to 'either/or' but rather express the applicability and rightness of both a 'yes-ness' and a 'no-ness' combined in the same subject of discussion. Further enriching explorations of other cultures may yield many more helpful ways of understanding mystical experiences – and the rest of our challenging world.[908]

Life is the only game in which the object of the game is to learn the rules.
– Ashleigh Brilliant

My experiences of living in several very different countries, of being a healer and healee, and my readings about other cultures have convinced me that unitary descriptions of reality simply do not do reality justice. There are juicy words and ideas in every language that are unique to its culture and can enrich those individuals who are open enough to look beyond their own.

To ride the pendulum away from the material world that is familiar and appears to be stable, and to enter realms that appear as varied and unstable as those of energy medicine and of our inner perceptions requires a measure of daring. This is a new/ancient frontier challenging each of us to explore, holding an openness to the duality of *danyet* as we pursue these explorations.

General lessons from quantum physics

Einstein's revolutionary theory, with time as a the fourth dimension and matter that can be understood as energy, were severely questioned and criticized by other mathematicians and scientists of his day. It was only with careful research over several decades that his theories came to be accepted. Students of healing face similar skepticism and rejection from modern science. It will take careful research to bridge the gaps of doubt in order to bring healing into the mainstream of Western medical practice.

Then, at the other end of the pendulum's traverse, we must be careful to keep hold of our sense of the mystical and not let healing become mechanized.

Beyond all our analogies, we must be true to the evidence of our inner investigations. Stanislav Grof and Joan Halifax[909] point out:

> It is essential that a paradigm emerges from the needs of our own discipline and attempts to build bridges to other disciplines rather than emulating them. The significance of new developments in physics for the study of consciousness lies, therefore, more in the destruction of the conceptual straitjackets of mechanistic Newtonian-Cartesian science than in the offer of a new mandatory paradigm.

Angels and quantum physics

Angels are suggested as possible metaphors for phenomena studied in quantum physics – by Matthew Fox, a British Episcopal priest, and Rupert Sheldrake, a biologist who developed a testable theory of morphogenetic fields that guide each species.[910] Both men review and analyze writings of three historic experts on angels: Dionysius the Areopagite of the 6th century, Hildegard of Bingen of the 12th century, and St. Thomas Aquinas of the 13th century.

They suggest that energy fields represent modern conceptualizations of the organizing principles of the universe. In earlier times, a soul or spirit of creation, the *anima mundi*, was believed to be the organizing principle of creation. This has been replaced by gravitational and electromagnetic fields.

Angelic hierarchies were said to exist as spheres within spheres, each contributing its influence to the other spheres inside and outside itself, and all influencing the world of Mankind. This parallels the modern views of interpenetrating energies, and of hierarchical levels of structure within living organisms, such as of atoms, molecules, chromosomes, cells, organs and organisms.

Fox and Sheldrake suggest several such parallels. For instance, they point out that angels connect us with 'The Being of Light' (God, as described by people who have had mystical experiences), where quantum physics speaks of a 'big bang' as the origin of the universe. Angelic realms have a nested hierarchy, and energy fields have serial levels of complexity and interpenetrate each other.

The most important contributions of Fox and Sheldrake are to point out how science, with its emphasis on linear analysis, misses awareness and ignores evidence of vitalistic processes in the universe.

> *The loss of mystery in the modern era is part of the shadow side of knowledge running around naked, looking for its power place, and not looking for wisdom. We have committed reductionism on mystery. Many people think when they hear the word mystery, it just means those scientific laws that we have not yet discovered, it's just a lacuna in our knowledge. But that's not what mystery means. Mystery is that dimension to reality that we encounter but do not alter.*
>
> – Matthew Fox

Quantum physics and the mystical in healing

> *[T]here is no conflict at all between science and spirituality. I think there is a conflict between the current scientific paradigm and spirituality but that's not science, that's just the belief system that science adheres to at the moment.*
>
> – Peter Russell

Observations from atomic physics have been used by numerous authors to suggest a theoretical basis for psi. The same explanations apply for healing.[911]

The mental state in which healing occurs has qualities of the mystical. It includes a sense of being one with the cosmos, or with the 'All.' Healers may be able to enter a reality in which they become one with the healee (along with becoming one with all of creation). LeShan has demonstrated clinically that the deliberate invocation of such visualizations can bring about healings, and this is one of the steps that healers use in the LeShan method of healing. Further evidence for the unity experienced in healing is found in healers' mirroring within their bodies symptoms that healees suffer;[912] in healers' observing details of healees' surroundings during distant healings[913]; in instances where a healee senses a healer's influence[914] or presence[915] during distant healings; and in the sense of the numinous associated with healings – both in healers and healees. Modern physics suggests that there may be elements of 'objective' reality to such a oneness.

Conversely, studies of healing will contribute to an understanding of other realities.

Mystics have told us that each of us has within us the total knowledge of all there is; that each of us in the microcosm of our being is a representation of the All. Healing gives us a doorway to the All, both for experience and understanding.

I truly resonate with the observations of Laurens van der Post,[916] on explorations of the atom and of the world within man:

> [A]t the point where our dreams vanish over the rim of sleep, we meet matter receding over the horizon and, in the process of the most powerful electronic microscope, behaving less like solid, predictable material but more as the swift changing texture of living thought. We pass from one to the other like Alice in Wonderland through a looking glass, to find that the objective mystery which faces us macrocosmically in the night skies above, confronts us macrocosmically in reverse. In the depths of our own mind... symbols, images, patterns of meaning with all the immense energies at their disposal, are constellated and in orbit and strangely akin to the minuscule solar systems, planets, Milky Ways, comets, nebulae and black holes of anti-matter, dynamic in the heart of the physical atom. How could two such discoveries coming at the same desperate moment in time, therefore, not be another of those strange affirmations of the symmetry of meaning?

The research evidence and subjective reports summarized thus far in this book strongly suggest that there are dimensions beyond our physical world to which we have access. For most of us, during physical life these are perceived only dimly through the filters of our unconscious minds, with all the distortions this entails. After we transition beyond physical existence there appears to be a return to unity with the All through small increments of personal growth, with occasional quantum leaps to new levels of awareness.

You might wonder if it isn't odd that so many scientists feel a connection with spiritual matters. Coming from the other direction, Gottfried Wilhelm Leibniz[917] observed: "It is God who is the ultimate reason of things, and the knowledge of God is no less the beginning of science than his essence and will are the beginning of beings."

Stanislav[918] observes, "I have not yet met a single individual who has had a deep experience of the transcendental realms and continues to subscribe to the worldview of Western materialistic science."

I strongly side with the validity of experiential explorations of mystical realms, complemented and supplemented by research that explores consensual validation of these reports.

> *If one wants to find out what lies beyond the frontier, the only way to do so is to go beyond it and see. On this journey one will do well to obtain both a map and a guide but one will have to travel every step by one's own efforts.*
>
> – Robert S. De Ropp

In summary

Conventional Western society craves linear explanations in order to feel comfortable with and accept hypotheses about the world. Quantum physics provides a variety of observations and theories relevant to mystical experiences that can fulfill this wish to parse the world into logical bits and pieces.

Quantum physics has demonstrated with rigorous scientific experiments that instant communication is possible between particles that are separated by any distance whatsoever; that the observer and the observed are not separable; and that there are many dimensions beyond the three physical ones, plus time, to which we commonly limit our consideration of the world.

These observations suggest that science may be arriving at a description of the world that is the same as that of mystics. Statements of mystics and of physicists about the world are in many cases indistinguishable from each other. Numbers of prominent physicists acknowledge a mystical quality to their work and to the world at large.

Let us proceed next to examine how spirituality and spiritual healing have been interpreted in Western society.

CHAPTER 11

Spiritual Healing and Spirituality

When the spirit in which you live is more important than the results of your living, you are spiritual. When the results are more important than the how you go about getting them, you are material.
            – W. Starcke

Science teaches us to see in order to believe. Spirit says believe and you will see...
            – Bernard and Barbara Siegel [919]

First, let us explore some of the perspectives on spirituality that arise from explorations in spiritual healing. Then we will consider various analyses of what spiritual awareness may be.

Spiritual healing is a term that has been used to denote a plethora of beliefs and practices, overlapping in many details, but often with particular meanings for specific religious or cultural groups. A representative sample is reviewed here. Spiritual healing is one of the commonest experiences I know that frequently opens into spiritual awareness. For this reason, a variety of perspectives on healing are reviewed and discussed. This chapter builds upon and confirms the research and anecdotal observations on transcendent and spiritual awarenesses reviewed in the previous chapters, and suggests further ways in which spirituality can be understood and can enhance our lives.

In Britain, *spiritual healing* is the most common popular term for practices that include prayer, mental intent, the laying-on of hands or a combination of these practices. It often is proffered in a context of religious beliefs, and is expected to bring out and to strengthen spiritual qualities in healers and healees as part of its effects. Outer expressions of spirituality may include adherence to religious tenets, engagement with religious rituals, attendance at church and involvement in altruism and good deeds. There may also be shifts towards greater belief in the existence of dimensions beyond the physical, ranging from linear reasoning through intuitive but vague faith, and on to absolute certainty that is supported by feeling, visions and messages from those dimensions, or by a sense of grace that strongly dominates and guides one's life.

Faith healing is also used by the lay public to cover the same healing spectrum. Many healers work from a place of absolute faith in a transcendent power, often within religious contexts. This label has misled many to believe that faith in a particular religion, in God and/or in the healer is required by healers and healees for healing to occur. Research with bacteria, plants, and animals performed by healers without religious reference[920] demonstrate that faith is unnecessary for healing to occur. This is not to say that faith is not important to those who believe in it. In fact, for them faith may be essential to healing themselves or others of illnesses believed to derive from sin or other religious causes.

In America, *spiritual healing* evokes images of revival meetings, with crowds charged to a high pitch of religious fervor; the lame dramatically throwing away their crutches; the preacher declaring another healing in the name of Christ... Oh, and pass the collections plate, by the way... It may also evoke associations of moral and financial scandals amongst some of the prominent media preachers.[921]

Having acknowledged the ambiguity in general usage, my personal preference is still for *spiritual healing*, because I find that healing opens healers and healees to transcendent awarenesses. This is one of the most important aspects of healing.

Perspectives on spiritual healing

> *Is that which is holy loved by the gods because it is holy,*
> *or is it holy because it is loved by the gods?*
> – Plato

Many and varied are the views on spirituality and spiritual healing.

Professor Robert Thouless, past President of the Psychology section of the British Association for the Advancement of Science and also of the Society for Psychical Research, presents a delineation of part of the territory that has been placed under the rubric of spiritual healing and of distinctions between this and other approaches to healing REF:

1. *Faith healing* addresses beliefs of healees, especially their religious articles of faith in the power of God to heal.

2. *Healing by prayer* relies on petitions to a higher power. These may be by healers or by any member of a religious congregation.

3. *Ritual healing* includes actions of a religious nature, which may include the laying-on of hands, reciting specific prayers for particular problems, visiting a shrine, etc. Subdivisions within this class include:

    a. The ritual act is performed by a person other than the patient, such as

        i. A religious official who carries out the healing act as a part of his ministry, the results of the act being attributed to his ministry alone; or

        ii. A person alleged to have the gift of healing, whether he be a minister or not.

    b. A ritual act is performed by the healee, and may include visits to a shrine, washings with water from a holy place, etc.

4. *Spirit healing*, in which the assumed agency is one or more discarnate spirits, whose aid is petitioned in effecting the healing. This is confusingly called 'Spiritual Healing' colloquially, though the same term is used to include instances (1-3) above.

Henry Goddard, at the end of the last century, reviewed evidence for the efficacy of faith cures, as in Thouless' categories above, (1) faith healing and (2) haling by prayer. Goddard distinguished several approaches:

1. *Mental Science* originated in the last century with the work of Phineas Quimby, the originator of the New Thought Movement. This is not affiliated with any religious organization. Quimby started with hypnotic cures but soon found them unnecessary. "[H]e simply sat by the side of his patient, convinced him that his disease was an error and 'established the truth in its place, that, if done, was the cure'." He said, "Now I deny disease as a truth, but admit it as a deception, started like all other stories without any foundation, and handed down from generation to generation till the people believe it, and it becomes a part of their lives. So they live a lie, and their senses are in it."

  He would occasionally manipulate the body of the patient, more to convince the patient that he was doing something effective than because he felt this was required.

2. *Christian Science* is an approach that was initiated by Mary Baker Glover Patterson Eddy, claiming divine inspiration. It is a paean to the ideal that mind is the source of all illness. If the patient can change his beliefs he can be cured. Christian Science is a religious movement. Its adherents eschew medical treatments, feeling that to use such treatments is to express disbelief in the powers and/or intentions of God.

3. *Divine Healing* includes prayer, laying-on-of-hands and rituals, in a religious setting. Goddard points out occasional doctrinaire attitudes of some of the proponents of divine healing, such as that

> ...when once a person has prayed for a healing it is dishonoring God to doubt the cure or to ask for a sign or symptom. The person must claim he

is healed and expect it. This accounts for the many people who claim to be healed but whose appearance contradicts their words.

4. *Hypnotism* is reviewed as related to the above belief systems.

Goddard noted that there were far more similarities than differences in the types of problems treated and in the results of treatments under these systems. Quantitative comparisons could not be made as statistics were not kept by therapists of the approaches (1-3) described above. Pain responded to all treatments rapidly and most satisfactorily. Goddard concludes that suggestion is the principle underlying all of these types of therapy. "In both hypnotism and Christian Science it is the fixed idea in the mind of the patient – placed there by the healer or operator, or suggested by a book or elaborated by the patient's own reasoning – that accomplishes the result through its tendency to 'generate its actuality'." He states in summary, however, that "... we do find sufficient evidence to convince us that the proper reform in mental attitude would relieve many a sufferer of ills that the ordinary physician cannot touch..."

Ailments treated in Goddard's review were predominantly psychosomatic problems that might respond quite readily to suggestion and/or placebos. Though it is hard to evaluate fully the cases he describes, it appears that some of them represented legitimate psi healing (i.e., more than placebo reactions). His inclusion of hypnotism with psi healing helps us appreciate the shifting sands in awareness of levels of healing and the generational fads of religious beliefs and medical diagnoses and practices.

Spirit healings   Numerous healers, especially in England and South America, believe that healing is brought about via the agency of discarnate spirits. Some gifted healers report having seen such spirits from childhood, even when they are in normal, waking states of consciousness.[922] Other healers learn to enter an Alternative State of Consciousness in order to communicate with spirits for diagnosis and treatment. This may be a momentary, partial shift of awareness, much as when one would go from viewing a movie to an awareness of an inner state of 'viewing' one's gut reaction to that movie; or the altered state may be a full trance that the healer enters spontaneously or with hypnotic induction.[923]

Some of the spirits are said to be the surviving entities of deceased physicians or others who were involved in healing when in the flesh. Some are alleged to be entities in the next world who are able and eager to act as guides to contact other spirits who have such knowledge.[924] It is said that particular spirits are available to particular healers because of resonances or *vibrations* of a favorable nature between the particular pair.

It is hard to know what to make of such claims by healers for contacts with spirits. The evidence is rather soft as presented by the healers themselves. Let us examine some of the better spirit healing literature, again without attempting a comprehensive survey.[925]

For instance, the late Gordon Turner, a noted British healer, felt that all healing has a spiritual basis. His usage of *spiritual healing* includes personal spirituality in addition to the assistance of spirit entities in healing. He comments on the difficulties a spiritual healer finds in explaining what he does (1969d):

> To speculate upon spiritual processes necessitates translating them into terms acceptable to physical consciousness; this in turn entails debasing the spiritual process that we are considering. Whilst it may be possible for the adept occultist so to elevate his mind that he can achieve a state of 'higher consciousness,' unfortunately the terminology does not exist to convey to other people these flashes of spiritual understanding.

Walt Whitman also commented on this difficulty:

> *When I undertake to tell the best I find I cannot.*
> *My tongue is ineffectual on its pivots,*
> *My breath will not be obedient to its organs,*
> *I become a dumb man.*[926]

Turner was born with gifts of seeing spirits and auras from early childhood, but not with gifts of healing. He brought out his healing powers through attendance at a spiritualist development circle, a séance group in which he first developed strong mediumistic abilities. Turner believed there are four categories of healing:[927]

1. *Spiritual healing* involves the beliefs that the power for healing comes from beyond one's consciousness and that one's actions are directed and/or controlled by outside 'intelligences'.

2. *Spirit operations* are performed by healers while in trance, at which time their actions are completely controlled by spirit entities. Diagnosis is often made without verbal inquiry about the healee's symptoms. Problems in the physical body amenable to surgery are then treated with operations that are performed upon the 'etheric' body. Turner describes such operations as appearing (to the non-mediumistic observer) to be a mime of an operation in the air above the healee. The healer performs this 'operation' on the auric, or energy body that surrounds the physical body. Turner reports that soreness and occasional skin redness resembling a healing scar may appear on the physical body of the healee at the site of the spirit operation. He claims that remarkable healings have taken place with these procedures, although he does not describe any.[928]

3. *Magnetic healing* is produced by energy from the healer's body. Magnetic healing overlaps spiritual healing and both may be used simultaneously so that it is impossible to tell which is causing the demonstrated effects. Turner feels that the hypnotic 'passes' of Mesmer and practices of radiesthesia (with pendulum or 'diagnostic box') belong to this category of healing. Turner notes that magnetic healers generally do not claim a spiritual source for their powers.

4. *Divine healing* involves a totally religious orientation, usually including the belief that the healing is produced by Christ. Turner notes that this form of healing introduces possible complications not associated with forms (1-3), primarily the induction of guilt over presumably unforgiven sins.

It is evident from his classification that Turner views spirits as a natural part of the cosmos. He does not feel that they need be interpreted within a particular religious orientation, although for some healers and healees this is the case.[929]

The late Harry Edwards was one of the most gifted and best known healers in England. An able politician, he was instrumental in getting the British National Health Service to permit healers to treat patients in 1,500 government hospitals. Edwards[930] believed that healing was spirit-directed:

> Nothing takes place by chance. As, therefore, law-governed forces control the universe, and ourselves within it, so must they also apply to spirit healing.
>
> This often occurs when all human skill has failed, and implies that wiser intelligences than those of man are responsible. Else whence comes the intelligent direction of those forces that have produced the healing?...
>
> The healing forces... also need intelligent direction. As man does not know the way to do this, their control can come only from discarnate sources...
>
> As man can direct a physical force, so it requires a spirit mind to direct a spirit force, for it belongs to the spirit realm and not to earth. So it is with the spirit healing forces; every act of healing demands independent, intelligent direction.
>
> To apply the right quality of healing force in its correct strength to a given human disharmony, intelligent direction is needed. As man has never possessed this knowledge, it cannot exist within the subconscious mind. The subconscious mind is the repository of experience. Because it has never known the way to motivate the spirit forces, the human mind cannot be responsible for the application and discrimination of these forces.
>
> We are, therefore, forced to the conclusion that the operating mind must be a spirit one: a mind that has acquired greater wisdom than man possesses. These spirit operators we call 'the healing guides.'
>
> The act of healing, which produces a change within the physical body, demands not only the knowledge of how to manipulate the metaphysical forces but also how to coordinate them with the physical forces that govern the human anatomy.[931]

Edwards presents a spiritualist's views of healing. His discussions and explanations of spiritual healing lack psychological sophistication and he does not consider alternative psychological interpretations of his observations – such as the powers of suggestion and the vast self-healing capacities that are discussed in detail in Healing Research, Volume II.

J. Bernard Hutton, a journalist, details the spiritual healings of Mrs. Leah Doctors, a British medium. Dr. Fu Lin Chang, her spirit guide, claims to have been a physician in Hong Kong in the fifteenth century. Chang explained to her how spirits help people on earth and are also able to help when they have just entered the spirit world and are often in a state of shock due to the newness and unfamiliarity of this transition. In the spirit world they also have hospitals.

> ... a person who has suffered a serious accident on earth and has lost a limb, often needs special treatment when he arrives in the spirit world. When the person 'dies,' he enters the spirit world with the loss of his limb indelibly branded on his mind. He does not realize that his spirit body is perfect. He therefore needs treatment while he adapts to his new spirit life...
>
>   But having seen so much suffering on earth, it had always been my hope that I would find a way to ease the suffering of those who had not yet entered the spirit world. This is not so easy as one might think. Spirit doctors can mingle with those on earth and are sometimes able to give them direct healing. But first, they must be able to establish the right kind of contact with them. If a spirit doctor wishes to provide an earthly being with continuous healing – which is often necessary in the treatment of 'incurable' diseases – it is essential for the spirit doctor to work through a suitable medium on earth. And it must be a medium whose vibrations are closely attuned to those of the spirit doctor so that he can work swiftly and effectively.[932]

Chang told Doctors he had had to spend many years preparing her, without her conscious awareness of this, for working with him. His preparation involved "synchronizing their vibrations until they blended satisfactorily." He was then able to transmit his healing powers through her. He himself had to learn special spirit methods of healing so that he could help people on earth. These required that he convert healing into rays that could be focused to be more effective.[933] He said that psychics could see the healing rays.

  Chang describes several ways in which rays are used to cure various diseases. Although he is the only spirit doctor controlling Mrs. Doctors, five other spirit doctors assist him. Mrs. Doctors says there are many aspects of Chang's work that he cannot explain because they would be incomprehensible in earthly terms.

  Chang describes the use of spirit knives and rays in various treatments and operations. He attributes the source of his healing power to God. Asked, "What is God?" he answered,

> Shall we say Mother Nature? ... God is the Ultimate Power. God is Spiritual Power. God is Divine Power. God is the Bright Light of all Sources of Understanding.[934]

Though Hutton does a creditable job describing the Doctors/Chang healings, the cases are reported without direct medical confirmation and often without precise diagnoses. They are thus open to laymen's distortions due to only partial understanding of medical processes.[935]

South American spiritual healing
Spiritual healing in South America is different from that in America and England. Stanley Krippner and Alberto Villoldo[936] describe the evolution of four of the Brazilian spiritist groups from origins in the culture of Yoruba slaves transported from West Africa in the sixteenth century.[937] Krippner is a widely traveled and widely published parapsychologist, Professor of Psychology at Saybrook Institute in San Francisco. Villoldo has conducted extensive field research on healing in Central and South America and is director of the Four Winds Foundation in San Francisco for the study of shamanism and healing.

1. *Candomble* was established in Brazil earlier than the others and has maintained more of the original Yoruba (West African) names for the lesser gods. Women lead religious services. Fortunes are told with the use of cowrie shells.

2. *Umbanda* is more Christianized, as in using Christian names for saints. Both men and women serve as priests. At religious services the priests and priestesses are said to 'incorporate' lesser spirits and are believed to be healers.

3. *Quimbanda* includes worship of harmful spirits and its practice is illegal under Brazilian law, in contrast to the other spirit religions that are protected under the law.

4. *Kardecism* also originated in Yoruba tradition but is mainly based on Allan Kardec's writings from France in the middle of the nineteenth century on 'spiritism.' Kardecism, also called Spiritism, maintained much of the Yoruba traditions, while eliminating elements that conflicted with more modern views.

> Kardec believed that the 'spirit' is enveloped in a semi-material body of its own which he named the 'perispirit.' This 'perispirit' is composed of a magnetic fluid (or 'aura') which contains a certain amount of electricity. It serves as an intermediary between one's 'spiritual body' and physical body. Thus Kardec stated that 'healing' can be accomplished by 'psychic healers' who send 'magnetic rays' from their fingertips into the 'auras' of ill persons. By using these 'magnetic passes,' a 'healer' can also 'magnetize' water which can be used for 'healing' purposes. 'Healers' may sometimes be mediums and communicate with various 'spirits,' but instead of orishas (Yoruba spirits) these entities are usually relatives or distinguished people, such as doctors, writers, and teachers.
>
> Kardec taught that when one's body is worn out, it is discarded and one's 'spirit' is freed in much the way that a fruit sheds its peel. Death,

according to Kardec, is like the setting aside of old clothing that is no longer of any use. The 'spirit' leaves the body, still sheathed in the 'perispirit' which constitutes for the 'spirit' a 'spiritual body' or 'etheric body.' It has a human shape because it once acted as a pattern or blueprint for the physical form. Ordinarily, the 'perispirit' remains invisible, yet it can momentarily be seen if a 'spirit' wills it. It is through the 'perispirit' that a 'spirit' acts upon matter, producing such phenomena as table-rapping.

Kardec thought that people who regarded 'spirits' as sources of absolute wisdom were making a grave mistake. Some 'spirits,' Kardec wrote, 'send us communications that are very sublime in their depth' yet 'there are others which are lowly and vulgar, trivial and deceiving...'[938]

Kardec believed that some mediums are also 'healers.'[939]

... the medium with 'healing' ability can help people either through prayers or by a 'laying-on' of hands. All devout Spiritists have this power to some extent and 'spirits' can often heighten their ability when it is needed.[940]

Discussion – Spirits in healing

Taken in isolation, reports of spirits intervening in human affairs might seem far-fetched. When viewed in the context of research from NDEs, apparitions, reincarnation, mediumistic and mystical experiences, spirits may not appear unlikely or impossible. If people are reborn after intervals of many years, it is possible that a spirit entity could be available in the interim between earthly lives for such tasks as are described by the various healers, clairsentients, and mediums.

Sensitives and mystics of various sorts have proposed cosmologies to explain spirits and angelic hierarchies.[941] All report that learning does not cease with death. Our surviving spirits continue our education in other-worldly schools and lessons, proceeding to ever more sophisticated and refined levels of education. One of the elective courses in this higher education may be to help from spirit dimensions to heal people who are still in the flesh.

It is hard to know what to make of the varying reports on what life after life may be like. They are similar to each other in basic outline but differ in many particulars. Perhaps each is merely focusing on a different aspect of learning activities in the afterworld or between-life existence. All the reports clearly suffer from difficulties of translating other-reality experiences – into sensory reality words and concepts. They may also be colored by the imperfections in the crystals of the beings who transmit the reports.

As water in a fountain rises as one stream but falls in many drops divided
by time and space, so are the revelations of the one stream of truth.
– Sufi Inayat Khan [942]

Why spirits are seen only by some healers is not clear. Perhaps it is a difficulty in bridging differences in levels of awareness, in dimensions, or in rates of vibrations. Perhaps some healers work with spirits and others with bioenergies.

As in other areas of healing, there is in spiritual healing a tremendous variation in practices and theories between the various healers, writers and researchers. The above provides a representative variety of views.[943]

Spirituality

There are a variety of perspectives for exploring spirituality.

Spirituality has been addressed in academic studies as *extrinsic* or *intrinsic.*[944] Extrinsic spirituality is expressed through religious affiliation and practice, which has been found to correlate with many aspects of health and illness. This is summarized below and discussed in great detail in the next chapter.

Intrinsic spirituality is a personal sense of being part of something greater than ourselves; of being participants in explorations of consciousness that are so vastly greater than the human mind can conceive that we are only barely able to grasp little whiffs of hints of being a part of this project. This is the aspect of spirituality that is addressed here, and for brevity's sake I will just use the term *spirituality* in the rest of this chapter with this meaning in focus.

Analyses of spirituality may take a variety of forms and perspectives. For many centuries, spirituality was discussed primarily within the contexts of religion and philosophy. Historically, in many religious contexts the focus is on elaborations of religious doctrines and explanations that adhere to a given religion's holy texts and teachings, which form the axioms of belief and faith upon which all discussions are permissible. Questioning the axioms is not permitted. Teachings of other religions may be acknowledged, but this usually is only for purposes of showing their flaws, errors and inferiority relative to the religion that is presenting its teachings.

Philosophy opened doors to questions about the axioms of religions. However, philosophy is also based on axioms of belief and has permissible and disallowed rules for building its reasoned analyses of explanations for hypotheses about the transcendent. An early example is Aristotle, who was a proponent of *teleology* – the presumption that there is a design and directing principle behind the processes of nature. He argued that "Nature adapts the organ to the function, and not the function to the organ." [945] Lucretius replied in support of philosophical naturalism, which argues that there are no principles underlying natural phenomena: "Nothing in the body is made in order that we may use it. What happens to exist is the cause of its use." [946]

Eastern religions take another approach. They teach ways in which people can explore spirituality experientially, especially through meditation. Meditation teachers know the steps and stages of meditative development and can guide students to connect with their own spiritual awareness.

In the simplest of terms, we can explore spirituality through head or heart; through logical, linear, reasoned knowing – through analyses of reports of perceptions and ideas *about* spirituality, or through direct, intuitive, gestaltic gnowing *of* spirituality. It is worth noting here that the term, *spirituality*, is derived from the Latin, *spiritus*, which means 'breath of life.' [947] The challenge is to describe and discuss a tangible quality of life that cannot be seen or measured.

David Aldridge does a marvelous job of summarizing a spectrum of perspectives on extrinsic spirituality. He starts with discussions of spirituality as a consideration of how people relate to a God who is outside of and distinct from themselves.[948]

Table III-4. Spirituality: meaning and unity	
Spirit refers to that noncorporeal and nonmental dimension of the person that is the source of unity and meaning, and 'spirituality' refers to the concepts, attitudes, and behaviors that derive from one's experience of that dimension. Spirit can be addressed only indirectly and inferentially, while spirituality can be understood and worked with in psychologic terms.	Hiatt 1986, p. 742
Not only of belief in God but of a relationship with a supreme power, often a relationship that includes prayer in some form. Others speak of the conviction that life has a purpose, of the search for meaning, of the attempt to interpret their present illness in a way that makes sense within their world-view.	Smyth and Bellemare 1988, p. 87
Spiritual... means in essence 'searching for existential meaning.' Spiritual beliefs may be expressed in religion and its hallowed practices, but a person can and often does have a spiritual dimension to his or her life that is totally unrelated to religion and not expressed or explored in religious practice.	Doyle 1992, p. 303
Definitions of spirituality... referred to a dynamic, principle, or an aspect of a person that related to God or god, other persons, or aspects of personal being or material nature... The spiritual dimension was used to refer to a quality beyond religious affiliation that is used to inspire or harmonize answers to questions regarding infinite subjects, e.g., meaning and purpose of life and one's relation to the universe.	Emblen 1992, p. 43
It is useful to think of spirit, spirituality, and religion as different points on a continuum. Spirit is the source dimension behind every personal or collective experience of spirituality. It is also the source dimension behind every religion. Spirituality can be considered closer to the source dimension than everyday religion that has moved far from the experience of spirit and primarily serves moral and social purposes. Spirit is said... to be the realm that unites us.	Lerner 1994, p. 115
(a) the need to find meaning, purpose and fulfillment in life, suffering and death, (b) the need for hope/will to live, (c) the need for belief and faith in self, others and God.	Ross 1994, p. 439
Spirituality is... the experiential integration of one's life in terms of one's ultimate values and meanings.	Muldoon and King 1995, p. 330
A quality that goes beyond religious affiliation, that strives for inspirations, reverence, awe and purpose... tries to be in harmony with the universe, strives for answers about the infinite, and comes into focus when the person faces emotional stress, physical illness or death.	McSherry and Draper 1997, p. 413
Spirituality is a belief system focusing on intangible elements that impart vitality and meaning to life events.	Joseph 1998, p. 220

Next, Aldridge brings us observations to consider spirituality as a transcendent aspect of ourselves.

Table III-5. Spirituality as transcendental	
Spirituality is defined in terms of personal views and behaviors that express a sense of relatedness to a transcendent dimension or to something greater than the self... Spirituality is a broader concept than religion or religiosity... Indicators of spirituality include prayer, sense of meaning in life, reading and contemplation, sense of closeness to a higher being, interactions with others and other experiences which reflect spiritual interaction or awareness. Spirituality may vary according to developmental level and life events.	Reed 1987 p. 336
Spiritual elements are those capacities that enable a human being to rise above or transcend any experience at hand. They are characterized by the capacity to seek meaning and purpose, to have faith, to love, to forgive, to pray, to meditate, to worship, and to seek beyond present circumstances.	Kuhn 1988 p. 91
The spiritual dimension of persons can be uniquely defined as the human capacity to transcend self, which is phenomenologically reflected in three basic spiritual needs: (a) the need for self-acceptance, a trusting relationship with self based on a sense of meaning and purpose in life; (b) the need for relationship with others and/or a supreme other (e.g. God) characterized by nonconditional love, trust, and forgiveness; and (c) the need for hope, which is the need to imagine and participate in the enhancement of a positive future. All persons experience these spiritual needs, whether or not they are part of a formal religious organization.	Highfield 1992 p. 3
Spiritual: pertaining to the innate capacity to, and tendency to seek to, transcend one's current locus of centricity, which transcendence involves increased love and knowledge. (p. 169)	Chandler, Holden, Kolander 1992
Six clear factors... appear to be fundamental aspects of spirituality... those of the journey, transcendence, community, religion, 'the mystery of creation,' and transformation.	Lapierre 1994 p.154
Spirituality... pertains to one's relationship with others, with oneself and with one's higher power, which is defined by the individual and need not be associated with a formal religion. (p. 287)	Berman Dixon 1998
Spirituality refers to the degree of involvement or state of awareness or devotion to a higher being or life philosophy. Not always related to conventional beliefs.	Lukoff *et al.* 1999 p. 65
Spirituality is rooted in an awareness which is part of the biological make-up of the human species. Spirituality is present in all individuals and it may manifest as inner peace and strength derived from perceived relationship with a transcendent God or an ultimate reality or whatever an individual values as supreme.	Narayana-samy 1999 p. 124

Aldridge suggests that beliefs in spirituality can be a motivating power or force, but his conceptualization is more of a mental construct than an actual, living Infinite Source with whom we can interact directly, and who can inspire us to reach beyond ourselves.

> *Religion encourages you to explore the thoughts of others and accept them as your own. Spirituality invites you to toss away the thoughts of others and come up with your own.*
> –Neale Donald Walsch [949]

Table III-6. Spirituality as power or force	
There are numerous meanings for the word spiritual; the most useful imply (Sims 1994) what a person lives for, their motivating force; the weakest, a nebulous power beyond description. Here are five aspects of meaning which the psychiatrist should consider:.. looking for the meaning in life... the interrelatedness of all... wholeness of the person, in which spirit is not separate from body or mind... what is seen as good, beautiful and enjoyable... the connection between god and man.	Sims 1994 p. 444
We propose a definition of 'spiritual' as a person's experience of, or a belief in, a power apart from their own existence. It may exist within them but is ultimately apart. It is the sense of relationship or connection with a power or force. It is more specific than a search for meaning or unity with others.	King and Dein 1998 p. 1259
The spirit refers to what is inside a person; what we would call thoughts, feelings, energy spirituality, the subjective viewpoint, mind, personality, psychology, or breath. But the spirit could also be outside a living person, and the implication would be that the internal spirit probably originated outside and invaded, so the person was 'inspired.'	Boyd 1995 p. 155

Finally, Aldridge surveys *postmodern* perspectives on spirituality, considering man as a part of nature.

Table III-7. Spirituality as postmodern	
Spirituality is regarded to be of human origin, not based on worship or creed, but paradoxically from something inherently within the self of a person, which symbolizes his or her spirituality in humanness. (p. 500)	Long 1997
Spirituality means freely interacting with the world on the basis of a system of ultimate values and meanings, whatever the source of those meanings... it involves interacting with the world not merely thinking about the world; that is, spirituality is concrete rather than abstract... the source of the ultimate values and meanings is not important. (p. 31) Spirituality... is rule-governed-behavior with the stipulation that the 'rule' is a belief that is evaluated as 'right' on the basis of a set of beliefs. (p. 47)	Reese 1997
There is another dimension called the non-observable, which is the source of religion's purpose and meaning. It is the failure to recognize the difference between the observable and the non-observable, confusing the one with the other or by denying one on behalf of the other, that confounds our understanding of religion. (p. 366)	Idinopulos 1998
Spirituality = any human practice which maintains contact between the everyday world and a more general meta-empirical framework of meaning by the way of individual manipulation of symbolic systems. (p. 147)	Hanegraaff 1999

For Aldridge, spirituality is an inspirational mental construct and belief that guides mortals to more noble, altruistic ways of relating to each other and to the world.

As numerous explorers in these realms have pointed out, linear, intellectualized definitions of spirituality tend to miss the mark in various ways. They are many steps removed from actual, immediately perceived experiences of spirituality that are described in personal spiritual experiences.

Qualitative studies

Joni Walton focuses on qualitative studies of spirituality. These are systematic, formal explorations of the beliefs, perceptions and subjective experiences of selected groups of people. Walton points out that spirituality can be awakened, nurtured and strengthened particularly through relationships. Connectedness to others may include family, friends, health care providers, church and social groups.[950] She observes that spiritual relationships can be of help by providing comfort, strength and healing energy to careseekers and caregivers.

Walton reviews the following variety of other sources that address this aspect of spirituality. Spiritual relationships are identified as the intrapersonal relationship to the self, as well as relationships with others, a higher power, and with aspects of one's environment that imbue life with meaning, awaken connections with inner strengths, feelings of inner peace and harmonious interconnectedness.[951] All relationships have the possibility of being spiritual, though not every relationship will be perceived as such. People's self-awareness and soul-searching will contribute to the depth and intimacy of their relationships.

Walton provides another range of definitions and descriptions of the spectrum of spirituality – derived by questioning people systematically about their views. (See Table III-8.)

Qualitative research[952] validates that spiritual relationships contribute to a sense of spirituality. Walton also surveys several clinical studies of spirituality.[953] Client-nurse interactions open many opportunities for spiritual relationships through mutual connectedness – experienced as compassion, trust, and shared consciousness in a caring environment.[954] Nurses can facilitate this by quieting and centering themselves, focusing on healing energy and setting the stage for the healings that listening, intimacy, and the ensuing development of trust can bring. Patients acknowledge these experiences help them to feel and cope better with the numerous challenges of dealing with painful and life-threatening illnesses, with the un-healing environments and routines of hospitals, and with treatments that are often addressed to their bodies but not to the rest of their being.[955]

For example, one study that explored the meaning of spiritual care with ten Christian volunteers identified relevant themes that included: finding higher meaning and purpose and facilitating transcendence of a situation, developing connectedness, and enabling hope. Participants perceived connection from the caregivers' understanding and accepting, and especially through sharing information about themselves.[956] In a different study of spiritual wellbeing in women in Appalachia, the core theme identified was feeling whole, which involved a sense of self and four facets of relationships: to a deity, to kin, to others, and to nature. The theme of self included purpose, satisfaction, inner strengths, responsibility, clearer values, personal identity, and service.[957] In well adults, a description of spirituality included "striving for and/or being infused with the reality of the interconnectedness among self, other human beings, and the Infinite that occurs during a depth experience and results in a life change." Awareness of one's interrelationship with the Infinite was facilitated by prayer, meditation and relaxation.[958] Nurse-family spiritual relationships were explored in a hospice setting. People felt the spiritual relationship was a journey, involving interconnectedness, enlightenment and mutuality, with a feeling of oneness which permanently transformed their lives. The spiritual relationship was experienced both by the hospice nurse and by the family as providing a profound source of meaning, each contributing the reciprocal "gift of self" to the other. They became "shining strangers' to one another, a term taken from religious philosophy of East and West that describes the unity of meaning.[959]

Table III-8. Spirituality as relationship - from qualitative studies *	
Spirituality is the intrapersonal relationship to the self, as well as relationships with others, a higher power, and with aspects of one's environment that imbue life with meaning, awaken connections with inner strengths, feelings of peace and harmonious interconnectedness.	Burkhardt 1989; Hungelmann et al; Reed
All relationships have a possibility of being spiritual, though not every relationship will be perceived as such. People's self-awareness and soul-searching will contribute to the depth and intimacy of their relationships.	Walton
Spirituality is a holistic, poly-dimensional humanistic experience which transcends ordinary experiences in physical, social, and psychological realms.	Elkins et al; Reed
Within holistic conceptualizations, spirituality cannot be experienced or isolated as separate parts.	Elkins et al; Granstrom; Mansen
Spirituality is a far broader term than religion, often including a humanistic orientation. People who are spiritual might or might not be religious. Religion includes frameworks for beliefs, values, behaviors, cultural and personal traditions, doctrines and rituals. Religion can contribute to individual spirituality but is distinctively different from spirituality.	Elkins et al; Emblen; Granstrom; Mansen; Reed
Components of spirituality may include meaning, purpose, and a life mission. Spirituality often includes the sense of being in touch with the sacred, with a unity or wholeness which enables people to find internal resources that can provide renewed energies, strengths, peace, hope and guidance.	Banks; Burkhardt 1989; Elkins et al; Granstrom; Highfield/Cason; Parse; Sodestrom/ Martinson
Connectedness to oneself and self-reflection enhances the intimate knowledge of oneself and of others, adding a mystical quality to relationships. This process of self-reflection and self-exploration can be initiated by traumas such as emotional, physical, or sexual abuse. Soul-searching, forgiving oneself, and re-establishing self love and relationships with others and with a higher power are then key to development of spiritual relationships.	Burkhardt 1994; Carper; Elkins; Huebner; Kendall; Kreidler
Caregiving relationships have the potential to open spiritual awareness and can be existentially nurturing.	Burkhardt 1989; Ellis; Granstrom; Reed; Paterson/ Zderad; Travelbee

*Abstracted from Walton.

Meditative perspectives on spirituality

Ken Wilber suggests definitions for spirituality based on meditative experiences.

1. *Spirituality represents the highest levels of any of various developmental lines*
   Within this perspective, spirituality develops in stages as people realize their maximum within any framework of development, such as "our highest cognitive capacities (e.g., transrational intuition), our most developed affects (e.g., transpersonal love), our highest moral aspirations (transcendental compassion for all sentient beings), our most evolved self (the transpersonal Self or supraindividual Witness), and so on." Here, spirituality reflects the highest stages of evolution on any of these developmental paths.[960]

2. *Spirituality represents the totality of the highest levels in all developmental lines*
   From this perspective, while spirituality unfolds within a given path of development in stages, the highest overall development of seekers on their personal paths is fundamentally individual and unique. Kathleen Moorfield suggests that Erik Erikson's stage of adult maturation, *generativity*, may fit this definition of spirituality. Generativity is a spans periods in adult years, manifesting as capacities that are cultivated and expressed through caring and loving behaviors that are for the benefit of others as well as for oneself. "The adult's awareness has moved beyond his ego, ethnicity and other self-identifications, and is now anchored in an awareness of the larger world's health and well-being." Moorefield, K.R.P. *An Innovative Look at Spirituality and Personality*, Unpublished dissertation for Ph.D. in Spirituality and Energy Medicine, Australia: Greenwich University 2002, 79.

3. *Spirituality is a distinct developmental line in and of itself*
   Numerous authorities propose a variety of stages of development for spirituality in it own right. Wilber's favorites are Daniel P. Brown and Jack Engler,[961] who documented parallels in stages of meditative development cross-culturally; and John Chirban, who found clear parallels in spiritual stages of development of Eastern Orthodox Christian saints. Others mentioned by Wilber in this category include Buddhist Highest Yoga Tantra, Helminiak, Yoga Sutras of Sanskrit Hinduism, Hazrat Inayat Kahn of the Sufi tradition, Mahamudra's Tibetan Mahayana Buddhism, Evelyn Underhill, and Visuddhimagga of Pali Theravada Buddhism.

4. *Spirituality as an attitude (such as love) which may be present regardless of one's developmental stage*
   This is the commonest definition of spirituality in popular usage. While there appears to be a consensus of acknowledgment of this description of spirituality, it is not defined sufficiently clearly to permit formal study. Wilber suggests this includes love, openness integration.[962] Moorfield points out that common definitions of spirituality may include: "a conception of the divine or of divinity; consciousness; a sense of meaning and purpose that life is worth living; compas-

sion, altruistic service and selfless concern often to the point of self-sacrifice; conscientiousness, morality, ethics, and responsible action; creativity, resourceful problem solving and the ability to handle life's uncertainties and ambiguities; a sense of faith and inner peace with one's self in the larger design of life; unconditional regard and love; a feeling of flow, interconnectedness and unity with nature, a Higher Power and/or others; forgiveness; optimism, free expression, play and enjoyment; an openness and nonjudgmental stance toward situations, self and others; a deep gratefulness for life; an appreciation of the mystery and vastness of the universe; beliefs in and personal experience of a primary, transcendent, numinous or nonmaterial reality; humility and an ease with learning; reverence for the holiness of all life; a commitment to sacred rituals and practices on a path of devotion; a sense of integrity and authenticity where inner values guide outer action; and, a life guided by ultimate concerns and a spiritually-centered organizing framework to understand human existence." [963]

Moorfield adds that these qualities and virtues provide guidelines for living a spiritual life, in addition to being goals to which one can aspire.

5. Spirituality is associated with peak experiences

Peak experiences clearly open into spiritual awareness but are states of consciousness rather than stages of development. They may evolve into enduring spiritual traits. [964]

Personal spirituality

My own belief is that spirituality is an awareness of a truly transcendent reality, in which we participate but of which we only have a dim and partial awareness from the vantage point of physical existence.

> We may be aware of a truth, yet until we have felt its force, it is not ours.
> To the cognition of the brain must be added the experience of the soul.
> – Arnold Bennett

Personal spirituality is experienced more through the heart and spirit than with the mind. It is an inner gnowing that carries a sense of realness that is qualitatively different from reality as known through the outer senses or logical reasoning. In the deeper experience of spirituality there is a sense of participating in the unconditional love and acceptance of the Infinite Source. Each of us manifests aspects of God into being through the manners in which we live our lives. This is more than just a perceived relationship that is created out of the beliefs and faith of the individual about the transcendent.

Western science generally distrusts individual, personal reports of spiritual experiences and prefers linear analyses of collected reports. By extracting common denominators from multiple reports, science hopes to provide some measure of assurance that we are not misled by wishful thinking, religious beliefs or stories from people who are mentally deranged. However, all the sophistication of philosophical, religious and analyses of meditative explorations of the transcendent does not (in my opinion) capture the essence of spirituality – in comparison with individual reports of personal spiritual awakenings.

Here is a description of a profound personal spiritual experience. Mellen-Thomas Benedict[965] is an artist who died of cancer in 1982. After being dead for more than an hour and a half, he returned to life, reporting that he had had a glorious Near-Death Experience.[966] He also connected with information that enabled him to advise on research in the mechanics of cellular communication and quantum biology, the relationship of light to life. He is developing methods of healing with light stimulation.

> The condition I had was inoperable, and any kind of chemotherapy they could give me would just have made me more of a vegetable. I was given six to eight months to live. I had been an information freak in the 1970's, and I had become increasingly despondent over the nuclear crisis, the ecology crisis, and so forth.
>
> So, since I did not have a spiritual basis, I began to believe that nature had made a mistake, and that we were probably a cancerous organism on the planet. I saw no way that we could get out from all the problems we had created for ourselves and the planet. I perceived all humans as cancer, and that is what I got. That is what killed me. Be careful what your world view is. It can feed back on you, especially if it is a negative world view. I had a seriously negative one. That is what led me into my death. I tried all sorts of alternative healing methods, but nothing helped. So I determined that this was really just between me and God. I had never really faced God before, or even dealt with God. I was not into any kind of spirituality at the time, but I began a journey into learning about spirituality and alternative healing. I set out to do all the reading I could and bone up on the subject, because I did not want to be surprised on the other side. So I started reading on various religions and philosophies. They were all very interesting, and gave hope that there was something on the other side.
>
> On the other hand, as a self-employed stained-glass artist at the time, I had no medical insurance whatsoever. So my life savings went overnight in testing. Then I was facing the medical profession without any kind of insurance. I did not want to have my family dragged down financially, so I determined to handle this myself. There was not constant pain, but there were black-outs. I got so that I would not dare to drive, and eventually I ended up in hospice care. I had my own personal hospice caretaker. I was very blessed by this angel who went through the last part of this with me. I lasted about eighteen months. I did not want to take a lot of drugs, since I wanted to be as conscious as possible. Then I experienced such pain that I had nothing but pain in my consciousness, luckily only for a few days at a time...
>
> I remember waking up one morning at home about 4:30 am, and I just knew that this was it. This was the day I was going to die. So I called a few friends and said goodbye. I woke up my hospice caretaker and told her. I

had a private agreement with her that she would leave my dead body alone for six hours, since I had read that all kinds of interesting things happen when you die. I went back to sleep.

The next thing I remember is the beginning of a typical Near-Death Experience. Suddenly I was fully aware and I was standing up, but my body was in the bed. There was this darkness around me. Being out of my body was even more vivid than ordinary experience. It was so vivid that I could see every room in the house, I could see the top of the house, I could see around the house, I could see under the house. There was this Light shining. I turned toward the Light. The Light was very similar to what many other people have described in their Near-Death Experiences. It was so magnificent. It is tangible; you can feel it. It is alluring; you want to go to it like you would want to go to your ideal mother's or father's arms. As I began to move toward the Light, I knew intuitively that if I went to the Light, I would be dead. So as I was moving toward the Light I said, "Please wait a minute, just hold on a second here. I want to think about this; I would like to talk to you before I go."

To my surprise, the entire experience halted at that point. You are indeed in control of your Near-Death Experience. You are not on a roller coaster ride. So my request was honored and I had some conversations with the Light. The Light kept changing into different figures, like Jesus, Buddha, Krishna, mandalas, archetypal images and signs. I asked the Light, "What is going on here? Please, Light, clarify yourself for me. I really want to know the reality of the situation." I cannot really say the exact words, because it was sort of telepathy.

The Light responded. The information transferred to me was that your beliefs shape the kind of feedback you are getting before the Light. If you were a Buddhist or Catholic or Fundamentalist, you get a feedback loop of your own stuff. You have a chance to look at it and examine it, but most people do not. As the Light revealed itself to me, I became aware that what I was really seeing was our Higher Self matrix... what I saw was that what we call our Higher Self in each of us is a matrix. It's also a conduit to the Source; each one of us comes directly, as a direct experience from the Source. We all have a Higher Self, or an oversoul part of our being. It revealed itself to me in its truest energy form. The only way I can really describe it is that the being of the Higher Self is more like a conduit...it is a direct connection to the Source that each and every one of us has. We are directly connected to the Source.

So the Light was showing me the Higher Self matrix. And it became very clear to me that all the Higher Selves are connected as one being, all humans are connected as one being, we are actually the same being, different aspects of the same being. It was not committed to one particular religion. So that is what was being fed back to me. And I saw this mandala of human souls. It was the most beautiful thing I have ever seen. I just went into it and, it was just over-whelming. It was like all the love you've every wanted, and it was the kind of love that cures, heals, regenerates.

As I asked the Light to keep explaining... I really wanted to know what the universe is about, and I was ready to go at that time. I said "I am ready, take me." ...

Now I came to this with my negative view of what has happen on the planet. So as I asked the light to keep clarifying for me, I saw in this magnificent mandala how beautiful we all are in our essence, our core. We are the most beautiful creations. The human soul, the human matrix that we all make together is absolutely fantastic, elegant, exotic, everything. I just cannot say enough about how it changed my opinion of human beings in that instant. I said, "Oh, God, I did not know how beautiful we are." At any level, high or low, in whatever shape you are in, you are the most beautiful creation...

The revelations coming from the Light seemed to go on and on, then I asked the Light, "Does this mean that humankind will be saved?" Then, like a trumpet blast with a shower of spiraling lights, the Great Light spoke, saying, "Remember this and never forget; you save, redeem and heal yourself. You always have. You always will. You were created with the power to do so from before the beginning of the world..."

The Light seemed to breathe me in even more deeply. It was as if the Light was completely absorbing me. The Love Light is, to this day, indescribable. I entered into another realm, more profound than the last, and became aware of something more, much more. It was an enormous stream of Light, vast and full, deep in the Heart of Life. I asked what this was...

I asked to see the rest of the Universe; beyond our solar system, beyond all human illusion...

Suddenly, I seemed to be rocketing away from the planet on this stream of Life. I saw the earth fly away. The solar system, in all its splendor, whizzed by and disappeared. At faster than light speed, I flew through the center of the galaxy, absorbing more knowledge as I went. I learned that this galaxy, and all of the Universe, is bursting with many different varieties of LIFE. I saw many worlds. The good news is that we are not alone in this Universe! As I rode this stream of consciousness through the center of the galaxy, the stream was expanding in awesome fractal waves of energy. The super clusters of galaxies with all their ancient wisdom flew by. At first I thought I was going somewhere; actually traveling. But then I realized that, as the stream was expanding, my own consciousness was also expanding to take in everything in the Universe! All creation passed by me. It was an unimaginable wonder! ...

As I passed into the second Light, the awareness came to me that I had just transcended the Truth... I found myself in a profound stillness, beyond all silence. I could see or perceive FOREVER, beyond Infinity. I was in the Void.

I was in pre-creation, before the Big Bang. I had crossed over the beginning of time - the First Word - the First vibration. I was in the Eye of Creation. I felt as if I was touching the Face of God. It was not a religious feeling. Simply I was at one with Absolute Life and Consciousness.

When I say that I could see or perceive forever, I mean that I could experience all of creation generating itself. It was without beginning and without end... I saw that the Big Bang is only one of an infinite number of Big Bangs creating Universes endlessly and simultaneously. The only images that even come close in human terms would be those created by supercomputers using fractal geometry equations.

The ancients knew of this. They said Godhead periodically created new Universes by breathing out, and de-creating other Universes by breathing in. These epochs were called Yugas. Modern science called this the Big Bang... I saw that each and every little piece of creation has the power to create. It is very difficult to try to explain this. I am still speechless about this.

It took me years after I returned to assimilate any words at all for the Void experience. I can tell you this now; the Void is less than nothing, yet more than everything that is! The Void is absolute zero; chaos forming all possibilities. It is Absolute Consciousness; much more than even Universal Intelligence.

Where is the Void? I know. The Void is inside and outside everything. You, right now even while you live, are always inside and outside the Void simultaneously. You don't have to go anywhere or die to get there. The Void is the vacuum or nothingness between all physical manifestations. The SPACE between atoms and their components...

So creation is God exploring God's Self through every way imaginable, in an ongoing, infinite exploration through every one of us. Through every piece of hair on your head, through every leaf on every tree, through every atom, God is exploring God's Self, the great "I am". I began to see that everything that is, is the Self, literally, your Self, my Self. Everything is the great Self. That is why God knows even when a leaf falls. That is possible because wherever you are is the center of the universe. Wherever any atom is, that is the center of the universe. There is God in that, and God in the Void...

I was in the Void and I was aware of everything that had ever been created. It was like I was looking out of God's eyes. I had become God... And suddenly I knew why every atom was, and I could see everything. The interesting point was that I went into the Void, I came back with this understanding that God is not there. God is here. That's what it is all about.

So this constant search of the human race to go out and find God ...God gave everything to us, everything is here - this is where it's at. And what we are into now is God's exploration of God through us. People are so busy trying to become God that they ought to realize that we are already God and God is becoming us. That's what it is really about.

When I realized this, I was finished with the Void, and wanted to return to this creation, or Yuga. It just seemed like the natural thing to do...

All energy this side of the Big Bang is light. Every sub-atom, atom, star, planet, even consciousness itself is made of light and has a frequency and/or particle. Light is living stuff. Everything is made of light, even stones. So everything is alive. Everything is made from the Light of God; everything is very intelligent...

Then the entire solar system appeared in the Light... I saw that the solar system we live in is our larger, local body. This is our local body and we are much bigger than we imagine. I saw that the solar system is our body. I am a part of this, and the earth is this great created being that we are, and we are the part of it that knows that it is. But we are only that part of it. We are not everything, but we are that part of it that knows that it is...

I was in this great Light of Love with the stream of life flowing through me. I have to say again, it is the most loving, non-judgmental Light. It is the ideal parent for this Wonder Child.

"What now?" I wondered.

The Light explained to me that there is no death; we are immortal beings. We have already been alive forever! I realized that we are part of a natural living system that recycles itself endlessly. I was never told that I had to come back. I just knew that I would. It was only natural, from what I had seen.

I don't know how long I was with the Light, in human time. But there came a moment when I realized that all my questions had been answered and my return was near. When I say that all my questions were answered on the other side, I mean to say just that. All my questions have been answered. Every human has a different life and set of questions to explore. Some of our questions are Universal, but each of us is exploring this thing we call Life in our own unique way. So is every other form of life, from mountains to every leaf on every tree.

And that is very important to the rest of us in this Universe. Because it all contributes to the Big Picture, the fullness of Life. We are literally God exploring God's Self in an infinite Dance of Life. Your uniqueness enhances all of Life...

As I began my return to the life cycle, it never crossed my mind, nor was I told, that I would return to the same body. It just did not matter. I had complete trust in the Light and the Life process. As the stream merged with the great Light, I asked never to forget the revelations and the feelings of what I had learned on the other side. There was a "Yes". It felt like a kiss to my soul.

Then I was taken back through the Light into the vibratory realm again...

I thought of myself as a human for the first time, and I was happy to be that. From what I have seen, I would be happy to be an atom in this universe. An atom. So to be the human part of God ... this is the most fantastic blessing. It is a blessing beyond our wildest estimation of what blessing can be. For each and every one of us to be the human part of this experience is awesome, and magnificent. Each and every one of us, no matter where we are, screwed up or not, is a blessing to the planet, right where we are.

So I went through the reincarnation process expecting to be a baby somewhere. But I was given a lesson on how individual identity and consciousness evolve. So I reincarnated back into this body. I was so surprised when I opened my eyes. I do not know why, because I understood it, but it was still such a surprise to be back in this body, back in my room with someone looking over me crying her eyes out. It was my hospice caretaker. She had given up an hour and a half after finding me dead. She was sure I was dead; all the signs of death were there - I was getting stiff.

We do not know how long I was dead, but we do know that it was an hour and a half since I was found. She honored my wish to have my newly dead body left alone for a few hours as much as she could. We had an amplified stethoscope and many ways of checking out the vital functions of the body to see what was happening. She can verify that I really was dead. It was not a Near-Death Experience. I experienced death itself for at least an hour and a half. She found me dead and checked the stethoscope, blood pressure and heart rate monitor for an hour and a half. Then I awakened and saw the light outside. I tried to get up to go to it, but I fell out of the bed. She heard a loud 'clunk,' ran in and found me on the floor.

When I recovered, I was very surprised and yet very awed about what had happened to me. At first all the memory of the trip that I have now was not there. I kept slipping out of this world and kept asking, "Am I alive?" This world seemed more like a dream than that one. Within three days, I was feeling normal again, clearer, yet different than I had ever felt in my life. My memory of the journey came back later. I could see nothing wrong with any human being I had ever seen. Before that I was really judgmental. I thought a lot of people were really screwed up, in fact I thought that everybody was screwed up but me. But I got clear on all that.

About three months later a friend said I should get tested, so I went and got the scans and so forth. I really felt good, so I was afraid of getting bad news. I remember the doctor at the clinic looking at the before and after scans, saying, "Well, there is nothing here now."

I said, "Really, it must be a miracle?" He said "No, these things happen, they are called spontaneous remission." He acted very unimpressed. But here was a miracle, and I was impressed, even if no one else was.

Which of the explorations of spirituality speaks to you more? For myself, Benedicts' report resonates the strongest, but I might tend towards discounting it to some extent without the masses of evidence reviewed earlier in this book.

Spirituality is an actual, participatory reality. Each of us IS a part of a transcendent reality, manifesting within ourselves both the awareness of the All and adding our personal contribution to the all. More on this in Chapter III-13.

> *If one took a cup of water from the ocean, all the waters of the world would have to move over to fill the gap. You are important; the world would not be the same without you.*
> – Alice Steadman [967]

Characteristics of spiritual experiences are virtually identical with those of the mystical experience (in Table III-4). It therefore seems highly likely that they are identical – but experienced, interpreted, and labeled by those who report having them as being different. The only item that appears to differ between the mystical and the spiritual interpretations of these noetic, transcendent awarenesses is number 7 from Table III-4. In the mystical experience this is *"Transiency – sustained for a limited period of time."* In the spiritual experience, this would more properly be labeled *Permanence* – participating in a continuity that transcends the time and space of personal existence; carrying a sense of transformation and connectedness with the All back into ordinary reality, following the spiritual experience.[968]

Assessments of spirituality

A variety of psychological tests have been devised to assess spirituality, though there are difficulties in examining transpersonal experiences and in defining them in scientific terminology.

1. These noetic, ineffable experiences must be translated into words and linear concepts so that quantifiable data can be collected. As we have seen from Tables III-4 to III-8, the broad range of interpretations may lead to conceptual choices in creating a psychological test that will make it difficult for others, who prefer a different definition of spirituality, to relate to tests based on different conceptual preferences.

2. The validity of self-reports as a basis for these data can be questioned.

3. One must be cautious in interpreting tests that are based on limited populations and may be colored by religious biases.

Nevertheless, there have been instruments developed which are validated and facilitate studies of individuals and groups.[969] Many are easy to score and can add to the theoretical and clinical explorations of transpersonal dimensions. An example of this is the study of McClain and colleagues, who demonstrated that spiritual wellbeing was the factor with greatest predictive value for assessing the coping abilities of patients in terminal care.

   My personal opinion is that these tests are extremely helpful in sociological studies and contribute to our understanding of how people report their spiritual experiences. But much as we would like to distill common denominators accurately defining spiritual experiences, I believe these efforts are of limited value because spiritual experiences are impossible to describe or define completely or adequately in words.

   I am in favor of the approach advocated by Jorge Ferrer. He suggests that each of us is a co-creator of spirituality through our experiences in transpersonal realms. Spirituality therefore cannot be described for yet another reason – it is a growing and evolving phenomenon, one which cannot be grasped in any permanent way through linear descriptions.[970]

Sometimes a visual symbol can bring a measure of clarity to a discussion. The ancient Sri Yantra is helpful here. (See Figure III-10.) It has a series of intersecting triangles, four pointing upwards, five downwards. Upwards triangles represent the masculine; downwards ones the feminine. The *bindu* dot in the center symbolizes the spiritual center of the universe, the All – the point where all contrasts and opposites meet and are experienced as parts of the unified whole.

Figure III-10. The Sri Yantra

If we consider each triangle to represent an aspect of spiritual awareness that is perceived by a different individual, each is different from the others. Though several may be identical in shape and size, each has its own orientation that makes it distinct from the other. Yet each contributes to the overall pattern, which is, for the most part symmetrical.

So it is with our co-creation of spiritual reality. Each of us contributes to the larger pattern of reality through our unique shaping of our personal slice of life – which is also a reflection of the whole of reality.

> ...I began to understand that the goal of psychic development is the self. There is no linear evolution; there is only a circumambulation of the self. Uniform development exists, at most, only at the beginning; later, everything points toward the center. This insight gave me stability, and gradually my inner peace returned. I knew that in finding the mandala as an expression of the self I had attained what was for me the ultimate. Perhaps someone else knows more, but not I.
>
> – Carl Jung [971]

Spiritual development

> *Give me your child between the ages of four and eight and he is mine forever after.*
>
> – Traditional wisdom of Jewish teachers

Children are traditionally educated in religious practices within their families, from the earliest ages. Where prayers are offered and rituals are practiced in healing manners, such as blessings over the meals, doing charitable acts, and praying for healing, these become routine parts of their lives forever after. Attitudes of reverence for that which we are given, and awarenesses of a power beyond ourselves become a natural part of the world for those blessed with a home with healing rituals. Illness is a challenge that brings out the best in family and community, with supportive visits, prayers, and healing. This is a spiritual experience of religion.

Where religious practice is a series of rituals empty of spiritual awareness, the child may still have a sense of community and rootedness in a historical tradition, but a sense of the beyond may be no more than an image of heaven and hell as preached at the congregation on days when one attends a house of worship out of duty – but without inner dedication to anything beyond oneself, other than to avoid the censure of the religious community for not attending services.

I digress to share my own experience of Judaism, which was in this category. I was raised in a home where we observed some of the *dos* and ignored most of the *don'ts* of our religion. I attended a Hebrew Jewish day school from second to eight grades – which followed a gently Orthodox (not rigid or punitive) Jewish tradition. For example, they tolerated my not wearing the ritual *tsitsit*, a miniature prayer shawl that boys and men wear as a sign of their covenant with their God, and handled my family's non-adherence to eating kosher food with gentle teasing.

Living in America, I was utterly bored by the mouthing of prayers and practice of rituals. The words were minimally relevant to my life, and the rituals brought me together for social activities that were stilted and not as interesting or exciting as other social gatherings. There was, however, a sense of community and an awareness of support – given an importance through stories of persecutions of my People through many centuries, and made very real and immediate by the Holocaust. This was very much a part of my family's awareness in the early years of my childhood that spanned much of World War II. Living in Israel from 1945-1949 and again from 1973-1979, I felt a much stronger communion with my People. The language we spoke, Hebrew, was the language of the Bible. Jewish holidays were national holidays. One of my favorite activities was to go on hikes with the Nature Protection Society, where lectures on flora and fauna were supplemented by Biblical stories of begats and battles and psalms. These made excursion into the hills and valleys of the Holy Land a trip through history as well as a trip through nature. But spirituality was not a part of the popular culture.

When I returned to Israel as an adult, I had the idealistic notion that the Orthodox Jews in Israel would be a spiritual people. I was disillusioned and disappointed to find many of them narrow, bigoted, sanctimonious and spiritually phony. They rigidly adhered to their rabbis' interpretations of Biblical law – concerning rituals. But cheating and lying were fine in business, and men had all the weight of a paternalistic rabbinical court on their side in marital disputes, while women were clearly second class beings, often viewed as chattel.

The short story is that I found very little of spiritual awareness in my religion, and less yet in my years of living in Israel.

Where religion is taught as avoidance of sins, with anticipations of dire, punitive retribution for moral transgressions, religion may become a prison and torture chamber rather than a greenhouse for spiritual blossoming. Illness may be interpreted as a lack of faith or as wages of sins, and chronic illness as a failure to repent or to have sufficient faith.

Where no religion is taught in childhood, it can be a challenge to develop spiritual awareness in later life. Many come to classes to study religion as adults, not realizing that they are learning *about* it rather than learning *it*. Without the inner awareness of being a part of something vaster than ourselves, developed as a natural part of growing up in a spiritual home, or at least in a religious home where the concepts of spirituality become a part of our perception of the world we live in, it may be difficult to waken to spirituality.

> *He to whom worshipping is a window,*
> *to open but also to shut,*
> *has not yet visited the house of his soul,*
> *whose windows are from dawn to dawn.*
>   – Khalil Gibran [972]

Yet Spirit moves in all beings, and even those who have no conscious awareness of it will often feel stirrings of something missing in their lives. This is clearly evidenced in the many who seek enlightenment in meditation, yoga, Eastern religions, peak experiences in sports, psychedelic openings to the transpersonal, poetry, music and other arts, deliberate lucid dreaming, explorations in transpersonal psychology studies, personal psychotherapy, out-of-body[973] and Near-Death Experiences.[974] Illness and other ill fortune may bring us to seek deeper meanings to our existence. Death of someone close to us often wakens questions of what happens to that spark of life which was embodied and now is no more. Bereavement apparitions, who visit two out of three people in mourning, convey informative messages but also, through the nature of this experience, confirm spiritual awarenesses.[975]

These spontaneous stirrings of spirituality tend to be more experiential, with direct awareness of the spiritual – not just thoughts *about* spirituality.

> *And because you cannot understand a God who will not act as*
> *humans would, you are lost. Your theology is your attempt to find your-*
> *self again.*
>   – Neale Donald Walsch [976]

Many come to spiritual awareness without conscious intent or searching. Some awaken to the deeper meanings of life through communing with nature. The miracle of life invites questions about who we are, how we got to be who we are, who is the Master Craftsman behind this wonderful world. Spontaneous awakenings occur without apparent rhyme or reason, as with Richard Bucke.[977] Kundalini energies may surge up the spine, unbidden, unexpected and sometimes disorienting – bringing with them a major spiritual opening.

Spiritual healing often connects healers and healees with spiritual aspects of their being. Beyond the fact that healing is often given for serious illness – which in and of itself raises spiritual awareness – healing facilitates alternative states of consciousness in which there is a sense of contact or communion with a vast reality beyond the everyday self.

Many of the views and beliefs on healing and spirituality held by healers and others rely upon the faith of the believer. Let us examine next what faith might include.

Faith

> *One cannot measure love with a ruler or scales.*
> *– Anonymous*

Joseph Campbell points out that a great deal of our materialistic distortions of religious and spiritual awarenesses may be due to a distancing from nature that is influenced by Judao-Christian tradition.

> [O]ur mainstream religions in the West are scriptural and were formulated a little over two thousand years ago in another place. Therefore, we have been unable to sanctify our land. Our land doesn't speak to us of the divine. Divine land is only over there in the Middle East... The Holy Land isn't in some other place. It's right in here – right inside each of us![978]

In religions that focus on ways to relate to nature and to the vital forces or gods of nature, people sense their own vital connection to nature. This has been lost for the most part in Western culture. Campbell continues:

> The gods are personifications of the energies that inform life – the very energies that are building the trees and moving the animals... The very energies that are in your body are personified by the gods. They're alive and well in everybody's life.
>
> Most traditions realize this – that deities are personifications, not facts... They are metaphors transparent to transcendence. But in our religious training we are not put in a position to understand how the gods are seen in other religious traditions so we have lost this language of the spirit...[979]
> ... When we forget the deities, we build a life on a program run by the head. The energies coming from the body are ignored and become threatening to the values, the head values, which we have chosen to live for...[980]

In industrial cultures, spirituality is compartmentalized – formalized in very limited religious practices, restricted to specific calendar days, differentiated and distanced from secularized life, and often denigrated by secular authorities as being *unscientific* and therefore not to be believed or relied upon.

Children often have direct awarenesses of spirituality. However, these are mostly discounted, discouraged and disparaged by our society, rather than being encouraged and nurtured.[981]

When we are raised in a society where linear, reductionistic approaches to life are emphasized to the exclusion of intuitive, meditative, and spiritual approaches, many are led to believe that they must justify their beliefs in the latter – as though inner awarenesses cannot be trusted. The degree of one's beliefs in spirituality in a materialistic context is a matter of faith, of trust – a matter of cognitive, reasoned opinion on what one has been taught, with a critical value judgment on the limited validity of one's inner perceptions and awarenesses.

> *Our whole business in this life is to restore to health the eye of the heart whereby God can be seen.*
> – St. Augustine

Specific stages of psychosocial development or *specific stages of spiritual conceptualization* may account for parts of the differences and conflicts in views on spiritual awarenesses. Successive stages of cognitive development, each with their increasing degrees of abstracting abilities, are well known to students of cognitive,[982] emotional/social[983] and moral[984] development. Until children reach a given age, they cannot conceive of certain abstractions. It may be that there are successive stages of development of inner awarenesses, or of learning to relate to these intuited perceptions and inner gnowings.

James Fowler describes six stages in the development of *faith*. He has validated these stages through research based on numerous interviews, using a standard series of questions that are extended to include open-ended questions. Fowler restricts himself to a definition of faith as *belief in the transcendent*.

> *Faith is the assured expectation of what is hoped for though not beheld.*
> – Bible [985]

I find Fowler's stages to be the most helpful in understanding a world that has distanced itself from spiritual awareness (although there are several other maps of spiritual development that may also be useful, and which I will review more briefly. I speculatively add my own observations, extending Fowler's discussion to consider how faith may develop when it includes *the experiences of transcendent worlds as gnostic realities* – to which we have access through inner, intuitive perceptions and experiences such as the out-of-body, near-death, pre-death experiences, spiritual healing, and more, as discussed in this volume and the earlier volumes of *Healing Research*. This is faith as gnosis – that is, based on personal awareness and mystical experiences rather than cognitive faith in truths of religious teachings. Within religious traditions this may be described as a *calling*.[986]

> *If God did not exist, it would be necessary to invent him.*
> – Voltaire

Stage 1. Intuitive-Projective Faith: Generally found in children between the ages of 2-6 years. Children at these ages are still developing their awarenesses of themselves and their relationships to the outside world. Fantasy and inner world perceptions may not be differentiated from perceptions of the outer world. In this stage the parents and other teachers introduce simple cultural explanations for everyday experiences. Children parrot the views they have learned but have little operational sense of their meanings.

Observations

It must be emphasized that this stage forms the basis in many ways for the development and unfolding of later stages. Fowler does not point this out, but it is commonly accepted that doctrinal templates are most readily implanted before the age of seven. As quoted above, in Judaism and other religions there is the understanding that younger children are impressionable and open to the imprinting of religious teachings. Parroting parental/family/cultural beliefs is a way of programming one's mind to believe the world is and should be the way one is taught. This then becomes "the way it's supposed to be."

This is a necessary part of the process of learning about the world. Whatever is learned at this age carries the imprint of faith – not just in religious matters, but in the faith one carries about the first imprints on the child-mind. These have the feeling of truth because they form the base for one's assumptions about how the world is and should be, and usually color all of one's subsequent learning – often in ways that are completely outside of conscious awareness. The software of the mind and the hardware of the brain are programmed through these initial processes of learning about the world.

A part of the basic teachings of childhood are the *meta-rules*, the rules about how rules are made and how they are allowed or not allowed to be questioned and changed. Where faith is taught as a rigid construct – as precepts and beliefs that are dictated by an outside authority and that cannot be questioned – then one is not allowed to change or adapt beliefs over time, either individually or collectively, unless told to do so by those who are the authorities in matters of faith. Where faith is taught as a flexible framework that can shift and accommodate to new individual and collective perceptions, to maturations in understandings, and to creative healing innovations, then faith can become a living, evolving engagement with inner and outer worlds.

As mentioned earlier, some parents raise their children without religious indoctrinations, with the intention of allowing them to develop their religious beliefs, affiliations and practices when they grow up. Adults from such backgrounds often end up seeking religious experiences intellectually, having difficulty in connecting with an emotionally satisfying affiliation to a faith. Those who persist in their searches may come into a richness unknown to them within their families of origin, satisfying inner needs for spirituality that are instinctive.

Fowler also does not address the 'clouds of glory,' which William Wordsworth pointed out are trailed into life by young children. Young children frequently have direct perceptions of energies surrounding the body.[987] (James Peterson found this in 20 percent of children he questioned.) They may spontaneously report memories of previous lives and of the period between lives, and a select few recall languages they never learned in their current lives.[988]. They may also perceive spirits and other-world entities[989] that appear to be aspects of a reality outside their imaginations. Children who have Near-Death Experiences are transformed by these.[990]

Adults have varying tolerance for children's claiming to perceive aspects of the world that most adults cannot perceive or explain, and that the adults may even fear. In turn, this can be confusing and distressing to the children, whose perceptions not only are not validated, but may be denied and dismissed. Children's reports of imaginary playmates and fantasy worlds may further confuse the children and the adults interacting with them. These playmates may be perceptions of spirit entities and dimensions beyond the physical – but might alternatively be vivid projections of the children's imaginations.

Some children will quietly maintain their awarenesses of other worlds and other lives but learn not to speak about them. These children are extremely grateful when they find adults who are accepting and understanding. Others are so frustrated at adults' denials of their perceptions that they end up denying them to themselves, repressing these awarenesses and forgetting they even had them.[991] Such latent awarenesses may remain simply as 'intuitive' impressions or may manifest in dreams. Sometimes, in the maturity and greater self-confidence of their adult years, they will again remember or perceive these awarenesses afresh.

Ken Wilber[992] notes that transpersonal aspects of a more advanced level of meditative spiritual development (Wilber's *centauric* level) have parallels with the pre-personal levels of development (under one year of age) as defined by Freud, *but emphasizes that these two states are clearly distinct.* Wilber points out that psychoanalysis has mistakenly presumed that transpersonal awareness represents a regression to infantile, wish-fulfilling fantasies – of an all-knowing, all-caring parental figure that is mistakenly projected as a God-figure. Wilber marshals reasons and evidence to refute this assertion, pointing out that distinct cognitive development occurs in children – from very primitive awareness to sophisticated understanding of the world. Transpersonal awarenesses in a person who has adult cognitive capacities is very different from the undifferentiated awareness of a young child.

What Wilber appears to miss is that children who are 2-4 years old may recall past lives and an existence between lives. These may be simple, factual memories, or may include advanced spiritual awarenesses, sometimes even with a sense of why they chose to incarnate into their family and their chosen or assigned tasks in this lifetime.[993]

Stage 2. Mythic-Literal Faith: Transition to this stage is brought about by the development of concrete operational thinking, whereby children stabilize their perceptions and conceptualizations of the physical and social worlds and learn to distinguish these from their internal worlds of fantasy. A well known milestone of this sort is children's relinquishing of the fantasy that they will marry mommy or daddy when they grow up, and then shifting to the understanding that they will marry someone *like* mommy or daddy.

Children in these latency years of seven to puberty learn the beliefs, stories, observances, moral rules and attitudes of their society. These are taken very literally, with no abstractions *about* what they are taught. Moral behavior tends to be interpreted concretely, with rewards and retributions anticipated in the forms of 'going to heaven if one behaves well;' 'an eye for an eye;' and other such precepts.

Many people remain comfortable with literal levels of explanations and with reliance on scriptural and other religious authorities to instruct and guide their faith and do not move to other levels of faith.

> *Every man takes the limit of his own field of vision for the limits of the world.*
>
> – Arthur Schopenhauer

Observations

Going beyond Fowler's discussion, this level offers a richness of tradition and draws from cultural wisdom that extends through many centuries. The teachings of Yahweh, Christ, Allah, Buddha and other religious luminaries, enriched by the teachings of disciples through the ages[994] can offer guidance and inspiration for a wonderful spiritual life. This can be a comfortable stage for a lifetime of spiritual development through studies of these teachings and living by these precepts.

> *Faith is the bird that feels the light and sings when the dawn is still dark.*
>
> – Rabindranath Tagore

However, there can be many negative aspects to remaining at this level of faith. In Western society the processes of socialization into religious teachings and intellectual teachings in schools – with the expectations of parents, peers, and teachers that fantasy worlds will be relinquished as one learns about the material, 'real' world – provide strong discouragements to children against trusting their perceptions of inner, intuitive, and personal spiritual awarenesses. For example, the numbers of children who report they see 'the colors around people' rapidly diminish with increasing age,[995] and similarly with those who recall past lives. Children who have personally 'seen the light' in Near-Death Experiences often learn to mute their sharing of these deeply meaningful and transformative awarenesses.[996] It is sad that Western educational systems systematically and rigidly emphasize linear, rational, reductionist (left brain hemisphere) aspects of cognition and ignore the intuitive, feeling, and creative (right brain) inner worlds. Frequent injunctions like 'stop daydreaming' are potently effective.

Yet another factor in reinforcing this level of faith is the separation of religious teachings from public school curricula in many Western countries. In the name of protecting children from indoctrinations in religious teachings, the development of personal spirituality and trust in this awareness are thereby precluded.

Clear and present dangers exist at this level of faith in adult life. Where the religious shepherds are invested with mantles of absolute spiritual authority, the flocks of congregants are taught to accept totally and obey the word of authority.

Figure III-11. Inner gnowing

While this may lead to greater moral and social good when the shepherds adhere to high moral and ethical standards, it may also lead to negative consequences when they are motivated to maintain and expand their power, or, worse, when they abuse their power individually (as in the sexual scandals of some Catholic clergy), or seek to establish their dominance over or oppress people who adhere to beliefs that differ from their own.

> *What concerns me is not the way things are,*
> *but the way people think things are.*
> – Epictetus [997]

In adult life, some individuals who have been at Stage 2 seek ways to develop their personal spiritual awareness and healing – through attending religious services, psychic development courses, practices of meditation, workshops on spiritual development, and other avenues to re-awaken and restore these personally enriching aspects of being.

Stage 3. Synthetic-Conventional Faith: Transition to this stage in puberty and teen years is stimulated by expanding horizons that extend beyond the family. There is also a cognitive development in the teen years that enables people to reason more abstractly. Contradictions become evident between various explanations for some of the deeper questions in life. There may be disillusionment with previously accepted literal explanations that are contradicted by scientific evidence or by explanations in other cultures that may appear equally valid. Faith – as belief in one's religious understanding of the world – must help to integrate one's diverse spheres of interaction with family, peers, school, employment, the media, and religion.

Teens are strongly oriented to peer opinions and values, expressed through individuals of one's personal acquaintance, of culturally valued traditional leaders or of personalities of media-mythic proportions. Faith is perceived in relationship to these individuals rather than as an abstract value system.

Observations
Teens are often faced with conflicting values between home and society at large. This is a test of their original faith, a decision point for remaining loyal to family teachings or relying on their personal judgment.

People with spiritual or psychic awarenesses often have great difficulties during this stage as they find themselves alienated from conventional 'crowd mentality.' They may doubt the reality and truth of their intuitively known realities under pressures to conform to their adolescent peer culture. Conversely, rebellions in their various forms may lead some teens to assert their rights to maintain their own views of reality. To some extent they may use adventures into the occult as counter-cultural vehicles in their explorations of growth into greater independence. Experimentation with hallucinogens and other mind-altering drugs may be a part of such rebellions.

The linear explanations stressed in Western thought are so powerfully reinforced in our educational system that they may be difficult to counter. Some will completely repress their intuitive sides. Others may retreat into reasoned agnostic positions that do not alienate them from their family and friends, and provide a measure of inner peace in the face of conflicts between their own perceptions and what most of their world tells them they ought to perceive or not perceive.

Fortunate are those whose parents encourage them to explore their outer and inner worlds, learning lessons and drawing conclusions for themselves.

> *When you give your children knowledge, you are telling them what you think. That is, you are telling them what they are supposed to know, what you want them to understand is true.*
> *When you give your children wisdom, you do not tell them what to know, or what is true, but, rather,* how to get to their own truth.
> – Neale Donald Walsch

More frequently, however, those who are open to awareness of other realities – when they are unwilling or unable to rationalize them away – find themselves isolated and lonesome because their views are not shared by their family and friends. They have to keep their intuitive awarenesses mostly to themselves to avoid rejection, ostracism or even persecution. On the positive side – sensitive people may develop trust and faith in their inner gnowing. On the negative side – they may question their intuitive abilities and spiritual awarenesses and dismiss these as fantasies, dampen or shut down their sensitivities or, worse, question their own sanity. They may also miss the opportunities for developing social skills or peer reflection that could help them sort out the many questions that are raised through spiritual awarenesses. They may also miss opportunities to discover the wonderful diversity in the ways spirit can manifest through different individuals and cultural traditions. In later years this can lead some individuals to intolerance for others' opinions and practices relating to psi and healing. In my experience, it is not rare to have psychics and healers claiming that their particular perceptions, inner guidance or cosmologies are THE best or the only correct ones.

> *The easy confidence with which I know another man's religion is folly teaches me to suspect that my own is also.*
> – Mark Twain

Stage 4. Individuative-Reflective Faith: Movement into this stage in late adolescence or at some point in adulthood is often stimulated by contradictions between authorities or by shifts in practices or policies that were previously construed as sacred and immutable. Shifts may be stimulated through encountering new belief systems as one enters different educational, work or geographic environments. Leaving home may bring about profound reassessments about values and practices, as people assume personal responsibility for their own decisions. Stimuli to shift into this stage may come when "... *the person must face certain unavoidable tensions: individuality versus being defined by a group or group membership; subjectivity and the power of one's strongly felt but unexamined feelings versus objectivity and the requirement of critical reflection; self-fulfillment or self-actualization as a primary concern versus service to and being for others; the question of being committed to the relative versus struggle with the possibility of an absolute.*" In this shift a person begins "*to take seriously the burden of responsibility for his or her own commitments, lifestyle, beliefs and attitudes.*" [998]

> *The faith that stands on authority is not faith.*
> – Ralph Waldo Emerson [999]

This stage represents a substantial shift – from defining one's role through one's relationship to others, to defining one's self through a *world view.* A "*capacity for critical reflection on identity (self) and outlook (ideology)*" is developed.[1000] A more individualized, personal system is synthesized. At this stage the world view is cognitive and critical and may tend to be exclusive and intolerant of contradictory views.

> *There is a strong craving for permanence, for certainty in a chaotic world, and many people prefer to look for it within a mathematical or scientific rather than a religious context. They are, perhaps, not aware that underlying both mathematics and religion there must be a foundation of faith which the individual must himself supply.*
> – Philip Davis and Reuben Hersh

Observations
People gifted with psi and healing abilities and spiritual awareness may at this level focus positively on their powers, and may apply and explore the personal benefits of their intuitive gifts as well as benefits that may be offered to others – as in psychic counseling and healing. On the negative side, some become inflated with their gifts, seeking personal aggrandizement through monetary gain, public recognition and satisfying their need for adulation by pushing healees to be healed rather than inviting them to change at a pace that is comfortable and in harmony with their psychological, developmental and social processes. Another danger for such individuals is in becoming ungrounded through dwelling too much in transpersonal realms; and yet another is the confusion of psychotic grandiosity – in which people imagine they are communicating with God or

Christ or other spiritual beings but actually are simply making these up in the context of an emotional breakdown.[1001]

People struggling with these issues may find psychological and social support in discussion groups and health awareness circles, various professional societies that study psychic and healing phenomena, in any of myriads of popular workshops or lectures on these subjects, or through enlightened psychological and psychiatric consultations.[1002]

I often have people tell me after lectures and workshops how much they appreciate learning that their intuitive, psychic, and healing abilities and spiritual awarenesses are not imaginary; how validating they find the experience of discussing these and the realization – through experiential demonstrations – that these are natural phenomena, available to most people who are open to exploring inner dimensions.

In religious contexts, validation may be found for such gifts within the beliefs and practices of particular sects. Healing services, spiritualist churches, and psychic development circles have been helpful in these regards. On the negative side, some religious groups may discourage, belittle, disparage, or even persecute those who listen to inner awarenesses rather than adhering to established credos. I know of several sensitive and highly gifted healers who were distressed and put off from participation in religious observances by reactions of fundamentalists – following simple healings which they gave for the relief of pains and other symptoms. Others have made similar observations.[1003] It takes a good measure of self-confidence and maturity not to be put off by confrontations with people who hold beliefs at the levels of stages 1-2[1004] and who insist that their way is THE way.

> *All great truths began as blasphemies.*
> – George Bernard Shaw

Stage 5. Conjunctive Faith: Inner voices start to speak to those who are open to developing further. At first this may be perceived as a feeling or cognitive dissatisfaction with limitations, contradictions, and paradoxes in the world views that were individually established but that are not sufficiently comprehensive to encompass the whole of reality. Intuitive awakening may extend to psychic and channeled awarenesses.[1005] This is a maturation that begins to tolerate a multiplicity of views that may cross several levels of abstraction, and indeed, several levels of realities. Symbols, stories, and myths from various traditions resonate within people and invite them to explore more deeply the mysteries and paradoxes of inner worlds.

Stage 5 is difficult to define. It is a state in which 'both and' feels more appropriate than 'either or.' It acknowledges the rightness of inner gnowings that are impossible to define adequately in linear terminology so that accommodations of cognitive paradigms are required in the process of exploring these inner realms. The inner gnowing may transcend linear logic and reason. Its rightness is self evident and convincingly apparent, despite the fact that it does not derive from reasoned hypotheses based on sensory data. A multidimensional approach to exploring reality develops. Earlier modes of analysis and reasoning are acknowledged as appropriate for particular stages of development and specific types of communication about the world. At the same time, an initiative is granted to the inner gnowing that informs and instructs its knowers rather than being deduced, built, or structured by them.

This is a new level of creativity. It is a relearning of the openness of the child in stage 1 to awarenesses of other worlds in which images and inner voices have their own life and may inform us constructively – just as outer sensory inputs may do. It is a 'second naiveté.' [1006] Here, however, it has a maturity that acknowledges the equal validity of other people's interpretations of their perceptions of these inner realities, from within their own cultural and experiential vantage points. *"[T]his stage's commitment to justice is freed from the confines of tribe, class, religious community or nation."* [1007]

In its positive aspects, this stage opens into creativity and to global ecumenism. In the negative, it can be overwhelming and paralyzing in its immensity and paradoxicality and may lead to passivity, complacency or withdrawal.

Do not believe in anything simply because you have heard it.
Do not believe in traditions because they have been handed down for many generations.
Do not believe in anything because it is spoken and rumored by many.
Do not believe in anything simply because it is found written in your religious books.
Do not believe in anything merely on the authority of your teachers or elders.
But after observation and analysis, when you find that anything agrees with reason,
and is conducive to the good and benefit of one and all,
then accept it and live to it.

                              – The Buddha [1008]

Observations

Those who open to the awareness of Stage 5 join the gifted minority in Western society who have not relinquished the awarenesses of other worlds that are present from Stage 1 – but were discounted and submerged under the pressures to learn the standardized descriptions and analyses of the outer sensory world.

Direct experiences of other realities – especially mystical, Near-Death and Pre-Death Experiences, Out-of-Body Experiences, bereavement apparitions, meditative, kundalini,[1009] and psychic experiences – may stimulate people to move into Stage 5.

While Stage 5 brings perceptions of other realities, it alternates between the inner and outer worlds. While the head and heart may be open to other planes of reality, the feet are still attracted to and maintain at least intermittent attachment with the ground. People at this stage may have a sense of being part of a vast, real-life play, guided through their inner awarenesses by intelligence from other dimensions.[1010]

On the other hand, staying 'grounded,' 'being real,' staying in the body and continuing to relate through linear reality with the material world at times when this is necessary appropriate may be a challenge, as one learns to navigate through transcendent dimensions in one' spiritual practice. The most important aspect is a working through of one's 'little ego' or 'little self,' letting go of old patterns of beliefs and social conformities that distance one from the transcendent, and learning to rely upon one's inner gnowing – while not becoming over-inflated with oneself. One learns to re-map inner and outer realities in the light of awarenesses from other dimensions. Through the relinquishing of old biases, beliefs and emotional scars, one allows the ego to become reconstituted within vastly broader and deeper awarenesses. One does not leave physical reality as long as one is still living the life of the flesh.

> *Before enlightenment, fetch wood and carry water.*
> *After enlightenment, fetch wood and carry water*
> – Zen teaching

Stage 6. Universalizing Faith: This stage "becomes a disciplined, activist *incarnation* – a making real and tangible – of the imperatives of absolute love and justice of which Stage 5 has partial apprehensions. The self at Stage 6 engages in spending and being spent for the transformation of present reality in the direction of a transcendent actuality." [1011] People at this stage inspire others through their living of their ideals of universal love, that transcend the accepted patterns of their society. Examples of people at this stage include Gandhi, Mother Theresa, and Martin Luther King, Jr. in his later years. This is not to say that people at Stage 6 are perfect but that they embody the striving towards the perfection of particular ideals.

> *When people ask me if I am religious, I tell them I love God far too much to be religious. "Oh, then you must believe in God?" they inevitably ask. "Of course not," I reply with a smile, "does a fish believe in water?" For me, God is all there is. What's to believe?*
>
> *Although the world's major religions all agree that God (however they define the term) is omnipresent, it seems that very few of their followers - including their clerical hierarchy - actually understand what omnipresence really means. And therein lies the source of the world's ills...*
>
> *... what is the purpose of naming him (or her or it) in the first place? Naming anything creates a subject/object relationship between you and the thing named, and that in and of itself means a separation. Every name of God, no matter how holy, drives a wedge between the creator and the created - which includes you and me. This separation is the primal breeding ground for fear, for we then see ourselves as tiny beings, abandoned (or evicted from Paradise) and living on the fringe of an incomprehensibly huge cosmos. It's no wonder most of humanity takes this whole God business so seriously – it appears to be no less than a matter of life and death.*

But what if the phrase "God is all that is" were literally true? This is what R. Buckminster Fuller must have understood when he said, "God, to me, it seems, is a verb not a noun."

...God is indeed a verb. He is not the creator. He is the ongoing unfoldment of creation itself. There is nothing that is not a part of this unfolding. Thus there can be nothing separate from God. God is infinite and infinity is One...

When we perceive God as a noun, we envision him as the creator, the architect of, and therefore separate from, his creation. Identifying ourselves as part of that creation, we see ourselves not only separate from our source but separate from each other and all other manifest things as well. This is the fatally flawed axiom underlying virtually all of the world's faiths. They may collectively call for love and peace, but the rampant divisiveness, greed, and competition that currently pervade human culture are the only inevitable outcomes of their separative philosophies.

Once I viewed God as a verb instead of a noun, my perception of life shifted. Everything around me, manifest or no, became God. There was only God. When someone spoke to me, it was with God's voice; when I listened, it was with God's heart. I invite you to try it. The small shift from noun to verb may well be the antidote to the forbidden fruit that banished us from Eden. As you begin to view God not as the creator but as the constantly changing dance of creation itself, you'll discover him in everything you see - including yourself. The old you - that fish swimming blindly in search of water - fades away as you dissolve into the simple meaning of it all. Perhaps, when your vision finally clears, you will find yourself living in the Promised Land that so many others are still praying for.

– Jean-Claude Koven

Observations

Children often have a personal spiritual awareness as well as a sense of moral values.[1012] This is a direct knowing of the transcendent, a gnosis rather than faith.

Similarly, at a certain stage of development, healers and psychics become directly aware of spirituality as a collective consciousness, a 'higher awareness' or of God. This higher awareness provides moral and practical guidance towards bettering the world in which we live. It may include awareness of *Gaia*, the geobiological system that comprises our planet. It may extend to include the material and spiritual universe in its entirety. Sensitive persons open to these levels of awareness are like brain cells in the mind of a higher consciousness. They are as individual waves upon the ocean – both having their own identities but also being a part of the vastness of the oceanic wholeness.[1013]

[Y]ou must remember that the air is precious to us, that the air shares its spirit with all the life it supports. The wind that gave our grandfather his first breath also receives his last sigh. And the wind must also give our children the spirit of life...

– Chief Seattle [1014]

Discussion

As we see in Fowler's stages and in my extensions of his discussions, faith in the existence of the Infinite Source can find expression in a spectrum of human relationships to oneself, to each other and to the transcendent. Where faith is narrowly focused, rigidly defined and exclusive, it is divisive: I am right and you are wrong. Exclusive faith may provide security in one's beliefs about one's beliefs, reinforced by social validations from like-minded members of one's community in beliefs, it casts doubts on all other beliefs. Rather than explore potential lessons in the diversity of beliefs, exclusive faith seeks to overcome and eliminate contrasting and conflicting views. Exclusive faith has been the single most destructive force in the history of mankind, generating more hatred and cruelty of humans against each other than any other single psychological and social factor.

In marked contrast, where faith is inclusive it acknowledges and accepts that one has a sense of the transcendent that is filtered through the prisms and facets of the crystal that is oneself, refracted into a rainbow of awarenesses, and is enriched by the different spectrum of refractions that others perceive through the crystals of their being. Inclusive faith generates love, acceptance, and healing among individuals and across cultures.

> *Begin with love, love for your life and love for the Creator that provided this to you as a gift. Then allow this love to slowly dissolve any fears or doubts that may encroach upon your simple desire to be of service. From the beginning of time it has always been faith that has connected souls to their source. Nothing more is required. The essence of spirituality is faith. It is this simple so that all may be able to experience its power. Yet faith must be exercised, brought to a place of maturity. You are in partnership with such a loving, boundless source that wishes only to show you what faith can accomplish. Each day make faith your friend. Faith is the true measure of spirituality.*
> *– Matthew Smith* [1015]

How can we understand the divergent pathways of exclusive and inclusive faith? In great part, the course of history in the abuses of exclusive faith has been shaped by leaders who strengthened the faith of their followers to believe in whatever the leaders taught them, in order to enhance and maintain the leaders' power. For instance, it has long been acknowledged that by keeping the focus of one's followers on perceived dangers from outside the community, leaders can strengthen their power and divert attention away from internal problems. Strongly encouraging followers to be faithful to the leaders' teachings and directives keeps their subjects under their power, especially when differences with 'others' (labeled as nonbelievers, heretics, infidels, or terrorists) are used as reasons to defend the faith and attack the 'others.' People are willing to cede their power to leaders who scare them and then promise to provide defenses against the declared enemies. An excellent recent example is George W. Bush who used the fear generated by the terrorist attacks in America to seize powers for the Federal government (through the Patriot Acts) while the majority of Americans agreed to cede their powers to him on his promises to protect them from terrorism. In the history of abuses of religious faith, the scapegoating of Jews is another such example.

People who are in Stages 1 and 2 of religious faith are for the most part content and happy to have leaders teach them tenets of faith that they can accept and adhere to. This becomes less possible as people move into Stages 3 to 6. At these levels, the focus shifts to faith in inner awarenesses.[1016]

Personality development and transcendent awareness

While the above considers stages of *faith*, other levels for consideration are the stages of psychological development in opening to spiritual awareness. Ken Wilber has some of the most detailed analyses of the unfolding of meditative awareness,[1017] and developmental stages in Zen cultivation are discussed by Kit.

The best and most detailed discussion of developmental stages in opening to transcendent awareness has been written by Jenny Wade,[1018] replete with quotes and references from numerous psychological studies.

Wade points out that we have to allow that there truly is a transcendent reality in order to examine this question – beyond just having faith. This is difficult to do from our starting point in material reality. Wade follows the reasoning of David Bohm, pointing out that we don't have to abandon our everyday, Newtonian understanding of the world when we explore the transcendent. The material world, or *explicate order*, is enfolded within the transcendent, *implicate order*.[1019] Both are accessible to us if we allow ourselves to open to them. However, many people do not develop beyond the more concrete stages of thinking in order to reach that level of readiness.

As in Fowler's analysis, Wade proposes stages of cognitive development, based on detailed analyses of theories proposed by psychologists in the last century.

1. Pre- and Perinatal Consciousness
A high level of transcendent awareness appears to exist while we are in the womb and around the time of birth.

People recall significant events that occurred prior to and around the time they were born when undergoing age regression during hypnotherapy and other forms of psychotherapy. They report details of their parents' arguments, their mother's emotional and physical traumas, their own difficulties in the process of being born, and even detail many casual circumstances surrounding their birth.[1020]

For instance, at the age of four years, a little girl reported that Cathy, the assistant midwife, had held her to her own breast to stop her crying. Not only was the memory accurate, but the child whispered this information to Cathy in the presence of others, out of apparent awareness that this was something that had left Cathy feeling guilty and uncomfortable – that her own mother had not been the first to suckle her. In another series of reports, children described in detail the precise steps in their birth, including people who had been present, instruments used, and the locale – including details unknown to their mothers.[1021]

2. Reactive Consciousness
Shortly after birth, infants become more focused on their physical selves and lose touch with transcendent reality.

3. Naïve Consciousness (till age 2)
The child learns to differentiate self from others. Transpersonal awareness is nil.

4. Egocentric consciousness (till age 4)
The child consolidates a sense of separate self, defined by conventional psychology primarily in cognitive terms and/or learning to achieve social fulfillment. The body appears material, thoughts appear immaterial. Linear time, with a past, present and future, is felt to be real, while transcendent time (the eternal *now*) is outside of conscious awareness. Past lives may be recalled till about age 4.[1022] Death is not understood as a finality, and there are fantasies that it can be outwitted. There is a tendency in Western culture for males to fixate at this level, especially those in lower socioeconomic classes.

5. Conformist Consciousness
This stage is typified by belonging and identifying with a group; reasoning is concrete and dualistic – either/or, black or white. Safety is sought through controlling others and the environment. The future is seen as an extension of the past. Death is an inevitable end to existence. Fears of death are mitigated by promises of an afterlife where conditions are linked to good or bad behaviors. Direct experience of the transcendent remains outside the framework of this level of awareness, where most people's development stops.

The following two stages are alternate pathways of further development.

6. Achievement Consciousness
More typical of males, focus is on manipulation of a world of objects external to the individual. Traditional Western schools emphasize linear thinking to prepare for better manipulation of the world, thereby decreasing right hemispheric activity that includes feelings, intuition and transcendent awareness. Success and power are the admired goals.

7. Affiliative Consciousness
This stage often develops out of disillusionment with Conformist Consciousness – much as Fowler's Individuative-Reflective Faith (Stage 4) develops out of Synthetic-Conventional Faith, (Stage 3). Patterns and similarities are favored over differences. This is not a naïve approach, as it has been prejudicially labeled by the predominantly analytical, linear, Western academic and social establishments. It is the right-brained awareness of intuitions and gestalts which appear from the left-brained, linear perspective to be il*logical* and un*reason*able.[1023] These criticisms are strengthened by the tendency at this stage to emphasize

relationships over reason, to prefer openness over closure, and to feel that love conquers all.

8. *Authentic Consciousness*

This stage, where right and left brain approaches are both honored, is achieved from either Achievement or Affiliative Consciousness. People at this stage have relinquished their ego defenses and are not bound by ego-motivated cognitions or perceptions. They are internally motivated towards personal growth and self-actualization. They identify themselves with the human race as a whole rather than with various social or societal subgroups. They are self-validating and do not rely on others for recognition. While pursuing their personal growth, they never do this at the expense of others, always seeking the highest good of all. They are able to empathize with and genuinely tolerate others' differences and limitations. Realizing that there are many paths to enlightenment, they are comfortable with the paradoxes and mysteries of life.

Peak experiences occur with increasing frequency as people become more congruent with authentic consciousness. Acknowledging that words are inadequate to describe the transcendent, they often rely on metaphors to express their awareness of the transcendent. Many come to feel that they have been born for a purpose and to fulfill a life mission even though they may not clearly perceive, comprehend, or be able to explain this. They feel intimately interconnected with other people and with nature.

9. *Transcendent consciousness*

Peak experiences are increasingly perceived as doorways and invitations – to detach from ordinary awareness on the one side, and to unite with the numinous, Absolute Reality on the other side. There is often a struggle to overcome the habits of perceptions and conceptualizations of earlier stages. Disciplined, meditative, spiritual practices may enable people to pass through that doorway. These steps often lead to alternative states of consciousness which are not sought for the thrill, beauty, or grandeur of peak experiences but are now understood to be vehicles for reaching into the transcendent. Awareness becomes that of being united with everything. This is often an exquisitely blissful state, frequently described as pure love, transcending space and time. Seekers on this path usually experience it intermittently, most often during their spiritual practices but also arising spontaneously at other times. Along with transcendent awareness, they often develop psi awarenesses and abilities to alter their body functions and to influence or even shape the environment through intentions that are activated in transcendent realities.

10. *Unity consciousness*

The ultimate state of enlightenment is a non-dual state in which there is the awareness of being united with the All. This is an all-inclusive state of integration of all levels of reality. Everything is *here* and *now*. Every vestige of dualism has been deconstructed and only the All remains. While it is rare for a person to dwell on the other side of the doorway to the transcendent, even one visit is transformative. Once having been there, a person is forever changed. With continued practice, Unity consciousness is often maintained for increasing lengths of time until finally one's ordinary consciousness becomes enlightened Unity consciousness. While there is no attachment to worldly suffering, an enlightened person still resonates with compassion to the suffering of others. All circumstances are greeted with equanimity and all people with unconditional acceptance and impartiality.

The perspectives of Unity consciousness are difficult to appreciate and understand from the vantage points of earlier stages. The dispassionate attitude of people at this level may be perceived by people at earlier stages as indifference, and they may question why the enlightened refrain from intervening to rescue people who are in trouble and distress. Their interventions are usually limited to sounding a note of Unity consciousness to which others can resonate. For example, Wade points out that Jesus had the ability to eliminate the hunger of the masses but did not do so, stating that worldly hardships are an essential aspect of life. Buddha, likewise, would not eliminate all suffering, teaching that one should seek to transform one's relationship to circumstances rather than changing the circumstances.

11. After-death consciousness
Wade appears to me weak only in this section of her discussion. While she does her consistently thorough job of summarizing reports from NDEs as evidence for After-death consciousness,[1024] she is not as strong in summarizing other evidence – as in apparitions, channeling and possession.[1025]

Wade is outstanding in her distillation of an enormous range of references that speak to her analysis of stages of development on the path to transcendent awareness. I cannot recommend her work highly enough.

Neurological studies and Fowler's stages of faith

Andrew Newberg,[1026] a radiologist at the University of Pennsylvania, has been exploring brain imaging in people who have practiced meditation for many years. His observations are based largely on Positron Emission Tomography (PET) scans, which reflect the current activity of the various portions of the brain. He suggests that Fowler's stages of faith may correlate with the development of the nervous system from childhood through old age.

1. Infancy: Neuronal development parallels Undifferentiated faith
Starting with a modest set of reflexes, brain functions rapidly mature throughout the first year of life.[1027] The higher cortex functions have not developed yet and there is limited integration of cognitive functions. By months 8-9 activity increases in the frontal lobes and related areas, in parallel with emerging cognitive and social development. After 2 years of age, brain scans qualitatively look like adult scans.

2. *Childhood: parallels with Intuitive-Projective stage*
Between the ages of 2-6 an enormous growth of functions is seen in the neocortex, along with increases in general brain metabolism. There is a rapid proliferation of neurons and interconnections between nerve cells. There are many potential pathways for various brain functions, paralleling the fluid cognitive processes typical of this age range.

3. *Childhood: Mythic-Literal stage*
Between ages 6-10 there is a decrease in the complexity of neuronal interconnections, with may be related to the establishment of habitual pathways of responses to stimuli.

4. *Adolescence to Early Adulthood: Synthetic-Conventional stage*
Between 11-20 overall brain metabolism starts to decrease. The decreases in numbers of connections between neurons continues as formal operational thinking and conformity to established norms develop. New ideas are assimilated but they are less likely to be foundation concepts.

5. *Adulthood: Individuative-Reflective stage*
Cognitive and emotional processes develop to their fuller potentials and with greater stability. New connections and terminations of connections are limited. This is a fairly steady state over several decades.

6. *Mid to Late Adulthood: Conjunctive Faith Stage*
Brain metabolic activity declines progressively from the age of 40. Without a person's awareness, this may contribute to disillusionment because striving to find answers does not appear to fulfill the promise of one's earlier expectations.

7. *Adulthood: Universalizing Faith stage*
Spiritual experiences and practices may contribute to this stage, in ways that we are just beginning to appreciate through our studies of brain maps in people who engage in spiritual practices.

   This type of experience probably develops from ways in which sensory and cognitive inputs are processed as they enter various parts of the brain that handle these inputs and the cognitive restructuring of what is perceived through the nerve messages to the brain. The normal decrease in nerve functions with age may contribute to such spiritual experiences occurring in older people.

   Newberg notes that in a gross way the brain scans in dementia resemble the brain scans of infants.

Observations: I believe Newberg's observations, based on PET scans of brain functions, may in many ways reflect stages of spiritual development. Two broad interpretations of these findings are possible: either the stages of faith are products of brain maturation, or maturation of faith and spiritual development is processed into conscious awareness in specific areas of the brain, which are altered by this process. The latter possibility is well supported by studies showing changes in the brain with the exercise of many physical and mental functions.

Not included in Newberg's analysis or theories are the validated reports of adults regarding detailed memories from the time of conception, though pregnancy, labor and delivery, and during infancy and early childhood. In my opinion, these appear to validate the theory that spirit is primary and the body an expression of spiritual awareness – rather than the reverse.

Personality types and stages of faith

In addition to developmental, logical, and social influences on the shaping of faith, there are factors of personality that must certainly contribute to how we choose to play the game of life. The Jungian polarities (formalized in the Myers-Briggs personality assessment)[1028] points out that people tend to favor one end of each of two polarities: Thinking $\leftarrow \rightarrow$ Feeling, and Outer Senses $\leftarrow \rightarrow$ Intuition. That is, we may be comfortable with thinking our way through situations while not being comfortable feeling our way through them (or vice versa). Similarly, we may be more comfortable sorting out our relationships with the world through inner, intuitive readings of what is going on rather than checking on our outer senses to determine how we should interact with the world (or vice versa).

Another polarity is that of introversion $\leftarrow \rightarrow$ extroversion; inner-directedness versus outer-directedness. We may be more inclined to attend to our personal perceptions, feelings, and assessments of the world, or we may rely more on interactions with the outer world to provide a sense of where we are in any given situation.[1029]

Other spiritual typologies of personality types have been suggested.

Danah Zohar and Ian Marshall have a marvelous discussion on J. L. Holland's six personality types and how they relate to religious beliefs and practices. While these have overlaps with the Jungian types, they are distinctly different. They are not mutually exclusive, and some people are found to score high on several of these, even when they are conceptualized as being polar to each other. These have been validated and widely used in the Holland[1030] vocational guidance test:

People with *conventional* personality type are precise, conforming and methodical. While devoted to detail and reliable, they may be rigid and defensive. About fifteen percent of people tested score highest within this category. Their opposite is the artistic type.

People with *social* personality type enjoy being with other people, are gregarious, kind, helpful, cooperative, and empathetic, found more in females. They are good teachers and therapists, responsible and idealistic. About thirty percent of people test highest on this category. Their opposite is the realistic type.

People with *investigative* personality type are devoted to investigating ideas, rational, analytical, and precise. They are wary of emotionality. They are introspective, independent, and prefer their own company. They make good researchers. About ten to fifteen percent of people tested fit in this category. Their opposite is the enterprising type.

People with *artistic* personality type are emotional, impulsive, and uninterested in dealing with routine, practical tasks. They are independent, imaginative, non-conformist, and attracted to the arts. About ten to fifteen percent of people test high in this category. Their opposite is the conventional type.

People with *realistic* personality type are practical, materialistic, frank, direct, reliable and thrifty, represented more in males. They are uncomfortable with social situations and intimate relationships. While they speak their own minds, they tend to conformity and can be rigid. About twenty percent test high on this type. Their opposite is the social personality.

People with *enterprising* personality type are ambitious, adventurous, optimistic, energetic and outgoing. They make good salespersons, supervisors, and businesspersons. They comprise ten to fifteen percent of those tested and their opposite is the investigative type.

Zohar and Marshall have devised a diagram in the form of a lotus flower, integrating the Holland and Jungian typologies, pointing out how people with each of these personality characteristics may experience and express their spirituality differently.

Such innate preferences must certainly shape our choices of where we settle in our relationship to faith in transcendent realities. If you are extroverted and more comfortable with thinking and your outer senses, you are more likely to favor a reasoned choice of faith and less likely to trust inner, intuitive knowing of a transcendent reality. Conversely, if you live through your inner world more strongly than through the outer world, you may choose to trust your personal, inner gnowing of spiritual realms.

Huston Smith proposes a somewhat different cosmology of spiritual personality types.

> ...In every sizable community one finds atheists who think that there is no God, polytheists who acknowledge many gods, monotheists who believe in a single God, and mystics who say that there is only God.
>
> These four ways of slicing the religious pie... are not explicitly articulated in the way theologies are. For the most part they pass unnoticed, for they leave no footprints in history and do not create headlines, as religions do when they collide. Yet the differences between the four spiritual personality types (as I am calling them) run deeper than theological differences, for they are grounded in human nature, whereas theological differences, being historical, come and go.[1031]

He pictures a stack of worlds inhabited by people who hold various views of the world. The atheists inhabit the bottom level, where only physical reality exists. Above them are other levels but each is separated from those above it by a one-way mirror. The atheists can see only their own level, reflected in the mirror of their beliefs that separates them from other awarenesses. Those who live in other belief worlds can see the atheists' world and the other worlds below theirs as well as their own. Each type argues that there is nothing beyond what they can see. Each believes that anything beyond their mirror is simply the creation of fantasy.

The atheist's world consists of physical matter. Mind is the product of the brain, and rational reasoning is the way one analyzes the world.

The polytheist's world includes gods, spirits of humans, and other discarnate entities. Western culture has converted these into channeled entities and a collective unconscious. Within organized religion there are angels and patron saints. These are experienced as much more real than the more abstract and distant holy trinity.

Smith observes that the 'Great Traditions' of the most recent millennia are monotheistic. God is "richly endowed with the finest qualities that human beings exemplify: wisdom, tenderness, mercy, compassion, creativity, love, and the like, which, elevated in degree, add up to glory. Love figures especially among these qualities…" [1032]

For the mystic, everything is a manifestation of God.

To appreciate the differences between these groups, Smith considers their attitudes towards values. For the atheist, value derives from experiences in the outer world. The polytheist has many more levels of values, including particularly good and evil, which are in conflict and either of which could gain the upper hand. The monotheist views evil as a schism with good, which is the original and stronger value. The polytheist sees all as good, all as being only a manifestation of God.

Logic is inadequate to comprehend and encompass the higher levels. These must be appreciated intuitively, through 'tacit knowing.'

Huston Smith has a marvelous gift of pattern recognition, a breadth and depth of familiarity with literature and the arts, a lifetime of experiences in investigating religions around the world, and a wonderful ability to explain and illustrate his points with an apt turn of phrase and lovely imagery. Smith's writing is all the more remarkable for his not himself connecting consciously with his spiritual awareness. By his own admission, he finds himself outside the levels where direct gnowing informs the world, having connected directly with spirituality only when using hallucinogenic drugs. Despite this handicap, his writings are among the clearest I have found in explaining some of the prevalent differences in spiritual awarenesses.

While there is no right or best way to parse the worlds that are beyond words, discussions leading to greater understanding of spiritual awareness are vital to our personal lives, and may be essential to our collective survival as a species – in view of the cultural and religious clashes that are fueling global conflicts. I return to Fowler's cosmology as a helpful way of viewing our world. [1033]

Societal stages of awareness parallel the stages of faith[1034]

I believe that the stages of faith that Fowler describes in individuals may be observed also in stages of societies' development of awareness and understanding about the spiritual world, In my extension of this discussion I use the term *faith* to indicate a belief that is based on inner gnowing (not just a reasoned belief about the validity of spiritual realities).

Stage 1. Intuitive-Projective Faith: Inner and outer worlds are not experienced as differentiated.

Nature is alive and animate, and people seek to find their proper places as an integral part of nature. The outer world includes nature devas and angels, spirits of ancestors, and one or more deities. All of these have a vital interest in the outer and inner worlds of living things and may interact with them. Conversely, each individual is intimately linked with these entities and may turn to them for help or may be required to respond to their wishes or even to their moods and whims.

The outer world reflects the inner. Omens and portents are seen in outer events. Divination helps in the interpretation of these reflections. Patterns or cracks that appear in bones thrown in the fire may portend the fates of men. Numerous other divination systems, such as the I Ching, Tarot, survive and flourish today, derived from this tradition.

In Stage 1 societal development of faith, the inner world reflects the outer. Dreams provide direction for people's relationships with the outer world. Visions are sought for guidance in important decisions. Mystical visions of respected shamans are accepted uncritically in explanations of questions about health, interpersonal relationships, and the relationships of people to their environment. This stage is a place of creativity.

Stage 2. Mythic-Literal Faith: The world is seen as having been created and defined by divine inspiration and interventions. The words of scriptural and personal authorities who claim to have received divine awakenings and messages are taken as literal truths. Adherence to these truths is mandatory and any questioning of these truths is heresy. People outside the chosen group are considered to be misguided. Polytheistic religions such as Hinduism are less intolerant of differing views of the realms of the spirits and deity than are monotheistic religions such as Christianity, Judaism and Islam.

Stage 3. Synthetic-Conventional Faith: Scientific methodology introduces an awareness of deductive investigation and reasoning about the outer world. Scientific approaches provide pragmatic and predictive methodologies and instruments for analyzing and manipulating the material world. These methods are applied towards reducing the unpredictabilities of life (such as illnesses) and conquering nature.

Science rejects Stages 1 and 2 as unreasonable. They are seen as lacking in sound bases for analysis by experimentation because they rely upon inner experiences that cannot be objectively studied. Authorities are to be respected only insofar as they base their teachings on experimental observations.

Stage 4. Individuative-Reflective Faith: An awareness is growing that science is not being true to its principles of reasoning objectively from evidence. Avenues of study that lie outside currently accepted paradigms are systematically denied research funds. Scientists who pursue such research are actively discouraged from doing so through peer pressure, limitations on their funding and threats to their professional advancement. Evidence that contradicts prevalent world views is not only rejected on the basis that it contradicts accepted theories but also is suppressed from publication. It would appear that much of modern science, which initially set out to explore the world objectively and correct its theories as new evidence was uncovered, has slipped backward into Stage 2, with a reliance on prevalent authorities and theories. Modern science has become largely a scientistic religion.

Those who remain true to Stage 4 principles do not reject evidence that contradicts prevalent world views. These scientists, philosophers and other independent thinkers seek to comprehend the world in the light of evidence that contradicts reductionistic, matter-bound observations and reasoning. Evidence from such areas as modern physics and psi phenomena is included in considerations of how the world functions. The analysis is still deductive and linear, based upon observations that are experimentally studied and statistically verifiable. Rupert Sheldrake's theory of morphogenetic fields is a good example of this stage.[1035]

Stage 5. Conjunctive Faith: Evidence from introspective, personal experiences is considered valid to understanding the world. Meditative, psychic, and spiritual truths are sought as sources for comprehending the cosmos. Acknowledgement is given to truths in all religions as long as they do not advocate harm to any living beings.

At the same time, analytical considerations are raised about whether subjective evidence might be colored by individual and cultural beliefs or even by mental derangement. Both left and right brain hemispheric modes of experience and analysis are welcomed.[1036]

Stage 6. Universalizing Faith: We are told by seers and mystics that we stand at the dawn of a new age of awareness. Primary, immediate perceptions of transcendent realities will be an integral part of everyday life. Individuals will sense themselves to be an integral part of Gaia, our geobiological planetary awareness. People will work for the common good, which they will perceive to be their own good, as they are a part of the All.

It seems we are coming full circle in Western society[1037] in moving from Stages 1 through 6. One may well question whether the excursion into linear reasoning over the past several centuries has been a positive or necessary contribution to societal development of awareness and expressions of faith. Some might feel it has been like being lost and wandering in a desert. My own impression is that we know the light only through its contrast with the darkness. Having explored the wonders of the reductionist, linear world and the mysteries of forgetfulness regarding spiritual dimensions, we can appreciate the transcendent dimensions all the more through these contrasts.

This discussion may seem highly theoretical, much like those of past centuries in which questions were pondered on a level of "How many angels can dance on the head of a pin?" This is far from the present case.

The effects on Gaia of our excursion into linear ways of relating to our planet are grossly evident. We have polluted our rivers, our earth, and our air, are exhausting our natural resources, and are decimating entire species irretrievably. Linear reasoning as the foundation for our individual and social lives has led us to measure and value our successes through material gains. Our linear reasoning leads us to focus on earning more, to collect more material possessions, to protect our personal and national turf against outsiders, and to seek our own gain at the expense of others who are less strong than ourselves. We cannot continue on this linear path without self-destructing.[1038]

I hope and pray that a return to greater spiritual awareness may help us change our course towards more intuitive and spiritual awarenesses of our relationships to ourselves, each other, and our planet in time to avoid an inevitable planetary disaster. This is not to say that we should abandon linear reasoning. Logic and common sense must balance our intuitive perceptions, which can mislead us for varieties of reasons.[1039]

Choices and consequences of where we elect to dwell *personally* in the stages of faith

If we live our lives by the firm rules of Stages 1 and 2, then our world has clear and sharp boundaries. We know the rules set out by our faith and we must obey them without question. Where loving and caring ethics are taught by our religion (and/or by our family's and community's interpretations of our religion), we may find nurturance for our emotional needs. Family ties and values are fostered as a matter of duty, creating a structure for support of every one of its members – with the broader religious community providing further support.

Where strict, harsh and repressive ethics are taught, we may find ourselves in perpetual guilt and shame, seeking material gains and power as sources of satisfaction in our lives.

> *In times long ago a couple would raise sheep for clothing and food. They spun the thread, wove the cloth and made the clothes; and the pride in all their achievements and their feeling of being needed was a bulwark against the emotional conflicts which this generation builds up.*
>
> *Now you can make a telephone call or push a button and all your bodily needs are cared for, and your soul feels cheated unless you find a non-material reason for being needed...*
>
> – Alice Steadman [1040]

However, rigid religious teachings may make it difficult to deal with emotional and relationship issues. We may feel that to be angry or to have other negative feelings is wrong or sinful and may seek to avoid awareness of feeling them.

Eugene Gendlin points out that we do many things to avoid dealing with our feelings because they make us uncomfortable. If they really make us uncomfortable, we may make a habit of avoiding particular ones, or may generalize and avoid feelings altogether. This works well to reduce our discomfort in the short run but leads to addictions of all sorts in the long run. Drinking, smoking, sex, shopping, compulsive working can all be ways of keeping our minds busy and avoiding feelings.

Peter Campbell and Edwin McMahon take Gendlin's work into spiritual dimensions. They point out that spirituality can function in the same way as any of these addictions. For instance, they warn about 'spiritualities of control.'

> There are spiritualities and spiritual exercises that can best be described as spiritualities of control. They easily become part of our arsenal of process-skipping devices. They protect us from change and, therefore, become a piece of the system that firmly locks addictive patterns in place. Their goal is not process but containment – the polar opposite of a healthy openness to grace.[1041]

Further problems arise at the boundaries of our religious community's interactions with the rest of the world. While firm faith in our religious beliefs works well within our own community, providing moral guidance and structure that maintain social order, this 'hardening of the oughteries' leads to serious conflicts when we are confronted by people of other faiths. This is all the more a problem when they, too, hold to Stage 1 or 2 belief systems.

This is the core issue that has placed the Christian Right and Muslim Fundamentalist communities in conflict. Each side is absolutely certain that it is right and the other is wrong.

Living in Stages 3, 4, and 5 invites increasing levels of personal spiritual awareness. This frees us to have personal choice in our lives, both in our spiritual and in our moral choices. It invites each of us to listen to our personal inner spiritual voice, connecting through our faith in the inner gnowing that whispers in our ears of the rightness and wrongness or our wishes, impulses and actions. Again, where we come from a place of heart, love, and compassion – doing to others as we would have them do unto us – we make this world an ever better place to live in. Each person in these levels takes responsibility for her or his own choices and thus has to bear the consequences and lessons of free will. Our personal spiritual lessons become ever more our own – rather than relying on obedience to articles of faith that were crafted many centuries ago and continue today to be decided by others for us.

> With this faith we will be able to hew out of the mountain of despair a stone of hope.
>
> – Dr. Martin Luther King, Jr. [1042]

While this may free us from rigid fundamentalist dictates, it leaves us open to the excesses of following our baser instincts, impulses and poor judgment – with no moral compass to guide us. Logic and reason may become our guiding star. This holds the danger of ignoring the guidance of our hearts and spirits, pursuing gods of mammon and power as our measures of personal achievement and. satisfaction. This has contributed to the excesses of the modern world's domination over nature – for the greedy benefits of human exploitation, at the cost of irreplaceable natural resources and irretrievable extinction of animal and plant species; and exploitation of the human resources of those in our own country and those in other nations who are at the mercy of people at the helms of ships of state and of multinational bulldozers – again greedily amassing monetary resources and exploiting the human resources that are helpless to defend against their depredations.

Sadly, the same depredations against nature and our fellow humans are often fostered by values supported and encouraged by Stage 1 and 2 faith. This occurs through the culture of elitism that follows from faith in being a 'chosen people' – which legitimates the exploitation and devastation of those who are 'others.' It is worsened by authoritarian styles of leadership that leave leaders and flock convinced that any questioning or opposition to their views are simply due to lack of faith in the beliefs of the chosen.

> *We should take care not to make the intellect our god; it has, of course, powerful muscles, but no personality.*
> — Albert Einstein

My personal preference is to work towards levels 5 to 6. I believe Western society as a whole has to do this – with much greater social responsibility, and to teach our children how to make ethical and moral choices with values built on personal spiritual awareness, if we want to have any hope of surviving.

As one approaches Stage 6, where one *is* part of everything – not just holding firm beliefs *about* being a child of the universe – then moral and ethical behaviors are a natural part of the way the world is and must be. One simply moves personally in the flow of that cosmic stream of love and compassion for every living thing – including Gaia and beyond. One is not separate from the rest of the world. Harming any part of the world would be unthinkable as this would be harming a part of oneself.

> *Faith is the opening of all sides and every level of one's life to the Divine in-flow.*
> — Rev. Martin Luther King Jr.

Choices and consequences of where we elect to dwell *collectively* in the stages of faith

Throughout history, collective beliefs have shaped societal perceptions, conceptualizations and interactions with the worlds of nature, nationality and spirituality. Today, our collective beliefs are crucial to the survival of life as we know it. Problems of overpopulation, depletion of resources, and pollution threaten to destroy our planet. The stages of faith that prevail may determine the outcome of how we face and deal with these challenges.

Where preferences have been towards Stages 1 and 2, authoritarian forms of government have prevailed. Kings and Caliphs, popes, mullahs and rabbis interpret religious doctrines and dictate moral and social rules, which then reflect into the social and economic attitudes and actions of cultural groups and nations. The leaders' benevolence or selfishness, wisdom or foolishness dictate and control to a great extent the ways in which their subjects act.

In monolithic and dictatorial systems, leaders will encourage perpetuation of Stage 1 and 2 beliefs as these help them to strengthen and maintain their personal and institutional powers. Meta-rules and regulations are developed that discourage any questioning of the leaders' decision-making powers or of their rights to enforce these.

With enlightened leadership, even though leaders rule through Stage 1 and 2 faith, entire civilizations may flourish and grow. The Egyptians, Mayans, Chinese, Japanese and Europeans have seen decades or even hundreds of years where peace prevailed, economies expanded and the arts and sciences blossomed under authoritarian rule. The danger, however, is that with self-seeking and selfish leadership, the rich and powerful may pursue ever more personal gains at the expense of their subjects, and ever more despotic control over them. Western societies appear to be moving in this direction.

Self-interests are dominant and held with Stage 1 and 2 levels of faith. We see this in most politicians, whose time frame and primary focus of concern ranges only as far as their next election, and in multinational corporations, whose motivation is to extract the greatest profits from their business. These politicians and corporations ignore the needs of the majority of people in their own nations and baldly exploit the resources of nations other than their own.

The further we move towards and into Stages 5 and 6 of faith the more we are likely to adopt and pursue a spiritual path of accepting and promoting the inherent worth, dignity, and brotherhood of mankind; of knowing that we are a part of Gaia and will only harm ourselves if we do not honor and protect her integrity.[1043]

The brain, the mind, and spirituality

> *If the human brain was so simple that we could understand it, we would be so simple that we couldn't.*
> — Emerson Pugh

Science has shown that various types of perceptions, emotions, and thoughts are associated with particular structures in the brain. Abnormalities in brain structure or in brain neurochemicals correlate with disturbances in sensory perceptions, feeling and thinking. Any of these may be altered by the introduction of drugs or by electrical stimulation of the brain. The mind is therefore believed by many to be solely the product of brain activity.

Healers, intuitives, meditators, and religions in many societies have suggested that mind and spirit exist as primary entities and forces, manifesting into the material world through the body.

Modern science has taken us away from the religious dogmas that dominated earlier centuries. In doing so, it has suggested that spirituality is an invention of religion, a series of pre-scientific myths created for lack of better alternatives to explain the processes of birth, nature, and death.

Danah Zohar and Ian Marshall suggest several points of reference along this spectrum:

Dualism proposes that there is a physical world, of which the brain is a part, and a completely separate world of consciousness. René Descartes is the most famous proponent of this view although he believed that God was the source of all consciousness. Modern proponents of this view, such as Sir John Eccles, a Nobel laureate in neurobiology, and Karl Popper, a philosopher, continue to suggest separate realms of matter and mind.

Eliminative materialism, championed by philosopher Daniel Dennett, holds that there is no consciousness outside of the activity of neurons in the brain. As there are billions of neurons, and countless interconnections between them, the sum of their collective activity is beyond calculation.

Soft materialists, such as Francis Crick, allow that consciousness exists as an entity of sorts but still tie it to brain functions. The brain is capable of abstractions beyond those of any computer ever devised, and more complex by far. At present we cannot explain the mind solely on the basis of neuronal function, but soft materialists believe that some day we will.

Property dualists propose that consciousness and matter may be two aspects of an underlying basic substance. Consciousness is the product of neuro-electrical oscillations, but still basically dependent on the activity of the material brain. Coherent neural oscillations at 40 Hz (cycles per second) frequencies are suggested to be a basis for universal consciousness, which would represent resonations of many brains at this frequency.[1044]

David Chalmers, following the theories of the philosopher, Bertrand Russell,[1045] suggest that *proto-consciousness* can be found as a fundamental property associated with all matter, similar to mass, location, charge and spin. Everything in the universe participates in consciousness as an inherent aspect of its being.

My own understanding of the universe has grown to include a universal, collective consciousness, based on the clear reports of countless gifted intuitives and healers, and on my own personal intuitive awareness.

Other scientists are focusing on parts of the brain that have been found to relate to spiritual awareness. Positron emission topography, a sophisticated way of obtaining images of brain activity, reveals that particular parts of the temporal lobes of the brain are active when our minds are focused on religious and spiritual issues.[1046] When some of these areas are stimulated by epileptic fits or by the insertion of electrodes into the brain, people report spiritual experiences. This is now being called *the God spot* of the brain.

This has led many researchers to assume that spirituality is simply the activity of these portions of the brain, including Zohar and Marshall.

> *Spiritual experiences are so consistent across cultures, across time, and across faiths that it suggests a common core that is likely a reflection of structures and processes in the human brain.*
> – David Wulff [1047]

Even though they go only this far in considering roots of spirituality, Zohar and Marshall have compiled a marvelous discussion of *spiritual intelligence*, suggesting that spiritual awareness derives from brain activity but that the sum of brain activity is more than the total of its parts. While they acknowledge the inspirational nature of spirituality, they ignore the evidence of mind extending beyond the brain – what Larry Dossey has termed *non-local consciousness*. They make no mention of the wealth of research, covered in earlier chapters of this book, suggesting that mind and spirit can exist separately from body and brain.

To summarize the brain-mind discussion succinctly: Materialism says that the brain creates the mind. Idealism proposes that mind creates all of matter, including the brain.

My own view is that the brain, along with the body, is like a TV set that transforms spiritual awareness/universal consciousness into personal awareness/ consciousness. None of the evidence of brain or chemical malfunctions disrupting consciousness contradicts this theory. If a transistor malfunctions in the TV set, then reception is impaired. This does not mean the TV set is the origin of the images on the screen. So it is with the brain and consciousness.[1048] The universality of spiritual experiences and the similarities in individual reports across diverse cultures suggest there is an objective validity to experiences of the transcendent.

Spirituality, religion and healing

Rachel Naomi Remen points out that it is difficult to define what 'spiritual' means by addressing it directly. It seems easier to point to what it is not.

The spiritual does not require definitions of morality and the rightness or wrongness of various issues. It is often attributed to divine prescriptions, but when one considers the range of cultural definitions of God's will, one may find this is more a reflection of cultural and social traditions. Religious views tend to be exclusive, suggesting that one view is right and another wrong.

> Yet the spiritual is profoundly non-judgmental and non-separative. The spiritual does not vary from time to time because it is not within time. Spirit is unchanging.[1049]

The spiritual does not require definitions of ethical values. These are society's applications of its moral codes in everyday life.

The spiritual may manifest through psychic awarenesses but it is not restricted to these perceptions. Psychic perceptions do not provide proof of spirituality because the spiritual is perceived and known in its own right. The spiritual refers to a direct awareness, an inner gnowing that

> ... is not separative. A deep sense of the spiritual leads one to trust not one's own lonely power but the great flow or pattern manifested in all life, including our own. We become not manipulator but witness.[1050]

Remen continues with the observation that religions may introduce one to spiritual awareness through teachings and practices.

> ... Religion is a bridge to the spiritual – but the spiritual lies beyond religion. Unfortunately in seeking the spiritual we may become attached to the bridge rather than crossing over it.
>   The most important thing in defining spirit is the recognition that spirit is an essential need of human nature. There is something in all of us that seeks the spiritual. This yearning varies in strength from person to person but it is always there in everyone. And so, healing becomes possible. Yet there is a culture-wide tendency to deny the spiritual – to delegate it at best, to ignore it at worst. In trying to point to it with a definition, I hope to initiate a kind of questioning of the role of spirit in health, in health care and in life.[1051]

Spirituality is an important aspect of spiritual healing. In all likelihood, every lesson in life is a step toward our spiritual development. When consciously perceived, spirituality may include: an intuitive acceptance of higher levels of awareness and an openness to exploring them; an awareness of a guiding, higher intelligence within oneself and of an all-knowing, all-loving intelligence beyond; a connectedness, respect and reverence for all living things; and/or a sense of duty to contribute in some way towards the betterment of the world. In years past, religious practices were the primary road to such inner awareness. Spiritual growth today (especially in the West) is often sought through meditative, yogic, transpersonal psychotherapeutic, psychedelic and other practices as well as through religious study and practices.

Biological energy interventions can lead to spiritual awareness. This can occur as a rising of *kundalini* energy, spontaneously or after practices of yoga and meditation. Eastern meditative and healing traditions tell us that kundalini is an energy residing at the base of the spine, coiled like a snake, ready to rise through the spinal cord when we reach a certain level of psychospiritual development.[1052] The rising of kundalini energy is a major spiritual transformation, usually accompanied by major spiritual awakenings, and often by intense physical symptoms as well (vertigo, headaches, pains, and other sensations in various parts of the body, and more). People who are not prepared or who do not understand kundalini processes may mistake this for a psychotic decompensation.

Both healers and healees often develop spirituality in the process of healing. The healer is healed along with the healee.[1053] In part, this is an aspect of meditative *centering*, or quieting of the mind, whereby healers enter healing states. In part it derives from the awe inspired by healings. More importantly, this draws from the deep inner rivers of cosmic love that accompany opening oneself to the All. Since healees experience this as well as healers, *healing engenders a spirituality in and of itself.* Healing also addresses spiritual levels of dis-ease, such as a lack of purpose or meaning in life. It engenders a spirituality through looking inward, through learning to trust the still, quiet voice inside that knows truths that are beyond linear truths.

Spatial metaphors are always dangerous, though unavoidable, in
Theology. In space if A is touching B then B must be touching A. In the
spiritual world this is not so. God is near me (or rather in) me, and yet
I may be far from God because I may be far from my own true self.
                                                                    – C. E. Rolt

We have tended in Western society to separate the physical body from the
transcendent spirit for several centuries. In many parts of the world, throughout
recorded history, a more wholistic view was held – addressing body, mind and
spirit as one entity.

> *The cure of a part should not be attempted without treatment of the whole.*
> *No attempt should be made to cure the body without the soul, and, if the*
> *head and body are to be healthy, you must begin by curing the mind. That*
> *is the first thing. Let no man persuade you to cure the head, until he has*
> *first given you his soul to be cured. For this is the great error of our day in*
> *the treatment of the human body, that physicians first separate the soul*
> *from the body.*
>   – Plato

That healing the body can lead to spirituality is seen most clearly in the
biofeedback therapy of Elmer and Alyce Green.[1054] They point out:

> At any level transformation may be usefully defined as a self-induced
> (autogenic) movement toward greater health – physical, emotional, mental,
> or spiritual... [O]n occasion a patient gets in touch with the deeper (higher)
> levels of being by contacting in themselves what seems to be the True Self
> (to use the Zen expression), and then they talk of spiritual feelings and
> insights.

The Greens base their understanding of this process in the Patanjali system of
yoga, in which

> [E]verything in the cosmos consists of mind and its modifications[1055]...
> [All] the body is in the mind, though not all the mind is in the body...
> [T]he various energies and substances are in reality a continuum...
> biofeedback-aided psychophysiologic training can 'open' the normally-
> closed body/emotions door in the brain which leads to awareness of
> normally- unconscious processes in the spectrum of being.
> Aurobindo... suggested that if we are embarrassed by the word *spirit*, then
> the thing to do is not use it. Instead think of spirit as the subtlest form of
> matter. On the other hand, he said, if we are not embarrassed by that word,
> then we can refer to 'matter' as the densest form of spirit.

Taking the reverse perspective, from a spiritual vantage point, the world we live
in is but a small part of a vaster, spiritual universe.

> *Matter is the vehicle for the manifestation of Soul on this plane of*
> *existence, and Soul is the vehicle on a higher plane for the manifestation*
> *of Spirit, and these three are a Trinity synthesized by Life, which pervades*
> *them all.*
>
> – Alice Bailey [1056]

My personal spiritual experiences

I have been disaffected with much of what I experience in conventional religious practices. I find many who are similarly disappointed with what they experience as unmeaningful, rote rituals and traditions devoid of spirituality in their churches and synagogues. Others are satisfied with their religious teachings and practices and draw deep and satisfying nurturance for their spiritual selves within these institutions.

> *Any religion...is for ever in danger of petrifaction into mere ritual and*
> *habit, though ritual and habit be essential to religion.*
>
> – T.S. Eliot [1057]

> *[E]very form of authoritarian or highly-organized society is inimical to*
> *individual spiritual evolution, because it prevents the individual person*
> *from expressing and therefore facing his true self from which experience*
> *alone comes the desire for his own spiritual growth.*
>
> – Joan Cooper [1058]

In contrast with this, my personal spiritual experiences have been wonderfully enriching. As I mentioned in the introduction, I was raised in a non-observant Jewish home, with religion experienced more as a cultural and historical tradition than a spiritual influence. This was reinforced by living in the secular sector of Israel for four years as a child and for six years as a parent. For most Israelis the Bible is just their local history book. It is marvelously grounding, however, to live in a land in which one's people put down historical roots over many centuries. My parents preferred to observe the 'Thou shalts' of Judaism and to ignore most of the religious (not the social) 'Thou shalt nots.' During my university and medical school years I became a Freudian agnostic, believing that God was the creation of man's reluctance to give up parental figures and to deny the finality of death.

A long series of life lessons gradually shifted my perceptions and beliefs. Particularly helpful have been: receiving psychotherapy, healing and intuitive readings; self-healing, especially with WHEE;[1059] being a psychotherapist, healer, lecturer and workshop leader – teaching what I am learning myself; reading omniverously; studying and participating in healing research; quenching a thirst for spirituality at the deep wells of my inner being through meditative practices, imbibing from the springs of experience of diverse cultural traditions. I find that participation in a group is helpful but that no one group seems to be just right for me all of the time. It is difficult for me to stay in touch with that edge of beingness that connects me with the All. At times repetitive rituals help; at other times these are too lullingly familiar and a change of routine brings me back to a connection with my higher self. Giving and receiving healing help me to connect with that higher level of being which I find deeply nurturing and satisfying.

I resonate with the views expressed by many spiritual teachers in Native American traditions. For instance, Carl Hammerschlag, a psychiatrist who works with Native Americans, writes:

> *Indians have a very different concept of where you worship. The whole earth is the temple. Any place you stand is a church. The tipi is a nesting enclosure on the Earth Mother's breast, a place of sharing among a small group. Here each can worship at his or her own time, as the heart directs, in his or her own language.*
>
> I sing my Jewish songs in the tipi, and I wear my father's prayer shawl, the one he wore at his bar mitzvah in Germany. My Indian friends say that it does not matter in what language you sing; there are always at least two people who understand – you and the Creator.[1060]

I do not recommend such a path for everyone. It may be that it is actually good only for a minority of people, perhaps those who are more inner-directed. I do recommend that people seek to make spirituality a part of their lives. I believe, along with many other healers, that the development of spirituality is the most important contribution of healing and that the physical effects of healing are of secondary importance.

I bring my spirituality into the therapy room as it feels appropriate. At first I did so with considerable hesitation. I was anxious that clients would find this strange and uncomfortable. The opposite has almost always been the case. People welcome discussions of their spiritual lives and draw great inspiration and strength from their inner wisdom, markedly facilitating their psychotherapy. This does not mean that I abandon the many and varied more conventional approaches in my practice. As detailed in *Healing Research,* vols. I and II, wholistic practice addresses body, mind, emotions, relationships (with other people and the environment) and spirit.

> *The physical body is the biofeedback mechanism of the soul.*
> – Len Wisneski

Spiritual transformations

Many believe that the attainment of spirituality can bring healings to the problems (material, physical, emotional, and social) of individuals and of mankind as a whole. Most healers can give examples of ordinary persons whose spirituality lifted them above their problems. There are also those whose spirituality permeates deeper into their beings and their relationships and leads to their relinquishing hurts and angers through forgiveness and love (not merely setting aside or burying their negative feelings), producing dramatic transformations in their personalities and inspiring others around them. There appears to be a common denominator here with the processes of psychotherapy and meditation – in a relinquishing of old habits of perception and reaction in order to allow space for unconditional acceptance and expressions of healthier and more healing responses.

One can misuse spirituality, seeking a *spiritual bypass* of problems. That is, people may be engaged in spiritual development but may ignore gross psychological challenges and relationship problems that could be the most important lessons for them in their lives. It is also possible to take a passive, fatalistic view, saying that misfortunes and evil are part of God's plan – using this as an excuse for not challenging negativity and evil in the world. The words of Alexander Pope[1061] confront this attitude:

> *Know then thyself, presume not God to scan;*
> *The proper study of mankind is man.*

One may engage in the rituals of religiosity rather than in spirituality or may compartmentalize spirituality to Sundays and holy days or to the healing sanctuary, but not alter one's selfish or even sinful pursuits on weekdays. On more subtle levels, when one is engaged in spiritual development and ignores one's *shadow* side, negativity may accumulate in the unconscious, lurking there till it finds targets for its expression.[1061] Worse, people may redirect and project their hurts and angers through the excuse of spirituality against others who do not share their views. There have probably been nearly as many killed in these misdirected perversions of spirituality as there have been from plagues and other illnesses.

> *The false God changes suffering into violence. The true God changes violence into suffering.*
>
> – Simone Weil

Modern day healers are not exempt from all of these pitfalls. Particularly dangerous is the allure of power through healing. Healers often go through stages where they enjoy showing off their powers, boosting their self-images and feeling special. Healing organizations may do much to promote the good that healing offers but the allure of power may also corrupt.

Teachers of healing are not exempt from these problems.

Jack Kornfield observed:

> Because awareness does not automatically transfer itself from one dimension of our life to another, compartments remain in the areas where our fears, our wounds, our defenses are deepest. Thus, we encounter graceful masters of tea ceremonies who remain confused and retarded in intimate relations, or yogis who can dissolve their bodies into light, but whose wisdom vanishes when they enter the marketplace.[1062]

There is a paradox in explorations of spirituality in the material world. We seek to become one with the All, yet can only know that oneness from contrast with the splits of good and evil, material and spiritual, and so on. Our experiences with the shadow can be what awakens us to the light.

Illness may bring us to find our spirituality by forcing us to become aware of the shadow within us:

> *... We humans, as microcosms, are reflections of the universe and contain the sum of all principles of being within our consciousness. Our path through the world of polarities obliges us to manifest these principles that are latent within us, so that we can become progressively more aware of ourselves with their aid. But recognition demands polarity, which in turn forces us constantly to decide. Every decision splits polarity into an accepted and a rejected pole. The accepted aspect is translated into behavior and so integrated at the conscious level. The rejected pole is banished to the shadows and compels our further attention by apparently coming back at us from 'out there.' Illness is a specific and very common expression of this general law. Under the terms of it, aspects of the shadow are precipitated into bodily form, where they are somatized as symptoms. Through the medium of the body, each symptom forces us, despite our best endeavors to the contrary, to manifest some principle that we have deliberately chosen not to live out, and so brings us back into balance. The symptom is the physical, bodily expression of whatever is lacking in our consciousness. The symptom makes us honest by making visible that which we have repressed.*
> – Dethlefsen and Dahlke [1063]

Numbers of psychotherapists, healers and researchers confirm this. They observe that people with cancer and other serious illnesses who seek understanding of their problems may find healing and spirituality growing through engagement with their inner searches for meanings behind their challenging life issues.[1064] Such healing may put them in touch with what their bodies are saying; with the psychological and relational issues around their symptoms; and with transpersonal awarenesses. The illness becomes a friend and wise counselor that stops them from being stuck in their habitual grooves of routines with only dim awareness of what they are about. Their illness forces them to reassess all aspects of their lives. It challenges them to seek, create, and sing their own song rather than to merely run on automatic pilot with their childhood programming, march to tunes chosen by others, keep in step with habits of internalized shoulds and shouldn'ts, or adhere to sacrificial niceties that are meant to please others rather than satisfy their own true needs. Their illnesses waken them to their inner demons of old hurts that were locked away, deep in the dungeons of their unconscious minds but that have gotten loose and are shouting and fighting to be released from their imprisonment.

Releasing the old behavioral patterns and hurts frees up energies to move forward with people's emotional, relational, and spiritual development. When their energies are not so invested in keeping their hurts from conscious awareness and preventing further anticipated hurts, they have the space to allow more positive experiences into their lives. Some of these may include spiritual awakening, especially when psi healing or simply confrontation with their mortality brings people in touch with their higher selves and with transpersonal awarenesses.

Broadening perspectives through spirituality

When we explore spirituality we begin to appreciate holographic ways of being in the world. If we are all subject to the influences of cosmic fields and energies, then the cosmos reciprocally is influenced by each element within it. Each individual healing thus brings the cosmos closer to being healed. One cannot remove a cup of hurt from the ocean of existence without every other atom of the waters in that infinite sea moving over to accommodate.[1065]

> *"I cannot define for you what God is," Jung wrote to me just before he died. "I can only say that my work has proved empirically that the pattern of God exists in every man, and that this pattern has at its disposal the greatest of all energies for transformation and transfiguration of his natural being. Not only the meaning of his life but his renewal and that of his institutions depend on his conscious relationship with this pattern in his collective unconscious."*
> — Laurens van der Post [1066]

The religious and philosophical questions of good and evil, light and darkness, positivity and negativity arise when healers approach problems of health and illness.

> *There can be the placing of a man in a sour and ill-favored soul when in more sunny ground he would never have succeeded in growing certain tendrils of the soul, the need for which he had failed to see until, through hardship, they began to spring forth, bringing unexpected beauty to his shape...*
> — Paul Beard [1067]

> *... Anger cannot occur unless you believe that you have been attacked, that your attack is justified in return, and that you are in no way responsible for it. Given these three wholly irrational premises, the equally irrational conclusion that a brother is worthy of attack rather than of love must follow. What can be expected from insane premises except an insane conclusion? The way to undo an insane conclusion is to consider the sanity of the premises on which it rests. You cannot be attacked, attack has no justification, and you are responsible for what you believe.*
> — A Course in Miracles

When people suffer from illness, they often wonder whether they might have brought their plight upon themselves through some wrongdoing or sin. Questions of good and evil must be considered in the context of one's basic assumptions about such issues. Shakespeare observed, "There is nothing good or bad, but thinking makes it so."

If illness is believed to be punishment for lack of religious faith, then only absolution and assertions and affirmations of faith within the religious fold can offer healing.

If illnesses are viewed as physical and/or energetic imbalances, then healing is the restoration of homeostatic balance – to the range of physiological functioning that is life-sustaining and required for life to proceed in a normal manner. This may be achieved through a boost to the body's defenses and coping mechanisms, or through the diminishing of harmful influences (such as a reduction in the potency of infecting organisms or environmental toxins). In this instance healing is the fixing of mechanical, biochemical, or energetic systems that have gone awry.

If illness is seen as divine punishment for moral, ethical, or religious transgressions, then healing may be a release from these punishments. This may occur through release of anger, jealousy and guilt; through healees reaching forgiveness towards themselves and others; and through forgiveness facilitated by the healer. Ultimately, people must forgive and thereby heal themselves.

> *Forgiveness can be a complex process. It's not something we decide to do as much as something we move toward or find ourselves growing into. No one should be told to forgive someone else or be expected to do so. Forgiveness involves a much deeper experience of finding inner peace along paths unique to each person.*
> – Kay Pranis et al. [1068]

The 12-step programs of Alcoholics Anonymous and related 'Anonymous' groups are outstanding examples of promoting spiritual awareness in these ways. [1069]

If illnesses are seen as messages from healees' unconscious minds, alerting the conscious mind to underlying dis-eases and tensions, then healing may be a release of old hurts that are stored in the unconscious, and an initiation of further emotional and social maturation.

> *What we call evil is simply ignorance bumping its head in the dark.*
> – Henry Ford

In either of the last two cases, healing heightens spiritual awareness. Many healers believe that this is the most important effect of healing.

> *Suffering is like the Grand Canyon. If we said, "It's so pretty, we must protect it from wind and storm," it would never be sculpted by the wind and we would never appreciate its beauty... If you don't suffer, you don't*

grow. You must experience sorrow, loss, tears and anger. Every time
you go through those, you grow, you progress. There is nothing more
important in life for your progress. No one will make progress if
everything is presented to him on a silver platter. No one.
– Elisabeth Kübler-Ross [1070]

Some have found it hard to believe in God when they see so much cruelty and suffering in the world. They ask, "How could there be a God if he allows terrible pain, like the Holocaust or like the slaughters of innocent men, women and children in Russia, Iran and Africa?"   Rabbi Harold Kushner has given much thought to these questions.

> ... I recognize His limitations. He is limited in what He can do by laws of nature and by the evolution of human nature and human moral freedom. I no longer hold God responsible for illnesses, accidents, and natural disasters, because I realize that I gain little and I lose so much when I blame God for these things. I can worship a God who hates suffering but cannot eliminate it, more easily than I can worship a God who chooses to make children suffer and die, for whatever exalted reason. [1071]

Western society tends to fear death as the *grim reaper* that terminates existence. Our materialistic culture teaches that our total existence will be reduced ultimately to ashes. Spiritual teachings, primarily through religious institutions, are denigrated as folk tales and wishful thinking. Little wonder that our society has a great fear of dying and of death – which are two distinct fears.

The fear of dying is often the greater one. We are usually carried off by illnesses, some of which may be uncomfortable or painful. Being afraid of dying, we tend to avoid being around those who are undergoing this transition. The dying are often taken to hospitals, not because there is much hope of keeping them alive but because people are afraid to be near them when they die. Never having witnessed the peace that the process of dying can bring, people are then afraid of death when their turn comes.

Life is real! Life is earnest!
And the grave is not its goal.
Dust thou art, to dust returned,
Was not spoken of the soul.
– Henry Wadsworth Longfellow [1072]

Death as a final termination of existence is usually a frightening prospect. Avoiding what we fear, we distance ourselves from anything that might remind us of death, particularly our own. This becomes a vicious circle, with fears increasing through such avoidances, leading to further avoidances. In traditional societies the family usually takes on the responsibility for preparing the body for burial or cremation. Death is thus a familiar, first-hand experience. In Western society our fears of death have spawned a major undertakers' industry that protects us from having to deal with dead bodies – but also keeps us from desensitizing ourselves from our fears of death.

He's not dead. He's electroencephalographically challenged.
– Anonymous

When we are not fearful of death and dying, life may be seen as a preparation for death. In such a context, we are encouraged to appreciate every living moment. The focus of Western society on doing rather than on being leaves little time for contemplation that opens into awareness of each moment. With this awareness, illness may be a healing of your spiritual being, reminding you to make the most of each moment of your limited time on earth. People with serious diseases have told me, "I've actually come to feel glad I have this illness. It has helped me reassess my priorities and to appreciate what is truly important." [1073]

For those who believe in an afterlife, death is merely a transition to another realm. Reports from NDEs, mediumistic communications, and reincarnation memories consistently describe death as a peaceful transition into gentler and more unconditionally accepting realms of being. Why the veils of forgetting keep us from full awareness of these other realms is still a mystery. Lucan[1074] suggests, "The gods conceal from men the happiness of death that they may endure life."

The existence of some sort of death and rebirth cycle appears likely if we accept the evidence from the research reviewed in this volume – on spiritual and mystical awarenesses through OBEs, pre-death, near-death and deathbed experiences, apparition and mediumistic research, and on reincarnation itself. Reincarnation suggests that each lifetime is a complex lesson. We are given series of challenges in actions, reactions and interactions with other people. If we make poor choices and hurt other people, we get to repeat the lessons in other lifetimes, often with the same persons but in reversed roles. If you were a domineering husband in a previous life, making your wife miserable with your demands, you might be a browbeaten housewife in this lifetime. Thus we may learn from counter-experiences about the pains we inflicted on others, and, at the same time, they may have the challenge of choosing forgiveness rather than hatred and revenge. If we meet these challenges successfully and learn our lessons thoroughly, we may advance in our inner development to the point that we no longer need or wish to incarnate, but may continue our lessons on purely spirit planes of existence.

God rewards us for successfully meeting a challenge by presenting us with a greater challenge.
– Anonymous

Illness, pain, suffering, evil and all the negatives of life take on very different perspectives if one accepts reincarnation. Karma, the lesson-debts/obligations carried over from one life to another, is a wonderfully wise teacher. Karma does not dictate the paths of our lives as some fatalists suggest. On the contrary, it offers us challenging choices. People commonly speak of *retributive* karma, in which we suffer the consequences of our sins from past lives. It is often more helpful to consider *restitutive* or *rebalancing* karma, in which we learn lessons in this life that help us to appreciate both sides of a situation or relationship.

After physical death the Being of Light is said to review people's performances in the classrooms of life. The review is made with unconditional acceptance, a love so great that it moves people to tears in the telling of it – after a Near-Death Experience. No judgments are made, except by each person upon her- or himself. All is simply grist for the mill on high.

Suicide and euthanasia are then options that might appear attractive under difficult and painful circumstances. As a psychiatric psychotherapist I have helped many people deal with suicidal thoughts. In many instances they reached a deeper place of understanding where suicide is no longer an attractive option. The despair of depression often lifts with psychotherapy and antidepressant herbs or medications, along with confrontations of relationships and situations that are stressful. Many have come back to me, saying, "I'm so glad I didn't pull the plug on my life! I can see now that I was scared of confronting my problems and didn't see another way out. I was so surprised when I did confront them that there actually were acceptable ways through or around my problems. Now I also see how much I would have hurt other people around me if I had done that. I have so much to live for now, that I didn't appreciate before!"

A few have done their best assessments and decided not to continue with the life of disappointments and tortures they were experiencing. While I don't encourage this choice, neither do I condemn it. I do everything I can to help look at current stresses, past traumas that have left emotional scars and vulnerabilities, and all the inner and outer resources that can be mustered. I discuss beliefs about the after-life, and the reports from mediums and Near-Death Experiencers who say this is something that is not viewed with favor on the other side. It is said that if you should suicide, you will have to come back again to learn the difficult lessons you have avoided by leaving physical existence prematurely. Lord Alfred Tennyson wrote, "Men, like soldiers, may not quit the post allotted by the Gods." [1075]

For some, the idea of reincarnation is alien or contrary to religious teachings. Evidence reviewed earlier in this book[1076] suggests that we are, indeed, born into a series of many lifetimes for lessons that help us to grow in psychological and spiritual wisdom. The choice of incarnating in each lifetime is partly our own, under the guidance of higher beings. We agree to be children to our parents and parents to our children so that we can give and receive lessons in honorable be-haviors, acceptance and forgiveness. All of this is done, ultimately, with deep love and unconditional acceptance by our higher Selves. It is our little selves that struggle and worry and fret and doubt and fear and vent angers and learn repen-tance and forgiveness and unconditional acceptance all over again.

Karma appears to be influenced by a collective consciousness that participates in the choices of birth and guides us through life, presenting ever greater challenges as we grow and advance in our development. Mystical traditions tell us that with-in this collective consciousness is the awareness of every sentience in the cosmos. This includes the physical cosmos and many dimensions beyond human ken.

Some of the patterns of this collective are intuited through channeled messages and synchronicities – those meaningful coincidences that invite us to look for deeper meanings in situations. Though detailed discussion of synchronicity is beyond the scope of this book, the observations of Jean Shinoda[1077] are apt.[1078]

> An uncanny, meaningful coincidence seems to lead to an awareness of an underlying connecting principle, as synchronistic events evoke an intuitively felt spiritual reality. Conversely, becoming spiritually centered, in touch with the Tao, is associated with the occurrence of positive synchronistic events. Being in touch with the Tao seems to prompt an easy flow of outer events *through* synchronicity. This is the message of religious teachings in both East and West: Seek spiritual values first; whatever is tangibly needed will follow after.

Increased spiritual awareness is felt by many to be another important contribution of healing – in social and economic arenas, on local, national, and global levels. When people open to their spiritual awareness, they feel themselves to be part of a larger whole, including their fellow human beings, other living thing, and Gaia, our planet. Healing on this level includes moral economic policies, respect for the environment, and re-sorting of priorities to include the addressing of spiritual issues in schools, social organizations, and government.

Katya Walter, in a brilliant discussion on the parallels between the genetic coding of DNA and the ancient Chinese divination in the I-Ching, observes,

> Hans Driesch in the 19th century developed a 'vitalist' theory which postulated that some non-physical cause must give life its vital force. He called it *entelechy*[1079] and said it holds a goal toward which the living system is directed. He said it's a non-spatial cause which is, however, enacted into space, and he pointed out that this unknown form of power doesn't contradict the second law of thermodynamics...[1080]
>
>   Unfortunately, in Driesch's day, the mind-bending quirkiness of quantum mechanics had not yet been discovered, and entrenched Newtonian physicists, with their emphasis on hard-headed reality, dismissed his vitalist idea as unsubstantiated wooly-mindedness.[1081]

Katya Walter argues convincingly for a return to acceptance of our intuitive, analog awarenesses. This is not to say that we should abandon linear logic. The best of both ways of experiencing and understanding the world comes from an 'analinear' blend of the two. Walter cites James Lovelock, who argues for an appreciation of humanity's intimate relationship with all the rest of the geobiological system of our planet, *Gaia*. Walter suggests that

> ... In a manner of speaking, we are bacteria in the belly of Gaia. And the scientific community at large is beginning to think that perhaps this may really be so.[1082]
>
> ... Along with living in the bosom of the world's physical body, analog cultures have felt cherished by a world soul, a tissue of invisible connection. Yet this connective, holistic mindset became disparaged in

Western culture ever since the Greek heyday of linear logic began to win out over the mystery cults.[1083]

Personal spiritual awareness brings us back to our connections with Gaia and with the vast realms of spirit that are beyond linear descriptions or explanations. Such awareness is every bit as valid as linear awareness. It puts us in touch with the cosmic awareness of the Infinite Source, and with a dim awareness that we are but a small – though significant – part of a much vaster plan than we shall ever know while we are in our earth bodies.

Societal spirituality

In the same way that individuals work through their karmic lessons families, societies, and global populations have their *collective spiritual development and karma.* There is a sense of a quickening awareness of these matters in modern society.

Out of pain and suffering grow spiritual awareness. Those societies where deep pains have been experienced will have greater collective openness to spirituality.

Our answers to questions of good and evil, pain and suffering, are to be found by looking inward to our higher selves that are aware of all we need to know. Yet this is a search that Western society has generally preferred to avoid and many people find so frightening that they seek every excuse not to look inward. Rabbinic lore holds that the truly brave man is the one who masters his inner spirit. Others have echoed this thought.

> *That is at bottom the only courage that is demanded of us: to have courage for the most strange, the most singular and the most inexplicable that we may encounter. That mankind has in this sense been cowardly has done life endless harm; the experiences that are called 'visions,' the whole so-called 'spirit-world,' death, all those things that are so closely akin to us, have by daily parrying been so crowded out of life that the senses with which we could have grasped them are atrophied. To say nothing of God.*
> – Rainer Maria Rilke [1084]

The idea of an all-knowing God is disturbing to some. "If God knows everything that will happen," they say, "doesn't that mean that every step we take is predetermined or predestined?" Life would indeed be a boring senseless play and we mechanical puppets upon its stage if this were so.

> *There once was an old man who said, "Damn!*
> *It is borne in upon me that I am*
> *An engine that moves*
> *In determinate grooves,*
> *I'm not even a bus, I'm a tram.*
> – Maurice Evan Hare

It seems far more reasonable that God gives us free will to make our choices, and does not interfere – even when we make outrageous errors – although God can see (as can humans sometimes – through precognitive glimpses) which choices we will make. Both ends of the spectrum of healings, the more dramatic ones and those which produce no apparent results, underline this view.

> *I dreamed I was in God's department store, where every one of His products were sold. I approached the sales clerk angel, saying, "I'm looking for the fruits of the spirit. Where can I find them?"*
> *"I'm sorry," said the angel, "but I can't help you."*
> *I was outraged. "I must have them." I shouted. "In place of injustice, hatred, killing and illness, I must find peace, healing, love, forgiveness, and acceptance. You must have these somewhere in God's store."*
> *The angel quietly answered, "We don't sell fruits. Only seeds."*
> – Anonymous

> *Life is like a game of cards. The hand that is dealt you represents determinism; the way you play it is free will.*
> – Nehru

> *Miracles are both beginnings and endings, and so they alter the temporal order. They are always affirmations of rebirth, which seem to go back but really go forward. They undo the past in the present, and thus release the future.*
> – A Course in Miracles

Healings that bring about very rapid effects, called *miraculous* healings by some, bring us to spirituality through their startling changes. Tumors and indolent, suppurating infections disappear instantaneously and totally. Broken bones are knit. People come out of comas, lose their paralyses and other neurological disorders. We find these healings so extraordinary that we feel only the intervention of God, Christ or some other heavenly spirit could have brought them about.

Healings that bring about no apparent results whatever may open us to question more deeply the meanings of life – thereby bringing us to another side of spiritual awareness.

Healings that bring about gradual or partial effects are, to my view, just as likely to enhance spiritual awareness – though this may occur at as gradual a pace as the healing changes that occur. Gradual healings challenge us to examine many aspects of our situation. These might include the multi-faceted relationships between people in need and their states of health and illness; their congenital endowments and family miasms; their relationships with infecting organisms and toxins in the environment; their bodies' homeostatic mechanisms (via the neuroendocrine and immune systems); their propensities to trauma and their bodies' natural mending abilities; their abilities to deal with growths gone awry; their mental attitudes, their emotional makeup and their social relationships; and their bodies' degenerations with aging. For, in truth, birth, growth, reproduction, and the transition through death are all miracles in their own right.

Spirituality in everyday life

In assessing and explaining our spiritual awarenesses we cannot be objective. It is impossible to free ourselves from our conceptual and physical limitations to know spirituality cognitively.

> *Man's mind is a mirror of a universe that mirrors man's mind.*
> – Joseph Chilton Pearce [1085]

The best way to know spirituality is through life's experiences, through our *beingness*, our inner gnowing of a deeper reality than that of our outer senses.

> *We can worship God by studying the beauty of His handiwork.*
> – Petrarch

Spirituality is compartmentalized into religious observances by many in Western society. Eastern meditation teachers say that at the end of spiritual development we return to our daily tasks of chopping wood and fetching water. If we are aware of our integral part in this mystery of life, of resonating in our every breath and thought with all of the cosmos, spirituality is in everything we are and do.

If life is a spiritual excursion of the soul into the material world, then all of life is a challenging lesson.

> *... We 'spiritualize' matter. We bring our spirit into the physical aspects of life.*
> – Barbara Brennan [1086]

> *Spirit, which is differentiated from soul in being both the ground and the goal of the process of human evolution, is all encompassing. It is already as it has always been. The spiritual journey is therefore described as one of eternal return, not to a prior condition in time, but to the awareness of unity in reality, despite the appearance of separation.*
> – Frances Vaughan [1087]

> *Whoever does not see God in every place does not see God in any place.*
> – Rabbi Elimelech

In summary

Personal spirituality is a sense of being part of something greater than ourselves. Spiritual healing is one of the paths that regularly open into spiritual awareness –

both in healers and healees. Inasmuch as it is impossible for words to adequately define spiritual experiences, a variety of perspectives provides a better approximation within linear conceptualizations of spirituality.

It may seem to some readers that in discussing spirituality I have gone way out on speculative limbs in this chapter. Let us climb down and ground ourselves in the next chapter in research which shows that religious affiliations and practices may be associated with benefits to our health.

CHAPTER 12

Research on Physical and Emotional Correlates of Religion and Spirituality

Religion and health: Is there an association, is it valid, and is it causal?

– Jeffrey Levin [1088]

The preceding chapters in this book are of great spiritual and philosophical interest. Though they are grounded in research, clearly related to healing, and of value to those exploring their spiritual development, the materialistic skeptic may still ask, "So what difference does any of this make in the physical world in which most of us live?"

First, it is of note that the majority of the US population considers religion to be of great importance to them. A US Gallup Poll reported in 1994 that 96 percent of persons over 18 years old believe in God or in a universal spirit; 90 percent pray; and over 40 percent attend church weekly. [1089]

Second, the majority of physicians in the US feel that religion is important to them and influences their practices. Farr Curlin and colleagues asked a statistical sampling of US physicians about the importance of religion in their lives. Of 2000 physicians surveyed, 90 percent attend religious services at least occasionally (vs. 81% of adults in the general population); 76 percent believe in God; 59 percent believe in some aspect of an afterlife; and 55 percent report their practice of medicine is influenced by their religious beliefs. Comparing this with general population surveys, physicians are more frequently affiliated with minority US religions, less prone to carry religious beliefs into other areas of life (58% vs. 73%); more likely to consider themselves as being *spiritual* rather than *religious* (20% vs. 9%), and more likely to report that they deal with major life problems without reliance on God (61% vs. 29%).[1090] (More on surveys below.)

Third, and most important as related to spiritual healing, Jeffrey Levin, Harold Koenig and colleagues[1091] show that religion is good for our health. They have collected remarkable surveys of hundreds of studies on correlations of religion with physical and emotional health. Most of this chapter is based on these summaries.

Historical Perspectives

A few notes on the social history of Western religion and spirituality are of interest.[1092]

Levin[1093] observes that Maimonides, Wesley, Freud, Jung, Bertrand Russell and other respected authorities identified religion as an influence on health that deserves careful scrutiny.

Emile Durkheim, a French sociologist, was the first to document epidemiological factors in mental health. He found different suicide rates in Protestants, Catholics and Jews. William James pointed out that religious experience could contribute to a 'Healthy Soul' or a 'Sick Soul.' The latter he graphically describes as "...positive and active anguish, a sort of psychic neuralgia wholly unknown to healthy life."

Malinowski delineates distinctions between magic, religion and science. Descartes' separation of mind from body helped shape Western beliefs that the physically measurable world could be believed and trusted, while the subjective, inner worlds could not be 'scientifically verified'. These were important trends in the development of Western civilization, leading to a distancing from religion and spiritual awareness.

At the same time, the industrial and scientific revolutions reinforced a focus on the material world, applying linear definitions, measurements, analyses and manipulations to master nature. The Protestant work ethic, especially through Calvinism, complemented and encouraged the rise of capitalism.[1094] Earning and material wealth became prevalent goals and measures of success.

Sigmund Freud's contribution to the move away from religion was considerable. He explained the belief in God as a projection of a wish for a Father to replace the parents lost when people grow up. Albert Ellis, an influential American psychologist who champions rationality and scathingly disparages subjective awareness, has been another influential exponent against religion. For many years, most American psychologists have similarly denigrated spirituality, accepting that God is the product of wishful thinking or fantasy.

These attitudes have become institutionalized in Western culture. Thinking and outer sensations have received the emphasis in governmental priorities. In social institutions such as schools and libraries, and through selective allocations of research funding, emphasis is given to linear, thinking topics – to the detriment of subjects such as the arts that focus on feelings and intuitions. In medical prioritizations the emphasis has been on physical health, giving minimal emphasis to quality of life on emotional and spiritual levels.

Carl Jung points out that individuals are generally polarized in their preferred modes of experience and expression. People tend towards one or the other of the polarities of thinking vs. feeling and outer senses vs. intuitive, inner senses.[1095] Western society has been so biased towards the thinking/sensation sides of these polarities that the topics of this volume of *Healing Research* are seen by many as second rate and even suspect as imaginary or wishful thinking.[1096] Quoting from Kaplan et al: "With rational ordering, as Geertz phrases it, 'the locus of sacredness was removed from the rooftrees, graveyards, and road-crossings of everyday life and put, in some sense, into another realm where dwelt Jahweh, Logos, Tao, or Brahman,' "[1097]

The trend away from religion is clearly exemplified by Karl Marx, who pointed out how suffering can be produced through social orders that emphasize religious practices. Yet Marx himself argues primarily through linear reasoning that epitomizes Western religious tradition. Carried to its extremes, this has produced the pain and chaos of witch hunts and the Communist experience.

Joseph Campbell, the marvelous master of mythology, pointed out that Western society has been conditioned and biased by monotheism towards *either/or* dichotomies in relating to religious issues. Judao/Christian/Muslim teachings are based on the Bible and Koran which teach that there is one omniscient and omnipotent God and that all other gods are false.[1098] Angels are accepted within these traditions only as messengers of God. Monotheism has led these religions to reject nature spirits as pagan beliefs. An example of this rejection is in monotheism's treatment of Pan, the king of nature spirits on earth. One of the common appearances of Pan is of a large, powerful creature with a human body above the waist, hairy legs and cloven hooves, two horns on his forehead, and a long tail. Christianity has used this very image to portray the Devil – certainly no coincidence.

In traditional cultures the spiritual is very much a part of everyday life. Inner experiences, rituals, and interactions with spirits and gods are as real as outer experiences.[1099]

Campbell (along with others[1100]) also pointed out that Western society is a *masculine-dominated*, mental creation that tends to put down and denigrate the feminine – and with it the feeling and intuitive sides of our relationships with ourselves, each other and the world at large. Campbell suggests that women do not need to compete as men do to assert themselves because in a very basic way – through their ability to bring forth life – they know their lives have the potential to be deeply meaningful. Men, on the other hand, have to create a reason to feel needed and important in life – hence competitiveness, self-interested politics, war and other masculine investments that are very unhealing.

With these attenuations of the vitalizing connection to the spirit inside oneself and in nature, Western culture has suffered an anomie, a lack of direction. Existential and transpersonal psychologies have sought to revitalize our awareness, reintroducing us to spirituality.[1101]

There is now a growing interest in the worlds of spirit and nature.[1102] In part this is fueled by population growth and wanton disregard for limitations of natural resources that threaten the balances of nature and our very survival on the planet. In part this is simply an awakening to the inner voices that speak to all of us if we but listen.[1103] Lorraine Canoe and Tom Porter observe:[1104]

> Righteousness occurs when the people put their minds and emotions in flow with the harmony of the universe and the intentions of the Good Mind, or Great Creator. The principles of righteousness demand that all thoughts of prejudice, privilege or superiority be swept away and that recognition be given to the reality that Creation is intended for the benefit of all equally – even the birds and the animals, the trees and insects, as well as human beings.

This historical review provides a background against which we may better appreciate the vast body of research on religion and healing that until recently has been unrecognized and undervalued by Western science.

Surveys on the importance of religion and spirituality

Surveys of the US population in general, and of people with health problems in particular, find that over 90% believe there is a transcendent Being.[1105] Most people who are ill would welcome their doctors asking them about their religious and spiritual wellbeing.[1106] A survey of family practice physicians showed that 96% feel that spiritual wellbeing is relevant to health.[1107] A Time/CNN poll in 1996 [1108] showed that 82% of Americans believe personal prayers can heal; 73% believe that praying for others is beneficial and can cure; and 77% believe God can help to cure serious illnesses.

A 1984 study showed that 19% of cancer patients supplemented their conventional medical treatments with prayer or spiritual healing.[1109] A survey of woman with breast cancer in support groups of the American Cancer Society found 88% believed Spiritual and religious practices contributed to their being able to cope better with their illness,[1110] Higher numbers yet reported praying to help deal with an acute illness. For instance, 96% of patients reported they prayed prior to surgery.[1111] Many wish that their doctors would pray for and with them.[1112]

Children are regularly taught about religion and spirituality. There is a growing awareness that these elements can be important in the treatment of children.[1113]

Research on religion and healing

Hundreds of studies have explored the relationships between religion and health.[1114]

Correlations of religion with health have been shown for: cardiovascular disease/hypertension,[1115] gastrointestinal disease,[1116] respiratory diseases,[1117] pain,[1118] renal dialysis,[1119] uterine cancer and other cancers,[1120] geriatrics,[1121] genetic abnormalities,[1122] social/psychological health,[1123] clergy,[1124] illness behaviors,[1125] preventive behavior,[1126] and more.[1127] The vast majority of studies show positive correlations of physical and emotional health with religion. For instance, Levin and Schiller[1128] conclude: "If a single statement were to be proffered characterizing the literature on religion and blood pressure, it would be that high religiosity (whether frequent attendance or high self-rating) is associated with lower pressure."

Negative effects may also be observed, especially with exaggerated religious involvement.[1129] Religion can be stressful when it makes excessively stringent demands upon its adherents.

Religion is commonly defined by researchers as *religious affiliation*. Many studies have shown differences between the health of members of various religions. For instance, Jews have been found to have a lower rate of uterine cancer. This is usually attributed to circumcision of Jewish males. Other such studies have focused on Seventh-Day Adventists,[1130] Mormons,[1131] Amish,[1132] Zulus[1133] and others.[1134] The conclusions of numbers of reviewers are that religious affiliation is generally correlated in a positive way with health.[1135] This holds true regardless of the many and varied criteria used by diverse researchers and reviewers in defining religiosity and regardless of disease factors examined.

In general, *the stricter the religions* (e.g., Jews,[1136] Mormons,[1137] Seventh-day Adventists,[1138] and clergy of all faiths[1139]), *the lower the risk of illness* was found. The reader is highly recommended to the original articles for further details and references.

The concept of *religiosity* is being refined,[1140] as it becomes apparent that affiliation alone is only a gross and limited definition of religious involvement.

Kimberly Sherrill and David Larson point out several behaviors, practices and attitudes within a religion that may influence health. For instance, religious *attendance* is a more reliable measure.[1141] A longitudinal study of 720 adults showed that attendance rather than affiliation was correlated with reduced psychological consequences of stress and physical problems.[1142] Out of 27 studies using *frequency of religious attendance* as the reference, 22 showed a positive, statistically significant relationship with health.[1143]

Measures of attendance, in turn, may be refined. David Williams observes that public religious involvements may include participation in meetings other than the principal weekly worship service, such as volunteer work, leadership roles and financial support.

Spiritual support (defined as distinct from social group support) is another salutary factor. For instance, spiritual support buffered parents' experience of the death of a child.[1144]

The *coping utility* of a religion may be expressed through feelings of enhanced control.[1145] This could be as *primary control*, in which people have improved tools for dealing with the world or *secondary control*, in which people modify their attitudes and perceptions. For example, J. Rodin showed that when older people's control over their activities was restricted, there were detrimental effects on their health.

Levin and Vanderpool[1146] point out (in a consideration of alternative explanatory hypotheses) that religion is *multifactorial*, including characteristics and benefits listed below.

Subjective religiosity may be distinct from outward behaviors.[1147] Gordon Allport suggested the distinction: 'institutionalized' vs. 'interiorized' religiosity. This may include people's assessments of the importance of religion or beliefs in specific teachings.[1148]   Addressing this factor, several reports suggest that behavioral correlates of religion, such as attendance and recitation of prayers, are more closely associated with health than subjective and attitudinal factors.[1149]

Researchers in gerontology and geriatrics have been more open to studying possible influences of religion on health than many other medical, sociological or psychological specialties.[1150] They find that "as adults age, formal or organizational religious involvement is strongly predictive of better health, happiness, and life satisfaction. Similarly, nonorganizational or private expressions of religiosity as well as positive subjective religious attitudes or beliefs are also promotive of health..."

Levin[1151] methodically considers whether these correlations are valid or merely chance associations. He states:

> In ruling out chance and bias...diversity and the sheer volume of studies may actually work to the advantage of validity. Since so many hundreds of studies have been published, and these overwhelmingly report statistically significant, positive religion-health associations or health differences across religious groups, and since most of these studies were epidemiologic censuses of entire populations or surveys of randomized samples, it is unlikely that this summary result is due solely to chance. At the level of individual studies, these results can probably be trusted, for the most part...
>
>   This diversity in studies suggests that bias may also be safely ruled out. A significant, positive religious effect on health was found in prospective and retrospective studies; in cohort and case-control studies; in studies of children and of older adults; in studies of U.S. White and Black Protestants, European Catholics, Parsis from India, Zulus from South Africa, Japanese Buddhists, and Israeli Jews, among others; in studies from the 1930s and studies from the 1980s; and in studies of self-limiting acute conditions, of fatal chronic diseases, and of illnesses with lengthy, brief, or absent latency periods between exposure and diagnosis and mortality.

Analyzing the correlations of religion with health

Can we consider the observed correlations between religion and health to be causal? On the way to answering this central question, Levin[1152] notes that there is no consensus amongst epidemiologists on the concept of causation in general (not just as related to studies of religion.[1153] Levin points out that some argue it is possible to refute hypotheses but never to prove them definitively.[1154] Verificationists seek to establish supporting evidence based on studies showing associations of characteristics or qualities which we could expect to identify in cause-and-effect relationships. [1155]

Levin and Vanderpool[1156] also caution that there is a wide gap between the average beliefs of scientists and those of the general population. About a decade ago, a survey of scientists in America showed that only 16 percent believed in life after death, contrasted with 67 percent among the general adult population[1157] and with 42 percent of those scientists who held this belief attending church or synagogue weekly or more often. In the general population there were 77 percent who believed in heaven, 58 percent in hell and 24 percent in reincarnation.[1158]

One must be cautious, therefore, in generalizing results from individual studies until their measuring criteria are validated through repeated and diversified studies.[1159]

So how do we decide whether the hundreds of studies on religion and health demonstrate *meaningful* correlations? A. Hill suggests nine qualities that could be expected in cause-effect relationships. Levin[1160] considers the cause-effect relationship between religion and health in the light of these qualities:

1. *Strength of effect.* Only a few studies address this factor. Comstock and Partridge studied whether infrequent church attendance may contribute to mortality. With certain diseases, people with infrequent church attendance could show nearly four times the mortality rates as people with frequent attendance. Comparing the health of clergy to the health of laypersons, King and Locke found significantly lower standardized mortality ratios for White Protestant clergy for all causes of deaths, total cancers, and cardiovascular-renal disease.

As Levin and Schiller[1161] point out, most studies considering this factor focus on the extremes of religious participation – either those with intense involvement or those lacking religious commitment. In the current state of our abilities to define religious parameters, this may be the principal way available to address this factor.

2. *Consistency.* There is robust evidence for this factor. Hundreds of studies have shown a positive relationship between religion and health, in a wide variety of research designs, conducted by numerous researchers in various countries, over several decades in the 20th century, focusing on numerous independent and dependent variables, considering subjects of diverse races, ethnicities, sex, age, social classes, nationalities, religious affiliations and illnesses.

3. *Specificity.* Religion clearly correlates with a broad spectrum of illnesses, relating to both morbidity and mortality. It is not restricted to a specific disease or type of problem.

4. *Temporality.* It has not been demonstrated with any certainty that religion as a variable precedes any effects on health. Most of the studies showing correlations between the two are retrospective or compare several groups cross-sectionally.

Levin[1162] points out that "it could be that increased disability leads to declines in religious attendance, rather than higher attendance leading to better health." Some of the studies of older populations are starting to address this question.[1163]

5. *Biological gradient.* A true effect ought to show greater results with greater inputs from a causal factor. Several studies suggest such an effect[1164] but these would require further verifications for any confidence in such an inference.

6. *Plausibility.* A causal correlation between religion and health is plausibly consonant with our understandings of health and illness from behavioral medicine, psychoneuroimmunology[1165] and social epidemiology.[1166] The social, behavioral and psychological aspects of religious involvement overlap broadly with aspects of these related fields of study that have demonstrated correlations between health and such factors as social support, addressing emotional and mental problems and the like.

7. *Coherence.* "According to Hill, a causal interpretation of an association[1167] 'should not seriously conflict with the generally known facts of the natural history and biology of the disease.' " Levin[1168] points out that this factor is impossible to assess, due to "the multiplicity of diseases and health outcomes for which a significant religious factor has been identified..."

I disagree with Hill's and Levin's assessments of this feature on two grounds. An a priori objection is that this feature would preclude any new discoveries in medicine. More relevant, an impressive body of evidence of research on healing[1169] demonstrates that focused thinking, meditation or prayer may influence health – despite the fact that psi healing is not generally accepted by conventional medicine.

8. *Experiment.* Levin mentions the experiment on distant healing by Byrd, showing highly significant effects on people hospitalized for cardiovascular problems, as "striking experimental evidence of a religiously oriented effect on health." He adds reservations: "...the nature of the exposure variable he studied (distant prayer) is substantively quite different from the other religious variables considered in this literature, namely public and private religious behaviors, attitudes, and affiliations. For these measures, no experimental evidence exists."

Many claim that healing by prayer is different from healing through wishes or meditations outside of a religious context. This contention is open to scientific investigation, though it is probable that alternative possibilities such as experimenter effects[1170] or super-ESP[1171] could not be ruled out. The study of Byrd satisfies everyone, as prayer healing was involved.[1172]

I repeat my differences with Levin here, as in (7) above, and add: It is clear that spiritual healing is not viewed by most sociologists[1173] and scientists as an actual, potent (rather than merely symbolic, metaphoric) intervention. Lionel Snell is an open minded representative of such critics. Snell analyzes a woman's use of the word 'energy' when she stated that she preferred the positive energy of a wood framed massage couch to one of metal:

I was amused by her use of the word 'energy', but that doesn't mean I rejected it. I understood perfectly clearly (if not precisely) what she meant by her words – and communication is the main job of language. She had used the word 'energy' in what I would describe as a magical rather than a scientific way...

A word does not need to *have* meaning in order to *convey* meaning....

To me scientific language is the use of words for the meaning they *have*, while magical language is the use of words for the meaning they *convey* as a metaphor...

Science is itself a good source of these magical metaphors. In the early nineteenth century magnetism caught the public imagination and a whole raft of magical theories of 'animal magnetism' and 'magnetic passes' were floated. Then science postulated an ether and spiritualists took up the idea of 'vibrations' and 'etheric' fields and forces. This century brought the idea of a fourth dimension, adding 'dimension' to the magical vocabulary. Now we have a spate of literature which weaves magical theories on the basis of quantum terminology.

If you insist on the original scientific meaning of these words, the result can be highly amusing. To the cynic it looks as if science has moved on and left a bunch of cranks trying to justify themselves in terms of outmoded terminology: sensitives wittering about 'etheric vibrations' at a time when the ether concept was no longer recognized by science; talk of 'higher' dimensions without any explanation of how a dimension can be 'high'; the phrase 'negative energies' when energy is normally recognized as a scalar quantity.

But if you admit the metaphorical use of these words the result is much more informative.

It is hoped that the four volumes of Healing Research can correct such disbeliefs in psi healing and the prejudices against the legitimacy of psi healing, energy medicine, and the validity of religion as very real and potent forces in the world. Levin suggests that we should establish a new specialty we could call *theosomatic medicine*.

One can only hope that more scientists will come to appreciate the power of prayer and will be more open-minded to new theories to explain this potent healing modality. It has been suggested that we may have to wait for the older generations to die off before these prejudices will be shifted in medical practice.

> *... I decided that not to employ prayer with my patients was the equivalent of deliberately withholding a potent drug or surgical procedure. I felt I should be true to the traditions of scientific medicine, which meant going through scientific data and not around it, no matter how uncomfortable it might be to do so and no matter how it might shake up one's favored beliefs. I simply could not ignore the evidence for prayer's effectiveness without feeling like a traitor to the scientific tradition.*
> – Larry Dossey [1174]

9. *Analogy.* That religion may influence health is supported by related psychosocial research. Religion may influence health via factors identical with or similar to those for which substantial bodies of research exist, as mentioned above.

Levin concludes:

> In summary, the question, 'Is it causal?', can be answered with a 'maybe'. Notwithstanding the falsificationist assertion that the answer, by definition, cannot ever be yes, examining the evidence in the light of Hill's guidelines is inconclusive but promising. Judging this literature in terms of consistency, plausibility, and analogy, the answer is yes. In terms of coherence, the answer is probably yes, but one cannot be certain. In terms of temporality and biological gradient, there is insufficient evidence, but recent gerontological findings may change this to a yes. In terms of strength and experiment, there is insufficient evidence. Finally, specificity does not seem to be applicable.

Levin concludes that there is reason to consider that a religious effect upon health may be causal on the basis of the numerous studies demonstrating correlations between religious affiliation and practice and health. This is without taking into consideration the masses of research on healing reviewed in Volume I of *Healing Research*, demonstrating that prayers and spiritual healing are potent interventions. Levin and associates have viewed religion as contributing primarily through psychological and social avenues to enhanced health. I believe that the research evidence suggests there are more direct effects through healing – as general prayer and in healings through prayer/meditation/wishes and the laying-on-of-hands. More on this below.

A spectrum of hypotheses could explain how religious affiliation might influence health, mostly in positive ways but occasionally also negatively, per Levin/Vanderpool[1175] and Levin.[1176] These hypotheses also point out many potential difficulties in clarifying such correlations.[1177]

1. *Behaviors* may be influenced through religious practices. These include various health-related proscriptions and prescriptions on diet, hygiene, intoxicants and exercise. These could, for instance, promote lower levels of blood pressure and diminish the incidence of some forms of cancers through reduced exposure to contributing risk factors.

2. *Hereditary endowments* of particular religious groups may contribute to lower or higher health risks with certain illnesses. It has been noted, for instance, that Jews have a lower incidence of cancer of the penis[1178] but higher risk for Tay Sachs disease, and Catholic nuns are at greater risk for developing breast cancer but lower risk for uterine cancer.[1179]

3. *Psychosocial influences* of religious practices may contribute to health. Religious rites of passage celebrate and validate psychosocial stages of life,

affirming a person's development of a sense of identify – both personally and as a member of a community. Participation in activities of religious congregations encourages social interactions, a sense of belonging, continuity of relationships amongst family and friends, and provides other planned and casual support systems.

Social support may benefit health[1180] by facilitating coping with stress and anger. This factor is repeatedly emphasized throughout the literature on religion and health. Less studied is the reverse. Enforced participation in religious services and rituals may be experienced by some as constrictive and may restrict opportunities for self-actualization.[1181]

4. *Psychodynamics of belief systems* may encourage peacefulness, develop self confidence or, conversely, engender guilt, depression and self doubt. For instance, the excessively striving person who has great difficulty relaxing (Type A personality) has been found to be more prone to cardiovascular disease, and the opposite (Type B) may be conducive to hypertension in unchurched or irreligious people.[1182] The Protestant work ethic may contribute to stress related illnesses. Calvinist or Wesleyan world views may be correlated with psychological parameters identified as *internal locus of control* wherein people view the world as internally directed.[1183] These parameters have been correlated with health-related behaviors.[1184] Socioeconomic status may influence studies, as people in lower socioeconomic groups more often pray privately, accept the doctrines of their religion and report personal religious experiences.[1185]

5. *Psychodynamics of religious rites*, both private and public, may contribute to diminishing anxieties, fears, loneliness, depression and the like,[1186] all of which are potential contributors to hypertension and its effects[1187] and other stress related illnesses.[1188] The benefits of religious rites may, for example, derive from suggestion, confession, peaceful atmospheres, a sense of mastery and empowerment, from socially sanctioned emotional releases[1189] and enhanced personal and group identity through religious socialization.[1190] One may readily postulate physiological mechanisms for some of these effects. Levin and Vanderpool[1191] suggest: "These positive effects may serve as sorts of psychic beta-blockers [medications that counteract effects of adrenalin] or emotional placebos that mitigate the body's attempt to elevate blood pressure."

I would add that numerous psychotherapeutic approaches introduce techniques and practices that parallel this psychodynamic religious factor: Autogenic Training and other relaxation therapies, meditation, Transpersonal Psychotherapies, Group therapies of all varieties, music therapy, etc.

Levin and Schiller[1192] point out that in secularized, Western society we must also consider the

" 'medical church' metaphor:... similarities between the institution of religion and the institution of medicine: surgery as initiation, hospitals as churches, medication as communion, suffering as sacrifice, anesthetization as ecstasy, the physician-patient transaction as informed by lay acknowledgement of 'apostolic' authority,' etc." [1193]

6. *Psychodynamics of faith* in religious beliefs and practices may enhance health, regardless of the effectiveness, per se, of these factors (4 and 5). The literature on placebo effects[1194] and the processes of psychoneuroimmunology[1195] are impressive testimonials on the contributions of self healing engendered by beliefs. People who believe that they are protected or healed through their religious affiliations and practices may derive immediate benefits through self-healing with prayers, anointing and other healing rituals.

7. *Epistemological confusion* (confusion about how we know what we know) may mislead us into believing that religious affiliation and practices contribute to health when in actuality there are other factors producing the observed results. One might, for instance, assume that religious attendance is an indicator of health promoting behavior. It could provide social support, calming from prayer and meditation, and cathartic rituals – all of which might contribute to lower blood pressure. On the other hand, the opposite might be true. Attendance might be associated with social obligation, enforced through guilt and fear which would raise blood pressure.[1196] We might also misinterpret the results of studies because of distortions introduced by self-selection of religious attenders. Consider the possibility that more frequent religious attendance might be motivated through the presence of illness and the seeking of divine healing. Conversely, attendance at religious services could be limited by physical disabilities. Levin and Vanderpool[1197] discuss many of these possible pitfalls.[1198]

8. *Measurement problems* may confuse the picture if researchers assume that various religious variables are uniformly present in diverse members of religious groups. Religious attendance, the most commonly used indicator of religiosity, is an example of such problems. Attendance may constitute entirely different meaning to various attenders, certainly between various religions but also within individuals of the same religion. Physical factors may also be at play in selecting people to attend or not. A person may be drawn to attend because of illness or prevented from attending because of severe disabilities.

9. *Analytical errors* may unwittingly creep into studies when clarifications are not made of factors such as the variability within the category of religious attendance. Or take another instance. Levin and Vanderpool[1199] note that "controlling for activity limitation[1200] often reduces the magnitude of associations between religious attendance and morbidity or poor health. Without collecting such data on functional health status or disability and then adjusting for these effects, significant associations between religious attendance and blood pressure may be spurious or tautological. That is, these associations may represent de facto correlations between lack of disabling morbidity and health, or, in other words, between health and health." Other such confounding variables between groups compared in various studies might include age and social class. These could be

the factors determining any observed differences rather than religious affiliation or attendance per se.

10. *Multifactorial explanations* may be more applicable than any single component of religion. Any combination of the above might apply, making it most difficult to obtain clear and valid assessments of the contributions of single factors. Summarized succinctly,[1201] such explanations could include:

> a. the affirming of a world-view that includes faith in some superempirical, usually supernatural being(s) or powers; b. rituals and ceremonious behaviors such as prayer, meditation, recitations, and rites; c. moral codes; d. distinctions between sacred and profane actions and objects;
> e. characteristic motivations and emotions; and f. ongoing social organizations that are usually long-lived and ethnically or regionally specific...[1202]
> [R]eligion's... greater, lasting, and stubbornly-persisting influence resides in the functions it fulfils... [R]eligion provides meaning, memory, systems of support, mutual aid, and a means of coping and comfort in the face of difficulty, disaster, and triumph... provisions which social epidemiologists have found to strongly benefit health... Furthermore, through teachers and prophets, religious traditions provide avenues of change, reform, and protest; and through rites of passage, religion serves to guide individuals from birth, through cycles of growth and maturity, to separation and death... Finally, by relating groups or peoples to that which is defined as absolute and supremely powerful, religious groups are elevated beyond a sense of helplessness, confusion and insignificance to levels of social control, empowerment, and mastery... effects which are believed to positively influence health...

11. *Superempirical or pantheistic influence(s)*, associated with religious beliefs and activated through practices and rituals, might bring about changes in health. Levin and Vanderpool observe: "This accessible, although presently immeasurable and ineffable, healing force or energy is attributed many names across various religious and mystical traditions: ether, *prana*, life force, *wakan*, Holy Spirit, *kundalini* energy, Christ Consciousness, *chi* or *ki,* eloptic energy, *baraka*, orgone, *ruakh*, huna, odic force, *mana*, second state energy, *Gestaltung*, the mitogenetic ray, *munia*, the It, *Odyle*, and so on." [1203]
Volumes I and II of *Healing Research* provide ample evidence that this may be a potent force for healing of physical, mental and emotional problems through self healing and with the help of healers.

12. *Supernatural influence(s)* that transcend our everyday world and/or may also be intimately a part of this world are recognized by all religions. Levin and Vanderpool feel that these transcendent influences cannot, by their nature, be measured in the everyday world.

I believe that evidence in this volume of *Healing Research* suggests that aspects of these influences may be measured through their effects upon the physical world, though the influencers themselves are beyond physical measurement.

Levin and Vanderpool seem to give greater weight or legitimacy to hypotheses (1) to (10), with their designation of multifactorial influences (10) – which apparently exclude superempirical and supernatural influences (11 and 12). I would include the latter two without question amongst the mulifactorial influences that can affect our health.[1204]

Religion as a subject for study

Despite the robust collection of evidence available, the medical and social sciences have generally avoided the pursuit of research on health correlates of religion.[1205] A number of factors contribute to this.

First are the historical trends of science away from religion, mentioned earlier. These beliefs bias Western scientists to consider religion as unimportant, irrelevant, unreal or unsuitable for scientific study.[1206]

Sherrill and Larson point out that there are strong influences on scientists to stay away from research on religion. In part this is a general problem of any new field of study. Initial results are inevitably partial, often contradicting previous expectations and findings, unsophisticated, not sharply focused and in need of replication and extension.[1207] Critics confuse 'studies that are fledgling' with 'studies that are flawed.' Critics then set up unrealistic standards to 'correct' the situation. Mentors in a new field are few if any and funding is limited. Those interested in the new field have to append the new subject to other areas of interest.

Sherrill and Larson point out that a strong 'anti-tenure-factor' comes into play in these processes. Academicians seem to have an unwritten rule that only one or two articles in 'fringe' areas of research are tolerated for any scientist. Any more than that can lead pioneering investigators to be labeled as 'fringe' themselves, to suffer peer disapproval and censure, and then to be denied grants and promotions.[1208]

Harold Koenig[1209] points out that skeptical doctors want studies that establish a causation between religion and health, not just studies that show correlations between the two. Others suggest that physician involvement in religion could be coercive, with patients feeling obliged to accept doctors' views along with the doctor's care that they need. There is also concern that doctors could engender guilt feelings in people who do not get well, blaming them for not having enough faith.[1210]

The similarities with healing research are readily apparent.[1211]

My personal belief is that there is in each of us the ability to perceive directly a connection, through our 'higher selves,' with something vast, eternal and awesome that is beyond words. The *process* of searching for this may be as helpful as the *content* of anything we may 'discover' or be able to translate into linear terminology.[1212]

I am your life. You are my expression. I am the vine, you are the branches.
I am the consciousness, you are my focus. There is no separation, except in
time, perhaps, and in my presence, time does not exist. I have the clarity
now, while you sleep yet in darkness. But I am calling you earnestly to
awaken. I would share with you the totality of my perceptions.
                                                    – Ken Carey [1213]

Suggestions from research on religion and health

The evidence from the many studies and reviews of the positive correlations of
religion with health should be made available to health care professionals, clergy
and educational institutions. This would facilitate their encouragement of people
to maintain or strengthen their religious affiliations as means of enhancing their
health. This would be especially relevant where social support and communal
involvement might be helpful, such as in community mental health care and
geriatrics.

Levin[1214] points out that further scientific enquiry should be directed towards
clarifying some of the alternative hypotheses listed above. He also cites Vaux,
who recommended many years ago that 'empirical studies of religion and health
need to better account for the interaction and interplay of biochemical,
endocrinological, metabolic, hormonal, and immunologic processes with social,
behavioral, and psychological patterns – a complex but intrinsic characteristic of
human beings.' In the frameworks of complementary/alternative medicine, we
are starting to make progress in these directions in studies of hypnotherapy,
biofeedback, psychoneuroimmunology, spiritual healing, applied kinesiology,
WHEE and varieties of other self-healing practices.[1215]

Religion and spirituality

Religions enrich our lives by providing a framework for thought and
action. We may take to a religion as a traveler who chooses a vehicle to
reach a destination. We may also choose a car or a horse carriage, mule or
camel back, ship or plane, and sometimes walk from place to place on our
own. There is variety in experience and enjoyment, and when one does a
little bit of each, one realizes that, depending on the context, one mode
may be better than another.

                                                    – Stacey Ake

Spiritual healing brings people in touch with their *personal* awareness of
spirituality. This bypasses the 'middle-man' of organized religion, providing an
immediate knowing of realities beyond our everyday world. For many, organized
religion may open doorways into these realms – through prayers, chants, rituals,
inspiring saints and the like. Religions offer us the experiences and practices of
many generations of spiritual seekers.

Prayer is the medium of miracles. It is a means of communication of the created with the Creator. Through prayer love is received and through miracles love is expressed.

– Course in Miracles.

Many, myself included, have found conventional religious affiliations to be more ritual than spiritual, more satisfying of social needs than of spiritual ones. As with all human experiences, one must sort out the wheat from the chaff, the truly spiritual from the ritual that is intended primarily for the perpetuation of that particular religious line of teaching and the maintenance of its teachers in roles of authority.

There is also the factor of socio-psychological evolution and growth over many centuries of religious practice. What may have been right for people hundreds or even thousands of years ago, might not be exactly right or relevant for people today.[1216]

There are also dangers in delving into personal spirituality. One may get lost in the transcendent, becoming 'ungrounded' and losing touch with the physical, emotional and social levels of existence. One may misguidedly believe that one has THE truth instead of an individual perception and interpretation of the truth that is subject to all the distortions of the frailties of human awareness. Because of these dangers, many feel safer to stay within the guidelines and confines of organized religion.

Again we approach questions that require far more space for adequate consideration than is possible here. Suffice it to say that religion may be good for your health on many levels.

My personal belief is that we come into this physical world for spiritual lessons. These lessons challenge us through all levels of our existence: the physical, emotional, mental, social and the more directly spiritual.

There is a phantom
in this painful dream
of who we wish we were -
the imagined self.
Don't be fooled
by a thought
into believing (another thought)
you are less
than God.

– Stephen Levine [1217]

Research in spiritual awareness and health

There is a wealth of research on meditative states, showing correlations with lower blood pressure, less need for pain medications in multitudes of conditions, enhanced stress management, and much more.[1218]

William Braud and Rosemarie Anderson discuss a spectrum of research approaches in transpersonal dimensions.

Surveys of people who have had Near-Death Experiences report anecdotally that their attitudes toward life are dramatically changed. They are more peaceful, have a clearer sense of their place in the world, and often commit themselves to working in spiritual ways. This would appear to be a fertile ground for further research on health correlates of spirituality.

While there is much focus in the complementary/alternative therapies community on addressing body, emotions, mind and spirit, only in the past few years has attention been given to researching spirituality per se as an avenue to health. This is a more specific focus than the much more general parameters of religious affiliation and practice, which could be helpful through social supports and other confounding factors mentioned earlier. However, as we have seen in the broad range of definitions of spirituality reviewed in Chapter III-11, there are many views and opinions on how to identify what is meant by spirituality. Unfortunately, this makes it difficult to know in many cases where the research articles belong in the spectrum of possible meanings of spirituality.

In summary

The majority of caregivers and careseekers agree that there is a place for considering religion and spirituality in health care. Hundreds of studies confirm that religious affiliation and practice are good for our health. However, it is unclear to what extent these are directly effective or whether social supports, a religious community and other related factors help to reduce stress or promote healthier lifestyles. Personal spirituality has only recently become a focus for study as a factor in promoting health. The numerous and varied definitions of spirituality may make it difficult to assess this factor as related to health. Researchers will have to carefully define their terms and hone their questionnaires to firm up this field of study.

Chapter 13

Participatory Spirituality

In the spacious mirror of reflective consciousness we begin to catch glimpses of the unity of the interwoven fabric of the cosmos and our intimate participation within the living web of existence. No longer is reality broken into relativistic islands of pieces. If only for a brief moment at a time, existence is glimpsed and known as a seamless totality. To explore our gradual awakening to the aliveness and unity of the universe... awakens the intuition that a living presence permeates the universe.

– Duane Elgin

Participatory spiritual awareness and healing

Jorge Ferrer, in a remarkably clear and lucid discussion of religion, philosophy and transpersonal psychology, points out that no religions can justify their basic tenets as anything other than articles of faith. All of the arguments between religions are conducted around elaborations of tenets that are presumed to be true and beyond questioning. Yet there is no way to prove that the basic beliefs of religion are true or valid.

Ferrer suggests that the only valid basis for spiritual belief lies in personal spiritual awareness, and that each of us is a co-creator of spiritual awareness as we explore the dimensions of spirituality. Within this view, spirituality is a dynamic, ever-evolving exploration of the transcendent rather than just a static, single truth that lies somewhere beyond full mortal awareness and comprehension, available only to speculative theorizing about its nature. Every person who experiences and explores spirituality is contributing to its collective reality. This does not mean that we fully comprehend the transcendent, which remains largely a mystery to our limited awareness.

My own belief has come to be that life was created by the Infinite Source as a way of understanding *knowing* through the contrast of forgetting our connections with Spirit and with the Infinite Source – which adds many dimensions to knowing, just as every yin adds to our appreciation of its contrasting yang. The Infinite Source is totally loving of its creations and leaves us free choice – to learn through our decisions, choices, successes and errors. Our soul connects us to the Infinite Source and to all of creation. It chooses lessons on the physical plane and in other dimensions, co-creating the evolving awareness of life in never-ending cycles of yang and yin; head and heart; hate and love; hurt and healing; anger and forgiveness; contraction and expansion. Lessons that are not completed and rounded out in one life are addressed in subsequent lives. Darkness, in the forms of anger, vengefulness and evil, is a stimulus and challenge to bring out more light and love. There is no single way that is the best way through these lessons. Each contributes to the wholeness of the All through our personal experiences and choices.

> *God created humankind so that humankind might cultivate the earthly*
> *and create the heavenly.*
>
> Hildegard of Bingen

So where does this leave us as individuals, struggling with our daily issues of making a living, building and maintaining nurturing relationships, and dealing with life's challenges? Robin Norwood[1219] has stated it nicely:

> *Every problem is an assignment from your soul. Therefore, acknowledge*
> *that a purpose is being served by your problem, your wound, your illness,*
> *your disability, your terminal condition, and try to align with it; that is,*
> *seek what it is trying to teach you. Remember that from the soul's perspec-*
> *tive, a change in consciousness is of far greater value than a 'cure'.*
> *Therefore, follow King Solomon's wise injunction: "With all your getting,*
> *get understanding." Make that understanding the object of your quest and*
> *be optimistic that you will be rewarded.*

Research at the personal edge of the mystery of transcendence

> *A Universe without and a Universe within. Our consciousness bridges the*
> *inner and outer worlds. The nature of that link reflects the beliefs, the*
> *thoughts, the feelings with which we meet our worlds. Yet what is closest to*
> *us is simply Mystery. Behind all words, behind all worlds, The Life that*
> *cannot be known. We dwell in the Wonder of Spirit and that Spirit speaks*
> *as well from the depths of our own beings. On this journey we are not*
> *alone in our questing for the One we are. That One speaks behind each*
> *sensation, each memory, each dream, and whispers through each relation-*

ship. We seek to open to the One we share. We yearn to know the One who calls through each meeting of I and Thou.

– Rabbi Theodore Falcon

If we take the view that each of us is a particle, however minute, in the corpus of the All, then each of us knows the All as a part of ourself and each of us contributes to the state of being of the All. This is more than a statement of faith. This can be researched, using accepted scientific methods that are detailed below.

Extensive research demonstrates that human consciousness can extend beyond our physical body and can interact with living organisms and with non-living parts of the world around us. Parapsychology has confirmed the existence of:

1. *Telepathy between one person and another* has been demonstrated in extensive experiments with highly significant results, performed by Joseph B. Rhine and Louisa E. Rhine at Duke University in North Carolina, and confirmed many times over by numerous researchers around the world over the better part of the last century.[1220] These studies confirm that people are able to acquire information directly from other people's minds. People can also transmit information via mind-to-mind communication. Distance does not appear to weaken telepathic effects even when thousands of miles separate senders and receivers.

Animal-human telepathy has been reported anecdotally and confirmed in fascinating studies – including dogs who behave in distinctive manners shortly before their owners return home, and telepathy with cats, birds and other species.[1221]

2. *Clairsentience:* Experiments with highly significant results have shown that some people obtain information about a person or object through extrasensory perception (ESP) not involving telepathy. This knowledge seems to come to the mind of the perceiver directly from the object. For instance, J. B. Rhine showed that there are people who can identify the order in which cards lie in a deck after the experimenter shuffled them face-down but before she turned them over.[1222] It has also been demonstrated in extensive experiments with highly significant results that people can know clairsentiently what is happening at a distant location without sensory cues or other contact (e.g., telephone or video) with that place.[1223]

In such cases telepathy could not have been involved. Clairsentient impressions may be perceived as sensory information (visual images, voices, smells, etc.) or as broader pictures and feelings, such as positive vibrations in a church, or negative vibrations in an empty room after an argument occurred there. They may be experienced as inner awarenesses or as images outside the perceiver.

3. *Precognition:* Gifted subjects are able to read the future for themselves or others. To initiate the perception they may hold an object belonging to a person, be in his presence, or be given her name. Intuitives can often give information about a person's or object's future or past. Laboratory subjects have been able to guess correctly the order of series of cards before they were shuffled[1224] and to describe places visited by experimenters before these places were selected.[1225]

4. *Psychokinesis* (also called *PK* or *telekinesis):* repeated, highly significant experiments have demonstrated that matter can be manipulated by the mind. Rhine asked subjects to roll the desired faces of dice (chosen by a random number table).[1226] Helmut Schmidt developed electronic random number generating (RNG) devices which subjects were able to influence.[1227] RNGs that function randomly when left alone, generating ones and zeros in chance patterns that average 50 percent ones and 50 percent zeros, deviate and produce significantly more ones or zeros when someone directs them to do so mentally. In another random model, a series of balls drops through a symmetrical pinball device that distributes them randomly when left alone, but deviates right or left when a person wills it to do so.[1228] PK has been repeatedly confirmed with RNGs based on electronic, mechanical, and even radioactive mechanisms.[1229]

Spiritual healing appears to be a sub-category of PK. A review of 191 controlled studies of healing – including humans, animals, plants, bacteria, yeasts, cells in laboratory culture, enzymes and more – found that 64 percent of the studies demonstrated significant results.[1230] A sub-set of this research examined mental influence on electrodermal activity, with astronomically significant results.[1231]

Collectively, these abilities (1-4) are called *extra-sensory perception (ESP), psychic* or *psi* abilities. People who have any one of these abilities often tend to have one or more of the others as well though they often excel in the one and may have only weak or occasional expressions of the remaining psi powers.

Psi awareness and communications have no apparent limits of distance or time. Studies of telepathy, clairsentience and PK over distances of hundreds of miles did not diminish the significance of the results.

> *When we try to pick up anything by itself, we find it hitched to everything else in the universe.*
> – John Muir

5. *Collective consciousness* is suggested to explain psi abilities and other manifestations of shared consciousness. In addition to the classical research in psi, fascinating early studies have been published on perturbations in human collective consciousness. Roger Nelson, Dean Radin and colleagues have repeatedly demonstrated that random number generators deviate from their normal random patterns during times when there are events of interest to large numbers of people.

> We have been collecting data from a global network of random event generators since August, 1998. The network has grown to about 65 host sites around the world running custom software that reads the output of physical random number generators and records a 200-bit trial sum once every second, continuously over months and years. The data are transmitted over the internet to a server in Princeton, NJ, USA, where they are archived for later analysis...
>
> The purpose of this project is to examine subtle correlations that appear to reflect the presence and activity of consciousness in the world.[1232]

Events that have registered include the Embassy bombings in Nairobi and Tanzania, on July 8, 1998; the visit of Pope John Paul II to the Middle East between March 21 and March 26, 2000; funeral ceremonies for Prime Minister Pierre Trudeau of Canada on October 3, 2000; and attacks on the World Trade Center on 9-11, to mention only a few. One might expect that the deviations would register primarily on local RNGs, but RNGs around the world register unusual readings during such events. The meaning of these perturbations is purely a matter of speculation at present. They are witnesses to effects of a global consciousness.

Collective consciousness has been observed in many instances of animal behaviors. The behaviors of insects in their hives seem particularly suggestive of a collective animal consciousness. The most striking example are the studies of termites. Sheldrake[1233] reports on termite mounds where a steel plate was pounded into a termite mound, dividing it into separated portions. The termites continued building their mound up higher around the plate. Tunnels were found in the newly extended portions of the mound that precisely matched each other in placement on each side of the plate. It is difficult to explain how these insects could have known how to match up the placement of their tunnels without a guiding collective consciousness in the mound.

Eugene Marais, in a fascinating study of African termites, brings us another such example. He found that if the queen in a termite mound was killed, all the termites which were in the mound and foraging in the fields around immediately stopped their activity even though they might be many yards away and completely out of any possible sensory contact with the queen.

The movements of schools of fish and flocks of birds likewise suggest a collective consciousness. The instantaneous changes in direction of hundreds of individual animals, moving in concert as a single, collective organism are well known but as yet poorly understood and far from being explained by any theories within conventional science. A collective consciousness appears to be a reasonable explanation, given that research has confirmed animal psi communications.

Animal-human telepathic communications[1234] extend the range and possibilities of collective consciousness to include all living beings.

It appears that individual humans can be in psychic communications with any and all other humans as well as with the inanimate world. This web of psi awareness creates, in effect, a collective consciousness that includes all living beings and all non-living matter on earth. This may explain the collective consciousness that has been acknowledged by Jung and his followers,[1235] and by anthropologists who have confirmed the existence of amazingly broad overlaps of mythic imagery in diverse cultures around the world.[1236] There is reason to believe this collective consciousness can and does extend to include the wider universe beyond our planet as well, though as yet no objective way has been devised for validation of such broader awarenesses.

While the concept of collective consciousness has classically been focused on human consciousness, theory and research suggest that all living organisms may participate in a vaster network of consciousness. Rupert Sheldrake's theory of morphogenetic fields, supported by his research, suggests that there are species-specific repositories of memories of individual members of that species, collectively available to each member of that species. These fields are hypothesized to guide the individual members of a species in their instinctual behaviors. The existence of a morphogenetic memory bank could explain how the experiences of individuals who discover better ways to cope can contribute to the collective consciousness of their species. A sparrow that discovers a new edible seed could thus share its knowledge with others of its species, and a wild goose can access its migration route through these morphogenetic fields. It is easy to see how this could apply to behavioral and social learning. Sheldrake suggests that this can equally apply to collective awareness of physical changes in the body of an organism that confers advantages for its survival.[1237]

Sheldrake has focused on the collective consciousness of single-species. There is every reason to expect that collective communications must occur between diverse species as well, considering the evidence from human-animal telepathic communications.[1238]

> *I live my life in widening circles*
> *that reach out across the world.*
> *I may not ever complete the last one,*
> *But I give myself to it....*
> *I have been circling for thousands of years,*
> *And I still don't know:*
> *Am I a falcon, a storm, or a great song.*
>
> – Rilke

6. *Biological energies* provide a basis for collective consciousness. *Healing Research, Volumes I and II,* review substantial bodies of research confirming the existence of bioenergy fields. These could provide nested hierarchies of information from individuals within a species, forming an aggregate of awarenesses and experiences that become a collective bioenergy field of consciousness[1239] – another way of acknowledging and explaining participatory intelligent design, which will be considered below.

Bioenergies link people with each other, guided by the intent of the healer and the receptivity of the healee. These have been reported to work primarily over short distances of several inches to several feet – the distance between the hands of a healer and the person or animal that is being given spiritual healing. Therapeutic Touch and Healing Touch have been the focus of the largest numbers of studies of this form of healing.[1240]

There is no clear limit to the distances through which bioenergies may act. For instance, Vladimir Safonov, a Russian healer, reports that he gives healing from any distance by visualizing the healee sitting in front of him and giving her a bioenergy treatment with his hands as though she were present.[1241] I know numbers of other healers who work in a similar manner, reporting that their hands become hot during these distant healings, just as they would with a laying-on of hands treatment.[1242]

7. *Spiritual awareness* is another layer of collective consciousness, as confirmed in the many studies of OBEs, NDEs, reincarnation memories and possession reviewed in this book, and through spiritual healing.[1243] People who have OBEs, sensitives who channel, and healers appear able to contact other living people anywhere in the worlds of the living and the deceased. Surviving spirits are reported by mediums and healers to be able to contact other spirits and living persons. While most of these reports focus on conscious, intentional communications, there is every possibility that similar communications are constantly present as a collective, unconscious web of interconnected awarenesses.

People report awareness of transcendent consciousness through meditation, prayer and spontaneous mystical experiences. They may encounter angels, luminary spirits surviving their earthly existence (Christ, Buddha, saints and other enlightened spirits) and God. Those who have experienced such encounters with transcendent consciousness often have no doubts that it is real. Modern science discounts these experiences as products of imagination, wishful thinking, projections born of religious faith and fervor or even as hallucinations of deranged minds. My personal belief is that these experiences of transcendent awareness are absolutely real – based on meditative, intuitive and healing experiences of my own and of others whom I respect.

The general consensus from these diverse observations is that our earthly awareness is actually very constricted and limited, compared to transcendent consciousness.[1244]

We live in illusion and the appearance of things.
There is a Reality.
You are that Reality.
Seeing this, you know that you are everything.
And being everything, you are no-thing.
That is all.
                                        – Kalu Rinpoche [1245]

There is thus a substantial collection of evidence from a variety of anecdotal and researched sources suggesting that human and non-human organisms are interlinked, individually and collectively, through a vast network of consciousness. Could this collective consciousness constitute a part of the Divine consciousness, much like the electrical activity of a brain cell participates in the awareness of the entire brain; and like a person participating in the culture and traditions of her nuclear and extended family, community, broader cultural group and the whole of humanity? While no objective proof of such a question appears possible, subjective reports from intuitives and healers are very much in line with this hypothesis. Jose Ferrer takes this a step further, suggesting that as each of us perceives transcendent realities through the lens of our being, we are co-creating the Divine.[1246]

Much of the enchantment of life lies in its mystery. The fact that most of us perceive and experience only dimly the Divine in ourselves and in the world around us provides a challenge for us to grow – to deepen our awareness and comprehension of our place in the cosmos.

> *The western world must be prepared to analyze religion as a phenomenon that does not necessarily explain the unanswered questions posed by the philosophical mind but that may, in itself, cause such questions to occur to all manner of people in a great variety of situations.*
> – Vine Deloria Jr.

> *Faith is an oasis in the heart which will never be reached by the caravan of thinking.*
> – Khalil Gibran [1247]

Taking our participatory spirituality a step further, we can ask, "Could our collective consciousness interact with reproductive and genetic processes, demonstrating thereby a participatory intelligent design on evolutionary processes?" Research suggests this is a distinct possibility.

Participatory intelligent design

> *God created man in His image and man returned the compliment.*
> – Jerome Lawrence/Robert E. Lee

Participatory intelligent design extends the theory of intelligent design discussed in the context of religious beliefs.[1248] It is based on research and promotes further research to confirm this theory. This theory does not rely on religious beliefs. Participatory intelligent design proposes that:

1. The enormous complexity of natural factors that are required for life to exist makes it highly unlikely (as in the theory of intelligent design) that life could evolve just by chance and by natural selection.

2. A guiding intelligence must have been present in order to create the universe as we know it (as in the theory of intelligent design).

3. Consciousness is an organizing principle in the universe that is continuously creating, guiding and shaping every aspect of the cosmos.
   Consciousness is constantly participating in the development of every aspect of the universe – from before the time of creation of the universe (as we speculate it may have come into being and in unfathomable ways that transcend our awareness), through the present time, and will continue to do so forever.

4. Addressing the world as matter, we may identify nested hierarchies of structure – ranging from subatomic levels and extending through atomic, molecular, chemical, protein, organelle, cellular, organ/tissue, and organismic levels. The

smaller sub-units combine to form the next larger units as we ascend the hierarchy of complexity. Participatory intelligent design is influenced by all of these levels and reciprocally acts upon all of these levels.

5. Addressing the world as energy, we may identify individual sub-entities of energetic nature, which interact with all other energetic sub-entities in the universe, both in nested energetic hierarchies and directly at each distinct level. Participatory intelligent design is influenced by all of these levels and reciprocally acts upon all of these levels.

6. Addressing the world as consciousness, we may identify individual sub-entities with consciousness which interacts with all other conscious sub-entities in the universe, both in nested energetic hierarchies and directly at each distinct level. Participatory intelligent design is influenced by all of these levels and reciprocally acts upon all of these levels.

7. Addressing the world as spirit, we may identify series of nested hierarchies of consciousness – encompassing every physical element, energy and unit of consciousness. Participatory intelligent design is influenced by all of these levels and reciprocally acts upon all of these levels.

Principles (5 – 7) may be distinctions that are peculiar to Western ways of conceptualizing the world. The true picture may be that all of these, and (4) as well, may be one combined form of existence.[1249] Participatory intelligent design both draws from and acts upon the combined aggregate of these levels. It also informs all levels (including levels that are beyond human ken) about the totality.

Several further propositions shape that which can be considered a part of participatory intelligent design.

8. There must be guidelines of some sort to assure us that personal spiritual awarenesses are reflections of the transcendent and are not in the spectrum of fantasies, denial of fears (especially of the presumed finality of death), wishful thinking, imagination, mental derangement or deliberate inventions that are born of motivations for gains (material or power) for individuals or special interest groups.

Ken Cohen[1250] suggests that we might take lessons in matters of ethical spiritual awareness from Native American traditions, which teach that true spirituality is known by its promotion of social cohesion. Similarly, conventional wisdom in Western spiritual healing teaches that we are best off when we petition the Transcendent for the highest good of all even when we are praying for the welfare of an individual.

Per earlier discussions,[1251] what people report to be mystical and spiritual experiences might even derive from psychotic, delusional projections rather than from awarenesses of the transcendent.

Considering all of the above, Principle 8 states: True personal spiritual awareness is known by its promotion of respect for individual perceptions, choices and actions as long as these do no harm and promote the good of all – including every living organism and so-called inanimate object on our planet, and Gaia, the totality of our planet itself.[1252]

9. While participatory intelligent design respects the right of every individual to interpret the worlds of matter and spirit as he chooses, it rejects any theory that is based on untestable and unprovable tenets. It accepts personal experience as experiential research.

These principles will help us to evaluate participatory intelligent design. Taking these into consideration, let us first examine further problems with evolution of various organisms as a manifestation of participatory intelligent design, and then expand our explorations both to the possibilities of more minute and more global and cosmic manifestations of these processes.

> *Strange is our situation here upon earth. Each of us comes for a short visit, not knowing why, yet sometimes seeming to a divine purpose. The important thing is not to stop questioning. Curiosity has its own reason for existing. One cannot help but be in awe when he contemplates the mysteries of eternity, of life, of the marvelous structure of reality. It is enough if one tries merely to comprehend a little of this mystery every day. Never lose a holy curiosity.*
> – Albert Einstein [1253]

Darwinian evolution: questions about genes, forms and functions[1254]

When we speak of intelligent design, most people focus on the question of whether Darwin's theory of selection of the fittest is adequate to explain evolution of species, or whether the intervention of a Deity is a more logical or reasonable hypothesis. Considerable evidence supports the Darwinian hypothesis that evolutionary shifts can occur through selection of forms and functions that provide greater adaptive benefits over long periods of time to various species in shifting environments. Over the last hundred and fifty years, modern science has tracked genetic shifts in insects, mammals, birds and plants, and over the last fifty years has also documented genetic shifts in bacteria, yeasts and other single-celled organisms and viruses. Various conditions that are stressful to a species frequently will produce mutations. For instance, when researchers develop new antibiotics, these will regularly produce strains of bacteria that are resistant to these antibiotics. It is clear that the strongest bacteria are selected until totally resistant strains are produced. The same is true of challenging conditions for other organisms.

Other evidence suggests that Darwinian selection may not be adequate to explain all of the observed genetic changes in various species – particularly over longer periods of time, and that intelligent design might provide more adequate explanations.

The genetic code as the language for a Divine instruction manual

The genetic code is an incredibly complex series of sequences of proteins, arranged in long chains. This code is the equivalent of a language for transmitting information from egg and sperm cells to the embryo that grows to reproduce another member of the species; to regulate biochemical processes within cells; to control the orderly growth of organisms; to repair damaged tissues; to fight infections; to reproduce more progeny; and to carry on the countless other processes required for life to continue.

Analysis of the four proteins that comprise the genetic code show that it is sequenced in the very same ways that some languages are sequenced.[1255] Scientists are proposing that the existence of a genetic 'language' therefore suggests a Creator who must have used that language in creating life.

Berney Williams[1256] points out that it is inaccurate to draw an analogy between the genetic code and language because this way of conceptualizing the world is a product of Western thinking, based on Latinate sentence structure. English language communicates through noun subjects, verb predicates and object predicates, suggesting *Actors → Actions → Receivers*. When we discuss the origins of the world, this creates in our Latinate-conditioned minds the images of a design (object) which must imply a designer (noun) to have created (verb) it. There is a hubris in assuming that this is THE way the world IS.

Williams suggests that we might examine the world through the mind of a Native American from the Hopi tribe.

> [T]he Hopi language is seen to contain no words, grammatical forms, constructions or expressions that refer directly to what we call 'time,' or to past, present, or future, or to enduring or lasting, or to motion as kinematic rather than dynamic (i.e. as a continuous translation in space and time rather than as an exhibition of dynamic effort in a certain process), or that even refer to space in such a way as to exclude that element of extension or existence that we call 'time,' and so by implication leave a residue that could be referred to as 'time.' Hence, the Hopi language contains no reference to 'time', either explicit or implicit.[1257]
>
> Thus, the Hopi language and culture conceals a METAPHYSICS, such as our so-called naive view of space and time does, or as the relativity theory does; yet it is a different metaphysics from either.[1258]
>
> The Hopi conceive time and motion in the objective realm in a purely operational sense – a matter of the complexity and magnitude of operations connecting events – so that the element of time is not separated from whatever element of space enters into the operations.[1259]

In Hopi, a man riding a horse are what they are doing. The man is not sitting on the horse, the horse is not carrying the man, and neither is traveling from one place to another. When people in modern Western culture see lightning we say that 'it' flashes. In Hopi, the lightning and the flashing are one, encompassed in a single word. B. L. Whorf observes,[1260]

Hopi can have verbs without subjects, and this gives to that language power as a logical system for understanding certain aspects of the cosmos. Scientific language, being founded on Western Indo-European and not on Hopi, does as we do, and sees sometimes actions and forces where there may be only states. For do you not conceive it possible that scientists as well as ladies with cats all unknowingly project the linguistic patterns of a particular type of language upon the universe, and SEE them there, rendered visible on the very face of nature? A change in language can transform our appreciation of the Cosmos.

As Williams cogently argues, a language "that emphasizes autonomous events, and sees 'objects' as collections of autonomous events as character attributes could bolster this 'living process creation' proposed as participatory intelligent design."[1261]

Considering the world through the concepts of twenty percent of the world population, Chinese culture can contribute further perspectives.[1262] *Yin* and *yang* are polar opposites that must be balanced in order for life to proceed in harmony. The term *yin* denotes the shady side of the slope, and may be associated with qualities of femininity, openness, passivity, receptivity, introversion, diminution, repose, weakness and coolness. *Yang* is the sunny side of the slope, and may be associated with the sun, masculinity, strength, brightness, assertiveness, movement, extroversion, growth and excitation.

In the body, the front is yin relative to the back; the upper portions of the body are yang relative to the lower parts; the inner organs are more yin than the outer aspects such as hair and skin. Yang disorders are characterized by fever, hyperactivity, heat and strong movements; yin illnesses include weakness, slowing down, feeling cold and lethargy.[1263]

Yin and yang complement each other. If yang is excessive, then yin will be too weak, and conversely.

In Chinese cosmology, causality is unimportant. It is the *pattern* of relationships which defines reality, and all reality is relative to the context which is under consideration.

> The philosopher Zou Yen...describes this idea this way: "Heaven is high, the earth is low, and thus [Heaven and Earth] are fixed. As the high and low are thus made clear, the honorable and humble have their place accordingly. As activity and tranquility have their constancy, the strong and the weak are thus differentiated... Cold and hot season take their turn... [Heaven] knows the great beginning, and [Earth] acts to bring things to completion... [Heaven] is Yang and [Earth] is Yin."
>
> Any Yin or Yang aspect can be further divided into Yin and Yang...
> – Kaptchuck [1264]

Coming from the other direction in our consideration of a possible language inherent in genetic codes, we find that protein transcription is not sequential.

Details for genetic directives for form and function are found in non-consecutive segments of gene sequences. Inferring that there is the equivalent of a language in these patterns of protein sequences may be premature. We are inferring a language from gene sequences because that is how our Western languages bias us to perceive the world.[1265]

All of these difficulties in interpreting the genetic code as a language still might not necessarily refute this argument for intelligent design. More below on problems in the languaging of genetic codes.

Further problems with Darwinian theory to explain evolution

Scientists are also questioning whether Darwinian selection is a sufficient explanation to account for *all* of the shifts that have occurred from the time of the spontaneous formation of proteins in the primordial chemical soup in the earliest eons of our planet; through incredibly complex aggregations of proteins into single-celled organisms; through the gathering of cells into collective communities that became multi-celled organisms; and then into the diversity of species that we have seen through archeological ages and into recent history.[1266]

Stephen Meyer, Director of Discovery Institute's Center for Science and Culture, has written an outstanding discussion exploring and explaining this controversy.[1267] He cites numerous critics who have questioned the adequacy of Darwin's theory to explain the range and rapidity of changes that have occurred in morphology as species developed on our planet.[1268]

Meyer focuses largely on the period in earth's history when the quantum developmental leap was made from very simple, mostly single-celled organisms, to increasingly complex animal life:

> ...the 'Cambrian explosion'... the geologically sudden appearance of many new animal body plans about 530 million years ago. At this time, at least nineteen, and perhaps as many as thirty-five phyla[1269] of forty total, made their first appearance on earth within a narrow five- to ten-million-year window of geologic time... Many new subphyla, between 32 and 48 of 56 total,[1270] and classes of animals also arose at this time with representatives of these new higher taxa [classifications of organisms] manifesting significant morphological innovations. The Cambrian explosion thus marked a major episode of morphogenesis in which many new and disparate organismal forms arose in a geologically brief period of time.

Meyer argues (convincingly, in my opinion) that Darwinian theory cannot adequately explain the following issues concerning selection of the fittest:

1. The complexity of protein structure
Many geneticists point out that it is highly improbable that a coherent, functional series of mutations could occur in any organism which would produce a totally new, viable, living organism. Genetic information is transmitted through a coded

series of proteins, called *bases*. Each base is an informational unit similar to a letter in the alphabet of genetic information. The genetic alphabet contains only four different bases.

A single gene contains more than 1,000 protein bases in a very specific sequence. Each unique series of bases in a gene dictates the instructions for whatever form or function is controlled by that gene in the organism. "A gene 999 bases in length represents one of 4^{999} possible nucleotide sequences" that are statistically possible. Making it more complex yet, each base is composed of twenty possible arrangements of amino acids (the building blocks of proteins). In a protein containing 333 amino acids, there are 20^{333} possible combinations of amino acids, of which that protein represents the one specific sequence that uniquely comprises that protein. Any of the other 20^{333} combinations will not produce that protein.

The likelihood of a mutation in one or more of the amino acids producing a viable new sequence in a single gene is so minutely small as to be nearly unimaginable. Any changes in the sequences of amino acids and proteins are more likely to produce a 'sentence' of genetic language that is not compatible with survival of the organism. This would be like putting a wrong letter or word into instructions for your computer. The new amino acid sequence would not fit with the rest of the biological computer's programs, and would jam up the biological informational programs of the cells.

2. The harmonious orchestrations of effects by multiple genes

The above relates to just a single gene. Many genes have to work together in harmony to orchestrate normal growth and ongoing biochemical functions in an organism. Evolutionary changes that would bring about a new structure such as a lung that breathes air in a fish, invent a feather on a reptile, or an eye in a worm would require enormous numbers of genetic mutations *that all have to work in harmony for the organism to survive.* The statistical probabilities of a whole series of such changes occurring simultaneously to produce such outcomes are astronomically small.

Meyer considers all of the above issues concerning mutations and then expands on the challenges faced by Darwinian theory to account for the explosion of new forms that occurred during the Cambrian geological period. During this period, very simple, single-celled creatures evolved into much more complex, multicellular organisms with differentiated structures and organs.[1271] The greater complexity in form and function must have been preceded by development of countless proteins, each of which would have to be far longer than 100 bases in order to orchestrate the numerous specialized functions required for the life of a multicellular organism.

Meyer focuses on one example, the enzyme lysyl oxidase. This is a complex protein that is needed to build connective tissues to support an organism's body structure. Lysyl oxidase which is found in living organisms today contains more than 400 amino acids. Lysyl oxidase is both extremely complicated (containing sequences of bases that never repeat) and very specific in its function. If we take estimates from laboratory mutation experiments on much shorter protein molecules, extrapolations suggest the likelihood of producing random proteins of this length that actually function is so minute that it appears absurd to suggest this could occur by chance. The length of time required would exceed the life of the entire universe.

Nevertheless, fossil data and molecular analyses demonstrate profound evolutionary changes during the Cambrian explosion, which was a far shorter period than the duration of the entire universe. Mutation rates for DNA are far too slow to produce the new genes and proteins required for building the animals that appeared in the Cambrian period.[1272]

To put it succinctly, Meyer concludes: Darwinian mechanisms address the "survival of the fittest, not the arrival of the fittest."

Atomic and subatomic particles and forces

> We had this old idea, that there was a universe out there, and here is man, the observer, safely protected from the universe by a six-inch slab of plate glass. Now we learn from the quantum world that even to observe so minuscule an object as an electron we have to shatter that plate glass; we have to reach in there... So the old word observer simply has to be crossed off the books, and we must put in the new word participator. In this way we've come to realize that the universe is a participatory universe.
> – John A. Wheeler

The guiding plan of design is also suggested on much more basic levels of exploration of our world. Our universe was created and is held together on atomic and molecular levels through a collection of fascinating coincidences. If the universe were not balanced precisely, as detailed below, I would not be here to write these words, nor would you be here to read them. The following are some observations gathered by Robert Newman, an astrophysicist at Cornell University, who is also a Professor at a Biblical Theological Seminary:[1273]

Four basic forces hold our universe together: a strong and a weak nuclear force; electromagnetism; and gravity. If these forces were not balanced precisely, life could not exist.

1. *Gravity* balances the speed of expansion of the entire universe. Astronomers have calculated that our universe is expanding, with indications that it all started with a 'big bang' about 15 billion years ago. While it was believed that the universe will eventually collapse upon itself, recent research shows that the expansion of the universe continues to accelerate, for reasons that are as yet unclear.[1274] Whatever the case, the density of matter in the universe lies within a precise balance between constant expansion and ultimate contraction. Following expansion for about 20 billion years, in order to remain today so close to this critical density, precise conditions must have existed in the initial instants of the big bang. At an almost unimaginable teeny tiny fraction of a second following the big bang (called the 'Planck time'),[1275] the precision of the density of the unimag-

inably compact universe had to be at a level of a single part in 10^{-60}. [1276] Had the density been the tiniest fraction of a percent higher at that instant, there would have been a rapid collapse of the universe, with no possibility for life as we know it to develop. Conversely, if the density had been the least bit lower, there would have been such a rapid expansion of the universe that no galaxies with stars and planets would have formed. Life is therefore the result of an incredible fine tuning of the density of matter and energy during the big bang. [1277]

2. *The strong nuclear force* makes an important contribution in the stars, wherein are created many basic chemical building blocks that are essential for life on earth. Life could not exist without a variety of heavy chemical elements, particularly carbon, oxygen and nitrogen. However, none of these were created in the big bang, which only created hydrogen, helium and several other very light elements. The remaining elements are produced within the stars, within which the laws of the weak and strong nuclear forces apply. If the strong force was 50 percent weaker, then carbon and iron would be unstable, making it impossible for proteins to develop. Were the strong force just 5 percent weaker, then there would be no deuterium, making it impossible for stars to burn as they do. Were the strong force just 5 percent stronger, then stars would burn much more intensely. The strong force must be precisely at the value it has in order to make the elements of stars stable, and in order to make it possible for biochemistry to produce and support life as we know it.

3. *The weak nuclear force* also makes essential contributions to our existence. Heavier elements are formed inside stars that are growing old. Without the weak force, the heavy elements would end up staying within the stars, unavailable to initiate and sustain life. As stars use up their fuel, they start to collapse, their temperatures rising dramatically and emitting increasing numbers of neutrinos. These neutrinos build up to the point that stars explode, spreading their heavy elements across the vastness of galactic space. These heavy elements then are incorporated in subsequent generations of stars and in the planets that circle them. This is how our earth acquired its heavy elements that are essential for life. Were the weak force weaker than it is, stars would not explode because their neutrinos would escape rather than contributing their explosive force, and the heavy elements would remain in the stars. Were the weak force stronger, then neutrinos would be unable to escape from stars, and likewise there would be no explosion and the heavy elements could not escape.

4. *Electromagnetism* is far stronger than gravity, [1278] but gravity is the force which acts across astronomical distances. Over these large distances, positive electromagnetic charges (mostly from protons), and negative charges (mostly from electrons, which are much smaller) exist in equal numbers, so they cancel each other out. No theory has been proposed to explain why the universe would contain positive and negative charges in perfect balance. This is all the more surprising, because our prevalent theories about the formation of the universe tell us that after the big bang protons were created much earlier than electrons. It is

utterly amazing to see that the total numbers of electrons and protons in the universe is matched better than one part times 10^{37}. [1279] If these universe these electromagnetic particles did not cancel out each other's effects, then all of the galaxies in the cosmos, with all of their stars and planets would be influenced far more by electromagnetic forces instead of by gravity, which would again create conditions in which life as we know it could not exist.

5. *Carbon* is required for the formation of proteins, DNA and RNA, the building blocks of all life on earth. Carbon is the only known element that links into chains of great length. The sole source for carbon in the universe is from stars. Carbon was formed in these stellar crucibles and dispersed over all of creation when stars exploded. Two coincidences have made carbon a common element instead of an extremely rare one. Carbon is created when three helium nuclei combine, and this combining of nuclei occurs very rarely, except at certain limited temperatures. If the temperature within stars were not exactly right for the formation of carbon, there would be no life as we know it. If the temperature required were only four percent lower, it would be very rare to find any carbon. A second saving grace is that a carbon atom can readily combine with a helium nucleus to create oxygen. Coincidentally, the energy needed for this combination is a little higher than for the creation of carbon and is thus a rare occurrence. If the required temperature were only half a percent higher, almost all of the carbon in stars would have been converted to oxygen. So if either parameter were just a little bit different, carbon would be very scarce and life forms as we know them could not have evolved on earth. [1280]

6. *Energy storage mechanisms* are required by living organisms in order to carry on life functions. Phosphorus appears to be a 'designer element' for living organisms because it alone among all the elements in existence can be combined to create various molecules which store energy efficiently. [1281] Lacking such these compounds, higher animal life would be impossible, because efficient energy storage is required for digestion, metabolism and mobility. [1282]

7. *Water* is composed of one oxygen and two hydrogen atoms. Water molecules are lighter than oxygen or nitrogen molecules, and should therefore exist as a gas at the temperatures on our planet that are so eminently suitable for life. Fortunately, two or three molecules of water join together loosely, making it a liquid at ordinary temperatures. Water forms the basis for cell plasma, animal blood and tree sap.

Another fortunate feature of water is that when it evaporates, the combined molecules separate from each other. This makes it possible to diffuse into the atmosphere so that water vapor does not lie on the surface of the earth as an unbreathable gas and stifle life.

Water also is a universal solvent, which can dissolve needed chemicals which can then circulate in cells, the bloodstream and in plant sap. Any other liquid which has the capacity to dissolve a similar range of substances is highly corrosive and would be deadly.

Water is also an unusual substance because it can absorb a great amount of heat with any change in temperature. It is therefore able to moderate the earth's climate. It also helps to stabilize body temperatures of humans and other animals.

Unlike most other substances, upon freezing it will expand rather than contracting. Ice, the expanded form of water, floats because it is lighter than liquid water. Oceans and lakes therefore do not freeze to the bottom, which would kill most marine creatures. Water expands in rock crevices as it freezes, thereby also helping to form soil by splitting up the rocks.[1283]

To Meyer's discussion above, Ervin Laszlo[1284] adds the following three observations:

8. "If the difference between the mass of the neutron and the proton were not precisely twice the mass of the electron, no substantial chemical reactions could take place."

9. If the electrical charges of protons and electrons were not exactly balanced, every bit of matter in the universe would be highly unstable and we would find nothing in the universe other than a uniform mixture of gases and radiation.

10. Uncountably enormous numbers of atoms had to come together to initiate the formation of stars and galaxies, on the order of 10^{16} suns. There is no theory to account for mechanisms whereby such an enormous quantity of atoms could have combined to form the universe we observe today. Random fluctuations of individual atoms provide no plausible explanation.

Our solar system

> [T]his most beautiful system of the sun, planets, and comets could only proceed from the counsel and dominion of an intelligent and powerful Being.
> — Isaac Newton

Coincidences within our solar system also create conditions required for life.

1. *Our sun* is the right size and we are the right distance from our sun. If the sun were only 20 percent larger (as are many of the suns in the universe) it would have consumed all its fuel in only four billion years. By this time in our sun's life, it would have been in a 'red giant' stage, and the earth would have been consumed in the expansion of the sun's fiery atmosphere. Had our sun been only 20 percent smaller, we would not have sufficient blue light for our plants to produce sugar and oxygen efficiently. Animals cannot produce either by themselves.

2. *The sun's luminosity is fairly constant.* If the sun's brightness varied too much, life would not survive. Our sun's luminosity has increased 25 percent over the last

four billion years, but plants appeared at just the right time to counterbalance the increased heat. As the sun became hotter, plants removed greater quantities of carbon dioxide from our atmosphere, replacing it with oxygen at precisely the right rate to dampen the greenhouse effect, while maintaining temperatures in a range that supports life.[1285]

3. *The earth is at the correct distance from the sun* to enable this response of our plants. Had the earth been five percent closer to the sun, the greenhouse effect early in earth's history would have exceeded the conditions that support plant life and we would not have any plants on earth. Without plants to reduce carbon dioxide, earth would be a furnace just like Venus. Had the earth been only one percent further away from the sun, an ice age would have prevailed due to colder temperatures two billion years ago, and our earth would be totally covered in ice today.[1286]

4. *Temperatures on earth* make this the only planet in our solar system that can support life as we know it. While temperatures vary between our poles and the equator, between summer and winter, and from the lowest to the highest points on the surface of our planet, the boiling point of water is exceeded only in volcanoes and geysers. While temperatures dip below freezing in winter and are constantly below freezing at the poles, our oceans never completely freeze over. We could not live on our neighboring planets: Venus averages around 900 degrees Fahrenheit. Mars barely gets above freezing even in midsummer at the equator. Earth alone has the right temperature range for life: warm enough for water to be liquid, cool enough that complex life molecules are not destroyed.

5. *The gravity on earth* holds the atmosphere at a pressure that supports life. If the earth were less massive, atmospheric pressure would not support life; if it were more massive, the atmosphere would be denser, creating a greenhouse effect in summer with temperatures too high for our survival.[1287]

6. *Oxygen* in the atmosphere on earth supports life. With only a few percent less oxygen, animals would not survive; with only a few percent more, plants would not survive.[1288]

These and other complex facts and balances of conditions in our universe are so unlikely to have occurred purely by chance that a guiding intelligence seems a far more likely explanation than mere chance.

Scientists are reluctant to consider that a Creator might have designed the universe, and have therefore proposed *the Anthropic principle*[1289] as a possible explanation for these many factors that appear to be incredible coincidences. The Anthropic theory suggests that we, as observers, are in some ways determining the way our universe exists.[1290] Clearly, life as we know it could not exist unless all of the factors detailed above and more are balanced precisely as they are. On the other hand, if life were impossible, we would not be present to observe this universe.

Conversely, observers will only exist in a universe where these many factors exist as they do in our universe. The theory that the orderliness of our universe is only some accident of human observation, is named the *weak Anthropic principle*. This theory still does not explain how the incredibly complex, astronomically unlikely probabilities detailed above could all have lined up and combined to make our world possible.

Going further along these lines, *the strong Anthropic principle* suggests that humanity itself in some way has influenced the world to take form with precisely the right conditions that allow life to exist. The basis for this is either that man is a part of God or that it is possible to influence events and bring about effects backward in time. [1291]

The Anthropic principle is consonant with the theory of participatory intelligent design. However, it merely acknowledges but does not explain any possible ways in which an intelligent agent could guide the formation and evolution of the universe.

Gaia, our planet

> *I will sing of*
> *well-founded Gaia,*
> *Mother of All,*
> *eldest of all beings,*
> *she feeds all creatures*
> *that are in the world,*
> *all that go upon the goodly land*
> *and all that are in the paths of the sea,*
> *and all that fly:*
> *all these are fed of her store.*
> — Homeric Hymn, 7th Century B.C.

The homeostatic mechanisms that maintain a steady environment conducive to life on our planet are astoundingly complex and remarkably successful. James Lovelock suggests that these salutary conditions have been created and are maintained through the collective participation of living organisms through the ages.[1292] He has called this ecobiological system *Gaia,* after the Greek earth goddess.[1293]

In his classic book, *Gaia, A new look at life on earth,* Lovelock notes the following impressive facts:[1294]

1. *Oxygen* is only present as a trace of the atmosphere on Mars and Venus. Lovelock estimates that Earth's atmosphere without life would similarly contain virtually no oxygen, whereas it presently contains 21 percent.

This level of oxygen is ideal for supporting living organisms. If the level increased any further it would be dangerous. For every one percent increase above our present level, there would be a seventy percent increase in the danger of forest fires started by lightning. At 25 percent and above, not much plant life would survive.[1295]

2. *Carbon dioxide* comprises 95 percent of the atmosphere on Venus and 96.5 percent on Mars. Lovelock estimates that Earth's atmosphere without life would contain 98 percent carbon dioxide instead of its 0.03 percent (in 1988).[1296]
   Since 1954, the amount of carbon dioxide in the atmosphere, measured in Hawaii, has increased by 3 percent each year, from between 310-320 parts per million to 370 parts per million in 2004.[1297]

3. *Methane* is found in the atmosphere at a concentration of 1.5 parts per million. The release of about a billion tons of methane annually is required to maintain this constant level in the atmosphere. In sunlight, oxygen reacts with methane to produce carbon dioxide plus water vapor. Yet the level of methane remains constant everywhere on our planet. Similarly, the oxygen used up in oxidizing the methane has to be replaced, requiring a minimum of 2 billion tons of oxygen annually. The fact that both of these gasses have remained in constant proportions in the atmosphere of our planet over millions of years is remarkable.[1298]

4. *The output of energy from the sun* has increased by 30 percent at a minimum over the three and a half billion years of the existence of life on the Earth. Going back to a time when there was thirty percent less solar heat, we would expect a mean temperature on Earth that is well under the freezing point of water. It would take only a two percent decrease in heat absorbed by one hemisphere in order to establish an Ice Age. If the climate on Earth were determined just by the sun's radiant heat, this planet would have been frozen over the first 1.5 billion years of life's existence. Archaeological records and the constant presence of life testify that such adversely cold conditions could not have existed.
   As noted earlier, Gaia has managed to maintain a constant range of temperatures during the 3.5 billion years of the existence of life on this planet. Calculations show that the interior heat of earth's molten core, maintained due to radioactive processes, could not account for the constant temperatures on the earth's surface. Lovelock cites two prevalent hypotheses for how Gaia may have maintained a warmer temperature in the early days of life: A darker overall color on earth would absorb more heat from the sun; and a higher percent of carbon dioxide would act like a blanket to warm the earth.[1299]

5. *Living organisms* on our planet play a major role in regulating these gasses (along with other processes that promote and maintain life). While it might seem far-fetched to suggest that a person, a plant or a fungus could contribute to the balance of planetary chemistry, Lovelock suggests very plausible mechanisms that explain how this is possible when one considers the large numbers of organisms on the planet – particularly our most numerous ones, the bacteria and other single-celled creatures.
   Lovelock views this as a strictly mechanistic theory, believing that naturally occurring processes account for the homeostatic mechanisms that maintain

conditions on Gaia which are conducive to life. He does not believe in any sort of vitalist theory that would suggest a consciousness to this system, which is the more commonly held view of Gaia today. Lovelock draws support for this view from the well established field of *cybernetics,* which focuses on "the self-regulating systems of communication and control in living organisms and machines."[1300] Within these self-regulating systems, one cannot define cause and effect. One cannot say whether the chicken is the egg's way of getting more eggs or vice-versa, and as Lovelock points out, this question has no relevance if one is studying the functions of the whole system.

Lovelock theorizes that life must extensively populate a planet in order to be capable of regulating the planetary chemical balances that maintain its climate. He notes that a diversity of life creates a more stable homeostatic system than would exist with limited numbers and types of organisms. A broad variety of predators and prey; vegetable food and foragers; organisms that populate diverse ecological niches and the Gaian chemicals that are available in these niches make it more possible for Gaia to develop corrective shifts for any imbalances that occur due to changes in any given part of the system.

How are these gasses maintained at their constant levels? Let's review some combinations of chemical and biological factors combining to make this possible.

Methane, commonly called marsh gas, is a biological product. It was initially believed to come mostly from intestinal gas[1301] of ruminant (cud-chewing) animals. It is now known that most of this gas is the product of bacterial fermentation in the mud and sediment of wet lands, marshes, river estuaries and sea beds. The amount of methane produced by microorganisms is amazingly large, approximately 500 million tons yearly.

When methane is produced by bacteria, it rises into the atmosphere. It seems to counterbalance oxygen in two ways: for the most part removing oxygen, but also returning a little to the atmosphere through different mechanisms. Some of it reaches the stratosphere where it is converted to water vapor and carbon dioxide. Methane is actually the principal source for water vapor in the higher layers of air surrounding the earth. The water in these outer reaches of the atmosphere eventually separates into its components of oxygen and hydrogen. Oxygen returns to earth, while hydrogen dissipates into space – creating a small but perhaps significant cumulative supplement of oxygen to the air over geologic time periods.

However, oxidation of methane lower in the atmosphere consumes a considerable quantity of oxygen, in the range of 1,000 megatons yearly. The complex chemical reactions involved proceed constantly in the atmosphere. Without methane in the air, the concentration of oxygen would increase by approximately one percent in as short a period as 24,000 years. This would be a very dangerous shift in the atmospheric balance of gasses, one that would be difficult for life forms to adjust to and to survive[1302].

The constant levels of oxygen present in the air over millions of years suggests that there must be an active regulating system to maintain this balance. This requires some way of sensing and acting upon any deviations from required oxygen concentrations in the atmosphere – neither of which control mechanisms has yet been discovered. This might be managed by production of methane and the burial of carbon from masses of plants that are washed into the beds of bodies of water. In the deep underwater mud, bacteria either convert it to methane or it remains buried. Therefore, any mechanisms which can shift this proportion can effectively regulate oxygen in the air. Perhaps when the air has too much oxygen, a warning signal might be amplified in the process of methane production, which would then move to rebalance the steady-state conditions by the increased production and release of methane gas into the air.

6. *Ammonia* is emitted into the atmosphere at a rate of about 1,000 megatons annually, entirely of biological origin. Ammonia strongly influences acidity in the environment. Ammonia is alkaline and is needed to balance the acids produced from the oxidation of sulphur and nitrogen. Precisely enough ammonia is produced by Gaia to maintain a slightly alkaline rainfall (pH near 8), which is optimal for life. If ammonia were not produced in adequate amounts, then rain would fall at an acid pH (close to 3), nearly as acid as vinegar.[1303]

7. *Nitrogen* has accumulated in the air because bacteria which release it from combination with other chemicals, along with other biological activities in living cells, produce an excess of this gas. It only gradually returns to its place of greatest concentration, in the sea, through inorganic mechanisms such as thunderstorms. Without life on our planet, the greater part of the nitrogen from the atmosphere would gradually combine with oxygen and be recycled back into the sea as nitrates. Nitrogen helps to stabilize our global climate by contributing the major portion of atmospheric density. This slow reacting gas is probably the best balance for the oxygen in the air, since a higher oxygen concentration would be disastrous. Furthermore, removing nitrogen from the sea and lessening the numbers of nitrate ions there, contributes to the challenging problem of keeping salinity sufficiently low enough to be compatible with life.[1304]

8. *The presence of oceans* is an important part of the homeostatic mechanisms of our planet. It appears that over the three and a half billion years of life on earth, while the sea level rose and fell as polar ice froze and remelted, and continents shifted around the surface of the planet, the total global water volume remained constant. Today the average ocean depth is around 2 miles.[1305]

9. *Silica* is assimilated by diatoms, which are single-celled or colonial algae that grow profusely in the sea during their brief lifespans in surface waters. Upon dying, they sink to the ocean bottom and their skeletons that contain silica become sediment, contributing approximately 300 million tons of silica rock to the ocean floor annually. In this way these microscopic organisms move silicon from the surface of sea waters, reducing the salinity of the sea.[1306]

These are but a few of the many facets of Gaia that exist in complex and delicate balances with each other. Lovelock believes that these intricately interdigitated, combinations of reactions which maintain constant temperatures, chemical balances and other conditions favorable to life have all occurred purely by chance.

Popular opinion has expanded Lovelock's theory of Gaia as a living geobiological entity that actively maintains her own homeostatic balance to support life, attributing to Gaia a sentience that Lovelock himself does not accept. This popular theory of Gaia is completely in line with the theory of participatory intelligent design. The nested consciousness of each individual organism participating in the ebb and flow of life on Earth could participate in and contribute to, as well as being guided by, the planetary consciousness. This would provide the missing link of a guiding consciousness to explain how the complex balances of chemicals and conditions favorable to life on earth are sensed and maintained – through appropriate biological responses of greater or lesser growth of organisms that produce needed chemicals or absorb and sequester excesses of the same materials. More on this in the discussion, below.[1307]

> *The Earth Goddess fashions the human body just as a potter fashions her pot.*
>
> Jukin proverb, Nigeria

Research suggesting human intelligent design

Jean-Baptiste Lamarck (1744-1823) proposed that the needs of a living organism could produce changes in its genetic makeup so that its form and function would mutate in a direction with desirable characteristics to help it survive better. He suggested that birds such as storks developed longer legs and webbed feet in response to their need to wade in shallow waters, not by selection of the fittest but in direct response to the need. No experiments were done at the time to confirm this theory.

Lamarck's theory was abandoned as the Darwinian theory of selection of the fittest became more accepted in the mid 19th century. A further blow to the Lamarckian theory came from August Weismann, a German biologist. Weismann proposed a germ-plasm theory to explain heredity. He asserted that the *soma* (body) is completely separate from *germ-plasm* (hereditary material). In support of his views, Weismann cut off the tails of several successive generations of mice. Not a single one was born tailless – suggesting that animals would not acquire a genetic change despite repeated external physical changes. As further evidence against Lamarckian genetics, he noted that circumcision of Jewish and Muslim boys did not produce children without foreskins. This argument was generally accepted and along with it, Darwinian theory was generally accepted.

It was only many years later that supporters of Lamarckian genetics pointed out that this was not a true test of Lamarckian theory because neither circumcision nor the cutting off tails of mice represent any inherent *need* of the organism. These are surgical interventions performed by others on the child or the mouse and therefore would not be expressed as a genetic change through Lamarckian mechanisms. In contrast, the existence of leaves on trees could create a biologically perceived need which would lead an animal to develop a long neck, eventually producing a giraffe that could reach this foliage.

In recent years, several other scientists have made similar observations. Stephen Gould suggested that the existence of a need in an animal species could lead to the development of physical characteristics that are of benefit to that species. In fact, characteristics have developed for which it would be very difficult to postulate explanations under Darwinian theory. Gould gives the example of the panda's extra, sixth digit on its forelimbs. This highly specialized thumb is extremely useful in splitting bamboo shoots, which are the principal item in the panda's diet. There is a very low probability of an extra digit developing by random mutations. A more likely hypothesis seems the mechanism of Lamarckian genetics.

Rupert Sheldrake proposes that a morphogenetic field could explain such phenomena. This is a psi field of species-specific, shared experiences. Individuals of a given species contribute their personal life experiences to this field of awareness, which then becomes available to other members of that species. This could explain the appearances of physical characteristics such as the camel's thick knee pads.

The theory of Lamarckian genetics has never gained general recognition or acceptance, despite these observations and studies that appear to support it. I believe there is reason to examine this evidence afresh. Let me start with the story of a remarkable person who was able single-handedly to demonstrate an ability to influence genetic development.[1308]

Luther Burbank was an American nurseryman who was able to produce remarkable numbers of new varieties of plants in the early 20th Century. He developed over 800 new varieties of fruits, vegetables, flowers, cacti and trees.

Ordinarily, it takes several decades of cross-fertilizations to develop a single new hybrid variety of a plant or animal. Specimens with desirable traits are cross-bred and re-crossed until the desired trait is strengthened. It is considered a notable achievement to produce a single new variety of a given species.

Burbank was able to bring out new traits in plants in just a few successive generations, over periods of only two to four years.[1309] His methods were based on more than just hybridization. Burbank would plant thousands of seeds. He would then select those plants with desirable new traits to inbreed until the new traits were breeding true (i.e., the plants were reproducing the new traits regularly and reliably). Thus far, the description sounds rather routine. However, let me quote Burbank describing his methods of selecting specimens and the rate at which he worked, in order to clarify the unusual range and nature of his abilities.

> From the first it has been my practice to mark selected individual plants by tying a strip of old white cloth on; this means that the marked plant is sacred... Plants that I could see would add nothing to my experiment, by any possibility, came up at once, or else were marked by my making a line in the bed with the toe of my shoe so that the men could take them out later... Now, when I had a very large project going on – a field or bed with thousands and thousands of varieties of individuals in it – I would have two or three of my helpers follow me and I would simply drop the 'neckties' on the superior plants or

those suited to my purpose, and put a shoc-mark against the worthless ones, about as rapidly as a man could walk along, and the men would do the tying and spade out and burn the condemned plants.[1310]

Burbank's neighbors thought he was most peculiar, if not actually crazy, because he regularly uprooted and burned large portions, sometimes the majority, of the plants he was growing. One might think at first that Burbank simply developed his powers of visual observation to such a high acuity that he could work this rapidly and accurately. Indeed, Burbank noted that his five senses were so acutely sensitive that he found some stimuli, such as certain music, painful. However, he himself adds:

Probably there is more to it than merely this sensory response in *me – it may be a sixth sense, it may be purely intuitive*[1311] – but I know that even those who have worked with me longest and have been closest to me, learning my methods and watching me in the gardens, have been unable to duplicate what I have done as a mere matter of routine, and with no thought as to how I did it. Some of the men who have worked for me have developed into good, sound, original, and even clever and successful plant developers. But as far as I have been able to observe they have not been able even to approach my own natural ability to choose between plants, and to choose, not one from a dozen, or a few here and there, but at wholesale – thousands of plants in a day out of tens of thousands growing in my experimental gardens.

Even close friends and observers have said what you, perhaps, are saying to yourself now; that is that I was bound to be right part of the time and that there is no way of telling how many poor selections I made through error nor how many perfect ones I caused to be destroyed. My friends were wrong, as you are. I made some mistakes, of course, but considering the number of plants I have selected in the course of sixty years as a plant breeder they are negligible. On the contrary, I will tell you a story, out of many such that are available, to show you how complete my gift is.[1312]

Burbank proceeds to tell of a friend, a judge who expressed skepticism regarding Burbank's ability to select plants correctly prior to their demonstrating the characteristics for which he was breeding them.

"Well, Judge," I said, "this selecting isn't being done by guesswork, though I suppose it looks like it. Why don't you take half a dozen of those condemned (plum) trees and plant them down on your Santa Clara Valley place, and find out for yourself whether I am right or wrong?"

He said he would like to make the test, and for good measure I insisted on his taking also six of the seedlings I had selected as the best varieties. So we dug the trees up carefully, packed them and shipped them to his home.

When the trees were bearing fruit, the Judge reported,

"Burbank, if any one had told me five years ago that selection could be done by a man almost at a trot, I would have said that he was crazy..."

He went on to admit that he had been wrong and that I had been right in every single case. He said that he had ordered his men to take out and burn all of the six trees I had condemned as seedlings, five years before, but that every one of the six I had chosen had proved perfect trees with beautiful luscious, well-developed fruit and plenty of it.[1313]

One might hypothesize that Burbank was simply gifted with precognition. His feats of hybridization would therefore have been merely (!) an enhanced and accelerated process of selection of seedlings – prior to their showing any hints of the desired new characteristics, such as flowers or fruits. However, some of Burbank's explanations for his success suggest that additional psi processes were involved.

... I have had as many as ten thousand separate and distinct experiments going on at one time. I have produced as many as five hundred varieties of plums on twelve trees in one short row.[1314] I have had in my gardens as many as eight thousand different varieties of roses, iris, or gladiolus. Every one of these was obtained by using natural processes or adaptations of them, and *every one was there because I needed it in my search for a definite quality or characteristic... I took Nature's mind and added to it my own, that knew exactly what it wanted and was in a hurry (comparatively speaking) to get it!*[1315]

Burbank was a staunch admirer of Darwin and credits him with the inspiration for developing many of his techniques. Nevertheless, he believed in Lamarckian inheritance of acquired characteristics.

I began with the cell, the fundamental unit of life: it was apparent from all I saw that the cell was influenced by environment, that those influences, if they persisted long enough – repetition, repetition, repetition – entered into the heredity, and that this heredity was the factor I had most to deal with in training plants to bend themselves to man's greater good...[1316]

One might wonder whether by 'repetition' Burbank referred merely to repeated generations of hybridization/selection. Although he does emphasize these mechanical processes,[1317] he clearly goes further towards human intelligent design in his beliefs.

... The fruit pit, bearing the seed, it is very difficult to break into; the soles of a man's feet are tough and of thickened skin; in each case the reason is, originally, that the seed must be honed against destruction by birds, the feet armored against thorns and pebbles and a nail in the shoe! Do you think these natural provisions are the result of chance?

Not at all...[1318]

Theoretical basis for participatory intelligent design

Burbank's incredible work invites us to ask, "How might one person have developed so many new varieties of plants?" I propose a hypothesis based on participatory intelligent design as an answer. In order to understand this theory, we must first review the basics of genetic reproduction. Our modern understanding of inherited characteristics dates back to an Austrian monk, Gregor Mendel, who studied close to 30,000 pea plants that he cross-bred between 1856 and 1863.

Mendel observed what happened when he cross-bred different colored pea plants. He found regular proportions of offspring with yellow and green peas in successive generations after crossing a green pea plant (which bred true for green – that is, always produced green peas) with a yellow pea plant (which bred true for yellow). The second generation peas were all green. Crossing pairs of plants grown from these peas, in the third generation he would obtain 3/4 green peas and 1/4 yellow peas.[1319]

Mendel figured out from these findings that there were dominant and recessive traits and that they came in pairs which could contain only green; only yellow; or one each of green and yellow. The yellow pea plants had a pair of these traits that were both yellow. The green peas could contain either both green, or one green and one yellow. Because the green was a *dominant* trait, it covered up the effects of the yellow trait in the second generation – where each plant progeny was receiving half of the influence from each parent plant. Thus, though all of the second generation plants had a *recessive* yellow trait, it did not show itself because the dominant green trait hid the yellow trait effects. In the third generation, 1/4 of the plants would have green traits only; 2/4 would have one green and one yellow; and 1/4 would have yellow traits only.[1320] (See Figure III-12)

Mendel observed that these discrete units of inheritance were passed in regular and constant proportions from one generation to another. It was only later that these units came to be called genes.

Figure III-12. Second generation cross-breeding

2nd GENERATION PARENT GENES	Green + Yellow ↓ ↓	
Green → + Yellow →	Green + Green	Yellow + Green
	Green + Yellow	Yellow + Yellow

3rd GENERATION PROGENY GENES

It has been subsequently confirmed that there are pairs of genes for each aspect of genetic inheritance, clustered in a series of chromosomes. Each chromosome may contain hundreds of genes. Modern gene research has identified the 'maps' for these series of gene pairs in humans and in numbers of other animals.

When egg and sperm cells are produced, the chromosomes in the parent cells line up in pairs and then separate into two half-sets of chromosomes, producing two eggs or two sperm cells, each of which contains half of the original set of chromosomes. (The cells with half of a chromosome set are called *haploid* cells.) Each egg and sperm cell has half the normal number of chromosomes for that organism – so that when they combine, the fertilized egg then has a normal number of chromosomes. If this did not happen, the fertilized egg would have double the number of chromosomes it should have, which would not be compatible with its survival.

This process of germ cell division is called *meiosis*. As the parent cells prepare for meiosis, pairs of chromosomes line up together and there is a random distribution of the genes between them.[1321] There is also a random distribution for which half of the pair of chromosomes (in the series of chromosomes present in the cell) goes into which haploid egg or sperm cell.[1322]

I suggest that intentional effects upon genetic inheritance can be explained on the basis of biological psychokinesis (PK) acting upon the process of meiosis. While we do not yet know the scientific mechanisms that would explain psi effects (any more than we know how to explain gravity), biological PK still provides a well studied and statistically validated mechanism that can help to explain such phenomena as Burbank's ability to produce these many new varieties of plants.

A robust body of research demonstrates that mental influence can produce highly significant deviations in random number generators (RNGs).[1323] The most common RNGs are electronic devices that function perfectly at random when left alone, generating ones and zeros in totally chance patterns that average out to 50 percent ones and 50 percent zeros. However, *RNGs will deviate and produce significantly more ones or zeros when someone directs them to do so mentally*. This has been repeatedly demonstrated with RNGs based on electronic, mechanical, and even radioactive mechanisms. The ability to influence RNGs may be a mechanism that could help to support and explain the theory of Lamarckian genetics.

The process of meiosis constitutes, in effect, a biological random number generator. Actually, the random distribution of genes between pairs of chromosomes in the process of meiosis, and the random distribution of halves of each pair into the haploid sperm and egg cells makes this a *double random number generator*.

Taking this information back to our discussion of Burbank's remarkable work may throw some light on how he was able to achieve so many new varieties of plants.

Burbank found that by cross-fertilizing between genetically diverse individuals of the same species (choosing specimens which possessed widely varying characteristics or which had simply been isolated geographically for long periods of time), he produced progeny in the third and later generations which were markedly more varied than the parent plants. This appears to be a possible method for increasing random options available during meiosis, upon which psi factors may operate to select new combinations for desired characteristics. In fact, his own words suggest that he was aware of this aid of psi influences:

> Crossing is done to secure a wealth of variation. By this means we get the species into a state of perturbation or *wabble*,[1324] and take advantage of the 'wabbling' to guide the life forces into the desired habits or channels.[1325]

> *[C]ombining heredities, by cross-pollinization, and thereafter selecting those individuals showing the strongest tendency toward my purpose, was one of the chiefest methods in my repertoire. It was here that there entered the one important process I relied on and which I had never seen stressed by any one before me – the repetition, repetition, repetition, of one influence on one plant for one purpose, time after time, day after day, generation after generation, patiently, tirelessly, without ever changing my idea or deviating from my plain course, until, in the end, the characteristic or quality or power I wanted in the plant was so firmly fixed in it – in its heredity, you see... that it could no more be bred out or dropped out or lost than could the plant's tendency to send its roots downward and its leaves upward.[1326]*

At first reading, it might appear that Burbank was indicating that he relied upon a single-minded focus on the processes of cross-breeding and selection of specimens from a pool of thousands of specimens for desired characteristics. Lest there be any doubt about Burbank's intended meaning, consider the following additional clarifications:

> *To Manly P. Hall, founder and president of the Philosophical Research Society of Los Angeles and a student of comparative religion, mythology and esoterica, Burbank revealed that when he wanted his plants to develop in some particular and peculiar way not common to their kind he would get down on his knees and talk to them. Burbank also mentioned that plants have over twenty sensory perceptions but, because they are different from ours, we cannot recognize them. "He was not sure," wrote Hall, "that the shrubs and flowers understood his words, but he was convinced that by some telepathy, they could comprehend his meaning."[1327]*

> *If we invite Mr. Thistle or Mr. Cactus into our gardens and patiently and earnestly teach and thoroughly convince him that all the marauding animals shall be kept out, it will not be very long before some members of his tribe will see fit partly to discard some of those exasperating pins and needles and put out a more civilized suit of clothes; and by further careful selection from this one varying individual others are produced which are absolutely spineless, to remain so as long as the marauding animals do not disturb them, often becoming useful members of our parks and gardens. It is great effort on the part of the plant to produce all these spines and when this effort is made unnecessary the plant will at once become more docile and pliable, and can*

be easily led into almost any useful occupation in which plants are employed.[1328]

"You have nothing to fear," I would tell them. "You don't need your defensive thorns I will protect you." Gradually the useful plant of the desert emerged in a thornless variety.[1329]

[T]he structural always follows the functional; in other words, the necessity of a thing is exhibited as functional and afterward the structure arises.[1330]

It would thus seem that Burbank was able to alter the genetic patterns of plants through persistent focus of his intent on desired characteristics. This would, by definition, be a form of biological psychokinesis.

Of additional note is the report that Burbank was a telepathic *sender*. He is mentioned as repeatedly being able to summon his sister from miles away telepathically. He is also said to have worked occasionally as a healer.[1331] These mentions of psi abilities add to the evidence (outside of Burbank's abilities to influence plant genetics), suggesting that there was much more to his methodology than mere cross-fertilizations and selections of desired specimens. He was apparently very reticent in discussing these aspects of his life, and the above are the only shreds of evidence I have been able to unearth relating to his psi abilities. It is probable that most people had difficulty just accepting him as the man of extraordinary natural abilities he was in plant cross-breeding. He probably would have had no desire to increase people's apprehensions by discussing matters which would have only raised further questions about his sanity.

Burbank lived at the time when railroads were opening new regional markets to farmers who previously had sold their produce locally. They wanted plants that could survive the time and traumas of travel from farm to distant markets, ripening along the way, without refrigeration. In response to their requests, he produced over 800 new varieties of plants to the orders of farmers and other nurserymen around the world, taking into consideration the desirability of complex sets of characteristics. These included: rate of growth; qualities of roots, trunk, height, branching, flowering, fruit (time of ripening, narrowness of range of individual ripenings within the group, size, shape, seed, color, texture, skin thickness, odor, flavor); productivity of plants; speed of reproduction; resistances (to cold, heat, insects, fungus); raw qualities (keeping fresh, surviving shipping, ripening in transit); and last, but certainly not least, cooking qualities. He was able by such methods to produce entirely new species, such as crosses between a plum and an apricot (a *plumcot*), which had previously been considered impossible to achieve.

His pet project was the spineless cactus. He hoped that this hardy plant would provide fodder in arid lands for animals that otherwise were unable to eat it.

It is ironic that although most of Burbank's new plant varieties continued to breed true indefinitely, the spineless cactus (about which he elaborated regarding apparent psi influence more than about other plants) did not. It reverted to producing spines several decades after his death. Evidence has also been presented by skeptics that spineless varieties existed prior to Burbank's and that his 'spineless' cacti still had little sharp spicules.

To build a thesis on the basis of one man's work must seem rather precarious, however unusual and successful he was. A few formal studies provide further evidence for the ability of individuals to influence inherited characteristics, in two papers from parapsychology research.

Carroll Nash[1332] tested the abilities of college volunteers with no known psi abilities to produce mutation of *Escherichia coli* bacteria from lac-negative to lac-positive forms in three culture tubes and to produce the reverse mutation in three tubes, with a further three tubes as controls (to be left unchanged). His subjects, who had no known psi or healing gifts, produced significant results.

> The mutant ratio of lac-positive to total bacteria was greater in the promoted than in the inhibited tubes...;[1333] less in the inhibited tubes than in the controls;[1334] and greater in the promoted tubes than in the controls, although not significantly so...
>
>   These results may also be interpreted to indicate selective *growth* of one type of bacterium over the other rather than mutation of one type into another. Were this the case, though, this would still be evidence for a biological PK effect, it would be irrelevant in evidence for environmental influence on genetics.

In a very different experiment, William Cox hypothesized that in families where there were several children of the same sex, there would be a motivation to produce a child of the opposite sex. He studied genealogies of families with either four boys or four girls to see whether there was a greater than chance occurrence of opposite-sex birth in the fifth child. He found a modestly significant greater incidence of boys born as fifth children after four girls,[1335] but the reverse did not prove significant.[1336]

The case of Paul Kammerer is also of interest and relevance.[1337] Kammerer had an unusual ability to breed amphibians and reptiles. He succeeded in raising varieties which no other zoologist had been able to breed previously in captivity. This may suggest no more than patience or especially tender, loving attention, which has been demonstrated in other laboratory workers to enhance the vitality and resistance of laboratory animals.[1338] However, inherent in such processes there may also be elements of spiritual healing.

In addition, Kammerer also explored the influence of environment on genetics. In simple experiments he placed salamanders with dark skins (with small yellow patches) in cages which had yellow earth. Successive generations of animals developed increasingly greater areas of yellow on their skin until they were soon mostly yellow. Conversely, in salamanders which started with mostly light skin, he was able to bring about development of greater areas of dark skin in successive generations by having them live in cages with black earth. There were no predators involved in these studies, so the development of skin colors – that would aid in camouflage for salamanders living in the wild – could not have been the product of Darwinian selection of individuals who survived the winnowing effects of predators.

Many of Kammerer's experiments were not repeated by others. He was discredited after World War I when a toad specimen from his laboratory was found to have been altered with India ink in a manner which suggested fraud – despite the fact that this same specimen had been carefully studied previously by other scientists and no questions of fraud whatsoever had been raised. Shortly after these accusations of fraud were made against him, Kammerer committed suicide. Subsequently, questions were raised in the scientific community as to whether the ink marks could have been made by a colleague in a deliberate attempt to discredit Kammerer.[1339]

Recently, Edward Skeele and colleagues have claimed there is evidence in studies of certain forms of genes[1340] that suggests genetic alterations which have been passed from parents to progeny. Experiments are in progress to explore this possibility.

Discussion on human influence on genetics

It appears probable from the above quotes that Burbank's methods involved biological PK. He seemed able to influence the genes of plants through his intention to produce new varieties. By increasing the range of variability or randomness of combinations of genetic materials (Burbank's *wabble*) through cross-fertilizations, he clearly would have introduced a more diversified gene pool from which to select and vary the cross-fertilizations. In addition, this might have increased the instability of the random processes during meiosis, which in turn may have increased his psi influence over these processes, tipping the balance of plant reproductive potential in desirable directions.

It is considered a creditable achievement to develop even one distinctly new variety of plant in a botanical career. To develop over 800 is astounding. The closest anyone else has come through modern methods of selective plant breeding is to produce about 100 new varieties of plants. It seems a reasonable hypothesis, in view of the above, that Burbank was gifted with biological PK ability.

The experiment of Nash on bacterial mutation could be explained, as he himself notes, by the alternative hypothesis that the *growth* of lac-positive and lac-negative bacteria might have been selectively enhanced. This possibility is supported by various studies of intentional effects on growth rates of plants, bacteria and yeasts. These demonstrate that growth can be enhanced and/or retarded.[1341] While it might seem difficult for PK to act selectively upon one class of bacterium growing together in a culture that also contains another variety of bacterium, this does not appear to contradict general observations of how psi can work. Psychics and healers can deliberately connect with a specific person, object or location that is thousands of miles away, representing one out of billions of possible people, items or places on the planet. Influencing specific single-celled organisms in a test tube may not be that different.

The study by Cox suggests that people can selectively favor the gender of their offspring when motivated to have a male child, but not with a female child. He presumed – but did not clarify through interviews – that those parents who had four sons were actually hoping for a daughter. The fact that boys and men are favored in many families over daughters might have produced these differences.

The Darwinian view that evolution is **determined** by environmental selection acting upon genetic endowment has been favored because it has the support of theories and research evidence. This has led to misperception that the Lamarckian hypothesis of environmental factors influencing genetic propensities is disproved. However, these theories are not mutually exclusive. *Both* may be correct. That is, Darwinian selection of the fittest genes may coexist with Lamarckian influences upon them. Western culture is a dichotomizing one. We tend to view issues as *either/or* rather than *both/and*. Even our language keeps us bound to this view. As mentioned earlier, in other languages, words acknowledge the oneness of contrasts. *Yin* and *yang* are polarities that are present in everything, and anything in the world can be yin relative to one thing and yin relative to another. In Russian, *da* is 'yes' and *nyet* is 'no;' and then there is the inclusive word, *danyet.*[1342]

> *And I have felt a presence that disturbs me with the joy of elevated thoughts;*
> *a sense sublime of something far more deeply interfused,*
> *whose dwelling is the light of setting suns, and the round ocean*
> *and the living air, and the blue sky, and in the mind of man;*
> *emotion and a spirit, that impels all thinking things,*
> *all objects of all thought, and rolls through all things.*
> *– William Wordsworth*

The Lamarckian hypothesis appears best supported by evidence from reports of Burbank's work. The work of Kammerer is also suggestive, though clouded by questions of possible fraud. No one disputed that Kammerer had an unusual gift for raising and breeding amphibians and reptiles in the lab. This in itself may represent a measure of psi ability. The production of the apparent genetic changes in the salamanders and frogs may have been due to psi talents in the experimenter which were not consciously utilized or even recognized by himself or others.

It is unfortunate that at the time that Kammerer and Burbank lived, in the early years of the 20th century, there were few who were open to exploration of psi phenomena. They had to work in isolation, eventually carrying much of their knowledge to the grave.

An alternative possibility to Burbank's influencing plants via biological PK is that he was able to select precognitively or clairsentiently those specimens which contained the characteristics he sought. It would appear unlikely, however, that this mode of selection could produce such large numbers of new plant varieties so quickly. Precognition or clairsentience do not appear to be reasonable alternative hypotheses for Nash's experiment or Kammerer's work.

Discussion on a conscious, living universe

The concept of *animism*, acknowledging there is a consciousness in nature, is not a new one. It is widely accepted in traditional societies and by Western intuitives and healers that absolutely everything is conscious. This includes all things that grow, reproduce and die (animals and plants) as well as all other things in the world (the land, individual rocks, bodies of water, the air, the heavenly bodies and every other object of our perceptions).[1343] Modern philosophers have dignified this awareness with various theories, such as *entelechy*, an inherent, goal-directedness in the universe;[1344] or *proto-consciousness* that is said to be an inherent property of every element in the universe.[1345]

My personal introduction to animism was through a visit to Findhorn – the community that was built on the north shore of Scotland. There, Peter and Eileen Caddy, who produced unusually large and healthy fruits, vegetables and flowers in a climate that is cold and inhospitable outside of the very short growing season. Their innovative ingredient was *talking to the plants and to the nature spirits who help them grow.* They acknowledged not only each and every element of the land and every living organism as sentient partners on their farm but also had names and vividly clear personalities for their cars and the communal dishwasher.

At first, I considered these to be quaint projections of people's fantasies, intuitive perceptions or simply folklore. Over the years, I read of others who shared these views and reported in detail their communications with cats, dogs, horses, trees, rocks and nature spirits. More importantly, I developed and learned to trust my own intuitive sensitivities and healing gifts, and was blessed to have meetings and healings with remarkable sensitives and healers in many lands. I have come to believe that we are all part of a vast consciousness which is beyond human comprehension and certainly incapable of description in human concepts.

Being a psychiatrist, and knowing all of the ways that I could deceive myself through wishful thinking, fantasies and anxieties, I wavered and vacillated for many years between accepting my intuitive understanding of the world and writing off these ideas as dreams and projections of my own mind. The evidence gathered in this book has helped me to know that I am at least not alone in holding these beliefs, and probably in the good company of people who engage the world on levels that transcend in very healing ways most of what I was taught in private and public schools, university, medical school, and extensive training and courses in psychiatry and continuing medical education.

Living in a society where we are taught that humans are the peak of the evolutionary tree, where it is presumed with great hubris that the earth was given to us to exploit in whatever manner serves our immediate needs and whims, it may be difficult to conceive of how we would fit into a world that is totally alive in its every element.

Ervin Laszlo points out that however diverse are the cells, tissues, organs and systems of an organism, essentially they act as a unified whole. He uses an analogy from Mae-Wan Ho, suggesting that all of these layers of elements perform together very much like a practiced jazz band in which each player spontaneously responds to the improvisations of the others. The organismic jazz band plays continuously throughout the life of the organism, expressing melodies and harmonies that characterize that organism through repetitive beats and rhythms, while interweaving endless variations. There are always new improvisations, with spontaneous shifts of tempos, keys and melodies in response to the demands of internal and external situations. An overall structure is evident but the artistic individuality is evident in the unending improvisations – with every single player, however major or minor in functional importance within the organism, reveling in their freedom to express their individuality while at the same time staying in perfect pace with the whole.[1346]

Laszlo is talking of the harmonious, nested hierarchies of elements and levels within a single human organism. The same applies as we extend our focus to include other nested hierarchies, such as groups of individuals, interactions with our immediate environment, Gaia as a planetary orchestra, the cosmic music of the spheres, and beyond into realms where the vibrations are of such a high level that they are beyond human capacity to hear (or indeed, even conceive or comprehend).

For those who live in a world that is alive in all its elements, we are in vital resonation with the totality; and conversely, every element in the totality is a vital part that resonates with us. To harm anything in the totality is to diminish a part of ourselves.

> *Great ideas, it has been said, come into the world as gently as doves.*
> *Perhaps then, if we listen attentively, we shall hear amid the uproar of*
> *empires and nations, a faint flutter of wings, the gentle stirring of life and*
> *hope. Some will say that this hope lies in a nation; others in a man.*
>   *I believe rather that it is awakened, revived, nourished by millions of*
> *solitary individuals whose deeds and works every day negate frontiers and*
> *the crudest implications of history. As a result, there shines forth fleetingly*
> *the ever-threatened truth that each and every man, on the foundation of his*
> *own suffering and joys, builds for all.*
>   *– Albert Camus*

This is how spiritual awareness can bring us into more conscious connection with the All and invites us to offer healing to the All. First and foremost, we can heal the part of the All where we have greatest influence and effect – healing ourselves as our contribution to the All. At the same time, we awaken to being interconnected with the world at large. To be inconsiderate to any aspect of the world is to harm a piece of the organism of which we are a part. To contribute to the growth, health and healing of any part is to enhance the world in which we participate.

Participatory intelligent design – in summary

> *Our true nature is far more ancient and encompassing than the separate*
> *self defined by habit and society.*
>   *We are as intrinsic to our living world as the rivers and trees, woven of*
> *the same intricate flows of matter/energy and mind. Having evolved us into*
> *self-reflexive consciousness, the world can now know itself through us,*

behold its own majesty, tell its own stories – and also respond to its own
suffering.
— Joanna Macy

In outline, here are the pieces of the puzzle of intelligent design:
   1. Incredible coincidences make life possible.
   2. Darwinian selection/evolution is inadequate to explain development of physical characteristics.
   3. Extrasensory perception (ESP), psychokinesis (PK) and healing enable human interactions with other organisms.
   4. The mind can influence random number generators (RNGs).
   5. When egg and sperm cells are formed in the process of *meiosis*, chromosomes and genes are randomly distributed – comprising a biological RNG.
   6. Collective consciousness exists.
   7. Each of us is a pixel in the cosmic screen of the universe; each of us contributes to the All.

The enormous coincidences that make life possible on earth suggest that a guiding intelligence must have been required to design our universe. There is an unbelievably minute probability of all of these factors lining up by chance to provide all of the conditions required for life. Fred Hoyle, a famous mathematician and cosmologist, suggests that the likelihood of life evolving just by chance would be the same as anticipating that a hurricane could rearrange a junk yard into a functioning airplane. There is, however, no logical, linear way to test, prove or disprove this hypothesis of the existence of an *Infinite Source* as the designer of the universe.

Assuming that a guiding intelligence does exist, there is similarly no way to define its nature – within the frameworks of Western science. There are no physical measures nor experiments we can perform to assess this guiding intelligence.

Science without religion is lame, religion without science is blind.
— Albert Einstein [1347]

Many have argued that this is a matter of religious belief, not a subject for scientific examination. As mentioned at the start of this discussion, speculations about a God based on religious teachings are matters of faith, not reason. Matters of faith are discussed in Chapter 12.

If, however, we accept that human consciousness is part of a vaster consciousness, we can begin to explore the possibility of participatory intelligent design – within the frameworks and limits of human consciousness. In the physical world we can see that an atom can be a part of a molecule, which is part of a protein, which is part of a cell, which is part of an organ, which is part of a unit of life that we identify as a person. Similarly, we can see that individual human consciousness may be a part of the collective consciousness of humanity, which is a part of the collective consciousness of all living things on this planet, which is part of a collective consciousness of all sentient awareness on this planet (to include all of nature, and all of our planet – as an organic, ecobiological system that many call *Gaia*). All of these are probably parts of further nested series of consciousness that culminate in the totality of consciousness which is the Infinite Source. While we may have glimmerings of individual awarenesses of the totality of which we are a miniscule part, we cannot perceive, much less comprehend, its totality (within linear, materialistic frameworks) any more than an atom understands the totality of the organism of which it is a part.

> *I suddenly realized it's all one, that this magnificent universe is a harmonious, directed, purposeful whole. That we humans, both as individuals and as a species are an integral part of the ongoing process of creation.*
>
> – Edgar Mitchell [1348]

Within personal spiritual awarenesses we may have glimmerings of perceptions and appreciations of some of the qualities and vastness of the Infinite Source. In the NDE, people experience encounters with a Being of Light or other perceptions of an omniscient, omnipotent, unconditionally accepting, totally loving presence. In meditative and mystical experiences, people may enter states in which they experience themselves as one with the All. [1349] While there is no proof through linear measurements that these numinous experiences represent valid perceptions of participation in the vastness of the All, their universality in the spectrum of human cultures around our planet suggest that they may be credible reports. If so, this would mean that each and every one of us is a part, however miniscule, of the Infinite Source.

If humans, limited as we are, can influence genetic processes through our intent, this suggests the possibility that the Infinite Source could do the same, on a much vaster and more comprehensive scale. Assuming that humans are somewhere along the spectrum between subatomic particles and very primitive cells in the Infinite Source, participating in the co-creative adventure called the mystery of life, then we may also participate in creating, maintaining, and evolving the universe of which we are a part. In nested hierarchies of co-creative intelligence, there may be layers of participatory intelligent design such as morphogenetic fields – each of which creates and guides the functions of specific nested levels of physical, mental, social and spiritual existence.

The vastness and complexity of evolution across planetary time clearly exceeds anything humankind could conceive or execute – in and of itself. We may, however, provide valuable feedback to the All about successful and failed evolutionary experiments in which we participate as a species.

> *The universe is not to be narrowed down to the limits of our own understanding, which has been the practice up to now, but our understanding must be stretched and enlarged to take in the image of the universe as it is discovered.*
>
> – Francis Bacon [1350]

Through our personal spiritual awareness, uniquely experienced by each of us in how we perceive our place as pixels in the holographic universe, and through the choices we make in living our lives, we shape and color our pixels, giving them the unique energies of our personality, attitudes, love and healing that we manifest into the world. Each pixel contributes to the whole picture that is the universe; each pixel in turn is perceived and experienced in the context of all the other pixels – particularly those in its immediate proximity. In the cosmic hologram of the All, each of us is a co-creator of the universe.

> *My view is that the ultimate verities will never be discovered in a test tube or a microscope. Can God be proven? No. But when one is in the presence of a liberated soul, proof no longer seems necessary, and all questions one came to ask seem answered by the silence.*
> – David Frank Gomes

Further research to test the Lamarckian hypothesis and participatory intelligent design

1. Cross-fertilization of plants, fruit flies, bacteria, viruses and other organisms can be random systems for experiments to explore influences of intent over genetic changes. The object will be to selectively influence successive generations to produce more individuals with particular characteristics. A simple, Mendelian cross-fertilization of green and white peas is within the reach of anyone with a garden plot. Laboratory studies of crosses of fruit flies or other organisms would produce quicker results as their breeding cycles are much shorter.

2. Refinements of Nash's experiment should be sought, wherein growth versus genetic influence can be distinguished.

3. Kammerer's experiments can be repeated, to include psi-gifted subjects who might contribute the crucial ingredient of biological PK into the experiment.
   The objection of conventional science that the experiment must be repeatable *by anyone* cannot be sustained when one appreciates that psi ability is not equally manifested in every individual. In fact, there is evidence from numerous studies of psi effects of believers and disbelievers in psi[1351] to suggest that skepticism may lead to a negative psi effect so that biologists seeking to disprove the Lamarckian hypothesis may be influencing their materials parapsychologically in accordance with their beliefs and producing null results. This may prove to be a confounding variable in modern genetics research.

4. Highly gifted botanists, nurserypersons, biologists and animal breeders who produce unusual results in their experiments may be:
   A. Studied for psi abilities, which might explain some of their gifts; and
   B. Encouraged to develop their talents as useful gifts rather than rejecting them as aberrations.

5. There are vast collections of research to show that the experimenter can influ ence the outcomes of scientific studies.[1352] The experimenter effect in research appears worth investigating, with psi factors in mind, as a model for participatory intelligent design at the human level of awareness/existence.

6. Highly gifted scientists in other fields may be similarly studied. Nikolas Tesla comes immediately to mind as an example of a scientist who might have been similar to Burbank in having psi gifts.[1353]

> *But what if, as the Sioux philosopher Vine Deloria Jr. says (from the perspective of that older, outlawed animist point of view),*[1354] *"the world is constantly creating itself because everything is alive and making choices that determine the future" ? Then creation (or evolution) is not something essentially over and done with; it's happening right now, all the time, in ways we can neither predict nor control, nor perhaps even comprehend. Everything, in other words, is conscious, alive, and free. Creation itself is 'heretical!'*
>
> – Joseph Felser [1355]

Practical approaches to planetary problems

> *All industrial systems and designs pale when compared to the efficiency of natural systems of production. Nothing does more with less. This knowledge makes nature the logical exemplar for an increasingly evolved form of commerce.*
>
> – Paul Hawken [1356]

Personal spirituality and participating in intelligent design enable us to sense our intimate connection with other people, with our environment and with the Earth as a whole. In addition to our work on ourselves, to be the best possible healing light that we can be in our immediate interactions, we can extend our healing influence to wider horizons.

One cannot consider the place of the human species in evolution without speculating on whether we are participating in a failing evolutionary experiment. If we do not halt overpopulation, exhaustion of resources and pollution of our planet, we are headed for suicidal extinction. While the healing of these suicidal tendencies is clearly a subject for many further books, a few words here feel appropriate.

> *The most meaningful activity in which a human being can be engaged is one that is directly related to human evolution. This is true because human beings now play an active and critical role not only in the process of their own evolution but in the survival and evolution of all living beings. Awareness of this places upon human beings a responsibility for their participation in and contribution to the process of evolution. If humankind would accept and acknowledge this responsibility and become creatively*

engaged in the process of metabiological evolution consciously, as well as unconsciously, a new reality would emerge, and a new age would be born.
                                                              – Jonas Salk

Paul Hawken, a green businessman, has written the best book I have ever found on the healing of the ecological dangers and disasters rampant on our planet, along with the most innovative approaches to dealing with them. I summarize here in some detail a range of his observations on the current destructive attitudes of business and government and his recommendations for restorative approaches for healing our physical and social environments. Unless otherwise indicated, the following materials (ending at the discussion) are a distillation of Hawken's observations.

Let us start with a simple definition of ecology. Ecology suggests ways to examine all of our economic and resource activities for their biological importance and impact rather than solely from the calculations of the potential monetary profits to be gained. The focus of ecology also extends beyond immediate gains to consider the impacts which our present lifestyle may have on future generations.

The focus of business has been narrowed through the years to concentrate primarily on the generation of profits. Corporations often show little or no consideration for any negative effects their products or the byproducts of their production may have, outside of gross liability for direct damages they may cause to people. In the native Hawaiian language there are 138 different words for falling rain, a witness to the profound importance of rain in the lives of these islanders. In contrast, business has just two words to describe profits: gross and net. No distinctions are made regarding how the profits were made. Business does not identify whether exploitation of people or the environment occurred, resource were depleted, communities were enhanced, lives were lost or whether consultants had to be hired to deal with executive stresses and outplacement services were required for victims of these problems. In other words, no attention is given to whether profits were of quality or mere quantity. In order for ecological awareness to shift, business must develop a new language that highlights new ways of seeing itself and its roles in relating to the environment.

How has this happened? How have the peoples of many nations allowed this to happen? There is an entrenched myth in industrial society that there are 'no limits.' This belief has grown so powerful that it seems ironically to be gaining in strength, a defensive denial that flies in the face of ever-growing evidence that we are reaching the limits of the carrying capacity of earth's resources. The myth of ever-expanding abundance through future advances in science and industry is not a theory supported by science, historical precedents or nature. It derives solely from self-interest; a wish to maintain what is by global standards an extravagant lifestyle. "Whether willfully ignorant or unabashedly hypocritical, at some point we must ask business to look candidly at the real world and see the skull-and-crossbones posted alongside ecological pathways, so that we can begin to create real solutions instead of illusory techniques of evasion..." [1357]

Hawken cites very pointed observations of Wendell Berry, an author and farmer:

The dilemma of private economic responsibility is that we have allowed our suppliers to enlarge our economic boundaries so far that we cannot be responsible for our effects on the world. The only remedy for this that I can see is to draw in our economic boundaries, shorten our supply lines, so as to permit us literally to know where we are economically. The closer we live to the ground that we live from, the more we know about our economic life; the more able we will be to take responsibility for it. The way to bring discipline into one's personal or household economy is limit one's economic geography.

Hawken asks a fascinating question: Could it be that we have been asking the wrong question, due to the confrontational nature of discussions between advocates for the interests of restoration and of business? We have focused on the question: "How can we save the environment?" Though it may sound at first ridiculous to both sides, the better question might be: "How can we save business?"

He notes that the ecological policies of big business are not a management problem but rather a design problem. While socially responsible business is starting to make significant efforts to reform the old, outmoded ethics of commerce, management persists unintentionally to give industry continued license to deplete resources and to ignore the consequences of their waste disposal on the environment. Their rationale is that by making whatever efforts they are advocating they are doing good. However, in countless minor and major ways they continue directly and indirectly to degrade the environment and to condone the policies that permit and perpetuate these abuses. This is as true of the well known ecologically sensitive businesses as it is of industries infamous for pollution.

Business has been extracting resources from nature in order to satisfy what is turning out to be an unsustainable and therefore transient period of materialistic wellbeing. Having reached and exceeded the limits of natural resources, we must now restore these, accept the limits of our world, and learn the restraints inherent in an ecologically sound relationship. Unless and until business wakes up to this, the relationship will remain predatory and destructive. "In order for free-market capitalism to transform itself in the century to come, it must fully acknowledge that the brilliant monuments of its triumph cast the darkest of shadows. Whatever possibilities business once represented, whatever dreams and glories corporate success once offered, the time has come to acknowledge that business as we know it is over. Over because it failed in one critical and thoughtless way: It did not honor the myriad forms of life that secure and connect its own breath and skin and heart to the breath and skin and heart of our earth." [1358]

We need to develop economics of *restoration* – the opposite of industrialization. Industrialization distanced the processes of production from the land and distanced people from the land. Consequently, economic values became separated and distanced from personal values. The result that we are living with today is an industrial economy, in which businesses exist to make money. Money is the principal focus of their existence. Their financing and growth depend upon their abilities to earn ever more income. In contrast, a restorative economy focuses on the integration with or replication of natural, cyclical systems as its approach to production and distribution. This approach programs industry to assure that every single product and by-product is accounted for ecologically in its manufactured forms prior to its production. The restorative economy combines ecology and commerce into a unified, sustainable project, taking full responsibility for every element of production and distribution.

A restorative economy would fundamentally alter many basic aspects of our present system: restoring our environment and making money will be the one and the same process. Business and restoration can be parts of a seamless web. This will take environmental protection out of its current reliance on charity, altruism, legislative battles and environmental activism. Until this occurs, restoration will remain subordinate as a neglected and abused afterthought to exploitative investment, industrial growth and inhuman technology. A "newborn literacy of enterprises" is proposed, to acknowledge that all of us are here together – at the mercy of nature and in the service of preserving nature and each other.

Of the largest 100 economies on our planet, 51 are multinational corporations while only 49 are nations. Hawken points out that the ever-increasing global power of corporations has sadly been lacking a comprehensive philosophy, has been devoid of any ethical construct, and has focused solely on accumulation of wealth as their reason for existence. It is difficult to identify principles which inform and guide corporations' commercial behaviors, though occasionally there appear random, self-proclaimed statements of ethics, without formula or rules for adherence to any principles, much less any mechanisms for enforcement. No one, from managers, to employees, customers and general public, takes responsibility.

The most detrimental aspect of our current economic system lies in the disconnect between the costs for destroying the earth and the prices set by industry. "Business has three basic issues to face: what it takes, what it makes, and what it wastes, and the three are intimately connected... An ecological model of commerce would imply that all waste have value to other modes of production so that everything is either reclaimed, reused, or recycled." [1359]

By calculating the costs for disposal of the by-products of manufactured and farm goods, it is possible to add these to the prices of durable goods, foods, chemicals and the like. This places the burden of costs on the consumer but also motivates the producer to be cost-conscious regarding wasteful processes and pollutants. Further along in the life of the products, it is also a motivation to reduce wastes and discards. A cyclical, restorative economy programs industry to assure that every single product and by-product is accounted for ecologically in its manufactured forms prior to its production.

I was pleased to fid that in Germany, these policies were initially advocated by ecologically conscious consumers. They refused to buy products that were sold in unnecessary packaging. Manufacturers responded appropriately and the practice of being ecologically responsible spread to the point that industries now pride themselves on planning thoroughly to minimize the pollution and wastes associated with their products. Many cars and other machines are now built with parts that are easily recycled at the end of the useful life of the car or other machine.

Hawken notes that businesses would not dream of relying on their capital reserves for ongoing operations. However, most businesses ignore this principle as related to depletion of reserves of energy and the environment – including vital animal and plant elements, and pollution that poison and destroy the environment. No culture can survive when it is constantly depleting its energy and resources capital. Therefore, green taxes are needed to stop the depletion of our world's resources. Green taxes will raise the costs of food and goods that include polluting fertilizers, pesticides and toxic industrial wastes as byproducts, thereby encouraging farmers and businesses to develop the best ways to stop their pollution.

When given the support of firm legislation, this also puts an end to the false economy of manufacturers cutting costs by disposing of pollutants in landfills – which leaves the manufacturer richer and the taxpayer footing the bills for medical costs incurred from pollutants and for cleaning up toxic wastes.

Consumers will not be paying higher costs in the overall economy because they will have lower health costs, lower insurance premiums, lower taxes to cover cleanups, increased economic output; and enhancements of the environment (rather than degradation) – thereby lowering costs of resources.

"The purpose of integrating cost into pricing is not to provide a toll road for polluters, but a pathway to innovation."[1360] The incentive for lowering costs is no different from the motivation presently operating in all businesses. However, with restorative pricing, producers' most efficient approaches to reduce their costs is not by shifting these to society at large, but to implement improved design and planning.

Hawken cites Dr. Karl-Henrik Robert, who uses "the Natural Step," asking easily answered systemic questions – eliciting surprisingly consensual accord, from such disparate organizations as Greenpeace, labor unions, leaders in industry and religion. For instance, in the example of DDT or any other long-lasting toxin, Robert asks six questions, to which the answers appear obvious to all: *Is DDT a natural product? No. Is DDT a stable chemical? Yes. Will it degrade into nontoxic materials? No. Can it accumulate in humans and animals? Yes. Can we predict what are safe tolerances? No. Is it reasonable to continue to spread DDT in the environment? Not if we wish to survive.*

Sustainability requires that the demands on the environment can be satisfied without diminishing the environment's capacity to provide for the needs of our children and grandchildren. The restorative economy golden rule is: Use only what you need, leave the world in a better state than you found it, harm no living thing or the environment, and make restitution for any damages you cause. Sustainability means you are not seeking to create a superior image, power, pizzazz, or other qualities that are not essential to their functions. Instead, your business is producing goods or services in ways that reduce all forms of environmental damage – including energy depletion, "distribution costs, economic concentration, soil erosion, atmospheric pollution, and other forms of environmental damage."[1361]

To finance changes, Hawken proposes that a universal tax levied on weapons manufacturers, administered by the United Nations, would finance the entire budget of the U.N. and would cover costs for worldwide restoration and peace-keeping efforts - including rescue and resettlement of refugees and other reparations to war victims. Higher weapons taxes would be a strong incentive for reducing arms purchases. This tax would help the world see that all of the suffering due to weapons is by far greater than any economic gains from its sale.

Environmental restoration could be promoted by a new US tariff status titled 'Most Sustainable Nation' (MSN), similar to the current 'Most Favored Nation.' MSN status would include lower tariffs or free trade with countries demonstrating sustainable husbanding of resources, restorative environmental policies, restrictions on worker exploitation, and confirmation that government officials were not selling public assets to exploitative industries. These countries would be granted greatest access to markets in industrial country.

However, Hawken suggests that we cannot solve global problems globally because they are actually global *symptoms* created by collections of local problems. It is actually the reductionist thinking which originated in the scientific revolution that has generated many of these problems, with the idealistic dreams that we could solve the problems of the world through 'conquering' nature and could create universally higher standards of living through industrialization of the world. We have had several centuries of assuming we could master nature and dominate the world, without taking into account the local needs of living systems. The harmonious functions of local cultures and traditions which had been successful in their environments for countless generations have been sacrificed for the promise enormous short-term profits (often defaulted) – leaving us the invoices for the damages produced through this short-sighted thinking and exploitative planning. The origins of our current ecological and social crises are thus imbedded in the mistaken beliefs of industrial commercial and economic theories.

As Lovelock points out, Gaia has survived and restored herself following numerous crises throughout geological time, witnessed by the sudden extinctions of groups of species and evolution and expansion of new species. Hawken observes that the Earth can be expected eventually to restore itself from the depredations of humanity. The essential question we must address in our communities and in our businesses is whether humanity is going to participate in this restoration or will be condemned by persistent ignorance to disappear from this earth.

Hawken summarizes his recommendations with two notes: First, we must live within our means. Second, we have to restore what we have lost.

Participatory planetary consciousness – for healing ourselves and our planet

We need to reinvent the human at the species level because the issues we are concerned with seem to be beyond the competence of our present cultural traditions, either individually or collectively. What is needed is something beyond existing traditions to bring us back to the most fundamental aspect of the human: giving shape to ourselves. The human is at a cultural impasse. In our efforts to reduce the other-than-human components of the planet to subservience to our Western cultural expression, we

have brought the entire set of life systems of the planet, including the
human, to an extremely dangerous situation. Radical new cultural forms
are needed. These new cultural forms would place the human within the
dynamics of the planet rather than place the planet within the dynamics of
the human.

– Thomas Berry [1362]

Humanity is facing a planetary crisis. As the world population grows, as resources dwindle and as pollution mounts, we are reaching the limits of sustainability for many animals, plants and other organisms on our planet. This could spell the end of life as we know it on this planet.

If we take spirituality to be an awareness of being part of a greater world beyond our individual, physical selves, then we can conceptualize the ways modern societies are relating to the world as a spiritual blindness. This is evidenced in a gross societal indifference to environmental degradation through exhaustion of resources and pollution. This spiritual blindness has allowed the situation to develop, to continue and to steadily worsen.

People's habits of perceptions and lifestyles are deeply ingrained, to the point that people feel as though their materialist understandings of the world represent the way 'reality' *is*. Most people do not realize that there are alternative ways of sensing, exploring and explaining the world – beyond the confines of our physical sensory reality. The current dominant Western culture is one that focuses primarily on the material world. We manipulate our resources and environment in the hopes of making our lives safer and more secure.

In focusing on our material standard of living as our primary activity in life, we get lost in the goal of constantly working towards earning more so we can buy more and have more material possessions. Rarely do we reach a point where we have enough – to allow us to pause and get off the treadmills of career and investments in the future, and to allow ourselves to enjoy what we have in the present.

The focus of Western culture on maintaining a high physical standard of living for Western countries leads us to squeeze out of our own environment and out of the rest of the world quantities of products and natural resources that cannot be sustained more than a few more years without exhausting the world's natural assets.

This process of supporting Western standards of living has also been devastating to people and nations with whom we trade. Viewed through the eyes of the non-affluent peoples of the world, industrial culture is an appealing dream – which the west has led them to believe they can aspire to achieve for themselves. This has misled people who were living in comfortable (though often modest) self-sufficiency, capable of supporting themselves in their local economy. The appeal of earning dollars to purchase Western goods has enticed whole nations to abandon their cultivation of food on self-sufficient family-owned plots of land, converting to cash crops in large, collective farms. This is fine when the prices for peanuts or soy are high in world markets, but devastating when the market prices dip. [1363]

Jack Manno and Ana Jamborcic observe:

> For every beneficial thing there is a point beyond which more is not necessarily better; where what is good for you in moderation gradually becomes harmful. This is not only true for the individual but also true of communities, nations and the planet. Whether we call it moderation, frugality or simple living, there is evidence to suggest restraint is good for health and wellbeing at every scale. The evidence for this article comes from data from a variety of sources that suggest that the relationship between growth in the consumption of resources and improvements in quality of life is subject to a threshold effect. Growth improves quality of life up to a point, until a threshold is reached where improvements in wellbeing begins to taper off (the point of diminishing marginal returns) and then may even decline. This relationship shows up in such areas as the relationship between Gross Domestic Product and national wellbeing, between income and satisfaction, energy consumption and welfare, health expenditures and health outcomes, and between personal consumption and personal health.
>
> Sufficiency and satiety may be the most important paths to health. Despite this, in many measures of consumption there is an increasing amount of scarcity and poverty on one end and growing profligacy and wealth on the other, with a shrinking middle zone of existence inbetween. The threshold effect suggests that it is at the middle levels of resource use where basic needs are met and there is enough for a range of personal growth opportunities, so that society gets the most health and well being for its resource use.
>
> The amount of productive land and sea area on the surface of the planet, when divided equally among the present world population, comes to slightly under 5 acres per person to produce what people need, and to absorb the waste products of their life style. The data in this article suggests that this level of resource use may be enough to live well. If so, our prospects for healing the planet rests on bringing the poorest up to that level while reducing the impact of the excesses allotted to the wealthiest. This article, based on the threshold effect, suggests that reducing our level of consumption may be beneficial to the planet as a whole, but also for our nations, our communities and our individual selves.

Those with eyes to look beyond the pursuit of immediate material gains see an end to the materialist dreams rapidly approaching.

> *Most people do not see that they are destroying their Earth – the very planet which gives them Life – because their actions seek only to enhance*

their quality of life. Amazingly, they are not far-sighted enough to observe
that short-term gains can produce long-term losses, and often do – and
will.

– Neale Donald Walsch [1364]

It cannot be more than a very few years before the planetary crunch of limited resources leads to a collapse of the grossly unreasonable Western standard of living.

  The only way I see to avert this planetary disaster is through increased personal spiritual awareness, to include our connection to each other and to Gaia.

May God bless us with discomfort at easy answers, half-truths,
and superficial relationships, so that we will live deep in our
hearts. May God bless us with anger at injustice, oppression, and
exploitation of people and the earth, so that we will work for jus-
tice, equity, and peace. May God bless us with tears to shed for
those who suffer, so we will reach out our hands to comfort them
and change their pain to joy. And may God bless us with the fool-
ishness to think that we can make a difference in the world, so we
will do the things which others say cannot be done. Amen.

– Prayer of the Interfaith Council
for Peace and Justice
Ann Arbor, Michigan

Personal spirituality can also help in addressing the very narrow range of focus of Western medical care. We are over-focused on the care and preservation of our physical body, investing enormous personal and collective resources to maintain and optimize physical health. We fight to prolong physical life and fight off death at all costs. This has been taken to such an extreme that thirty percent of our healthcare budget is invested in the last thirty days of life – to little avail for those who are suffering terminal illnesses. Often this is achieved at the cost of prolonging misery rather than enhancing the quality of life that people would choose for the end of their physical existence in this lifetime. In the blinkered obsession with fighting to prolong physical life, we battle against death but lose sight of the goal of having a good life and a gentle passing from this life to the next.

My personal experiences of spirituality

I continue to peel the Sisyphean onion of life, learning my lessons – which often come in small and large doses of reminders to let go of thinking and knowing, and to open my heart and intuition and spirit to deeper gnowings. I am reminded of this continuing quest when I am moved by the little everyday kindnesses of people towards each other; by the creativity and nobility of people in the creative arts; by resonating with the pain of people oppressed by other people; by the beauties of nature; by the pain of seeing and sensing Gaia exploited, polluted and her magnificent material and spiritual munificence ignored; by the nobility and love of humans who transcend their life challenges; by appreciating the miracles of existence as a piece of the All, seeking my way home.

In Summary

Participatory spirituality acknowledges that each of us has a place in the creation of reality. Our influence upon the world extends far beyond the realities we generate – through our personal physical, psychological, and social interactions with the world and our reactions to these through our body, emotions and mind. Each of us is also a particle and wavicle in the nested hierarchies of spiritual existence. We can contribute light or darkness to the All through our choices in acting and responding to the challenges in our lives.

The most important question we might be asking ourselves is, "What are we each doing with the choices given us in the dramas of our lives? What are we contributing to the All?

Conclusions

This is my understanding of how it works. In the Beginning there was the Void; and the Void was filled with the All-There-Is, therefore, nonVoid. Perhaps in the Void the Unseen Mystery experienced loneliness, breathed a sigh, and thus was born the God and the Goddess, yin and yang, father and mother, masculine and feminine, the man and woman in all of us. The wings of the bird carry positives and negative charges, male and female. Likewise, it takes two wings to fly to the spaces of the Great Mystery.
— Oh Shinnah [1365]

The whole is more than the sum of the parts.
— Aristotle [1366]

Spiritual elements in healing

Spiritual dimensions are perceived intuitively by many who participate in healing. The closer one is to the material world in energy fields and concepts, the more the evidence can be documented and is amenable to measurements. As one moves into reports that are derived from more intuitive awarenesses, especially where these relate to spirit worlds, the evidence is less and less appropriate for numerical analyses. Here the subjective reports demonstrate broad overlaps but still have sufficient differences between them to make it difficult or impossible to analyze them in linear terms. One cannot appreciate a place from maps, verbal descriptions, poetry or pictures nearly to the same degree as one can from visiting the place itself.

We must be cautious in exploring these realms that we do not take any evidence to be THE truth. As mortals, we are bound to limited perceptual capacities and limiting linear concepts for describing and analyzing these.

A part of the numinous nature of the spiritual is its mystery, which requires an element of trust and faith as we explore and experience these realms.

> *God could cause us considerable embarrassment by revealing all the secrets of nature to us: we should not know what to do for sheer apathy and boredom.*
> — Goethe

Despite these difficulties, research evidence strongly suggests that:

1. Many people are aware of a spirit existence for themselves and for others.

2. There is a remarkably coherent pattern across the diverse areas of spirituality research. There are few contradictions (and these are relatively minor) raised by reports from studies of OBE, NDE, apparitions and nature spirits, possession, reincarnation, meditative and mystical experiences. This is all the more remarkable when one considers the general consistency of reports in these areas from around the world.

3. Attuning ourselves to our spirituality can deepen our appreciation and enjoyment of life and our participation in it.

4. The spirit existence appears to those who experience it to be more real and enduring than physical existence.

Research on spirituality is important, but it can only serve to confirm or deny that which we know intuitively within ourselves. First and foremost it reveals that spiritual awareness is available to most of us though it may require practices, such as meditation, yoga, prayer and the like, to develop it. This is good news to those who are open to pursuing such paths.

It is discomforting, even frightening news to some organized religions who teach that spiritual awareness and healing are only to be done within the confines of their own religious beliefs and practices, under the dictates of their leaders.

> *There's a divinity that shapes our ends,*
> *Rough-hew them how we will.*
>
> – William Shakespeare (*Hamlet*)]

My personal path of spiritual awareness

I have come a long way in opening to my personal spirituality. In everyday life, I am still working on deepening my meditation practice, refining my intuitive and healing skills, exploring and teaching others to do the same. My sense of the spiritual is that I am serving a higher purpose, of which I am but dimly aware. A major part of my life lesson seems to be to deepen my own personal spiritual awareness so that I may more clearly and consistently be a catalyst for others to do the same.

I still struggle some of the time with my left-brained, thinking ways of perceiving and relating to the world. I have come to realize that I have deep layers of distrust in letting go of my sense of left-brained knowing and of my false sense of being in control – so that I can learn to trust fuly in the inner gnowing, my higher Self, and the Infinite Source as the deeper sources of wisdom and guidance for my life.

Accepting our personal powers to connect with the spiritual and to heal

> *Those who do not have power over the story that dominates their lives –*
> *the power to retell it, rethink it, deconstruct it, joke about it, and change it*
> *as times change – truly are powerless, because they cannot think new*
> *thoughts.*
>
> – Salman Rushdie

Personal spirituality opens us to awareness of our interconnectedness with our higher selves, with each other, and with *Gaia*, our planetary ecobiological system. When we are spiritually awake we become aware that we are integrally related to all of creation. Any threat or harm to other living things or to the environment is a threat to ourselves. We are part of everything and everything is part of us. Caring for other people and for our environment is caring for ourselves. Harming others or the environment is harming ourselves. Ethical, caring, loving behavior becomes a natural part of existence.

> *I am I plus my surroundings, and if I do not preserve the latter*
> *I do not preserve myself.*
>
> – José Ortega y Gasset [1367]

Being an integral part of the All offers each of us a unique perspective on transcendent realms. Accepting the validity of personal spirituality then may present a challenge in that there are as many views of transcendent reality as there are reports about it. This may be a healthy observation to take on board, although it may be as viewed from conventional, linear, Western reality as a difficult truth to have to accept. Our greatest challenge and the most promising way forward may be to shift our awareness and our ways of relating to the world, integrating personal spirituality not only into our personal lives, but also into our culture as a whole. Then, our relationships with each other and with our planet will reflect our oneness with the All.

> *[W]e possess only partial truth. Truth is like a gigantic diamond that fell to*
> *earth aeons ago and broke into pieces. The pieces were scattered all over*
> *the earth, but when the natives in a particular region found a piece, they*
> *mistook it for the whole diamond. Furthermore, even if we were to bring*
> *the pieces together, we still would have only a fragmented diamond.*
>
> – A. Reza Arasteh & Anees A. Sheikh [1368]

Most importantly, personal spiritual awareness and healing reconnect us with our awareness and powers to participate in the creation of the realities of our world. Healing calls our awareness to the miracle of existence. It opens our inner doors to the mysteries of the infinite – within ourselves and in the wider world beyond.

> *There is One Holy Book, the sacred manuscript of nature, the only scrip-*
> *ture which can enlighten the reader...*

It is when the eye of the soul is opened and the sight is keen that the Sufi can read the divine law in the manuscript of nature.
                                              – Hazrat Inayat Khan

The great thing about science is that the questions are so much more important than the answers. Almost any scientist can find an answer if he/she can only find a good question. I think that theology tends to make the mistake of straining for answers, even answers that claim to be final. Science lives with the questions. All its answers are tentative, and breed further questions. The really great questions – those a bright child might ask – are never finished answering.
                                              – George Wald

It may be that when we no longer know what to do, we have come to our real work, and when we no longer know which way to go, we have begun our real journey.
                                              – Wendell Berry

Wind and spirit, earth and being, rain and doing, lightning and awareness imperative, thunder and the word, seed and sower, all are one: and it is necessary only for man to ask for his seed to be chosen and to pray for the sower within to sow it through the deed and act of himself, and then the harvest for all will be golden and great.
                                              – Laurens van der Post [1369]

WE ARE CO-CREATORS OF OUR OWN LIVES,
OF OUR COLLECTIVE HUMAN EXISTENCE,
AND OF THE CONTINUED EXISTENCE OF GAIA.

Glossary

Akashic Records – Records in spirit or psychic realms that contain all the information about everything that ever was or will be; in essence, a cosmic library.

The All – The totality of the universe in all its manifestations, from physical to spiritual, and extending beyond human awareness and comprehension.

Alternative State of Consciousness (ASC) – A state of awareness that is different from everyday perceptions of the outer world through the five senses of sight, sound, smell, taste and touch. In such a state, perceptions and associated thoughts are often processed in ways that differ from the linear, reasoned mental processes. Intuition, imagery, and gestaltic/wholistic analyses of perceptions often are the primary modes of processing awarenesses. *Alternative term: Altered State of Consciousness.*

Amino acids – The building blocks of proteins.

Apophatic – Identifying that which *is not* Divine as a way of approaching some semblance of defining what *is* Divine.

Apport – A physical materialization produced by a medium.

ASC – See *Alternative State of Consciousness.*

Base – A coded series of proteins that are the building blocks of genes.

Bioplasma – This is a suggested biological parallel with plasma from the world of physics. Plasma is a fourth state of matter (after solid, liquid, and gas). In physics, plasma is found only at very hot temperatures. In biology it is allegedly present at normal temperatures, and is hypothesized to be a basis for life

Channeling – See *Mediumship.*

Clairsentience – Knowledge about an animate or inanimate object, without the use of sensory cues (also called psychometry). This may be perceived as visual imagery (clairvoyance), auditory messages (clairandience), or other *internal* sensory awareness, such as taste, smell, or a mirroring of bodily sensations from another person.

Confidence – Belief based on experience of previous experiences, events and results

Control group – In a research study, the comparison group, equivalent in as many characteristics as possible to the treatments group.

Cross-correspondences – Spirit communications through separate mediums, who did not know of each other, producing separate, fragmentary messages from two spirits. The fragments make sense only when combined later by investigators.

Cryptomnesia – Memory which actually comes from outside sources, such as the media or from stories told by family and friends, but which a person mistakenly recalls as having occurred to themselves, personally.

Cupping – A glass is inverted against the skin with burning cotton inside it (often placed on top of a coin that insulates the skin from the burning cotton). The fire uses up the oxygen and thereby creates a vacuum within the glass, which then acts like a suction cup to draw out blood from a superficial cut in the skin – along with negative energies that are associated with diseases. In some cases, no cuts are made, and the cupping is intended to draw out negative bioenergies alone.

Deductive reasoning – Logical thought leading from the general to the more specific

Double-blind study – Research study in which neither the patients nor the experimenters treating or assessing the patients know who is receiving the experimental treatment and who is in the control group.

Emic – Explanation that acknowledges that peoples from cultures other than our own, behaving in manners that are different from ours, usually have their own legitimate cultural explanations for their beliefs and behaviors. (Contrasted with *etic*)

Entheogen – Mind-altering drug used to awaken spiritual awareness.

Epistemology – The science dealing with origins and methods of knowledge, particularly relating to limits and validity of theories.

Etic – Explanations based on Western convictions that modern science can provide "objective" explanations for every phenomenon - within the frameworks of Western scientific paradigms. (Contrasted with *emic*)

ESP – See *Extrasensory Perception.*

Extrtasensory Perception – Telepathy, clairvoyance, pre- and retro-cognition.

Faith – Belief without preliminary factual basis in the material world; also a meta-belief in the validity of another belief.

Gnosis/Gnowing – Direct, intuitive knowledge which often carries with it an inner, numinous sense of certainty about its validity. This is an awareness through the intuitive, right brain for some; for others a knowing felt in the heart rather than in the head. To those who have experienced gnosis, it may feel even more real than physical reality, which, in comparison, is sometimes described as an illusion.

Hermeneutics – The science, methodology and art of interpreting scripture.

Hologram – 3-dimensional photographic image in which any portion of the negative contains the entire picture.

Homeostatic mechanisms – Mechanisms that maintain a constant environment that is conducive to life, within living organisms and on our planet.

Inductive reasoning – Logical thought leading from the specific to the more general

Ineffable – Beyond description in ordinary language.

Intercessory prayer – Prayer specifically for healing.

Intuition – Thought without underlying logical basis. The use of intuition alone does not imply that facts were gathered with other than the five usual senses. Intuition, of itself, is neutral… not necessarily spiritual. One can think intuitively about science or mathematics, for example. Intuition can have several layers, including:

- pattern recognition based on pervious experiences with situations that are similar to the current one;
- psychic (psi) impressions deriving from telepathy, clairsentience, precognition and retrocognition
- bioenergy perceptions acquired through interactions of one person's biological energy field(s) with the field(s) of other living beings and non-living things.
- spiritual awareness, derived from transpersonal consciousness

Kundalini – Energies (described initially in Eastern traditions) originating at the base of the spine, which may rise up the spine as a part of a bioenergetic process of spiritual awakening.

Lucid dreaming – Dreams in which the dreamer feels awake and is in conscious control of the progress and unfolding of the dream experience.

Mediumship – Psychic perceptions of spirits and communications with them.

Metaphysical thought – Speculations on primary causes and ultimate significance of the world beyond its measurable and testable limits. Metaphysics addresses 'why' things are and makes value assessments of thought and actions. In some cases the reasoning is inductive, that is from personal experience which is positive, intuitive, or first person: *gnosis*. In most cases, the reasoning is deductive, usually based upon assumptions derived from cultural or religious traditions or another person's *gnosis*.

Morphogenetic field – Proposed by Rupert Sheldrake, this is an aggregate of individual experiences that resides in a field of consciousness related to a given species. Individuals contribute to this memory field and can draw from it, as for intuitive guidance.

Morphology – Shape and structural design of the body.

Mystical – Transpersonal awarenesses that arise spontaneously or through meditative and other practices, which are beyond ordinary explanations. See also *Spiritual*.

NDE – Near-Death Experience.

Nested hierarchy – Serial levels of matter, information, energy and organization in which an individual item contributes to a more complex structure or organization, which in turn contributes to a yet more complex structure or organization. (For example, in a living body, the energy field of an atom contributes to the field of the molecule of which it is a part; the molecule contributes to the field of the protein of which it is a part; the protein contributes to the field of the tissue of which it is a part; etc. etc. On social levels, an individual is a part of a family, which is part of a local community, which is part of a regional community, which is part of a nation, which is part of the global community.)

Noetic – Awarenesses beyond description in linear words and concepts, derived from spiritual awareness, gnosis.

Obsession – See *Possession*

Ontology – Metaphysical study of the theories of basic reality or pure being.

Peritonitis – Infection in the abdominal cavity.

Phyla – Major divisions of living organisms, such as Porifera – sponges; Nematoda – earthworms; Chordata – vertebrate animals (including man).

Possession (Obsession) – When a discarnate entity has taken over (*possessed* or *obsessed*) the mind and/or body of an individual for its own purposes

Precognition – Knowledge of a future event prior to its occurrence.

PS-I – Manipulations by the psychic surgeon only in the aura or astral body, which is secondarily presumed to effect changes in the physical body

PS-II – Manipulation by the psychic surgeon of the healee's physical body.

Psi (Psychic or Extra-Sensory Perception) – Thought or experience based on information or sensory awarenesses gathered without the use of the five usual senses: Including telepathy, clairsentience, precognition and retrocognition. Once within the unconscious or conscious mind, this information may be processed logically or intuitively. Psi may represent the most primitive or generalized form of knowing. Indications are that it is often an inherited capacity and can improve with use. It can also be a learned skill, as most people have some measure of psi ability. Examples: auric vision, telepathy, remote viewing, psychometry, psychokinesis (PK).

Psi healing – See *Spiritual healing.*

Psychometry – See *Clairvoyance.*

Reductionistic – Presuming that everything can ultimately be explained by dissecting it into ever more basic components and analyzing it into ever finer details; at the same time overlooking or denying that the whole can be more than the sum of its parts.

Religion – Organized religion grows out of spiritual experience as a way of perpetuating and passing on *gnosis* to those who are not primary experiencers. It may or may not foster or encourage or welcome individuals other than the founders of the religion to themselves question basic assumptions, traditions or values. The more distant a religion is from a sense of personal experience with its basic truths, the more likely it will be to insist on absolute adherence to its fundamental doctrines and tenets as a way to insure that its followers do not deviate or stray from its central teachings – or from those who hold offices in the religious hierarchy. Some religions require their adherents to demonstrate their faith by exhibiting prescribed behaviors (example: speaking in tongues, walking on burning coals, handling poisonous snakes without being harmed); passing tradition-based rituals or tests of knowledge or skill (catechism or Bar Mitzva); or being "born again." These are types of group-acknowledged and accepted *gnosis* and are usually rigidly adhered to within a particular group. For example, one would not usually speak in tongues in a Catholic Church service or be expected to sit in silent meditation for many hours in a Jewish synagogue observance.

Retrocognition – Knowledge of a past event, without use of sensory cues.

Scientism (Science as a religion) – Modern science adopted as a religion, assuming it has the ultimate answers to explain life, the universe and everything; resisting or even refusing to consider alternative theories; used to discount observations and theories that are not currently popular, such as psi abilities and transpersonal awarenesses.

Séance – A session in which a medium channels information from spirits.

Soteriology – Theology dealing with salvation, particularly relating to Jesus Christ

Shadow – Those parts of our unconscious mind that we would rather not be aware of, including major and minor traumatic experiences, feelings which we find uncomfortable, self-doubts and misgivings we would rather not perceive, and the like.

Soul – That part of a person which survives death integrates aspects of the person's most recent personality with their eternal Self. (Some prefer to call this part the *spirit.* See also *spirit* for my explanation of my preference for *soul* here and *spirit* there.)

Spirit – That part of a person which survives death and still retains aspects of the person's personality. (Some prefer to call this part the *soul.* I prefer *spirit* because of the popular use of this term to denote those who have passed on but return to communicate through channeled messages or as apparitions. See also *soul.*)

Spiritual – Transpersonal awarenesses arising spontaneously or through meditative and other practices, beyond ordinary explanations, and to which are attributed an inspiring and guiding meaningfulness, often attributed to a Deity. See also *Mystical.*

Spiritual gifts (Sitvas, Charisms) – Extraordinary abilities that may be acquired suddenly or as a result of spiritual practices, such as prolonged meditation or vision quests. For example: healing through touch or at a distance; prophesy; discernment of discarnate spirits; levitation; bilocation.

Spiritual healing – A systematic, purposeful intervention by one or more persons intending to help another living being (person, animal, plant, or other living system) by focused intention, hand contact, or movements of the hands around the body to improve their condition. Spiritual healing is brought about without conventional energetic, mechanical, or chemical interventions. Some healers attribute spiritual healings to God, Christ, other 'higher powers,' spirits, universal or cosmic forces or energies, bioenergies or forces residing in the healer, psychokinesis (mind over matter), or self-healing powers or energies latent in the healee. Psychological interventions are inevitably part of spiritual healing (as they are with every clinical intervention), but spiritual healing adds many dimensions to interpersonal healing factors.

Spirituality – Spirituality has many facets. It is an individual's basic quest or understanding of ultimate meanings and values in life. Spirituality often results from primary experience, *gnosis*, which may be stimulated by strongly positive, traumatic or transformational life occurrences, such as dramatic loss and grief; near death experiences, bereavement apparitions and channeled encounters with spirits, psychic or even psychotic episodes; and other encounters beyond ordinary experience. These may include healing crises and transformations. Spirituality often includes a sense of participating in a reality that is vaster than can be comprehended by human awareness, that is self-aware, totally loving and unconditionally accepting.

Sweetening spiral – When a positive action draws a positive response, which encourages further positive actions, etc. The opposite of a *vicious circle*.

Synchronicity – Meaningful coincidences that appear to suggest a hidden or guiding order of collective awareness in the world.

Teleology – The study of final causes; the study of actions as they relate to their utility or ends; activity leading towards achievement of goals; an attribution of purpose in the natural processes of nature.

Telepathy – The transfer of thoughts, images or commands from one living being to another, without use of sensory cues.

Theodicy – Questions and speculations on how a loving, benevolent God could permit evil in the world.

Traditional societies – Non-industrial societies in which there are unbroken traditions of personal spiritual awareness and healing.

Transpersonal – Awarenesses that extend beyond the body, often associated with feelings of being in touch with spiritual dimensions.

Transcendent – Relating to realities that are perceived as being outside of the physical world (but may include the physical), associated with a consciousness that is vastly higher and wiser than that of humanity.

Transpersonal – Awareness extending beyond people's physical boundaries.

VOT – Voices on Tape, apparently from transpersonal sources.

Xenoglossy – Speaking in a language that has not been learned in the current lifetime.

Appendix - Resources

Here are resources focused on personal spirituality.

**Association for Research and
Enlightenment (ARE)**
http://www.edgarcayce.org
Edgar Cayce readings

Rev. Rosalyn L. Bruyere
Healing Light Center Church
261 E. Alegria #12
Sierra Madre, CA 91024
(818) 306-2170
Workshops

**Consciousness Research and Training
Institute**
Joyce Goodrich, PhD
325 W. 68 Street, Box 9G
New York, NY 10021
Training in LeShan (distant) healing, re-
search, periodic newsletter

Council for Healing
http://councilforhealing.org/
Network of individual healers and healing
organizations promoting understanding of
healing and access to healing

Healing Touch
Colorado Center for Healing Touch
12477 W. Cedar Drive, Suite 202
Lakewood, Colorado 80228
(303) 989-7982 Fax 980-8683
HTIheal@aol.com
Training, certification, referrals, research

**University of Spiritual Healing and
Sufism**
P.O. Box 688
Angwin, CA 94508
(707) 965-0400 ext 21 Fax 965-4101
Workshops, 4-year course. Director -
Ibrahim (Robert) Jaffe, MD

Kahuna healing
Aloha International
P.O. Box 665
Kilauea, HI 96754
Tel/Fax (808) 828-0302

Lucidity Institute
http://www.lucidity.com
Information about lucid dreaming

Meditation
Transcendental Meditatio
www.tm.org
Classes, resources, research
List of meditation resources
www.realization.org/page/doc0/doc0025.
TM

Monroe Institute
Workshops, guided sessions in Out-of-
Body Experiences (OBE)
www.monroeinstitute.com

Prayer healing

List of prayer groups
http://freehealing.org/links.html

Christian based distant healing, not restricted to Christian healees
Drhugh@netzero.net

White Eagle Lodge
http://www.whiteagle.org/firstpage.htm

Qigong

American Association of Acupuncture and
Oriental Medicine
433 Front Street
Catasaugua, PA 18032
(610) 226-1433
www.qigonghealing.com
Information, referrals

American Foundation of Traditional
  Chinese Medicine
505 Beach Street
San Francisco, CA 94133
(415) 776-0502

Qigong Institute
561 Berkeley Avenue
Menlo Park, CA 94025
www.qigonginstitute.org
qi@qigonginstitute.org
Qigong Database of annual China conference abstracts, Kenneth Sancier, PhD

Qigong Research and Practice Center
P.O. Box 1727
Nederland, CO 80466
Tel/Fax (303) 258-0971
www.qigonghealing.com
Workshops, consultations - Ken Cohen

Tao and Zen Research Center
5910 Amboy Road
Staten Island, NY 10309
(718) 967-4624   Fax 356-1922

French qigong resources
www.zhanzhuanggong.bizland.com/
www.iquebec.com/qigongetcancer/
Moderator - Claude Fournier

Reiki

American International Reiki Association
2210 Wilshire Blvd. #831
Santa Monica, CA 90403
(310) 788-1821

American Reiki Master Association
Box 130
Lake City, FL 32056
(904) 755-9638

International Center for Reiki Training
21421 Hilltop Street
Southfield, MI 48034
(248) 948-8112   (800) 332-8112
www.reiki.org
Workshops, newsletter, referrals

Int'l Association of Reiki Professionals
P.O. Box 481
Winchester, MA 01890
(781) 729-3530 Fax: (781) 721-7306
www.iarp.org info@iarp.org
Reiki Alliance
P.O. Box 41
Cataldo, ID 83810
(208) 682-3535

Shamanic healing

Foundation for Shamanic Studies
P.O. Box 1939
Mill Valley, CA 94942
(415) 380-8282
Information, referrals - Michael Harner

Four Winds Society
P.O. Box 1493
Pacific Palisades, CA 90272
(310) 454-0444 Fax - (310) 230-0905
Information on Inka shamanism, work-
shops - Alberto Villoldo

Ruth Inge Heinze, PhD
Center for South & Southeast Asia Studies
2321 Russell St. #3A
Berkeley, CA 94705
Annual conference, proceedings

Foundation for Shamanic Studies
P.O. Box 1939
Mill Valley, CA 94942
(415) 380-8282
Information, referrals

Foundation for Shamanic Studies
P.O. Box 670, Belden Station
Norwalk, CT 06852
(203) 454-2827
Information

Therapeutic Touch

**Therapeutic Touch™ (TT™) and
Nurse Healers Professional Associates
International (NH-PAI)**
P.O. Box 158
Warnerville, NY 12187-0158
Phone: (518) 325-1185 Toll Free (877)
32NHPAI
Fax: (509) 693-3537
www.therapeutic-touch.org
NH-PAI@therapeutic-touch.org
Promotes holistic approaches and complementary therapies, including TT.
Training, certification in TT.

Therapeutic Touch Network Ontario
P.O. Box 85551
875 Eglinton Ave
W. Toronto M6C 4A8
Canada
(416) 65-TOUCH
http://www.therapeutictouchnetwk.com/
ttno.membership@sympatico.ca
Information, referrals, malpractice insurance for recognized practitioners

**SPIRITUAL EMERGENCIES/
EMERGENCES**

Second Aid
England
www.secondaid.net   enquiries@secondaid.net
Spiritual wounds and scars, self-help,
healing and counseling
Led by Judy Fraser

Spiritual Emergence Network (SEN)
California Institute of Integral Studies
1453 Mission Street
San Francisco, CA 94103
 (415) 648-2610
www.realization.org/page/doc0/doc0027.h
tm (Accessed 3/28/06) SEN@CIIS.edu
Information and referrals for help with
existential and/or spiritual
crisis and related problems

Barbara Brennan School of Healing
500 N.E. Spanish River Boulevard
Suite108
Boca Raton, FL 33431-4559
(800) 924-2564
Intensive, modular 4-year course, referrals

Touching Spirit Center LLC
Litchfield, CT
www.touchingspirit.org
Workshops, training, Instructor - Elizabeth
Stratton

**GRADUATE PROGRAMS
INCLUDING TRANSPERSONAL
STUDIES
Some with distant learning programs**

Academy of Intuition Medicine
PO Box 1921 Mill Valley, CA 94942
415.381.1010 Fax: 415.381.1080
Francesca McCartney, PhD
Founder, President
www.intuitionmedicine.org

Atlantic University
P.O. Box 595
67th St. & Atlantic Ave.
Virginia Beach, VA 23451
(804) 428-3588

**California Institute of Integral Studies
(CIIS)**
1453 Mission Street
San Francisco, CA 94103
(415) 575-6150
Spirit, intellect, and wisdom in service to
individuals, communities, and the Earth

Energy Medicine University
PO Box 1921 Mill Valley, CA 94942
USA
Phone: 415.381.1010 Fax: 415.381.1080
Francesca McCartney, PhD
Founder, President
www.intuitionmedicine.org

Holos University Graduate Seminary (HUGS)
5607 S. 222nd Road
Fair Grove MO, 65648
Tel. 888-272-6109   Fax: 888-528-0746
www.HUGS-edu.org
http://holosuniversity.org/
MA and PhD of Theology, distant learning

Institute of Transpersonal Psychology
744 San Antonio Road
Palo Alto CA 94303
(650) 493-4430   Fax 493-6835
Psychological research and education, probing the mind, body, spirit connection

John F. Kennedy University
12 Altarinda Road
Orinda, California 94563-2603
800.696.   http://www.jfku.edu
Degree programs in holistic studies, psychology, more.

Lesley College
29 Everett St.
Cambridge, MA 02138
(617) 349-3700

Naropa University
2130 Arapahoe Ave.
Boulder, CO 80302
(303) 444-0202   Fax 444-0410
Transpersonal, contemplative, somatic psychology; Buddhist, environmental studies, and more.

Ontario Institute - Studies in Education
University of Toronto
252 Bloor St. W.
Toronto, Ontario, Canada MSS 1V6
(416) 923-6641

Pacifica Graduate institute
249 Lambert Rd.
Carpinteria, CA 93013
(805) 969-3636

Rosebridge Graduate School of Integrative Psychology
1040 Oak Grove Road #103
Concord, CA 94518
(510) 689-0560

Salve Regina University
Holistic Counseling Program
100 Ochre Road
Newport, RI 02840
(401) 847-6650   http://www.salve.edu/
Holistic Counseling

Saybrook Graduate School and Research Center
450 Pacific Ave., 3rd Floor
San Francisco, CA 94133-4640
(800) 825-4480 (415) 433-9200
Psychology, Human Science.
Organizational Systems Inquiry

Southwestern College
PO. Box 4788
Santa Fe, NM 87502
(505) 471-5756

Stare University of 'West Georgia
Carrollton, GA 30118
(914) 967-6080

SUNY Empire State College
617 Main St.
Buffalo, NY 14203
(716) 853-7706

The Union Institute
440 East McMillaan St.
Cincinnati, OH 45206
(513) 861-6400

MAGAZINES AND JOURNALS

Caduceus Magazine
http://www.caduceus.info/

International Journal of Healing and Caring – on line
www.ijhc.org

Science & Spirit
http://www.science-spirit.org

Science & Theology News
http://www.stnews.org/index.php

Notes

Prologue

1 Other noteworthy books by Sacks: *The Man Who Mistook His Wife for a Hat; Awakenings* (see also film with this title).
2 Sacks, p. 107.
3 Sacks, p. 108.
4 Sacks, p. 111.
5 I take God to be an omniscient, omnipotent consciousness that has participated in the creation of the universe in ways that are beyond our comprehension and that granted humans free choice to learn from our mistakes. Everything in the universe is part of God. More on spiritual issues in Chapters III-8, 9, 10, 11, 12, 13 and Conclusion.

Introduction

6 See more on the history of **spiritual healing and energy medicine within western science** in the Introduction to Volume I.
7 The term *psi*, from the Greek letter Ψ is used in parapsychology to denote powers of telepathy, clairsentience, pre- and retro-cognition, and psychokinesis (mind influencing matter). More on this later in the introduction.
8 While skeptics continue to make many false claims about the lack of evidence for psi effects, the Parapsychological Association has for many decades been accepted as an affiliate of the American Association for the Advancement of Science (AAAS), which could not fault the meticulous body of research on psi. There are chairs in parapsychology at the University of Utrecht in the Netherlands, Edinburgh University in Scotland, and, Lund University in Sweden.
9 **Spiritual healing** is reviewed in Volume I; **bioenergies** are discussed in Chapter II-3.
10 In Greek mythology, Sisyphus was a crafty, deceitful man who even cheated death when it came for him. In punishment, the gods set him the endless task of rolling a giant boulder up a hill, only to have it roll down again and again, requiring that he roll it back up each time.
11 Senge 1990, 142.
12 www.micro.magnet.fsu.edu/primer/java/scienceopticsu/powersof10/index.html (Accessed 3/14/06).
13 Confucius, Attributed.
14 For instance, R. Sloan, a professor at Columbia University, published an article in the prestigious medical journal, *Lancet*, in which he disparaged the studies which correlate religious affiliation and practice with better health. See Sloan; Sloan et al 2000; 2001.
15 German acknowledges this too in the vernacular of *ja-ein*, the combination of *ja* and *nein*.
16 Gender neutrality is promoted in these books through random alternations of masculine with feminine pronouns.
17 Walsch 1997, p. 80.
18 More on **stages of development of faith** in Chapter III-11.
19 New Thought churches are much closer to my views of spirituality, but their numbers are as yet rather small.
20 Joseph Campbell 1989a.
21 An acknowledgment of being a part of all creation – the earth, the waters, the sky and every living thing within them, and also a part of the unseen worlds of spirit. "All my relations" is a parallel in usage with "Amen" at the end of a ceremony or prayer.
22 van der Post 1988, p. 72.

23 I take this from the terms, *gnosis* and *gnostic*, but avoid the original terms because they have too many historical and religious associations that would be distracting to my discussion of personal spirituality.

24 **Gnowing** is a direct, intuitive knowledge which often carries with it an inner, numinous sense of certainty about its validity. This is an awareness through the intuitive, right brain for some; for others a knowing felt in the heart rather than in the head. To those who have experienced gnosis, it may feel even more real than physical reality, which, in comparison, is sometimes described as an illusion.

25 The spirit may travel away from the physical body, as in Out-of-Body Experiences.

26 Some have used these terms with opposite meanings: *Soul* referring to the energetic component that survives death and *spirit* denoting that part which is eternal and which retains the lessons of the various souls in their series of incarnations. I prefer the use I have indicated in the text because, in common usage, we 'give up the spirit' when we die; and a *spirit* can be a ghost, or a surviving entity that speaks through a medium (discussed in Chapter III-5).

27 See **right and left brain ways of knowing the world** in Chapter II-1. The intuitive gnowing of the heart is described and discussed by Gibran 1923.

28 See Galapagos; Loy for details.

29 I use my initials where the quotation is new to Healing Research, Volume III, to avoid confusion with sources other than this volume.

30 See **correlations between religion and health** in Chapter III-12.

31 **Bereavement apparitions** are discussed in Chapter III-4.

32 See review of **astrology** in Chapter II-4.

33 Felser, p. 100-101.

34 Where quotes expand on a point discussed in the text, they are in normal font; where they illustrate or counterpoint the text poetically, humorously or metaphorically they are in italics.

Chapter 1: Out-of-Body Experiences

35 Ecclesiastes 12:6.

36 On **consciousness outside the body** see: Alvarado 1997; Crookall 1972; O. Fox (earliest modern writing); Frost; Gabbard; C. Green 1973; Greenhouse; Irwin 1985; 1987; Mitchell; Monroe; Muldoon; Powell; Rogo 1978; 1983; Osis 1979; Osis/McCormick; Rogo 1978; Swann; Tannous.

37 e.g. MacManaway, described in Chapter I-1.

38 Kelsey/Grant.

39 von Franz 1987.

40 e.g. David-Neel.

41 Modern investigations of OBEs in the laboratory, often labeled *remote viewing*, are discussed below.

42 Hart 1954; Irwin 1980; Sheils.

43 On OBEs in the blind see also Irwin 1987; Krishnan.

44 Monroe; Muldoon; Rogo 1983.

45 Rogo 1978; Targ/Harary.

46 Jahn/Dunn 1987.

47 Rogo 1978.

48 Psi perceptions of items in the room which are not designated by experimenters as *targets for that experiment* are given little value in psi research because they cannot be quantified and are not part of the designated research protocol.

49 Easily hypnotized people who exhibit psi abilities are discussed in Chapters II-1; I-3.

50 Tart 1968.

51 Tart 1969.

52 For further psychophysiological studies of OBEs see Alvarado; Krippner 1996; McCreery/Claridge; Morris et al 1978; Osis/Mitchell 1977; Palmer 1979; Tart 1967; Twemlow 1977.

53 Palmer 1979.
54 **Remote viewing in the military** is reported in McMonaegle. See also journal at www.emergentmind.org/journal.htm.
55 For further research reports see: Osis 1972; 1980; Osis/Haraldsson 1976; Osis/Mitchell; Tart 1968.
56 Alvarado 2003.
57 Tart 1967; 1968; 1969; Morris et al; Osis/Mitchell.
58 McCreery; Palmeri 1978.
59 Todd/Dewhurst 1955.
60 Tart 1995.
61 Palmer 1979; Tart 1967; 1968.
62 Kelzer.
63 Tart 1968.
64 More observations on the blind are presented in the following chapter, on the Near-Death Experience.
65 Rogo 1978.
66 See **summaries of psi research** in Edge; Nash 1978; 1984; Radin.
67 More on quantum physics in chapter III-9.
68 See **Kirlian photography** in Chapter II-3.
69 Markides 1987, p. 51.

Chapter 2: Near-Death and Pre-Death Experiences

70 Baden/Hennessee; Carr 1993; Milbourne 1979.
71 Morse 1999.
72 Those who believe in survival of the spirit may prefer *passed on* to *died*.
73 Anonymous 1992.
74 Hennessee 1989; Carr 1993; Milbourne 1979.
75 Ring, p. 145- 146.
76 Flynn, 1986; Grey, 1985; Musgrave, 1997; Ring, 1980, 1984; Sutherland, 1992; Tiberi, 1993.
77 S. Levine 1984, p. 76.
78 Bailey/Yates.
79 More following this quote of Benedict in Chapter III-11.
80 Holk.
81 Royce.
82 Heim.
83 Fenwick 2002; Parnia et al 2001a; b.
84 (p < 0.0001).
85 See deathbed and bereavement apparitions in Chapter III-4.
86 Blackmore 1984.
87 Ring 1980.
88 Ring 1980, 1984; Morse/Perry 1990; Ossis/Haraldson 1977; Moody 1975, 1977.
89 Morse with Perry 1990.
90 Devinsky; Dewhurst; Gloor; Mandell; Mendez; Morgan 1990; Morse 1992; Palmini; Penfield 1955; Penfield/Rasmussen; Persinger.
91 Morse cites Tipler. See also discussion on mystical experiences and quantum physics, respectively, in Chapters III-9 and III-10.
92 Atwater 2001.
93 Penfield 1975.
94 Gregory; Sacks; Senden; Valvo.
95 *U.S. News & World Report* 1997.
96 Morse with Perry, 1990.

97 Other helpful **NDE references**: *Anabiosis* - publication of the International Association for Near-Death Experiences (IANDS, at the University of Connecticut); Anonymous 1992, Atwater (children); Benedict (personal experience, detailed other-world descriptions); Carr; Gallup; Gibson; M. Grey 1985; Greyson 1983; 1990; Greyson/Bush; Greyson/Flynn; Greyson/Harris; Greyson/Stevenson 1980; Kelleher; Kubis/Macy; Kubler-Ross 1981; Lorimer 1990; Lundahl; Lundahl/Widdison; Lundahl, et al; Moody; Moody with Perry; Olson/Dulaney; Palmer; Morse; Morse/Perry 1990; 1992; 1994; Randles/Hough; Rawlings; Ring 1980; 1982; 1984; Ring/ Rosing; Ring/Valarino; Ritchie 1978; 1991; Roberts/Owen; Sabom; Serdahely; Simpson (Nursing); Sabom; Simpson (nursing); Walker/Serdahely (historical discussion of research, per Bockris); Zaleski.

Awareness of people in spirit waiting to be born: Wambach 1981; Gabriel/Gabriel 1992; Lundahl 1992.

On the **transformative aspect of the NDE** Flynn 1986; Ring 1984; Sutherland 1990.

Gallup reports a widening acceptance of NDE in America.

Rogo 1984; Siegel/Hirschman discuss **drug-induced experiences resembling the NDE**.

Rogo 1970 1972 discusses the other-wordly *music of the spheres* phenomenon. A last classic relating to this subject is The Tibetan Book of The Dead (Evans-Wentz translation recommended); Rinpoche. R. Siegel presents the theory that NDE experiences represent dissociative hallucinations.

Unusual book on resurrection reports: A. Herbert.

Websites with NDE references: www.near-death.com; www.iands.org/bib.html; Health care provider references www.seattleiands.org/htm/biblio1.htm

98 Carr; Greyson 1990; Ring 1980, 1984; Ring/Rosing; Sabom; Serdahely 1991; Zaleski; Pas-richa/Stevenson 1986 (As summarized by Wade 1996).

99 Wade 1996.

100 Morse 1994.

101 More on pre-death experience in R. Smith.

102 Osis/Haraldsson 1977.

103 Gallup/Proctor, as reported in Bockris.

104 Evans-Wentz; Rinpoche.

105 Bockris confuses and combines (3) and (4).

106 M. Gray; Rawlings 1978; 1993; Rinpoche; Swedenborg 1970.

107 Rawlings 1978, cited in Bockris.

108 Kübler-Ross 1991.

109 Morse 1994.

110 On **theories of disordered, diseased or dying brain to explain NDE's**: Blackmore 1992; Broughton 1991; Kurtz 1985; Milbourne 1979; Noyes/Kletti; Rodabough 1985; E. Rodin; Siegel 1977, 1980; Wilson 1982; Zaleski 1987.

111 Devinsky; Dewhurst; Gloor; Mandell; Mendez; Morgan 1990; Morse 1992; Palmini; Pen-field 1955; Penfield/Rasmussen; Persinger.

112 Atwater 2001.

113 Morse cites Tipler. See also discussion on mystical experiences and quantum physics, re-spectively, in Chapters III-9 and III-10.

114 Newberg/Iversen; Newberg et al 2001.

115 **Endorphins** are naturally-occurring, morphine-like substances in the brain that have tranquilizing properties similar to opiates.

116 Lenz.

117 C. Green 1968; LaBerge 1988, 1990, 1993; LaBerge/Rheingold.

118 C. Green 1968.

119 Kirtley.

120 Blackmore 1993.

121 Greyson 2000.

122 S. Levine 1984.

123 Melvin Morse with Paul Perry 1994, p. 165.

124 See mystical experiences in Chapter III-9; Spiritual experiences in Chapter III-11.
125 See deathbed and bereavement apparitions in Chapter III-4.
126 Greaves 1980.

Chapter 3: Reincarnation

127 **Famous people who reported past life experiences or interest and belief in these**:
Louisa May Alcott, Elizabeth Barrett Browning, Charles Dickens, Arthur Conan Doyle, George
Elliot, Ralph Waldo Emerson, Victor Hugo, David Hume, William James, Henry Wadsworth
Longfellow, John Masefield, Edgar Allen Poe, Nevil Shute, Alfred Lord Tennyson, Henry
David Thoreau, Leo Tolstoy, Voltaire, Walt Whitman, John Greenleaf Whittier.
Notable figures from the past include: Cicero, Plato, Pythagoras, Lao Tse.
For further discussions of **experiences from past lives that appear to produce psychological
problems in present lives**, see Cockell; Fiore 1978; Goldberg; Grossi; Lucas; McClain; Modi;
Shiffrin; Sutphen/Taylor. Schlotterbeck compares past life therapy with other psychotherapies.
*Talents developed as apparent result of reincarnation memories or such memories evoked under
hypnosis* are mentioned in Feldman with Goldsmith; Ostrander and Schroeder. Venn has
an excellent discussion of *criticisms of hypnotically induced reincarnation memories.* J. Roberts 1973; 1984 has *fictionalized descriptions of reincarnation and spirit guidance* experiences
across several lifetimes.
128 Chadha/Stevenson; Stevenson 1974a. See also reports from other researchers on spontaneous reincarnation memories: Christie-Murray 1988; Wilson 1982; Rogo 1985.
129 Stevenson 1974b; 1984; Stevenson/Pasricha.
130 Stevenson 1995; 1997.
131 Pasricha 1998.
132 Stevenson 1997.
133 Gershom 1992; 1996.
134 More on **Jewish views of the afterlife** in Raphael.
135 Ash 1967.
136 Lucas 1993a; b; McClain.
137 B. Weiss 1994; 1995; 1996.
138 B. Weiss 1994, p. 117.
139 C. Snow 1989.
140 Chapter III-5.
141 Chapter III-6.
142 Beard 1980; Bodine; Newton; Newton/Duff; Steinpach
143 Stevenson 1961; 1974a.
144 See also **vicarious traumatization** in the discussion below, under Other Psychological
explanations for past life reports.
145 Zolik.
146 Laszlo, p. 161-162.
147 See also Chari for another helpful discussion on **psi and reincarnation**.
148 **Psychic surgery** is discussed in Chapter 7
149 Spirit guides are discussed in Chapters 5 and 6; with examples of spirit guides for healing
in Chapter I-1.
150 More on **possession** in Chapter III-6.
151 Ivanova 1978 describes similar **'parapictography'** in trance states.
152 Rinpoche.
153 See discussion of Stevenson's research in Chapter III-3.
154 Bache; Chamberlain 1981; 1987; 1988a; b; Cheek 1986; 1992; Grof/Halifax 1985; Restak;
Schindler; Van Husen; Verny/Kelly.
155 Leader et al. 1982; Madison, Adubato and Madison 1986.
156 See Chapter II-1 for a fuller discussion of **suggestion under hypnosis**.

157 Rosenthal 1974; 1978.

158 A delightful group of these suggestions is found in Haley 1973. Two examples are quoted in Chapter II-1.

159 On **neurolinguistic programming (NLP)** see Bandler/Grinder.

160 See Chapter II-1 for explanations of various reinforcements that can shape people's behaviors.

161 See Chapter II-1 for discussion of suggestion and experimenter effects.

162 See more on **possession** in Chapter III-6.

163 See Chapter I-3; II-1 for discussions of **psi with hypnosis.**

164 Wilson/Barber.

165 Dingwall 1968; LeCron.

166 See Chapter I-3 on **remote viewing**.

167 Questions regarding apparent **reincarnation phenomena as possible super-psi effects** are also discussed by Chari; Gauld 1976; 1977; Jacobson; Murphy 1973.

168 Weiss 1994; 1995; 1996.

169 Woolger, considering **past life recall from a Jungian perspective**, also suggests that such memories may be more psychological truths than literal truths.

170 On multiple personality see Allison; Crabtree; Sliker.

171 Joy, p. 159.

172 Benor 1992b; Von Franz 1980.

173 Shapiro, p. 294.

174 Woolger 1993.

175 Michael Newton has extensive discussions on life between lives.

176 See LeShan 1976, Chapter IV-2, on **other realities**.

177 See also discussion of **Visualization** in Chapter II-2; **Thought forms** in Besant/Leadbeater.

178 Joseph Campbell 1989b, p. 57-58.

179 Desoille p. 59.

180 Desoille p. 59-60.

181 Desoille p. 60.

182 Benor et al., 2001.

183 They may experience this as Christ, Buddha, Allah, God, or whatever form feels best to them.

184 Gary Zukav 1990, p. 36.

185 On **mythic realities** see LeShan 1974; 1976, reviewed in Chapter IV-2; and on reworking psychological problems through **visualizations** see Chapter II-2.

186 See discussion of *Conjuring up Philip* in Chapter 5.

187 D. Scott Rogo 1985.

188 The greater bulk of this literature was published after Rogo's untimely death.in 1990, at the age of 40.

189 Carl Jung 1964, p. 69.

190 Carl Jung 1965, p,. 318.

191 Brugh Joy's 1990.

192 Jane Roberts 1975.

193 Jane Roberts 1973; 1984.

194 Wesselman (1996; 1999; 2001), an anthropologist, has another series of books on visions of a future reincarnation that resonates forwards and backwards in time.

195 Willis Harman 1994.

196 Frances Vaughan 1995, p. 93.

197 **Karma** and related matters are discussed further in Chapters III-8; III-11, along with other aspects of religion, spirituality and healing.

198 For further general reading on **reincarnation** see: Blythe; Cerminara; Challoner 1969; Cohen 1975; J. Cooper; Head/Cranston (reports and opinions from around the world); Holzer 1974(a); Leek 1974, Moody 1996; Mullen; Pasricha; Pasricha/Stevenson 1986; Rivas (Nether

lands cases); Rogo 1985; Stemman 1997; Stevenson 1977; TenDam; Wambach, 1979; Wolf 1970. On Xenoglossy: Stevenson/Pasricha; Tipler; Whitton. Ivanova 1986(b) reports on reincarnation memories that apear to herself as healer and to her healees during healings. Guirdham 1970; 1974 are worth mentioning as suggestive case histories, but unsatisfactory because he has refused to share case material with other professionals (see discussion of Rogo 1985). The Reincarnation Library of Aeon Publishing Co. in Mamaroneck, NY. is a book club specializing in reincarnation.

Chapter 4: Apparitions, Nature Spirits and Angels

199 Paris Flammonde p. 14.
200 See expanded statement of Norwood in Chapter II-8.
201 Discussed in other chapters in this book.
202 More on theodicy in Chapters III-8; III-9; III-13.
203 Whitaker, p. 117.
204 Whitaker, p. 120-1.
205 On **bereavement apparitions** see also Amatuzio; Baden/Hennessee; Longman et al; Rees on bereavement apparitions/hallucinations.
206 See descriptions and explanations of spirits participating in the healings of Harry Edwards in Chapter I-1.
207 Targ/Katra 1998, p. 273.
208 H. Hart/E. B. Hart 1933; 1956.
209 See also G. Prince for collective/reciprocal sightings of apparitions.
210 Hart/Hart 1933.
211 Hart/Hart 1933.
212 Weiss 1995, p. 133.
213 Forman 1981b; Gribbin.
214 Smyth 1981; 1983.
215 On **spirits appearing in photographs** see Gettings 1978; Goodman 1982a; Holzer 1969; Permutt; The Unexplained.
216 Hufford 1982.
217 Kant, p. 92.
218 Kant, p. 88.
219 Jung 1920.
220 S. Johnson 1791.
221 See Chapter I-3 for more on **clairsentient perceptions**.
222 See more on thought forms under **visualization** in Chapter II-2.
223 Markides 1991 p. 210.
224 Gurney, et al.; L. Rhine 1961.
225 See more on **possession** in Chapters III-5 and III-6.
226 **Reincarnation** and **karma** are discussed in Chapter III-3; III-8.
227 Further discussions on **apparitions** may be found in Anderson 1984; Bayless 1973; Broad 1962; Currie; Devers; Durville; H. Evans 1982; 1986; Gauld 1977; Goldsmith; Greber; Guggenheim/Guggenheim; Jacobson; Lawson; LaGrand; MacKenzie 1971; Moody/Perry 1993; Nesbitt; G. Prince (consensual perceptions of spirits); Rogo 1973; Tyrrell 1953; West 1960. Photographs on which spirit forms can be seen are presented in: Fukurai; Gettings; Goodman 1982a; b; Holzer 1969; Permutt. Smyth describes phantom ships, aircraft and a London bus; J. Webster; Wiseman. More on **Voices OnTapes** in Bander; Rogo and Bayless; *Unlimited Horizons*; on spirit telephone calls in Rogo and Bayless. Vargas, et al. present a **psychiatric survey of bereavement apparitions**. **Interactive ghosts**, labeled 'timeslips' are discussed in Forman 1981a; b; c; d; 1982a; b; 1983. More on time in Shallis.
228 Patience Worth/Irving Litvag p. 239.
229 See Chapter III-3 on **Reincarnation**.

230 **Religious views of survival** and **spirituality** in Chapter III-8, III-9 and III-11; See especially: Foundation for Inner Peace; Kornfield; Rinpoche; F. Vaughan; Wilber.

231 Evans-Wentz 1977; Hawken; van Gelder. Again, we have the emic and etic approaches to consider in examining reports from traditional societies.

232 Married name Kunz; co-developer of Therapeutic Touch healing with Dolores Krieger.

233 See discussion of **clairsentience**, the ability to perceive objects directly through extrasensory perception (ESP) in Chapter I-3.

234 Van Gelder, p. 62.

235 Van Gelder, p. 63.

236 Van Gelder, p. 64.

237 Hawken.

238 Hawken.

239 Hawken, p. 146.

240 M. Wright, p. 1.

241 M. Wright, p. 17-18.

242 **Biblical references to angels** are listed at http://www.geocities.com/missus_gumby/angels.htm.

243 Watts, Attributed.

244 Godwin; Monroe in Jovanovic.

245 Pruitt, p. 63.

246 Pruitt, p. 66.

247 Pruitt, p. 66-7.

248 Hebrews 13:2.

249 Jovanovic 1995.

250 See Chapter III-2 on the NDE.

251 Other books on **Angels**: Davidson (bibliography 25pp!); R. Hauck; Muolenburgh 1992; 1993; Isaac; Lewis/Oliver; Maclean; J. Price; Singh; Steiger; Sutherland. On **nature spirits** see Hawken; Thompkins 1997; Chapters III-8.

252 Hayward.

253 Price, p. 101.

254 2 Kings:7:5-7.

255 2 Kings:7:15.

256 Moolenburgh, p. 96.

257 Moolenburgh, p. 195.

258 Moolenburgh, p. 201.

259 Moolenburgh, p. 42.

260 Moolenburgh, p. 43.

261 The rays were described by Dwal Khul, a Tibetan Master, in the Alice Bailey books in the 1930's and 1940's. *Esoteric Psychology 1* was dictated to Alice Bailey by Dwal Khul while Alice was in New York in 1936 and Dwal Khul was in Tibet. There are 7 rays. A ray is a force, power or energy. The 7 rays are: 1. Will or power; 2. Love or Wisdom; 3. Adaptability or Active Intelligence; 4. Harmony, Beauty or Art; 5. Concrete Knowledge or Science; 6. Abstract Idealism and Devotion;

7. Ceremonial Order and Synthesis

262 I have put forth Godwins views in an order that is slightly different from the original.

263 On **collective consciousness** see Benor 2003; Jung 1953-1979; 1964; 1993. On morphogenetic fields see Sheldrake.

264 See Chapters II-2; III-5 on **creating realities through visualizations**.

265 See brief discussion on multiple personalities in Chapter II-1; Allison; Crabtree.

266 Lilly, p. 227.

267 See Chapter II-1 on **psychological defense mechanisms.**

268 Lilly.

269 On **alternate realities** see LeShan 1974; 1976, reviewed in Chapter IV-2.

270 Atlantis and Lemuria are said to have been very advanced civilizations that existed before recorded history. For reasons that are not clear, knowledge of their cultures was lost. People have reported memories of incarnations in these lands.

271 Godwin, p. 215.

272 Godwin, p. 239.

273 Godwin, p. 244.

274 **Morphogenetic fields** are discussed in Chapter II-3 and IV-2.

275 M. Fox/Sheldrake, p. 39.

276 More on the discussions of Fox/Sheldrake in Chapter III-10, including details from writings of St. Thomas Aquinas and Hildegard of Bingen, the other two experts discussed in their book.

277 Bacon 1620b.

278 Psalm 91:9-12.

279 **Muscle testing** and **dowsing** as ways of connecting with intuitive awareness are discussed in Chapters II-1; II-2 and (II-5 – Popular edition).

280 Godwin, p. 206.

281 van Gelder, p. 117.

282 Owen/Sparrow.

283 Peterson 1987; Price.

284 See discussion on **mystical experiences** in Chapter III-9.

285 More on angels in Chapter III-8.

Notes: Chapter 5 - Mediumistic (Channeled) Experiences

286 Wickland, p. 16.

287 Angelo.

288 Angelo, p. 77.

289 On **spirit materializations** see: Fuller 1978; Greber; Haraldsson; Pulos /Richman; Von Schrenk-Nötzing.

290 Angelo; Edwards; Hutton.

291 See **psychic surgery** in chapter III-7.

292 See Osty for detailed descriptions of these PK phenomena. It would be impossible to determine whether the PK effects are due to spirits or to the psi abilities of the medium or sitters.

293 See discussion on **possession** in the following chapter.

294 Moody 1992.

295 Shapiro 1995.

296 Schwartz 2002.

297 The mediums studied by Schwartz included: George Anderson, Laurie Campbell, John Edward, Anne Gehman, Susan Northrop.

298 Roberts 1974.

299 Roberts 1974, p. 324-5.

300 **On distinguishing the qualities and credibilities of mediumistic transmissions** see Beard 1988; J. Cooper; Klimo; Northage.

301 Gardner Murphy 1961.

302 Besant/Leadbeater 1908. See discussion on this in Bockris.

303 Chapman 1973; 1978.

304 See description of **Chapman's psychic surgery** in Chapter 7.

305 Gauld 1977; 1982.

306 Super-psi would require the participants in séances to obtain their information entirely via their own telepathy, clairvoyance and pre- or retro- cognition. In the instances of cross-correspondences, this would have to occur in their unconscious minds, with some participant(s) organizing which materials are transmitted by and to which participants. While not

inconceivable, this does stretch the bounds of requirements for unconscious collaborations on psi channels. See Gauld 1977; 1982 for a good discussion on **super-psi.**

307 von Franz 1980, p. 41-2.

308 Turner 1970.

309 See also in Chapter III-7 (from Stelter) descriptions of Crawford's application of dye to ectoplasm, with transfer of this dye to the skin of the medium after the ectoplasm was reabsorbed by the medium.

310 See reviews of Crawford's work in Barham 1988a; b; similar work in Brookes-Smith 1975. Other reports of **materializations** in Stemman 1982b; materialization of fillings in teeth Fuller; Stemman 1983a.

311 Further descriptions of **table tilting research** are presented and/or reviewed in Barham; Batcheldor 1966; 1984; Brookes; Brookes-Smith; Crookes; Isaacs; Osty 1923; 1933; Richards. See Pearsall for a more general discussion on this subject. See Ellison 1981 for photos of the Philip Séance group and of a levitated table. See more on the Philip experiments in Chapter I-2. See *Spiritual Scinetist* for reports from a parapsychology group in England which has been persuing this line of research in the past few years, with claims for impressive results.

312 Owen/Sparrow 1984; Ellison 1981; Gauld 1982.

313 Senkowski 1990.

314 **VOT publications**: Bander; D. Ellis; Estes; Fuller 1985/6; Meek 1982; Raudive; Rogo/Bayless; H Schaefer; S. Smith 1977; K. Webster; Welsh. More on instrumental transcommunication (ITC) at Bray; Chisholm; Findlay; Fuller 1986; Keen/Ellison/Fontana; Kubis; Macy; Rinaldi (list of EVP sites); Solomon/Solomon. *Unlimited Horizons* is a newsletter devoted to VOT phenomena.

315 D. Ellis 1978.

316 Bander.

317 Friedrich Jurgenson 1969.

318 Orso 1985a; b; MacRae.

319 Trajna; A. MacRae; Senkowski 1989

320 VOT mainly since 1980.

321 Estes; Fuller 1985/6; Meek 1988; Uphoff 1988; K. Webster.

322 Instrumental Transcommunication www.worlditc.org

323 Rinpoche.

324 Kelsey/Grant, p. 217-218.

325 Beard 1966; 1980.

326 Other mediums have described various levels of spiritual existence: Blavatsky; Crookall; Currie; Meek.

327 I use 'the All' as a global term to include your higher self, spirit, soul, and the unseen but very present worlds beyond ordinary consciousness, extending to and including the Infinite Source.

328 On life in spirit existence see Kubis; Randles; Ring/Valarino; Van Ness.

329 van Gelder.

330 More on nature spirits and angels in Chapter 4.

331 Castaneda; Harner.

332 Benor 2003.

333 Samuel 1:28.

334 Benor 1986.

335 On the **nature of and views from spirit worlds** see Angelo; P. Beard; Carey, J. Cooper; Foundation for Inner Peace; Gibson; H. Greaves; Markides 1985; 1987; 1991; Melton; Malz; Newton; Singh; S. Smith 1977; Turoff; on the **transition into spirit through death** see Rinpoche.

336 On **mediumship** see Berg; Bjorling (bibliography); Bolendas; Carington 1935; Gray; Hastings; Kardek; Oppenheim; Soal; Stemman 1982; Storm; Trick; Tyrell. For classical descriptions the famous D. D. Home see Zorab. For healers who work with spirit guides see: Edwards; Fuller; D. Stein. Interesting **channeled materials** are presented by: Beard; Carey;

Course in Miracles; Greaves; J. Roberts; E. Green 2001 (explanations of Alzheimer's disease by the channeled spirit of Green's wife, who spoke through her own physical body). Harris 1983; Hicks (more channeled materials from Seth). For further descriptions of **shamanism** see Eliade; Grauds; Halifax; Harner; Heinze; Isberg (journeying); Krippner/Welch (outstanding academic work); Sifers (counseling); Tress (imagery); Whitaker. Castaneda's books (apparently fictionalized) on a modern day Mexican shaman are good reads and true to shamanic practices and experiences of Western students of shamanism. **Fake mediums** who deliberately defraud a gullible public are discussed by Keene; Rogo 1982; 1983B. **Fake healers** are described by Bishop; Randi 1986; 1987.

337 E. Glenn presents a qualitative study from Jungian perspectives on soul retrieval.

338 Cooper; Greaves.

339 On creating realities see Chapter II-2 on **visualization**.

340 For discussions on **survival of death** see Beard 1966; Lorimer 1986; Ritchie; C. Wilson 1987.

341 Kübler Ross in Jovanovic, p153.

342 Vargas, et al.

343 e.g. Kelsey/Grant; Worrall/Worrall; Turner 1970.

344 Kelsey/Grant, p. 212.

345 Peterson 1987.

346 More on **death** in chapter III-8.

347 See discussion on **mystical experiences** in Chapter III-9.

348 Beard 1980, p. 115.

349 Palmstierna, p. 249-50.

350 van der Post 1994, p. 71.

351 See more full discussion on **cautions in accepting mediumistic readings** later in this chapter.

352 Asquith 1937.

353 H. Smith 1965.

354 See Benor 1992 for an example of the **difficulties in translating clairsentient diagnostic perceptions into linear language**.

355 Charles Tart 1975b.

356 See Chapter 1 on Out-of-Body Experience (OBE) research.

357 See Chapter III-10 on **convergences of physics and mysticism**

358 LeShan 1974.

359 Eisenbud 1983; Frank 1974.

360 Laing 1960.

361 On **fears of psi influence** and how we repress and deny these see section on reasons healing and psi have not been accepted, Chapter IV-3; Benor 1990a; Eisenbud 1983; Tart. 1986b.

362 Cincinatti in 1967.

363 Vargas, et al.

364 See more on **bereavement apparitions** in Chapter 4.

365 Dingwall 1974; Vasiliev; and others present experiments demonstrating **hypnotic induction at a distance**; while Merker 1971; von Urban 1958 describe instances of the Indian rope trick as an example of this. See discussion in Chapter II-1, Hypnosis; Visualization in Chapter II-2.

366 Whitmont 1993, p. 45.

367 Benor 2005.

368 e.g. Daskalos (Markides); Kahuna healers (M. Long).

369 **Psychic surgery** is described in Chapter III-7. M. Long is the earliest reference to this connection of mediumistic materializations with psychic surgery. See also Insall on Isa Northage, a medium who is said to have materialized a spirit psychic surgeon.

370 More on materializations in psychic surgery in Chapter III-7.

Notes: Chapter 6 – Possession

371 Dethlefsen/Dahlke; Markides.

372 See Chapter III-6 on **Possession**.

373 More on **mystical experiences** in Chapter III-9.

374 Matthew 8:16.

375 **Poltergeist** means *mischievous spirit*. This term is used to indicate movement of objects without physical intervention of a person. While it may occur during possession, it occurs far more commonly in the presence of agitated people who externalize their stresses unconsciously in this way, with no apparent involvement of spirits.. See Chapter I-3 for a discussion of Poltergeist, or Random Spontaneous Psychokinesis (RSPK) phenomena. References: Bayless 1967; Fodor 1958; Goss; Gould/Cornell; Groff 1999; Houran/Lange; Podmore; Rogo 1974b; Roll 1972; Thurston.

376 Rogo 1974b; 1988.

377 Allison, p. 196.

378 Allison, p. 197.

379 Allison, p. 198.

380 Allison, p. 198.

381 Allison, p. 199.

382 For more on **multiple personality disorder and possession** see Coons; Kenney; Whiteman; C. Wilson 1987. A fascinating side note comes from a pair of British healers who have worked for years together, reciting the 91st psalm in their exorcism rituals. They find that the King James version is effective, while the New English version is not. Whether this reflects the beliefs and preferences of the healers, morphogenetic fields or something else would be a challenge to sort out.

383 Wickland, p. 29.

384 Wickland, p. 17.

385 See Chapter II-4 on **Dowsing**, which involves the use of a pendulum or dowsing rod to provide feedback from the dowsers' unconscious mind on the questions they ask.

386 **Kahuna healers** are described by Max Freedom Long, reviewed in detail in Chapter I-1.

387 Kiskos, personal communications.

388 Krippner/Villoldo 1976a; 1986.

389 'Magnetic field' here refers to the bioenergy field.

390 Krippner/Villoldo, p. 132-134.

391 Villoldo/Krippner 1987, p. 41-2.

392 Hammerschlag, p. 111.

393 Of related interest and overlapping with multiple personality disorders and dissociation: 1. Eye Movement Desensitization and Reprocessing (EMDR) is pioneering treatment of dissociative disorders (Shapiro). 2. Applied Kinesiology is identify discrete traumas that produce learning disabilities and to release these (Krebs). Kinesiology appears to have a potential for identifying etiologies of problems, which might include possession. More on this, including cautions in interpreting intuitive impressions, in Chapter II-1 and II-2. 3. Transpersonal psychology has identified mental state-specific learning (Tart).

394 See Chapter II-2, Benor et al 2001 on **visualizations involving unconditional love and acceptance** for dealing with fears. These visualizations may often take the form of monsters that seem bent on possessing us.

395 Mother Meera, Attributed.

396 For further discussion on **psi** and **psychopathology**, see Chapters I-3; II-1; Mintz with Schmeidler.

397 For more on **Possession** see Allison; Balducci; W. Baldwin; Barnes; Barlow, et al.; Crabtree; W. J. Finch; Fiore 1995; Giel, et al.; Martin; Modi; J.W. Montgomery; Naegeli-Osjord; Nicola; Nevus; Oesterreich; Pattison, et al.; Peck; J. Perry; Prince 1966; Ross/Stalstrom; Ste

venson/Pasricha et al 1989;-E. Taylor 1983; Van Dusen; C. Ward; L. Watkins.. D. W. Long describes a medium who paints with the aid of alleged possession by famous artists.

Chapter 7: Psychic Surgery

398 M. Long 1976; 1978.
399 These are categories of Motoyama and of Stelter.
400 Many healers state that the bioenergy body is the template for the physical body.
401 **Spiritual healing** is reviewed in detail in Chapters I-1; I-4; I-5.
402 **Psi phenomena** are discussed in Chapter I-3.
403 The **energy body** and **biological energy fields** are discussed in Chapters II-2 to II-4.
404 L. Watson 1975.
405 L. Watson 1975, p. 227-230.
406 Naegeli, cited in L. Watson 1975, p. 231.
407 L. Watson 1975, p. 231.
408 Case report taken from T. Valentine.
409 L. Watson 1975, p. 234.
410 L. Watson 1975, p. 234-235.
411 L. Watson 1975, p. 235.
412 L. Watson 1975, p. 234.
413 L. Watson 1975, p. 233-4.
414 L. Watson 1975, p. 236, citing Meek 1973.
415 L. Watson 1975, p. 236-7.
416 Chesi 1981.
417 I (DB) have also seen videotapes of Sison's cotton wool disappearing into the body. These were taken in the Philippines by Sigfried Pracher, of London.
418 Chesi 1981, p. 65.
419 Chesi 1981, p. 205-7.
420 Fuller, 1975.
421 Fuller 1975, p. 43.
422 Fuller 1975, p. 44-5.
423 Fuller 1975, p. 51.
424 Puharich 1972.
425 Alternate spelling to Altimiro, apparently.
426 Fuller, p. 53.
427 See Chapters III-3; IV-2 on **organizing fields**.
428 Greenfield/Rauscher, 1985.
429 **Dr. Fritz** has worked through several people in Brazil. See Maki.
430 The observations in this book are as helpful today as they were when it was written, 30 years ago.
431 Meek, p. 103.
432 Meek, p. 104.
433 Meek, p. 105.
434 Meek, p. 111.
435 Meek, p. 120-121.
436 Seutemann, in Meek, p. 89.
437 Seutemann, in Meek, p. 90.
438 Seutemann, in Meek, p. 91.
439 Seutemann, in Meek, p. 92.
440 Seutemann, in Meek, p. 92-93.
441 Seutemann, in Meek, p. 93.
442 Seutemann, in Meek, p. 94.
443 Millner/Smart.

444 Throughout the psi and healing literature, it is noted that skeptics appear to inhibit the appearance of the phenomena. This was true as well for mediums and in the structured séance phenomena of Batcheldor and those who replicated his model.

445 Motoyama, 1978b.

446 Motoyama's **chakra** observations are briefly described in Chapter II-2.

447 Stelter prefers the term 'psi' healing.

448 See discussions on **bioplasma** in Chapters II-4; IV-2.

449 See descriptions of **mediumistic materializations** in Chapter 5. M. Long proposes the same theory to account for materializations in healing.

450 See also in Chapter III-5 descriptions of Crawford's experiments with clay as a marker for ectoplasm extruded from the medium's body.

451 More on **firewalking** in Chapter IV-3; Nordland; Vilenskaya 1985f; 1991.

452 Kervran, 1972. See Chapters III-3; IV-2 on **organizing fields**.

453 Stelter provides no sources for his observations attributed to Baranger and von Herzeele.

454 Uphoff/Uphoff, 1975.

455 Seutemann, in Uphoff/Uphoff, 1975, p. 108.

456 Sherman, 1967.

457 Decker, in Sherman, p. 58.

458 Decker, in Sherman, p. 59.

459 Decker, in Sherman, p. 68.

460 Decker, in Sherman, p. 68.

461 Agpaoa died in the mid 1980's, middle-aged and still a much-studied but controversial figure to Western science.

462 Licauco, p. 10.

463 Licauco, p. 9-10.

464 Licauco, p. 13.

465 Licauco, p. 15-16.

466 Licauco, p. 26.

467 Licauco, p. xix.

468 Lourival, in Anne Dooley, p. 135-7.

469 Alokazov et al.

470 For **more on PS II** see: Chesi 1981 (the best illustrated); Don/Moura; Dooley; Folz; Gray; Krippner/Villoldo 1976; 1987; Lava and Aranetta; Motoyama 1977; 1978(b); Ormond/McGill; Sladek; Stemman 1983; Tabori/Raphael; J. Thomas; Valentine. Lava/Araneta are worthy of mention but very sketchy.

471 Walter and Mary Jo Uphoff, 1975.

472 Uphoff/Uphoff, p. 106. No reference is given for van Leeuwen, presumably cited in Tenhaeff.

473 Maurice Barbanell, 1954.

474 Chapman, 1973.

475 Uphoff/Uphoff, p. 103-4. For further descriptions of Chapman's work see Chapman 1973; 1978; Harvey 1981.

476 Roy Stemman, 1983b.

477 Stemman may be quoting from an article by Thompson.

478 See similar observations in Insall, excerpted in Stemman 1982.

479 David St. Clair, 1979.

480 St. Clair, p. 98-99.

481 St. Clair, p. 111-112.

482 St. Clair, p. 113.

483 St. Clair, p. 239-40.

484 St. Clair, p. 266-7.

485 St. Clair, p. 243-255.

486 St. Clair, p. 251-252.

487 St. Clair, p. 267.

488 Bragdon; M. Thomas.

489 Hoy is quoted also in Meek. I prefer the Zetetic Scholar version for contrast with the other reports I quote because it is more trenchantly critical. The Zetetic Scholar was dedicated to questioning the validity of parapsychological phenomena. See also Nolen 1984 for descriptions of sleight of hand in psychic surgery. See Rogo for descriptions of filmed Philippine PS fakes. Lincoln/Wood present a case where PS did not help and where laboratory studies did not confirm the healer's legitimacy. On the wealth of **rigorous studies in parapsychology research** see Edge et al; Nash/Nash; Radin 1997.

490 Thoreau 1850.

491 Puharich 1983.

492 Valentine, p. 113-4.

493 Valentine, p. 119-120.

494 Referencing an article by Merker.

495 Valentine, p. 116.

496 Valentine, p. 135-6.

497 Valentine, p. 133.

498 See **deliberately caused bodily damage (DCBD)** in Benor 1993/4; Dossey 1998c; Malacz.

499 Vilenskaya 1985f; 1991.

500 Schwarz.

501 **Unusual human abilities** are discussed in Chapter II-1.

502 Brennan; Krieger; Safonov; Turner 1974; others in Chapter I-1.

503 Brennan 1989.

504 Brennan 1990.

505 St. Clair 1974.

506 See Chapter I-3 for more on **PK**.

507 Isaacs 1981.

508 **Stigmata** are wounds appearing in people's flesh in places that mimic the wounds of Christ. See: Dietz; Lifschutz; McCaffery; Starr; Stelter.

509 Motoyama 1978b.

510 On **peculiarities of alternative states of consciousness** see Tart; LeShan reviewed in Chapter IV-2; Eisenbud 1967, reviewed in Chapter I-1.

511 Licauco; Motoyama; Stelter.

512 See also discussion on **possible hallucinations under hypnosis**, Chapter II-1; **Visualization** in Chapter II-1 and II-2.

513 On **thoughtography** see Chapter IV-3; Eisenbud 1967.

514 Lincoln and Wood; Motoyama; Naegeli; Valentine; others.

515 Starr.

516 The sheep-goat effect is discussed in Chapter I-3.

517 More on **spiritual aspects of healing** in Chapters III-8, 11.

518 For a brief, tongue-in-cheek but still scientific discussion of bees' flight, see D. Watson.

Chapter 8: Religions and Healing

519 Conference on psychic surgery organized by Siegfried Pracher.

520 On **self-correcting movements of healees during healing** see Margaret; Caine; Tinworth, described in Chapter I-1; Aho.

521 See Dowling; West 1957; and discussion in Chapter I-5.

522 Goethe 1832.

523 See LeShan 1976 on **alternate realities**, Chapter IV-2.

524 Felser, p. xx.

525 Fox/Sheldrake, p. 81.

526 For references on Shamanism see endnote 333 in Chapter III-5.

527 Slomoff.

528 Siegel 1986; 1990.529 Karr 1849.

530 Einstein 1979.

531 See Volume II on **energy medicine**.

532 Kornfield 1996, p. 217.

533 L. Smith, p. 22 – 23.

534 Bazak.

535 For reports that suggest that healing may be conveyed via **amulets, saints' relics** and other 'vehicles' for healing, see Chapter I-1, Estebany; I-4, Grad 1965; Martel (in Bloomfield 1990; Graves); IV-3; Chapters I-1 and I-5 on

536 For **Biblical references to healing** see Healing Research, Volume 1, Appendix A.

537 Oxford English Dictionary.

538 Harvey 1983.

539 Stanford, p. 24-5.

540 On personal spiritual development from a Christian perspective see also Marion. On feminine perspectives on spirituality see Andreev. On Christian ethics see Penelhum.

541 MacManaway, p. 24.

542 MacManaway with Turcan is an excellent brief overview of healing and of the influences of politics on public attitudes towards, and acceptance of, healing and related phenomena. See also Bek/Pullar; D. J. West 1957 for another discussion on the history of the church and healing.

543 MacManaway, p. 24.

544 Macmanaway, p. 24.

545 See Heinemann for a psychoanalytic discussion of the killing of women as witches.

546 Valea, p. 176.

547 Montefiore p. 161. SeeValea for a different interpretation of these historical notes.

548 Deuteronomy 10:12.

549 MacNutt, p. 9.

550 MacNutt, p. 162.

551 MacNutt, p. 163.

552 Rogo 1982.

553 Rogo 1982, p. 265.

554 Rogo 1982, p. 268.

555 Rogo 1982, p. 271.

556 On non-healers demonstrating **successful healing** see especially Braud 1989; Nash 1982; 1984; Chapters I-4; I-5 on numerous other studies where healers demonstrated effects.

557 A broad sampling of healing reports is presented in Chapters I-1; I-5.

558 MacNutt 1987, p146.

559 See research on **vehicles conveying healing** in Chapters I-4; I-5; anecdotes in Chapter I-1; discussion in IV-3.

560 Sheldrake 1981.

561 Sheldrake's **morphogenetic fields** are reviewed in Chapter IV-2.

562 More on **Lourdes and other shrines** in Chapters I-1; IV-3.

563 More on **linger effects** in Chapter IV-3; Cahn/Muscle; Watkins/Watkins 1974.

564 Wells/Watkins.

565 **Pre- and retro-cognition** are discussed in Chapters I-3 and IV-3.

566 Schmidt.

567 See discussions of **apparitions** in Chapter III-4.

568 See Edwards's report (1968) of a healing that apparently occurred prior to his receiving the request, summarized in Chapter I-1.

569 Cramer; Merker; Von Urban, briefly reviewed in Chapter III-7.

570 Owen/Sparrow. The **Philip phenomena** are reviewed in Chapters III-5; I-3; **Visualization** in II-2.

571 See discussion on **angels and other apparitions** in Chapter III-4.

572 Browne 1716.

573 See G. Barna for a 'categorization of American spirituality.'

574 Bosman.

575 Markides 1991, p. 196.

576 B. Russell 1928.

577 Popper 1945.

578 More on **fundamentalism as articles of faith** in Chapter III-11.

579 Summary from discussion of H. Smith 1965.

580 In the Pali texts of Theravada Buddhism

581 More on the **cosmologies of Ken Wilber** in Chapters II-1; IV-2.

582 Literally, *atman* means *breath* and is used for the ultimate essence of beingness, in many ways equivalent to *soul*. In Hebrew, *ruach* means wind and means spirit.

583 The 'Thotrol' is the Tibetan book of living and dying; Evans-Wentz; Rinpoche.

584 Wilber 1980, p. 175.

585 Rama 1980.

586 Gardner/Gardner, p. xvi.

587 Beard 1966, p. 171.

588 Plato, in *Laws*.

589 See Chapter III-3 on **reincarnation**.

590 Markides 1991.

591 Chitrabhana, in Gardner and Gardner (See Chapter I-1); Daskalos, in Markides.

592 Bach 1977, p. 121.

593 On **Neurotheology** see discussion later in this chapter.

594 Zukav 1989.

595 Buddha, Kalama Sutra.

596 On **Buddhist spiritual paths** see discussion under meditation in Chapter II-1; H. Smith 1965; Spalding; Wilber 1980.

597 Apraia/Lobsang; Vigne are particularly clear and cogent in discussing this avenue to spiritual awareness.

598 For discussions and **research on the health benefits of meditation** see Murphy/Donovan 1995; 1997; Chapters II-1 and II-2. For early research on brain activity changes with meditation see Newburg et al.

599 For discussions on **meditation as *centering*** and on **accessing other levels of reality** see Chapters I-1; III-9; III-10; IV-2; IV-3.

600 On **bodymind awareness and cellular memories of traumas** see Chapter II-1, and on various forms of psychotherapy that can address and release these see Chapter II-1; on bodymind therapies with similar results, Chapter II-2.

601 The **frailties and fallibilities of spiritual teachers** discussed with trenchant sensitivity in Kornfield 1993.

602 On **psychotherapy and spiritual healing** see my discussion in Chapter I-1, also at www.wholistichealingresearch.com/Articles/PsychotherSH.asp and www.wholistichealingresearch.com/Articles/SpirHealPT.asp.

603 Krippner/Welch. More on shamanism in Chapters I-5; II-2; III-5; IV-3.

604 Hoffman; Horgan; Masters/Houston; Nichols; Stafford/Golightly; Stillman/Wilette; and see also articles in *Journal of Psychoactive Drugs*.

605 Matthew Smith 2004, p. 113.

606 Van Gelder is the gifted intuitive and healer who was co-founder of Therapeutic Touch. See Van Gelder 1978.

607 Others who describe awareness of **animism**: Bortoft; T. Brown 1979; 2001; Cowan; Hawken 1978; Pelikan; Pogacnik 1997; 2001; Roads; Somé 1994; Thompkins 1997; M.S. Wright; and see discussion of nature spirits in Chapter III-4.

608 This survey is conducted annually by the Graduate Center of the City University of New York.

609 Kosmin/Mayer; American Atheists.

610 D. P. Miller.

611 Szasz 1973.

612 Katz.

613 Dawkins 1996, p. 132-133. See also Dawkins 1986.

614 Many attribute this to Mary Frye.
www.businessballs.com/donotstandatmygraveandweep.htm (accessed 11/27/05)
Quoting from the following blog: www.everything2.com/index.pl?node_id=841955
"A copy of 'Do not stand at my Grave and Weep' was found in an envelope left by a young British soldier, Stephen Cummins, who was killed on active service in Northern Ireland. The envelope was to be opened by his parents in the event of his death. Along with the poem were photos and a letter. The immediate thought was that the soldier himself had penned it; this has since been proven wrong. There are many suggestions that have been floated regarding the true author, including Joyce Fossen, Albert Spengler, Gwyndion Perderwen and Mary Frye. There is also a possibility that it was written originally by Navajo Indians. It is the "the most re-quested English language poem of the past sixty years. I also believe that it is quite possibly the most beautiful."
"This song was recorded by Lizzie West as 'Prayer,' on her Holy Road: Freedom Songs album, which isn't as bad as the title sounds like it would be."

615 Bacon 1625.

616 Tennyson 1850.

617 Rilke 1934.

618 Darrow 1925.

619 See more on **reasons why healing and psi have not been accepted** in Benor 1990a; Chapter IV-3.

620 There is a form of agnosticism that comes with deep meditation, differing from the agnos-ticism described here. After prolonged practice of meditation, one may come to an awareness that there is nothing one can know other than that one is observing transient perceptions and thoughts.

621 Newberg et al, p. 7.

622 Newberg et al 2001. See also discussion of **neurohormonal and other physical and psy-chological theories to explain mystical experiences,** in Chapter III-9.

623 More on **neurotheology** at Carter/Frith; Joseph et al; McKinney; Persinger www.innerworlds.50megs.com/#articles; Winkelman 2000 (neurotheology and shamanism).

624 Tart 1995. Tart adds to this introduction: "Incidentally, I want to assure you that this is not an attack on Christianity, only an educational exercise." This Creed is quoted with the kind permission of the author. For the original Nicene creed see www.mit.edu/~tb/anglican/intro/lr-nicene-creed.html. In personal communication Tart added the clarification that this Creed is not his personal belief.

625 Einstein 1941.

626 Bockris has excellent discussions on the issues of **scientism**.

627 An example in point is the discussion on intelligent design (ID). Here is an idea seeking geneticists to study it, as discussed in Chapter III-13. The American Association for the Ad-vancement of Science (AAAS) has taken a firm stance against ID.
"AAAS Board Resolution on Intelligent Design Theory
  The contemporary theory of biological evolution is one of the most robust products of scien-tific inquiry. It is the foundation for research in many areas of biology as well as an essential element of science education. To become informed and responsible citizens in our contempo-rary technological world, students need to study the theories and empirical evidence central to current scientific understanding.
  Over the past several years proponents of so-called 'intelligent design theory,' also known as ID, have challenged the accepted scientific theory of biological evolution. As part of this effort they have sought to introduce the teaching of 'intelligent design theory' into the science curric-ula of the public schools. The movement presents 'intelligent design theory' to the public as a

theoretical innovation, supported by scientific evidence, that offers a more adequate explanation for the origin of the diversity of living organisms than the current scientifically accepted theory of evolution. In response to this effort, individual scientists and philosophers of science have provided substantive critiques of 'intelligent design,' demonstrating significant conceptual flaws in its formulation, a lack of credible scientific evidence, and misrepresentations of scientific facts.

Recognizing that the 'intelligent design theory' represents a challenge to the quality of science education, the Board of Directors of the AAAS unanimously adopts the following resolution:

Whereas, ID proponents claim that contemporary evolutionary theory is incapable of explaining the origin of the diversity of living organisms;

Whereas, to date, the ID movement has failed to offer credible scientific evidence to support their claim that ID undermines the current scientifically accepted theory of evolution;

Whereas, the ID movement has not proposed a scientific means of testing its claims;

Therefore Be It Resolved, that the lack of scientific warrant for so-called 'intelligent design theory' makes it improper to include as a part of science education;

Therefore Be Further It Resolved, that AAAS urges citizens across the nation to oppose the establishment of policies that would permit the teaching of 'intelligent design theory' as a part of the science curricula of the public schools;

Therefore Be It Further Resolved, that AAAS calls upon its members to assist those engaged in overseeing science education policy to understand the nature of science, the content of contemporary evolutionary theory and the inappropriateness of 'intelligent design theory' as subject matter for science education;

Therefore Be Further It Resolved, that AAAS encourages its affiliated societies to endorse this resolution and to communicate their support to appropriate parties at the federal, state and local levels of the government.

Approved by the AAAS Board of Directors on 10/18/02"

628 See a list of such scientist in a footnote in Chapter III-10.

629 On **spiritual awareness and healing** see Chapter III-11.

630 Grof 1998, p. 213.

631 In this chapter and the last one I deviate from the pattern of sharing my personal views at the end of the chapter because they feel more relevant within the text.

632 The three dimensions of space plus the dimension of time.

633 More on the **overlaps of quantum physics with mystical awareness** in Chapter III-10. On the problems of perceptions and conceptualizations across dimensions, see Abbot; Rucker.

634 More on **collective consciousness** and **transpersonal psychology** in Chapters III-10; II-1; IV-2; IV-3.

635 van der Post 1988, p. 85.

636 USA TODAY/Gallup.

637 McElroy 2002, p. 71.

638 Pratt, p. 8.

639 Somé 1993.

640 Cohen 2003, p. 254.

641 On **archetypes** see especially the writings of Jung. Chopra 2003 suggests ways to activate and invite positive archetypal energies into our lives.

642 Grad 1965a/1976; Saklani.

643 Grad 1965a/1967.

644 Sheldrake 1981.

645 On **mudras** see Hirschi; Mesko; Trumpa.

646 See **dynamic healing** in Chapter I-1, including Tinworth, 'Margaret' and Cain.

647 Sheldrake 1981; 1987.

648 See previous note.

649 On **rituals** see Chordas/Gross; Feinstein/Krippner; Geisler 1984; 1985a; 1985b; Hammerschlag/Silverman; Lantz (women's archetypal myths); Linn/Linn; Somé.

650 Shakespeare *Hamlet*.

651 Foster; Poloma/Gallup.

652 Dossey 1993.

653 Randall-May.

654 Ten Psalms are recommended for healing: 16, 32, 41, 42, 59, 77, 105, 137, 150 (from L. Smith).

655 Levine 1984, p. 108.

656 See research on healing, including vehicles for healing, below.

657 Proverbs 20:15.

658 Greenbaum, p. 98.

659 Greenbaum, p. 95.

660 Greenbaum, p. 167.

661 More on **Spiritual Awareness and Healing** in Chapter III-11.

662 Talmud. More on Jewish views of the afterlife in Raphael; on Jewish mysticism see D. Cooper.

663 See Snow for an outstanding example of prayer healing.

664 Randall-May.

665 Much can be said about the ethics of prayers and distant/absent healing. See website of the Council for Healing for a detailed distillation of Codes of Conduct and Standards for Practice of a spectrum of healing organizations: www.councilforhealing.org.

666 Significnce levels ranged from p < .05 to p < .002.

667 'Intercessors' were 35% non-denominational, 27% Episcopalian, and the rest Protestant or Roman Catholic. Prayers were sent on a regular basis over the 28 days after hospital admission, which covered patients' complete hospital stay in 95 percent of cases.

668 On the scale developed by Byrd, no significant differences were found between groups, although a trend was seen favoring the prayer group.

669 Because of immune system impairments, people with AIDS are subject to multiple, unusual infections, particularly in their lungs and on their skin.

670 All healers had at least five years' experience, including treatment of AIDS, and were accustomed to sending distant healing. Healers had only the first names and photographs of five of the subjects.

671 CD4 white cell counts and scores on the other psychological tests did not differ significantly between the two groups.

672 Atwater, 2001.

673 Atwater 2001, p. 41-42. For more on prayer see Bridges; Byrd; Clark 1995a; 1995b; A. Davis; T. Davis; Guiley; W. Harris et al; E. Jackson; King/Bushwick; Kleissler; Kowey et al; Levin 1996a; C. S. Lewis; Lipinski; Loehr; MacNutt 1987; Mains/Bell; G. Marwick; McGarey; Mosley/Hill; Poloma; Prell; Randall-May; J. Richardson 1995; Rogo 1986; Roth; Windget.

674 Aviles et al; Bernardi et al; Dusek et al; Ernst; Krucoff et al; Krucoff et al; Leibovici; Matthews et al; Matthews et al; Roberts et al; Saudia et al. The study by Cha et al has been seriously questioned and its validity is in doubt, per Solfvin et al.

675 Loehr.

676 *Blinds* are carefully controlled conditions under which the healers, the healees and the researchers do not know who is being sent prayers. This is the best way known to study the effects of prayers while minimizing the possibilities that the effects would be caused by suggestion. See further discussions on research designs at www.wholistichealingresearch.com/Research/RschTop.asp

677 Benor 2001a; b.

678 Spindrift, Inc. 1993.

679 Extensive research with teachers, doctors and other caregivers shows that their expectations can subtly but potently influence the outcomes of their work and studies. For instance, if a teacher is led to believe that Sally has a high IQ (when she actually has an average IQ), then Sally is likely to do better in her studies and to receive higher grades. Much more on suggestion and expectation effects in Chapter II-1.

680 A **morphogenetic field** is an energetic summation of similar experiences within a given species that appears to facilitate members of that species in being able to be successful in the same experience. Research has shown, for instance, that when the solution to a puzzle is shown on TV, it becomes easier for the next batch of people tested with that puzzle to find the solution and they do so more quickly, per Sheldrake 1981/1987. More on **theories to explain healing** in Chapter IV-2. Larry Dossey 2001, in an excellent discussion on spirituality in the medical arts, and Jeffrey Levin 1995, in a marvelous article on how prayer heals, also consider some of these possibilities.

681 See Chapter IV-2 for theories to explain healing.

682 See discussion of **meditation and its benefits** in Chapter II-1; II-2; benefits of religious affiliation and practice in Chapter III-12.

683 Tennyson 1869.

684 **Health benefits of religious affiliations and practices** are reviewed in Chapter III-12.

685 K. Cohen 2003, p. 27-28

686 Proust 1921.

687 Instructions are continued in the footnotes lest your say to yourself that you might have absorbed some of these suggestions subliminally from the page under Step 1.

Step 2. Start to picture to yourself that your feet are connecting with Mother Earth. You might feel that roots are extending from your feet, going deep into the earth. Sense the earth energies rising through your feet, into your legs, into your body. Feel how these healing energies reach every particle of your being. Feel them concentrate particularly in your heart. Now sense that you are projecting the loving, healing energies from your heart to the same person. Do not 'push the river' by picturing that these energies are changing the person to whom they are sent. (Their needs and wishes for changing or staying as they are should be respected.) Picture that you are projecting love, support, healing, unconditional acceptance, or any other qualities that might be helpful to that person, allowing that they may accept just as much of these qualities as they need at this time. Spend as long as feels intuitively right to you in feeling that you are projecting healing to that person. Do not read further until you have done Step 2.

Step 3. Now invite the Infinite Source (you might address God, Christ, Buddha, Allah, your higher self, or just a cosmic source of very strong energies) to connect with you through the top of your head. Sense the energies from the infinite source coming through your head, into your body. Feel how these healing energies reach every aspect of your being. Feel them concentrate particularly in your heart. Now sense that you are projecting the loving, healing, unconditionally accepting energies from your heart to the same person. Spend as long as feels intuitively right to you in feeling that you are projecting healing to that person.

When you have finished this exercise, take some time to reflect upon the differences you perceived between the three steps. I believe that through stepwise exercises of this sort we can begin to appreciate some of the qualities of spiritual awareness.

688 Gurdjieff refined this form of meditation, described well by Tart 1986.

689 See further discussion on **meditation** in Chapter II-2; other ways of meditating in II-5 (Popular edition); **fantasy inner journeys** in IV-2.

690 Khan 1996, p. 199.

691 Satchidananda, p. 226.

692 Course in Miracles, Manual for Teachers, p. 73.

693 Grof 1998.

694 This is my interpretation of the admonition against allowing women into the mystical garden. In the days when these admonitions were given, there was no psychological conceptualization of problems, and few ways to deal with emotional breakdowns.

695 Mentioned above under Eastern views of healing

696 Paley 1835.

697 Darwin 1859.

698 The CRSC is sponsored by the Discovery Institute, a conservative think tank based in Seattle.

699 *Healing Research,* Volume I reviews 191 controlled studies, published prior to 2001. Of these, 64 percent overall demonstrate significant results; 37 studies meet rigorous criteria for scientific studies and demonstrated significant results.

700 On paradigm shifts see T. Kuhn.

701 In 1982 it took me six months of discussion with a hospital research board to get approval for a double blind, controlled study of spiritual healing in surgical patients. At each monthly meeting they were approving other studies that included experimental drugs, surgical techniques and radiotherapy approaches – each of which carried distinct risks to health and life. Despite the fact that their remit was only to determine the safety of a research procedure, they would not approve a study of healing that carried absolutely no risks to the patients other than disappointment that they might find themselves in a control group rather than in an experimental group that would receive the treatment. (The latter is an argument actually raised by this Institutional Review Board in objecting to this study, despite the fact that this factor was present in every other controlled study – of conventional medical modalities – that they were approving.)

702 I encountered this issue when seeking assistance in studying healing effects on water. I could not find an expert in spectroscopy to measure ultraviolet changes in the spectrum of healer-treated water because these scientists feared that a publication on this subject that included their name would mean the end of their career.

703 Monroe 1994.

704 Behe 2002. See also Behe 1996; 1999.

705 Behe 1996 adds several further examples of **irreducibly complex systems**: Various organisms that shoot darts or hot water for attack and defense. Behe 2002 points to yet another, similar example: the complex series of chemical reactions that enable blood to clot.

706 Meyer's discussion is well referenced, for anyone wishing to delve into questions about Darwinian theory in greater depth.

707 Discussion in this section also following much of Meyer's analysis.

708 Axe; Eden; Denton; Perutz/Lehmann.

709 Eden; Lovtrup; Schutzenberger.

710 For more on intelligent design see J. Keen; Thaxton.

711 Moolenburgh, p. 56.

712 See discussions of self-healing in Chapters II-1; IV-3.

713 Shapira, p. *xv.*

714 Ecclesiastes 3:1-8.

715 See Chapter IV-3 for tables and discussions on physical world, psychological, bioenergetic and spiritual **factors influencing healing.**

716 *Avodah Zarah* 56a.

717 Volf.

718 Gershom 1992; 1996.

719 Gershom 1996.

720 Gershom 1996, p. 9-10.

721 **Inspirational readings**: L. Jampolsky; Personal odysseys: Baisley; J. Rogers;

722 T. Moore, p. 165.

723 Sherman. Gordon, quoted in Hawken 1993, p. 17.

724 Polkinghorne presents an excellent series of discussions on religious and scientific analyses of God's love and explanations of how God might allow evil to exist.

725 Grof 1998, p. 114.

726 Grof 1998, p. 116.

727 Wade 1996, p. 217.

728 e.g., The Gospel of Matthew 4:3, 26:11; The Gospel of Mark 14:7; The Gospel of Luke 4:3; Gospel of John 12:8.

729 Pranis et al, p. 19-20.

730 An interesting note on this issue is sounded through the recently publicized Gospel of Judas, in which it is clarified that Christ invited Judas to betray him. www.tertullian.org/rpearse/manuscripts/gospel_of_judas/#English%20Translation (Accessed 3/8/06)

731 More on shamanic teachings in Chapter I-5; II-2; III-5; IV-3.

732 Targ/Harary.

733 Kübler-Ross 1969.

734 Kübler-Ross 1981.

735 Henslee et al.

736 Maslow 1971.

737 Levine, 1984, p. 31.

738 Althouse, p. 93-5.

739 Siegel 1986, p. 77.

740 M. Bowen.

741 R. Benor.

742 R. Benor.

743 Alder 1876.

744 Levine 1984, p. 82.

745 van der Post 1963.

746 Steadman, p. 20.

747 Rinpoche; Wilber 1980.

748 On **intuitive and mediumistic perspectives on death** see for instance, Beard; Lambillion 2001; more in Chapter III-5.

749 See **Visualization** in Chapter II-2 and footnote 13 in Chapter III-3; also III-2; III-5; III-7.

750 Personal transpersonal and spiritual awareness are discussed in Chapter III-11.

751 Readings on **dealing with death** – Al-Ghazali (Islamic); Al-Haddad (Islamic); Althouse; R. Benor 2001; Boerstler; D. Callahan (research); Cosgrove; Doctor-Healer Network Newsletter; Field/Cassel; Foos-Graber (annotated bibliography); Grad 1980; Grof 1994; Grof/Halifax 1977; Hick; M.E.M. Jackson; J. James/Cherry; Kaufman (hospital caregivers and careseekers deal with death); Kirkpatrick; Krammer; Krishnamurti; Kubler-Ross 1969; 1975; 1975; Kuhl; Levine 1984; 1986; 1987; M. Murphy 1988; Nuland; Osler; Plotnikoff 2000a; Rinpoche; Rando; X. Rose; St. Aubyn; Sacred Heart Medical Center (No One Dies Alone); Sanders; Sarnoff-Schiff; Schneiderman; Seibert; K. Singh; R. Smith; Twycross (palliative care); Worden. For **bereavement** – Bowen; Cogrove; L. Greene/Landis; James/Cherry; Kubler-Ross; Murphy 1988; Rando; X. Rose; St. Aubyn; Sanders; Sarnoff Schiff; Schneidman; Seibert; R. Smith; Wilber 1991; Worden. **Advance directives** - Larson/Eaton. On **dealing with illness and tragedy** - Kushner; On **prayer** - Dossey 1993; 1996; 1998d; Jackson. On **healing and prayer** - Dossey 1993; 1996; Randall-May; E. Salmon; **Deathbed visions** – Barrett; Morse/Perry; Wills-Brandon. On **bereavement apparitions, spirit survival** – Amatuzio (A pathologist/coroner's report); Gallup 1982; Kennedy (imagined and possibly real); LeGrand; G. Mullin (on related Tibetan traditions); Rinpoche; Vargas, et al. (a psychiatric survey showing 65% of bereaved reporting a sense of survival); *The Tibetan Book of the Dead* (Evans-Wentz translation is excellent). **Euthanasia/Physician assisted suicide** - Bachman; Chin et al. On **Pentecostal Catholic beliefs and practices** - Chordas; McGuire; Gross. On **Charismatic spiritual gifts** - Sneck. On a **healing attributed to Blessed John Ogilvie** - Hickey/Smith. On **Christian theology and psi** - Heaney; Ikin. On **Christianity and science** - Blazer; Jaki. On **historical Jesus** - Lüdman; Schweitzer. On the **resurrection as a possible apparition occurrence** - Heaney; On **Judaism and psi** - Bazak. On folk medicine in **Jewish tradition** - Zimmels. On **religion and psi** - Broad 1953. On **Imagery in religion** - Capon; Dupré. **Research on clinical effects of prayer**: Byrd; Harris et al; Joyce/Welldon (p. oor); Loehr; Sicher et al; Spindrift. **Feminine spiritual awareness** S. Anderson. **Secular spirituality** Van Ness. For a **spectrum of spiritual traditions** see Foundation for Inner Peace; Hixon; A. Huxley 1944; 1954; R. Lawlor; McGaa/Man; Somé; Villoldo/Jendressen; Chasin. **General references**

on spirituality C. Beck, Morrison; Nh'at Hanh; Metzner. On **Psychotherapy and spiritual awareness** see Cortright; Dethlefsen/Dahlke; Dossey 1989; 1996; Green/Green; Grof 1975; 1985; Grof/Bennett; Grof/Grof 1995; Leskowitz; Levine 1984; 1986; 1987; 1991. R. Mann; J. Nelson; J. Perry; Steere. On **dangers in spiritual explorations** see Wolinsky.

Chapter 9: Mystical Experiences

752 Einstein 1979, p. 108.

753 Jung, Attributed.

754 In sociology, this is called an *etic* view – Explanations based on Western convictions that modern science can provide 'objective' explanations for every phenomenon - within the frameworks of Western scientific paradigms. This is contrasted with the *emic* view – Explanations that acknowledge that peoples from cultures other than our own, behaving in manners that are different from ours, usually have their own legitimate cultural explanations for their beliefs and behaviors.

755 I use the term g*nostic*, with a small 'g' as a generic term for a person who possesses inner spiritual awareness, not to be confused with Gnostic as used to identify early Christian mystics.

756 Horgan, p. 4.

757 More on Darwinian evolution and intelligent design in Chapters III-8 and III-13.

758 Horgan, p. 23.

759 See discussions of Wilber's views in Chapters II-1; with brief mentions in this volume, especially Chapters III-11; III-3; and this chapter.

760 See discussion of **Neurotheology** in chapter III-8.

761 Jensine.

762 Persinger 1987.

763 Horgan, p. 101.

764 Horgan, p. 103. I omit discussion of Horgan's interview with Susan Blackmore, a psi skeptic, for the same reason that I don't dwell on his views about psi. I am impressed that the thousands of meticulous studies of psi over the last century, validated by the American Association for the Advancement of Science, are adequate proofs for its existence. This evidence is reviewed in Chapter I-3.

765 'Explantory gap' was coined by a philosopher, Joseph Levine, in 1983 – per Horgan p. 137.

766 Horgan, p. 137.

767 Horgan, p. 128.

768 More about Zen and the brain in Austin 1998.

769 Horgan, p. 129, with quotes from Austin, p. 470-472.

770 Horgan, p. 130.

771 Caldwell; Castaneda; DeRopp; Grinspoon/Bakalar; Grof 1980 (psychotherapy); Halpern (alcoholics); Hoffmann; Masters/Houston; Nichols; Pahnke; H. Smith 2000; Strassman; Tart 1969; Vollenweider.

772 Grof 1980.

773 Holotropic breathing involves deep, rapid breathing that induces ASCs, often with recollection of birth memories.

774 2 Corinthians 12:1-4.

775 More on spiritual vs. mystical experiences in Chapter III-11.

776 Horse-drawn wagon.

777 In Hinduism, the ultimate reality that underlies the universe, from which everything originates and to which it returns.

778 Bucke, p. 9-10.

779 See discussions on the **ineffability of the mystical** experience later in this chapter.

780 Dossey 1996; Jackson

781 More on **meditation** in Chapter II-2; Kornfield; Wilber.

782 See crisis induced mystical experiences as **Near-Death Experiences** in Chapter III-2; **apparitions** in Chapter III-4.

783 On **experiential spiritual quests** see Matthiessen; Persig; Villoldo/Krippner

784 On **psychic experiences** see Chapter I-3; on **spiritual experiences** see Chapters III-1 - III-8.

785 Murphy/White.

786 On **kundalini energies** see: Galbraith 1998; 1999; 2000; Greenwell; C. Hill 1990; Jung 1932; Khalsa 1990; Mookerjie; Sanella; Selby; K. Thomas 2000; J. White 1990.

787 These are technically termed *entheogenic* plants and chemicals, suggesting in the roots of the word, 'God-containing' or 'God-enabling' (H. Smith 2000).

788 Bradley 1893.

789 Underhill, Attributed.

790 See Ferrer (masterful analysis of philosophical views of transpersonal realms); also Maslow for more on this.

791 It is obvious that diverse interpretations and usage of *mystical* and *spiritual* make it impossible to draw firm and clear lines between these terms. Spiritual experiences of religious luminaries are often labeled in ways that contradict my usage here (e.g. *Christian mystics*). I trust that my definitions and discussions will clarify my usage.

792 I am embarrassed by my scientistic colleagues who have espoused and defended many of the theories of science with all the rigidities of religious fanatics, who refuse to consider new theories and rigidly defend their own.

793 Clarke; Gersten; Lukoff et al 1992 ; 1998 (DSM IV diagnosis of 'Religious or Spiritual Problem'); J. Nelson. See also Spiritual Competency Resource Center.

794 **Psi** is discussed in Chapter III-13; I-3.

795 I am indebted to Owens; Pahnke; Prince/Savage, upon whose outlines I have expanded. W. James and Underhill are the original sources for many of these observations.

796 Owens.

797 Pahnke.

798 On **meditative techniques** see Chapters II-1; II-2; Goleman; LeShan.

799 Neihardt, p. 36.

800 Jung, attributed.

801 McFadden, p. 11.

802 Owens.

803 Pahnke.

804 Satprem 1981, p. 47-8.

805 Dethlefsen/Dahlke; Grof.

806 Schnabel 1958.

807 Satprem 1981.

808 LeShan 1974a; 1976.

809 Hirshberg/Barasch, p. 135.

810 Goleman.

811 A most exquisite paean to the treasure in a transient relationship is the vignette in the last chapter of Laurens van der Post 1963, on a personal relationship between a man and a woman following a brief encounter.

812 G. Knight, p. 156.

813 D. Knight, p. 156.

814 Some of the **dangers inherent in meditation** are explied by LeShan 1974b.

815 Dossey 2001.

816 *Spontaneous remission* is another such convenient label, which in its vagueness allows doctors to feel they have identified a cause for unusual recuperations from illness – without having to study them further to identify other possible causes for such remissions that might challenge conventional understanding of health and illness. Much more on spontaneous remissions and self-healing in Chapter II-1.

817 See discussions in Chapter IV-3, under **reasons healing has not been accepted**; Benor 1990a; Tart 1986b.

818 The obvious parallel is of Newtonian physics with quantum physics, discussed next and in Chapter IV-2.

819 Course in Miracles; Kornfield.

820 A *sweetening spiral* is where a positive action draws a positive response, which encourages further positive actions, etc. (Isn't it a sad commentary on our society that we haven't developed a commonly accepted term for the opposite of a vicious circle?) More on this in Chapter II-1; II-5 (popular edition).

821 In California the Spiritual Emergence Network; in England, Second Aid. See Appendix, Resources.

822 Roberts 1972, p. vii.

823 On **reincarnation** see Chapter III-3.

824 The reports of reincarnation memories that arise spontaneously in young children, as well as those arising in NDEs, hypnosis, and other forms of psychotherapy (see, e.g. Botkin) deserve to be addressed as any other phenomenon of nature that can be observed and studied.

825 Beard; J. Roberts.

826 Greaves.

827 **Apparitions, angels and nature spirits** are reviewed in Chapter III-4.

828 Ferrer 2002.

829 e.g. Aurobindo; Blavatsky; Campbell 1978; 1989; Greaves 1977; Roberts 1974; Satprem; H Smith.

830 Quoted by Ring 1984, p. 57-8.

831 Attributed.

832 Quoted by Ring 1984, p. 151.

833 Lehmann.

834 Lukoff.

835 Szasz 1984. Here is yet another example of society's rejection of that which deviates from the conventional norm.

836 Allison labels this the 'inner self helper.'

837 Wilber 1980.

838 See **Wilber's meditation cosmologies** in Chapter II-1. Jack Kornfield presents an excellent discussion on the benefits of psychotherapy and meditation, separately and combined. He has excellent discussions, with a wealth of experience as a meditator and teacher of meditation on the clear distinctions between psychopathology and enlightenment.

839 Wade 2004.

840 Oddly, and without adequate explanation, numerous people also report synesthesias without any drug ingestion. It is simply the way their nervous system works. See www.mixsig.net (Accessed 4/6/06).

841 Newberg et al. More on Neurotheology in Chapter III-8.

842 Blundell; J. Brown; Cade/Coxhead; Hutchison 1986; Kasamatsu/Hirai; M. Winkelman; Murphy/Donovan; Smith 1984. Lipton 2005 reports that during peak experiences, gamma waves (>35Hz) have been recorded.

843 Greaves.

844 See Chapter III-2.

845 Mookerjee.

846 Kellogg et al.

847 Knoll/Kugler; Oster.

848 Hedges.

849 More on the relationship of mystical awareness to quantum physics in the following chapter.

850 LeShan; Goodrich.

851 See reviews of research on intuitive perceptions in Benor 2001a; b.

852 Schwartz et al.

853 More on **mystical experiences** in Anonymous 1960; Anonymous 1973; Bohm 1957; 1980; Bolen; Briggs and Peat; Burr; Carey; Church/ Sher; Coxhead; Dossey 1993; Ferguson; Green 1972; 1986; Heron; James; LeShan 1974; 1976; Morse/ Perry 1994; Needleman; Peat; Tart 1975a; b; 1981; Underhill; F. Vaughan; Von Franz 1980; 1987; Weber 78; Zukav 1979; 1990. Tweedie gives a picture of the process of learning to be a Sufi Master. On Gaia, the geobiological ecosystem as an entity for contemplation see Lovelock; P. Russell.

854 For more on this issue see discussion on spirituality in chapter III-11, and on personal spiritual awareness in Chapter III-13.

855 There may also be surprises in studying transcendent aspects of water crystals. Emoto has shown that mental intent, prayers, positive thoughts and feelings, music and other factors may influence the formation of the shapes of snowflakes.

856 Matthew 18:2-3.

857 Luke 17:21.

858 William Blake.

859 Quoted in Matthiessen.

860 Heisenberg 1958.

861 Schrödinger, p. 176.

862 Eddington, p. 150.

863 Einstein 1949, p. 12-13.

864 Wheeler/ Zurek 1983, p. 194.

865 Capra; Zukav 1979. See also: F. Wolf; Jahn/ Dunne 1988, for research on **mind-matter interactions** and theories to begin to explain these. Jahn/ Dunne have gathered a marvelous collection of mystical quotes of physicists 1983; 1988. Interesting references on **quantum physics and mystical awareness**: Bohm 1957; 1980; Bockris; Cole; Dossey 1982; Goswami 1979; 1995; B. Greene; N. Herbert 1985; 1993; Kaku; Laszlo; V. Mansfield; Nadeau/ Kafatos; Schrödinger 1992; Walker; Wheeler; Wheeler/ Zurek; Wilber 1984. On the reductionist view that the brain is the product of chance evolutionary events, with theories supported by quantum physics see Satinover.

866 Chew 1968, p. 765.

867 Zukav 1979, p. 331.

868 In addition to classical, Euclidian geometry, there are **non-Euclidian geometries**. These include several distinct systems for calculating spatial relationships, each differing from (and contradicting) the others. For instance, in Reimannian geometry, lines extended to infinity form circles, because space is curved.

869 Capra, citing a quotation of Margenau from Schilpp, p. 250.

870 Capra, p. 163.

871 Capra, quoting Needham, p. 458.

872 Quotes above from Capra, p. 68-69.

873 Capra, quoting Chuang Tsu, ch. 22.

874 Capra, p. 137-138.

875 Bohm/Hiley, pp. 96, 102, quoted in Capra.

876 Aurobindo 1957, p. 993, quoted in Capra.

877 Nagarjuna, p. 138, quoted in Capra.

878 Capra, p. 138-9.

879 Stapp, p. 1310, quoted in Capra.

880 Heisenberg 1958, p. 107.

881 Jeans 1943.

882 Jahn/ Dunne 1988, p. 316.

883 Another physicist, Elizabeth Rauscher 1983, presents a technical discussion on how laws of physics might be compatible with psi.

884 More on **holographic reality** in Chapter IV-2; Benor 1983; Bohm 1980; Dossey 1982; 1984; Talbot.

885 See discussion in Chapter III-8 on mystical experiences in the light of psi phenomena.

886 Cited in Jahn/ Dunne 1984; Laszlo; 1987; Wilber 1984, 1985.

887 Tiller 1997; Tiller et al 2001a; b; c.
888 Tiller 2003a; b.
889 Tiller 2003a.
890 Tiller, 2003a.
891 On the unlimited 'zero point' energies that are postulated to exist in the 'emptiness' of space see Cole; M. King.
892 Laszlo, p. 83-84.

Chapter 10: Quantum Physics Converges with the Mystical

893 See more on the physical aspects of these theories in Chapter IV-2.
894 Dossey 1996, p. 80.
895 Russell 2000.
896 Wilber 1985.
897 H. Smith 1958.
898 Markides 1987, p. 6.
899 My personal struggles with reaching into the mystical realms through outer and inner questing may well reflect my Jungian polarities (iNFj). My sharing these explorations here is in no way intended to indicate that these are the preferred or better paths. See discussions on Jungian polarities and life-path preferences in Chapter II-1; Buddhist views of different paths to enlightenment in Chapter II-8.
900 de Broglie, p. 280.
901 Rudolf Rucker explains how intrusions from dimensions beyond the three we are used to may appear just as strange to those of us not educated to conceptualizing four and more dimensions.
902 Various writers have started to help us move us in this direction: Capra; Dossey 1982; LeShan 1974a; Laszlo; Zukav 1979.
903 Dossey 1982 explains the mathematical proofs of Kurt Gödel that indicate the limitations of such an approach. Hofstadter's summary is more complete, but also more difficult to follow.
904 Tart 1975a; b.
905 More on personal spirituality in Chapter III-13.
906 Rumi, Attributed.
907 The similar example of **Chaos theory** is presented by Gleick. For other discussions of integration of the mystical in the modern world see Berman; LeShan 1974a; Taub-Bynum; von Franz.
908 See C. J. Moore for a delicious **collection of terms from a spectrum of languages**, where no equivalent term exists in other languages. Hampden-Turner for a kaleidoscopic review of **ways of perceiving the world**.
909 Grof/ Halifax, p. 72-73.
910 **Morphogenetic fields** are discussed in Chapter II-3 and IV-2.
911 **Theories** dealing directly **with healing** are considered in Chapter IV-2.
912 This form of healer resonance with healee symptoms has been termed a *telesomatic reaction* by Berthold Schwarz 1967.
913 **Healers whose clairsentience extends to the physical surroundings of healees** during absent healing include Safonov; Ivanova; others described in Chapter I-1.

Chapter 11: Spiritual healing and spirituality

914 Goodrich.
915 MacManaway.

916 van der Post 1976, p. 61-62.
917 Leibniz 1687.
918 Grof 1998, p. 254.
919 Siegel/ Siegel, p. 210.
920 See **research on healing** in Chapters I-4; I-5.
921 Randi 1986; 1987.
922 e.g., Joan Grant (Kelsey/ Grant); Olga Worrall (Worrall/ Worrall); Turner 1970.
923 These usually call themselves *spiritual* healers, though Thouless' term, *spirit* healers is more appropriate.
924 Greaves 1977.
925 See review of **Apparitions** in Chapter III-4; **Mediumistic phenomena** in III-5.
926 See also discussions on the ineffability of the mystical experience in Chapter III-9.
927 Turner, 1974.
928 For descriptions of such **psychic surgery** see Chapter III-7.
929 See further descriptions of Turner's healing work in Chapters I-1 and I-5; his reports of aura changes during healing in Chapter II-3. See also discussions below on the broad spectrum of religious beliefs associated with healings. While Turner focuses on healings through Christ, others have experienced healings through God, Mary, saints, angels and other transcendent agents for healing.
930 Edwards, 1945.
931 See Denham for further descriptions of Edward's work; P. Miller; Barbanell for biographies of Edwards; and further brief excerpts from Edwards in Chapter I-1.
932 Hutton, p. 46-7.
933 **Cosmic healing rays** are mentioned by A. Bailey; Tansley; others. These are said to relate not only to individual healings but also to evolution and healing of society and the cosmos.
934 Hutton, p. 52.
935 See Bishop for a skeptic's view of the Doctors/Chang healing team.
936 Krippner/ Villoldo 1976/1986.
937 Quotes from the 1976 edition.
938 Krippner/ Villoldo 1976/1986, p. 119.
939 Krippner/ Villoldo 1976/1986, p. 122.
940 Krippner/ Villoldo 1976/1986, p. 124. Krippner/ Villoldo 1983 add some embellishments to their reports in their book. See other good descriptions of **Brazilian spiritists** in Bramly 1977; Bronson 1985a; 1985b; St. Clair 1970.
941 On the **cosmologies of spirit worlds** see A. Bailey; Cerutti; Greaves 1977; Karagulla; Kelsey and Grant; Pettit Neal and Karagulla; Roberts 1972; 1973; 1974; Sarayadrian.
942 Inayat Khan, p7.
943 There is a seemingly endless collection of books on **spirit healing**. I mention here a smattering of references that I came across without systematic efforts to seek and sift out all the available sources. General: Angelo; Barbanell 1954; 1969; Beard; Crookshank; Desmond; DiOrio; Doniger; Hood; Hortsmann; Ikin 1937; Lester; Montague; Oursler; Richmond 1890; Slomoff; Storm; Warner; Wolfe 1959; Wolff 1969; and Young 1960; 1981. On **children's spirituality** see Coles. See Favazza on **psychotherapy in religious terms** and metaphors; on spirituality in psychotherapy see Fleischman; Grof/ Grof; Myss 1996; Parnell 1996; 1997. Bender discusses **dangers of spiritualism**. Hickey and Smith describe Blessed John Ogilvie, who is credited with healings when his name is invoked in prayer. Melton has a 75-page list of **references on spirit and spiritual healing**. On **transpersonal psychology** see Boorstein; Cortright; Ferrer (personal spirituality); Firman/ Gila; Grof/ Grof; R. Mann; J. Nelson; J. Perry; Steere; Wullimier; and Chapter II-1. On **spirituality as in healing into wholeness** see Faivre/ Needleman; Feldman/ Kornfield; Sol. Gordon; S. Harrison; Myss 1996; Pachalski; S. Roman; Ruiz; Siblerud; E. Taylor 1997; Underhill 1993; Walsch/ Riccio 1997. For **spiritual IQ** see Zohar.

944 On **extrinsic and intrinsic spirituality** see McBride. Allport makes similar distinctions, using the terms *institutionalized* and *internalized religion.*

945 De partib, cited in Wikipedia.

946 De nat. rerum, cited in Wikipedia.

947 Elkins, et al.

948 Tables from Aldridge 2000, with the kind permission of the author and publisher, Jessica Kingsley.

949 Walsch, p. 80.

950 Burkhardt 1989.

951 Burkhardt 1989; Hungelmann et al; Reed.

952 Grounded theory and phenomenological studies.

953 The following summaries are abstracted from Walton.

954 Camp; Schubert/ Lionberger.

955 Camp.

956 Conco.

957 Barker.

958 Burns.

959 Stiles.

960 Wilber suggests in this category the works of Alexander; Cook-Greutner; Wade. I agree with Moorfield that Maslow appears to be in this category as well. "Maslow and those who advance his thinking believe that every healthy person has an inherent capacity to value, cultivate and integrate all aspects of the self, to fully self-actualize, and to transcend the needs of the self. On this path, people may or may not have peak experiences (a phenomena discussed later in this chapter), although peak experiences are thought to expose other layers of reality that once seemed unknown, impossible or unavailable. Yet self-actualization and self-transcendence are not the only fruits; the process of striving alone is thought to cultivate the person's spiritual muscle." Moorefield, p. 77.

961 Brown 1977; 1981; Brown/ Engler; Wilber/ Engler/ Brown.

962 Wilber 2000, p. 133-134.

963 Moorfield, p. 87-89.

964 On **peak experiences** see Maslow 1964; Murphy/ White; Wade 2004.

965 www.mellen-thomas.com

966 www.nderf.org/mellen_thomas_nde.htm

967 Steadman, p. 4.

968 For many, *spirituality* is an 'S-word' that is not spoken because it raises negative associations. It is often the same with *God.* It used to be the case with *love* but this has shifted in the past two decades to be more acceptable.

969 **Tests that are free of religious assumptions** include: Spirituality Index of Well-Being (Daaleman et al); The Spirituality Scale (Delaney); Self-Expansiveness Level Form (Friedman); Spirituality Assessment Scale (Howden); Spiritual Orientation Inventory (Elkins et al); Mystical Experiences Scale (Hood); Index of Core Spiritual Experience (Kass et al); Peak Experiences Scale (Mathes et al); Underwood/ Teresi; Index of Core Spiritual Experiences/ INSPIRIT (VandeCreek et al.). On **spirituality within religious frameworks**:. The Spiritual Involvement and Beliefs Scale (Hatch RL, et al); Intrinsic Religious Motivation Scalee (Hoge). For excellent reviews and discussions of assessments instruments for spirituality see Braud 1995; Kass; D. Macdonald et al. 1995; 1999a; b. On taking a spiritual history see Maugans.

970 More on **personal spiritual awareness** in Chapters III-8; III-12.

971 Jung 1965, p. 196-197.

972 Gibran 1923.

973 See OBE in Chapter III-1.

974 See NDE in Chapter III-2.

975 See apparitions in Chapter III-4.

976 Walsch 1997, p. 41.

977 See notes on Bucke in Chapter III-9, under mystical experiences.

978 Campbell, p. 27-8.

979 Campbell, p. 28.

980 Campbell, p. 29. See more on **Campbell's views of Western distancing from the mystical** in Chapter III-12.

981 On **children's spirituality** see Coles; Harroll; Pearce 2002; Trent, Walsch/ Riccio 1998.

982 Piaget.

983 E. Erikson.

984 Kohlberg.

985 Hebrews 11:1.

986 Hillman; Spangler 1996.

987 See discussion of **auras** and **biological energy fields** in Chapters II-2 and II-3.

988 See **research on reincarnation** in Chapter III-3; recall of past life languages in Stevenson 1987.

989 Kelsey/ Grant; Worrall/ Worrall.

990 Morse/ Perry 1990.

991 On the **waning of children's intuitive capacities as they grow older** see Hahn; Peterson 1975; 1987; Williams 1983; Witkin/ Goodenough. On social discouragements that inhibit psi see Broughton; Kurtz. [Needs smaller font-don't seem to be able to do 10.5 on my computer].

992 Wilber 1980.

993 See discussion of reincarnation memories in Chapter III-3.

994 H. Smith 1965 presents the best cross-cultural summary I've found.

995 Peterson 1975; 1987.

996 Morse/ Perry 1990.

997 Epictetus (55-135) Quoted in DiCarlo, p 1.

998 Fowler, p. 182.

999 Emerson 1841a.

1000 Fowler, p. 182.

1001 The **distinction between true transcendent awarenesses and psychotic decompensations** may be difficult to determine in some cases. See Clarke; Gersten; Lukoff et al 1992 ; 1998 (DSM IV diagnosis of 'Religious or Spiritual Problem'); J. Nelson.

1002 In California the Spiritual Emergence Network; in England, Second Aid. See Appendix, Resources.

1003 e.g. Lukoff, et al.

1004 Torpey.

1005 For examples of **psychic and spiritual awakenings** see: Angelo; M. Bach; Bucke; Carey 1982; 1988; 1991; Foundation for Inner Peace; Heron; Karagulla; Moody 1975; 1988; 1993; Morse/ Perry 1990; 1994; Norwood; Roud; Weiss; Chapter III-2 on the NDE.

1006 Ricoeur.

1007 Fowler, p. 198.

1008 Buddha, in the Kalama Sutra.

1009 On **Kundalini** experiences see: Galbraith 1998; 1999; 2000; Greenwell (best overall ref); C. Hill 1990; Jung 1932; Khalsa 1990; Mookerjie; Sannella; Selby; K. Thomas 2000; J. White 1990.

1010 Joy 1990.

1011 Fowler, p. 200.

1012 Coles.

1013 More on **mystical experiences and views of wholeness** in Chapter III-9 and III-10.

1014 Chief Seattle 1854.

1015 M. Smith, p. 45.

1016 In a much simpler analysis of faith, Matthew Smith suggests, "...*The Urantia Book* describes two kinds of faith: that of the child, pure and simple, the kind that heavens open for; and that of the full-grown man, robust and confident, the kind that takes leaps into the unknown."

1017 Wilber's stages of meditative awareness are detailed in Chapter II-1.

1018 Wade 1996.

1019 See chapter III-10 for discussion on Newtonian and Quantum physics and how these help us appreciate the explicate and implicate orders of reality.

1020 On pre-birth and perinatal memories see Bache; Chamberlain 1981; 1987; 1988a; b; Cheek 1986; 1992; Grof 1985; Grof/ Bennett; Grof/ Halifax 1985; Restak; Schindler; Van Husen; Verny/ Kelly.

1021 Example of Cathy from Chamberlain 1988a.

1022 Stevenson 1987; Stevenson/ Pasricha.

1023 See discussion on **right and left brain function** in Chapter II-1.

1024 NDEs are discussed in Chapter II-2.

1025 Reviewed in Chapters III-4, 5 and 6.

1026 Newberg 2005.

1027 Particularly in the sensorimotor cortex, thalamus, cerebellum and brain stem.

1028 Briggs-Myers/ Myers; Keirsey/ Bates; Quenk. On the Meyers-Briggs test and spirituality see Goldsmith.

1029 Michael/ Norrisey discuss Jungian personality types and prayer preferences.

1030 Holland 1958.

1031 H. Smith 2001, p. 234.

1032 H. Smith 2001.

1033 On psychological analyses of spiritual awarenesses see also Boyer.

1034 A version of this discussion was published in Benor (2003a).

1035 Sheldrake 1981/1987.

1036 See discusssion of **right and left brain hemispheric functions** in Chapter II-1.

1037 It would be fascinating to consider the stages of faith from Hindu and Buddhist perspectives, but this is beyond the scope of the present discussion.

1038 Berry; Carson; Hawken.

1039 For discussions of **intuition** see Chapters II-1; II-2; II-5 (Popular edition).

1040 Steadman, p. 15.

1041 Campbell/ McMahon, p. 189.

1042 King, Jr. 1963.

1043 Bunyard; Hawken 1993; Lovelock 1991; Margulis/ Sagan; Watson/ Lovelock.

1044 Chalmers discusses the views of the property dualists.

1045 B. Russell 1927.

1046 Newberg; Persinger 1987; Ramachandran/ Blakeslee.

1047 Wulff, in Begley/ Reagan 2002, p. 62.

1048 These are not new or original observations. W. James and Tiller, among others, have used this radio/ TV analogy.

1049 Remen, p. 63.

1050 Remen, p. 63.

1051 Remen, p. 63.

1052 On kundalini see endnote 995. Kripinanda tells us that Masons speak of the energy, or Spirit, that rises through the spinal column..The Hopi Indians, of North America, have always known about kundalini.

1053 R. Moss.

1054 E. Green/ A. Green 1984.

1055 Taimni.

1056 Bailey, p. 80.

1057 Eliot 1927.

1058 Cooper, p. 17.

1059 WHEE is the Wholistic Hybrid derived from Eye Movement Desensitization and Reprocessing (EMDR) and Emotional Freedom Techniques (EFT). It is a method I put together that is incredibly potent and rapidly effective for self-healing. WHEE releases old hurts, facilitates inner child work, and enables transformations of negative feelings and beliefs into positive ones. http://www.wholistichealingresearch.com/selfhealingwheeandother.html

1060 Hammerschlag, p. 59.

1061 Pope 1733.
1062 Kornfield 1993, p. 249.
1063 Dethlefsen/ Dahlke, p. 42-3.
1064 On **spirituality, especially arising with illness** see also Bakken; Barasch; Dethlefsen/ Dahlke; Dossey 1991; 1993; 1996; D. Evans; Greenwood/ Nunn; Hirshberg/ Barasch; B. Joy 1990; S. Levine 1984; 1986; 1987; Martsolf/ Mickley; Siegel. On nursing and spirituality: Burkhardt. On **transpersonal psychology** see Chapter II-1.
1065 Image borrowed from Steadman.
1066 van der Post 1976, p. 216.
1067 Beard, p. 172.
1068 Pranis et al, p. 42.
1069 Green, et al; Mason.
1070 Kübler-Ross, in Jovanovic, p. 151.
1071 Kushner, p. 134.
1072 Longfellow 1838.
1073 Dethlefsen/ Dahlke; Levine 1984; 1986; 1987; Siegel 1986, 1990; Wilber.
1074 Lucan, in Bolander, p. 74.
1075 Tennyson 1868.
1076 Chapters III-2, III-3, III-5, III-6.
1077 Jean Shinoda 1979, p. 97.
1078 More on **synchronicity** in Chapter IV-2.
1079 More on **entelechy**, an inherent, goal-directedness in the universe, in Whitmont.
1080 The second law of thermodynamics states that 'everything runs down,' i.e. entropy increases with time.
1081 Katya Walter, p. 135.
1082 Katya Walter, p. 135.
1083 Katya Walter, p. 136. See more about **Gaia and a guiding intelligence in nature** in Barrow/ Tipler; Lovelock; Sahtouris/ Lovelock; and discussion in Chapter III-13.
1084 Rilke p. 67.
1085 Pearce 2002.
1086 B. Brennan 1993, p. 93.
1087 F. Vaughan 1995, p. 49.

Chapter 12: Research on physical and emotional correlates of religion and spirituality

1088 Levin 1993a.
1089 Princeton Religion Research Center.
1090 Curlin et al.
1091 For **reviews of studies of religion and health**: Jarvis/ Northcutt; Koenig 1997; Koenig et al 2001 (the most comprehensive review); Levin 1988; 1993a; 1994 (extensive refs); 1999 (extensive refs); Levin/ Schiller; Levin/ Vanderpool 1987 (extensive refs); 1989; 1992; Mueller et al (discussion of a series of reviews); Schiller/ Levin; Witter, et al.
1092 Taken primarily from Kaplan et al.
1093 Levin 1993.
1094 Weber 1979.
1095 More on the **Jungian polarities** in Chapters II-1 under *personality development*; IV-3, under *reasons healing has not been accpeted*. See especially Von Franz 1971; Figure II-1.
1096 See Sachs; Prologue/ Epilogue of this volume.
1097 Kaplan et al: 1989.
1098 More on **Campbell's views of the demystification of religion** in Chapter III-11.
1099 McFadden; Somé.

1100 Diamond/ Ornstein; Merchant 1980; 1992; Reuther; Seager; Schaef; Swimme/ Swimme.

1101 On **transpersonal psychology** see Assagioli; Berman, Bolen 1979; Boorstein; Carey; Dass 1985; 1996; Dass/ Gorman; Dethlefsen/ Dahlke; Dossey 1989; 1991; Firman; Fromm; Goleman, et al.; Green/ Green 1984; 1986; Grof/ Halifax; Jung 1967a; b; S. Levine 1984; 1986; 1987; 1991; R. Maslow; R. Moss 1981; 1986; 1987; Needleman; Pearce; Satprem 1968; Tart 1975b; Taub-Bynum; Underhill; Von Franz 1980; 1987; Watts; Wilber 1979; Wilber, et al. 1986; Wolman/ Ullman.

1102 Lovelock; Schumacher.

1103 On **intuition** see: Benor 2002 (extensive references); Carey; Inglis; McFadden.

1104 Church/ Sherr p. 21.

1105 Gallup 1990; King/ Bushwick; Maughans/ Wadland.

1106 Daaleman/ Nease; Ehman, et al; King/ Bushwick.

1107 M. Ellis et al.

1108 Yankelovich.

1109 Cassileth et al.

1110 Johnson et al.

1111 Saudia et al.

1112 In 1996 a national survey, 64% of Americans stated they felt doctors should pray with their patients if they request this (Wallis). A study of hospital patients (King/Bushwick) found that 70% believed their physicians ought to consider patients' spiritual needs; 48% would have liked their physicians to pray with them, and 37% would have liked their doctors to discuss their religious beliefs with them. A CBS survey in 1998 found that 80% would welcome their doctors praying with them (Hyde). Despite the importance attributed to religion and spirituality, patients report that their needs in these areas are often ignored (King/ Bushwick; Maugans/ Wadland; Fitchett, et al.). This is clearly an area of patient care that deserves more attention, both in clinical practice and research. On **blending of medical, psychological and religious approaches in clinical settings** see also: Baider, et al (melanoma); Bergin (psychotherapy); S. Carroll (alcoholism); Daaleman/ Nease; Dossey 1996; Ehman et al; Fitchett et al; Fulton; Gallup 1990; Gorsuch 1995 (substance abuse); Holland, et al (melanoma); J. King/ Bushwick; Koenig et al 1989 (elderly patients); Larimore ; Larson/ Milano; Lefavi; P. Levin et al 1997; Lewis; Marwick; Maugans (taking a spiritual history); Maugans/ Wadland; McKee/ Chappel; Mueller et al; Neeleman (psychiatry); Olive; Plotnikoff 2000b; Osler; Post, et al; Prioreschi (the supernatural in Hippocratic medicine); Qureshi (transcultural); Schlitz et al; Schreiber; Sloan (opposing spiritual questioning in medical practice); Swinton; Sulmasy; Tart 1997; Thoresen/ Harris; Trout; Yawar. On **spirituality in nursing practice** Dyson, et al; Golberg; MacRae.

1113 L. Barnes, et al.

1114 For reviews and references on **specific illness and religion** see Koenig et al 2001; Levin 1994; Levin/ Schiller 1987.

1115 **On religion and cardiovascular disease/ hypertension**: Armstrong et al (vegetarian Seventh-Day Adventists); Comstock 1971 (attendance); Comstock/ Tonascia; Friedlander/ Kark; Kaplan 1976, Levin et al 1988 (social/ psychological explanations); Levin/ Schiller (higher cardiovascular problems in Jews); Levin/ Vanderpool 1989 (review - hypertension); Marmot/ Syme (belief in importance of religion); Scotch 1960; 1963; (Zulu hypertension); Scotch/ Geiger (psychological/ sociocultural factors).

Included in these studies are assessments of overall mortality; arteriosclerotic heart disease; degenerative heart disease; infarction, prevalence, atherosclerosis, rheumatic/ non rheumatic; hypertension; angina; aortic calcification; endocarditis; and cholesterol levels (Levin/ Schiller 1987).

1116 On **religion and gastrointestinal disease**: Birnbaum ea al (Ashkenazi Jews); Monk et al 1969a; b (colitis/ enteritis in Jews).

1117 On **religion and respiratory diseases** see Dysinger et al; Kahn, et al; Lemon/ Walden.

1118 Zborowski.

1119 O'Brien.

1120 On **religion and uterine cancer**: (Kennaway; Levin/ Schiller 1987). **Other cancers**: Gardner/ Lyon 1982a; b; Enstrom et al (gradient per involvement); Troyer (loWest rates among behaviorally strict).1118 On **religion and geriatrics**: Idler; Koenig et al; Levin 1989; 1994;Moberg 1953a; b.

1121 On **religion and geriatrics**: Idler; Koenig et al; Levin 1989; 1994;Moberg 1953a; b.

1122 On **religion and genetic abnormalities**: Krupp et al (Tay-Sachs disease).

1123 On **religion and social/psychological health**: Griffith et al 1980; 1984; Kiev 1964 (folk psychiatry); Krause/ Tran (self esteem/ mastery); La Barre (confession/ catharsis in American Indians); Levin 1993b (age and mystical/psi experiences); Levin et al 1988 (type A behavior); Levin/ Schiller 1987; Jenkins/ Pargament; Kaplan/ Johnson (Navaho psychotherapy); McIntosh/ Spilka (control); Pargament et al (locus of control); Jenkins (life change/ stress).

1124 On **health/ mortality of clergy**: Fecher; King/ Bailar; King/ Locke; Levin/ Schiller 1987; Locke/ King.

1125 On **religion and illness behaviors**: Mechanic; O'Brien; Zborowski.

1126 On **religion and preventive behaviors**: Studer/ Thornton (contraception); Suchman' (illness).

1127 Levin/ Schiller 1987.

1128 Levin/ Schiller 1987.

1129 On **deleterious effects of exaggerated religious involvement** see Asser/ Swan (child deaths from medical neglect); MacDonald/ Luckett; Cavenar, et al; on **religion as a stressor** through guilt/anxiety see B. Kaplan.

1130 Stanton.

1131 West et al.

1132 Hamman/ Barancik/ Lilienfeld.

1133 Scotch 1963.

1134 Levin/ Vanderpool 1992.

1135 Levin ; Levin ; Levin ; Levin ; Levin ; Levin 1994; Levin and Schiller 1987; Levin/ Vanderpool 1987; Levin/ Vanderpool 1989; Levin/ Vanderpool 1992; Martin/ Carlson.

1136 Friedlander/ Kark.

1137 Gardner/ Lyon 1982a; 1982b.

1138 Armstrong/ Van Merwyk/ Coates.

1139 King/ Locke.

1140 **Western traditions** - Clements; Koenig/ Smiley/ Gonzales; **Eastern** - Rama; **Folk** - Krippner/ Welch; Sempebwa.

1141 For discussions on **religious attendance** see Larson et al 1986; Levin/ Schiller; Levin/ Vanderpool 1987 (review 27 studies); Koenig 1997; Williams et al.

1142 D. Williams.

1143 Levin/ Vanderpool 1989.

1144 Maton.

1145 McIntosh/ Spilka.

1146 Levin/ Vanderpool 1992.

1147 Weber 1979.

1148 D. Williams. See also: On **subjective assessments of religion** see Levin/ Markides; Williams. On the Religious Orientation Scale (ROS) see Allport; Allport/ Ross; Kirkpatrick; Kirkpatrick/ Hood (criticisms) Stark/ Glock (criticisms). On religion and the Multidimensional Health Locus of Control scales: Levin/ Schiller; Sloan; sloan et al 1999; Wallston/ Wallston. Gorsuch 1984 cautions about measuring religious variables.

1149 Ellison/ Gay; Gartner et al.

1150 Levin 1994b.

1151 Levin 1994a.

1152 Levin 1994a.

1153 Rothman.

1154 Susser.

1155 A. Hill; Labarthe/ Stallones.

1156 Levin/ Vanderpool 1992.

1157 Gallup/ Proctor.

1158 Gallup/ Gallup.

1159 Glock developed **five distinct religious dimensions**: ideological (religious beliefs); ritualistic (religious practice); experiential (religious feelings); consequential (generalized effects of religion in a person's life); and intellectual (religious knowledge). Hilty/ Morgan/ Burns found Glock's typology to be the most frequently used by sociologists. Silverman surveys 462 references on questionnaires and other measures applied in social studies of religion. An 11-dimensional construct is proposed by King/ Hunt 1972; 1975. For more on **measuring religious involvement** see Chatters et al; Fukuyama; Glock/ Stark; Silverman; Williams.

1160 Levin 1994a.

1161 Levin and Schiller 1987.

1162 Levin 1994a.

1163 Levin/ Vanderpool 1989.

1164 Gardner/ Lyon 1982a; b.

1165 On **behavioral medicine** and **psychoneuroimmunology** see Chapters II-1 and II-2.

1166 Labarthe/ Stallones.

1167 Differences between a possible salutary factor and a disease.

1168 Levin 1994a.

1169 See review of 191 **controlled studies of healing** in Chapter I-4.

1170 On **experimenter effects** see discussions of suggestion and placebo in Chapter II-1.

1171 On super-ESP see Chapter I-3. Briefly, this is ESP which is directed by the unconscious mind of a person, but may still produce potent effects without the person's awareness.

1172 Byrd.

1173 On **sociologists' views of spiritual healing** see Finkler; Krippner/ Welch; on New Age approaches see English-Lueck; McGuire; on the supernatural see Merrill.

1174 Dossey 1993, p. xviii.

1175 Levin/ Vanderpool 1989.

1176 Levin 1994b.

1177 **Other theoretical papers on religion and health**: Idler; Levin / Vanderpool 1989; 1992; Vaux.

1178 Travers.

1179 Rigoni-Stern.

1180 On **religion and social support** see Broadhead, et al; Kaplan, et al; Koenig et al 1988; Martin; Maton. Williams 1994 points out that most of the focus is on *primary* prevention in the supportive influences of religion, i.e. how religion may enhance environmental conditions. There is room to consider *secondary* prevention - decreasing the duration of illness with early diagnosis and treatment; and *tertiary* prevention - reducing debilities of illnesses and disabilities.

1181 Levin 1994b.

1182 Levin, et al, 1988.

1183 Jeynes; Levin/ Schiller 1986.

1184 Wallston/ Wallston. See also: on **psychodynamics of belief systems** see Williams. On **fundamentalism**, with dogmatic, simplistic attitudes that include high intolerance for uncertainty and ambiguity see Hartz/ Everett. A measurement for tolerance of ambiguity is suggested by King/ Hunt 1975; Hilty et al.

1185 On **socioeconomic status** and reporting religious experience see Goode; Stark/ Bainbridge; D. Williams.

1186 Yinger.

1187 Scotch/ Geiger.

1188 On **religion and stresses, both positive and negative effects,** see Avison/ Turner; Brown/ Harris; Craig/ Brown; Brown et al; Dohrenwend/ Dohrenwend; C. G. Ellison; Kaplan et al; Landerman, et al; Lin/ Ensel; Mirowsky/ Ross; Morris/ Blake/ Buckley; Mueller, et al; Pearlin; Ramirez 1988;Ross 1990; Selye; Shaver et al; Tausig; Wetherington/ Kessler; Williams; Williams et al..

1189 Kiev; La Barre; V. Turner.

1190 On **enhanced socialization** see Williams. A spiritual well-being scale (SWBS) has been developed by Ellison/ Smith and Maturity of Faith scales by Benson/ Elkin.

1191 Levin/ Vanderpool 1989.

1192 Levin/ Schiller 1987.

1193 Levin 1983; Mendelsohn; Pitts/ Schiller; Szasz.

1194 **Placebo effects** are discussed in Chapter II-1. See especially White/ Tursky/ Schwartz.

1195 **Psychoneuroimmunology (PNI),** the influence of the mind upon the nervous and immune systems is discussed in Chapter II-1. See especially Achterberg; Simonton, et al, also considered in the same chapter under **Visualization.**

1196 Kaplan.

1197 Levin/ Vanderpool 1987.

1198 On **selection biases** in religious research see Galanter/ Buckley; Ullman 1988; Williams.

1199 Levin/ Vanderpool 1987.

1200 Levin/ Markides 1985; Levin 1989.

1201 Levin/ Vanderpool 1992.

1202 Alston; Levin/ Vanderpool 1987.

1203 Ludzia; R. Wilson. See also list of names for healing energies in I-Introduction; J. White.

1204 For more on **spirituality and religion in clinical practice** see: J. Campbell, 2001; Dona-hue; Dossey 1993; Gartner, et al; Henry/ Henry; Idler/ Kasl; Lerner; Meador/ Koenig; Oates 1971; 1987; Shafranske; Sperry; Worthington et al.

1205 Larson et al survey *systematic reviews* **of research on religion.** Systematic reviews examine the frequency of inclusion of this topic amongst all the articles in a given time period. Here are the percents of articles in which religion is considered in the principal journals of Psychiatry (2.5%), Family Practice (4.8%), Gerontology/Geriatrics (3.6%), Psychology (0.5). Only 5% of Pastoral Care articles included analyses of effects of religion.

1206 Levin 1994b.

1207 Craigie et al demonstrate this process with research on religion. They surveyed 52 articles in the *Journal of Family Practice,* finding 64 'uses of religious variables'. Of 16 that referred to religious denominations, 16 demonstrated neutral outcomes. Of 27 using dimensions such as 'relationship with God' and 'social support', 24 (89%) showed positive associations with religion.

1208 See also Engelhart/ Caplan for similar discussions.

1209 Harold Koenig 2001a.

1210 See discussion of guilt and blame associated with spirituality and health, discussed in Chapter II-8.

1211 Fears of healing and psi are discussed in Chapter IV-3, under **reasons healing has not been accepted.**

1212 See Chapter III-9 on **mystical experiences.**

1213 Carey 1982, p. 68.

1214 Levin 1993.

1215 See *Healing Research* Volumes I, II and IV; Benor 1992.

1216 Jaynes.

1217 S. Levine 1991, p33.

1218 Murphy/ Donovan 1995; 1997.

Chapter 13: Participatory spirituality

1219 Norwood 1994, p. 205.

1220 See Honorton 1985 for a meta analysis of 28 studies reporting actual hit rates, of which 23 had hit rates above chance expectation. Statistical analyses of the combined hit rates for the 28 studies showed odds against chance of ten billion to one. See summaries and discussions of telepathy research in: Edge, et al; Nash 1986; Radin 1997; J.B. Rhine; L. Rhine 1961; 1967.

1221 Sheldrake 2000.

1222 See Milton 1985 for a meta analysis of a variety of clairsentient techniques (card guessing, ganzfeld sessions, remote viewing), including millions of individual trials in hundreds of studies produced a statistically significant overall effect with odds of 10 million to 1 above chance. See review and discussion of clairsentience in: L. Rhine 1961; 67.

1223 See Honorton 1977 for a meta-analysis of 16 studies of remote viewing, 8 with significant effects; the overall statistical significance of the 16 studies was 476 million to 1 above chance. See discussions of remote viewing in: Jahn/ Dunne 1987; Puthoff/ Targ; Schmidt; others in Edge et al.

1224 See Honorton and Ferrari 1989 for a literature survey that identified all 'forced-choice' experiments 1935 to 1987, including 309 studies in 113 articles by 62 different investigators. There were nearly 2 million individual trials, with over 50,000 subjects. Methods ranged from ESP cards to fully automated, computer-generated, randomly presented symbols. The intervals between guesses and generation of future targets ranged from milliseconds to a year. A meta-analysis of the 309 studies found the odds against chance of were 1025 (ten million billion billion) to one. For discussion of precognition research see: L. E. Rhine 1961.

1225 Jahn/ Dunne 1987.

1226 See Radin/ Ferrari, 1991 for a meta-analysis of 73 publications by 52 investigators 1935 - 1987, including 2,569 people, 2.6 million dice throws in 148 experiments. The number of dice tossed per study ranged from 60 - 240,000; number of participants per study between 1 and 393. In all the experimental studies, the overall hit rate 51.2%. These were compared with 31 control studies in which there were 150,000 dice throws where no mental influence was applied. The overall hit rate in all *control* studies 50.02 was percent, and the confidence interval well within chance expectation; overall odds against chance 2:1. The odds against chance in comparing the two groups was over 1 billion to 1.

1227 See Radin 1997; Radin/ Nelson, internet reference, for a meta-analysis of PK on RNGs that identified 152 references 1959 to 1987; covering 832 studies by 68 investigators. Of these, 597 experimental studies (258 in a long-term investigation at the Princeton University PEAR laboratory) and 235 control studies (127 PEAR lab). Overall results comparing experimental and control series found the odds against chance were greater than 1 trillion to one. Control results well within chance levels, odds 2:1 Overall experimental effect, per study, about 51%, where 50 percent would be expected by chance. For descriptions and discussions of PK on RNGs see: Jahn/ Dunn 1987; Schmidt 1974.

1228 Jahn/ Dunn 1987.

1229 Interestingly, there are people whose influence on RNGs produces significant deviations but in the direction *opposite* to that which they intend. See Jahn/ Dunn 1987.

1230 Spiritual healing research is reviewed in *Healing Research, Volume 1*.

1231 *Psychokinesis (PK) on living systems* is called the allobiofeedback model, with feedback given to healer, not to subject of distant mental influence. See Braud/ Schlitz 1989; 1991 for a meta-analysis of 400 individual sessions, in which they found an average effect size of 53% vs. 50% for chance, with odds of 1.4 million to 1 above chance.

1232 Global Consciousness Project; Princeton Engineering Anomalies Research.

1233 Sheldrake 2000.

1234 Sheldrake 2000.

1235 Jung 1953-1979; 1964; 1965; 1993; von Franz 1980.

1236 Frazer has an encyclopedic collection of myths and customs in cultures around the world, relating to the priesthood of Diana at Aricia, in Italy. The priest in this tale maintains his post as king, reigning from the proximity to a specific tree in a sacred grove, only as long as no aspirant to the position kills him. As this tale had no precedent in Greek or Roman mythology, Frazer set out to discover its origins. In a scholarly exploration over three decades and 12 volumes of collected myths, Frazer details with closely similar elements in myths from Europe, North and South America, Asia, Africa and Australia. Frazer discusses the origins of the overlaps, but does not venture beyond speculations based on cognitive storytelling and cultural myth-making based on everyday experiences in the physical world.

Jung expanded on these cross-cultural overlaps (from Frazer and from his own broad reading in mythologies of many cultures), proposing a collective consciousness. Classical Jungian teachings do not include discussions of psi and formal scientific research of the collective unconscious.

If one reads Frazer from the emic perspective (acknowledging that traditional cultures have valid reasons for their beliefs and practices), and with awareness of the spirits that may be associated with the animate and so-called inanimate world, then much of the Jungian basis for speculating on the collective consciousness through shared imagery is weakened. What appear to be mythic knowledge and beliefs shared through a collective consciousness are actually common, direct awarenesses of the interconnection of all things through bioenergies, telepathy, clairsentience, pre- and retrocognition and the animation of the entire world. More on this in the discussions of participatory intelligent design.

Here we enter the worlds of channeled reports of intelligence on planets in distant stars and the visits of aliens in UFOs ñ which may contain more than small elements of truth but which are outside the scope of this volume.

1237 Sheldrake 1981/1987 also considers contributions of morphogenetic fields in maintaining and adapting the physical form of living organisms, as will be considered further, below.

1238 Sheldrake 2000 has an excellent collection of anecdotes and reviews of studies that demonstrate animal-human communications.

1239 For example, an individual is a part of a family, which is part of a local community, which is part of a regional community, which is part of a nation, which is part of the global community. Communications between individuals and groups at various levels occur through exchanges of spoken and written words, as well as through psi – which can extend forwards and backwards in time.

1240 TT and HT studies are reviewed in *Healing Research, Volume 1.*

1241 Safonov in Chapter I-1.

1242 Another recent example is Steven Gaynor, a podiatrist/ foot surgeon who practices as a healer.

1243 Spiritual healing is reviewed in *Healing Research, Volume 1.*

1244 On **transcendent awarenesses** see: Aurobindo; Bailey; Beard; Berman, Bolen 1979; Boorstein; Bucke; Carey; Dass 1985; 1996; Dass/ Gorman; Dethlefsen/ Dahlke; Dossey 1989; 1991; Firman; Fromm; Goleman, et al.; Green/ Green 1984; 1986; Grof/ Halifax; W. James; Kornfield 1993; Kübler-Ross 1991; S. Levine 1984; 1986; 1987; 1991; R. Maslow; T. Moore; R. Moss 1981; 1986; 1987; Needleman; J. Pearce 1981; 2002; Ring 1980; 1984; J. Roberts 1972; 1973; 1974; 1975; Satprem; Tart 1975b; Taub-Bynum; Underhill 1960; 1993; van Gelder; Von Franz 1980; 1987; Watts; Wilber 1979; Wilber, et al. 1986; Wolman/ Ullman.

1245 Kalu Rinpoche, Attributed.

1246 Ferrer, reviewed in Chapters III-8; III-11.

1247 Gibran, Sand and Foam.

1248 Intelligent design is discussed in Chapter III-8.

1249 More on this below, in the discussion of a possible 'language' of gene sequencing.

1250 K. Cohen 2005.

1251 See Chapter III-8 for a discussion on mystical vs psychotic experiences.

1252 Sensitives report that there is no such thing as inanimate matter. Every rock and drop of water and breeze has its own special sentience. More on Gaia, below.

1253 Einstein quote from internet source, see References. See also the report of Mellen-Tomas Benedict in chapter III-11 on perceiving the infinite.

1254 The initial discussion is taken largely from R. Newman 2005, an astrophysicist at Cornell University who is also a Professor at a Biblical Theological Seminary, and a proponent of Biblical creative design. It is supplemented from a variety of other sources.

1255 Thaxton; Yockey.

1256 B. Williams 2005.

1257 Whorf, p. 57-8.

1258 Whorf, p. 58.

1259 Whorf, p. 63.

1260 Whorf, p. 262-263.

1261 Williams 2005.

1262 This discussion on Chinese perspectives is taken from Chapter II-2.

1263 Cohen 1997; Kaptchuck.

1264 Kaptchuck, p. 9.

1265 Sapir/ Whorf.

1266 Acknowledging that there are many fewer species today than two centuries ago – due to their failure to survive the stress of man's depredations of our planet.

1267 Meyer 2005.

1268 Questioning Darwinian explanations: Becker/ Lonnig; Carroll; Conway 2000; 2003; Morris 2000; 2003; Erwin; Gilbert et al; Goodwin; Lonnig/ Saedler; Miklos; Shubin/ Marshall; Stadler et al; Thomson; J. Valentine; Wagner; Wagner/ Stadler; Webster/ Goodwin.

1269 *Phyla* are major divisions of living organisms, such as Porifera – sponges; Nematoda – earthworms; Chordata – vertebrate animals (including man).

1270 Meyer, 2003.

1271 For fossil details of the Cambrian period see
www.fossilmall.com/Fossil_Archive/Western_Fossils/Cambrian_Animals/
Cambrian_Biota.htm.

1272 Ohno, cited in Meyer 2005.

1273 While Newman is a Biblical Creationist, his summary is an excellent presentation of the scientific evidence for intelligent design.

1274 Laszlo has the clearest discussion that I've found on these topics.

1275 10^{-43} seconds.

1276 This is a fraction with a 1 in the numerator and 10 with 60 zeros after it in the denominator.

1277 Davies; Boslough, cited in Newman.

1278 Gravity is weaker by 10^{37} than electromagnetism.

1279 Weinberg, cited in Newman.

1280 Hoyle, cited in Newman.

1281 Adenosine Triphosphate (ATP) and adenosine diphosphate (ADP) store energy for such biological processes as metabolizing food, transporting biochemicals across cell membranes and contracting muscles.

1282 From Newman.

1283 For more on these subjects see Hayward, cited in Newman.

1284 Laszlo, p.64.

1285 Gingrich; M. Hart 1982; 1989, cited in Newman.

1286 M. Hart 1979, cited in Newman.

1287 M. Hart 1979; 1982; cited in Newman.

1288 M. Hart 1979; 1982; cited in Newman. For additional evidence of this sort, see H. Ross. Further discussion on the steady percent of oxygen in Earth's atmosphere below.

1289 Barrow/ Tipler.

1290 Newman is again succinct and clear in exploring the Anthropic theory in the context of intelligent design.

1291 Newman proposes that the God of the Bible is suggested as the creator of the universe and is a far stronger theory than the Anthropic Principle. He cites Barfield; Wenham for discussions supporting this view.

1292 Lovelock first proposed the Gaia hypothesis in 1972. Lovelock 1988 notes that as early as 1785 James Hutton, a Scottish scientist who is credited with founding the study of geology, suggested that Earth is a 'superorganism' that should be studied as one would explore the physiology of any living organism. Edward Seuss first used the term 'biosphere' in 1875. Vladimir Ivanovich Vernadsky, a Russian geologist, gave this word its modern meaning. Lovelock reports 1988 that he was unaware of these earlier references.

1293 James Lovelock, a British chemist, together with Lynn Margulis, a US biologist, developed the Gaia theory in the mid 1960s and 1970s.

1294 Some of these items overlap with the discussion of intelligent design from the perspective of the solar system.

1295 Lovelock, p. 65.

1296 Lovelock, p. 36.

1297 See Keeling Curve for figures on Carbon Dioxide increases in Hawaii. See R. Sanders on the global warming effects of increased carbon dioxide. The U.S. Energy Information Administration has an explanation of carbon dioxide increases in the atmosphere, but the official governmental line is that "we don't know what the effects might be." www.eia.doe.gov/oiaf/1605/ggccebro/chapter1.html

1298 Lovelock, p. 67-69.

1299 Today's global warming is attributed by most earth scientists to the increase in man's production of carbon dioxide, per the figures noted in the text in (2) of this discussion.

1300 *Cybernetics* is derived from *kubernetes,* the Greek word for 'steersman.' Lovelock (1979, p. 44) sees this as a very apt derivation in the case of Gaia, "since the primary function of many cybernetic systems is to steer an optimum course through changing conditions towards a predetermined goal."

1301 More commonly called *farts*.

1302 Lovelock, p. 68.

1303 Lovelock, p. 72.

1304 Lovelock, p. 72-73.

1305 Lovelock, p. 79.

1306 Lovelock, p. 88.

1307 I found it at first surprising that the above, along with further, more detailed evidence gathered by Lovelock has not been included in the Creationists' arguments for intelligent design. On second thought, however, it would appear that the counter-arguments of Lovelock which propose a naturalistic approach to these intricate balances of chemicals in our environment might not forward the goals of the Creationists.

Popular opinion has expanded Lovelock's theory of Gaia as a living geobiological entity that actively maintains her own homeostatic balance to support life, attributing to Gaia a sentience that Lovelock himself does not support. This, too, might not suit the arguments of Creationists, and may further explain why they have not used this evidence in advocating for the teaching of intelligent design in schools.

1308 The discussion of Luther Burbank's work presented below was originally presented at the annual meeting of the Society for Psychical Research in the UK in 1987, and a revised version of this presentation is in Benor 1988.

1309 Burbank with Hall; Clampett; Dreyer; Tompkins/ Bird; Whitson et al; Yogananda.

1310 Burbank/ Hall, p. 53.

1311 Italics inserted.

1312 Burbank/ Hall, p. 52.

1313 Burbank/ Hall, p. 54.

1314 Burbank would graft diverse varieties of fruit branches onto the trunk of a solidly established tree, thereby shortcutting the necessity of raising a tree from seed in order to obtain its fruits. He could produce new varieties through careful cross-pollination of the flowers.

1315 Burbank/ Hall, p. 44. Italics added.

1316 Burbank/ Hall, p. 88. Italics added.

1317 Burbank/ Hall, p. 76.

1318 Burbank/ Hall, p. 95.

1319 In following generations he found different but regular and predictable proportions of green and yellow peas.

1320 Many years later, it was discovered that pea plants have 7 chromosome pairs. Mendel studied seven characteristics of peas: seeds (round/wrinkled; coat color, color of storage material within) and characters in the plant (distribution of flowers, shape and color of the pods, length of stem). He was unusually lucky in his choices, because peas have only 7 chromosomes, and several of the traits he chose were governed by the same chromosome; but the relevant genes were located far enough apart along the chromosome chain of proteins that they produced their influences essentially independently of each other. This allowed Mendel to observe dominant/recessive crossbreeding influences in proportions that were consistent for each of the traits he was studying.

1321 For instance, Mendel observed that any one characteristic (such as pea seed color) was independent of any other characteristic (such as length of stalk).

1322 These studies led to what are now known as *Mendel's Laws of Heredity*.

1. The sex cell of an animal or plant may contain either of two factors (alleles) for different traits but cannot contain both factors required to express the traits.

2. Any given characteristics are inherited independently from other characteris-tics (*the law of independent assortment*).

3. Every inherited characteristic is determined by two genes, one from each parent, and in many cases one will be dominant and the other recessive (*the law of dominants and recessives*).

1323 Jahn/ Dunne 1987; Nelson/ Radin 1987; Radin; Schmidt 1974.

1324 Italics added.

1325 Jordan, p. 204.

1326 Burbank and Hall, p. 107. Italics inserted.

1327 Tompkins and Bird, p. 133; similar citation of Hall in Kraft/ Kraft 1959, p 131.

1328 Harwood, p 662.

1329 Yogananda 1983, p. 41.

1330 Burbank with Hall, p. 97.

1331 Kraft/ Kraft, p. 126-129.

1332 Nash 1984.

1333 $p < .005$, two-tailed.

1334 $p < .02$, two-tailed.

1335 $p < .04$, two-tailed.

1336 As a second control, Cox examined the frequency of families with a boy or girl as first born, followed by four children of the opposite sex, finding no significant deviations from chance expectations in these control series.

1337 Koestler; S. Silverman.

1338 Dossey 1982, p 61-2.

1339 Koestler; S. Silverman.

1340 Retrogenes.

1341 For healing effects on plant growth: Grad 1963; 1964a; b; 1965/1976; Macdonald, Dakin et al 1975; Saklani 1988; 1990. Bacteria: Nash 1982. Yeasts: Barry; Haraldsson/ Thorsteinson; Tedder/ Monty. See Chapter I-4 for critiques of these studies. For anecdotal reports of extensive studies of plant growth see Loehr.

1342 German also acknowledges this duality in the combination of *ja* and *nein*, as *jain*.

1343 See discussion of animism in Chapter III-8; Bortoft; T. Brown 1979; 2001; Cowan; Hawken 1978; Pelikan; Pogacnik 1997; 2001; Roads; Somé 1994; Thompkins 1997; M.S. Wright; and see discussion of nature spirits in Chapter III-4.

1344 Dreisch; Whitmont.

1345 Chalmers; B. Russell 1927.

1346 See further quotes from Laszlo on the similarities of living organisms with quantum systems in Chapter III-10.
1347 Einstein 1941.
1348 E. Mitchell, quoted in DiCarlo, p. 17.
1349 See descriptions of the NDE in Chapter III-2; angelic encounters in III-3; meditative experiences in II-1; III-8; mystical experiences in III-9.
1350 Bacon, in DiCarlo, p. 35.
1351 In psi research, believers have been nicknamed *sheep* and disbelievers *goats*. Numerous studies confirm that sheep produce psi effects at significantly better than chance levels, which goats produce psi effects significantly more poorly than chance. More on sheep/goat effects in Palmer, 1971; 1972; Lovitts; reviewed in Chapter I-3.
1352 Rosenthal; Rosenthal/ Rubin; Solfvin.
1353 Tesla developed a variety of electrical devices that produced unusual effects that no one to date has been able to explain. See Seifer.
1354 Deloria 1999, p. 46.
1355 Felser, p.74-75.
1356 Hawken 1993, p. 20.
1357 Hawken 1993, p. 33.
1358 Hawken 1993, p. 6.
1359 Hawken 1993, p. 12.
1360 Hawken 1993, p. 83.
1361 Hawken 1993, p. 139.
1362 Berry 2005, 578.
1363 Schumacher.
1364 Walsch 1997, p. 52.
1365 Oh Shinnah 1991, p. 151.
1366 Aristotle 384-322 BC.
1367 Ortega y Gasset 1914.
1368 Arasteh/ Sheikh p. 149.
1369 Laurens van der Post 1963.

References

A

AAAS.
www.aaas.org/news/releases/2002/1106id2.sht
ml (Accessed 11/28/05)

Abbott, Edwin A. *Flatland: A Romance of Many Dimensions*, New York/ London: Barnes & Noble/ Harper & Row 1983 (Orig. 1963).

Achterberg, Jean/ Lawlis, Frank. Letters: Human research and studying psychosocial interventions for cancer, *Advances* 1992, 8(4), 2-4.

Adler, Felix (Founder of the Ethical Culture Movement). In: Begley/ Reagan 2002, 80.

Agnellet, M. *I Accept These Facts: The Lourdes Cures Examined*, London: 1958.

Aho, Marja-Leena. *Gift of Healing*, Portland, OR: LifeTime Publishing 1996.

Ake, Stacey. www.metanexus.net, 5/28/02.

Alder, Felix. Attributed

Aldridge, PhD. *Spirituality, Healing and Medicine: Return to the Silence*, Philadelphia/ London: Jessica Kingsley 2000.

Alighieri, Dante. *The Divine Comedy*, Canto XXViii, Paradise, Trans. John Ciardi 1987.

Allison, Ralph B. The possession syndrome on trial, *American J Forensic Psychiatry* 1985, 611, 46-55.

Allison, Ralph/ Schwarz, Ted. *Minds in Many Pieces*, New York: Rawson, Wade 1980.

Allport, Gordon W. *The Nature of Prejudice*, Garden City, NY: Anchor 1958.

Althouse, Lawrence W. *Rediscovering the Gift of Healing*, Nashville, TN: Abington 1977.

Alvarado, Carlos S. Mapping the characteristics of out-of-body experiences, *J the American Society Psychical Research* 1997, 91(1), 16-32.

Alvarado, Carlos. Out-of-body experiences, In: Cardeña, E/ Lynn, SJ/ Krippner, S, eds. *Varieties of anomalous experiences*, Washington, DC: American Psychological Association 2000, 183-218.

Alvarado, Carlos. Personal communication 2003.

Amatuzio, Janis. *Forever Ours: A Forensic Pathologist's Perspective on Immortality and Living – A Collection of Real-Life Stories*, Minneapolis: Midwest Forensic Pathology, P.A,

3960 Coon Rapids Blvd., LL21, Coon Rapids, MN 55433 www.foreverour.com

Ameen, Abu'l-Mundhir Khaleel ibn Ibraaheem. *The Jinn and Human Sickness: Remedies in the Light of the Qur'aan & Sunnah*, Riyadh: Darussalam 2005.

Amen, Daniel G. *Healing the Hardware of the Soul: How Making the Brain-Soul Connection Can Optimize Your Life, Love, and Spiritual Growth*, New York: Simon & Schuster/The Free Press 2002.

American Atheists. Survey indicates more Americans 'without faith'
www.atheists.org/flash.line/atheist4.htm
(Accessed 9/26/05)

Amundson, Ron. The hundredth monkey phenomenon, *Skeptical Inquirer* 1985, 9(4), 348-356.

Anandarajah, G/ Hight, E. Spirituality and medical practice: Using the HOPE questions as a practical tool for spiritual assessment, *American Family Physician* 2001, 63(1), 81-9.

Anandarajah, G/ Stumpff, J. Integrating spirituality into medical practice: a survey of FM clerkship students, *Family Medicine* March 2004, 36(3), 160-1.

Anderson, George/ Barone, Andrew. *Walking in the Garden of Souls: George Anderson's Advice from the Hereafter for Living in the Here and Now*, New York: GP Putnam's Sons/ Penguin 2001.

Anderson, Rodger. Psychometry or survival? Part I, *Parapsychology Review* 1984, 15(3), 6-8.

Anderson, Sherry Ruth/ Hopkins, Patricia. *The Feminine Face of God*, New York: Gill & Macmillan 1996.

Andrade, HG. *A Corpuscular Theory of Spirit*, Sao Paulo: Privately published 1968.

Andreev, Daniel. *The Rose of the World*, Hudson, NY: Lindisfarne 1998.

Andreson, Jensine. Meditation meets behavioral medicine, *J Consciousness Studies* 2001, 7(11-12), 32.

Angell, Marcia. *The Truth About the Drug Companies: How They Deceive Us and What to Do About It*, Random House 2004.

Angelo, Jack, *The Healing Spirit: The Story of Dennis Barrett*, London: Rider 1990.

Anonymous. In: Evans-Wentz, WY, ed. *The Tibetan Book of the Dead, or the After-Death Experiences on the 'Bardo' Plane, According to*

Lama Kazi Dawa- Samdup's English Rendering, New York/London: Oxford University 1960.

Anonymous. In: Johnston, William, ed. *The Cloud of Unknowing and the Book of Privy Counselling*, Garden City, NY: Image/ Doubleday 1973.

Anonymous. NDEs and the not-close-to death experience, *Vital Signs*, 1992, 1(3), 11-15.

Antonio, Don. Quoted in Grauds, p. 94.

Apraia, Joseph/ Lobsang, Rapgay. *Eastern Wisdom for Western Life*, Newleaf 2000.

Aquinas, St Thomas. www.aquinasonline.com.

Aquinas, St. Thomas. *Summa Theologiae I*, question 51, answer 2.

Armstrong, B/ Van Merwyk, AJ/ Coates, H. Blood pressure in Seventh-Day Adventist vegetarians, *American J Epidemiology* 1977, 105, 444-449.

Armstrong, Karen. *The Battle for God*, New York: Ballantine 2000

Ash, Sholem. *The Nazarene*, New York: Carroll and Graf 1967.

Asquith, Margot. In: Channon, Chips, *Diary* 20 Dec. 1937.

Assagioli, Roberto. *Psychosynthesis,* London: Turnstone 1965.

Asser, Seth M/ Swan, Rita. Child fatalities from religion-motivated medical neglect, *Pediatrics* 1998, 101(4), 625-629 (31 refs).

Atwater, PMH. *Children of the New Millenium.* New York: Three Rivers 1999.

Atwater, PMH. *Coming Back to Life: The After-Effects of the Near-Death Experience*, New York: Citadel/ Kensington 2001.

Aurelius, Marcus. *Meditations.*

Aurobindo, Sri. *The Mind of Light*, New York: Dutton 1953.

Aurobindo, Sri. *The Synthesis of Yoga*, Pondicherry, India: Aurobindo Ashram 1957.

Austin, James. *Zen and the Brain*, Cambridge, MA: MIT 1998.

Aviles, Jennifer M, et al. Intercessory prayer and cardiovascular disease progression in a coronary care unit population: A randomized controlled trial, *Mayo Clinic Proceedings* 2001, 76, 1192-1198.

Avodah Zarah 56a, cited in Greenbaum, p. 185

Axe, DD. Extreme functional sensitivity to conservative amino acid changes on enzyme exteriors. *J Molecular Biology* 2000, 301(3), 585-596.

Azuma, Nagato/ Stevenson, Ian. 'Psychic surgery' in the Philippines as a form of group hypnosis, *American J Clinical Hypnosis* 1988, 31(1), 61- 67.

Azuonye, Ikechukwu Obialo. A difficult case: Diagnosis made by hallucinatory voices, *British Medical J* 1997, 315, 1685-1686.

B

Bach, Marcus. *Spiritual Breakthroughs for Our Time*, Garden City, NY: Doubleday, 1965.

Bach, Richard. *Illusions*, Delacorte/ Eleanor Friede 1977.

Bach, Richard. *Jonathan Livingston Seagull*, London: Pan 1976.

Bache, CM. *Lifecycles: Reincarnation and the Web of Life*, New York: Paragon House 1990.

Bachman JG/ Alcser KH/ Doukas DJ, et al. Attitudes of Michigan physicians and the public toward legalizing physician-assisted suicide and voluntary euthanasia. *New England J Medicine* 1996, 334(5), 303-9.

Bacon, Francis. *Novum Organum* 1620.

Bacon, Francis. Of Atheism, In: *Essays* 1625.

Bacon, Francis. In: DiCarlo 1996, p. 35.

Baden, MM/ Hennessee, JA. *Unnatural Death: Confessions of a Medical Examiner*, New York: Random House 1989.

Baer, RA. Mindfulness training as a clinical intervention: A conceptual and empirical review, *Clinical Psychology: Science and Practice* 2003, 10, 125–143.

Baider L, et al. The role of religious and spiritual beliefs in coping with malignant melanoma: an Israeli sample. *Psycho-Oncology.* 1999, 8, 27-35.

Bailey, Alice A. *Esoteric Healing, V.VI*, New York: Lucis 1972.

Bailey, Lee Worth/ Yates, Jenny. *The Near-Death Experience: A Reader*, New York: Routledge 1996.

Baisley, Barbara. *No Easy Answers: An Exploration of Suffering*, Epworth 2000.

Bakken, Kenneth L. *The Call to Wholeness: Health as a Spiritual Journey*, New York: Crossroad 1985.

Balducci, Corrado. Parapsychology and diabolic possession, *International J Parapsychology* 1966, 8, 193-212.

Ball, Philip. *Critical Mass: How One Thing Leads to Another*, New York: Farrar, Straus and Giroux 2004.

Bander, Peter. *Carry on Talking*, Garrards Cross, UK: Colin Smythe 1972.

Bander, Peter. *Voices from the Tapes,* New York: Drake 1973.

Bandler, Richard/ Grinder, John. *Frogs into Princes: Neurolinguistic Programming,* Moab, Utah: Real People 1979.

Barbanell, Maurice. *Harry Edwards and His Healing,* London: Psychic Book Club 1953.

Barbanell, Maurice. *Saga of Spirit Healing,* London: Spiritualist 1954.

Barbanell, Maurice. *I Hear a Voice: A Biography of E.G. Fricker the Healer,* London: Spiritualist 1962.

Barbanell, Maurice. *Spiritualism Today,* London: Herbert Jenkins 1969.

Barfield, Kenny. *Why the Bible is Number 1: The World's Sacred Writings in the Light of Science,* Grand Rapids: Baker 1988.

Barham, Allan. Dr. W. J. Crawford, his work and his legacy in psychokinesis, *J the Society PsychicalResearch* 1988(a), 55, 113-138.

Barham, Allan. The Crawford legacy, part II: Recent research in macro-PK with special reference to the work of Batcheldor and Brookes-Smith, *J the Society PsychicalResearch* 1988(b), 55, 196-207.

Barker, ERD. *Being whole: Spiritual well-being in Appalachian women: a phenomenological study,* Unpublished doctoral dissertation, Austin: University of Texas at Austin 1989.

Barlow, DH/ Abel, GC/ Blanchard, E. B. Gender identity change in a transsexual: an exorcism, *Archives of Sexual Behavior* 1977, 6, 387-395.

Barna, George. *The Index of Leading Spiritual Indicators,* Dallas: Word Publishing 1996.

Barna Group. *Annual Barna Group survey describes changes in America's religious beliefs and practices,* 2005. www.barna.org/FlexPage.aspx?Page=BarnaUpdate&BarnaUpdateID=186 (Accessed 9/26/05).

Barnes, Linda, et al. Spirituality, religion, and pediatrics: intersecting worlds of healing, *Pediatrics* 2000, 104(6), 899-908 (162 refs).

Barnes, NJ. Lady Rokujo's ghost: spirit possession, Buddhism, and healing in Japanese literature, *Lit. Med.* 1989, 8, 106-121.

Barnett, Libby/ Chambers, Maggie/ Davidson, Susan. *Reiki Energy Medicine : Bringing Healing Touch into Home, Hospital, and Hospice,* Rochester, VT: Healing Arts 1996.

Barondess, Jeremiah A. The impossible in medicine, In: Davis/ Park.

Barrett, Sir William. *Death-Bed Visions,* London: Methuen 1926.

Barrie, JM. *Peter Pan* (1928), New York: Bantam 1983.

Barrington, Mary Rose. A slip in time and place, *Fate,* 1985 (Oct), 88-94.

Barrow, John D/ Tipler, Frank J. *The Anthropic Cosmo-logical Principle,* Oxford University 1986.

Barry, J, General and comparative study of the psychokinetic effect on a fungus culture, *J Parapsychology* 1968, 32, 237-243.

Bartlett, John/ Kaplan, J, ed. *Bartlett's Familiar Quotations,* New York: Little, Brown & Co. 1992.

Batcheldor, KJ. Report of a case of table levitation and associated phenomena, *J the Society PsychicalResearch* 1966, 43(729), 339- 356.

Batcheldor, KJ. Contribution to the theory of PK induction from sitter-group work, In: Roll, WG/ Beloff, J/ White, R, eds. *Research in Parapsychology* 1982, Metuchen, NJ: Scarecrow 1983, 45-61. (Also in: *J the American Society PsychicalResearch* 1984, 78(2), 105-132.)

Bayless, Raymond. *The Enigma of the Poltergeist,* New York: Ace 1967.

Bayless, Raymond. *Apparitions and the Survival of Death,* New York: Citadel 1973.

Bazak, Jacob. *Judaism and Psychical Phenomena,* New York: Garrett, 1972.

Beard, Paul. *Survival of Death: For and Against,* London: Hodder & Stoughton 1966.

Beard, Paul. *Living On,* London: Allen and Unwin 1980.

Beard, Paul. The sitter's task and responsibility, *Light* 1988, 108(2), 66-74.

Beck, Charlotte Joko. *Nothing Special: Living Zen,* San Francisco: Harper San Francisco 1993.

Becker, H/ Lonnig, W. Transposons: Eukaryotic, In: *Nature Encyclopedia of Life Sciences* vol. 18, London: Nature Publishing Group 2001, 529-539.

Bedi, Ashok. *Path To The Soul,* York Beach, ME: Weiser Books 2000.

Beesley, Ronald. *Service of the Race,* Speldhurst, England: White Lodge 1972.

Begley, Sharon/ Reagan, Michael, ed. *Inside the Mid of God: Images and Words of Inner Space,* Philadelphia, PA: Templeton Foundation Press, 2002.

Behe, Michael J. *Darwin's Black Box,* NY: Free Press 1996.

Behe, Michael J. *Darwin's Breakdown,* Touchstone, July-August 1999.

Behe, Michael J. The Challenge of Irreducible Complexity, *Natural History Magazine*, April 2002 www.actionbioscience.org/evolution/nhmag.ht ml.

Bek, Lilla/ Pullar, Philippa. *The Seven Levels of Healing*, London: Century 1986.

Belinfante, Frederik Jozef. In: John Barrow, *The World Within the World*. Cited in Satinover, Jeffrey. *The Quantum Brain: The Search for Freedom and the Next Generation of Man*, New York: John Wiley & Sons 2001.

Bender, H. Emotional dangers of spiritualism, *Tomorrow*, 1960, 8(4), 53-60.

Benedict, Mellen-Thomas. (NDE report, Accessed 9/12/03) www.nderf.org/mellen_thomas_nde.htm

Bennett, Arnold. Attributed.

Benor, Daniel J. Intersections of holography, psi, acupuncture and related issues, *American J Acupuncture* 1983, 11(2), 105-118.

Benor, Daniel J. The overlap of psychic "readings" with psychotherapy, *Psi Research*, 1986, 5(1,2), 56-78.

Benor, Daniel J. Lamarckian genetics: theories from psi research and evidence from the work of Luther Burbank, Weiner, DH/ Morris, RL, *Research in Parapsychology* 1987, Metuchen, NJ and London: Scarecrow 1988, 166-170. Revised version at www.WholisticHealingResearch.com/Articles/ Burbank.htm

Benor, Daniel J. A psychiatrist examines fears of healing, *J the Society PsychicalResearch* 1990(a), 56, 287-299.

Benor, Daniel J. The implications of $E = mc^2$ for healing and parapsychology, *Scientific and Medical Network Newsletter*, 1990(b), April, 12-14. www.WholisticHealingResearch.com/Articles/ Einstein.htm

Benor, Daniel J. Little deaths of daily life, *Doctor-Healer Network Newsletter* 1992(a), No. 4, 7-8.

Benor, Daniel J. Lessons from spiritual healing research & practice, *Subtle Energies*, 1992(b), 3(1), 73-88.

Benor, Daniel J. Intuitive diagnosis, *Subtle Energies* 1992(c), 3(2), 41-64. www.WholisticHealingResearch.com/Articles/ IntuitDx.htm

Benor, Daniel J. Spiritual healing and psychotherapy, *The Therapist* 1994, 1(4), 37-39 www.WholisticHealingResearch.com/Articles/ SpirHealPT.htm

Benor, Daniel J. Spiritual healing: a unifying influence in complementary therapies, *Complementary Therapies in Medicine* (UK), 1995(a), 3(4), 234-238 www.wholistichealingresearch.com/Articles/Un ifying.htm

Benor, Daniel J. Medical Student Health Awareness: The Louisville Program for Medical Student Health Awareness, *Complementary Therapies in Medicine*, 1995(b), 3(2), 93-99.

Benor, Daniel J. *Healing Research: Volume I, Spiritual Healing: Scientific Validation of a Healing Revolution*, Southfield, MI: Vision Publications 2001(a).

Benor, Daniel J. *Healing Research: Volume I, Professional Supplement*, Southfield, MI: Vision Publications 2001(b).

Benor, Daniel J. Psychotherapy and spiritual healing, In: Benor, Daniel J, *Healing Research*, Volume I, Chapter 1 (revised ed), Southfield, Michigan: Vision Publications 2001(c) (Earlier version in *Human Potential* (UK), Summer 1996, 13-16. www.wholistichealingresearch.com/Articles/ PsychotherSH.htm

Benor, Daniel J. Intuition (Editorial), *International J Healing and Caring – On line* 2002, 2(2), 1-17.

Benor, Daniel J. Developing faith in the transcendent (Editorial), *International J Healing and Caring–On Line* May, 2003(a), 3(2).

Benor, Daniel J. Collective consciousness (Editorial) *International J Healing and Caring–On line* 2003(b), 3(3) www.ijhc.org/Members/Journal/3-3Articles/ EdmuseTx-3-3.asp

Benor, Daniel J. Darkness and Light: Perspectives through the yin-yang symbol (Editorial), *International J Healing & Caring – On line* 2004, 4(1), 1-20.

Benor, Daniel J/ Stumpfeldt, Dorothea von/ Benor, Ruth. EmotionalBodyProcess, Part I - Healing Through Love, *International J Healing and Caring – On line* 2001, V.1 www.ijhc.org/ Journal/ 0601articles/ love-I-1.html

Benor, Ruth. Healing unto death, In: Benor, Daniel J, *Healing Research: Volume I, Spiritual Healing: Scientific Validation of a Healing Revolution*, Southfield, MI: Vision Publications, 2001, 132-138.

Bentov, Itzak, *Stalking the Wild Pendulum: On the Mechanics of Consciousness*, New York: E.P. Dutton 1977.

Beresford, John Davys. *The Case for Faith Healing*, London: Allen and Unwin 1934.

Berg, Dorothy A. A modus operandi of trance communication: a comparison of theories, *J the American Society PsychicalResearch* 1951, 45, 17-36.

Bergin AE/ Jensen JP. Religiosity of psychotherapists: a national survey. *Psychotherapy* 1990, 27, 3-7.

Berman, E/ Merz, JF/ Rudnick, M/ Snyder, RW/ Rogers, KK/ Lee, J/ Johnson, D/ Mosenkis, A/ Israni, A/ Wolpe, PR/ Lipschutz, JH [University of' Pennsylvania]. Religiosity in a hemodialysis population and its relationship to satisfaction with medical care, satisfaction with life, and adherence, *American J Kidney Diseases* September 2004, 44(3), 488-97.

Berman, Morris. *The Reenchantment of the World*, New York: Bantam 1984.

Bernardi, Luciano, et al. Effect of rosary prayer and yoga mantras on autonomic cardiovascular rhythms: comparative study, *British Medical J* 2001, 323, 1446-1449.

Bernstein, Morey. *The Search for Bridey Murphy,* New York: Doubleday 1978.

Berry, Thomas. 'Reinventing the human, In: Schlitz, Marilyn/ Amorok, Tina, with Micozzi, Marc S. *Consciousness & Healing: Integral Approaches to Mind-Body Medicine*, St. Louis, MO: Elsevier/ Churchill Livingstone 2005, 578.

Berry, Wendell. Conservation is good work, *The Amicus J* Winter 1992, 33.

Bertalanffy, Ludwig von. General systems theory and psychiatry, In: Arieti, Sylvano, ed, *American Handbook of Psychiatry, Vol. I, Chapter 51*, New York: Basic Books 1974, 1095-1117.

Berwick, Peter R/ Douglas, Robert R. Hypnosis, exorcism and healing: a case report, *American J Clinical Hypnosis* 1977, 20(2).

Besant, Annie/ Leadbeater, CW. *Occult Chemistry*, Madras, India: Thosophical 1908; London 1919; Madras 1951.

Besant, Annie/ Leadbeater, CW. *Thought-Forms*, Wheaton, IL: Quest/ Theosophical 1971, Orig. 1925. Reprinted with permission of The Theosophical Publishing House, Adyar, Madras 600 020, India.

Bird, Christopher. *The Divining Hand: The Five Hundred Year Old Mystery of Dowsing*, New York: EP Dutton 1979.

Bishop, G. *Faith Healing: God or Fraud?* Los Angeles: Sherbourne 1967.

Blackmore, Susan. Postal survey of OBEs and other experiences. *J the Society Psychical Research*, 1984, 52, 225-244.

Blackmore, Susan. Glimpse of an afterlife or just the dying brain? *Psi Researcher* 1992, 6, 2-3.

Blackmore, Susan. *Dying to Live* London: Grafton 1993.

Blake, William. Attributed.

Blatty, William Peter. *The Exorcist,* New York: Bantam/ Harper & Row 1971; New York: HarperCollins 2000 (reissue)

Blavatsky, Helena P. Quote from: deZirkoff, Boris, ed, *Collected Writings 1874-1890*, V.I-XII, Wheaton, IL: Quest/Theosophical.

Blavatsky, Helena P. *The Secret Doctrine*, Vols. I and II, Pasadena, CA: Theosophical University Press 1973.

Blazer, Dan. *Freud vs. God: How Psychiatry Lost Its Soul & Christianity Lost Its Mind.* InterVarsity Press 1998.

Bloomfield, Bob. *Linda Martel: Little Healer,* Tasburgh, UK: Pelegrin Trust/ Pilgrim 1990.

Blumrich, Josef F. *Spaceships of Ezekiel*, New York: Bantam 1974.

Blythe, Henry. *The Three Lives of Naomi Henry: An Investigation into Reincarnation,* New York: Citadel 1956.

Bockris, John O'M. *The New Paradigm: A Confrontation Between Physics and the Paranormal Phenomena*, College Station, TX: D&M Enterprises 2004. (Caution: Many errors in this book in names, references.)

Bodine, Echo. *Echoes of the Soul: The Soul's Journey Beyond the Light – Through Life, Death, and Life After Death*, Novato, CA: New World 1999.

Boerstler, Richard W. *Letting Go: A Holistic and Meditative Approach to Living and Dying,* Watertown, MA: Associates in Thanatology 1982.

Bohm, David. *Causality and Chance in Modern Physics*, London: Routledge and Kegan Paul 1957.

Bohm, David. *Wholeness and the Implicate Order*, London: Routlege and Kegan Paul 1980.

Bohm, David/ Hiley, B. On the intuitive understanding of nonlocality as implied by quantum theory, *Foundations of Physics* 1975, 5, 96, 102.

Bolen, Jean Shinoda. *The Tau of Psychology: Synchro-nicity and the Self,* New York: Harper & Row 1979.

Bolendas, Joa (Hill, John, Trans.). *Alive in God's World: Human Life on Earth and in Heaven*, Great Barrington, MA: Lindesfarne 2001.

Bolton, Brett. *Edgar Cayce Speaks*, New York: Avon 1969.

Boorstein, Seymor. *Clinical Studies in Transpersonal Psychotherapy,* New York: State University of New York 1997.

Borelli, Marianne/ Heidt, Patricia, eds. *Therapeutic Touch,* New York: Springer 1981, 129-137.

Bortoft, Henri. *The Wholeness of Nature: Goethe's Way toward a Science of Conscious Participation in Nature,* Herndon, VA: Steiner/ Anthroposophic 1996.

Bosman, John-Eduard. *Some are not healed: the theory-practice tension regarding the healing ministry in a Pentecostal church* (Practical Theology), D.TH. University of South Africa 1997.

Botkin, Allan L. The induction of after-death communications utilizing eye-movement desensitization and reprocessing: a new discovery, *J Near-Death Studies,* Spring 2000, 18(3).

Botkin, Allan L/ Hogan, R. Craig. *Induced After-death Communication: A New Therapy for Healing Grief And Trauma,* Charlottesville, VA: Hampton Roads 2005.

Bowen, Charles. Psychic surgery and healing by UFO's: Is there a link? (Book Review of "Beyond the Senses", *Flying Saucer Review* 1969, 17(4), 23.

Bowen, Murray. Family reaction to death, In: Guerin, Philip J. Jr. *Family Therapy: Theory and Practice,* New York: Gardener/ John Wiley 1976, 335-348.

Boyer, Pascal. *Religion Explained, or The Mental Instincts that Fashion Gods, Ghosts and Ancestors,* Random House (UK) and New York: Basic Books (USA) 2001.

Bradley, FH. *Appearance and Reality* 1893.

Bragdon, Emma. *Spiritual Alliances: Discovering the Roots of Health* Woodstock, VT: Lightening Up Press 2003.

Bramly, Serge. *Macumba: The Teachings of Maria-Jose, Mother of the Gods,* New York: Avon 1977.

Braud, William. Distant mental influence of rate of hemolysis of human red blood cells, In: Henkel, Linda A/ Berger, Rich E, eds. *Research in Parapsychology 1988,* 1989, 1-6.

Braud, William. *Information on standardized assessments of possible relevance for research in transpersonal psychology, spirituality, and related areas,* Institute of

Transpersonal Psychology, April 22, 1995. www.itplibrary.org/resources/tests.htm.

Braud, William/ Anderson, Rosemarie. *Transpersonal Research Methods for the Social Sciences: Honoring Human Experience,* Thousand Oaks, CA: Sage 1998.

Bray, Shirley. *A Guide for the Spiritual Traveler,* Cleveland, Queensland, Australia: Scroll 1990.

Brennan, Barbara. *Hands of Light,* New York: Bantam 1987.

Brennan, Barbara. Personal communication 1990.

Brennan, Barbara. *Light Emerging,* New York: Bantam 1993.

Bridges, Holly. *A Circle of Prayer, Coming Together to Find Spirit, Caring, and Community.* Berkeley, California: Wildcat Canyon Press, 1997.

Briggs, John/ Peat, F. David. *Turbulent Mirror: An Illustrated Guide to Chaos Theory and the Science of Wholeness,* New York: Harper Collins 1990.

Briggs-Myers, Isabel/ Myers, Peter B. *Gifts Differing: Understanding Personality Type,* Consulting Psychologists Press 1995.

Brilliant, Ashleigh. www.ashleighbrilliant.com

Broad, CD. *Religion, Philosophy and Psychical Research,* London: Routledge and Kegan Paul 1953.

Broad, CD. Theoretical points arising: theories about collective and reciprocal hallucinations, In: *Lectures on Psychical Research,* London: Routledge and Kegan Paul; New York: Humanities 1962.

Broadhead, WE, et al. The epidemiologic evidence for a relationship between social support and health, *American J Epidemiology* 1983, 117, 521-537.

Bronowski, Jacob. *A Sense of the Future,* Cambridge: MIT Press 1977.

Bronson, Matthew. Healing voices of Brazil, *Association for the Anthropological Study of Consciousness Newsletter* 1985(a), 1(2), 3-5.

Bronson, Matthew. Brazilian spiritist healers, *Shaman's Drum* 1985(b), 3, 23- 28.

Brookes-Smith, Colin. Paranormal electrical conductance phenomena, *J the Society PsychicalResearch* 1975, 48, 73-86.

Brookes-Smith, Colin/ Hunt, DW. Some experiments in psychokinesis, *J the Society PsychicalResearch* 1970, 45, 265-280.

Brooks, Gwendolyn. *A Street in Bronzeville* 1945.

Broughton, RS. *Parapsychology: The Controversial Sci-ence,* New York: Ballantine 1991.

Brown, Ellen. *Forbidden Medicine,* Murrieta, CA: Third Millenium 1998.

Brown, JA. Relationships between phenomena of consciousness and interhemispheric brain-wave patterns during nonordinary states of consciousness, *Ph.D. dissertation*, San Francisco: Saybrook Institute 1986, 301.

Brown, Rosemary. *Unfinished Symphonies*, New York: William Morrow 1971.

Brown, Tom (As Told to William J. Watkins). *The Tracker: The True Story of Tom Brown, Jr.,* New York: Penguin 1979.

Brown, Tom. *Grandfather: A Native American's Lifelong Search for Truth and Harmony with Nature*, New York: Penguin 2001.

Browne, Thomas. *Christian Morals* 1716. (From Oxford 1998).

Brussat, Frederic/ Brussat, Mary Ann. *Spiritual Literacy: Reading the Sacred in Everyday Life*, NY: Touchstone/ Simon & Schuster 1998.

Bucke, Richard Maurice. *Cosmic Consciousness*, New York: Dutton 1923 (Orig. 1901).

Buddha. Attributed.

Budzynski, TH. Clinical applications of non-drug-induced states, In: Wollman, BB/ Ullman, M, eds. *Handbook of States of Consciousness*, New York: Van Nostrand Reinhold 1986.

Buhlman, William L. *The Secret of the Soul: Using Out-of-Body Experiences to Understand Our True Nature*, HarperSanFrancisco 2001.

Bunyard, P. *Gaia in Action: Science of the Living Earth*, Floris Books 1996.

Burbank, Luther with Hall, Wilbur, *The Harvest of the Years*, Boston and New York: Houghton Mifflin 1921.

Burkhardt, MA. Spirituality: An analysis of the concept, *Holistic Nursing Practice,* 1989, 33(3), 69-77.

Burkhardt, MA. Becoming and connecting: Elements of spirituality for women, *Holistic Nursing Practice* 1994, 8(4), 12-21.

Burkhardt, Margaret A. Reintegrating spirituality into healthcare, *Alternative Therapies* 1998, 4(2), 128-27.

Burns, P. *The experience of spirituality in the well adult: A phenomenological study*, Unpublished doctoral dis-sertation, Texas Women's University 1989.

Burr, Harold. *Blueprint for Immortality*, London: Neville Spearman 1972.

Butler, Samuel. *Notebooks* 1912.

Byrd, Randolph C. Positive therapeutic effects of intercessory prayer in a coronary care population, *Southern Medical J* 1988, 81(7), 826-29.

C

Cade, C. Maxwell/ Coxhead, N. *The Awakened Mind: Biofeedback and the Development of Higher States of Awareness*, New York: Delacorte Press/ Eleanor Friede 1978.

Callahan D. Death and the research imperative. *New England J Medicine* 2000, 342, 654-6.

Camp, PE. *Having faith: Experiencing coronary artery bypass grafting*, Unpublished doctoral dissertation, University of Alabama, Birmingham 1991.

Campbell, Joseph. *The Masks of God*, New York: Penguin 1978.

Campbell, Joseph. *This Business of the Gods*, Caledon East, Ontario, Canada: Windrose Films 1989.

Campbell, Joseph. *Thou Art That: Transforming Religious Metaphor*, CA: New World Library 2001.

Campbell, Joseph with Moyers, Bill. *The Power of Myth*, London: Doubleday/ Transworld 1989.

Campbell, Peter A/ McMahon, Edwin M. *Bio-Spirituality: Focusing as a Way to Grow* (2nd ed), Chicago, IL: Loyola 1997 (orig. 1985).

Camus, Albert. *The Artist and His Time* (Autobiography) www.azer.com/aiweb/categories/topics/Quotes/quote_camus.html (Accessed 12/14/05)

Canoe, Lorraine/ Porter, Tom. Sounding a basic call to consciousness, In: McFadden, p. 21.

Capon, Robert Farrar. *The Fingerprints of God: Tracking the Divine Suspect through a History of Images*, Grand Rapids, MI: William Eerdmans 2000.

Capra, Fritjof. *The Tao of Physics*, Boulder, CO: Shambala 1975.

Carey, Ken. *The Starseed Transmissions*, New York: HarperCollins 1991 (orig. 1982).

Carey, Ken. *Return of the Bird Tribes*, New York: Talman 1988.

Carey, Ken. *Starseed: The Third Millennium*, Harper SanFrancisco 1991.

Carington, Whately. The quantitative study of trance personalities, *Proceedings of the Society PsychicalResearch* 1935, 43, 319-361.

Carr, C. Death and near-death: A comparison of Tibetan and Euro-American experiences, *J Transpersonal Psychology* 1993, 25(1), 59-110.

Carroll, RL. Towards a new evolutionary synthesis, *Trends in Ecology and Evolution* 2000, 15, 27-32.

Carroll S. Spirituality and purpose in life in alcoholism recovery. J Studies Alcoholism 1993;54:297-301.

Fulton, Ruth Ann B. Spirituality and nursing education, In:

Carson, Rachel. *Silent Spring*, New York: Houghton Mifflin 2002 (orig. 1962).

Carter, Rita/ Frith, Christopher Donald. *Mapping the Mind*, University of CA Press 2000.

Cassileth, BR/ Lusk, EJ/ Strouse, TB/ Bodenheimer, BJ. Contemporary unorthodox treatment in cancer medicine: a study of patients, treatments, and practitioners. *Annals Internal Medicine* 1984, 101(1), 105-112.

Castaneda, Carlos. *Tales of Power*, New York: Simon & Schuster 1974. (Fictionalized stories apparently based on various true shamanic experiences.)

Catholic Conference. *Study Text II: Anointing and Pastoral Care of the Sick*, Washington, D.C. Publications Office, U.S. Catholic Conference, 1973 (quoted in MacNutt).

Cavallini, Giuliana. *Saint Martin de Porres*, Rockford, IL: Tan 1979.

Cavenar, JO/ Spaulding, J. Depressive disorders and religious conversions, *J Nervous and Mental Disease* 1977, 165, 209-212.

Cayce, Hugh Lynn. *Gifts of Healing*, Virginia Beach, VA: Association for Research & Enlightenment, n.d.

CBS. Survey cited at www.restministries.org/admin-media.htm (Accessed 6/20/04)

Cerminara, Gina. *Many Lives, Many Loves*, New York: New American Library 1974.

Chadha, NK/ Stevenson, Ian. Two correlates of violent death in cases of the reincarnation type, *J the Society PsychicalResearch* 1988, 55, 71-79.

Challoner, HK. *The Wheel of Rebirth*, Wheaton, IL: Quest/ Theosophical 1969.

Challoner, HK. *The Path of Healing*, Wheaton, IL: Quest/ Theosophical 1972.

Chalmers, David J. Moving forward on the problem of consciousness, *J Consciousness Studies* 1997, 4(1), 3-46. www.consc.net/papers/moving.html (Accessed 1/3/06)

Chamberlain, DB. Birth recall in hypnosis, *Birth Psychology Bulletin* 1981, 2(2), 14-18.

Chamberlain, DB. Consciousness at birth: The range of empirical evidence, In: Verny, TR, ed. *Pre- and Perinatal Psychology: An Introduction*, New York: Human Science 1987, 69-90.

Chamberlain, DB. *Babies Remember Birth: And Other Amazing Scientific Discoveries About the Mind and Personality of Your Newborn*, Los Angeles: Tarcher 1988a.

Chamberlain, DB. The mind of the newborn: Increasing evidence of competence, In: Fedor-Freybergh, P/ Vogel, MLV, eds. *Prenatal and Perinatal Psychology and Medicine: Encounter with the Unborn, A Comprehensive Survey of Research and Practice*, Park Ridge, NJ: Parthenon 1988b, 5-22.

Chapman, George. *Extraordinary Encounters*, Aylesbury, Bucks, England: Lang 1973.

Chapman, George (As told by Stemman, Roy). *Surgeon From Another World*, London: W. H. Allen 1978.

Chari, CTK. Paranormal cognition, survival and reincarnation, *J the American Society PsychicalResearch* 1962, 5, 158-183.

Chasin, Esther G. *Mitzvot as Spiritual Practices: A Jewish Guidebook for the Soul*, Northvale, NJ: Jason Aronson 1997.

Chatters, LM/ Levin, JS/ Taylor, RJ. Antecedents and dimensions of religious involvement among older Black adults, *J Gerontology: Social Sciences* 1992, 47, S269-278.

Cheek, David B. Prenatal and perinatal imprints: Apparent prenatal consciousness as revealed by hypnosis, *Pre- and Peri-Natal Psychology J* 1986, 1(2), 97-110, 302.

Cheek, David B. Are telepathy, clairvoyance and "hearing" possible in utero? Suggestive evidence as revealed during hypnotic age-regression studies of prenatal memory, *Pre- and Peri-Natal Psychology J* 1992, 7(2), 125-137, 302-303.

Chesi, Gert. *Faith Healers in the Philippines*, Austria: Perlinger 1981.

Chew, GF. 'Bootstrap:' A scientific idea? *Science* 1968, 161, 762-5.

Chibnall, JT/ Bennett, ML/ Videen, SD/ Duckro, PN/ Miller, DK. Identifying barriers to psychosocial spiritual care at the end of life: a physician group study, *American J Hospice & Palliative Care* 2004, 21(6), 419-26.

Chin AE/ Hedberg K/ Higginson GK/ Fleming DW. Legalized physician-assisted suicide in Oregon – the firstyear's experience. *New England J Medicine* 1999, 340, 577-83.

Chinese painter, 14th Century. Quoted in Matthiessen.

Chisholm, Judith. *EVP and Transcommunication Society for the UK and Ireland*, www.psychicworld.net/evp3.htm (Accessed 5/2/05)

Chisholm, Judith. *Voices from Paradise—How the dead speak to us*, Charlbury, UK: Jon Carpenter 2000. www.psychicworld.net/ (Accessed 5/2/05)

Chiu, L/ Emblen, JD/ Van Hofwegen, L/ Sawatzky, R/ Meyerhoff, H [University of British Columbia]. An integrative review of the concept of spirituality in the health sciences, *Western J Nursing Research* 2004, 26(4), 405-28.

Chopra, Deepak. *How to Know God*, NY: Harmony/ Random House 2000.

Chopra, Deepak. *The Spontaneous Fulfillment of Desire: Harnessing the Infinite Power of Coincidence*, New York: Harmony Books 2003.

Chordas, TJ/ Gross, SJ. Healing of memories: Psychotherapeutic ritual among Catholic Pentacostals, *J Pastoral Care* 1976, 30, 245-257.

Christie-Murray, D. *Reincarnation: Ancient Beliefs and Modern Evidence*, Garden City Park, NY: Avery 1988, 303.

Church, Dawson/ Sherr, Alan. *The Heart of the Healer*, New York: Aslan 1987.

Clampett, Frederick W. *Luther Burbank, "Our Beloved Infidel." His Religion of Humanity*, Westport, CT: Greenwood 1926.

Clark, Glenn. *The Soul's Sincere Desire*, Minneapolis, Minnesota: Macalester Park Publishing Company 1995(a).

Clark, Glenn. *Two or Three Gathered Together*, Minneapolis, Minnesota: Macalaster Park Publishing Company 1995(b).

Clarke, Isabel. Madness and mysticism: clarifying the mystery, *Network* 2000, 72, 18.

Clarke, Isabel. *Psychosis and Spirituality*, London/ Philadelphia: Whurr 2001.

Clements, WM, ed. *Religion, Aging and Health: A Global Perspective*, compiled by the World Health Organization, New York: Haworth 1989.

Coan, R.W. *Human Consciousness and Its Evolution – A Multidimensional View*, Westport, CT: Greenwood 1987.

Cockell, Jenny. *Yesterday's Children*, London: Piatkus 1993.

Cohen, Daniel. *The Mysteries of Reincarnation*, New York: Dodd, Mead & Co. 1975.

Cohen, Kenneth. *The Way of Qigong: The Art and Science of Chinese Energy Healing*, New York: Random House 1997.

Cohen, Kenneth. *Honoring the Medicine: Native American Healing*, New York: Ballantine 2003.

Cohen, Kenneth. Personal communication 2005.

Cole, KC. *The Hole in the Universe: How Scientists Peered Over the Edge of Emptiness and Found Everything*, Orlando, FL: Harcourt 2001.

Coles, Robert. *The Spiritual Life of Children*, Boston: Houghton Mifflin 1990.

Colgrove, Melba/ Bloomfield, Harold H/ McWilliams, Peter. *How To Survive the Loss of a Love*, New York: Bantam 1976.

Comstock, GW. Fatal arteriosclerotic heart disease, water hardness, and socio-economic characteristics, *American J Epidemiology* 1971, 94, 1-10.

Comstock, GW/ Partridge, KB. Church attendance and health, *J Chronic Diseases* 1972, 25, 665-672.

Comstock, GW/ Tonascia, JA. Education and mortality in Washington County, Maryland, *J Health and Social Behavior* 1977, 18, 54-61.

Conco, D. Christian patients' views of spiritual care, *Western J Nursing Research*, 1995, 17(3), 266-276.

Constantinides, P. Women heal women: spirit possession and sexual segregation in a muslim society, *Social Science and Medicine*, 1985, 21(6), 685-692.

Conway, Morris S. Evolution: bringing molecules into the fold, *Cell* 2000, 100, 1-11.

Conway, Morris S. Cambrian "explosion" of metazoans and molecular biology: would Darwin be satisfied? *International J Developmental Biology* 2003, 47(7-8), 505-515.

Coons, PM. Multiple personality: diagnostic considerations, *J Clinical Psychiatry* 1980, 41(10), 330-336.

Cooper, Rabbi David. *God is a Verb, Kabbalah and the Practice of Mystical Judaism.* New York: Riverhead Books 1997.

Cooper, Joan. *The Ancient Teaching of Yoga and the Spiritual Evolution of Man*, London: Research 1979.

Cortright, Brant. *Psychotherapy and Spirit; Theory and Practice in Transpersonal Psychotherapy.* State University of New York Press 1997.

Cowan, Eliot. *Plant Spirit Medicine: The Healing Power of Plants*, Orem, UT: Granite 1999.

Cox, William E. The influence of "applied psi" upon the sex of offspring, *J the Society PsychicalResearch* 1957, 39, 65-77.

Coxhead, Nona. *The Relevance of Bliss*, New York: St. Martin's 1986.

Crabtree, Adam. *Multiple Man: Exploration in Possession and Multiple Personality*, New York and London: Holt, Rinehart & Winston 1985.

Cramer, Marc. The rise and fall of the rope trick, *The Unexplained* 1981, 5(56), 1101-1105.

Crawford, WJ. *The Psychic Structure of the Goligher Circle*, New York: Dutton 1921.

Crick, Francis.*The Astonishing Hypothesis*, London/ New York: Simon & Schuster 1994.

Croke, Piers. A shower of roses, *The Unexplained* 1981, 3(36), 704-707.

Crookall, R. *Casebook of Astral Projection,* New York: University Books 1972.

Crookall, Robert. *The Supreme Adventure,* Cambridge: James Clarke 1974.

Crookes, William. Notes on seances with D. D. Homes, *Proceedings of the Society Psychical-Research,* 1889-1890, 6, 98.

Crookes, William. *Researches in the Phenomena of Spiritism,* W. London: The Psychic Bookshop 1926.

Crookshank, FG. *Diagnosis and Spiritual Healing,* London: Kegan Paul, 1927.

Curlin, Farr A, et al. Religious Characteristics of U.S. Physicians: A National Survey. *J General Internal Medicine* 2005, 20(7), 629.

D

Daaleman, TP/ Frey, BB. The spirituality index of well-being: a new instrument for health-related quality of-life research, *Annals of Family Medicine* 2004, 2(5), 499-503.

Daaleman, TP/ Nease, DE, Jr. Patient attitudes regarding physician inquiry into spiritual and religious issues, *J Family Practice* 1994, 39, 564-568.

Daaleman, TP et al. The spirituality index of well-being: development and testing of a new measure, *J Family Practice* 2002, 51(11), (36 refs).

Dalai Lama, His Holiness. *Ethics for the New Millennium,* New York: Riverhead Books, Penguin Putnam 1999, 22-23.

Daniel, Alma/ Wyllie, Timothy/ Ramer, Andrew. *Ask Your Angels: A practical guide to working with the messengers of Heaven to empower and enrich your life,* NY: Ballantine 1992.

Darrow, Clarence. Speech at the trial of Thomas Scopes, 15 July 1925, 41/ 21.

Das, Lama Surya. *Letting Go of the Person You Used to Be: Lessons on Loss, Change, and Spiritual Transforma-tion,* Lama Surya Das, Broadway 2003.

Dass, Ram, In: Elliott, William. *Tying Rocks to Clouds,* New York: Image/ Doubleday 1996, 61-75.

Dass, Ram/ Gorman, Paul. *How Can I Help? Stories and Reflections on Service,* New York: Knopf/ London: Rider 1985.

David-Neel, Alexandra. *Magic and Mystery in Tibet,* New York: Viking/ Penguin 1956.

David-Neel, Alexandra. Psychic phenomena in Tibet, *Psychic,* Sep Oct 1971, 3(2), 18-20.

Davidson, Gustav. *Dictionary of Angels,* New York: Free Press/ Macmillan 1967 (bibliography 25 pp).

Davies, Paul. *The Mind of God: The Scientific Basis for a Rational World,* New York: Simon and Schuster.

Davis, Avram. *The Way of Flame. A Guide to the Forgotten Mystical Tradition of Jewish Meditation.* San Francisco: Harper, 1996.

Davis, Philip J/ Park, David. *No Way: The Nature of the Impossible,* New York: W. H. Freeman 1987.

Davis, Thomas N III. Can prayer facilitate healing and growth? *Southern Medical J* 1986, 79(6), 733-735.

Dawkins, Richard. *The Blind Watchmaker,* London: Longmans 1986.

Dawkins, Richard. *River Out of Eden: A Darwinian View of Life,* New York: Perseus Books 1995.

de Broglie, Louis. *Matter and Light: The New Physics,* Translated by W. H. Johnston, New York: W. W. Norton 1939 (from Jahn/ Dunne 1983).

De nat. rerum, IV, 833; cf. 822-56, cited in Wikipedia www.en.wikipedia.org/wiki/Teleology (Accessed 1/20/06)

De partib., animal., IV, xii, 694b; 13, cited in Wikipedia www.en.wikipedia.org/wiki/Teleology (Accessed 1/20/06)

Dearmer, Perey. *Body and Soul,* London: Pitman 1912.

Delaney. The Spirituality Scale: development and psychometric testing of a holistic instrument, *J Holist Nurs.* 2005, 23, 145-167.

Deloria, Vine Jr. Attributed.

Denham, Charles. Harry Edward's 40 years of healing, In: Fate Magazine (Orig. January 1973), *Exploring the Healing Miracle,* Highland Park, IL: Clark 1983.

Dennett, Daniel C. *Consciousness Explained,* Boston: Little Brown 1991, 304.

Denton, M. *Evolution: a theory in crisis,* London: Adler & Adler 1986.

DeRopp, Robert. *Drugs and the Mind,* New York: Dell 1976.

Descartes, René. *Meditations,* New York: Bobbs-Merrill 1960.

Desmond, Shaw. *Healing: Psychic and Divine,* London: Rider 1956.

Desoille, Robert. *The Directed Daydream,* New York: Psychosynthesis Research Foundation 1966. Translated from French original *Réveil Dirigé.*

Dethlefsen, Thorwald. *Voices From Other Lives: Reincarnation as a Source of Healing,* New York: M. Evans/ Lippincott 1977.

Dethlefsen, Thorwald/ Dahlke, Rudiger. *The Healing Power of Illness: The Meaning of Symptoms and How to Interpret Them.,* Longmead, UK: Element 1990. Orig. German 1983, Trans. Peter Lerresurier.

Deverell, Doré. *Light Beyond the Darkness,* Edinburgh, Scotland: Clairview 2000.

Devers, Edie. *Goodbye Again: Experiences with Departed Loved Ones,* Kansas City, MO: Andrew and McMeel 1997.

Devine, Jennifer A, et al. Fisheries: Deep-sea fishes qualify as endangered, *Nature* 2006, 439, 29-29

Devinsky, O, et al. Autoscopic phenomena with seizures, *Archives of Neurology* 1989, 46, 1080-1088 (from Morse 1998).

Dewhurst, K/ Beard, A.W. Sudden religious conversions in temporal lobe epilepsy, *British J Psychiatry* 1970, 117, 487-507 (from Morse 1998).

Diamond, Irene/ Ornstein, Gloria Feman, eds. *Reweaving the World: The Emergence of Ecofeminism,* San Francisco: Sierra Club 1990.

DiCarlo, Russell E. *Towards a New World View: Conversations at the Leading Edge,* Erie, PA: Epic Publishing 1996.

Dickinson, Emily. Quote at www.pprsites.tripod.com/ pprquotes/PPR-Quotes-Ecstasy.htm (Accessed 9/8/03).

Dietz, PA. (Stigmatization produced by Paul Diebel), *Tidschrift voor Parapsychologie,* 1930/ 31, 3, 145-155 (Dutch). (From abstract in *Parapsychology Abstracts International* 1985, 3(2), No. 01378).

Dillion, Louise Hahn. Experience and insights in mystical theology, *Network* 2000, 72, 51.

Dingwall, Eric John. *Abnormal Hypnotic Phenomena: A Survey of 19th Century Cases,* London: Churchill 1968.

Dingwall, Eric John. The end of a legend: a note on the magical flight, *Parapsychology Review* 1974, 5(2), 1-3.

DiOrio, RA with Gropman, D. *The Man Beneath the Gift: The Story of My Life,* New York: William Morrow 1980.

Don, Norman S/ Moura, Gilda. Trance surgery in Brazil, *Alternative Therapies* 2000, 6(4), 39-48.

Doniger, Simon, ed. *Healing: Human and Divine,* New York: Association Press 1957.

Dooley, Anne. *Every Wall a Door: Exploring Psychic Surgery and Healing,* New York: Dutton 1974. Copyright (c) by Anne Dooley. Reprinted by permission of the publisher, E.P. Dutton, a division of New American Library.

Dossey, Larry. *Space, Time and Medicine,* Boulder, CO: Shambala 1982.

Dossey, Larry. *Beyond Illness: Discovering the Experience of Health,* Boulder and London: Shambala 1984.

Dossey, Larry. *Recovering the Soul: A Scientific and Spiritual Search,* New York/ London: Bantam 1989.

Dossey, Larry. *Meaning and Medicine: A Doctor's Tales of Breakthrough and Healing,* New York: Bantam 1991.

Dossey, Larry. *Healing Words: The Power of Prayer and the Practice of Medicine,* New York: HarperSanFrancisco 1993.

Dossey, Larry. *Prayer is Good Medicine,* HarperSanFrancisco 1996.

Dossey, Larry. Canceled funerals: A look at miracle cures, *Alternative Therapies* 1998a, 4(2), 10-18; 116-119 (34 refs).

Dossey, Larry. The Right Man syndrome: skepticism and alternative medicine, *Alternative Therapies* 1998b, 4(3), 10-18; 116-119 (91 refs).

Dossey, Larry. Deliberately caused bodily damage, *Alternative Therapies* 1998c, (5), 11-16; 103-111.

Dossey, Larry. *Be Careful What You Pray For, You Just Might Get It,* HarperSanFrancisco 1998d.

Dossey, Larry. *Reinventing Medicine Beyond Mind-Body to a New Era of Healing,* San Francisco: Harper 1999.

Dossey, Larry. Spirituality, science and the medical arts, *Subtle Energies* 2001, 12(1), 1-16.

Dowling, St. John. Lourdes cures and their medical assessment, *J the Royal Society of Medicine* 1984, 77, 634-638.

Driesch, Hans. *Science and Philosophy of Organisms,* London: Black 1908.

Dreyer, Peter, *A Gardner Touched with Genius: The Life of Luther Burbank,* New York: Coward, McCann & Geoghegan 1975.

Dupré, Louis K. *Symbols of the Sacred,* Grand Rapids, MI: William Eerdmans 2000.

Durkheim, E. *The Elementary Forms of Religious Life,* London: Allen & Unwin 1915.

Durville, H. Experimental researches with phantoms of the living, *Annals of Psychical Science* 1908, 7, 464-470.

Dysinger, PW, et al. Pulmonary emphysema in a nonsmoking population, *Diseases of the Chest* 1963, 43, 17-26.

Dyson, J/ Cobb, M/ Forman, B. The meaning of spirituality: a literature review, *J Adv Nursing* 1997, 26, 1183-8.

The Doctor-Healer Network Newsletter, Issue No. 4, Winter 1992-3 (Articles on dealing with death and bereavement, including 'healing unto death'.)

E

Eadie, Betty J. *Embraced by the Light* Piatkus 1993

Early, Loretta F/ Lifschutz, Joseph E. A Case of Stigmata, *Archives of General Psychiatry* 1974, 30, 197-202.

Eaton, Evelyn. *I Send a Voice*, London and Wheaton, IL: Quest/ Theosophical 1978.

Eccles, JC. *Evolutions of the Brain: Creation of the Self*, London: Routledge 1989, 304.

Eddington, Arthur. *Space, Time and Gravitation*, Cambridge: University Press 1978 (from Jahn/ Dunne).

Eden, Donna/ Feinstein, David/ Garten, Brooks/ Myss, Carolyn. *Energy Medicine*, New York: Tarcher 1999.

Eden, M. The inadequacies of neo-Darwinian evolution as a scientific theory, In: Morehead, PS/ Kaplan, MM, eds. *Mathematical Challenges to the Darwinian Interpretation of Evolution,* Wistar Institute Symposium Monograph, New York: Allen R. Liss 1967, 5-12.

Edge, Hoyt L, et al. *Foundations of Parapsychology: Exploring the Boundaries of Human Capability,* Boston & London: Routledge and Kegan Paul 1986.

Edwards, Harry. *The Science of Spirit Healing*, London: Rider, Approx. 1945 (No copyright date given).

Edwards, Harry. *The Evidence for Spirit Healing*, London: Spiritualist 1953.

Edwards, Harry. *Thirty Years a Spiritual Healer*, London: Herbert Jenkins, 1968.

Egbert, N, et al. A review and application of social scientific measures of religiosity and spirituality: assessing a missing component in health communication research, *Health Communication* 2004, 16(1), 7-27.

Ehman, J et al. Do patients want physicians to inquire about their spiritual or religious beliefs if they become gravely ill? *Arch Intern Med* 1999, 159, 1803-1806.

Eick, JJ, et al. Incidental roentgenographic demonstration of multiple metallic foreign bodies with an unusual etiology, *J Louisiana State Medical Society* 1982, 134, 10-11.

Einstein, Albert. *Science, Philosophy and Religion: a Symposium* 1941.

Einstein, Albert. In: Schilpp, PA, ed. *Albert Einstein: Philosopher-Scientist*, Evanston, IL: Library of Living Philosophers/ Menasha, WI: George Banta 1949.

Einstein, Albert, In: Barnett, L. *The Universe and Dr. Einstein* (rev. ed.) New York: William Morrow/ Bantam 1979.

Einstein, Albert. "Strange is our situation..." (undated) Cited at www.nicklewis.smartcampaigns.com/taxonomy _ menu/6/61 (Accessed 1/4/06)

Einstein, Albert. *Out of My Later Years*, rev. reprint ed., Secaucus, NJ: Citadel 1956 (Quoted in Jahn and Dunne).

Eisenbud, Jule. *The World of Ted Serios*, New York; Pocket Books 1967.

Eisenbud, Jule. *Parapsychology and the Unconscious*, Berkeley, CA: North Atlantic Books 1983.

Eliade, Mircea. *Shamanism: Archaic Techniques of Ecstacy,* Trans: W. Trask, London: Routledge and Kegan Paul 1970.

Eliot, TS. *Selected Essays*, 1927.

Elkins, DN. Psychotherapy and spirituality: Toward a theory of the soul, *J Humanistic Psychology*, 1995, 35(2), 78-96.

Elkins, DN/ Hedstrom, LJ/ Hughes, LL/ Leaf, JA/ Saunders, C. Towards a humanistic-phenomenological spirituality: Definition, description, and measurement, *J Humanistic Psychology*, 1988, 28(4), 5-18.

Elliott, G. Maurice. Spiritual healing, *Parapsychology Foundation Newsletter* 1960 (Jul-Aug), 4-6.

Ellis, Albert. Psychotherapy and atheistic values, *J Consulting and Clinical Psychology* 1980, 48, 635.

Ellis, David J. *The Mediumship of the Tape Recorder*, Pulborough, W. Sussex 1978.

Ellis, MR, et al. Addressing spiritual concerns of patients: family physicians' attitudes and practices, *J Family Practice* 1999, 48, 105-109.

Ellison, AJ. A romantic fiction, *The Unexplained*, 1981, 5(52), 1021-1025.

Emblen, JD. Religion and spiritually defined according to current use in nursing literature, *J Professional Nursing* 1992, 8, 41-47.

Emerson, Ralph Waldo. Circles, In: *Essays* 1841a.

Emerson, Ralph Waldo. The over-soul, in *Essays* 1841b, 158/ 8

Emmons Robert A. *The Psychology of Ultimate Concerns: Motivation and Spirituality in Personality*, New York: Guilford Press 2003.

Emmons, RA, et al. Assessing spirituality through personal goals: Implications for research on religion and subjective well-being. *Social Indicators Research* 1998, 45, 391-422.

Emmons, RA/ McCullough, ME. Counting blessings versus burdens: An experimental investigation of gratitude and subjective well-being in daily life. *J Personality and Social Psychology* 2003, 84(2), 377-389.

Emoto, Masaru. *Messages from Water*, Volume 1 (Half-facing pages in Japanese) www.cocreah.com/messages_from_water%20article.htm

Engelhardt, H, et al. *Scientific Controversies - Case Studies in the Resolution and Closure of Disputes in Science and Technology*, Cambridge, England: Cambridge University 1987.

English-Lueck, JA. *Health in the New Age: A Study in California Holistic Practices*, Albuquerque, NM: University of New Mexico 1990.

Enstrom, JE. Cancer mortality among Mormons, *Cancer* 1975, 36, 825-841.

Erikson, Erik. *Childhood and Society*, New York: Norton 1963.

Erwin, DH. Macroevolution is more than repeated rounds of microevolution, *Evolution & Development* 2000, 2, 78-84.

Estes, J Worth. *The Medical Skills of Ancient Egypt* Canton, MA: Science History Publications/ USA.

Estes, SW. *Voices of Eternity*, New York: Ballantine/ Fawcett Gold Medal 1988.

Evans, Donald. *Spirituality and Human Nature*, Albany, NY: SUNY 1993.

Evans, Hilary. *Spontaneous sightings of seemingly autonomous entities: A comparative study in the light of experimental and contrived entity fabrications*, Presentation at the 25th annual convention of the Parapsychological Association/ 100th convention of the Society PsychicalResearch at Cambridge 1982.

Evans, Hilary. *Visions, Apparitions, Alien Visitors: A Comparative Study of the Entity Enigma*, Wellingborough, Northamptonshire, England: Aquarian 1986.

Evans-Wentz, WY. *The Tibetan Book of the Dead, Third Edition*, London: Oxford University Press 1972.

Evans-Wentz, WY. *The Fairy-Faith in Celtic Countries*, Gerards Cross: Colin Smythe 1977.

F

Faivre, Antoine/ Needleman, Jacob, eds. *Modern Esoteric Spirituality*, London: SCM 1993.

Falcon, Rabbi Theodore. Excerpt from *High Holidays: Prayers and Meditations* 2005.

Favazza, Armando R. Modern Christian healing of mental illness, *American J Psychiatry* 1982, 139(6), 728-735.

Fecher, CJ. History of health studies, In Nix, JT/ Fecher, CJ, eds. *Stamina for the Apostolate*, Washington, DC: Center for Applied Research in the Apostolate 1970, 3-14.

Feilding, Everard. *Sittings With Usapia Palladino*, New Hyde Park, New York: University Books 1963.

Feinstein, David/ Krippner, Stanley. *The Mythic Path: Discovering the Guiding Stories of Your Past - Creating a Vision for Your Future*, New York: Tarcher/ Putnam 1997.

Feldman, Christina/ Kornfield, Jack. *Stories of the Spirit, Stories of the Heart: Parables of the S;piritual Path from Around the World*, HarperSnaFrancisco 1991.

Feldman, David Henry with Goldsmith, Lynn. *Child Prodigies and the Development of Human Potential*, New York: Basic Books 1986.

Felser, Joseph. *The Way Back to Paradise: Restoring the Balance between Magic and Reason*, Charlottesville, VA: Hampton Roads 2005.

Fenwick P. Near death experiences in cardiac arrest: visions of a dying brain or visions of a new science of consciousness. *Resuscitation* 2002, 52, 5-11.

Ferguson, Marilyn. *The Aquarian Conspiracy: Personal and Social Transformation in the 1980's*, Los Angeles, CA: J.P. Tarcher/ Houghton Mifflin 1976.

Ferrer, Jorge N. *Revisioning Transpersonal Theory: A Participatory Vision of Human Spirituality*, Albany, New York: State University of New York Press 2002.

Ferrini, Paul. *Love Without Conditions: Reflections of the Christ Mind*, South Deerfield, MA: Heartways 1994.

Field, Marilyn J/ Cassel, Christine K, eds. *Approaching Death: Improving Care at the End of*

Life, (Institute of Medicine Publication) Washington, DC: National Academy 1997.

Fields, Rick. *Chop Wood, Carry Water*, Los Angeles, CA: Jeremy Tarcher 1984.

Finch, WJ "Bill." *Pendulum and Possession*, Sedona, AZ: Esoteric Publications 1975.

Findlay, Arthur. *On the Edge of the Etheric— The Afterlife Scientifically Explained*, London: Psychic Press Limited 1970 (Orig. 1931).

Finkler, Kaja. *Spiritualist Healers in Mexico*, South Hadley, MA: Bergin and Garvey 1985.

Finucane, Ronald C. Faith healing in medieval Europe: miracles at saints' shrines, *Psychiatry* 1973, 36(3), 341-346.

Fiore, Edith. *You Have Been Here Before*, New York: Ballantine 1978.

Fiore, Edith. *The Unquiet Dead: a Psychologist Treats Spirit Possession*, New York: Ballantine Books 1995.

Fiori, KL, et al. Spiritual turning points and perceived control over the life course, *International J Aging & Human Development* 2004, 59(4), 391-420.

Firman, John/ Gila, Ann. *The Primal Wound; A Transpersonal View of Trauma, Addiction and Growth*, State University of New York 1997.

Fitchett, G, et al. The religious needs and resources of psychiatric inpatients. *J Nerv Ment Dis* 1997, 185, 320-326.

Fitchett, G, et al. Religious struggle: prevalence correlates and mental health risks in diabetic, congestive heart failure, and oncology patients, *International J Psychiatry & Medicine* 2004, 34(2), 179-96.

Flammonde, Paris. *The Mystic Healers*, New York: Stein & Day 1975.

Flynn, Charles P. *After the Beyond*, Englewood Cliffs, NJ: Prentice-Hall 1986.

Fodor, Nandor. *On the Trail of the Poltergeist*, New York: Ciltadel Press 1958.

Fodor, Nandor. *Encyclopedia of Psychic Science*, USA: University Books, Inc. 1966 (large no. of people catalogued).

Fogg, SL, et al. An analysis of referrals to chaplains in a community hospital in New York over a seven year period, *The J Pastoral Care & Counseling*: *JPCC* 2004, 58(3), 225-35.

Folz, Joe. *Psychic Healers of the Philippines*, Logos, NJ: Bridge 1981.

Foos-Graber, Anja. *Deathing: An Intelligent Alternative for the Final Moments of Life*, York Beach, ME: Nicholas Hays 1989.

Ford, Debbie. *The Dark Side of the Light Chasers: Reclaiming Your Power, Creativity, Brilliance, and Dreams*, NY: Riverhead 1998.

Ford, Henry. *Observer* (UK) 16 March 1930.

Forman, Joan. *The Mask of Time*, London: Corgi 1981(a).

Forman, Joan. When time slips, *The Unexplained* 1981(b), 3(33), 646-649; 700.

Forman, Joan. Leaps into the future, *The Unexplained* 1981(c), 3(35), 699-700.

Forman, Joan. Time out of mind, *The Unexplained* 1981(d), 4(38), 756-760.

Forman, Joan. Future shock, *The Unexplained* 1982(a), 9(102), 2026-2029.

Forman, Joan. This is how it will be, *The Unexplained* 1982(b), 9(103), 2047-2049.

Forman, Joan. Ghoules of tomorrow, *The Unexplained* 1983, 11(127), 2535-2537.

Forth, Sarah. Healing the earth as we heal ourselves, *Doctor-Healer Network Newsletter* Winter 1993-4, No. 7, 18-20.

Fosar, Grazyna/ Bludorf, Franz. *The Biological Chip in our Cells: Revolutionary results of modern genetics,* www.fosar-bludorf.com/index_eng.htm (search archives for "The Biological Chip in our Cells").

Foster, Richard J. *Coming Home: An Invitation to Prayer*, Bloomington MN: Garborg's Heart 'n Home 1993.

Foundation for Inner Peace. *A Course in Miracles*, London and New York: Arkana 1985.

Fowler, James W. *States of Faith: The Psychology of Human Development and the Quest for Meaning*, New York: HarperSanFrancisco 1982.

Fox, Matthew. Quote from Fox/ Sheldrake, p. 134.

Fox, Matthew/ Sheldrake, Rupert. *The Physics of Angels: Exploring the Realm where Science and Spirit Meet*, HarperSanFrancisco 1996.

Fox, Oliver. *Astral Projections*, Hyde Park, NY: University Books 1962. (Cf. Original article in the *Occult Review* 1920.)

Frank, Jerome. *Persuasion and Healing*, New York: Schocken 1961.

Frankl, Viktor E. *Man's Search for Meaning*, London: Hodder Stoughton 1964.

Franklin, Benjamin. "Work as though..." Attributed.

Frazer, Sir James George. *The Golden Bough*. New York: MacMillan 1960.

Friedlander, Y/ Kark, JD. Familial aggregation of blood pressure in a Jewish population sample in Jerusalem among ethnic and religious groupings, *Sociology and Biology* 1984, 31, 75-90.

Friedman, HL. The Self-Expansiveness Level Form: A conceptualization and measurement of a transpersonal construct. *J Transpersonal Psychology* 1983, 15(1), 37-50.

Frost, Gavin/ Frost, Yvonne. *Astral Travel*, York Beach, ME: Samuel Weiser 1982.

Frye, Mary Elizabeth. 1932 www.eir.library.utoronto.ca/rpo/display/poem26 70.html (Accessed 1/12/05)

Fukurai, T. *Edinburgh, Scotland: Clairvoyance and Thoughtography*, New York: Arno 1975. (Orig. London: Rider 1931)

Fukuyama, Y. The major dimensions of church membership, *Review of Religious Research* 1961, 2, 154-161. (From Williams 1994).

Fuller, JG. *The Ghost of 29 Megacycles*, London: Souvenir 1985/ New York: Signet 1986.

Fuller, John G. *Arigo: Surgeon of the Rusty Knife*, New York: Simon and Schuster 1975 (Copyright 1974 John G. Fuller; Reprinted by permission of Harper & Row, Publishers, Inc).

Fuller, John G. *The Ghost of Flight 401*, Berkley, CA: Berkley Publishing 1978.

G

Gabbard, Glen O. *With the Eyes of the Mind*, New York: Praeger 1984.

Gabriel, M/ Gabriel, M. *Voices from the Womb*, Lower Lake, CA: Aslan 1992.

Galapagos, Barnabus. 1999-2002, The Flying Turtle Company, LLC. (7/25/03) www.ftexploring.com/askdrg/askdrgalapagos.html

Galbraith, Jean. Spontaneous rising of kundalini energy: pesudo-schizophrenia or spiritual disease? *Network: The Scientific and Medical Network Review* (UK) 1998, 67, 29.

Galbraith, Jean. Is Spiritual experience up spine always a benign process? Can it teach us anything new about spiritual pathways? *Network: The Scientific and Medical Network Review* (UK) December 1999, 71.

Galbraith, Jean. *Erratum* for Gabraith 1999, *Network: The Scientific and Medical Network Review* (UK) 2000, 72, 29 (corrections in table showing results of survey).

Gallup G. *Religion in America: 1990*, Princeton, NJ: Princeton Religious Research Center 1990.

Gallup, G/ Gallup, A. Church attendance, membership still important in US, poll says, *Houston Post* December 18, 1988, A-30.

Gallup, George Jr. with Proctor, William. *Adventures in Immortality: A Look Beyond the Threshold of Death*, New York: McGraw-Hill 1982.

Gallup Organization. Gallup social and economic indicators: religion; 1939-1999. (Accessed 8/30/00) www.gallup.com/poll/indicators/indreligion.asp

Gardner, JW/ Lyon, JL. Cancer in Utah Mormon women by church activity level, *American J Epidemiology* 1982(a), 116, 258-265.

Gardner, JW/ Lyon, JL. Cancer in Utah Mormon men by lay priesthood level, *American J Epidemiology* 1982(b), 116, 258-265.

Gardner, Nancy/ Gardner, Esmond. *Five Great Healers Speak Here*, Wheaton, IL: Quest/ Theosophical 1982.

Gardner, Rex. *Healing Miracles: A Doctor Investigates*, London: Darton, Longman and Todd 1986.

Garner, Jim. Spontaneous regressions: scientific documentation as a basis for the declaration of miracles, *Canadian Medical Association J* 1974, 111, 1254-1264.

Gauld, Alan. ESP and attempts to explain it, In: Thakur, S, ed. *Philosophy and Psychical Research*, London: Allen and Unwin 1976, 17-46.

Gauld, Alan. Discarnate survival, In: Wolman, Benjamin B, ed. *Handbook of Parapsychology*, New York: Van Nostrand Reinhold 1977.

Gauld, Alan. *Mediumship and Survival: A Century of Investigation* London: Heinemann 1982.

Gaynor, Steven. *From Physician to Healer: A doctor's encounters with spiritual healing*, Lake Worth, FL: Center for Light 2005.

Geisler, Patrick V. Batcheldorian psychodynamics in the Umbanda ritual trance consultation, Part I, *Parapsychology Review* 1984, 15(6), 5-9.

Geisler, Patrick V. Batcheldorian psychodynamics in the Umbanda ritual trance consultation, Part II, *Parapsychology Review*, 1985(a), 16(1), 11-14.

Geisler, Patrick V. Parapsychological anthropology II: a multi-method study of psi and psi-related processes in the Umbanda ritual trance consultation, *J the American Society Psychical-Research*, 1985(b), 79(2), 113-166.

Gendlin, Eugene T. *Focusing*, New York: Bantam 1981.

Gershom, Yonassan, *Beyond the Ashes*, Virginia Beach, VA 1992.

Gershom, Yonassan. *From Ashes to Healing*, Virginia Beach, VA 1996.

Gersten Dennis. *Are You Getting Enlightened or Losing Your Mind? A Spiritual Program for Mental Fitness*, New York: Random House 1997.

Gettings, Fred. *Ghosts in Photographs*, New York: Harmony 1978.

Gevitz, Norman, ed. *Other Healers: Unorthodox Medicine in America*, Baltimore: Johns Hopkins University 1988.

Gibran, Khalil. *The Prophet*, New York: Knopf 1923.

Gibran, Khalil. *Sand and Foam*, New York: Knopf 1926.

Gibson, Arvin. *Glimpses of Eternity: NDE*, Bountiful, UT: Horizon 1992.

Giel, R.; Gezahegn, Y/ van Luijk, JN. Faith healing and spirit possession in Ghion, Ethiopia, *Social Science and Medicine* 1968, 2(1), 63-76.

Gilbert, SF/ Opitz, JM/ Raff, RA. Resynthesizing evolu-tionary and developmental biology, *Developmental Biology* 1996, 173, 357-372.

Gingrich, Owen. Let there be light: modern cosmogony and Biblical creation, In: Frye, Roland Mushat, ed. *Is God a Creationist?* New York: Charles Scribner's Sons 1983, 132-133.

Giovetti, Paola. *Angels: The Role of Celestial Guardians and Beings of Light*, York Beach, ME: Samuel Weiser 1993.

Gleick, James. *Chaos: Making a New Science*, New York: Viking/ Penguin 1987.

Glenn, Elizabeth F. *Shamanism and Healing: a Phenomenological Study of Soul Retrieval* (Alternative Medicine), The Fielding Institute 1995.

Global Consciousness Project
www.noosphere.princeton.edu (Accessed 1/16/06)

Gloor, P, et al. The role of the limbic system in experimental phenomena of temporal lobe epilepsy, *Annals of Neurology* 1982, 23, 129-144 (from Morse 1998).

Goddard, Henry H. The effects of mind on body as evidenced by faith cures, *American J Psychology* 1899, 10, 431-502.

Godwin, Malcolm. *Angels: An Endangered Species*, New York: Simon & Schuster 1990/ London: Boxtree 1993.

Goethe, Johann Wolfgang von. The Earth Spirit, *anima mundi*, in Faust 1832 (Translation: Dennis Stillings).

Goldberg, B. *Past Lives, Future Lives: Accounts of Regressions and Progressions Through Hypnosis*, Van Nuys CA: Newcastle 1982.

Goldsmith, Joel S. *The Art of Spiritual Healing*, New York: Harper and Row 1959.

Goldsmith, Malcolmm. *Knowing Me Knowing God: Exploring Your Spirituality With Myers-Briggs*, Abingdon 1997.

Goleman, Daniel. *The Meditative Mind - The Varieties of Meditative Experience*, Tarcher 1988.

Goleman, Daniel. *Destructive Emotions: A Scientific Dialogue with the Dalai Lama*, New York: Bantam 2003.

Goleman, Daniel. *Healing Emotions: Conversations with the Dalai Lama on Mindfulness, Emotions, and Health*, Boulder, CO: Shambhala 2003.

Goleman, Daniel/ Smith, Huston/ Dass, Ram. Truth and transformation in psychological and spiritual paths, *J Transpersonal Psychology* 1985, 17(2), 183-214.

Gomes, David Frank. Attributed.

Goodman, Felicitas. Body posture and the religious altered state of consciousness: an experimental investigation, *J Humanistic Psychology* 1986, 26(3), 81-118.

Goodman, Felicitas. *Ecstasy, Ritual, and Alternate Reality: Religion in a Pluralistic World*, Indiana University 1992. (See also Gore/ Goodman)

Goodman, Felicitas/ Nauwald, Nana. *Ecstatic Trance: New Ritual Body Postures*, Binkey Kok; Workbook edition 2003.

Goodman, Frederick. Unexpected developments, *The Unexplained* 1982(a), 8(95), 1881-1885.

Goodman, Frederick. An enterprising spirit, *The Unexplained* 1982(b), 9(97), 1930-1933.

Goodrich, Joyce. *Psychic Healing - A Pilot Study*. Doctoral dissertation, Graduate School, Yellow Springs, Ohio 1974.

Goodrich, Joyce. Studies in paranormal healing, *New Horizons* 1976, 2, 21-24.

Goodrich, Joyce. The psychic healing training and research project, In: Fosshage, James L/ Olsen, Paul, *Healing: Implications for Psychotherapy*, New York: Human Sciences Press 1978, 84-110.

Goodwin, BC. *How the Leopard Changed Its Spots: The Evolution of Complexity*, New York: Scribner's 1995.

Gordon, Sherman. *Commencement Address*, California School of Professional Psychology, 1986.

Gordon, Sol. *When Living Hurts*, New York: Union of American Hebrew Congregations 1985.

Gore, Belinda/ Goodman, Felicitas. Ecstatic Body Postures: Alternate Reality (Workbook edition), Bear & Co 1995. (See also Goodman)

Gorsuch, RL. Measurement: the boon and bane of investigating religion, *American Psychological* 1984, 39, 228-236.

Gorsuch RL. Religious aspects of substance abuse and recovery. Journal of Social Issues. 1995, 5, 65-83.

Goss, Michael. *Poltergeists: An Annotated Bibliography of Works in English, circa 1880-1975*, Metuchen, NJ and London: Scarecrow 1979.

Goswami, Amit. *The Concepts of Physics*, Heath 1979.

Goswami Amit. *The Self-Aware Universe: How Conscious-ness Creates the Material World*, New York: Tarcher 1995.

Gould, A/ Cornell, AD. *Poltergeist*, London: Routledge and Kagen Paul 1979.

Gould, Stephen Jay, *The Panda's Thumb: More Reflections in Natural History*, New York/ London: W. W. Norton 1980.

Govinda, Lama Angarika. *The Way of the White Clouds*, Boulder, CO: Shambhala 1971.

Govinda, Lama Angarika. *Foundations of Tibetan Mysticism*, New York: Weiser 1974.

Grad, Bernard. A telekinetic effect on plant growth I. *International J Parapsychology* 1963, 5(2), 117-134.

Grad, Bernard. A telekinetic effect on plant growth II. Experiments Involving Treatment of Saline in Stoppered Bottles, *International J Parapsychology* 1964(a), 6, 473-498.

Grad, Bernard. A telekinetic effect on plant growth III. Stimulating and inhibiting effects, *Research Brief Presented to the Seventh Annual Convention of the Parapsychological Association, Oxford University*, Oxford, England Sep 1964(b).

Grad, Bernard R. Some biological effects of laying-on of hands: a review of experiments with animals and plants, *J the American Society PsychicalResearch* 1965(a), 59, 95-127 (Reproduced in: Schmeidler, Gertrude, ed. *Parapsychology: Its Relation to Physics, Biology, Psychology and Psychiatry*, Metuchen, NJ: Scarecrow 1976).

Granstrom, S. Spiritual care for oncology patients, *Topics in Clinical Nursing,* 1985, 7(1), 39-45.

Grauds, Connie. *Jungle Medicine*, San Rafael, CA: Center for Spirited Medicine.

Graves, Charles. *The Legend of Linda Martel*, London: Icon 1968.

Gray, Isa. *From Materialization to Healing: Evidence of Both*, New York: Regency 1972.

Gray, Margot. *Return from Death*, London: Arkana 1985.

Greaves, Helen. *Testimony of Light*, Suffolk, England: Neville Spearman 1980.

Greber, Johannes. *Communications with the Spirit World*, Teaneck, NJ: Johannes Greber Memorial Foundation 1933.

Green, Celia. *Lucid Dreams,* Oxford, UK: Institute for Psychical Research 1968.

Green, Celia. *Out of the body experiences*, New York: Ballantine 1973.

Green, Elmer. Biofeedback training and yoga: Imagery and healing, *Conference on Psychic Healing and Self Healing Sponsored by the Association for Humanistic Psychology*, May 1972.

Green, Elmer E. Biofeedback, consciousness and human potential, *Perkins J*, 1986, 39, 22-31.

Green, Elmer. *The Ozawkie Book of the Dead: Alzheimer's isn't what you think it is!* Los Angeles: Philosophical Research Society 2001, Parts 1, 2, 3.

Green, Elmer/ Green, Alyce. Biofeedback and transformation, *American Theosophist* 1984, 72, 142-152.

Green, William Michael. *The Therapeutic Effects of Distant Intercessory Prayer and Patients' Enhanced Positive Expectations on Recovery Rates and Anxiety Levels of Hospitalized Neurosurgical Pituitary Patients: A Double-blind Study,* Doctoral dissertation, California Institute of Integral Studies, San Francisco, 1993.

Greenbaum, Avraham. *The Wings of the Sun*, New York/ Jerusalem: Breslav Research Institute 1995.

Greene, B. *The Fabric of the Cosmos: Space, Time, and the Texture of Reality*, New York: Knopf 2004.

Greene, Lorri A/ Landis, Jacquelyn. *Saying Goodbye to the Pet You Love: A Complete Resource to Help You Heal*, New Harbinger Press 2002.

Greenfield, Sidney M. The return of Dr. Fritz: spiritist healing and patronage networks in urban, industrial Brazil, *Social Science and Medicine* 1987, 24(12), 1095-1108.

Greenhouse, Herbert B. *The Astral Journey*, New York: Avon 1974.

Greenwell, Bonnie. *Energies of Transformation: A Guide to the Kundalini Process*, Cupertino, CA: Shakti River Press/ Transpersonal Learning Services 1990.

Greenwood, Michael. *Braving the Void: Journeys into Healing*, Victoria, B.C. Canada: Paradox 1998.

Grey, Margot. *Return from Death*, Boston, MA: Routledge and Kegan Paul/ Arkana 1985.

Greyson, Bruce. The Near-Death Experience Scale: construction, reliability and validity, *J Nervous and Mental Disorders* 1983, 140, 612-620.

Greyson, Bruce. Near-Death Encounters With and Without Near-Death Experiences: Comparative NDE Scale Profiles, *J Near-Death Studies* 1990, 8(3), 151-161.

Greyson Bruce. Dissociation in people who have near-death experiences: out of their bodies or out of their minds? *Lancet* 2000, 355(9202), 460-3.

Greyson, Bruce/ Bush, NE. Distressing Near-Death Experiences, *Psychiatry* 1992, 55, 95-100.

Greyson, Bruce/ Flynn, Charles, eds. *The Near Death Experience: Problems, Prospects, Perspectives*, Springfield, IL: Thomas, 1984.

Greyson, Bruce/ Harris, Barbara. Clinical approaches to the near-death experiencer, *J Near-Death Studies* 1987, 6(1), 41-52.

Greyson, Bruce/ Stevenson, Ian. Near-Death Experiences, *J the American Medical Association*, 1979, 242, 265-267.

Gribbin, John. *Time Warps*, NY: Delacorte/ Eleanor Friede 1979.

Grof, Stanislav. *Realms of the Human Unconscious*, New York: Viking 1975.

Grof, Stanislav. *LSD Psychotherapy*, Pomona, CA: Hunter House 1980.

Grof, Stanislav. *Beyond the Brain: Birth, Death and Transcendence in Psychotherapy*, Albany: State University of New York Press 1985.

Grof, Stanislav. *Books of the Dead: Manuals for Living and Dying*, New York: Thames & Hudson 1994.

Grof, Stanislav. *The Cosmic Game: Explorations of the Frontiers of Human Consciousness*, Albany: State University of New York 1998.

Grof, Stanislav. *The Holotropic Mind*, San Francisco: Harper 1999.

Grof, Stanislav/ Bennett, HZ. *The Holotropic Mind: The Three Levels of Human Consciousness and How They Shape Our Lives*, San Francisco: Harper 1990.

Grof, Stanislav/ Grof, Christina. *Spiritual Emergency: When Personal Transformation Becomes a Crisis*, New York: Putnam/ England: Thorsons 1995.

Grof, Stanislav/ Halifax, Joan. *The Human Encounter with Death*. New York: Dutton 1977.

Grof, Stanislav/ Halifax, Joan. *Beyond the Brain: Birth, Death and Transcendence in Psychotherapy*, New York: State University of New York 1985.

Grossi, Ralph. *Reliving Reincarnation Through Hypnosis*, Hicksville, NY: Exposition Press 1975.

Grossman, Cathy Lynne. Charting the unchurched in America, *USA Today*, 3/7/2002, www.usatoday.com/life/2002/2002-03-07-no-religion.htm (Accessed 9/26/05)

Guggenheim, Bill/ Guggenheim, Judith. *Hello from Heaven*, New York: Bantam 1997. www.after-death.com/

Guiley, Rosemary Ellen. *Prayer Works*, Unity 1998.

Guirdham, A. *The Nature of Healing*, London: Allen and Unwin 1964.

Guirdham, Arthur. *The Cathars and Reincarnation*, London: Neville Spearman 1970.

Guirdham, Arthur. *We Are One Another*, Jersey, Channel Islands: Neville Spearman 1974.

Gurney, Edmund/ Myers, Frederic WH/ Podmore, Frank. *Phantasms of the Living, Vol. 1*, London: Society PsychicalResearch 1886.

H

Haldane, John Burton Sanderson. *Possible Worlds and Other Essays*, London: Chatto & Windus 1927.

Haley, Jay. *Uncommon Therapy*, New York: Balantine 1973.

Halifax, Joan. *Shaman: The Wounded Healer*, New York: Crossroads 1982.

Hall, Manley Palmer. *Healing: The Divine Art*, Los Angeles: Philosophical Research Society, 1943.

Hamman, RF/ Barancik, JI/ Lilienfeld, AM. Patterns of mortality in the Old Order Amish, *American J Epidemiology* 1981, 114, 845-861.

Hammerschlag, Carl A. *Dancing Healers: A Doctor's Journey of Healing with Native Americans*, HarperSanFrancisco 1989.

Hammerschlag, Carl A/ Silverman, Howard D. *Healing Ceremonies: Creating Personal Rituals for Spiritual, Emotional, Physical, and Mental Health*, New York: Perigee/ Berkeley 1997.

Hampden-Turner, Charles. *Maps of the Mind*, New York: MacMillan 1982.

Haraldsson, Erlendur. *Miracles Are My Visiting Cards*, London: Century 1987.

Haraldsson, E/ Thorsteinsson, T. Psychokinetic effects on yeast: an exploratory experiment, In: Roll, WC/ Morris, RL/ Morris, JD, eds. *Research in Parapsychology 1972*, Metuchen, NJ: Scarecrow Press 1973, 20-21.

Hare, Maurice Evan. *Limerick* 1905.

Harman, Willis. The re-emergence of the survival question, *Noetic Sciences Review*, 1994 (Winter), No. 32, 33.

Harner, Michael. *The Way of the Shaman*, New York: Bantam/ Harper and Row 1980.

Harpur, Tom. *The Hidden Fire: A Practical and Personal Approach to Awakening a Greater Intimacy with God*, Kelowna, British Columbia, Canada: Northstone/ Wood Lake 1998.

Harris, Melvin. *Investigating the Unexplained*, Buffalo, NY: Promethius 1986.

Harris, Melvin. Once in a lifetime, *The Unexplained* 1983, 12(136), 2710-2713.

Harris, William S, et al. A randomized, controlled trial of the effects of remote, intercessory prayer on outcomes in patients admitted to the coronary care unit, *Archives of Internal Medicine* 1999, 159(19), 2273-2278.

Harrison, Steven. *Doing Nothing: Coming to the End of the Spiritual Search*, NY: Crossroad 1997.

Harroll, David, *Spiritual Parenting: A Loving Guide for the New Age Parent*, Marlow 1990.

Hart, Hornell. ESP projection spontaneous cases, *J American Soc. Psych. Research* 1954, 48, 121-146.

Hart, Hornell. Six theories about apparitions, *Proceedings of the Society PsychicalResearch* 1956, 50, 153-239.

Hart, Hornell. *The Enigma of Survival*, Springfield, Illinois: C.C. Thomas 1959. Quotes by courtesy of the publisher.

Hart, Hornell/ Hart, EB. Visions and apparitions collectively and reciprocally perceived, *Proceedings of the Society PsychicalResearch* 1933, 41, 205-249.

Hart, Michael. Habitable zones about main sequence stars, *Icarus* 1979, 37, 351-357.

Hart, Michael. Atmospheric evolution, In: Michael H/ Zuckerman, Ben, eds. *Extraterrestrials, Where Are They?* New York: Pergamon 1982, 156.

Hartwell, John/ Janis, Joseph/ Harary, Blue. A study of the physiological variables associated with Out-of-Body experiences, In: Morris, JD/ Roll, WG/ Morris, RL. *Research in Parapsychology, 1974*, Metuchen, NJ: Scarecrow 1975, 127-129.

Harvey, Andrew, ed. *The Essential Mystics: The Soul's Journey into Truth*, NY: Castle/ Book Sales 1996.

Harvey, Andrew. *The Direct Path : Creating a Personal Journey to the Divine Using the World's Spirtual Traditions*, NY: Broadway Books 2001.

Harvey, David. Taking the Cain cure, *The Unexplained* 1982, 9(108), 2154-2157.

Harvey, David. Healing at a stroke, *The Unexplained* 1983, 13(153), 3046-3049.

Harvey, David. *The Power to Heal: An Investigation of Healing and the Healing Experience*, Wellingborough, Northamptonshire, England: Aquarian 1983.

Harwood, William S. A wonder-worker of sciences: An authoritative account of Luther Burbank's unique work in creating new forms of plant life, *Century Magazine* 1906, 656-667, 821-837.

Hasted, John. *The Metal-Benders*, Boston: Routledge and Kegan Paul 1981.

Hastings, Arthur. *With the Tongues of Men and Angels: A Study of Channeling*, San Francisco: Holt, Rinehart, Winston 1991.

Hatch RL, et al. The Spiritual Involvement and Beliefs Scale. Development and testing of a new instrument. *J Family Practice* 1998, 46, 476-86.

Hauck, Rex, ed. *Angels, the Mysterious Messengers*, New York: Ballantine 1994.

Havel, Václav. [modern science...] Politics and conscience, *Living in Truth*, London: Faber and Faber 1987.

Havel, Vaclav. *Speech at Independence Hall*, Philadelphia, July 4, 1994, excerpted in *The New York Times*, July 8, 1994, A.27.

Hawken, Paul. *The Magic of Findhorn*, Fontana/ Collins 1978.

Hawken, Paul. *The Ecology of Commerce: A Declaration of Sustainability*, NY: HarperCollins 1993.

Hawken, Paul, et al. *Natural Capitalism: Creating the Next Industrial Revolution*, New York: Little, Brown & Co. 1999.

Hawking, Stephen. *A Brief History of Time*, New York: Bantam 1988.

Hawthorne, Nathaniel. In: Bolander, p. 87.

Haynes, Renee. Faith healing and psychic healing: are they the same? *Parapsychology Review* 1977(a), 8(4), 10-13.

Hayward, Captain Cecil Wightwick. *This England* 1982 (Quoted by Price, 1994).

Head, Joseph and Cranston, SL, eds. *Reincarnation: The Phoenix Fire Mystery*, New York: Julian 1977.

Heaney, John J. *The Sacred and the Psychic: Parapsychology and Christian Theology*, New York: Paulist/ New Jersey: Ramsey 1984.

Hebda, Hillard. *An Inquiry into Unorthodox Healing: Psychic Healing and Psychic Surgery*, M.A. Thesis, Governors State University (Human Learning and Development), 1975, (Abstract from *Parapsychology Abstracts International*, 1983, 1(2), No. 479. 58 Refs.).

Hedges, Ken. Phosphenes in the context of Native American art, *American Rock Art* 1982, 7-8, 1-10.

Heider, John. *The Tao of Leadership*, Atlanta, GA: Humanics New Age 1985.

Heifetz, Harold, ed. *Zen and Hasidism*, Wheaton, IL: Quest/ Theosophical 1978.

Heilferty, CM. Spiritual development and the dying child: the pediatric nurse practitioner's role, *J Pediatric Health Care* 2004, 18(6), 271-5.

Heim, A. The experience of dying from falls (Trans. Noyes, R & Kletti, R.) *Omega* 1972, 3, 45-52. (Orig. Notzen uber den tod durch absturz, *Jarbuch des Schweizer Alpenclub* 1892, 27, 327-333.)

Heinemann, Evelyn. *Witches – A Psychoanalytical Exploration of the Killing of Women*, Free Association Books 2000.

Heinze, Ruth-Inge, ed. *Proceedings of the Third International Conference on the Study of Shamanism and Alternate Modes of Healing*, Berkeley: University of California 1986.

Heisenberg, Werner. *Physics and Philosophy: The Revolution in Modern Science*, New York: Harper and Brothers 1958.

Heisenberg, Werner. *Physics and Beyond*, Translated by Pomeranz, AJ, New York: Harper & Row 1971.

Henry, James D/ Henry, Linda. *Reclaiming Soul in Healthcare*, Chicago: AHA Press Health Forum 1999.

Henry, JP. The relation of social to biological processes in disease, *Social Science and Medicine* 1982, 16, 369-380.

Henslee, JA, et al. Impact of premonitions of SIDS on grieving and healing, *Pediatric Pulmonology* 1993, 16, 393.

Herbert, Fr. Albert J. *Raised from the Dead: True Stories of 400 Resurrection Miracles*, Rockford, IL: Tan 1986.

Herbert, N. *Quantum Reality: Beyond the New Physics*, New York: Anchor Books 1985.

Herbert, N. *Elemental Mind and the New Physics*, New York: Dutton 1993.

Heron, John. *Confessions of a Janus-Brain: A Personal Account of Living in Two Worlds*, London: Endymion 1987.

Hiatt, JF. Spirituality, medicine and healing, *Southern Medical J* 1986, 79(6), 736-743.

Hick, John H. *Death and Eternal Life*, New York: Harper and Row 1976.

Hickey, Des/ Smith, Gus. *Miracle*, London: Hodder and Stoughton 1978.

Hicks, Abraham-Esther. *The Science of Deliberate Creation*, Abraham-Hicks Publications www.abraham-hicks.com, (830) 755-2299 (Channels Seth).

Highfield, M/ Cason, C. Spiritual needs of patients: Are they recognized? *Cancer Nursing*, 1983, 6(3), 187-192.

Hildegard Schaefer. (Translator: Heidemarie Hallmann) *The Bridge Between Earth and Beyond*, www.worlditc.org (eBook).

Hill, AB. The environment and disease: Association or causation? *Proceedings of the Royal Society of Medicine* 1965, 58, 1217-1219.

Hill, Christopher. *Is kundalini real?* In: White, John 1990, 106-119.

Hillman, James. *The Soul's Code: Character, Calling and Fate*, New York: Random House 1996.

Hirschi, Gertrud. *Mudras, Yoga in Your Hands*, New York: Samuel Weiser 2000.

Hirshberg, Caryl/ Barasch, Ian Mark. *Remarkable Recoveries*, New York: Riverhead 1995.

Hitt, Jack. This Is Your Brain on God, *Wired* November 1999, 7(11). Trans-cranial magnetic stimulation produces experiences described as spiritual awarenesses. www.wired.com/wired/archive/7.11/persinger_pr.html.

Hixon, Lex. *The Heart of the Koran*, Wheaton, IL: Theosophical 1988/ New Delhi: Goodword 1998.

Hodge. D. Working with Hindu clients in a spiritually sensitive manner, *Social Work* 2004, 49(I), 27-38.

Hoffmann, Albert. *LSD: My Problem Chilc*, Los Angeles: Tarcher 1983.

Hofstadter, Douglas. *Godel, Escher, Bach*, New York: Vintage 1979.

Hoge, DA validated Intrinsic Religious Motivation Scale, *J the Scientific Study of Religion* 1972, 11:369-76.

Holland JC, et al. The role of religious and spiritual beliefs in coping with malignant melanoma, *Psycho-Oncology*. 1999;8:14-26.

Holland, John L. *Making Vocational Choices: A Theory of Vocational Personalities and Work Environments*, Lutz, FL: Psychological Assessment Resources 1997.

Hollenweger, WJ. *The Pentecostals*, Minneapolis, MN: Augsburg 1972.

Holzer, Hans. *Psychic Photography*, London: Souvenir 1969.

Holzer, Hans. *Born Again: The Truth About Reincarnation*, New York: Pocket/ Doubleday 1974.

Homeric hymn. www.kheper.net/topics/Gaia/goddess.htm (Accessed 11/13/05).

Honorton C. Psi and internal attention states, In: *Handbook of Parapsychology*, Wolman, BB, ed. New York: Van Nostrand Reinhold 1977.

Honorton C. Meta-analysis of psi ganzfeld research: A response to Hyman, *Journal of Parapsychology* 1985, 49, 51-91.

Honorton C, Ferrari, DC. Future telling: A meta-analysis of forced-choice precognition experiments, 1935-1987, *Journal of Parapsychology* 1989, 53, 281-308.

Hood, Mariya. *Magic Power to Heal*, Hicksville, New York: Exposition 1976.

Horgan, John. *Rational Mysticism: Dispatches from the Border between Science and Spirituality*, New York, New York: Houghton Mifflin 2003.

Horstmann, Lorna. *An Introduction to Spiritual Healing*, London: Rider 1968.

Houran, J/ Lange, R, eds. *Hauntings and Poltergeists*, London: McFarland 2001.

House, JS/ Landis, KR/ Umberson, D. Social relationships and health, *Science* 1988, 241, 540-545.

Houskamp, BM/ Fisher, LA/ Stuber, ML. Spirituality in children and adolescents: research findings and implications for clinicians and researchers, *Child Adolescent Psychiatric Clinics of North America* 2004, 13(1), 221-230.

Howden, J. *Development and psychometric characteristics of the Spirituality Assessment Scale*, Unpublished doctoral dissertation, Texas Woman's University, Denton 1992.

Howton, Richard. *Divine Healing and Demon Possession*, London: Ward, Lock and Co., 1909.

Hoy, David. Psychic surgery: hoax or hope?, *Zetetic Scholar* 1981, 8, 37-46.

Hoyle, Fred. *The Intelligent Universe*, London: Michael Joseph 1983.

Hubbard, Elbert. *The Note Book* 1927.

Hufford, David. Christian religious healing, *J Operational Psychiatry* 1977, 8(2), 22-27.

Hufford, David J. *The Terror That Comes in the Night*, University of Pennsylvania Press 1982.

Hungelmann, J/ Kenkel-Ross, E/ Klassen, L/ Stollenwerk, RM. Spiritual well-being in older adults: Harmonious inter-connectedness, *J Religion and Health* 1985, 24, 147-154.

Hunt, Diana/ Hait, Pam. *The Tao of Time: Time management for the real world - a right-brain approach that gives you the control you need and the freedom you want*, London/ New York: Fireside/ Simon & Schuster 1990.

Hurley, J. Finley. *Sorcery*, Boston & London: Routledge and Kegan Paul 1985.

Hutchison, M. *Megabrain: New Tools and Techniques for Brain Growth and Mind Expansion*, New York: Ballantine 1986, 308.

Hutton, J. Bernard. *The Healing Power: The Extraordinary Spiritual Healing of Mrs. Leah Doctors and 'Dr. Chang,' Her Spirit Guide*, London: Leslie Frewin 1975.

Huxley, Aldous. *The Perennial Philosophy*, New York: Harper and Row 1944.

Huxley, Aldous. *The Doors of Prception*, New York: Harper 1954.

Huxley, Francis. The miraculous Virgin of Guadalupe, *International J Parapsychology* 1959, 1(1), 19-31.

Huxley, Francis. Unusual methods of healing, *J the British Society of Dowsers* 1964, 18(123), 4-6.

Huxley, TH. The coming of age of the origin of species, in *Science and Culture and Other Essays* 1881.

I

Idler, E/ Kasl, S. Religion, disability, depression, and the timing of death, *American J Sociology* 1992, 97, 1052-1079.

Idler, EL. Religious involvement and the health of the elderly: some hypotheses and an initial test, *Social Forces* 1987, 66, 226-238.

Ikin, A. Graham. *New Concepts of Healing: Medical, Psychological and Religious*, New York: Association Press 1956/ London: Hodder & Stoughton 1955.

Inglis, B/ West, R. *The Unknown Guest: The Mystery of Intuition* London: Coronet 1989.

Insall, GSM. *A Path Prepared*, London: Allan Macdonald 1849.

Insel, PM/ Moos, RH. *Health and the Social Environment*, Lexington, MA: D.C. Heath & Co. 1974.

Irwin, Harvey J. *Psi and the Mind: an Information Processing Approach*, Metuchen, NJ: Scarecrow 1979.

Irwin, Harvey. Out of the body down under: Some cognitive characteristics of Australian students reporting OBEs, *J the Society PsychicalResearch* 1980, 50, 448-459.

Irwin, HJ. Out-of-body experiences in the blind. *J Near-Death Studies*, 1987, 6(1), 53-60.

Isaac, Stephen, ed. *Angels of Nature,* Wheaton, IL: Quest 1995.

Isaacs, Julian. The Batcheldor approach: some strength and weaknesses, *J the American Society PsychicalResearch*, 1984, 78(2), 123-132.

Isberg, Brooke. *The Circles of Life: The Experience of Healing through the Use of the Shamanic Journey*, London: Union Institute 1997.

Ivanova, Barbara. Psychography in the USSR, *International J Paraphysics*, 1978, 12(3/4), 81-84.

Ivanova, Barbara. Incarnation-regressions: informational, educational and healing effects, *Psi Research*, 1986a, 5(1/2), 16-28.

Ivanova, Barbara. Reincarnation and healing, *Psi Research*, 1986b, 5(1/2), 28-33.

J

Jackson, Edgar N. *Understanding Prayer*, New York: World Publishing Co. 1986.

Jackson, ME Mueller. The use of Therapeutic Touch in the nursing care of the terminally ill person, Chapter 7 (pp. 72-79), In: Borelli, MD/ Heidt, P, eds. *Therapeutic Touch: A Book of Readings*, New York: Springer 1981.

Jacobson, Nils O. (Trans. from Swedish - La Farge, S.) *Life without Death? On Parapsychology, Mysticism and the Question of Survival*, London: Turnstone 1974.

Jahn, Robert/ Dunn, Brenda. *On the Quantum Mechanics of Consciousness with Application to Anomalous Phenomena: Appendix B: Collected Thoughts on the Role of Consciousness in the Physical Representation of Reality*, Princeton, NJ: Princeton Engineering Anomalies Research Laboratory 1983 (rev. ed. 1984).

Jahn, Robert/ Dunn, Brenda. *The Margins of Reality*, San Diego: Harcourt, Brace Jovanovich 1987. (9pp refs)

Jaki, Stanley L. *The Savior of Science*, 2nd ed. Grand Rapids, MI: William Eerdmans 1988.

Jamal, Tranvir. *Complementary Medicine: A Practial Guide*, England: Butterworth Heinemann 1997.

James, JW/ Cherry, F. *The Grief Recovery Handbook: A Step by Step Program for Moving Beyond Loss,* New York: Perennial/ Harper and Row 1988.

James, William. *Varieties of Religious Experiences*, New York/ London: Collier/ Macmillan 1961 (Orig. 1902).

Jampolsky, Lee J. *Smile for No Good Reason*, London: Hampton Roads 2000.

Jang, T/ Kryder, GD/ Char, D/ Howell, R/ Primrose, J/ Tan, D. Prehospital spirituality: how well do we know ambulance patients? *Prehospital & Disaster Medicine* 2004, 19(4), 356-61.

Jarvis, GK/ Northcutt, H.C. Religion and differences in morbidity and mortality, *Social Science and Medicine* 1987, 25, 813-824.

Jaynes, Julian. *The Origin of Consciousness in the Breakdown of the Bicameral Mind*. Boston, MA: Houghton Mifflin 1976.

Jeans, James. *Physics and Philosophy*, Cambridge University 1943 (from Jahn/ Dunne 1983).

Jenkins, CD. Psychosocial modifiers in response to stress, In: Barrett, JE et al., eds. *Stress and Mental Disorder*, New York: Raven 1979.

Jenkins, RA/ Pargament, KI. Cognitive appraisals in cancer patients, *Social Science and Medicine* 1988, 26, 625-633.

Jeynes, WH. *Religion, Education and Academic Success*. Greenwich, CT: Information Age 2003.

Jimenez, Juan Ramon/ Maloney, Dennis/ Wright, James. *Light and Shadows: Selected Poems and Prose* (Translator Bly, Robert), White Pine 1987.

Johnson, Phillip E. *Darwin on Trial,* Downers Grove, IL: InterVarsity Press, 2nd edition 1993.

Johnson, Samuel, in Boswell, James. *Life of Samuel Johnson* 1791.

Johnson, SC/ Spilka, B. Coping with breast cancer: the roles of clergy and faith, *J Religion Health* 1991, 30(1), 21-33.

Jones, FC/ Twemlow, SW. Psychological and demographic characteristics of persons reporting "OBE Experiences," *Hillside J Clin. Psychiatry* 1948, 6, 105-15.

Jordan, David Starr, Some experiments of Luther Burbank, *Popular Science Monthly* 1905 (Jan), 201-225.

Joseph, Arthur Samuel. *The Sound of the Soul: Discovering the Power of Your Voice*, Deerfield Beach, FL: Health Communications 1996.

Joseph, Rhawn/ Newberg, Andrew/ Alper, Matthew/ James, William/ Neitzshe, Friederich/ d'Aquili, Eugene G/ Persinger, Michael/ Carol Albright. *NeuroTheology: Brain, Science, Spirituality, Religious Experience*, San Jose, CA: University Press 2003.

Joubert, Joseph. Cited in Reagan, Michael, ed. *Reflections on the Nature of God*, Radnor, PA: Templeton Foundation Press/ Lionheart Books, Ltd. 2004, 50.

Jovanovic, Pierre. *An Inquiry into the Existence of Guardian Angels: A Journalist's Investigative Report*, New York: M. Evans 1995.

Joy, Brugh. *Avalanch*, New York: Ballantine 1990.

Joyce, CRB/Welldon, RMC. The objective efficacy of prayer: a double-blind clinical trial, *J Chronic Diseases* 1965, 18, 367-77.

Jukin proverb, Nigeria. Internet passalong.

Jung, Carl. The psychological foundations of belief in spirits, *Proceedings of the Society PsychicalResearch* 1920, 31.

Jung, Carl. *The Collected Works of CG Jung*, 20 vols. Bollingen Series XX, Hull, RFC, trans/ Read, H, et al., eds. Princeton, NJ: Princeton University 1953-1979.

Jung, Carl. *Man and His Symbols*, Garden City, NY: Windfall/ Doubleday 1964.

Jung, Carl. *Memories, Dreams, Reflections*, New York: Vintage 1965.

Jung, Carl. *The Archetypes and the Collective Unconscious, Collected Works*, V.9 Part I, Princeton, NJ: Princeton University 1969.

Jung, Carl. *Psychology and the Occult*, London: Ark/ Routledge 1993.

K

Kaku, Michio. *Hyperspace: A Scientific Odyssey Through Parallel Universes, Time Warps, and the 10th Dimension*, Anchor 1995.

Kant, Immanuel. *Dreams of a Spirit-Seer, Illustrated by Dreams of Metaphysics* translated by Goerwitz, E. New York/ London: (publisher not named) 1990 (quoted in Jung 1982)

Kaplan, BH. A note on religious beliefs and coronary heart disease, *J Surgical Cardiology and Medical Association*, 1976 (Feb) Suppl. 60-64.

Kaplan, BH/ Cassel, JC/ Gore, S. Social support and health, *Medical Care Supplement* 1977, 15, 47-58.

Kaptchuk, Ted J. *The Web That Has No Weaver*, New York: Congdon and Weed 1984.

Karagulla, Shafica. *Breakthrough to Creativity: Your Higher Sense Perception*, Santa Monica, CA: DeVorss 1967.

Kardek, Allan. *The Book on Mediums*, New York: Weiser 1970.

Karlen, Barbro. *And the Wolves Howled*, Hemdon, VA: Clairview/ Temple Lodge 2000.

Karr, Alphonse. *Les Guêpes*, January 1849.

Kasamatsu, A/ Hirai, T. An electroencephalographic study on the Zen meditation, In: Tart, CT, ed. *Altered States of Consciousness*, Garden City, NY: Anchor Doubleday 1969, 501-514, 309.

Kass, JD. Contributions of religious experience to psychological and physical well-being: research evidence and explanatory model, *Care Giver J* 1991, 8, 4-11.

Kass, JD, et al. Health outcomes and a new index of spiritual experience, *J the Scientific Study of Religion* 1991, 30, 203-11.

Kassy, Karen Grace. *Ihealth Intuition: A Simple Guide to Greater Well-Being*, Center City, MN: Hazelden 2000

Kaufman, Sharon R. *...And a Time to Die: How American Hospitals Shape the End of Life*, New York: Scribner 2005.

Keats, John. *Lamia* 1820.

Keeling, Charles David. The breathing of Gaia www.calspace.ucsd.edu/virtualmuseum/climate change1/05_3.shtml (Accessed 10/1/05)

Keen, Jeffrey. *Consciousness, Intent, and the Structure of the Universe*, Victoria: Trafford/Jeffrey Keen 2005.

Keen, Montague/ Ellison, Arthur/ Fontana, David. *The Scole Report*, Society PsychicalResearch 1999.

Keene, M. Lamar, as told to Spraggett, Allen. *The Psychic Mafia*, New York: Dell 1976.

Keirsey, David W/ Bates, Marilyn. *Please Understand Me: Character and Temperament Types*, Prometheus Nemesis 1985.

Keirsey. *Spiritual healing personality profile*. www.keirsey.com/personality/nfip.html

Kellehear, Allan. *Experiences Near Death: Beyond Medicine and Religion*, New York: Oxford University 1996.

Kelsey, Denys/ Grant, Joan. *Many Lifetimes*, Garden City, NY: Doubleday 1967.

Kelsey, Morton. *Healing and Christianity (In Ancient Thought and Modern Times)*, New York: Harper and Row 1973.

Kelzer, Kenneth. *The Sun and the Shadow: MyExperiment with Lucid Dreaming*, Virginia Beach, VA: A.R.E. 1987.

Kendall, J. Wellness spirituality in homosexual men with HIV infection, *J American Nursing AIDS Care,* 1994, 5(4), 28-34.

Kendler, KS/ Liy, XQ/ Gardner, CO/ McCullough, ME/ Larson, D/ Prescott, CA. Dimensions of religiosity and their relationship to lifetime psychiatric and substance use disorders. *American J Psychiatry* 2003, 160(3), 496-503.

Kennaway, EL. The racial and social incidence of cancer of the uterus, *British J Cancer,* 1948, II, 177-212.

Kennedy, Alexandra. *Your Loved One Lives on Within You,* New York: Berkley 1997.

Kenny, MG. Multiple personality and spirit possession, *Psychiatry* 1981, 44, 337-358.

Kertzer, David. *Ritual, Politics and Power,* reprint edition, Yale University Press 1989.

Khalsa, MSS/ Gurucharan Singh/ Khalsa, Sadhu Singh. Kundalini energy, In: White, John 1990, 254-290 (50 refs).

Khan, HA, et al. Association between reported diet and all-cause mortality: 21 year follow-up on 27, 530 adult Seventh-Day Adventists, *American J Epidemiology* 1984, 119, 775-787.

Khan, Hazrat Inayat. *One of the ten thoughts which form the foundation of Sufism* www.psychcentral.com/psypsych/Hazrat_Inayat _Khan

Khan, Hazrat Inayat. *There is one holy book...* www.ruhaniat.org/readings/10-3Commentary.php (Accessed 12/5/05)

Khan, Pir Vilayat Inayat. *Introducing Spirituality into Counseling and Psychotherapy,* Santa Fe, NM: Omega 1982.

Khan, Pir Vilayat, in Elliott, William. *Tying Rocks to Clouds,* New York: Image/ Doubleday 1996, 192-202.

Khan, Sufi Inayat. *The Bowl of Saki,* undated.

Kierkegaard, Soren. Attributed.

Kiev, Ari, ed. *Magic, Faith and Healing: Studies in Primitive Psychiatry Today,* New York: Free Press/ Macmillan 1964.

Kiev, Ari. *Curanderismo: Mexican-American Folk Psychiatry,* New York: Free Press 1968.

Kimball, Gayle. *Essential Energy Tools: How to Develop Your Clairvoyant and Healing Abilities,* Chico, CA: Equality 2001.

King, DE, et al. Implementation and assessment of a spiritual history taking curriculum in the first year of medical school, *Teaching & Learning in Medicine* Winter 2004, 16(I), 64-68.

King, DE/ Bushwick, B. Beliefs and attitudes of hospital inpatients about faith healing and prayer, *J Family Pract* 1994, 39, 349-352.

King, Frances. The word made flesh, *The Unexplained,* 1982, 8(85), 1690- 1693.

King, H/ Bailar, JC. The health of the clergy: a review of demographic literature, Demography 1969, 6, 27-43.

King, H/ Locke, FB. American White Protestant clergy as a low-risk population for mortality research, *J the National Cancer Institute* 1980, 65, 1115-1124.

King, Martin Luther Jr. "I Have A Dream" speech, delivered on the steps at the Lincoln Memorial in Washington D.C. August 28, 1963.

King, Martin Luther Jr. *Strength to Love,* New York: Fortress (Orig. 1963) 1986.

King, Moray B. *Tapping the Zero-Point Energy,* Provo, UT: Paraclete 1992.

King, Moray B. *Quest for Zero Point Energy Engineering Principles for Free Energy,* Kempton, IL: Adventures Unlimited 2002.

Kirkpatrick, Bill. *Going Forth, a Practical & Spiritual Approach to Dying & Death,* Darton, Longman, and Todd Ltd. 1997.

Kirtley, DD. *The Psychology of Blindnessi,* Chicago: Nelson-Hall 1975.

Kit, Wong Kiew. *The Complete Book of Zen,* Boston, MA: Tuttle/ London: Periplus Editions 2002.

Kleijnen, Jos/ Knipschild, Paul/ Ter Riet, Gorben. Clinical Trials of Homeopathy, *British Medical J* 1991, 302, 317-322.

Kleissler, Thomas A/ LeBert, Margo A/ McGuiness, Mary C. *Small Christian Communities: A Vision of Hope.* Mahwah, NJ 1991.

Klimo, Jon. *Psychics, Prophets and Mystics: Receiving Information from Paranormal Sources,* London: Aquarian/ Grafton/ Harper Collins 1991 (US edition: *Channeling,* Los Angeles: Tarcher).

Klopstock, Friedrich. In: Lombroso, C. *The Man of Genius* 1891.

Knight, Damon. *Charles Fort: Prophet of the Unexplained,* London: Golancz 1971.

Koenig, Harold. *Is Religion Good for Your Health? The Effects of Religion on Physical and Mental Health,* Harrington Park 1997.

Koenig, Harold G. *The Healing Power of Faith: Science Explores Medicine's Last Great Frontier,* New York: Simon/ Schuster 1999.

Koenig, Harold G. Religion, Spirituality, and Medicine: How Are They Related and What Does It Mean? *Mayo Clinic Proceedings* 2001, 76, 1189-1191.

Koenig HG, Bearon LB, Dayringer R. Physician perspectives on the role of religion in the physician–older patient relationship. *J Family Practice* 1989;28:441-8.

Koenig, HG/ George, LK/ Titus, P. Religion, spirituality, and health in medically ill hospitalized older patients, *J the American Geriatrics Society* April 2004, 52(4), 554-62.

Koenig, Harold G/ McCullough, Michael E/ Larson, David B. *Handbook of Religion and Health*, Oxford University 2001.

Koenig, HG/ Smiley, M/ Gonzales, JP. *Religion, Health and Aging*, New York: Greenwood 1988.

Koestler, Arthur, *The Case of the Midwife Toad*, New York:Random House 1971.

Kohlberg, Lawrence. Stage and sequence: the cognitive developmental approach to socialization, in Goslin, David A, ed. *Handbook of Socialization Theory and Research*, Chicago: Rand McNally 1969.

Kornfield, Jack. *A Path With Heart: A Guide Through the Perils and Pitfalls of Spiritual Life*, New York: Bantam 1993.

Kornfield, Jack. In: Elliott, William. *Tying Rocks to Clouds*, New York: Image/ Doubleday 1996, 215-222.

Kosmin, Barry A/ Mayer, Egon. American Religious Identification Survey (ARIS). www.gc.cuny.edu/faculty/research_briefs/aris/a ris_index.htm (Accessed 9/26/05)

Koss, JD. Expectations and outcomes for patients given mental health care or spiritist healing in Puerto Rico, *American J Psychiatry* 1987, 144(1), 56-61.

Koven, Jean-Claude. *Where in God's name did we go wrong?* www.goingdeeper.org/articles/110.php (Accessed 2/18/06)

Kowey, Peter R/ Friehling, Ted D/ Marinchak, Roger A. Prayer meeting cardioversion, *Annals of Internal Medicine* 1986, 104(5), 727-728.

Kraft, Ken/ Kraft, Pet. *Luther Burbank, The Wizard and the Man*, New York: Meredith 1967.

Krammer, Kenneth. *The Sacred Art of Dying: How World Religions Understand Death*, Paulist Press, 1988.

Krause, N/ Tran, TV. Stress and religious involvement among older blacks, *J Gerontology: Social Sciences* 1989, 44, S4-13.

Krieger, Dolores. The relationship of touch, with intent to help or to heal, to subjects' in-vivo hemoglobin values, In: *American Nurses' Association 9th Nursing Research Conference, San Antonio, TX 1973*, Kansas City, MO: American Nurses' Association 1974, 39-58.

Krieger, Dolores. *The Therapeutic Touch: How to Use Your Hands to Help or Heal,* Englewood Cliffs, NJ: Prentice-Hall 1979.

Krippner, Stanley. A pilot study in ESP, dreams and purported OBEs, *J Society PsychicalResearch* 1996, 61, 88-93.

Krippner, Stanley/ Villoldo, Alberto. Spirit healing in Brazil, In: Fate Magazine, *Exploring the Healing Miracle* Highland Park, IL: Clark 1983 (Orig. *Fate*, Mar 1976).

Krippner, Stanley/ Villoldo, Alberto. *The Realms of Healing*, Millbrae, CA: Celestial Arts 1976; 3rd. Ed. Rev. 1986.

Krippner, Stanley/ Welch, Patrick. *Spiritual Dimensions of Healing: From Native Shamanism to Contemporary Health Care*, New York: Irvington 1992.

Krishna, Gopi. The sudden awakening of kundalini, In: White, John 1990, 198-209.

Krishnamurti, J. *The Urgency of Change*, New York/ London: Perennial/ Harper & Row 1970.

Krishnamurti, Jiddu. *On Living and Dying, First Series*, San Francisco: Harper San Francisco 1992.

Krishnan, V. *OBEs in the blind*, J Near Death Studies, 1987, 7(2), 134-139.

Krupp, MD/ Schroeder, SA/ Tierney, LM, Jr. *Current Medical Diagnosis & Treatment 1987*, Norwalk, CT: Appleton & Lange 1987.

Krystal, Phyllis. *Cutting the Ties that Bind*, London: Sawbridge 1986.

Kubis, Pat. *Conversations Beyond the Light with Departed Friends and Colleagues by Electronic Means.* Boulder, CO: Griffin 1995.

Kubis, Pat/ Macy, Mark. *Conversations Beyond the Light*, England: Grail 1995.

Kübler-Ross, Elisabeth. *On Death and Dying*, New York: Macmillan 1969.

Kübler-Ross, Elisabeth. *Death: The Final Stage of Growth*, Englewood Cliffs, NJ: Prentice-Hall 1975.

Kübler-Ross, Elisabeth. *Living with Death and Dying*, New York: Macmillan 1981; London: Souvenir 1982.

Kübler-Ross, Elisabeth. *On Life After Death*, Berkeley, CA: Celestial Arts 1991.

Kuhlman, Kathryn. *I Believe in Miracles*, New York: Pyramid 1969.

Kuhn CA. spiritual inventory of the medically ill patient. *Psychiatric Medicine* 1988, 6(2), 87-100.

Kuhn, Thomas S. *The Structure of Scientific Revolutions*. Chicago, IL: University Of Chicago 1996.

Kunz, Dora, ed. *Spiritual Aspects of the Healing Arts*, Wheaton, IL: Theosophical 1985.

Kunz, FL. *The Quest for the Quiet Mindi*, Wheaton, IL: Quest/ Theosophical 1956.

Kurtz, Paul, ed. *A Skeptic's Handbook of Parapsychology*, Buffalo: Prometheus 1985.

Kurtz, Paul. *The Transcendental Temptation: A Critique of Religion and the Paranormal*, Buffalo, NY: Promethius 1986.

Kushner, Harold S. *When Bad Things Happen to Good People*, New York: Schocken 1981.

Kyle, David. *Human Robots and Holy Mechanics: Reclaiming Our Souls in a Machine World*, Portland, Oregon: Swan-Raven & Co. 1993.

L

LaBarre, W. Confession as cathartic therapy in American Indian tribes, In: Kiev, A, ed. *Magic, Faith and Healing*, Free Press 1964, 36-49.

Labarthe, DR/ Stallones, RA. Epidemiologic inference, In: Rothman, KJ, ed: *Causal Inference*, Chestnut Hill, MA 1988, 119-129.

LaBerge, Stephen. *Lucid dreaming*. Los Angeles: J. P. Tarcher 1985.

LaBerge, Stephen. The psychophysiology of lucid dreaming. In J. Gackenbach & S. LaBerge, eds. *Conscious mind, sleeping brain: Perspectives on lucid dreaming* (pp. 135-153). New York: Plenum 1988.

LaBerge, Stephen. Lucid dreaming: Psychophysiological studies of consciousness during REM sleep, In: Bootsen, RR/ Kihlstrom, JF/ Schacter, DL, eds. *Sleep and Cognition*. Washington, D.C. American Psychological Association 1990, 109-126.

LaBerge, Stephen. Physiological studies of lucid dreaming. In Antrobus, J/ Bertini, M, eds. *The Neuropsychology of Dreaming Sleep,* Hillsdale, NJ: Erlbaum 1993, 289-303.

LaBerge, S/ Rheingold, H. *Exploring the World of Lucid Dreaming*. New York: Ballantine 1990.

LaGrand, Louis E. *After-death Communication: Final Farewells*, St. Paul, MN: Llewellyn 1997.

Laing, Ronald D. *The Divided Self,* London: Tavistock 1960.

Lambillion, Paul. *Being Loving is Being Healthy: Self Healing through the Power of Love*, Romford, England: L. N. Fowler 1987.

Lambillion, Paul. *Auras and Colours:: A Guide to Working with Subtle Energies,* Gateway 2001.

Lange, Walter R. *Healing Miracles: The Story of the St. Rupertus Spring and its Miraculous,*

Health-Giving Water, Brooklyn, NY: Walter R. Lange 1977.

Lantz, Jamie Elizabeth. *The Therapeutic Value of Women's Ritual* (Archetypes, Myths), MA Thesis, Prescott College 1996.

Lao Tsu. Attributed.

Larcher, Hubert. Sacred places and paranormal cures, *Revue Metapsychique* 1981, 15(4), 19-28.

Larimore, WL, et al. Should clinicians incorporate positive spirituality into their practices? What does the evidence say? *Annals of Behavioral Medicine* 2002, 24(1), 69.

Larson, David B/ Milano, Mary A. Greenwold. Are religion and spirituality clinically relevant? *Mind/ Body Medicine* 1995, 1(3), 147-157.

Larson, David B/ Sherrill, Kimberly A/ Lyons, John S. Neglect and Misuse of the R Word, In: 1994b, 178-195.

Larson, DB, et al. Systematic analysis of research on religious variables in four major psychiatric Journals, 1978-1982, *American J Psychiatry* 1986, 143, 329-334.

Larson EJ/ Eaton TA. The limits of advance directives: a history and assessment of the Patient Self-Determination Act. *Wake Forest Law Review* 1997, 32, 349-93.

Laszlo, Ervin. *Science and the Akashic Field: An Integral Theory of Everything*, Rochester, Vermont: Inner Traditions 2004.

Lava, Jesus B/ Araneta, Antonio S. *Faith Healing and Psychic Surgery in the Philippines* (Rev. ed.), Manila: Araneta University Campus/ AIA Press 1986.

Lava, Jesus B/ Araneta, Antonio S. *Faith Healing*, Manila: Philippine Society Psychical Research Foundation 1987.

Lawlor, Robert. *Voices of the First Day: Awakening in the Aboriginal Dreamtime*, Rochester, VT: Inner Traditions 1991.

Lawrence, DH. Letter to J. Middleton Murry, 2 February 1923, 114/70

Lawrence, Jerome/ Lee, Robert E. *Inherit the Wind*, New York: Random House 2003.

Lawson, Lee. *Visitations from the Afterlife: True Stories of Love and Healing* HarperSanFrancisco 2000.

Leadbeater, CW. *Man Visible and Invisible*, Wheaton, IL: Quest 1969 (Orig. 1902).

Leader, LR, et al. The assessment and significance of habituation to a repeated stimulus by the human fetus, *Early Human Development* 1982, 7, 211-219; 310.

LeCron, Leslie. Hypnosis and ESP, *Psychic* 1970, August.

Leder, Drew. Spooky actions at a distance. physics, psi, and distant healing, *J Alternative and Complementary Medicine* 2005, 11(5), 923–930.

Lee, Gypsy Rose. Attributed, 186/39.

Leek, Sybil, *The Story of Faith Healing*, New York: Macmillan 1973.

Leek, Sybil, *Reincarnation: The Second Chance*, New York: Bantam 1974.

Lefavi, Robert. *Reasons to Believe: A Journey of Spiritual Awareness in the Modern World*, Pasadena, CA: Hope Publishing House 1999.

Lehmann, HE. Pharmacotherapy of schizophrenia, In: Hoch, PH/ Zubin, J, eds. *Psychopathology of Schizophrenia*, New York: Grune & Stratton 1966.

Leibniz, Gottfried Wilhelm. *Letter on a General Principle Useful in Explaining the Laws of Nature* 1687.

Leichtman, Robert R/ Japiske, Carl. The nature and purpose of the emotions, *J Holistic Medicine* 1984, 6(2), 148-160.

Lemon, FR/ Walden, RT. Death from respiratory system disease among Seventh-Day Adventist Men, *J the American Medical Association* 1966, 198, 117-126.

Lenz, Frederick. *Life-Times: True Accounts of Reincarnation*, Indianapolis, In: Bobbs-Merrill 1979.

Lerner, Michael. *Spirit Matters*, Hampton Roads Publishing 2000.

LeShan, Lawrence. *The Medium, The Mystic and The Physicist: Toward a General Theory of the Paranormal*, New York: Ballantine 1974(a). (Copyright 1966, 1973, 1974 by Lawrence LeShan. Quotations by permission of Viking Penguin, Inc.)

LeShan, L. *How to Meditate*, New York: Bantam 1974b.

LeShan, Lawrence. *Alternate Realities*, New York: Ballantine 1976.

Leskowitz, Eric D, ed. *Transpersonal Hypnosis: Gateway to Body, Mind, and Spirit*, New York: CRC 2000.

Lester, RM. *Towards the Hereafter: With Special Inquiry into Spiritual Healing*, New York: Citadel Press 1957.

Leuret, Francois/ Bon, Henri. *Modern Miraculous Cures: A Documented Account of Miracles and Medicine in the 20th Century*, New York: Farrar, Straus and Cudahy 1957.

Levesque, GV. *Miracle Cures for the Millions*, New York: Bell 1966.

Levin, Jeffrey S. *Medicalization and Religion*, MPH Thesis, University of North Carolina School of Public Health 1983.

Levin, Jeffrey S. Religious factors in Aging, adjustment and health: a theoretical overview, *J Religion and Aging* 1989, 4(3/4), 133-146.

Levin, Jeffrey S. Age differences in mystical experience, *Gerontologist* 1993, 33(4), 507-513.

Levin, Jeffrey S. Religion and health: is there an association, is it valid, and is it causal?, *Social Science and Medicine* 1994a, 38, 1474-1482.

Levin, Jeffrey S. *Religion in Aging and Health: Theoretical Foundations and Methodological Frontiers*, London/ Thousand Oaks, CA: Sage 1994b.

Levin, Jeffrey S. How prayer heals: A theoretical model, *Alternative Therapies in Health and Medicine* 1996a, 2(1), 66-73.

Levin JS. How religion influences morbidity and health: reflections on natural history, salutogenesis and host resistance. Social Science and Medicine 1996b, 43, 849-64.

Levin JS et al. Religion and spirituality in medicine: research and education. *J American Medical Association* 1997, 278, 792-3.

Levin, Jeffrey S. *God, Faith and Healing*, New York: Wiley 1999.

Levin, JS/ Jenkins, CD/ Rose, RM. Religion, Type A behavior, and health, *J Religion and Health* 1988, 27, 267-278.

Levin, Jeffrey S/ Markides, KS. Religion and health in Mexican Americans, *J Religion and Health* 1985, 24, 60-69.

Levin, Jeffrey S/ Markides, Kyriakos S. Religious attendance and subjective health, *J Scientific Study of Religion* 1986, 25, 31-40.

Levin, Jeffrey/ Schiller, Preston L. Religion and the Multidimensional Health Locus of Control scales, *Psychological Reports* 1986, 59, 26.

Levin, Jeffrey S/ Schiller, Preston L. Is there a religious factor in health? *J Religion and Health* 1987, 26(1), 9-35 (215 refs).

Levin, Jeffrey S/ Vanderpool, Harold Y. Is frequent religious attendance really conducive to better health?: Toward an epidemiology of religion, *Social Science and Medicine* 1987, 24(7), 589-600 (85 refs).

Levin, Jeffrey S/ Vanderpool, Harold Y: Is religion therapeutically significant for hypertension?, *Social Science and Medicine* 1989, 29(1), 69-78 (65 refs).

Levin, Jeffrey S/ Vanderpool, Harold Y. Religious factors in physical health and the prevention of illness, In: Pargament, Kenneth I/ Maton, Kenneth I/ Hess, Robert E, eds. *Religion and Prevention in Mental Health: Research,*

Vision, and Action, London/ New York: Haworth 1992.

Levine, Joseph. Materilism and qualia: the explanatory gap, Pacific Philosophical Quarterly 1983, 64, 354-361.

Levine, Stephen. Meetings at the Edge: Dialogues with the Grieving and the Dying, the Healing and the Healed, New York/ London: Anchor/ Doubleday 1984.

Levine, Stephen. Who Dies? An Investigation of Conscious Living and Conscious Dying Bath, England: Gateway 1986.

Levine, Stephen. Healing into Life and Death, Garden City, New York: Anchor/ Doubleday 1987.

Levine, Stephen. Guided Meditations, Explorations and Healings, New York/ London: Anchor/ Doubleday 1991.

Lewis, CS. Letters to Malcolm: Chiefly on Prayer, New York: Harcourt Brace Jovanovich 1964.

Lewis, James R/ Oliver, Evelyn Dorothy. Angels A to Z, Detroit, MI: Visible Ink 1996.

Lewis, Pamela J. A review of prayer within the role of the holistic nurse, J Holistic Nursing 1996, 14(4), 308-315.

Lewith, George, et al. Complementary Medicine: An Integrated Approach, Oxford, England: Oxford Medical 1996.

Library of Excerpts. Hopi: Heterochronic Patterns, www.humanevolution.net/a/hopi.html (Accessed 10/1/05)

Licauco, Jaime T. The Truth Behind Faith Healing in the Philippines, Manila, Philippines: Metro Manila 1981.

Lifschutz, Joseph E. Hysterical stigmatization, American J Psychiatry 1957, 114, 527-531.

Lilly, JC. The Deep Self, New York: Simon and Schuster 1977.

Lincoln, PJ/ Wood, NJ. Psychic surgery: A serological investigation, Lancet 1979, 1, 1197-1198.

Linn, Denise with Meadow Linn. Quest – A Guide for Creating Your Own Vision Quest, New York: Ballantine 1999.

Linnard-Palmer, L/ Kools, S. Parents' refusal of medical treatment based on religious and/or cultural beliefs: the law, ethical principles, and clinical implications, J Pediatric Nursing October 2004, 19(5), 351-56.

Lipinski, Boguslaw. Report on the unknown tyupe of energy recorded in Medjugorje during prayers in March 1985, Psi Research 1986, 5(1,2), 239-240.

Lipton, Bruce H. The Biology of Belief: Unleashing the Power of Consciousness, Matter and Miracles, Santa Rosa, CA: Mountain of Love/ Elite Books 2005.

Litvag, Irving. Singer in the Shadows: The Strange Story of Patience Worth, New York: Macmillan 1972.

Locke, FB/ King, H. Mortality among Baptist Clergymen, J Chronic Disease 1980, 33, 581-590.

Lockley, Martin. A broader look at the spiritual emergence experience: implications for consciousness studies, Network 2000, 72, 30.

Loehr, Franklin. The Power of Prayer on Plants, New York: Signet 1969.

Long, Donna Wilson. The Discarnate masters of Luiz Antonio Gasparetto, Shaman's Drum 1986, 5, 32-37.

Long, Max Freedom. The Secret Science Behind Miracles, Marina Del Rey, CA: DeVorss 1976 (Orig. 1948).

Long, Max Freedom. Recovering the Ancient Magic, Cape Girardeau, MO: Huna 1978 (Orig. 1936).

Longfellow, Henry Wadsworth. A psalm of life 1838.

Longman, AJ/ Lindstrom, B/ Clark, M. Sensory-perceptual experiences of bereaved individuals, American J Hospice Care 1988, July/August, 42-45.

Lonnig, WE/ Saedler, H. Chromosome rearrangements and transposable elements, Annual Review of Genetics 2002, 36, 389-410.

Lorimer, David. Survival? Body, Mind and Death in the Light of Psychic Experience, London: Routledge & Kegan Paul 1986.

Lorimer, David. Whole in One, London: Arkana/ Penguin 1990.

Lovelock, James. Gaia: A New Look at Life on Earth, Oxford, England: Oxford University Press 1979 (reprinted 1995).

Lovelock, James. The Ages of Gaia: A Biography of Our Living Earth. Oxford/New York: Oxford University 1988.

Lovelock, James E. Healing Gaia, Harmony Books 1991.

Lovelock, James. The Earth is about to catch a morbid fever that may last as long as 100,000 years, The Independent—Online Edition, 16 January 2006. www.comment.independent.co.uk/commentators/article338830.ece (Accessed 2/1/06)

Lovitts, Barbara E. The sheep-goat effect turned upside down, J Parapsychology 1981, 45, 293-310.

Lovtrup, S. Semantics, logic and vulgate neo-darwinism, *Evolutionary Theory* 1979, 4, 157-172.

Loy, Jim. *A Bee Can't Fly?* 1996, (Accessed 7/25/03) www.jimloy.com/ physics/ bee.htm

Lucas, Winafred Blake. *Regression Therapy: A Handbook for Professionals, Vol. I: Past Life Therapy*, Crest Park, CA: Deep Forest 1993a.

Lucas, Winafred Blake. *Regression Therapy: A Handbook for Professionals, Vol. II: Special Instances of Altered State Work*, Crest Park, CA: Deep Forest 1993b.

Lüdman, Gerd. *Jesus After 2000 Years*, SCM 2000.

Ludzia, LF. Life Force: The Secret of Empowerment, St Paul, MN: Llewellyn 1987.

Lukianowicz, N. 'Autoscopic Phenomena,' *AMA Archives of Neurology and Psychology* 1958, 80(2), 199-220.

Lukoff, David. The diagnosis of mystical experiences with psychotic features, *J Transpersonal Psychology* 1985, 17(2), 155-181.

Lukoff, D/ Lu, F/ Turner, R. From spiritual emergency to spiritual problem: The transpersonal roots of the new DSM-IV category. *J Humanistic Psychology*, 1998, 38(2), 21-50.

Lukoff, David/ Turner, Robert/ Lu, Francis. Transpersonal psychology research review: Psychoreligious dimensions of healing, *J Transpersonal Psychology* 1992, 24(1), 41-60 (51 refs).

Lundahl, C, ed. *A Collection of Near-Death Research Findings: Scientific Inquiries into the Experiences of Persons Near Physical Death*, Chicago, IL: Nelson-Hall 1982.

Lundahl, CR. Near-death visions of unborn children: Indications of a pre-earth life, *J Near-Death Studies* 1992, 11(2), 123-128.

Lundahl, Craig R/ Widdison, Harold A. *The Eternal Journey: How Near-Death Experiences Illuminate Our Earthly Lives*, New York: Warner Books 1997.

Lutgendorf, SK, et al. Religious participation, interleukin-6, and mortality in older adults, *Health Psychology* September 2004, 23(5), 465-75.

M

MacDonald, CB/ Luckett, JB. Religious affiliation and psychiatric diagnoses, *J Scientific Study of Religion* 1983, 22, 15-37.

MacDonald, Douglas A/ Friedman, Harris L/ Kuentzel, Jeffery G. A survey of measures of spiritual and transpersonal constructs: Part one – research update, *The J Transpersonal Psychology* 1999(a), 31(2), 137-154; Part two – additional instruments, *The J Transpersonal Psychology* 1999(b), 31(2), 155-177.

MacDonald, Douglas A/ LeClair, Laura/ Holland/ Cornelius J, et al. A survey of measures of transpersonal constructs, *The J Transpersonal Psychology* 1995, 27(2), 171-239.

MacDonald, R/ Dakin, HS/ Hickman, JL. Preliminary studies with three alleged 'psychic healers,' In: Morris, JD/ Roll, WG/ Morris, RL, eds. *Research in Parapsychology 1976*, Metuchen, NJ/London: Scarecrow 1977.

MacKenzie, A. *Apparitions and Ghosts: A Modern Study*, London: Barker 1971.

Maclean, Dorothy. *To Hear the Angels Sing*, Hudson, NY: Lindisfarne 1990.

MacManaway, Bruce with Turcan, Johanna. *Healing: The Energy That Can Restore Health*, Wellingsborough, Northamptonshire, England: Thorsons 1983.

MacNutt, Francis. *Healing*, Notre Dame, Ave Maria Press 1974.

MacNutt, Francis. Healing prayer, In: *Church and Sherr* 1987, 143-153.

MacRae, Alexander. Some findings related to the electronic voice phenomenon, *Psi Research* 1984, 3(1), 36-46.

Macrae, Janet A. *Nursing as a Spiritual Practice: A Contemporary Application of Florence Nightingale's Views*, New York: Springer 2001.

Macy, Joanna/ Brown, Molly Young, Six principles for reconnecting to the earth, Adapted from *Coming Back to Life*, Gabriola Island, BC, Canada: New Society 1998. www.care2.com/channels/solutions/self/1746 (Accessed 12/14/05)

Macy, Mark H. *Miracles in the Storm: Talking to the Other Side With the New Technology of Spiritual Contact*, New York: New American Library 2001.

Macy, Mark/ Erhardt, Rolf-Dietmar. Instrumental Transcommunication, www.worlditc.org/

Madison, LS/ Adubato, SA/ Madison, JK, et al. Fetal response decrement: True habituation? *J Develomental and Behavioral Pediatrics* 1986, 7(1), 14-20, 311.

Mains, David and Steve Bell. *Two are Better Than One. A Guide to Prayer Partnerships That Work*. Sisters, Oregon: Multnomah School of the Bible 1991.

Major, Ralph Hermon. *Faiths that Healed*, New York: Appleton-Century, 1940.

Maki, Masao. *In Search of Brazil's Quantum Surgeon: The Dr. Fritz Phenomenon*, San Francisco, CA: Cadence 1998.

Malacz, WP. Deliberately caused bodily damage (DCBD) phenomena: a different perspective, *J the Society PsychicalResearch* 1998, 62, 434-444.

Malinowski, B. *Magic, Science, and Religion*, Garden City, NY: Doubleday 1948 (Orig. 1925).

Mallasz, Gitta. *Talking with Angels*, Zurich: Daimon Verlag 1988.

Malz, Betty. *My Glimpse of Eternity*, New York: Chosen 1977.

Mandell, Arnold J. Toward a psychobiology of transcendence: God in the brain, in Davidson, Richard J/ Davidson, Julian M, eds. *The Psychobiology of Consciousness*, New York: Plenum 1980.

Mann, Ronald L. *Sacred Healing; Integrating Spirituality with Psychotherapy*, Blue Dolphin 1998.

Mann, Thomas. *Dr. Faustus*, quoted in Dossey 1998, p.18 (from Ruthven, M. *Torture: The Grand Conspiracy*, London: Weidenfield/ Nicolson 1978).

Manno, Jack/ Jamborcic, Ana. Sufficiency and simple living: The Path to Personal and Global Well-Being, *International J Healing and Caring 1*, 2005, 1-8.

Mansen, TJ. The spiritual dimension of individuals: Conceptual development, *Nursing Diagnosis*, 1993, 4(4), 140-147.

Marais, Eugene: *The Soul of the White Ant*. London: Cape 1971.

Margulis, L/ Sagan, D. *Slanted Truths: Essays on Gaia, Evolution and Symbiosis*, New York 1997.

Margolies, Morris B. *A Gathering of Angels: Angels in Jewish Life and Literature*, New York: Ballantine 1994.

Marion, Jim. *Putting on the Mind of Christ: The Inner Work of Christian Spirituality,* London: Hampton Roads 2000.

Markides, Kyriakos. *The Magus of Strovolos: The Extraordinary World of a Spiritual Healer*, London & Boston: Arkana 1985.

Markides, Kyriakos. *Homage to the Sun: The Wisdom of the Magus of Strovolos*, New York & London: Arkana 1987.

Markides, Kyriakos. *Fire in the Heart: Healers, Sages and Mystics*, London: Arkana/ Penguin 1991.

Marmot, MG/ Syme, SL. Acculturation and coronary heart disease in Japanese-Americans, *American J Epidemi-ology* 1976, 104, 225-247.

Martin, JE/ Carlson, CR. Spiritual dimensions of health psychology, In: Miller, R/ Martin, JE, eds. *Behavior Therapy and Religion*, Newbury Park, CA: Sage 1988, 57-110.

Martin, Malachi. *Hostage to the Devil: The Possession and Exorcism of Five Contemporary Americans,* Harper SanFrancisco 1992.

Marwick, Charles. Should physicians prescribe prayer for health? Spiritual aspects of well-being considered, *J American Medical Association*, 1973, 273(20), 1561-1562.

Maslow, Abraham. *Religions, Values and Peak-Experiences*, Columbus, OH: Ohio State University 1964.

Maslow, Abraham, *The Farthest Reaches of Human Nature,* New York: Viking 1971.

Maslow, Abraham. *Motivation and Personality*, in Frager, R/Fadiman, J/ McReynolds, C/ Cox, R, eds. (rev. ed.), New York: Harper & Row 1987.

Mason, Daniel Aloysius. *The Psychological and Spiritual Principles of the Twelve Steps of Alcoholics Anonymous*, Ph.D. Union Institute 1998.

Mason, RC/ Clark, G/ Reeves, RB/ Wagner, B. Acceptance and healing, *J Religion and Health* 1969, 8, 123-142.

Masters, Robert EL/ Houston, Jean. *The varieties of psychedelic experience*, New York: Delta 1967.

Mathes, EW/ Zevon, MA/ Roter, PM/ Joerger, SM. Peak experience tendencies: Scale development and theory testing. *J Humanistic Psychology* 1982, 22(3), 92-108.

Maton, KI. The stress buffering role of spiritual support, *J Scientific Study of Religion* 1989, 28, 310-323.

Matthiessen, Peter. *The Snow Leopard: The Astonishing Spiritual Odyssey of a Man in Search of Himself,* New York: Bantam/ Viking Penguin 1978.

Maugans, TA.The SPIRITual history, *Arch Fam Med* 5, 1996, 11-6.

Maugans, TA/ Wadland, WC. Religion and family medicine: A survey of physicians and patients, *J Family Practice* 1991, 32, 210-213.

Maxwell, J. Nursing's new age? *Christianity Today* 1996, 40(3), 96-99.

McAll, Kenneth. *Healing the Family Tree*, London: Sheldon 1982.

McCaffery, John. *Tales of Padre Pio, The Friar of San Giovanni*, Garden City, NY: Image/

Doubleday 1981. (Orig. *The Friar of San Giovanni*, U.K. Darton, Longman & Todd 1978.)

McCaffrey, AM/ Eisenberg, DM/ Legedza, AT/ Davis, RB/ Phillips, RS. Prayer for health concerns: results of a national survey on prevalence and patterns of use, *Archives Internal Medicine* April 2004, 164(8), 858-62.

McClain, CS, et al. Effect of spiritual well-being on end-of-life despair in terminally-ill cancer patients, *Lancet* 2003, 361(9369), 1603-7.

McClain, Florence. *A Practical Guide to Past Life Regression*, St. Paul, MN: Llewellyn 1985.

McClure, Kevin. Fire within and without, *The Unexplained* 1981, 4(38), 750- 753.

McClure, Kevin. Miracles of the Virgin, *The Unexplained*, 1983, 11(131), 2614-2617.

McCreery, C./ Claridge, G. A study of hallucinations in normal subjects II.
Electrophysiological data, *Personality and Individual Differences* 1996, 21, 749-758.

McCullough, ME/ Emmons, RA/ Tsang, J. The grateful disposition: A conceptual and empirical topography. *J Personality and Social Psychology* 2002, 82, 112-127.

McCullough, ME/ Emmons, RA/ Tsang, J. Gratitude in intermediate affective terrain: Links of grateful mood to individual differences and daily emotional experience. *J Personality and Social Psychology* 2004, 86(2), 295-309.

McDougall, W. Fourth report on a Lamarckian experiment, *British J Psychology* 1938, 28, 321-345.

McElroy, Susan Chernak. *Heart in the Wild*, New York: Ballatine Books, 2002, 71.

McFadden, Steven. *Profiles in Wisdom: Native Elders Speak about the Earth*, Santa Fe, NM: Bear & Co. 1991.

McGaa, Ed/ Man, Eagle. *Mother Earth Spirituality: Native American Paths to Healing Ourselves and Our World*, San Francisco: HarperCollins 1990.

McGarey, Gladys Taylor with Jess Stearn. *The Physician Within You, Medicine for the Millennium*. Deerfield Beach, Florida: Health Communications 1997.

McGuire, M. Health and spirituality as contemporary concerns, *Annals of the American Academy of Political and Social Science* 1993, 527, 144-154.

McGuire, Meredith B. *Pentecostal Catholics*, Philadelphia: Temple University 1982.

McIntosh, D/ Spilka, B. Religion and physical health: the role of personal faith and control beliefs, *Research in the Social Scientific Study of Religion* 1990, 2, 167-194.

McKee, DD/ Chappel, JN. Spirituality and medical practice. *J Fam Pract* 1992, 35, 201; 205-8.

McKinney, Laurence O. *Neurotheology: Virtual Religion in the 21st Century,* Cambridge, MA: American Institute for Mindfulness 1994.

McKnight, Rosalind A. *My Out-of-Body Explorations with Robert A. Monroe*, London: Hampton Roads 1999.

McMoneagle, Joseph. *Mind Trek: Exploring Consciousness, Time, and Space through Remote Viewing*, Hampton Roads 1993.

McMoneagle, Joseph. *Ultimate Time Machine: A Remote Viewer's Perception of Time and Predictions for the New Millennium,* Hampton Roads 1998.

McSherry, W/ Draper, P. The spiritual dimension: why the absence within the nursing curricula? *Nurse Education Today* 1997, 17, 413-417.

Mechanic, D. Religion, religiosity and illness behavior, *Human Organization* 1963, 22, 202-208.

Meek, George W (ed). A study of psychic surgery and spiritual healing in the Philippines, Privately printed 1973 (Cited in L. Watson 1975, p. 236.

Meek, George W. *Healers and the Healing Process*, Wheaton, IL: Theosophical Publishing House 1977. (Quotes reprinted by permission of publisher. Copyright George W. Meek, 1977.

Meek, George W. *Spiricom -- An Electromagnetic-Etheric Systems Approach to Communications with Other Levels of Human Consciousness*, Franklin, NC: Metascience 1982.

Meek, George W. Report from Europe, *Unlimited Horizons Newsletter* 1988, 6(1).

Mellen, Thomas
www.nderf.org/mellen_thomas_nde.htm

Melton, J. Gordon. *A Reader's Guide to the Ministry of Healing*, Evanston, IL: Academy of Religion and Psychical Research 1973 (75 pp. refs.).

Mendel, Gregor. Experiments on plant hybridization, *Read at the meetings of the Natural History Society of Brunn February 8th, and March 8th 1866*
www.mendelweb.org/Mendel.html
(Accessed 9/2/05).

Mendel.
www.en.wikipedia.org/wiki/Mendelian_inheritance (Accessed 9/2/05).

Mendelsohn, RS. *Confessions of a Medical Heretic*, New York: Warren 1979.

Mendez, MP, et al. The relationship of epileptic auras and psychological attributes, *J Neuropsychiatry and Clinical Neuroscience* 1996, 8, 287-292 (from Morse 1998).

Merchant, Carolyn. *The Death of Nature: Women, Ecology and the Scientific Revolution*, San Francisco: Harper & Row 1980.

Merchant, Carolyn: *Radical Ecology: The Search for a Liveable World*, New York/ London: Routledge 1992.

Merker, Mordecai M. Telepathy: A lawyer's analysis of the Indian rope trick, *Parapsychological Review* 1971, 2(6), 20-22.

Merrill, GG. Health, healing and religion, *Maryland State Medical J* 1981, 30, 45-47.

Mesko, Sabrina. *Healing Mudras: Yoga forYour Hands*, New York: Ballantine/ Wellspring 2000.

Metzner, Ralph. *The Unfolding Self: Varieties of Transformative Experience*, Novato: Origin 1998.

Meyer, Stephen C. DNA and the origin of life: Information, specification and explanation, In: Campbell, JA/ Meyer, SC, eds. *Darwinism, design and public education*, Lansing, MI: Michigan State University Press 2003, 223-285.

Meyer, Stephen C. Intelligent Design: The Origin of Biological Information and the Higher Taxonomic Categories, *Proceedings of the Biological Society of Washington* 2005, 117(2), 213-239.
www.discovery.org/scripts/viewDB/index.php?command=view&id=2177 (Accessed 9/5/05).

Michael, Chester P/ Norrisey, Marie C. *Prayer and Termperament: Different Prayer Forms for Different Personality Types*, Charlottesville, VA: Open Door 1991.

Miklos, GLG. Emergence of organizational complexities during metazoan evolution: Perspectives from molecular biology, palaeontology and neo-Darwinism, *Mem. Ass. Australas. Palaeontols* 1993, 15:7-41.

Milbourne, C. *Search for the Soul: An Insider's Report on the Continuing Quest by Psychics and Scientists for Evidence of Life After Death*, New York: Crowell 1979.

Miller, D. Patrick. Spirituality Up, Religion Down in America 2005.
www.infoshop.org/inews/article.php?story=200 50705225244714 (Accessed 9/26/05)

Miller, John (Jack) P/ Nakagawa, Yoshira. *Nurturing Our Wholeness: Perspectives on Spirituality in Education*, Brandon, VT: Foundation for Educational Renewal 2002.

Miller, Paul. *Born to Heal: A Biography of Harry Edwards, the Spirit Healer*, London: Spiritualist Press 1969 (Orig. 1948).

Mills, A, et al. Replication studies of cases suggestive of reincarnation by three independent investigators, *J the American Society PsychicalResearch* 1994, 88, 207.

Milner, Dennis. *The Loom of Creation*, London: Neville Spearman 1970.

Milton J. A meta-analysis of waking state of consciousness, free-response ESP studies. In Zingrone, NL/ Schlitz, MJ, eds. Research in parapsychology 1994, 31-34, Lanham, MD: Scarecrow Press 1995.

Mintz, Elizabeth E with Schmeidler, Gertrude R. *The Psychic Thread*, New York: Human Sciences 1983.

Mir, Maria/ Vilenskaya, Larissa. *The Golden Chalice*, San Francisco, CA: H. S. Dakin.

Mitchell, Edgar. In DiCarlo, p. 17.

Mitchell, Janet Lee. *Out-of-Body Experiences: A Handbook*, Jefferson, NC: McFarland 1981.

Moberg, DO. The Christian religion and personal adjustment in old age, *American Sociological Review* 1953a, 18, 87-90.

Moberg, DO. Church membership and personal adjustment in old age, *J Gerontology* 1953b, 8, 207-211.

Modi, Shakuntala. *Remarkable Healings: A Psychiatrist Discovers Unsuspected Roots of Mental and Physical Illness*, Charlottesville, VA: Hampton Roads 1998.

Monk, M, et al: An epidemiological study of ulcerative colitis and regional enteritis among adults in Baltimore - II. *Gastroenterology* 1969a, 56, 847-857.

Monk, M, et al: An epidemiological study of ulcerative colitis and regional enteritis among adults in Baltimore - III. *J Chronic Diseases* 1969b, 22, 565-578.

Monroe, Robert A. *Journeys Out of the Body*, Garden City, NY: Anchor 1973.

Montagno, Elson de A. Clinical parapsychology: The spiritist model in Brazil, In: Weiner, Debra H/ Radin, Dean I, eds. *Research in Parapsychology 1985*, Metuchen, NJ and London: Scarecrow 1986, 171-172.

Montefiore, Hugh. Is the philosophy of reincarnation compatible with Christianity? *J Religion and Psychical Research* 2002, 25(3), 158-166.

Montello, Louise. *Essential Musical Intelligence: Using Music as Your Path to Healing, Creativity, and Radiant Wholeness*, Wheaton, IL: Quest/ Theosophical 2002.

Montgomery, John Warwick, ed. *Demon Possession*, Minneapolis, MN: Bethany Fellowship 1976.

Montgomery, Ruth. *Born to Heal*, New York: Popular Library 1973.

Moody, Raymond A. *Life After Life*, New York: Bantam 1975.

Moody, Raymond A. *Reflections On Life After Life*, San Francisco: Cameron 1977.

Moody, Raymond A. Family Reunions: Visionary encounters with the departed in a modern-day psychomanteum, *J Near-Death Studies* 1992, 11, 83-121.

Moody, Raymond A/ Perry, Paul. *The Light Beyond*, New York: Bantam 1988.

Moody, Raymond A/ Perry, P. *Reunions: Visionary encounters with departed loved ones*, New York: Villard 1993.

Mookerjee, Ajit. *Tantra Art: Its Philosophy and Physics*, Basel, Paris, New Delhi: Ravi Kumar 1983.

Mookerjee, Ajit. *Kundalini: The Arousal of the Inner Energy*, Destiny/ Inner Traditions International 1991.

Moolenburgh, HC. *Meetings with Angels*, (Trans. from Dutch by Langham, Tony/ Peters, Plym) Saffron Walden, England: C.W. Daniel 1992.

Moore, Christopher J. *In Other Words: A Language Lover's Guide to the Most Intriguing Words Around the World*, New York: Levenger/ Walker & Co. 2004.

Moore, Thomas. *The Re-Enchantment of Everyday Life*, New York, New York; Harper Collins 1996.

Moorefield, Kathleen Renee Patin. *An Innovative Look at Spirituality and Personality*, Unpublished dissertation for Ph.D. in Spirituality and Energy Medicine, Australia: Greenwich University 2002.

Morris, RL/ Harary, SB/ Janis, J/ Hartwell, J/ Roll, WG. Studies of communication during out-of-body experiences, *J American Society PsychicalResearch* 1978, 72, 1-21.

Morrison, Scott. *Open and Innocent: The Gentle, Passionate Art of Not-Knowing*, 21st Century Renaissance 1997.

Morse, Melvin with Perry, Paul. *Closer to the Light: Learning from the Near-Death Experiences of Children*, New York: Ivy 1990.

Morse, Melvin with Perry, Paul. *Parting Visions: An Exploration of Pre-Death Psychic and Spiritual Experiences*, New York: Villard/ Random House 1994.

Morse, Melvin. The right temporal lobe and associated limbic lobe structures as the biological interface with an interconnected universe, *Network* 1998, 68, 3-7.

Morse, Melvin, et al. Childhood Near Death Experiences, *American J Diseases of Childhood* 1986, 140, 110-114 (from Morse 1998).

Morse, Melvin/Neppe, V. Near Death Experiences (letter), *Lancet* 1991, 337-386.

Mosley, Glenn/ Hill, Joanna. *The Power of Prayer around the World*, Templeton Foundation 2000.

Moss, Richard. *The Black Butterfly: An Invitation to Radical Aliveness*, Berkeley, CA: Celestial Arts 1986.

Moss, Thelma/ Schmeidler, Gertrude R. Quantitative investigation of a 'haunted house' with sensitives and a control group, *J the American Society PsychicalResearch* 1968, 62, 399-410.

Mother Teresa. Attributed.

Motoyama, Hiroshi. Excerpts from lecture on 'psychic surgery,' *International Association for Religion and Parapsychology Newsletter*, Dec 1977.

Motoyama, Hiroshi with Brown, Rande. *Science and the Evolution of Consciousness, Ki and Psi*, Brookline, MA: Autumn 1978(a).

Motoyama, Hiroshi. Tony Agpaoa's psychic surgery and its mechanisms, *Religion and Parapsycholog*, Encinitas, CA: International Association for Religion and Parapsychology 1978(b).

Motoyama, Hiroshi. *Theories of the Chakras: Bridge to Higher Consciousness*, Wheaton, IL: Theosophical 1981.

Motoyama, Hiroshi. *Karma & Reincarnation*, London: Piatkus 1992.

Mourning Dove. Quote from *Native American Wisdom*, Philadelphia/ London: Running Press 1994, p.111.

Mueller, Paul S/ Plevak, David J/ Rummans, Teresa A. Religious involvement, spirituality, and medicine: Implications for clinical practice, *Mayo Clinic Proceedings* 2001, 76, 1225-1235 (105 refs).

Muktananda, Swami. Sensual excitement, In: White, John, 1990, 167-168.

Muldoon M/ King N. Spirituality, health care, and bioethics. *J Relig Health* 1995, 34(4), 329-349.

Muldoon, Sylvan/ Carrington, H. *The Projection of the Astral Body*, New York: Samuel Weiser 1970.

Mullen, Karl E. *Reincarnation*, London: Psychic 1970.

Mullin, Glenn H. *Death and Dying: The Tibetan Tradition*, Boston, MA: Arkana 1986.

Muolenburgh, HC. *Meetings with Angels*, Trans. from Dutch by T. Langham/ Plym Peters, Saffron Walden, England: C.W. Daniel 1992.

Muolenburgh, HC. *Handbook of Angels*, Trans. from Dutch by Amina Marix-Evans, Saffron Walden, England: C. W. Daniels 1993.

Murphet, H. *Sai Baba, Man of Miracles*, India: Macmillan 1972.

Murphet, H. *Sai Baba, Avatar*, India: Macmillan 1978.

Murphy, Gardner. *Challenge of Psychical Research*, New York/ London: Harper Colophon 1970.

Murphy, Gardner. A Carringtonian approach to Ian Stevenson's "Twenty Cases Suggestive of Reincarnation," *J the American Society PsychicalResearch* 1973, 67(2), 117-129.

Murphy, M/ Donovan, S. *The Physical and Psychological Effects of Meditation: A Review of Contemporary Meditation Research with a Comprehensive Bibliography 1931-1988*, San Rafael: Esalen Institute, Study of Exceptional Functioning 1988, 312.

Murphy, Michael. *The Wisdom of Dying: Practices for Living*, Longmead, England: Element 1988.

Murphy, Michael/ Donovan, Steven. *Physical and Psychological Effects of Meditation*, New York: Tarcher/ Putnam 1995.

Murphy, Michael/ Donovan, Steven. *The Physical and Psychological Effects of Meditation: A Review of Contemporary Meditation Research With a Comprehensive Bibliography,* 1931-1996. San Rafael.CA: Esalen Institute of Exceptional Functioning 1997.

Murphy, Michael/ White, Rhea A. *In the Zone: Transcendent Experience in Sports*, New York: Penguin 1995.

Musgrave, C. The near-death experience: A study of spiritual transformation. *J Near-Death Studies* 1997, 15(3), 187-202.

Myers, AT/ Myers, FWH. Mind-cure, faith-cure and the miracles of Lourdes, *Proceedings of the Society PsychicalResearch* 1894, 9, 160- 209.

Myers, FWH. *Human Personality and its Survival of Bodily Death*, New York: Longmans Green 1903.

Myss, Caroline. *Anatomy of the Spirit: The Seven Stages of Power and Healing*, New York: Harmony 1996.

N

Nadeau, R/ Kafatos, M. *The Non-local Universe: The New Physics and Matters of the Mind*, New York: Oxford University 1999.

Naegeli, H. Die 'Tricks' der Geist-Operateure, *Esotera* 1973, 24, 685.

Naegeli-Osjord, Hans. *Possession and Exorcism*, Oregon, WI: New Frontiers Center 1988.

Nagarjuna, quoted in TRVMurti. *The Central Philosophy of Buddhism*, London: Allan & Unwin 1955.

Naparstek, Belleruth. *Your Sixth Sense: Unlocking the Power of Your Intuition*, New York: HarperCollins 1997.

Naranjo, Claudio. Drug-induced states, In: Wolman/ Ullman 1986, 365-394.

Narayanasamy A. A review of spirituality as applied to nursing. *International J Nursing Studies* 1999, 36, 117-125.

Nash, Carroll B. *Science of Psi: ESP and PK*, Springfield, IL: C.C. Thomas 1978.

Nash, Carroll B. Psychokinetic control of bacterial growth, *J Society PsychicalResearch* 1982, 51, 217-221.

Nash, Carroll B. Test of psychokinetic control of bacterial mutation, *J American Society PsychicalResearch* 1984, 78(2), 145-152.

Nash, Carroll B, *Parapsychology: The Science of Psiology*, Springfield, IL: Charles C. Thomas 1986.

Nash, CB/ Nash, CS. The effect of paranormally conditioned solution on yeast fermentation, *J Parapsych-ology* 1967, 31, 314.

Neal, Emily Gardiner. *The Healing Power of Christ*, New York: Hawthorne 1972.

Neal, James H. *Jungle Magic: My Life Among the Witch Doctors of West Africa*, New York: Paperback 1969.

Needham, J. *Science and Civilisation in China*, vol. III, Cambridge, England: Cambridge University 1956.

Needleman, Jacob, *A Sense of the Cosmos*, London: Arkana 1988.

Neeleman T/ King MB. Psychiatrists' religious attitudes in relation to their clinical practice: a survey of 231 psychiatrists. *Acta Psychiatr Scand* 1993, 88(6),420-4.

Neher, Andrew. *The Psychology of Transcendence*, Englewood Cliffs, NJ: Spectrum/ Prentice-Hall 1980.

Neihardt, John G. *Black Elk Speaks*, New York: Washington Square 1972, 36.

Nelson, John E. *Healing the Split; Integrating Spirit Into Our Understanding of the Mentally Ill*, State University of New York Press 1994.

Nelson, Roger/ Radin, Dean. When immovable objections meet irresistible evidence, *Behavioral & Brain Sciences* 1987, 10, 600-601.

Nesbitt, Mark. *Ghosts of Gettysburg: Spirits, Apparitions and Haunted Places of the Battlefield*, Gettysburg, PA: Thomas 1991.

Netherton, M/ Shiffrin, N. *Past Lives Therapy*, New York: Ace 1978.

Nevus, John. *Demon Possession and Allied Themes*, Chicago, IL: Revell (no date).

Newberg, Andrew B. Developmental spirituality: A neuropsychological model, Presentation at 8th Annual Spirituality Research Symposium, *The Spiritual Care of Hospitalized Children & Their Families*, Department of Pastoral Care, UPHS, Office of the Chaplain and The Pediatric Advanced Care Team at CHOP, June 9, 2005.

Newberg, Andrew/ D'Aquili, Eugene/ Rause, Vince. *Why God Won't Go Away: Brain Science & the Biology of Belief,* New York: Ballantine 2001.

Newberg, AB/ Iversen J. The neural basis of the complex mental task of meditation: neurotransmitter and neurochemical considerations, *Medical Hypotheses* 2003, 61(2), 282-291.

Newman, Robert C. *A Designed Universe* 2005. www.ibri.org/Tracts/dsgntct.htm (Accessed 8/5/05).

Newton, Isaac. [1687] In: Hutchins, RM, ed., General Scholium, *Mathematical Principles of Natural Philosophy*, Chicago: Great Books of the Western World, 1952, 369 (from Thaxton).

Newton, John. *Journey of Souls: Case Studies of Life Between Lives*, St. Paul, MN: Llewellyn 2001 (orig. 1994).

Newton, Michael. *Journey of Souls: Case Studies of Life Between Lives*, St. Paul, MN: Llewelyn Publications 2001.

Newton, Michael/ Duff, Michael. *Destiny of Souls: New Case Studies of Life Between Lives,* St Paul, MN: Llewellyn 2000.

Newton-Smith, WH. *The Structure of Time*, London: Routledge and Kegan Paul 1984.

Nhat Hanh, Thich. *Peace is Every Step: The Path of Mindfulness in Everyday Life*, New York: Bantam Books 1991.

Nicola, Rev. John J. *Diabolical Possession and Exorcism*, Rockford, IL: Tan 1974.

Nolen, William A. *Healing: A Doctor in Search of a Miracle*, New York: Random House 1974.

Nolen, William A. Psychic healing, In: Abell, George O/ Singer, Barry, *Science and the Para-*

normal NY: Charles Scribner's Sons, 1984, 185-194.

Nordland, Rod. The firewalkers of Fiji: Faith and a nip of 'kava,' *Philadelphia Inquirer* Apr 16 1982, p. 2.

Norris, CM. *Concept Clarification In Nursing*, Rockville, MD: Aspen Systems Corp. 1982.

Northage, Ivy. Levels of communication, *Light* 1988, 108(2), 62- 65.

Norwood, Robin. *Why Me? Why This? Why Now?* London: Century 1994.

Noyes, R/ Kletti, R. Panoramic memory: A response to the threat of death, *Omega* 1977, 8, 181-194.

Nuland, Sherwin B. *How We Die*, New York: Knopf, 1994.

O

O'Brien, ME. Religious faith and adjustment to long-term hemodialysis, *J Religion and Health*, 1982, 21, 68-80.

Oesterreich, Traugott K. *Possession and Exorcism (Among Primitive Races, in Antiquity, the Middle Ages, and Modern Times)*, New York: Causeway 1974 (Orig. titled, *Possession: Demoniacal and Other* 1921).

Oh Shinnah. Odyssey of a warrior woman, In: *McFadden* 1991.

Ohno, S. The notion of the Cambrian pananimalia genome, *Proceedings of the National Academy of Sciences* 1996, 93, 8475-8478.

Olive, KE. Physician religious beliefs and the physician-patient relationship: a study of devout physicians. *Southern Medical J* 1995; 88(12), 1249-55.

Ólaoire, Seán. Presentation at Healing Research Conference, Boston, 1997, Personal communication 1997.

Olson, Melodie/ Dulaney, Peggy. Life satisfaction, life review, and near death experiences in the elderly, *J Holistic Nursing*, 1993, 11(4), 368-382.

On healing unto death, *The Doctor-Healer Network Newsletter*, Winter 1992-3, Issue No. 4.

Oppenheim, Janet. *The Other World: Spiritualism and Psychical Research in England 1850-1914*, Cambridge, England: Cambridge University 1985.

Ormond, Ron/ McGill, Ormond. *Into the Strange Unknown*, CA: The Esoteric Foundation 1959.

Ornstein, Robert/ Thompson, Richard. *The Amazing Brain*, Boston: Houghton Mifflin 1984.

Orr, Leonard/ Ray, Sondra. *Rebirthing in the New Age*, Millbrae, CA: Celestial Arts 1977.

Orso, Renato. Analisi elettroacustica delle voci, *Informazioni J. Psicofonia* 1985a, 7(2), 22-25.

Orso, Renato. *Esecuzione dei sonogrammi rilasciato al Signor R. Orso*, Istituto Elettrotechnico Nazionale Torino, Certificato 8 Ottobre 1985b.

Ortega y Gasset, José. *Meditaciones del Quijote* 1914.

Osis, Karlis. *Deathbed Observations of Physicians and Nurses*, New York: Parapsychology Foundation 1961.

Osis, Karlis. New OBE experiments, *American Society PsychicalResearch* 1972, 14.

Osis, Karlis. What did the dying see? *American Society PsychicalResearch Newsletter* 1975, 24, 1-3.

Osis, Karlis. Insider's views of the OBE: A questionnaire survey, In: Roll, W. G., *Research in Parapsychology 1978* Metuchen, NJ: Scarecrow 1979, 50-52.

Osis, Karlis. Current research in OBE experiences, *American Society PsychicalResearch Newsletter* 1980, 6.

Osis, Karlis/ Haraldsson, Erlendur. OBE in Indian Swamis: Sathya Sai Baba and Dadaji, *Research in Parapsychology*, 1976.

Osis, Karlis/ Haraldsson, Erlendur. *At the Hour of Death*, New York: Discus/ Avon 1977.

Osis, Karlis/ McCormick, Donna. Kinetic effects at the ostensible location of an out-of-body projection during perceptual testing, *J the American Society PsychicalResearch* 1980, 74, 319-329.

Osis, Karlis/ Mitchell, Janet L. Physiological correlates of reported out-of-body experiences, *J Society PsychicalResearch* 1977, 49, 525-536.

Osler, William. The faith that heals, *British Medical J* 1910, i, 1470-2.

Osty, Eugene. *Supernormal Faculties in Man*, Translated by deBrath, S, London: Methuen 1923.

Osty, Eugene. *Supernormal Aspects of Energy and Matter*, Translated by Besterman, Theodore, London, Society PsychicalResearch 1933.

Oursler, Will. *The Healing Power of Faith*, New York: Hawthorn 1957.

Ovid. *Ars Amatoria* 17.

Owen, Iris M with Sparrow, Margaret. *Conjuring Up Philip: An Adventure in Psychokinesis*, New York: Harper and Row 1976.

Owen, Iris/ Sparrow, Margaret. Personal Communication, 1984.

Owens, CM. The mystical experience: facts and values, In: White, J. *The Highest State of Consciousness*, Garden City, NY: Anchor/ Doubleday 1972.

Owens, JE/ Cook, EW/ Stevenson, I. Features of "near-death experience" in relation to whether or not patients were near death, *Lancet* 1990, 336, 1175-1177.

Oxford. *Essential Quotations dictionary, American Edition*, New York, NY: Berkeley 1998.

P

Pahnke, WN. Drugs and mysticism, In: White, J., *The Highest State of Consciousness*, Garden City, NY: Anchor/ Doubleday 1972.

Paige, Leroy (Satchel). American baseball player, In: *Begley/ Reagan*, 2002, 108.

Paley, William. *Natural Theology*, Boston: Gould, Kendall and Lincoln 1835.

Palmer, Greg. *Death: The Trip of a Lifetime*, HarperSanFrancisco 1993.

Palmer, John. Scoring in ESP tests as a function of belief in ESP. Part I: The sheep-goat effect, *J the American Society PsychicalResearch* 1971, 65, 373-408.

Palmer, John. Scoring in ESP tests as a function of belief in ESP. Part II, Beyond the sheep-goat effect, *J the American Society PsychicalResearch* 1972, 66, 1-26.

Palmer, John. ESP and out-of-body experiences: EEG correlates. In Roll, WG, ed. *Research in parapsychology* 1978, Metuchen, NJ: Scarecrow Press 1979, 135-138.

Palmini, A/ Gloor, P. The localizing value of auras in partial seizures, *Neurology* 1992, 42, 801-806.

Palmstierna, Eric. *Widening Horizons*, John Lane, The Bodley Head, 249-50.

Pannikar, R. *Myth, Faith and Hermeneutics*, New York: Paulist 1979, p. 98.

Pargament, KI/ Brannick, MT/ Adamakos, H/ Ensing, DS/ Keleman, ML/ Warren, RK/ Falgout, K/ Cook, P/ Myers, J. Indiscriminate proreligiousness: Conceptualization and measurement, *J for the Scientific Study of Religion* 1987, 26, 182-200.

Pargament, Kenneth I/ Koenig, Harold G/ Tarakeshwar, Nalini/ Hahn, June. Religious Struggle as a Predictor of Mortality Among Medically Ill Elderly Patients: A 2-Year Longitudinal Study, *Archives of Internal Medicine* 2001, 161, 1881-1885.

Pargament, KI/ Koenig, HG/ Tarakeshwar, N/ Hahn, J. Religious coping methods as predictors of psychological, physical and spiritual outcomes among medically ill elderly patients: a two-year longitudinal study, *J Health Psychology* November 2004, 9(6), 713-30.

Parnell, Laurel. Eye Movement Desensitization and Reprocessing (EMDR) and spiritual unfolding, *J Transpersonal Psychology*, 1996, 28, 129-153.

Parnell, Laurel. *Transforming Trauma*, New York: Norton 1997.

Parnia S, et al. A qualitative and quantitative study of the incidence,features and aetiology of near death experiences in cardiac arrest survivors. *Resuscitation* 2001, 48, 149-156.

Parnia S, et al. Near-death experience in survivors of cardiac arrest: a prospective study in the Netherlands. *Lancet* 2001, 358, 2039-2045.

Parse, RR. *Man-Living-Health: A Theory of Nursing*, New York: John Wiley 1981.

Pascal, Blaise. Commemoration of Osmund, Bishop of Salisbury.

Pasricha, Satwant. *Claims of Reincarnation: An Empirical Study of Cases in India*, New Delhi: Harman 1990.

Pasricha, Satwant K. Are reincarnation type cases shaped by parental guidance? An empirical study concerning the limits of parents' influence on children, *J Scientific Exploration* 1992, 6(2), 167-180.

Pasricha, Satwant K. Cases of the reincarnation type in Northern India with birthmarks and birth defects, *J Scientific Exploration* 1998, 12(2), 259-293.

Pasricha, Satwant/ Stevenson, Ian. Near-death experiences in India: A preliminary report, *J Nervous and Mental Disease* 1986, 175, 165-170.

Pattison, E Mansel/ Kahan, Joel/ Hurd, Gary S. Trance and possession states, in Wolman, BB/ Ullman, M, eds. *Handbook of States of Consciousness*, New York: Van Nostrand Reinhold 1986, 287-310.

Paul, Stephen C/ Collins, Gary Max. *Inneractions: Visions to Bring Your Inner and Outer Worlds into Harmony*, HarperSanFrancisco 1992.

Pearce, Ian. Medicine, religion and healing, *Healing Review*, Summer 1981, England: National Federation of Spiritual Healers, 10-13.

Pearce, Joseph Chilton. *The Bond of Power*, New York: Dutton 1981.

Pearce, Joseph Chilton. *The Biology of Transcendence: A Blueprint of the Human Spirit*, Rocherster, VT: Park Street 2002.

Pearsall, Ronald. *The Table-Rappers*, New York: St. Martin's 1972.

Peat, F. David. *Synchronicity: The Bridge Between Matter and Mind*, New York and London: Bantam 1987.

Peat, F. David. Towards a process theory of healing: energy, activity and global form, *Subtle Energies* 1992, 3(2), 1-40.

Peck, M. Scott. *People of the Lie*, New York: Simon & Schuster 1983.

Pelikan, Wilhelm. *Healing Plants: Insights through Spiritual Science*, Georgetown, Ontario: Mercury 1997.

Pellerin, Cheryl. *Trips*, New York: Seven Stories Press 1998.

Penelhum, Terence. *Christian Ethics and Human Nature*, SCM 2000.

Penfield, W. The role of the temporal cortex in certain psychical phenomena, *J Mental Science* 1955, 101, 451-465 (from Morse 1998).

Penfield, W. *The Mystery of the Mind: A Critical Study of Consciousness and the Human Brain*, Princeton: Princeton University Press 1975.

Penfield, W/ Rasmussen, T. *The Cerebral Cortex of Man: a Clinical Study of Localization Of Function*, New York: Macmillan 1950, 162-181 (from Morse 1988).

Penn, William. *No Cross, No Crown*, 1669.

Permutt, Cyril. *Beyond the Spectrum: A Survey of Supernormal Photography*, Cambridge, England: Patrick Stephens 1983.

Perry, John Weir. *Trials of the Visionary Mind; Spiritual Emergency and the Renewal Process*, State University of New York Press 1999.

Perry, Michael, ed. *Deliverance: Psychic Disturbances and Occult Involvement*, London: SPCK 1987.

Persinger, Michael A. *Neurophysiological Bases of God Beliefs*, Westport, CT: Praeger 1987.

Persinger, Michael A. Michael Persinger has a vision - the Almighty isn't dead, he's an energy field: Your mind is an electromagnetic map to your soul. *Wired* Nov 1999, Issue 7.11

www.wired.com/ wired/ archive/ 7.11/ persinger_pr.html. See also www.laurentian.ca/ neurosci/ persinger.html.

Perutz, MF/ Lehmann, H. Molecular pathology of human hemoglobin, *Nature* 219, 1968, 902-909.

Peters, Larry. *Ecstasy and Healing in Nepal*, Malibu, CA: Undena 1981.

Peterson, James W. *The Secret Life of Kids*, Wheaton, IL: Quest/ Theosophical 1987.

Peterson, James W. Extrasensory abilities of children: An ignored reality? *Learning* December 1975, 10-14.

Phillips, Jan. *God Is at Eye Level: Photography as a Healing Art*, Wheaton, IL: Quest 2000.

Phoenix: New directions in the study of man, *J the Association for Transpersonal Anthropology.*

Piaget, Jean. *The Child and Reality*, New York: Penguin 1976

Pierrakos, John C. *Human Energy Systems Theory: History and New Growth Perspectives*, New York: Institute for the New Age of Man 1976.

Pirsig, Robert M. *Zen and the Art of Motorcycle Maintenance*, New York/ London: Bantam 1975.

Pitts, JR/ Schiller, PL. *Marginality, structural differenti-ation and professionalization*, Presented at the Annual Meeting of the American Sociological Association 1978.

Plato. *Euthyphro.*

Plato. *Laws*, Book X; quoted in Head, Joseph/ Cranston, S.L. *Reincarnation*, Quest 1961, 557.

Playfair, Guy Lyon. Twenty years among the tables, *Psi Research* 1985a, 4(1), 96-107.

Plotnikoff, Gregory A. In search of a good death: the spiritual dimension, *Minnesota Medicine* May 2000a, 83. www.mmaonline.net/publications/MnMed2000/May/Plotnikoff.cfm (Accessed 3/9/06).

Plotnikoff, Gregory A. Should medicine reach out to the spirit? Understanding a patient's spiritual foundation can guide appropriate care, *Postgraduate Medicine* 2000b, 108(6).

Podmore, Frank. Poltergeists, *Proceedings of the Society PsychicalResearch* 1896, 12, 45-115.

Pogacnik, Marko. *Nature Spirits & Elemental Beings: Working with the Intelligence in Nature*, Forres, Moray, Scotland: Findhorn 1997.

Pogacnik, Marko. *Daughter of GAIA: Rebirth of the Divine Feminine*, Forres, Moray, Scotland: Findhorn 2001.

Polkinghorne, John, ed. *The Work of Love: Creation as Kenosis*, Grand Rapids, MI: Eerdmans 2001.

Poloma, Margaret M/ Gallup, George H Jr. *Varieties of Prayer: A Survey Report*, Philadelphia, PA: Trinity Press 1991.

Pope, Alexander. *An Essay on Man*, Epistle 1733, 2, 208-214.

Popper, Karl R. *The Open Society and its Enemies*, 5th ed. Princeton, NJ: Princeton University (Orig. 1945) 1966.

Popper, Karl R/ Eccles, John C. *The Self and Its Brain*, Berlin, Heidelberg, London, New York: Springer-Verlag International 1977, 120.

Post, Stephen G, et al. Physicians and patient spirituality: Professional boundaries, competency, and ethics, *Annals of Internal Medicine*, 2000, 132, 578-583.

Poulton, Kay. *Harvest of Light: A Pilgrimage of Healing*, London: Regency 1968.

Powell, AE. *The Astral Body*, Wheaton, IL: Theosophical Publishing House 1972. Powell, LH/ Shahabi, L/ Thoresen, CE. Religion and spirituality, *American Psychologist* 2003, 58(1), 36-52.

Pranis, Kay/ Stuart, Barry/ Wedge, Mark. *Peacemaking Circles: From Crime to Community*, St. Paul, MN: Living Justice Press 2003.

Pratt, Christina. Ritual and ceremony, *American Holistic Medical Association Newsletter*, Summer 2005, VIII (3), 8.

Prell, Riv-Ellen. *Prayer and Community. The Havurah in American Judaism*. Detroit, Michigan: Wayne State University Press 1989.

Price, HH. Haunting and the 'psychic ether' hypothesis, *Proceedings of the Society PsychicalResearch* 1938-1939, 45, 317-328.

Price, Hope. *Angels: True Stories of How They Touch Our Lives*, London: Pan/ Macmillan 1994.

Price, John Randolph. *The Angels Within Us: A Spiritual Guide to the Twenty-Two Angels that Govern Our Lives*, New York: Fawcett Columbine 1993.

Prince, GR. *The Enchanted Boundary*, Boston: Boston Society PsychicalResearch 1955.

Prince, R/ Savage, C. Mystical states and the concept of regression, in White, J. *The Highest State of Conscious-ness*, Garden City, NY: Anchor/ Doubleday 1972.

Prince, Raymond, ed. Trance and possession states, *Proceedings of the Second Annual Conference of the R. M. Bucke Memorial Society*, 4-6 March 1966, Montreal.

Prince, Raymond. Fundamental differences of psychoanalysis and faith healing, *International J Psychiatry* 1972, 10(1), 125-128.

Prince, Walter Franklin. Two cures of 'paranoia' by experimental appeals to purported obsessing spirits, *Psychoanalytic Review* 1969, 56, 57-86.

Princeton Engineering Anomalies Research www.princeton.edu/~pear/5.html (Accessed 1/16/06).

Princeton Religion Research Center. *Religion in America*, Princeton: The Gallup Poll 1996.

Proust, Marcel. *Guemantes Way*, 1921.

Pruitt, James. *The Complete Angel: Angels Through the Ages - All You Need to Know*, New York: Avon 1995.

Puchalski, CM. The role of spirituality in health care, *Baylor University Medical Center Proceedings* 2001, 14, 353-357.

Puchalski. CM. Spirituality in health: the role of spirituality in critical care, *Critical Care Clinics* 2004, 20(3), 487-504, x.

Puharich, Andrija. Protocommunication, *Parapsychology Today: A Geographic View. Proceedings of International Conference*, New York: Parapsychology Foundation 1973, 224-249.

Puharich, Andrija. Pachita: Instant surgeon, *The Unexplained* 1983, 13(154), 3074-3077 (Quotes by permission of Orbis Publishing Ltd., London).

Puharich, Henry K. The work of the Brazilian healer Arigo, In: *The Varieties of Healing Experience*, Los Altos, CA: Academy of Parapsychology and Medicine 1972.

Pulos, Lee/ Richman, Gary. *Miracles and Other Realties*, San Francisco: Omega Press 1990.

Puthoff, H. E./ Targ, R. A, A perceptual channel for information transfer over kilometer distances: Historical perspective and recent research, *Proceedings of the IEEE* 1976, 64, 329-354.

Q

Quenk, Naomi L. *Essentials of Myers-Briggs Type Indicator Assessment (Essentials of Psychological Assessment Series)*, New York: John Wiley & Sons 1999.

R

Radin DI/ Ferrari DC. Effects of consciousness on the fall of dice: A meta-analysis, *Journal of Scientific Exploration* 1991, 5, 61-84.

Radin, Dean. *The Conscious Universe*, New York: HarperCollins 1997.

Radin, D. For whom the bell tolls: A question of global consciousness, *IONS Noetic Sci Rev* 2003, 63, 8–13, 44–45.

Radin, D. *Global Consciousness: Seeking for Whom the Bell Tolls. Exploring Mind-Matter Interactions on a Global Scale*, www.experiencefestival.com/a/Global_Consciousn ess/ id/9788 (accessed 2/26/06).

Radin D/ Nelson, R. Meta-analysis of mind-matter interaction experiments: 1959 to 2000 www.boundaryinstitute.org/articles/rngma.pdf (Accessed 2/26/06)

Raikov, Vladimir L., Artificial reincarnation through hypnosis, *Psychic* Jun 1971.

Rama, S. *A Practical Guide to Holistic Health*, Honesdale, PA: Himalayan International Institute 1978.

Rama, Swami. *Freedom from the Bondage of Karma*, Honesdale, PA: Himalayan 1980.

Ramachandran, VS/ Blakeslee, Sandra. *Phantoms in the Brain*, London: Fourth Estate 1998.

Ramondetta, LM/ Sills, D. Spirituality in gynecological oncology: a review, *International J Gynecological Cancer* March-April 2004, 14(2), 183-201.

Randall-May, Cay. *Pray Together Now: How to Find or Form a Prayer Group*, Boston, MA: Element 1999.

Randi, James. "Be healed in the name of God!" an expose of the Reverend W. V. Grant, *Free Inquiry* 1986 (Spring), 8-19.

Randi, James. *The Faith Healers*, Buffalo, NY: Promethius 1987.

Randles, Jenny/ Hough, Peter. *The Afterlife: An Investigation into the Mysteries of Life After*, London: Piatkus 1993.

Rando, Therese A. *How to Go On Living When Someone You Love Dies*, New York: Bantam Books 1991.

Raudive, Konstantine. *Breakthrough: An Amazing Experiment in Electronic Communication with the Dead*, Gerrards Cross, UK: Colin Smythe 1971.

Rauscher, Elizabeth A. The physics of psi phenomena in space and time, Part I. Major principles of physics, psychic phenomena and some physical models, *Psi Research* 1983, 2(2), 64-87; Part II. Multidimensional geometric models, *Psi Research* 1983, 2(3), 93-120.

Rauscher, Elizabeth. Psi applications: Alternative healing techniques in Brazil, *Psi Research* 1985, 4(1), 57-65.

Rawlings, Morris. *Beyond Death's Door*, Nashville, TN: Thomas Nelson 1993.

Ray, Kane. *Religion: The Paradigm of Self-Deception*, Bloomington, In: AuthorHouse 2004.

Reagan, Michael, ed. *Reflections on the Nature of God*, Radnor, PA: Templeton Foundation Press/ Lionheart Books, Ltd. 2004, 48.

Reed, PG. Spirituality and well-being in terminally-ill, hospitalized adults, *Research in Nursing & Health* 1987, 10(5), 335-344.

Rees, WD. The bereaved and their hallucinations, In: Schoenberg, B et al., eds. *Bereavement and Its Psycho-logical Aspects*, New York: Columbia University 1975.

Religious Education Association. *Faith development in the adult life cycle*, Minneapolis: Religious Education Association of the United States and Canada 1987.

Remen, Rachel Naomi. On Defining Spirit, *Noetic Sciences Review* 1993, 27, 40.

Restak, RM. *The Infant Mind*, Garden City, NY: Doubleday 1986.

Reuther, Rosemary Radford. *Gaia and God: An Ecofeminist Theology of Earth Healing*, New York: HarperSanFrancisco 1992.

Rhine, JB. *Extrasensory Perception*, Boston: Branden 1964.

Rhine, Louisa E. *Hidden Channels of the Mind*, New York: William Morrow 1961.

Rhine, Louisa E. *ESP in Life and Lab: Tracing Hidden Channels*, New York: MacMillan 1967.

Rhine, Louisa E. *Mind Over Matter*, New York: Collier 1970.

Richards, John Thomas. *SORRAT: A History of the Neihardt Psychokinesis Experiments*, Metuchen, NJ: Scarecrow 1982.

Richardson, Jan L. *Sacred Journeys. A Woman's Book of Daily Prayer*. Nashville, Tennessee: Upper Room Books, 1995.

Ricoeur, Paul. *The Symbolism of Evil*, trans. Emerson Buchanan, Boston: Beacon 1967

Rigoni-Stern. Nota sulle richerche del dottor fanchou intorno la frequenza del cancro, *Annali Universitatis Medicina* 1844, 110, 484-503.

Rilke, Rainer Maria. *Letters to a Young Poet*, M. D. Herter Norton, trans., New York: W. W. Norton 1934.

Rinaldi, Sonia. ITC association of Brazil (Associacao Nacional de Transcomunicadores), *List of EVP sites*, www.ringsurf.com/netring?ring=EVP_ITC;id=9 ;action=list (Accessed 5/2/05).

Ring, Kenneth. *Life at Death: Scientific Investigation of the Near-Death Experience*, New York: Coward, McCann & Geoghegan 1980.

Ring, Kenneth. *Heading towards Omega: In Search of the Meaning of the Near-Death Experience*, New York: William Morrow 1984.

Ring, K/ Cooper, S. Near-death and out-of-body experiences in the blind: A study of apparent eyeless vision, *J Near Death Studies*, 1997, 16, 101-1047.

Ring, K/ Rosing, CJ. The omega project: An empirical study of the NDE-prone personality, *J Near-Death Studies* 1990, 8(4), 211-239.

Ring, Kenneth/ Cooper, Sharon. *Mindsight*, William James Centre for Consciousness Studies, UK 1999.

Ring, Kenneth/ Valarino, Evelyn Elsaesser. *Lessons from the Light*, Insight 1998.

Rinpoche, Sogyal. *The Tibetan Book of Living and Dying*, New York: HarperSanFrancisco 1992.

Riscalla, Louise Mead. A study of religious healers and healees, *J the American Society for Psychosomatic Dentistry and Medicine* 1982, 29(3), 97-103.

Ritchie, George G. *Return from Tomorrow*, New York: Chosen 1978.

Ritchie, George G. *My Life After Dying*, Norfolk, VA: Hampton Roads 1991.

Rivas, Titus. Three cases of the reincarnation type in the Netherlands, *J Scientific Exploration*, 2003, 17(3), Article 6. www.scientificexploration.org/jse/abstracts/v17 n3a6.php (Accessed 1/11/06)

Roads, Michael J. *Talking with Nature: Journey into Nature*, Novato, California: New World Library 2003.

Roberts, Estelle. *Fifty Years a Medium*, London: Corgi/ Transworld, 1969.

Roberts, Glenn/ Owen, John. The near-death experience, *British J Psychiatry* 1988, 153, 607-617.

Roberts, Jane. *Seth Speaks*, Englewood Cliffs, NJ: Prentice-Hall 1972.

Roberts, Jane. *The Education of Oversoul 7*, New York: Pocket 1973.

Roberts, Jane. *The Nature of Personal Reality*, Englewood Cliffs, NJ: Prentice- Hall 1974 (Quotes reprinted by permission of the publisher).

Roberts, Jane. *Dialogues of the Soul and Mortal Self in Time*, Englewood Cliffs, NJ: Prentice-Hall 1975.

Roberts, Jane. *Oversoul Seven and the Museum of Time*, Englewood Cliffs, NJ: Prentice-Hall 1984.

Rodabough, T. NDEs: Examination of the supporting data and aternative explanations, *Death Studies* 1985, 9, 95-113.

Rodin, Ernst A. The reality of death experiences, *J Nervous and Mental Disease* 1980, 168(5), 259-263.

Rodin, J. Aging and health: Effects of the sense of control, *Science* 1986, 233, 1271-1276.

Rogers, John. *Dying to Live*, Minerva 200.

Rogo, D. Scott, ed. *Mind Beyond the Body: The Mystery of ESP Projection*, New York: Penguin 1978.

Rogo, D. Scott/ Bayless, Raymond. Psychic surgery, *J the Society PsychicalResearch* 1968, 44, 426.

Rogo, D. Scott. Photographs by the mind, *Psychic* Apr 1970(a).

Rogo, D. Scott. *NAD: A Study of Some Unusual "Other World" Experiences*, NY: University 1970(b).

Rogo, D. Scott. *A Psychic Study of 'The Music of the Spheres' (NAD, Volume II)*, Secaucus, NJ: University Books 1972.

Rogo, D. Scott. *Man Does Survive Death*, Secaucus, NJ: Citadel 1973.

Rogo, D. Scott. Possession and parapsychology, *Para-psychology Review* 1974(a), 5(6), 18-24.

Rogo, D. Scott. Psychotherapy and the poltergeist, *J the Society PsychicalResearch* 1974(b), 47, 433-447.

Rogo, D. Scott/ Bayless, Raymond. *Phone Calls from the Dead: The Results of a Two-Year Investigation into an Incredible Phenomenon*, Englewood Cliffs, NJ: Prentice-Hall 1979.

Rogo, D. Scott. *Miracles: A Parascientific Inquiry into Wondrous Phenomena*, New York: Dial 1982.

Rogo, D. Scott. *Leaving the Body: A Complete Guide to Astral Projection*, Englewood Cliffs, N.J. Prentice-Hall 1983(a).

Rogo, D. Scott. In pursuit of the healing force, In: *Fate Magazine, Exploring the Healing Miracle*, Highland Park, IL: Clark 1983(b) (Orig. *Fate Magazine* Mar. 1983).

Rogo, D. Scott. Experiencing death through drugs, *Fate* May 1984(a), 88-93.

Rogo, D. Scott. Ketamine and the Near-Death Experience, *Anabiosis* 4, 1984(b), 87- 96.

Rogo, D. Scott. *The Search for Yesterday: A Critical Examination of the Evidence for Reincarnation*, Englewood Cliffs, NJ: Prentice-Hall 1985.

Rogo, D. Scott. The power of prayer, *Fate* 1986 (Aug), 43-50.

Rogo, D. Scott. *The Infinite Boundary: Spirit Possession, Madness and Multiple Personality*, Wellingborough, Northants. England: Aquarian/ Thorsons; New York: Dodd, Mead 1988.

Roll, William G. *The Poltergeist*, Garden City, NY: Doubleday 1972.

Roll, William/ Montagno, Elson/ Pulos, Lee/ Giovetti, Paola. *Physical Mediumship: Some Recent Claims*, Presentation at 100th Society PsychicalResearch and 25th Parapsychological Association Conference, Aug 1982.

Roman, Sanaya. *Spiritual Growth: Being Your Higher Self*, Tiburon, CA: H. J. Kramer 1989.

Romanyshyn, Robert. *The Soul in Grief: Love, Death and Transformation*, Berkeley, CA: Frog 1999.

Rose, Xenia. *Widow's Journey A Return to Living*, Human Horizons Series. ISBN 0-285-65098-X.

Rosenberg, Carol, ed. *Your Daily Diary and Health J: Helping You Live Your Best Life*, North Bergen, NJ: Basic Health Publications 2004, 180.

Rosenberg, Marshall B/ Leu, Lucy, eds. *Nonviolent Communication: A Language of Life: Create Your Life, Your Relationships, and Your World in Harmony with Your Values*, Puddledancer Press.

Rosenthal, R. *On the Social Psychology of the Self-Fulfilling Prophecy: Further Evidence for Pygmalion Effects and Their Mediating Mechanisms*, New York: MSS Modular Publications 1974, Module 53, 1-28.

Rosenthal, R/ Rubin, DR. Interpersonal expectancy effects: The first 345 studies, *The Behavioral and Brain Sciences* 1978, 3, 377-415.

Ross, Hugh. *The Fingerprint of God*, Whitaker House, 1989.

Ross, Michael W/ Stalstrom, Olli W. Exorcism as psychiatric treatment: a homosexual case study, *Archives of Sexual Behavior*, 1979, 8(4), 379-383.

Roth, Ron. *The Healing Path of Prayer*. New York: Harmony Books, 1997.

Rothman, KJ. Inferring causal connections - habit, faith or logic? in Rothman, KJ, ed. *Causal Inference*, Chestnut Hill, MP Epidemiology Resources 1988, 3-12.

Roud, Paul C. *Making Miracles: An Exploration into the Dynamics of Self-Healing*, Wellingborough, England: Thorsons 1990.

Royce, D. The near death experience, a survey of clergy attitudes and knowledge, *J Pastoral Care* 1985, 39, 31-42.

Rucker, Rudolf VB. *Geometry, Relativity, and the Fourth Dimension*, New York: Dover 1977.

Ruiz, don Miguel. *The Four Agreements: A Practical Guide to Personal Freedom, A Toltec Wisdom Book*, San Rafael, CA: Amer-Allen 1997.

Rushdie, Salman. One thousand days in a balloon, In: Rushdie, Salman. *Imaginary Homelands: Essays and Criticism 1981-1991*, New York/London: Penguin 1992, 430-439.

Russell, Bertrand. *The Analysis of Matter,* London: Kegan Paul 1927.

Russell, Bertrand. *Sceptical Essays*, London: Unwin (Orig. 1928) 1960. (From Oxford 1998)

Russell, Peter. Quoted in *Newsletter of the Consciousness Research and Training Project* 1998, 12(1), 3.

Russell, Peter. Mysterious light: a scientist's odyssey, *Noetic Sciences Review* 1999, No.50.

Russell, Peter. The mystery of consciousness and the meaning of light, *Newsletter of the Consciousness Research and Training Project* 2000, 9(1), 7.

Rydberg, V. Source of quote lost.

S

Sancta Clara, Abraham a. (Attributed).

Sabom, Michael B. *Recollections of Death*, New York: Harper and Row 1982.

Sacks, Oliver. *A Leg to Stand On*, London: Picador/ Pan 1986.

Sacred Heart Medical Center. *No One Dies Alone: A Guide for Creating & maintaining a Volunteer Companion Program for Dying Hospital Patients*, Eugene, OR: Sacred Heart Medical Center, 1255 Hilyard Street, Eugene, OR 97401 www.peacehealth.org

Safonov, Vladimir. Personal experience in psychic diagnostics and healing, In: Vilenskaya, Larissa, *Parapsychology in the USSR, Part III*, San Francisco: Washington Research Center 1981, 42-45.

Sahtouris, Elisabet/ Lovelock James E. *Earthdance: Living Systems in Evolution*, iUniverse.com 2000.

Saklani, Alok. Preliminary tests for psi-ability in shamans of Garhwal Himalaya, *J Society PsychicalResearch* 1988, 55(81), 60-70.

Saklani, Alok. Psychokinetic effects on plant growth: further studies, In: Henkel, Linda A.

and Palmer, John, *Research in Parapsychology 1989* 1990, 37-41.

Salk, Jonas. *Anatomy of Reality: Merging of Intuition and Reason (Convergence Series)*, New York: Columbia University 1983.

Salmon, EH. *He Heals Today: A Healer's Case-Book*, Worcs, England: Arthur James/ London: Purnell & Sons 1951.

Salmon, J. Warren, ed. *Alternative Medicines: Popular and Policy Perspectives*, New York: Methuen/ London: Tavistock 1984.

Samuel, Andrée/ Kiskos, Julika. Clinical psychology and levels of reality: Part II: ESP as an aid to psychotherapy in some psychological disorders, *Proceedings 4th International Conference on Psychotronics Research*, Sao Paulo, Brazil 1979, 347-351.

Sanders, Catherine M. *Surviving Grief and Learning To Live Again*, New York: John Wiley & Sons 1992.

Sanders, Robert. Faster carbon dioxide emissions will overwhelm capacity of land and ocean to absorb carbon 02 August 2005 www.berkeley.edu/news/media/releases/2005/0 8/02_carbon.shtml (Accessed 10/1/05)

Sandner, Donald. Navaho symbolic healing, *Shaman's Drum* 1985, 1, 25-30.

Sandweiss, Samuel H. *Spirit and the Mind*, San Diego, CA: Birth Day 1985.

Sanford, Agnes. *The Healing Light*, St. Paul, MN: Macalester Park 1949.

Sanford, John A. *Healing and Wholeness*, New York: Paulist 1977 (not psychic healing).

Sannella, Lee. *Kundalini - Psychosis or Transcendence?* San Francisco: H. S. Dakin 1978.

Sapir, Edward/ Whorf, Benjamin Lee. The Sapir-Whorf hypothesis, www.venus.va.com.au/suggestion/sapir.html (Accessed 10/1/05).

Saraydarian, H. *The Science of Meditation*, Agoura, CA: Aquarian Educational Group 1971.

Sargant, William. *The Mind Possessed*, New York: Penguin 1974.

Satchidananda, Swami. In: Elliott, William. *Tying Rocks to Clouds*, New York: Image/ Doubleday 1996, 223-235.

Satinover, Jeffrey. *The Quantum Brain: The Search for Freedom and the Next Generation of Man*, New York: John Wiley & Sons 2001.

Satprem. *Sri Aurobindo, or the Adventure of Conscious-ness*, New York: Harper and Row 1968.

Satprem. *The Mind of the Cells, or Willed Mutation of Our Species* (Translated from French by

Mahak, Francine and Venet, Luc), NY: Institute for Evolutionary Research 1981.

Sattar, SP/ Ahmed, MS/ Madison, J/ Olsen, DR/ Bhatia, SC/ Ellahi, S/ Majeed, F/ Ramaswamy, S/ Petty, F/ Wilson, DR. Patient and physician attitudes to using medications with religiously forbidden ingredients, *Annals Pharmacotherapy* November 2004, 38(II), 1830-5.

Saudia, TL/ Kinney, MR/ Brown, KC, Young-Ward, L. Health locus of control and helpfulness of prayer, *Heart Lung* 1991, 20(1), 60-65.

Schatzman, Morton. *The Story of Ruth*, New York: Putnam 1980.

Schiller, Preston L/ Levin, Jeffrey S. Is there a religious factor in health care utilization? A review, *Social Science and Medicine* 1988, 27, 1369-1379.

Schilpp, PA, ed. *Albert Einstein: Philosopher-Scientist,* Evanston, IL: Library of Living Philosophers/ Menasha, WI: George Banta 1949.

Schindler, S. A new view of the unborn: Toward a developmental psychology of the prenatal period, In: Fedor-Freybergh, P/ Vogel, MLV, eds. *Prenatal and Perinatal Psychology and Medicine: Encounter with the Unborn, A Comprehensive Survey of Research and Practice*, Park Ridge, NJ: Parthenon 1988.

Schlitz, M/ Radin, D/ Malle, BF/ Schmidt, S/ Utts, J/ Yount, L. Distant healing intention: definitions and evolving guidelines for laboratory studies, *Altern Therapies* 2003, 9(3), A37.

Schlotterbeck, Karl. *Living Your Past Lives*, New York: Ballantine 1987.

Schmeidler, Gertrude. *Personal Communication* 1987.

Schmidt, Helmut. PK effect on pre-recorded targets, *J American Society PsychicalResearch* 1976, 70, 267-291.

Schnabel, Artur. Quoted in *Chicago Daily News,* June 11, 1958.

Schneider, Stephen H et al., eds. *Scientists Debate Gaia: The Next Century*, Boston, MA: MIT 2004.

Schneidman, Edwin. *Voices of Death*, New York Harper & Row 1980.

Schreiber K. Religion in the physician-patient relationship. *JAMA* 1991;266(21), 3062-3066.

Schrödinger, Erwin. *What Is Life? and Mind and Matter*, Cambridge: Cambridge University 1967, 1992.

Schubert, PE/ Lionberger, HJ. Mutual connectedness, *J Holistic Nursing,* 1995, 13(2), 102-116.

Schumacher, EF. *Small Is Beautiful: Economics as if People Mattered*, New York: Harper-Collins 1989.

Schutze, Barbara. Group counseling, with and without the addition of Intercessory prayer, as a factor in self-esteem, *Proceedings of the 4th International Conference on Psychotronic Research, Sao Paulo, Brazil,* 1979.

Schutzenberger, M. Algorithms and the neo-Darwinian theory of evolution, In: Morehead, PS/ Kaplan, MM eds., *Mathematical challenges to the Darwinian interpretation of evolution,* Wistar Institute Symposium Monograph, New York: Allen R. Liss 1967, 73-75.

Schwartz, Arthur J. The nature of spiritual transformation: a review of the literature 2000. http://www.metanexus.net/spiritual_transformation/research/literature_review.html   (Accessed 3/8/06)

Schwartz, Gary E/ Russek, Linda G/ Beltran, Justin. Interpersonal hand-energy registration: evidence for implicit performance and perception, *Subtle Energies* 1995, 6(3), 183-200.

Schwartz, Gary. *The Afterlife Experiments*, Pocket Books, 2002.

Schwarz, Berthold E. Possible telesomatic reactions, *J Medical Society of New Jersey* 1967, 64, 600-603.

Schwarz, Berthold E. Ordeal by serpents, fire and strychnine, *Psychiatric Quarterly* 1970, 34, 405-429.

Schweitzer, Albert. *The Quest for Historical Jesus*, SCM 2000 (orig. 1906).

Scotch, NA. A preliminary report on the relation of sociocultural factors to hypertension among the Zulu, *Annals of the New York Academy of Science* 1960, 84, 1000-1009.

Scotch, NA. Sociocultural factors in the epidemiology of Zulu hypertension, *American J Public Health* 1963, 53, 1205-1213.

Scotch, NA/ Geiger, HJ. The epidemiology of essential hypertension II: psychological and sociocultural factors in etiology, *J Chronic Diseases* 1963, 16, 1183-1213.

Scott, Walter. In: *Bolander* p. 74.

Seager, Joni. *Earth Follies: Coming to Feminist Terms with the Global Environmental Crisis*, New York/ London: Routledge 1993.

Seattle, Chief. *Speech to governor of Washington Territory*, 1854.

Seibert, Dinah, et al. *Are You Sad too? Helping Children Deal with Loss and Death*, Santa Cruz, CA: ETR Associates 1993.

Seifer, Marc J. Wizard: The Life and Times of Nikola Tesla : Biography of a Genius, New York: Citadel 1998.

Selby, John. *Kundalini Awakening: A Gentle Guide to Chakra Activation and Spiritual Growth,* New York: Bantam 1992.

Selden, John. *Table Talk* 1689.

Sempebwa, JW. Religiosity and health behaviour in Africa, *Social Science and Medicine* 1983, 17, 2033-2036.

Seneca. *Epistles* 22: 17

Senge, Peter M. The Fifth Discipline, New York: Currency/ Doubleday, 1990.

Senkowski, Ernst. *Instrumentelle Trenskommunikation - Dialog mit dem Unbekamten* (German), Frankfurt a. M. R. G. Fischer 1989.

Senkowski, Ernst. Personal communication 1990.

Serdahely, William J. A comparison of retrospective accounts of childhood near-death experiences with contemporary pediatric near-death experience accounts, *J Near-Death Studies* 1991, 9(4), 219-224.

Serdahely, William. *J Near Death Studies* 1992, 10(3), 171-182.

Setzer, J Schoneberg. The God of Ambrose Worrall, *Spiritual Frontiers* 1983, 15(2), 15-22.

Seutemann, Sigrun. Report on Philippine surgery performed by Tony Agpaoa, June 1973, Appendix in: Millner, Dennis/ Smart, Edward. *The Loom of Creation,* New York: Harper and Row 1976.

Sexson, SB. Religious and spiritual assessment of the child and adolescent, *Child & Adolescence Psychiatric Clinics of North America* January 2004, 13(I), 35-47, vi.

Shafer, Mark G. PK metal bending in a semiformal group, In: *Research in Parapsychology 1980,* Metuchen, NJ: Scarecrow 1981, 33-35.

Shallis, Michael. *On Time,* New York: Schocken 1983.

Shapira, Rabbi Kalonymus Kalman. *To Heal the Soul,* Northvale, NJ: Jason Aronson 1995.

Shapiro, Francine. *Eye Movement Desensitization and Repatterning,* New York: Guildford 1995.

Shealy, C Norman/ Myss, Caroline. *AIDS: Passageway to Transformation,* Walpole, NH: Stillpoint 1987.

Sheehan, Molly. *A Guide to Green Hope Farm Flower Essences,* P.O. Box 125, Meriden, NH 03770, 1998.

Sheikh, Anees A/ Sheikh, Katharina S, eds. *Eastern and Western Approaches to Healing: Ancient Wisdom and Modern Knowledge,* New York: John Wiley & Sons 1989.

Sheils, Dean. A cross-cultural survey of beliefs in out-of-the-body experiences, *J the Society PsychicalResearch* 1978, 49, 697 (Cited in L. Watson, *Supernature II*).

Sheldon, Michael. How Joan was cured at Lourdes, In: *Fate Magazine, Exploring the Healing Miracle,,* Highland Park, IL: Clark 1983 (Orig. *Fate Magazine* Feb. 1955).

Sheldrake, Rupert. *A New Science of Life: The Hypothesis of Formative Causation,* Los Angeles: Tarcher 1981; Rev. ed. 1987.

Sheldrake, Rupert. *Dogs That Know When Their Owners Are Coming Home: And Other Unexplained Powers of Animals,* New York: Three Rivers 2000.

Sherman, Harold. *Wonder Healers of the Philippines,* Los Angeles: DeVorss 1967.

Sherrill, Kimberly A/ Larson, David B. Antitenure factor in religious research, In: *Levin* 1994b, 149-177.

Shiffrin, Nancy. Past Lives, Present Problems, *Human Behavior Magazine* Sep 1977, 6(9).

Shiflett, Samuel C. Effect of Reiki treatments of functional recovery in patients in poststroke rehabilitation: A pilot study, *The J Alternative and Complementary Medicine* 2002, 8(6), 755-763.

Shreve-Neiger, AK/ Edelstein, BA. Religion and anxiety: a critical review of the literature, *Clinical Psychology Review* August 2004, 24(4), 379-397.

Shubin, NH/ Marshall, CR. Fossils, genes, and the origin of novelty, In: Deep time, *The Paleontological Society* 2000, 324-340.

Siblerud, Robert. *The Science of the Soul: Explaining the Spiritual Universe,* Sacred Science 2000.

Siegel, Bernard/ Siegel, Barbara. Doctors, patients and inner wellness, In: Church/ Sher, p.197-211.

Siegel, Bernie S. *Love, Medicine & Miracles: Lessons Learned About Self- Healing from a Surgeon's Experience with Exceptional Patients,* New York: Harper and Row 1986.

Siegel, Bernie. *Peace, Love & Healing: Bodymind Communication & the Path to Self-Healing,* London: Rider 1990.

Siegel, RK/ Hirschman, AE. Hashish Near-Death Experiences, *Anabiosis,* 1984, 4, 69-86.

Siegel, Ronald K. The psychology of life after death, *American Psychologist* 1980, 35(10), 911-931.

Sieveking, Paul. One in life and death, *The Unexplained* 1981, 5(89), 1174- 1177.

Sifers, Sarah Cruse. *The Use of Shamanic Counseling by Counselors and Clients: An Exploration of a Spiritual Movement*, University of Utah 1998.

Silverman, Steve. *Paul Kammerer: How one toad destroyed one man's entire career* www.home.nycap.rr.com/useless/kammerer/ (Accessed 9/3/05)

Silverman, W. *Bibliography of measurement techniques used in the social sicentific study of religion*, Psychological Documents, Ms. 2539, Hicksville, NY: American Psychological Association 1982.

Simpson, Suzanne M. Near death experience: A concept analysis as applied to nursing, *J Advanced Nursing*, 36(4), 520-526 (28 refs).

Singh, K. *The Crown of Life*, Delhi: Ruhani Satsang 1973.

Singh, Kathleen Dowling. *The Grace in Dying: A Message of Hope, Comfort, and Spiritual Transformation*, San Francisco/New York: HarperCollins 1998.

Skinner, Stephen. *The Living Earth Manual of Feng Shui: Chinese Geomancy*, London, Boston: Routledge and Kegan Paul 1982.

Sladek, Martin. *Two Weeks with the Psychic Surgeons*, Chicago: DOMA 1976.

Sliker, Gretchen. *Multiple Mind: Healing the Split in Psyche and World*, Boston/ London: Shambhala 1992.

Sloan, Richard P. Should physicians prescribe religious activities? *New England J Medicine* 2000, 342(25), 1913-1916.

Sloan Richard P, at al. Religion, spirituality, and medicine. *Lancet* 1999, 353, 664-7.

Sloan, Richard P, et al. Without a prayer: Methodological problems, ethical challenges, and misrepresentations in the study of religion, spirituality, and medicine, in Plante, Thomas G/ Sherman, Allen, eds. *Faith and health: Psychological perspectives*, New York, NY: Guilford Press 2001, 339-354.

Sloan, RP/ Bagiella, E/ Powell, T. Religion, spirituality, and medicine, *Lancet* 1999, 353(9153), 664-667

Slomoff, Daniel A. Traditional African medicine: voodoo healing, In: Heinze, Ruth-Inge, ed. *Proceedings of the 2nd International Conference on the Study of Shamanism*, Santa Sabina Center, San Rafael, CA 1985.

Slomoff, Danny. Ecstatic spirits: A West African healer at work, *Shaman's Drum* 1986, 5, 27-31.

Smith, A. *The Mind*, New York: Viking 1984, 316.

Smith, Huston. *The Religions of Man*, New York: Harper/ Colophon 1965.

Smith, Huston. *Forgotten Truth: The Primordial Tradition*, New York: Harper/ Colophon 1977.

Smith, Huston. *Cleansing the doors of Perception*, New York: Tarcher 2000.

Smith, Huston. *Why Religion Matters: The Fate of the Human Spirit in an Age of Disbelief*, New York: Harper SanFrancisco 2001.

Smith, Linda L., *Called Into Healing*, Arvada, Colorado: HTSM Press, 2000.

Smith, Martin. *Find Me In The River*, by singing group *Curious?* UK: Music 2001. www.delirious.org.uk/lyrics/songs/findmein.html   Quoted in Walton, Brad. *How Does the Heart Know Love?* Edina, MN: Beaver's Pond Press, 23.

Smith, Matthew. *The Soul Knows: A Path of Listening*, Vancouver: Matthew Smith 2004. www.trafford.com/robots/04-0962.html

Smith, Rodney. *Lessons from the Dying*, Boston: Wisdom 1998.

Smith, Susy. *The Enigma of Out-of-Body Travel*, New York: Signet 1965.

Smith, Susy. *Voices of the Dead?* New York: New American Library 1977.

Smyth, Frank. Ghosts without souls? *The Unexplained* 1981, 3(28), 550-553.

Smyth, Frank. Ghosts of the air, *The Unexplained* 1983, 11(125), 2498-2450.

Smyth P/ Bellemare D. Spirituality, pastoral care, and religion: the need for clear distinctions. *J Palliative Care* 1988, 4(1-2), 86-8.

Sneck, William Joseph. *Charismatic Spiritual Gifts: A Phenomenological Analysis*, Washington, D.C. University Press of America 1981.

Snell, Lionel. I love your energy, baby, it's so relaxing, *Caduceus* 1993, No. 22, 3.

Snow, Chet. *Mass Dreams of the Future: Do we face an apocalypse or a global spiritual awakening? The choice is ours, Featuring hypnotic future-life progressions by Helen Wambach*, Crest Park, CA: Deep Forest 1993.

Snow, Robert L. *Looking for Carroll Beckwith: The True Story of a Detective's Search for His Past Life*, St. Martin's Press 1999.

Snow, Tiffany. *The Power of Divine: A Healer's Guide--Tapping into the Miracle*, San Diego: Spirit Journey Books 2004.

Soal, SG. A report on some communications received through Mrs. Blanche Cooper, *Proceedings of the Society PsychicalResearch* 1925, 35, 471-594.

Sodestrom, K/ Martinson, I. Patients' spiritual coping strategies: A study of nurse and patient perspectives, *Oncology Nursing Forum,* 1987, 14(2), 41-46.

Solfvin, Gerald F. Psi expectancy effects in psychic healing studies with malarial mice, *European J Parapsychology* 1982(b), 4(2), 160-197.

Solfvin, Gerald F/ Leskowitz, Eric/ Benor, Daniel J. Questions concerning the scientific credibility of wound healing studies authored by Daniel P. Wirth, www.wholistichealingresearch.com/Wirthq.asp.

Solomon, George F. The emerging field of psychoneuroimmunology, with a special note on Aids, *Advances* 1985, 2(1), 6-19.

Solomon, Grant/ Solomon, Jane/ Scole Experimental Group. *The Scole Experiment, Scientific Evidence for Life After Death,* London: Piatkus 1999.

Solomon, Paul. The triune concept, In: *Albright and Albright* 1981.

Somé, Malidoma Patrice. *Ritual: Power, Healing, and Community,* New York: Penguin/Arkana 1997; Portland, OR: Swan Raven & Company 1993.

Somé, Malidoma Patrice. *Of Water and the Spirit: Ritual, Magic, and Initiation in the Life of an African Shaman,* New York: Tarcher/ Putnam 1994.

Sorrell, Stephanie June. The Medicine Angel, *Caduceus* 1995. (With the kind permission of the author and Caduceus)

Spalding, Baird T. Life and Teaching of the Masters of the Far East, New York: DeVorss 1962.

Spangler, David. *The Laws of Manifestation,* Forres, Moray, Scotland: Findhorn Foundation 1975.

Spangler, David. *The Call,* New York: Riverhead 1996.

Spanos, Nicholas P. Past-Life Hypnotic Regression: A Critical Review, *Skeptical Inquirer* 1987-8, 12(2), 174-180.

Spenser, Edmund. *Epithalamion,* Book I, Canto 9, 40.

Spindrift, Inc. *The Spindrift Papers* (Spindrift Research, c/o Bill Sweet, 500 Huntington Commons Road, # 447, Mount Prospect, Illinois 60056 (www.xnet.com/ ~spindrif) 1993.

Spiritual beliefs and the dying process. The Nathan Cummings Foundation and Fetzer Institute. New York: October 1997.

Spiritual Competency Resource Center www.internetguides.com/dsm4/wwwlib.asp

Spiritual Frontiers Editor. Research report: Setzer's sanctuary effect, *Spiritual Frontiers* 1980, 12(1), 20-23.

Spiritual Scientist, Street Farmhouse, Scole, Diss, Norfolk IP21 4DR, England. Reporting on table tilting/ rapping and other spirit manifestations.

Spraggett, Allen. *Kathryn Kuhlman: The Woman who Believed in Miracles,* New York: World 1970.

St. Aubyn, L. *Today is a Good Day to Die,* Bath, UK: Gateway 1991

St. Clair, David. Spiritism in Brazil, *Psychic* Dec 1970, 2(3), 8-14.

St. Clair, David. *Psychic Healers,* New York: Bantam/ Doubleday 1979 (Orig. 1974).

Stadler, BMR/ Stadler, PF/ Wagner, GP/ Fontana, W. The topology of the possible: formal spaces underlying patterns of evolutionary change, *J Theoretical Biology* 2001, 213:241-274.

Stanford Encyclopedia of Philosophy. *Mysticism,* www.plato.stanford.edu/entries/mysticism/.

Stanton, H. *Bibliography of Health Research on Seventh-Day Adventists,* Wahroonga, NSW, Australia: Adventist Health Department 1989.

Stapp, Henry P. S-matrix interpretation of quantum theory, *Physical Review* 1971, Vol. D3, 1303-1320.

Stapp, Henry P. Quantum physics and the physicist's view of nature, In: *The World View of Contemporary Physics,* Richard E. Kitchener, ed. Albany: State University of New York Press 1988.

Starcke, W. *Homesick for Heaven,* Buerne, TX: Guadalupe 1988.

Starhawk (pseud. for Simos, Miriam). *Dreaming the Dark: Magic, Sex & Politics,* Boston: Beacon 1982.

Starr, Bill. Sister Lucy heals for Christ, In: *Exploring the Healing Miracle,* Highland Park, IL: Clark 1983 (Orig. *Fate Magazine* Aug. 1975).

Staudacher, C. *Beyond Grief: A Guide for Recovering from the Death of a Loved One,* USA: New Harbinger 1987 London: Condor/Souvenir 1988.

Steadman, Alice. *Who's the Matter With Me,* Marina del Rey, CA: DeVorss 1969.

Stearn, Jess. *Edgar Cayce -- The Sleeping Prophet,* New York: Bantam 1967.

Steele, Edward J/ Lindley, Robyn A/ Blanden, Robert V. *Lamarck's Signature : How Retrogenes Are Changing Darwin's Natural Selection*

Paradigm, Jackson, TN: Perseus Books Group 1999. (reviewed at www.home.wxs.nl/~gkorthof/kortho39.htm; Accessed 1/16/06)

Steere, David A. *Spiritual Presence in Psychotherapy; A Guide for Caregivers.* Brunner/ Mazel 1997.

Steffen, Sylvester L. *Religion & Civility: The Primacy of Conscience,* Bloomington, In: AuthorHouse 2004.

Steiger, Brad. *Guardian Angels and Spirit Guides,* New York: Plume/ Dutton Signet/ Penguin 1995.

Stein, Diane. *Psychic Healing with Spiritual Guides and Angels,* Freedom, CA: Crossings 1996

Steinpach, R. *How is that we live after death and what is the meaning of life?* Stuttgart, Germany; Stiftung Gralsbotschaft 1980.

Stelter, Alfred. *Psi-Healing,* New York: Bantam 1976.

Stemman, Roy. This too, too solid flesh, *The Unexplained* 1982(a), 8(83), 1846-1849 (Quotes by permission of Orbis Publishing Ltd., London).

Stemman, Roy. Apports, *The Unexplained* 1982(b), 8(91), 1806-1809.

Stemman, Roy. New teeth for old, *The Unexplained* 1983(a), 12(139), 2770-2773.

Stemman, Roy. Surgeon from the other side, *The Unexplained,* 1983(b), 12(142), 2838-2840.

Stevens, Jay. *Storming Heaven,* New York: Grove 1987.

Stevenson, Ian. *The evidence for survival from claimed memories of former incarnations,* Winning Essay of the Contest in Honor of William James 1961 (Published in 2 parts in *J the American Society PsychicalResearch* April and July 1960).

Stevenson, Ian. *20 Cases Suggestive of Reincarnation,* Charlottesville, VA: University of Virginia 1974(a).

Stevenson, Ian. *Xenoglossy: A Review and Report of a Case,* Charlottesville, VA: University of Virginia 1974(b).

Stevenson, Ian. Research into the evidence of man's survival after death: A historical and critical survey with a summary of recent developments, *J Nervous and Mental Diseases,* 1977, 165(3), 152-170.

Stevenson, Ian. *Unlearned Language: New Studies in Xenoglossy,* Charlottesville, VA: University of VA 1984.

Stevenson, Ian. *Children Who Remember Previous Lives: A Question of Reincarnation,* Charlottesville, VA: University of Virginia 1987.

Stevenson, Ian. A new look at maternal impressions: an analysis of 50 published cases and reports of two recent examples, *J Scientific Exploration* 1992, 6(4), 353.

Stevenson, Ian. *Reincarnation and Biology: A Contribution to the Etiology of Birthmarks and Birth Defects, Vols. I and II,* Westport, CT: Greenwood 1995.

Stevenson, Ian. *Where Reincarnation and Biology Intersect,* Westport, CT: Praeger 1997.

Stevenson, Ian/ Pasricha, Satwant. A case of secondary personality with xenoglossy, *American J Psychiatry* 1979, 136, 1591-1592.

Stevenson, Ian, et al. Deception and self-deception in cases of the reincarnation type: seven illustrative cases in Asia, *J the American Society PsychicalResearch* 1988, 82, 1.

Stevenson, Ian, et al. A case of the possession type in India with evidence of paranormal knowledge, *J Scientific Exploration* 1989, 3(1), 81-101.

Stiles, MK. The shining stranger: Application of the phenomenological method in the investigation of the nurse-family spiritual relationship, *Cancer Nursing* 1994, 17(1), 18-26.

Stone, Irving. *The Agony and the Ecstasy,* New York: Signet 1961.

Storm, Howard. *My Descent into Death,* Edinburgh, Scotland: Clairview 2000.

Storm, Stella, ed. *Philosophy of Silver Birch,* London: Spiritualist 1969.

Storr, Anthony. *Feet of Clay,* New York: Free Press 1996.

Strassman, Rick. *DMT: The Spirit Molecule,* Rochester, VT: Park Street 2001.

Stuber, ML/ Houskamp, BM. Spirituality in children confronting death, *Child & Adolescent Psychiatric Clinics of North America* January 2004, 13(1), 127-36, viii.

Studer, M/ Thornton, A. Adolescent religiosity and contraceptive usage, *J Marriage and the Family* 1987, 49, 117-128.

Suarez, M/ Raffaelli, M/ O'Leary, A. Use of folk healing practices by HIV-infected Hispanics living in the united states, *AIDS Care* 1996, 8(6), 683-690.

Suchman, E. Sociomedical variations among ethnic groups, *American J Sociology* 1964, 70, 319-331.

Sufi saying. Anonymous.

Sugrue, Thomas. *There is a River,* New York: Dell 1970.

Susser, M. Falsification, verification and causal inference in epidemiology, In: Rothman, KJ, ed. *Causal Inference*, Chestnut Hill, MA 1988, 33-57.

Sutherland, C. *Transformed by the Light: Life After Near-Death Experiences*, Sydney, Australia: Bantam 1992.

Sutherland, Cherie. *In the Company of Angels,* Bath, UK: Gateway 2001.

Sutphen, Dick. *Past Lives, Future Loves*, New York: Pocket/ Simon and Schuster 1978.

Sutphen, Dick/ Taylor, Lauren Leigh. *Past-Life Therapy in Action*, Malibu, CA: Valley of the Sun 1983.

Swan, Jim. Sacred places in nature: Is there a significant difference? *Psi Research* 1985, 4(1), 108-117.

Swedenborg, Emanuel. *Heaven and Hell*, New York: Swedenborg Foundation 1970.

Swedenborg, Emanuel. Quoted in Reagan, Michael, ed. *Reflections on the Nature of God*, Radnor, PA: Templeton Foundation Press/ Lionheart Books, Ltd. 2004, 48.

Swimme, Brian/ Berry, Thomas. *The Universe Story*, New York: HarperSanFrancisco 1992.

Swinton, John. *Spirituality and Mental Health Care, Rediscovering a 'Forgotten' Dimension*, London: Jessica Kingsley 2001.

Szasz, Thomas. *The Second Sin*, 1973.

Szasz, Thomas S. *The Theology of Therapy: The Breach of the First Amendment through the Medicalization of Morals,* NYU Review of Law and Social Change 1975, 5, 127-135.

Szasz, Thomas S. *The Theology of Medicine*, Baton Rouge: Louisiana State University 1977.

Szasz, Thomas. *The Myth of Mental Illness*, New York: HarperTrade 1984.

T

Tabori, Paul/ Raphael, Phyllis, eds. *Beyond the Senses*, London: Souvenir 1971.

Tagore, Rabindranath. Attributed quote.

Talbot, Michael. *The Holographic Universe*, New York: HarperPerennial 1991.

Tannous, A. *Beyond Coincidence*, Garden City, NY 1976.

Tansley, David V with Rae, Malcolm and Westlake, Aubrey T. *Dimensions of Radionics: A Manual of Radionic Theory and Practice for the Health Care Professional*, Hengiscote, England: Health Science Press 1977.

Targ, Russell/ Harary, Keith. *The Mind Race: Understanding and Using Psychic Abilities*, New York: Villard 1984.

Targ, Russell/ Katra, Jane. *Miracles of Mind*. Novato, California: New World Library 1998.

Tart, Charles T. A second psychophysiological study of out-of-the-body experiences in a gifted subject, *International J Parapsychology* 1967, 9, 251-258.

Tart, Charles T. A psychophysiological study of out-of-the-body experiences in a selected subject, *J the American Society PsychicalResearch* 1968, 62, 3-27.

Tart, Charles T. A further psychophysiological study of out-of-the-body experiences in a gifted subject, In: Monroe, Robert A/ Roll, W/ Morris, R/ Morris, J, eds. *Proceedings of the Parapsychological Association* 1969, 6.

Tart, Charles T. *Transpersonal Psychologies*, New York: Harper and Row 1975(a).

Tart, Charles T. *States of Consciousness*, New York: E.P. Dutton 1975(b).

Tart, Charles T. Causality and synchronicity: Steps toward clarification, *J the American Society PsychicalResearch* 1981, 75, 121-141.

Tart, Charles T. *Waking Up*, Boston: New Science/ Shambhala 1986(a).

Tart, Charles T. Psychics' fears of psychic powers, *J American Society PsychicalResearch* 1986(b), 80(3), 279-292.

Tart, Charles T. *Consciousness: A Psychological, Transpersonal and Parapsychological Approach,* Paper presented at the Third International Symposium on Science and Consciousness in Ancient Olympia, 4-7 January, 1993.

Tart, Charles T. Toward the objective exploration of non-ordinary reality, *J Transpersonal Psychology* 1995, 27(1), 57-67.

Taub-Bynum, E Bruce. *The Family Unconscious: An Invisible Bond*, Wheaton, IL: Quest/ Theosophical 1984.

Taylor, Eugene. *William James on Exceptional Mental States*, New York: Scribner's, 1983 (Reviewed by Rogo, DS in *Fate*, Nov. 1984).

Taylor, Eugene. *A Psychology of Spirtiual Healing*, West Chester, PA: Chrysalis 1997.

Taylor-Reilly, David/ Taylor, Morag A. The difficulty with homeopathy: A brief review of principles, methods and research, *Complementary Medical Research* 1988, 3(1), 70-78 (57 refs).

Tedder, W/ Monty, M. Exploration of long-distance PK: A conceptual replication of the influence on a biological system, In: Roll, WG, et al., eds. *Research In Parapsychology 1980*, Metuchen, NJ: Scarecrow 1981, 90-93.

Teilhard de Chardin, Pierre. *The Phenomenon of Man*, New York: Perennial 1976.

TenDam, H. *Exploring Reincarnation*, London: Penguin 1990.

Tenen, Stan. *Geometric Metaphors of Life*, Meru Foundation, Dept. G, P.O. Box 1738, San Anselmo, CA 94979. (video)

Tenhaeff, WHC. *Telepathy and Clairvoyance*, Springfield, IL: Charles C. Thomas 1972 (From Uphoff/ Uphoff 1975).

Tennyson, Alfred Lord. *In Memoriam* 1850.

Tennyson, Alfred Lord. *Lucretius* 1868.

Thaxton,Charles B. DNA, Design and the Origin of Life, *Origins*, www.origins.org/articles/thaxton_dnadesign.html#text7 (Accessed 8/6/05).

Thomas, Jesse. *Psychic Surgeon*, London: Arthur Barker 1957.

Thomas, Mark. *John of God: Visiting Joao de Deus at Casa de Dom Inacio*, Abadiania, Goias, Brasil, Video by Mark Thomas, 2002. $20 + P&H   Vision Thang Pty Limited, PO Box 2007, Clovelly NSW 2031 Australia www.visionthang.tv

Thomson, KS. Macroevolution: The morphological problem, *American Zoologist* 1992, 32, 106-112.

Thoreau, Henry David. *Diary*, 11 November 1850.

Thornton, Francis Beauchesne. *Catholic Shrines in the United States and Canada*, New York: Wilfred Funk 1954.

Thornton, John F. Rossiter. From The Prayer Wheel. 2006. www.theprayerwheel.com

Thoresen CE/ Harris AH. Spirituality and health: what's the evidence and what's needed? *Annals of Behavioral Medicine* 2002, 24(1), 3-13.

Thouless, Robert H. Experiments in spiritual healing, In: *Proceedings of Four Conferences of Parapsychological Studies*, New York: Parapsychology Foundation 1957, 50-52 (Also in: Newsletter of the Parapsychology Foundation 1955, 2(2), 5-7).

Thurston, Herbert. *Ghosts and Poltergeists*, Chicago: Henry Regnery 1954.

Thurston, Herbert. *The Physical Phenomena of Mysticism*, London: Burns Oates 1952.

Tiller, William A. *Science and Human Transformation: Subtle Energies, Intentionality and Consciousness* 1997.

Tiller, William A. Conscious Acts of Creation: The Emergence of a New Physics, *International J Healing and Caring – on line* 2003(a), 3(1), 1-21.

Tiller, William A. Towards a Quantitative Model of Both Local and Non-Local Energetic/ Information Healing, *International J Healing and Caring – on line* 2003(b), 3(2), 1-12.

Tiller, William A/ Dibble, Walter E/ Kohane, Michael J. *Conscious Acts of Creation: The emergence of a New Physics*, Walnut Creek, CA: Pavior 2001(a).

Tiller, William A/ Dibble, Walter E/ Kohane, Michael J. Exploring robust interactions between human intention and inanimate/ animate systems, Part I: experimental, *Frontier Perspectives* 2001(b), 9(2), 6-21.

Tiller, William A/ Dibble, Walter E/ Kohane, Michael J. Exploring robust interactions between human intention and inanimate/ animate systems, Part II: Theoretical, *Frontier Perspectives* 2001(c), 10(1), 9-18.

Tipler, Frank J. *The Physics of Immortality: Modern Cosmology, God and the Resurrection of the Dead*, New York/ London: Anchor/ Doubleday 1994.

Todd, John/ Dewhurst, Kenneth. The double: Its psychopathology and psychophysiology, *J Nervous and Mental Diseases* 1955, 122,

Tompkins, Peter/Bird, Christopher, *The Secret Life of Plants*, New York/ London: Harper & Row 1972, 126-134.

Torpey, Debbie. Compassionate understanding, *Cooperative Connection: Newsletter of the Nurse Healers Professional Associates, Inc.* 1995, 16(3), 1.

Trajna, Carlo M. *Ignoto chiama uomo*, Firenze (Salani) 1980.

Transkommunikation, Gesellschaft fur Psychobiophysic e.V., Eichendorffstrasse 19, D-6500 Mainz, Germany.

Travers, B. Observations on the local diseases termed malignant, *Medical and Chirurgical Transactions* 1837, 17, 737.

Trent, John et al., eds. *Guide to the Spiritual Growth of Children*, Tyndale House 2000.

Tress, Lynn Suzanne. *A Cross-Cultural Comparison of Imagery Techniques Utilized by Shamans and their Implications for Clinical Psychotherapy*, PsyD, Miami Institute of Psychology of the Caribbean Center for Advanced Studies 1999.

Trevino, Carlos. 'Possession,' psychiatry and psi, *Psi Reasearch* 1983, 2(2), 97-101.

Trick, OL. Psychological studies of two mediums, *J Parapsychology* 1966, 30, 301-302 (Abstract).

Troyer, H. Review of cancer among 4 religious sects: evidence that life-styles are distinctive sets of risk factors, *Social Sciences and Medicine*, 1988, 26, 1007-1117.

Trungpa, Chogyam. *Mudra*, Boston: Shambhala 1978.

Turner, Gordon. Psychic energy is the power of life (Part 4 of 4-Part Series), *Two Worlds* (Oct) 1969, 302-303.

Turner, Gordon. *An Outline of Spiritual Healing*, London: Psychic Press 1970.

Turner, Gordon. *A Time to Heal: The Autobiography of an Extraordinary Healer*, London: Talmy, Franklin 1974.

Turner, VW. An Ndembu doctor in practice, in Kiev, A, ed: *Magic, Faith and Healing*, Free Press 1964, 230-262.

Turoff, Stephen. *Seven Steps to Eternity*, Edinburgh, Scotland: Clairview 2000.

Twain, Mark. "Man is a Religious..." *The Lowest Animal* 1897.

Twain, Mark. "The altar cloth..." *The Notebook* 1898.

Tweedie, Irina. *The Chasm of Fire: A Woman's Experience of Liberation through the Teachings of a Sufi Master*, Longmead, England: Element 1988.

Twemlow, SW. Epilogue: Personality file. In: Monroe, R. *Journeys Out of the Body*, New York: Doubleday 1977 (pp. 275-280).

Tyrrell, GNM. A communication introduced in automatic script, *J the Society PsychicalResearch* 1939, 31, 91-95.

Tyrrell, GNM. *Apparitions*, New York: Macmillan 1953.

Chang Tzu. In: Kaptchuk, p. 139.

Chuang Tzu. Trans. James Legge, arranged by Clae Waltham. New York: Ace 1971.

U

The Unexplained, The unexplained psychic photo file, *The Unexplained* 1983, 11(124), 2470-2473.

U.S. Energy Information Administration www.eia.doe.gov/oiaf/1605/ggccebro/chapter1. html

U.S. News & World Report, "Is There Life After Death?" March 31, 1997, 58-64.

Underhill, Evelyn. *Mysticism: A Study in the Nature and Development of Man's Spiritual Consciousness*, London: University/ Methuen 1960 (Orig. 1911).

Underhill, Evelyn. *The Spiritual Life*, London: Oneworld 1993 (Orig. 1936); Harrisburg, PA: Morehouse 1955 (Orig. Hodder & Stoughton 1937).

Underwood, LG/ Teresi, JA. The daily spiritual experience scale: development, theoretical description, reliability, exploratory factor analysis, and preliminary construct validity using health-related data, *Annals of Behavioral Medicine* 2002, 24(1), 22-33.

Unlimited Horizons, Metascience, P.O. Box 737, Franklin, NC 28734 (Newsletter about voices on tapes).

Uphoff, Walter H. 'Psychic surgery:' a reply to Loren Parks, *Artifex* 1986, 5(2), 1-6.

Uphoff, Walter H. *New Frontiers Newsletter* 1988, Nos. 26/ 27.

Uphoff, Walter/ Uphoff, Mary Jo. *New Psychic Frontiers: Your Key to New Worlds*, Gerards Cross, England: Colin Smythe 1975.

Uphoff, Walter/ Uphoff, Mary Jo, *Mind over Matter: Implications of Masuaki Kiyota's PK Feats with Metal and Film for: Healing, Physics, Psychiatry, War and Peace, Et Cetera*, Oregon, WI: New Frontiers Center 1980.

V

Valea, Ernest. Reincarnation and Christianity: a possible marriage? *J Religion and Psychical Research* 2002, 25(3), 167-176 (good web refs).

Valentine, JW. *On the origin of phyla*, Chicago: University of Chicago Press 2004.

Valentine, Tom. *Psychic Surgery*, New York: Pocket 1975 (Quotes with permission of Contemporary Books, Inc., Chicago. Copyright T. Valentine 1973).

van der Post, Laurens. *The Seed and the Sower*, London: Hogarth/ Penguin 1963.

van der Post, Laurens. *Jung and the Story of Our Time*, New York: Hogarth/ Penguin 1976.

van der Post, Laurens. *Yet Being Someone Other*, New York: Hogarth/ Penguin 1982.

van der Post, Laurens. *A Walk with a White Bushman*, New York: Penguin 1988.

van der Post, Laurens. *The Voice of the Thunder,* New York/ London: Penguin 1994.

Van Dusen, W. *Spirits in Madness*, New York: Sweron Long Foundation 1998.

Van Dyke, Henry. In: Bolander p. 74.

van Gelder, Dora (Kunz). *The Real World of Fairies*, Wheaton, IL: Quest/ Theosophical 1978.

van Husen, JE. The development of fears, phobias, and restrictive patterns of adaptation following attempted abortions, *Pre- and Perinatal Psychology J* 1988, 2(3), 179-185.

van Lommel, Pim, et al. Near-death experience in survivors of cardiac arrest: a prospective study in the Netherlands, *Lancet* 2001, 358, 2039-2045.

Van Ness, Peter, ed. *Spirituality and the Secular Quest*, England: SCM 1996.

VandeCreek, L/ Ayres, S/ Bassham, M. Using INSPIRIT to conduct spiritual assessments, *J Pastoral Care* 1995, 49, 83-9.

Vargas, Luis A, et al. Exploring the multidimensional aspects of grief reactions, *American J Psychiatry* 1989, 146(11), 1484-9.

Vasiliev, Leonid L. *Mysterious Phenomena of the Human Psyche* (Translated from Russian), New Hyde Park, NY: University Books 1965.

Vasiliev, LL. *Experiments in Distant Influence: Discoveries by Russia's Foremost Parapsychologist*, New York: Dutton 1976. Previously published as *Experiments in Mental Suggestion* (rev. ed.), Hampshire, England: Gally Hill Press/ Institute for the Study of Mental Images 1963. (See also review of the latter by Rush, JH)

Vaughan, Alan. *Incredible Coincidence: The Baffling World of Synchronicity*, Scranton, PA: Harper and Row 1979.

Vaughan, Frances. *The Inward Arc*, Nevada City, CA: Blue Dolphin 1995.

Vaux, K. Religion and health, *Preventive Medicine* 1976, 5, 522-536.

Venn, Jonathan. Hypnosis and the reincarnation hypothesis: A critical review and case study, *J the American Society PsychicalResearch* 1986, 80(4), 408-425.

Verny, Thomas/ Kelly, John. *The Secret Life of the Unborn Child*, New York: Dell 1986.

Versluis, Arthur. *Wisdom's Children*, Albany, NY: SUNY 1999.

Vigne, Jacques. *Indian wisdom, modern psychology and Christianity*, www.anandamayi.org/ devotees/ jv

Vilenskaya, Larissa. Firewalking and beyond, *Psi Research* 1985, 4(2), 89-109.

Vilenskaya, Larissa. *Firewalking*, Falls Village, CT: Bramble 1991.

Villoldo, Alberto. *Shaman, Healer, Sage: How to Heal Yourself and Others with the Energhy Medicine of the Americas*, New York: Harmony 2001.

Villoldo, Alberto/ Jendresen, Erik. *Dance of the Four Wind: Secrets of the Inca Medicine Wheel*, Rochester, VT: Destiny 1995.

Villoldo, Alberto/ Krippner, Stanley. *Healing States: A Journey into the World of Spiritual Healing and Shamanism*, New York: Fireside/ Simon and Schuster 1987.

Virtue, Doreen. *Healing with the Angels*, Carlsbad, CA: Hay House 1999.

Volf, Miroslav. (Accessed 12/19/05) www.titusonenine.classicalanglican.net/?p=750 3

Voltaire. Épîtres no. 96, "A l'Auteur du livre des trois imposteurs"

Von Franz, Marie-Louise. *On Divination and Synchronicity: The Psychology of Meaningful Chance*, Toronto: Inner City 1980.

Von Franz, Marie-Louise. *On Dreams and Death: A Jungian Interpretation* (Translated from German), Boston and London: Shambhala 1987.

Von Schrenk-Nötzing, A. *Phenomena of Materialization: A Contributions to the Investigation of Mediumistic Teleplastics*, Ayer Co., November 1975.

Von Urban, R. *Beyond Human Knowledge*, New York: Pageant 1958.

W

Wade, Jenny. *Changes of Mind: A Holonomic Theory of the Evolution of Consciousness*, Albany: State University of New York Press 1996. (22 pp refs, 21 pp notes)

Wade, Jenny. *Transcendent Sex: When Lovemaking Opens the Veil*, New York: Pocket 2004.

Wagner, GP. What is the promise of developmental evolution? Part II: A causal explanation of evolutionary innovations may be impossible, *J Experimental Zoology (Mol. Dev. Evol.)* 2001, 291, 305-309.

Wagner, GP/ Stadler, PF. Quasi-independence, homology and the Unity-C of type: a topological theory of characters, *J Theoretical Biology* 2003, 220, 505-527.

Wald, George. (Nobel Laureate and Harvard Professor Emeritus in Biology). Attributed.

Walker, B/ Serdahely, W. *J Near Death Studies*, Winter 1990, 105.

Wallis, C. Faith and healing, *Time* June 24, 1996, 58-64.

Wallston, BS/ Wallston, KA. Locus of control and health: a review of the literature, *Health Education Monographs* 1978, 6, 106-117.

Walsch, Neale Donald. *Conversations With God: An Uncommon Dialogue*, Charlottesville, VA: Hampton Roads Publishing Company, Inc., 1997.

Walsch, Neale Donald/ Riccio, Frank. *The Little Soul and the Sun: A Children's Parable Adapted from Conversa-tions With God*, Hampton Roads 1998.

Walsh, Roger/ Vaughan, Frances. *Paths Beyond Ego: The Transpersonal Vision* (A New Consciousness Reader), Tarcher 1993.

Walter, Katya. *The Tao of Chaos: DNA and the I Ching. Unlocking the Code of the Universe*, Rockport, MA/ Shaftesbury, England: Element 1994.

Walton, Brad. *How Does the Heart Know Love?* Edina, MN: Beaver's Pond Press Wambach, Helen, *Reliving Past Lives: The Evidence Under Hypnosis*, New York: Harper and Row 1978.

Wambach, Helen. *Life Before Life*, New York: Bantam 1979.

Ward, Colleen. Spirit possession and mental health: A psycho- anthropological perspective, *Human Relations* 1980, 33(3), 149-163.

Warner, David. Search for a Healer, *Fate*, May 1984, 78-84.

Wasserman, Gerhard D. *Shadow Matter & Psychic Phenomena*, England: Mandrake of Oxford 1993.

Watkins, John G/ Watkins, Helen H. Hypnosis, multiple personality, and ego states as altered states of consciousness, In: Wolman/ Ullman, 133-158.

Watkins, L. *The Real Exorcists*, London: Methuen 1983.

Watkins, Mary M. *Waking Dreams*, New York: Harper and Row 1977.

Watkins, PC/ Woodward, K/ Stone, T/ Kolts, RL. Gratitude and happiness: development of a measure of gratitude, and relationships with subjective well-being. *Social behavior and Personality* 2003, 31(5), 431-451.

Watson, AJ/ Lovelock, JE. Biological homeostasis of the global environment: the parable of Daisyworld, *Tellus* 1983, 35B:284.

Watson, David. The Flying Turtle (c) Ask Dr. Galapagos www.ftexploring.com/askdrg/askdrgalapagos.html (Accessed 8/15/03)

Watson, Lyall. *The Romeo Error: A Matter of Life and Death*, New York: Anchor/ Doubleday 1975.

Watson, Lyall. *Lifetide*, New York: Bantam/Simon & Schuster 1979.

Watts, Alan. Attributed.

Weber, Renee. The enfolding-unfolding universe: a conversation with David Bohm, *ReVision* Summer/ Fall 1978, 24-51.

Weber, Renee. Philosophical foundations and frameworks for healing, *ReVision*, 1979, 2(2) (also in: Borelli and Heidt, *Therapeutic Touch*, New York: Springer 1981, 13-39).

Webster, G/ Goodwin, B. *Form and transformation: generative and relational principles in biology*, Cambridge: Cambridge University Press 1996.

Webster, H. *Taboo, A Sociological Study*, Stanford, CA: Stanford University 1942.

Webster, James. *Life is for Ever*, Brooklyn, NY: Woodside 2000.

Webster, Ken. *The Vertical Plane*, London: Grafton 1989.

Weinberg, Steven. *The First Three Minutes*, New York: Bantam 1979.

Weiss, Brian. *Many Lives, Many Masters*, New York: Simon & Schuster 1988/ London: Piatkus 1994.

Weiss, Brian. *Through Time into Healing*, London: Piatkus 1995.

Weiss, Brian. *Only Love is Real*, New York: Warner/ London: Piatkus 1996.

Wells, Roger/ Watkins, Graham. Linger effects in several PK experiments, In: Morris, JD/ Roll, WG/ Morris, RL. *Research In Parapsychology 1974*, Metuchen, NJ and London: Scarecrow 1975, 143-147.

Welsh, William Addams. *Talks with the Dead*, New York: Pinnacle 1975.

Welwood, John. *Toward a Psychology of Awakening*, London:Shambhala 2002, 4-5.

Wenham, John. *The Easter Enigma*, Grand Rapids: Zondervan 1983.

West, DJ. The investigation of spontaneous cases, *Proceedings of the Society PsychicalResearch* 1948, 264-300.

West, DJ. *Eleven Lourdes Miracles*, London: Helix 1957.

West, DJ. Visionary and hallucinatory experiences: A comparative appraisal, *International J Parapsychology* 1960, 2, 89-100.

West, DW/ Lhon, JL/ Gardner, JW. Cancer risk factors: an analysis of Utah Mormons and non-Mormons, J National Cancer Institute 1980, 65, 1083-1095.

Westerbeke, Patricia/ Gover, John/ Krippner, Stanley. Subjective reactions to the Phillipino 'healers:' A questionnaire study, In: Morris, JD/ Roll, WG/ Morris, RL, eds. *Research in Parapsychology 1976*, Metuchen, NJ: Scarecrow 1977, 70-71.

Wheeler, John A. The universe as a home for man, *American Scientist* 1974, 62, 683-691.

Wheeler, John A. In Buckley, Paul/ Peat, F David. *A Question of Physics*, London: Routledge and Kegan Paul 1979.

Wheeler, John A/ Zurek, WH. *Quantum Theory and Measurement*, Princeton, NJ: Princeton University 1983.

Whitaker, Kay Cordell. *The Reluctant Shaman: A Woman's First Encounters with the Unseen Spirits of the Earth*, SanFrancisco: Harper 1991.

White, EB. Coon Tree, in *Essays of E.B. White*, New York: HarperPerennial 1999.

White, John, ed. *The Highest State of Consciousness*, Garden City, NY: Anchor/ Doubleday 1972.

White, John, *Kundalini: Evolution and Enlightenment*, New York: Paragon 1990; Anchor 1979.

White, L/ Tursky, B/ Schwartz, GE, eds. *Placebo: Theory, Research and Mechanisms*, New York: Guildford 1985.

White, Ruth/ Swainson, Mary. *The Healing Spectrum*, Suffolk, England: Neville Spearman, 1979.

Whiteman, JHM. A firsthand experiential view of 'multiple personality' and possession. *J Society Psychical Research* 1966, 61(845), 193-210.

Whitman, Walt. Quote from 'Song of Myself', in *Leaves of Grass*.

Whitmont, Edward C. *The Alchemy of Healing: Psyche and Soma*, Berkeley, CA: Homeopathic Education Services and North Atlantic Books 1993

Whitson, John: John, Robert and Williams, Henry Smith, eds. *Luther Burbank, His Methods and Discoveries and Their Practical Application, Prepared from His Original Field Notes Covering More than 100,000 Experiments Made During Forty Years Devoted to Plant Improvement*, New York/ London: Luther Burbank Society 1915, Vols 1-XII.

Whitton, Joel L. Xenoglossia: A subject with two possible instances, *New Horizons* 1977, 2(4), 18-26.

Whorf, BL. Language, Thought & Reality. MIT Press: Cambridge 1956, 57-8. (as quoted at Library of Excerpts www.humanevolution.net/a/hopi.html Accessed 10/4/05).

Wickland, Carl A. *Thirty Years Among the Dead*, London: Spiritualist 1968 (Orig. 1924). (Quotes by permission of Psychic News, London.)

Wilber, Ken. *The Atman Project: A Transpersonal View of Human Development*, Wheaton, IL: Quest 1980.

Wilber, Ken. *No Boundary: Eastern and Western Approaches to Personal Growth*, Boulder, CO: Shambala 1981.

Wilber, Ken. *Are the Chakras real?* In: White, John 1990, 120-131.

Wilber, Ken. *Grace and Grit: Spirituality and Healing in the Life and Death of Treya Killam Wilber*, Boston, MA: Gill and Macmillan 1991.

Wilber, Ken. *Integral Psychology: Consciousness, Spirit, Psychology, Therapy*, Boston: Shambhala Publications 2000.

Wilber, Ken, ed. *Quantum Questions: Mystical Writings of the World's Great Physicists*, Boston: Shambhala 1984, 2001.

Wilber, Ken/ Engler, Jack/ Brown, Daniel P. *Transformations of Consciousness: Conventional and Contemplative Perspectives on Development*, Boston: New Science Library/ Shambhala 1986.

Williams, Berney. Personal communication 2005.

Williams, David R. Measurement of religion, In: Levin 1994, 125-148.

Williams, David, et al. Religion and psychological distress in a community sample, *Social Science and Medicine* 1991, 32, 1257-1262.

Wills-Brandon, Carla. *One Last Hug Before I Go: The Mystery and Meaning of Deathbed Visions*, Deerfield Beach, FL: Health Communications 2000.

Wilson, Colin. *Afterlife: An Investigation of the Evidence for Life After Death*, London: Dolphin/ Doubleday 1987.

Wilson, CWM. The association between allergic disease, entities, multiple personalities, and medical dowsing, *Alternative Medicine* 1987(a), 2(3/4), 215-227.

Wilson, CWM. Entity possession: a dcausative factor in disease, *Psionic Medicine* 1987(b), 6(23), 4-21.

Wilson, I. *All in the Mind: Reincarnation, Hypnotic Regression, Stigmata, Multiple Personality, and Other Little Understood Powers of the Mind*, Garden City, NY: Doubleday 1982.

Wilson, RA. *Wilhelm Reich in Hell*, Phoenix, AZ: Falcon 1987.

Wilson, Sheryl C/ Barber, Theodore X. The fantasy-prone personality: Implications for understanding imagery, hypnosis and parapsychological phenomena, *Psi Research* 1982, 1(3), 94-116.

Windget, Terry. *Complete Book of Christian Prayer*. New York: Continuum Publishing 1996.

Winkelman, Michael. Trance states: A theoretical model and cross-cultural analysis, *Ethos* 1986, 14(2), 174-203; 319.

Winkelman, Michael. *Shamanism: The Neural Ecology of Consciousness and Healing*, Bergin & Garvey 2000.

Wise, Charles C. Jr. Some problems of spiritualist healing, *Spiritual Frontiers* 1972, 4(4), 219-228. (Quotes by permission of the quarterly *J Spiritual Frontiers Fellowship*, 10819 Winner Road, Independence, MO 64052; "SFF does not necessarily share all of the views stated by the writers of its Journal.")

Wiseman, Richard, et al. An investigation into alleged 'hauntings,' *British J Psychology* 2002, 94(2), 195-211.

Wisneski, Len. Personal communication 2003.

Witter, RA, et al. Religion and subjective well-being in adulthood: a quantitative synthesis, *Review of Religious Research* 1985, 26, 332-342.

Wolf, FA. *Taking the Quantum Leap: The New Physics for Nonscientists*, San Francisco: Harper & Row 1981 (Cited in Levin 1995).

Wolf, William. Are we ever reborn? *J for the Study of Consciousness* 1970, 3(2), 137-148.

Wolfe, D. Richard. Faith healing and healing faith, *J the Indiana State Medical Association* 1959, 52(4), 567-576.

Wolff, William. *Healers, Gurus, and Spiritual Guides*, Los Angeles: Sherbourne 1969.

Wolinsky, Stephen. *The Dark Side of The Inner Child*, Brable Books 1993.

Wolman, Benjamin, B/ Ullman, Montague, eds. *Handbook of States of Consciousness* New York: Van Nostrand Reinhold 1986.

Woodbury, Tony. Eskimo words for 'snow,' www.ecst.csuchico.edu/~atman/Misc/eskimo-snow-words.html (Accessed 10/1/05)

Woolger Roger. Tracing the Karmic Source of Prenatal Programmes. In Winafred B Lucas, ed. *Regression Therapy: A Handbook for Professionals*, Vol. 2; Deep Forest Press 1993, 32-37.

Woolger, Roger. *Other Lives, Other Selves: A Jungian Psychotherapist Discovers Past Lives*, New York: Dolphin/ Doubleday 1987.

Worden, William J. *Grief Counseling and Grief Therapy: a Handbook for the Mental Health Practitioner*, New York: Springer 1991.

Wordsworth, William. *Ode: Intimations of Immortality from Recollections of Early Childhood* 1807.

Worrall, Ambrose A/ Worrall, Olga N. *The Gift of Healing*, New York: Harper and Row 1965.

Worrall, Ambrose A/ Worrall, Olga N. with Oursler, Will, *Explore Your Psychic World*, New York: Harper and Row 1970 (Quotes reprinted by permission of the publishers.)

Wright, Lorraine M. *Spirituality, Suffering, and Illness: Ideas for Healing*, Los Angeles: F. A. Davis 2004.

Wright, Machaelle Small. *Co-Creative Science: A Revolution In Science Providing Real Solutions For Today's Health & Environment*, Warrenton, VA: Perelandra, Ltd 1997.

Y

Yankelovich Partners. Telephone poll for *Time/CNN*, June 12-13 1996, from *Time*, June 1996, 58-62.

Yawar, Athar. Spirituality in medicine: what is to be done? *J the Royal Society of Medicine* 2001, 94, 529-533.

Yinger, JM. *The Scientific Study of Religion*, London: Macmillan 1970.

Yockey, Hubert P. Self organization Origin of Life Scenarios and Information theory, *J Theoret. Biol.* 1981, 91, 13. (cited in Thaxton).

Yogananda, Paramahansa, *Autobiography of a Yogi*. Los Angles: Self-Realization Fellowship 1983, 411-417.

Yogananda, Paramahansa. *God Talks with Arjuma--The Bhagavad Gita: Royal Science of God-Realization. The immortal dialogue between soul and spirit. A new translation and commentary* (2 volumes). Los Angeles, CA: Self-Realizations Fellowship 1995 (3880 San Rafael Ave., Los Angeles, CA 90065-3298).

Young, Alan. *Spiritual Healing: Miracle or Mirage*, Marina del Rey, CA: DeVorss 1981.

Young, Lawrence. To Go Boldly Forth...Leading the Future" Keynote speech, 1999 National Conference Director of the Paul Robeson Cultural Center at Pennsylvania State University www.mortarboard.org/1news013.html (Accessed 7/25/03)

Young, Richard K/ Merberg, Albert L. *Spiritual Therapy*, New York: Harper and Row 1960.

Yram (pseudo for Marcel Forhan). *Practical Astral Projection*, New York: Weiser 1972. Bokris, John O'M. *The New Paradigm: A Confrontation Between Physics and the Paranormal Phenomena*, College Station, TX: D&M Enterprises 2004.

Z

Zaleski, Carol. *Otherworld Journeys: Accounts of Near-Death Experiences in Medieval and Modern Times*, New York: Oxford University 1987.

Zammit, Victor. *A Lawyer Presents the Case for the Afterlife: Irrefutable Objective Evidence*, www.victorzammit.com/book/index.html (Accessed 5/2/05)

Zborowski, M. Cultural components in responses to pain, *J Social Issues* 1952, 8, 16-30.

Zimmels, HJ. *Magicians, Theologians and Doctors: Studies in Folk Medicine and Folk Lore as Reflected in the Rabbinical Responsa 12th-19th Centuries*, London: Edward Goldston and Sons 1952.

Zohar, Danah/ Marshall, Ian. *SQ: Spiritual Intelligence, the Ultimate Intelligence*, New York: MacMillan 2000.

Zolik, ES. An experimental investigation of the psychodynamic implications of the hypnotic 'previous existence' fantasy, *J Clinical Psychology* 1958, 14, 179.

Zorab, GAM. The sittings with D. D. Home at Amsterdam, *J Parapsychology* 1970, 34, 47-63.

Zukav, Gary. *The Dancing Wu Li Masters*, New York: William Morrow 1979.

Zukav, Gary. *The Seat of the Soul*, New York/ London: Fireside/ Simon & Schuster 1990.

Index

Daniel J. Benor, MD, ABHM, enjoys sharing his ongoing search for ever more ways to peel the onion of life's resistances. His goal is to reach the gnowing (with the inner knowing of truth which has the feel of rightness) that we are all cells in the body of the Infinite Source.

While his unique area of expertise is spiritual awareness and healing, his principal work is through wholistic healing – addressing spirit, relationships (with people and the environment), mind, emotions and body. He teaches WHEE, a method he developed for rapid, easy, potent self-healing for children and adults dealing with PTSD and other forms of stress, psychological and physical pain, low self-esteem, cravings and other issues.

By training, Dr. Benor is a wholistic psychiatric psychotherapist. His psychotherapy blends elements from intuitive and spiritual awareness, spiritual healing (as in Reiki and Therapeutic Touch), WHEE - Wholistic Hybrid derived from Eye Movement Desensitization and Reprocessing (EMDR) and Emotional Freedom Technique (EFT), transactional analysis, gestalt therapy, hypnotherapy, meditation, imagery and relaxation, dream analysis, and other approaches. He has taught this spectrum internationally for 25 years to people involved in wholistic, intuitive, and spiritual approaches to caring, health and personal development.

Dr. Benor founded The Doctor-Healer Network in England and North America. He is the author of Healing Research, Volumes I-IV and many articles. He edits and publishes the peer reviewed International Journal of Healing and Caring - On Line (www.ijhc.org) and moderates www.WholisticHealingResearch.com, a major informational website on spiritual awareness, healing and CAM research, including his personal blog.

Dr. Benor appears internationally on radio and TV. He is a Founding Diplomate of the American Board of Holistic Medicine ABHM), and Coordinator for the Council for Healing, a non-profit organization that promotes awareness of spiritual healing (www.councilforhealing.org).